# STORM KING'S THUNDER

# CREDITS

**Lead Designer:** Christopher Perkins
**Story Design:** Jenna Helland, Adam Lee, Christopher Perkins, Richard Whitters
**Additional Design:** Mike Mearls
**Managing Editor:** Jeremy Crawford
**Editors:** Kim Mohan, Michele Carter
**Editorial Assistance:** Matt Sernett, Chris Dupuis, Ben Petrisor, Sean K Reynolds, Stan!
**Story Consultant:** R.A. Salvatore
**D&D Lead Designers:** Mike Mearls, Jeremy Crawford

**Art Director:** Kate Irwin
**Additional Art Direction:** Shauna Narciso, Richard Whitters
**Graphic Designer:** Emi Tanji
**Cover Illustrator:** Tyler Jacobson
**Interior Illustrators:** John-Paul Balmet, Beet, Mark Behm, Eric Belisle, Jedd Chevrier, Olga Drebas, Michael Dutton, Wayne England, Lars Grant-West, Lake Hurwitz, Tyler Jacobson, Julian Kok, Olly Lawson, Christopher Moeller, Scott Murphy, Chris Rahn, Ned Rogers, Chris Seaman, Richard Whitters
**Cartographers:** Jared Blando, Will Doyle, Jason A. Engle, Lee Moyer, Christopher Perkins, Mike Schley

**Project Manager:** Heather Fleming
**Product Engineer:** Cynda Callaway
**Imaging Technicians:** Sven Bolen, Carmen Cheung, Kevin Yee
**Art Administration:** David Gershman
**Prepress Specialist:** Jefferson Dunlap

**Other D&D Team Members:** Greg Bilsland, John Feil, Trevor Kidd, Christopher Lindsay, Shelly Mazzanoble, Hilary Ross, Liz Schuh, Nathan Stewart, Greg Tito, Shawn Wood

*Disclaimer: Creatures and objects in this adventure are bigger than they appear. No giant beanstalks were damaged and no golden geese were harmed in the making of this book.*

The following D&D books provided material and inspiration:

Baker, Richard, Christopher Perkins, and others. *Princes of the Apocalypse.* 2015.
Baur, Wolfgang, Steve Winter, and others. *Hoard of the Dragon Queen.* 2014.
Bonny, Ed, Jeff Grubb, Rich Redman, Skip Williams, and Steve Winter. *Monster Manual II.* 2002.
Boyd, Eric L. *City of Splendors: Waterdeep.* 2005.
Cordell, Bruce R., Ed Greenwood, and Chris Sims. *Forgotten Realms Campaign Guide.* 2008.
Doyle, Will. "King of the Wolves." *Dungeon* 220. 2013.
Greenwood, Ed. *Volo's Guide to the North.* 1993.
Greenwood, Ed, and Jason Carl. *Silver Marches.* 2002.
Greenwood, Ed, with Sean K Reynolds. "Wyrms of the North: Iymrith." *Dragon* 242. 1997.
Greenwood, Ed, Sean K Reynolds, Skip Williams, and Rob Heinsoo. *Forgotten Realms Campaign Setting.* 2001.
Jaquays, Jennell, writing as Paul Jaquays. *The Savage Frontier.* 1988.
Kenson, Steve, and others. *Sword Coast Adventurer's Guide.* 2015.
Salvatore, R.A., James Wyatt, and Jeffrey Ludwig. *Legacy of the Crystal Shard.* 2013.
Schend, Steven E., and Thomas M. Reid. *Wyrmskull Throne.* 1999.
Selinker, Michael. "Lear the Giant King." *Dungeon* 78. 2000.
Winninger, Ray. *Giantcraft.* 1995.

**Playtesters:** Teos Abadia, Robert Alaniz, Jay Anderson, Christopher Arroyo, Paul Baalham, Henry Bangsberg, Dave Bendit, Stacy Bermes, Brian Boring, Mik Calow, Joseph Chora, Mitch Clark, Justin Clift, Jacob Ela, Jason Fransella, Gregory L. Harris, Adam Hennebeck, Mary Hershey, Sterling Hershey, Justin Hicks, Bruce Higa, Chris Hodge, Eric Hufstetler, Joe Hughes, Paul Hughes, Donald Jacobs, Chris Jacobsen, Evan Jorstad, James Jorstad, Alex Kammer, Steven C. Knight, Yan Lacharité, Jon Lamkin, Majorie Lamkin, Randy Lenius, Mike Liebhart, Tom Lommel, Michael Long, Jonathan Longstaff, Keith Loveday, Joyce McCosco, Paul Melamed, Mark Meredith, Lou Michelli, Mike Mihalas, Daren Mitchell, Albert Paoletti, Clint Pushee, Rob Quillen II, Karl Resch, Sam Robertson, Steve Roe, Jeremy Schaefer, Robert Schwartz, Arthur Severance, Ray Slover Jr., Caoimhe Snow, Keaton Stamps, David "Oak" Stark, David Steele, Kyle Turner, Angel Uribe, Will Vaughan, Shane Walker, Morgan Wessler, Keoki Young

## ON THE COVER

Heir to the Wyrmskull Throne, and indeed all of giant-kind, the storm giant Serissa stands amidst the clouds, in the shadow of her mighty father, King Hekaton. Her contentious elder siblings, Mirran and Nym, occupy the forefront of this tempestuous illustration by the esteemed Tyler Jacobson.

620B86690001001 EN
ISBN: 978-0-7869-6600-4
First Printing: September 2016

9 8 7 6 5

# CONTENTS

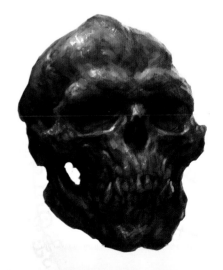

# Dramatis Personae

The main members of the adventure's cast of characters are listed here in alphabetical order for easy reference.

| Major NPC | Description | More Information |
| --- | --- | --- |
| Alastrah | Cloud giant infant daughter of Countess Sansuri | Chapter 9 ("Lyn Armaal," area 23) |
| Augrek Brighthelm | Dwarf sheriff's deputy in Bryn Shander | Chapter 2 ("Bryn Shander," area B1), stat block in appendix D |
| Beldora | Human spy for the Harpers in Bryn Shander | Chapter 2 ("Bryn Shander," area B7), stat block in appendix D |
| Braxow | Stone giant thane in Maelstrom | Chapter 10 ("Maelstrom," area 14) |
| Brimskarda | Fire giant duchess and wife of Duke Zalto | Chapter 8 ("Ironslag," area 31) |
| Cinderhild | Adolescent fire giant daughter of Duke Zalto | Chapter 8 ("Ironslag," area 26B) |
| Claugiyliamatar | Reclusive ancient green dragon in the Kryptgarden Forest | Chapter 3 ("Kryptgarden Forest") |
| Cog | Hill giant guard in Maelstrom | Chapter 10 ("Maelstrom," area 15) |
| Cressaro | Cloud giant castellan of Lyn Armaal | Chapter 9 ("Lyn Armaal," area 14) |
| Cryovain | Adult white dragon chained aboard the *Krigvind* | Chapter 7 ("The *Krigvind*") |
| Darathra Shendrel | Human lord protector of Triboar | Chapter 2 ("Triboar," area T1), stat block in appendix D |
| Darz Helgar | Retired human member of a Waterdhavian thieves' guild | Chapter 2 ("Triboar," area T2), stat block in appendix D |
| Duvessa Shane | Human town speaker of Bryn Shander | Chapter 2 ("Bryn Shander," area B5), stat block in appendix D |
| Eigeron | Cloud giant ghost | Chapter 4 ("Eye of the All-Father," area 11) |
| Felgolos | Adult bronze dragon imprisoned by Countess Sansuri | Chapter 9 ("Lyn Armaal," area 8) |
| Ghelryn Foehammer | Dwarf smith and owner of Foehammer's Forge in Triboar | Chapter 2 ("Triboar," area T18), stat block in appendix D |
| Guh | Hill giant chief based in Grudd Haug | Introduction ("The Giant Lords"), chapter 5 ("Grudd Haug," area 2) |
| Harshnag | Legendary good-aligned frost giant adventurer | Chapter 3 ("Harshnag") |
| Hekaton | Storm giant king abducted by the Kraken Society | Introduction ("King Hekaton and His Daughters"), chapter 11 ("The *Morkoth*," area 3) |
| Hellenhild | Frost giant jarl in Maelstrom | Chapter 10 ("Maelstrom," area 14) |
| Isendraug | Adult white dragon confined to Svardborg | Chapter 7 ("Svardborg," area 4E) |
| Iymrith | Ancient blue dragon stirring up trouble among the storm giants | Introduction ("Iymrith"), chapter 4 ("Encounter with Iymrith"), chapter 10 ("Maelstrom," area 15), chapter 12 ("Iymrith's Lair," area 3), stats in appendix C |
| Kaaltar | Cloud giant infant son of Countess Sansuri | Chapter 9 ("Lyn Armaal," area 23) |
| Kayalithica | Stone giant thane based in Deadstone Cleft | Introduction ("The Giant Lords"), chapter 6 ("Deadstone Cleft," area 14) |
| Kella Darkhope | Zhentarim spy hiding in the Nightstone Inn | Chapter 1 ("Nightstone," area 8F) |
| Khaspere Drylund | Human noble and member of the Kraken Society | Chapter 11 ("The *Grand Dame*") |
| Klauth | Meddlesome ancient red dragon in Klauthen Vale | Chapter 3 ("Klauthen Vale") |
| Lifferlas | Awakened tree in Goldenfields | Chapter 2 ("Goldenfields," area G6), stat block in appendix D |
| Markham Southwell | Human sheriff of Bryn Shander | Chapter 2 ("Bryn Shander," area B6), stat block in appendix D |
| Miros Xelbrin | Human proprietor of Northfurrow's End, an inn in Goldenfields | Chapter 2 ("Goldenfields," area G8), stat block in appendix D |
| Mirran | Evil storm giant and eldest daughter of King Hekaton | Introduction ("King Hekaton and His Daughters"), chapter 10 ("Maelstrom," area 14) |
| Moog | Upset hill giant | Chapter 3 ("Old Tower") |

| Major NPC | Description | More Information |
|---|---|---|
| Morak Ur'gray | Dwarf innkeeper imprisoned in the Dripping Caves | Chapter 1 ("Dripping Caves," area 4) |
| Narth Tezrin | Human proprietor of the Lion's Share, a store in Triboar | Chapter 2 ("Triboar," area T6), stat block in appendix D |
| Naxene Drathkala | Human mage of the Watchful Order of Magists and Protectors | Chapter 2 ("Goldenfields," area G8), stat block in appendix D |
| Nimir | Storm giant sent to kill Iymrith | Chapter 12 ("Finding Iymrith"), stat block in appendix D |
| Nym | Evil storm giant and second daughter of King Hekaton | Introduction ("King Hekaton and His Daughters"), chapter 10 ("Maelstrom," area 14) |
| Oren Yogilvy | Halfling musician staying at Northfurrow's End | Chapter 2 ("Goldenfields," area G8), stat block in appendix D |
| Orlekto | Storm giant sent to kill Iymrith | Chapter 12 ("Finding Iymrith"), stat block in appendix D |
| Othovir | Human owner of Othovir's Harness Shop in Triboar | Chapter 2 ("Triboar," area T11), stat block in appendix D |
| Pow Ming | Human mage and head of security aboard the *Grand Dame* | Chapter 11 ("The *Grand Dame*") |
| Rool | Orc assassin and first mate of the *Morkoth* | Chapter 11 ("The *Morkoth*") |
| Sansuri | Cloud giant countess based in Lyn Armaal | Introduction ("The Giant Lords"), chapter 9 ("Lyn Armaal," area 8) |
| Serissa | Storm giant and youngest daughter of King Hekaton | Introduction ("King Hekaton and His Daughters"), chapter 10 ("Maelstrom," area 15) |
| Shaldoor | Storm giant sent to kill Iymrith | Chapter 12 ("Finding Iymrith"), stat block in appendix D |
| Shalvus Martholio | Human shepherd and Zhentarim spy | Chapter 2 ("Goldenfields," area G5), stat block in appendix D |
| Sir Baric Nylef | Human knight of the Order of the Gauntlet in Bryn Shander | Chapter 2 ("Bryn Shander," area B8), stat block in appendix D |
| Sirac of Suzail | Human son of Artus Cimber living in Bryn Shander | Chapter 2 ("Bryn Shander," area B4), stat block in appendix D |
| Slarkrethel | Spellcasting kraken of the Trackless Sea | Introduction ("The Kraken Society"), chapter 11 ("The Kraken Cometh") |
| Storvald | Frost giant jarl based in Svardborg | Introduction ("The Giant Lords"), chapter 7 ("The *Krigvind*") |
| Tartha | Fire giant duchess in Maelstrom | Chapter 10 ("Maelstrom," area 14) |
| Tholtz Daggerdark | Human archmage and captain of the *Morkoth* | Chapter 11 ("The *Morkoth*") |
| Thullen | Cloud giant count and brother of Countess Sansuri | Chapter 9 ("Lyn Armaal," area 28) |
| Tug | Hill giant guard in Maelstrom | Chapter 10 ("Maelstrom," area 15) |
| Urgala Meltimer | Human proprietor of Northshield House, an inn in Triboar | Chapter 2 ("Triboar," area T10), stat block in appendix D |
| Uthor | Storm giant imperator and castellan of Maelstrom | Chapter 10 ("Maelstrom," area 15) |
| Vaal | Cloud giant count in Maelstrom | Chapter 10 ("Maelstrom," area 14) |
| Vaasha | Storm giant sent to kill Iymrith | Chapter 12 ("Finding Iymrith"), stat block in appendix D |
| Xolkin Alassandar | Half-elf leader of the Seven Snakes mercenary band | Chapter 1 ("Seven Snakes") |
| Zaltember | Adolescent fire giant son of Duke Zalto | Chapter 8 ("Ironslag," area 18) |
| Zalto | Fire giant duke based in Ironslag | Introduction ("The Giant Lords"), chapter 8 ("Ironslag," area 28) |
| Zephyros | Eccentric cloud giant wizard | Chapter 1 ("Tower of Zephyros") |
| Zi Liang | Human acolyte of the Harvesthome Abbey | Chapter 2 ("Goldenfields," area G7), stat block in appendix D |

# Introduction

**Y**OU ARE ABOUT TO EMBARK ON A GREAT adventure that pits heroes against giants bent on reshaping the world. *Storm King's Thunder* is a DUNGEONS & DRAGONS adventure for four to six player characters. You can start the adventure with 1st-level characters or 5th-level characters. Either way, the characters should reach at least 11th level by the adventure's conclusion. Because giants figure prominently in the story, at least one character should be able to speak and understand the Giant language.

The adventure takes place in the Forgotten Realms, specifically in a region known as the Savage Frontier, in the northwest corner of the continent of Faerûn. Nonetheless, you can easily adapt the adventure to your home campaign by changing the names of various locations and factions.

We recommend that you read the entire adventure before attempting to run it. This introduction begins with an "Adventure Background" section that summarizes the events that set the adventure in motion. The "Running the Adventure" section tells you everything you need to know to run the adventure smoothly. That section also presents guidelines for character level advancement, outlines the flow of the adventure, and describes its major challenges. Once you've reviewed this material and are ready to run the adventure, proceed with chapter 1, "A Great Upheaval," if the characters are starting at 1st level, or chapter 2, "Rumblings," if they are starting at 5th level.

## Adventure Background

The Savage Frontier (also known as the North) is a cold, rugged, sparsely populated land of snow-capped mountains, rocky hills, sprawling forests, and foggy vales. Isolated strongholds, ancient burial mounds, and the ruins of many forgotten empires dot this vast landscape. Bounded by the Sea of Swords to the west and the desert of Anauroch to the east, the Savage Frontier extends as far north as Icewind Dale and as far south as the town of Daggerford. Old roads stretch across this great expanse, linking the dwarven strongholds and mines in the mountains to the coastal settlements, frontier towns, and fortified outposts of humans and other folk. These roads are long, lonely, or poorly defended, making them dangerous to traverse. In fertile valleys, towns and cities have sprung up, separated by dozens if not hundreds of miles of untamed wilderness haunted by hostile Humanoids and monsters.

Evil dragons stirred into action by their dark queen, Tiamat, threatened the settlements of the Savage Frontier for a time. Ultimately, they were defeated and forced to withdraw to their lairs, while Tiamat was banished to the Nine Hells. Fear of the dragons' wrath has faded quickly with the coming of a new threat: giants. The peoples of the North are no strangers to giant incursions. Frost giants have long claimed the Spine of the World as their demesne, and hill giants are known to scrounge for food in the untamed hills. But now, in the past couple of months, giants of every kind have emerged from their strongholds in force to threaten civilization as

## Giant Runes

BLOD
(BLOOD RUNE)

SKYE
(CLOUD RUNE)

DOD
(DEATH RUNE)

WYRM
(DRAGON RUNE)

UVEN
(ENEMY RUNE)

ILD
(FIRE RUNE)

VENN
(FRIEND RUNE)

ISE
(FROST/ICE RUNE)

HAUG
(HILL RUNE)

FERD
(JOURNEY RUNE)

KONG
(KING RUNE)

STIG
(LIGHT RUNE)

LIV
(LIFE RUNE)

FJELL
(MOUNTAIN RUNE)

HELLIG
(SACRED RUNES)

SKOLD
(SHIELD RUNE)

STEIN
(STONE RUNE)

UVAR
(STORM RUNE)

KRIG
(WAR RUNE)

VIND
(WIND RUNE)

FIGURE 0.1: GIANT RUNES

never before—and not just frost giants and hill giants, but also stone giants, fire giants, and cloud giants. All of the giants are in an uproar. Reports of giant attacks throughout the North have reached the coastal cities of Luskan, Neverwinter, and Waterdeep, stoking fears that the giants are waging war against humans, dwarves, elves, and other small folk.

## THE ORDNING

Giant society (such as it is) is defined in large part by the ordning, a caste system imposed upon the giants by their gods, chief among them Annam the All-Father. The ordning determines where a giant stands among his or her ilk. Traditionally, storm giants have stood at the top of the ordning. Tall and powerful, they struggle to keep the weaker races of giants from despoiling the realms of small folk and sparking conflict. The greatest storm giants are powerful seers, skilled at identifying and interpreting cosmic signs and divine omens. The aloof and aristocratic cloud giants, one step below the storm giants, rarely condescend to deal with lesser giants or small folk. Extravagance defines their culture and their place in the ordning. Below them are the tyrannical, warmongering fire giants and the merciless, predatory frost giants. Fire giants rank themselves by their forging skill, whereas frost giants rank themselves by their martial prowess. Near the bottom of the ordning are the xenophobic stone giants, who mostly live underground and regard the surface world as a realm of dreams. How well they sculpt stone determines their place among their peers. The lowest and smallest of the true giants are the hill giants, as gluttonous as they are loathsome. Hill giants are dullards who live in fear of their more powerful giant cousins. In hill giant society, the biggest rule.

Dragons are the ancient enemies of giants. Thousands of years ago, the last great empire of giants—Ostoria—fell after a long and brutal conflict with dragons. Little of Ostoria remains in what is now called the Savage Frontier. The civilizations of small folk have taken over the land once ruled by giants. Although evil giants make occasional forays into territory settled by small folk, their ambitions have long been curtailed by their lack of cohesion and the imposition of good-aligned storm giants and cloud giants whose memories of ancient, glorious Ostoria have faded over time.

The recent efforts by dragons to bring Tiamat into the world (as told in the adventure *Tyranny of Dragons*) and the attempts by small folk to thwart them so upset the giant gods that Annam the All-Father shattered the ordning between the giants to break his "children" out of their complacency, pitting the six giant types against one another while keeping some semblance of order within each type. In so doing, Annam has spurred cloud, fire, frost, stone, and hill giants to challenge the established hierarchy and reforge their destiny. All the giants sensed the upheaval instantly, and now the giant types fiercely compete against one another, striving to create a new ordning through their deeds and accomplishments. These giants' calamitous endeavors have not only put the settlements of humans and other small folk in jeopardy but also attracted the attention of the giants' ancient enemies—the dragons—who will not abide the rise of another giant empire.

Small folk can only speculate as to the cause of the giants' unrest. It remains to be seen whether the old ordning between the giant types will be restored, or whether a new hierarchy will replace the old one, knocking the storm giants from their lofty perch.

FROM LEFT TO RIGHT: KING HEKATON, QUEEN NERI, MIRRAN, NYM, AND SERISSA

# KING HEKATON AND HIS DAUGHTERS

Prior to the shattering of the ordning, King Hekaton was arguably the most powerful of all storm giants. From Maelstrom, his citadel deep within the Trackless Sea, he presided over a court that included representatives of every race of giant, from mighty storm giants to lowly hill giants. He used the power of the *Wyrmskull Throne*—a gift given to him by his wife—to keep the more unruly giants in line.

For as long as Hekaton had reigned, fear of the king's wrath and respect for the ordning was enough to keep lesser giants from rising up against him. But in recent years, King Hekaton had become convinced that the age of the giants was past, as evidenced by the growing distance between the giants and their gods. Annam the All-Father didn't answer prayers, and his divine offspring—the lesser giant gods—were out of touch, constantly waging war against one another on the Outer Planes. Hekaton came to believe that the giants were no longer the rightful masters of the world.

Then, several months ago, Hekaton's fear became reality when the ordning was shattered. The king was profoundly shaken by the realization that storm giants might lose their apex status among giants. In the aftermath of the upheaval, he did his utmost to hold his court together, bullying weaker giants into submission.

Hekaton's wife, Queen Neri, was particularly fond of the small folk. She visited them often in the years before the ordning was sundered, rising up out of the sea to meet them on the shores of the Sword Coast. Neri continually urged her husband to respect the civilizations of the small folk and leave them alone, if he could not countenance forming alliances with them. Hekaton, inherently distrustful of the small folk, wanted nothing to do with them, but he respected his wife's desire to treat with them on occasion.

Neri continued to visit the small folk from time to time even after the upheaval—until the day came when she failed to return from one of her trips to the Sword Coast. Hekaton's younger brother, Imperator Uthor, commander of the king's garrison, found Neri's corpse shortly thereafter on a small island where she had been known to meet with humans. It was clear that she had been killed by small folk, and Hekaton wept for days before threatening to unleash his vengeance on the unsuspecting coastal territories.

Uthor couldn't calm his brother's rage, so he turned to Princess Serissa, the king's youngest daughter, for help. Serissa, who shared her mother's affection for small folk and who stood next in line to inherit the *Wyrmskull Throne*, urged her father to uncover the truth before lashing out at anyone he encountered. Hekaton was swayed by his daughter's levelheadedness and wisdom, and once his hurricane-like anger ran its course, he set out to learn how his wife met her end. Unfortunately for the king, he was blind to enemies not only in his court but also in his family.

The seeds of discontent in Hekaton's family were sown more than a year before the ordning was shattered, when the king divined that his two eldest daughters, Mirran and Nym, were unfit to rule, and saw signs that pointed to Serissa, his youngest daughter, as his most worthy successor. Mirran was tempestuous and prone to emotional outbursts, while Nym was the opposite—as cold and unloving as the sea. While Hekaton adored them both, he doubted their ability to keep the lesser giants in line, so he named Serissa as his heir apparent.

Mirran and Nym abided by his decision, but nevertheless their unhappiness was clear. Secretly, they blamed their mother for persuading their father to pass them over. Their blame was unfounded, in fact; Queen Neri had actually warned her husband against making any such pronouncement. Mirran and Nym seethed inside but were too terrified of their father to do anything, until a recent arrival to Maelstrom named Iymrith wormed her way into Hekaton's court and goaded them into action.

The elder sisters, acting in accordance with Iymrith's counsel, are responsible for both Neri's death and Hekaton's disappearance. Mirran and Nym got their revenge against Neri by plotting—with Iymrith's help—to have her assassinated. Then they urged their father to hunt down the small folk who killed their mother and fed him false information on the whereabouts of the assassins, to throw the king off track and put him in peril.

In the wake of Hekaton's disappearance, turmoil engulfed his court. After nearly a month of waiting for him to come back, Serissa reluctantly claimed her father's throne at Imperator Uthor's urging.

## MIRRAN AND NYM

King Hekaton's eldest daughter, Mirran, is a spoiled brat with the forcefulness and unpredictability of a typhoon. She covets the power of the *Wyrmskull Throne* and believes it rightfully belongs to her. She is angry with her parents for placing Serissa next in the line of succession, and she has made her feelings plain. Mirran believes she is destined to rule and has seen signs that reinforce her belief. Once she claims the throne, Mirran expects all other giants to kneel before her. She plans to use her newfound power to resurrect the ancient empire of Ostoria, sweeping away the cities and kingdoms of the small folk.

If Mirran is the blustery gale of an ocean storm, then Nym is the undercurrent. King Hekaton's middle child is cold and calculating. She has always felt neglected by her parents, in part because Mirran was so demanding and Serissa so young. In truth, King Hekaton and Queen Neri loved Nym as much as they adored their other daughters, but they found her distant and difficult to please. Nym wants Mirran to seize the throne—and then, when Mirran makes enemies at every turn and proves to everyone that she is unfit to rule, Nym plans to supplant her. She has received omens that support her bid for power. Unlike her blustery older sister, Nym is worried about the consequences of the dissolution of the ordning. Nonetheless, Iymrith has convinced her that she has an important destiny to fulfill, and that the gods will reward her if she brings about the return of Ostoria.

From left to right: Iymrith, Chief Guh, Thane Kayalithica

## Serissa

When King Hekaton disappears, Princess Serissa finds herself thrust into power. Unable to find her father and fearing that he might be dead, Serissa can imagine her political influence evaporating quickly. Several giant lords previously under her father's thumb have abandoned her court and set out to impress the gods in ways that could all but destroy the civilizations of the small folk. Serissa fears warfare among the six giant races as they strive to outdo one another, perhaps in the process reigniting the ancient conflict between giants and dragons. The princess-regent knows that her older sisters envy and despise her, but it has never occurred to her that they were involved in their mother's death or their father's kidnapping. Other than Iymrith and her Uncle Uthor, there are few giants Serissa feels she can trust.

Hekaton left behind a piece of regalia called the *Korolnor Scepter*, a magic item that allows its owner to harness the powers of the *Wyrmskull Throne*. In accordance with her father's wishes, Serissa has claimed the scepter and the throne. Even with the throne's magic at her command, she feels adrift. Serissa wants to reach out to the small folk for help in finding her father, because she knows that despite their size, they are capable of great feats of heroism. But Iymrith and Uthor have advised Serissa to steer clear of them. Uthor believes (incorrectly) that an alliance with the small folk would further anger Annam the All-Father, while Iymrith wants the giants and the small folk to annihilate one another.

Serissa values the counsel of her advisors, but she has her own mind. She wants to see her faith—and her mother's faith—in the small folk vindicated, so she leaps at any opportunity to use small folk to find her father, who she believes has the power to set things right. She is hoping for a cosmic sign to validate her beliefs, but time is not on her side.

## Iymrith

Iymrith is an ancient blue dragon who can assume the form of a storm giant. In this guise, she has infiltrated Hekaton's court. While concealing her true nature and agenda from the giants, Iymrith offers counsel to Princess Serissa and at the same time secretly feeds the anger and jealousy of Serissa's older siblings, with the ultimate goal of thrusting the giants into war with the small folk. The dragon also wants to wrest the *Wyrmskull Throne* from the storm giants and add it to her trove.

The disguised dragon put Mirran and Nym in contact with representatives of Slarkrethel, a legendary kraken that haunts the Trackless Sea. These small folk belong to a secret yet widespread organization called the Kraken Society. Using information given to them by the evil storm giant sisters, Kraken Society operatives ambushed and killed Queen Neri. Iymrith then planted rumors in the storm giant court that the queen had been assassinated by the Lords' Alliance, a confederacy of cities and settlements populated by small folk and scattered throughout the North. The Lords' Alliance represents one of the greatest threats to dragons in Faerûn, so Iymrith is keen to bring about its end.

## The Giant Lords

Convinced that King Hekaton is dead or otherwise out of the picture, five giant lords have struck out into the world to reshape the ordning through their deeds, each hoping to be elevated by the gods to the pinnacle of giantkind.

### Chief Guh

Guh, a gluttonous hill giant chief, has raised an enormous timber steading in the hills northeast of Goldenfields, in the central Dessarin Valley. Comfortably housed within her lair, Guh has instructed her husbands

FROM LEFT TO RIGHT: JARL STORVALD, DUKE ZALTO, COUNTESS SANSURI

to bring her all the food they can carry. Her plan is to consume all that is brought before her and grow to immense size. When she becomes the largest giant in the world, Guh believes the gods will reward her and elevate hill giants to the top of the ordning. Guh has spent the past four months gorging herself, while nearby ranches, farmsteads, and orchards have been pillaged. Not content with the amount of food hoarded thus far, Guh's mates move to attack nearby settlements and plunder their fields and storehouses.

## THANE KAYALITHICA

After fleeing Hekaton's court, Kayalithica, an inscrutable stone giant thane, withdrew to her canyon sanctuary of Deadstone Cleft. There, in its hallowed halls, she hoped to elevate her people to the top of the ordning by first seeking divine inspiration. Deadstone Cleft is hidden within the Graypeak Mountains, east of Delimbiyr Vale and the High Forest, and northeast of the mining settlement of Llorkh. After weeks of meditation, Kayalithica concluded that the small folk had corrupted the dreams of all giants by building their wretched settlements on the bones of ancient Ostoria. She intends to wipe the land clean of their "filth," thus restoring the "dream world" to its rightful state. Kayalithica's stone giants strike forth from Deadstone Cleft to destroy the works of humans, dwarves, and elves, then return to carve the tales of their accomplishments into the walls for the gods to see and admire.

## JARL STORVALD

Storvald, a fierce and adventurous frost giant jarl, traveled to the coldest reaches of the Sea of Moving Ice to reclaim Svardborg, the ancestral home of his forebears. He found a nest of white dragon eggs within the iceberg fortress and successfully enslaved a mated pair of white dragons by holding their eggs hostage. Within a mat-

ter of months thereafter, he also freed several gigantic longships from the ice and sent his giant raiders out to attack smaller ships and plunder their supplies, as well as to pillage wood from the mainland to repair the damaged ships and lodges of Svardborg.

Storvald has childhood memories of a legend about the Ice That Never Melts—a powerful, frost-coated golden ring that can freeze the oceans and blanket the world in mountains of snow. Small folk know this artifact by another name: the *Ring of Winter*. The ring, which grants immortality to its wearer, was last seen in the possession of a human adventurer (and former Harper) named Artus Cimber. Guided by magical runes of tracking, Storvald plans to find the ring and bring about the Age of Everlasting Ice, thus ensuring his place at the top of the ordning. Storvald procured a drop of Cimber's blood from a Zhentarim wizard named Nilraun, and used the drop to empower his runes. Unbeknown to Storvald, the runes are steering the frost giants not to Artus Cimber but to other, closer individuals who carry the Cimber bloodline—Artus's living relatives, most of whom know nothing about the *Ring of Winter*'s whereabouts.

## DUKE ZALTO

Zalto, a fire giant duke, believes that he can become the ruler of all giants by slaughtering their ancient enemies: dragons. Duke Zalto has set his minions to the task of finding and unearthing fragments of a dragon-slaying colossus called the Vonindod ("titan of death"). Pieces of it were lost in battle, while the rest was dismantled at the end of the ancient war between giants and dragonkind. Once all the pieces are found, Zalto plans to reforge the Vonindod and unleash it on the world. Beneath the Ice Spires lies an ancient fire giant forge called Ironslag. Unfortunately for Zalto, Ironslag's forges aren't hot enough to repair the colossus. The duke, undaunted, plans to steal Maegera, the fire primordial trapped in the subterranean dwarven fortress-city of Gauntlgrym, and trap it within Ironslag's adamantine forge. The dwarves rely on Maegera to heat their own forges. Hesitant to storm the dwarven fortress, Zalto has met with drow representatives of House Xorlarrin, who know the layout of Gauntlgrym well. With their aid, the fire giant duke plans to imprison Maegera in an *iron flask* and transport the primordial to Ironslag—a goal easier imagined than accomplished.

## COUNTESS SANSURI

Sansuri, a vainglorious cloud giant countess, is one of several cloud giant nobles who have retreated to their cloud castles and embarked on expeditions to map the present-day Sword Coast in search of long-lost Ostorian treasures and battlegrounds. Like archaeologists, they seek to uncover secrets of the past and retrieve relics of their ancient history to impress the gods. Sansuri, a powerful wizard, is searching for something more: a long-lost trove of dragon magic, hidden away by her ancestors. Once cloud giants knock storm giants from the pinnacle of the ordning, she plans to use her newfound magic to destroy her rivals as well as Hekaton's court. But the countess is not happy at present, because her search for the lost trove has not been going well. Frustrated, Sansuri has used powerful magic and guile to capture a bronze dragon named Felgolos. She is torturing the wyrm for information. The dragon's terrible roars can be heard emanating from Sansuri's cloud castle for miles in every direction.

# FACTIONS IN THE NORTH

The giants' plots have far-reaching consequences for the Savage Frontier and the peoples who live there. Giant castles in the clouds have been seen drifting overhead, casting ominous shadows on the settlements of the North. Caravans and farmsteads have come under attack. Frost giant longships have begun terrorizing the Sword Coast. Various organizations throughout the North are justly concerned, and some have important roles to play in events yet to unfold.

---

### CREATING NEW GIANT LORDS

This adventure focuses on the machinations of a few giant lords, but they aren't the only evil giants vying for glory and their gods' admiration. Other giant lords might be engaged in foul plots throughout the North. Here are a few examples of lords you could create:

- A cloud giant wizard planning to cast an apocalyptic spell using a large obsidian rock called a nightstone (see chapter 1) as a material component.
- A fire giant duchess paying hobgoblin warlords to raze northern settlements.
- A frost giant jarl using an *orb of dragonkind* to lure dragons to its iceberg fortress to be slaughtered.
- A stone giant thane trying to awaken the tarrasque, which slumbers in the Underdark.
- A hill giant chief with a *headband of intellect* performing rituals that can transform people into pigs.

---

## THE HARPERS

The Harpers are spellcasters and spies who covertly oppose the abuse of power, magical or otherwise. Working alone or in small cells, they gather information throughout Faerûn, discern the political dynamics within each region, and help the weak, the poor, and the oppressed, acting openly only as a last resort.

The Harpers were instrumental in defeating Tiamat and ending the tyranny of dragons, and with reports of giant attacks on the rise, they see giants as an emergent threat to peace in the North. The Harpers don't know why the giants are becoming so active all at once, or what their ultimate goals are. As yet, no major towns or cities have come under attack, although the Harpers expect that situation to change. Harpers are eager to recruit adventurers to help them combat the giant threat.

## THE LORDS' ALLIANCE

Various settlements of the North have banded together to form the Lords' Alliance, a shaky coalition that proactively eliminates threats to their mutual safety and prosperity. Alliance leaders are often contentious, while their operatives seek honor and glory for themselves and their respective lords. Key representatives of the Lords' Alliance include the canny Lord Dagult Neverember of Neverwinter, the resplendent Lady Laeral Silverhand of Waterdeep, the grave Lord Taern Hornblade of Silverymoon, and the willful Queen Dagnabbet of Mithral Hall.

With the aid of adventurers, the Lords' Alliance thwarted Tiamat and her dragons. Alliance members aren't about to let giants run roughshod over their settlements and plunder their farmsteads. Alliance members call on adventurers of every stripe to attack and kill giants on sight, promising rewards of 200 to 500 gold pieces for each giant head brought to their gates.

Rumors that the Lords' Alliance was behind King Hekaton's disappearance have not yet reached the alliance leaders. Were the alliance to learn of these rumors, its leaders would quietly investigate the veracity of the claims while publicly dismissing them.

## THE EMERALD ENCLAVE

The Emerald Enclave is a group of wilderness survivalists who preserve the natural order by rooting out unnatural threats. They struggle to keep civilization and the wilderness from destroying each other, and they help others survive the natural perils of the Savage Frontier.

As sightings of giants become more common, members of the Emerald Enclave begin to realize something is afoot. Hill giants laying waste to vast tracts of forest, stone giants leveling homesteads, frost giants endangering mountain passes, and fire giants rounding up slaves and putting grasslands and forests to the torch are enough to invoke the enclave's wrath.

## THE ORDER OF THE GAUNTLET

Members of the Order of the Gauntlet seek to protect others from the depredations of evildoers. Placing their faith in deities such as Torm, Helm, and Tyr, they bring the strength of their faith, their hearts, and their weapons to bear against villainy.

Knights of the order and their loyal squires can be found throughout the North, gathering information on the giants, searching for their lairs, and aiding in the defense of settlements.

## THE ZHENTARIM

The Zhentarim, also known as the Black Network, is an unscrupulous shadow network that seeks to expand its influence and power base throughout the North. Its members crave wealth and personal power, though the public face of the organization appears much more benign, offering the best mercenaries money can buy. Adventurers allied with the Zhentarim are free to profit as they see fit, either by helping or hindering the giants.

The Black Network has spies and operatives in every major northern settlement, and it doesn't wish to see its footholds destroyed by rampaging giants. As it strives to protect its holdings, the Zhentarim also wants to understand the giants' motivations. The leaders of the Black Network are open to the possibility of establishing trade relations with the giants or bribing them, if necessary, to ensure their own continued wealth and prosperity. At the same time, the Zhentarim profits by selling the services of mercenaries to those who can't defend themselves.

## THE KRAKEN SOCIETY

Far from being a benevolent faction, the Kraken Society is a group of spies, smugglers, slavers, and assassins. Only the society's leaders know that the founder of their organization is Slarkrethel, a magic-using kraken that lives in the depths of the Trackless Sea.

Krakens are forsaken creations of the gods, left behind after a cosmic war that ushered in the dawn of the civilized world. Ancient beyond reckoning, Slarkrethel longs to rejoin its creators in the heavens. For tens of thousands of years, the kraken has been searching tirelessly for a long-lost path to divine ascendancy. In the meantime, its stretches its tentacles across Faerûn, laying low powers that might one day threaten it.

Worship of Slarkrethel began hundreds of years ago on the Purple Rocks. The humans who inhabit these islands cast their young into the sea as part of a ritual to appease Slarkrethel. These sacrificed offspring resurface and return to their villages years later as adults, albeit with piscine deformities. When they reach the end of their natural life span, they return to the sea and their fearsome master. The inhabitants of the Purple Rocks otherwise eke out quiet lives, unaware of the kraken's vast spy network on the mainland.

The Kraken Society's widespread organization wasn't born at the Purple Rocks, but in the cities of the North. The psychic abilities of the kraken are so great that it can reach out to creatures on land up and down the Sword Coast. Over the years, it has telepathically lured exiles, outcasts, and lost souls to its organization with the promise of a better life. Its agents are evil and grasping. When they are not gathering information for the kraken, they lurk in the shadows and indulge in activities befitting their evil nature.

Slarkrethel was old when the giants and dragons waged war against each other forty thousand years ago,

### TENDAYS AND THE ROLL OF YEARS

In the Forgotten Realms setting, a week is ten days long and is referred to as a tenday. There are three tendays per month, and twelve months in a year. For more information on the calendar of the Forgotten Realms, see "The Calendar of Harptos" sidebar in chapter 1 of the *Dungeon Master's Guide*.

This adventure isn't set at a specific time but is assumed to take place sometime after 1485 DR, the Year of the Iron Dwarf's Vengeance, during which a horde of orcs waged war on the North before being driven back into the mountains. This conflict is referred to in this adventure as the War of the Silver Marches. The years that follow the Year of the Iron Dwarf's Vengeance have similarly colorful names:

1486 DR, the Year of the Nether Mountain Scrolls
1487 DR, the Year of the Rune Lords Triumphant
1488 DR, the Year of Dwarvenkind Reborn
1489 DR, the Year of the Warrior Princess
1490 DR, the Year of the Star Walker's Return
1491 DR, the Year of the Scarlet Witch
1492 DR, the Year of Three Ships Sailing
1493 DR, the Year of the Purple Dragons

and the kraken aims to rekindle that war and destroy the cities of the Sword Coast in the process. When Iymrith reached out to its agents for assistance, Slarkrethel instructed its devotees to humor the dragon by capturing Hekaton, the storm giant king, after slaying his queen. Iymrith wants Hekaton kept alive so that he can't be resurrected and so that he can be held for ransom if her plans are thwarted.

A seafaring Kraken Society wizard named Tholtz Daggerdark has turned his ship, the *Morkoth*, into a floating prison. King Hekaton lies bound and chained within, unable to escape without aid. The ship circles the islands of the Trackless Sea, far from prying eye

# RUNNING THE ADVENTURE

To run this adventure, you need the fifth edition *Player's Handbook*, *Dungeon Master's Guide*, and *Monster Manual*. Take a few minutes to reread the section on giants in the *Monster Manual*, since it contains important information about giants. The *Sword Coast Adventurer's Guide*, while not required reading, has extensive information on the Sword Coast and the North that can help you flesh out the adventure's default setting. It also presents new character backgrounds that work well for this adventure.

Text that appears in a box like this is meant to be read aloud or paraphrased for the players when their characters first arrive at a location or under a specific circumstance, as described in the text.

The *Monster Manual* contains stat blocks for most of the monsters and NPCs found in this adventure. When a monster's name appears in **bold** type, that's a visual cue pointing you to the creature's stat block in the *Monster Manual*. Descriptions and stat blocks for new monsters appear in appendix C. If a stat block is in appendix C,

NOBODY WINS WHEN
GIANTS FIGHT.

the adventure's text tells you so. That appendix also provides new action and trait options for the giants in the *Monster Manual*—options that you're free to use or ignore when running this adventure.

Spells and nonmagical objects or equipment mentioned in the adventure are described in the *Player's Handbook*. Magic items are described in the *Dungeon Master's Guide*, unless the adventure's text directs you to an item's description in appendix B.

## Adventure Synopsis

Figure 0.1 is a flowchart that illustrates the intended flow of the adventure. It also shows the level for which each chapter is designed.

The adventure begins with chapter 1. The adventurers arrive at the fortified village of Nightstone, shortly after a cloud giant attack. After securing the settlement, the characters locate several missing villagers in a monster-infested cave complex north of the village. The chapter concludes with the characters rescuing the villagers and gaining a quest that leads them to one of three locations: Bryn Shander, Goldenfields, or Triboar. Zephyros, a friendly cloud giant wizard, offers to transport them to their destination with the aid of his flying tower. En route, the characters fend off a group of evil air cultists as well as a Lords' Alliance strike team that mistakes Zephyros for a hostile threat. After delivering the characters to their intended destination, Zephyros bids the party farewell before taking his leave.

In chapter 2, the characters defend Bryn Shander, Goldenfields, or Triboar against a giant attack. Quests gained at the end of the battle prompt them to explore more of the Savage Frontier. The characters eventually cross paths with another friendly giant: a frost giant adventurer named Harshnag. These events are described in chapter 3.

In chapter 4, Harshnag leads the characters to a temple under the Spine of the World, wherein they consult a divine oracle. The oracle requires that the adventurers retrieve some lost relics buried under Uthgardt ancestral mounds scattered throughout the North. If the adventurers complete the oracle's quest, it tells them what must be done to end the giant threat. As the characters leave the temple for the last time, Iymrith appears and attacks them. Harshnag holds the ancient blue dragon at bay while the adventurers escape with or without the aid of mysterious dragon cultists and an airship.

Chapters 5 through 9 describe the lairs of five giant lords threatening the North. Players choose which giant lord they wish to confront. This villain has a *conch of teleportation* that the characters need to reach Maelstrom, a storm giant stronghold in the depths of the Trackless Sea. Chapter 10 describes the politically charged court of the storm giants and the challenges faced by its current ruler, Princess Serissa.

If the characters earn Serissa's trust, she tasks them with finding her father, King Hekaton. The search for Hekaton is handled in chapter 11. Once freed from captivity, he joins forces with the party to slay the dragon Iymrith in chapter 12. If Hekaton survives this final battle, he reclaims his throne. Otherwise, his daughter Serissa becomes queen. In either event, the storm gi-

ants forge an alliance with the small folk against the enemies of giantkind: dragons. This act might be enough to restore the ordning as it was, or the future of the ordning might remain an open question in your campaign.

Once Iymrith is defeated, the storm giants are happy to let the characters deal with the remaining evil giant lords as they see fit.

*Storm King's Thunder* is not a "ticking clock" adventure, meaning that the characters are under no pressure to end the giant threat quickly. The plots of the giant lords take months to unfold, giving the characters time to explore the North, travel from place to place, and entertain distractions.

Some players might feel a sense of urgency and stick to the main story line as much as possible, missing out on many elements of the adventure. Others might be willing to follow loose threads and stray from the main story, hoping to take the adventure in interesting new directions. The adventure allows for a fair amount of wandering. If you begin to think the party has wandered too far away from the main plot, you can use Harshnag (see chapter 3) to help steer characters back to the main story. You can also have the characters meet faction members (see the "Factions in the North" section) who can provide a sense of growing urgency and point characters in the right direction.

### Starting at 5th Level

You can begin the adventure with 5th-level characters by skipping over chapter 1 and starting in one of the three locations described in chapter 2. Appendix A suggests ways in which you can transition characters from the D&D *Starter Set* adventure or one of several other D&D adventures to chapter 2 of *Storm King's Thunder*.

### Character Advancement

Rather than have you track experience points, this adventure assumes that the characters gain levels by accomplishing certain goals. At the end of each chapter is a "Character Advancement" sidebar, which tells you the circumstances under which the characters advance in level. The adventure flowchart (figure 0.1) shows what level the characters are expected to be when they begin each chapter. Once they reach 9th level, they don't advance to 10th level until they've completed the goals in both chapters 10 and 11.

Of course, you can ignore these milestones and track XP as normal.

## Deadly Encounters

Many of the encounters in this adventure are deadly by design. They test the players' ability to make smart, informed decisions under pressure. A deadly encounter might be the only encounter the characters have on a given day (and assumes the party is at full strength), or it might be so overwhelming that the characters are expected to avoid combat at all costs.

A total-party kill ("TPK") need not herald the end of the campaign. Giants and other intelligent creatures are fond of taking prisoners. The first time a TPK occurs, you can have the characters miraculously awaken as prisoners with 1 hit point each. Give them every chance

# ADVENTURE FLOWCHART

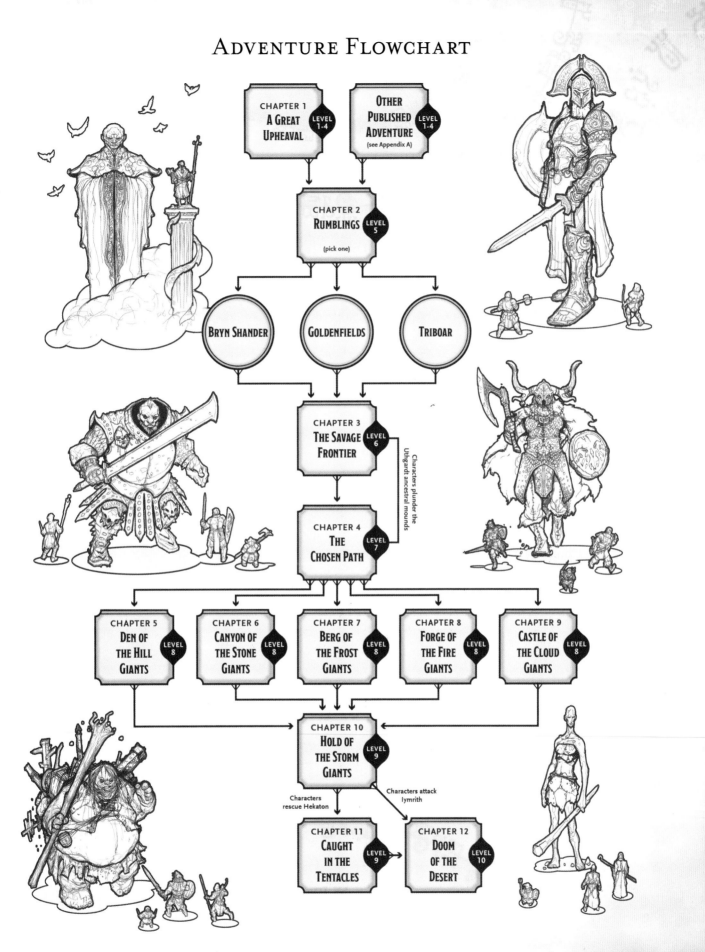

**CHAPTER 1**
**A GREAT UPHEAVAL** — LEVEL 1-4

**OTHER PUBLISHED ADVENTURE** — LEVEL 1-4
(see Appendix A)

**CHAPTER 2**
**RUMBLINGS** — LEVEL 5
(pick one)

**BRYN SHANDER**

**GOLDENFIELDS**

**TRIBOAR**

**CHAPTER 3**
**THE SAVAGE FRONTIER** — LEVEL 6

Characters plunder the Uthgardt ancestral mounds

**CHAPTER 4**
**THE CHOSEN PATH** — LEVEL 7

**CHAPTER 5**
**DEN OF THE HILL GIANTS** — LEVEL 8

**CHAPTER 6**
**CANYON OF THE STONE GIANTS** — LEVEL 8

**CHAPTER 7**
**BERG OF THE FROST GIANTS** — LEVEL 8

**CHAPTER 8**
**FORGE OF THE FIRE GIANTS** — LEVEL 8

**CHAPTER 9**
**CASTLE OF THE CLOUD GIANTS** — LEVEL 8

**CHAPTER 10**
**HOLD OF THE STORM GIANTS** — LEVEL 9

Characters rescue Hekaton

Characters attack Iymrith

**CHAPTER 11**
**CAUGHT IN THE TENTACLES** — LEVEL 9

**CHAPTER 12**
**DOOM OF THE DESERT** — LEVEL 10

FIGURE 0.2: ADVENTURE FLOWCHART

to escape their captors. If necessary, use NPCs such as Zephyros, the cloud giant wizard in chapter 1, to help them get out of tight spots. With luck, the players will take the hint and be wary of repeating the experience.

# Treasure

*Storm King's Thunder* contains a generous amount of treasure. This section provides guidance on how to handle certain kinds of treasure found in this adventure.

## Random Coin Amounts

The number of coins in a creature's hoard is often represented as a die expression with a multiplier. For example, a giant might have 3d6 × 100 gp in a sack. To determine the number of coins in the sack, roll 3d6 and multiply the result by 100 to get a number between 300 and 1,800. Instead of rolling to determine the number of coins, you can pick an amount that falls within the specified range. If the characters have more loot than they known what to do with, take the minimum. If they seem light on treasure, take the average (in this case, 1,000 gp) or the maximum.

## Random Magic Items

Sometimes a treasure hoard contains one or more magic items determined by rolling on the magic item treasure tables in chapter 7 of the *Dungeon Master's Guide*. When determining a random magic item, roll a d100 (or have a player roll for you) and consult the specified table in the *Dungeon Master's Guide*. If your players have a "wish list" of magic items, or you think a particular item might be useful to the party, you can forgo the roll and select an item from the table. For example, if the characters find a magic item tied to Magic Item Table B, and the party is light on water-breathing magic heading into chapter 10, you might decide that the item is a *potion of water breathing* or a *cloak of the manta ray*, both of which appear on Magic Item Table B in the *Dungeon Master's Guide*.

## Giant-Sized Treasures

Scattered throughout the adventure are art objects crafted to giant scale, including giant-sized pieces of jewelry, articles of clothing, and room decor. Although such art objects are often quite valuable, their size and weight make them difficult to transport. Characters must decide for themselves whether it's worth the trouble to carry these items. If the characters get greedy, use the variant encumbrance rules in the *Player's Handbook* to track what they can reasonably carry.

## Giants' Bags

In addition to treasure, giants often possess mundane items that they carry around in leather sacks or store in old chests. As the characters loot corpses and plunder giant hoards, throw in a few items chosen or rolled randomly from the Items in a Giant's Bag table. Items that are not giant-sized are sized for Small or Medium characters.

## Items in a Giant's Bag

| d100 | Item |
|---|---|
| 01–02 | Handaxe blade (used as a hand chopper) |
| 03–04 | Dented metal helm (used as a bowl) |
| 05–06 | Moldy and stinky wheel of cheese |
| 07–08 | Giant-sized shabby cloak (wool or hide) |
| 09–10 | Giant-sized bone comb |
| 11–12 | Iron cooking pot |
| 13–14 | Giant-sized drinking horn |
| 15–16 | Giant-sized skinning knife |
| 17–18 | Haunch of meat |
| 19–20 | Mangy fur pelt |
| 21–22 | Small bag of salt |
| 23–24 | Giant-sized pair of old sandals |
| 25–26 | Giant-sized waterskin (full) |
| 27–28 | Cask of ale (half empty) |
| 29–30 | Giant-sized necklace made of bones (hill), stone beads (stone), dragon fangs (frost), iron ingots (fire), feathers (cloud), or starfish (storm) |
| 31–32 | 5-foot length of chain |
| 33–34 | 1d6 Humanoid skulls |
| 35–36 | Bag of dried mushrooms |
| 37–38 | 50-foot coil of hempen rope |
| 39–40 | 3-foot-tall idol depicting Grolantor (hill), Skoraeus Stonebones (stone), Thrym (frost), Surtur (fire), Memnor (cloud), or Stronmaus (storm) |
| 41–42 | 1d6 dead trout |
| 43–44 | Dented steel shield |
| 45–46 | Wooden oar |
| 47–48 | Empty wooden barrel |
| 49–50 | 30-foot-long hempen rope tied to a wooden bucket |
| 51–52 | Bundled-up tent |
| 53–54 | Riding saddle |
| 55–56 | Stuffed animal |
| 57–58 | Live animal (chicken, goat, pig, or sheep) |
| 59–60 | 1d6 moldy loaves of bread |
| 61–62 | 6-foot-long wooden fence post |
| 63–64 | Wooden door with twisted iron hinges |
| 65–66 | Empty wooden chest (unlocked) |
| 67–68 | Rocking chair |
| 69–70 | Painted rocking horse or wooden toboggan |
| 71–72 | 1d6 dragon scales |
| 73–74 | Carved stone statue of a dwarf or human |
| 75–76 | Wooden mannequin or target dummy |
| 77–78 | Coffin or small casket |
| 79–80 | Cauldron or giant-sized kettle |
| 81–82 | Giant-sized smoking pipe |
| 83–84 | Bronze gong |
| 85–86 | Iron bell (with or without its clapper) |
| 87–88 | Beehive |
| 89–90 | Giant-sized drum |
| 91–92 | Carved wooden statue of an elf or halfling |
| 93–94 | Uprooted shrub or berry bush |
| 95–96 | 10-foot-long hempen rope tied to a rowboat anchor |
| 97–98 | Wagon wheel |
| 99–00 | Tombstone |

# CHAPTER 1: A GREAT UPHEAVAL

THIS CHAPTER IS DESIGNED TO ADVANCE A party of 1st-level characters to 5th level. The characters gain levels by accomplishing various goals, which are summarized in the Character Advancement sidebar at the end of the chapter. If the characters are already 5th level, skip ahead to chapter 2, "Rumblings," using the information in appendix A if the characters are transitioning from another published adventure to this one.

Nightstone is a fortified settlement located a few miles south of the Ardeep Forest, in the untamed hills between Waterdeep and Daggerford. A lonely wooden signpost, standing where the trail to Nightstone meets the High Road, points the way to the settlement.

Nightstone's closest neighbors are the elves of the Ardeep Forest. Hunters from Nightstone have incurred the elves' wrath on multiple occasions. However, elves are the least of the settlement's problems, as fledgling heroes who come to Nightstone in search of adventure quickly discover.

The characters are traveling to Nightstone for one or more of the following reasons:

- The characters have heard rumors of goblins terrorizing the settlement. The High Steward of Nightstone, Lady Velrosa Nandar, is a Waterdhavian noble. She is reportedly offering a reward to anyone willing and able to deal with the goblin threat.

- Nightstone is a popular retreat for wealthy nobles who wish to hunt in the Ardeep Forest. Adventurers can earn good money by offering their services as guards on a hunt.
- The residents of Nightstone have a longstanding and seemingly irreconcilable conflict with their northern neighbors, the elves of the Ardeep Forest. Lady Velrosa Nandar has been searching for skilled mediators to help resolve the dispute.
- The Nightstone Inn is renowned for its food and cozy guest rooms. The dwarf innkeeper, Morak Ur'gray, has a fondness for adventurers and a nose for lucrative adventuring opportunities.

You can create other adventure hooks using the information presented in this chapter about Nightstone.

When you and the players are ready to get underway, read:

> You've been traveling along the High Road for days. As evening approaches, you spot a wooden signpost next to a trail that heads north into the hills. Nailed to the post are three arrow-shaped signs. The two marked "Waterdeep" and "Daggerford" follow the High Road but point in opposite directions. The third, marked "Nightstone," beckons you to follow the trail. If memory serves, Nightstone is roughly ten miles up the trail.

# NIGHTSTONE

Read the following boxed text as the characters approach Nightstone. You can adjust the boxed text for the time of day or night when the party arrives.

> After following the trail for ten miles, you hear the ringing of a bell. The sound grows louder as Nightstone comes into view. A river flows around the settlement, forming a moat. The village itself is contained within a wooden palisade, beyond which you see a windmill, a tall steeple, and the high-pitched rooftops of several other buildings. Apart from the ringing of the bell, you detect no other activity in the village. The trail ends before a lowered drawbridge that spans the moat. Beyond the drawbridge, two stone watchtowers flank an open gap in the palisade.
>
> South of the village and surrounded by the river moat is a cone-shaped, flat-topped hill on which stands a stone keep enclosed by a wooden wall. The keep, which overlooks the village, has partially collapsed. A wooden bridge that once connected the keep to the village has also partially collapsed.

Nightstone got its name from a massive chunk of obsidian that once stood in the middle of the village square. The obsidian megalith had strange glyphs carved into it and radiated magic under the scrutiny of *detect magic* spells, but its properties and purpose couldn't be ascertained. The villagers assumed it was a relic of some bygone age or kingdom and left it alone.

Three days ago, a cloud giant castle passed over Nightstone and dropped large rocks on the settlement and its keep. Unable to defend themselves against the bombardment, villagers who weren't killed in the attack lowered the drawbridge and fled into the nearby hills, taking refuge in some caves. Once the village was abandoned, four cloud giants descended from the sky, uprooted the nightstone, and bore it back to their castle for further study, believing it to be an Ostorian artifact. The cloud castle then drifted away with its prize.

The villagers were surprised to find a clan of goblins and an allied pair of ogres lurking in the caves. The villagers were ambushed, captured, and brought before Hark, the goblin boss. Hark interrogated them, learned of the giant attack on Nightstone, and sent a band of goblins to plunder the abandoned village. Characters who capture and interrogate these goblins can learn where the villagers are located.

The following warning signs indicate that all is not well in Nightstone:

- The drawbridge (area 1) is lowered, and the perimeter watchtowers (area 2) are unguarded.
- The temple bell (area 5) won't stop ringing.
- The keep (area 14) and the bridge that connects it to the village (area 11) have partially collapsed.

Goblins are scouring the village for treasure. They have unwisely spread themselves thin, providing adven-

## NIGHTSTONE: GENERAL FEATURES

Nightstone is a motte-and-bailey fortification built on the Ardeep River. The settlement's general features are summarized here.

***Bailey.*** A 15-foot-high wooden palisade encloses the village bailey. The palisade's logs rise to sharpened points, and the gaps between the logs are sealed with tar. The palisade and its stone watchtowers (see area 2) can't be climbed without the aid of climbing gear or magic, such as a *spider climb* spell.

All the buildings in the village except the watchtowers are made of wood and have steep, shingled rooftops. Muddy paths connect them.

***Moat.*** Water from the river fills the moat to a depth of 15 feet. The moat is 30 feet wide, narrowing to a width of 20 feet under the drawbridge (area 1). The moat is home to schools of trout.

***Motte.*** The keep overlooking the village stands atop a constructed, funnel-shaped hill called a motte. The rocky slopes of the motte are covered with loose shale, and scaling these slopes without climbing gear requires a successful DC 20 Strength (Athletics) check.

Encircling the motte's keep is an 8-foot-high stone parapet with a 15-foot-high outer curtain wall made of thick wooden planks perforated with shuttered archer windows. The outer walls of the keep are made of smooth, tightly fitted stone bricks. The keep and the outer curtain wall can't be climbed without the aid of climbing gear or magic, such as a *spider climb* spell.

***Rocks.*** As the characters explore Nightstone, they see ample evidence of the giants' attack: rocks embedded in the earth, holes punched through rooftops, shattered wreckage, and dead villagers buried under piles of debris. The cloud giants' rocks are 3 feet in diameter and weigh 500 pounds each.

turers with an opportunity to pick them off one or two at a time. A goblin that is alone and outnumbered might try to flee if it takes damage, at your discretion. If possible, the goblin retreats to the temple (area 5). See the "Nightstone: General Features" sidebar for information about the settlement. Map 1.1 shows its layout. The sections that follow describe locations on that map.

## 1. DRAWBRIDGE

The drawbridge is lowered when the party first arrives. It is 20 feet long, 10 feet wide, and made of sturdy oak planks. Iron chains bolted to the drawbridge connect to winch mechanisms in the nearby watchtowers (area 2a).

### FOOTPRINTS

Characters who search the area west of the drawbridge see several humanoid tracks in the grass and dirt. A successful DC 15 Wisdom (Survival) check reveals that most of the tracks (made by several dozen fleeing villagers) lead north. A successful check also reveals smaller humanoid tracks (made by roughly a dozen goblins) heading from the north toward the drawbridge, as well as two sets of unusually large wolf tracks (made by the worgs in area 3) heading in the same direction.

## 2. WATCHTOWERS

Seven stone watchtowers stand along the village perimeter. Each tower is 20 feet tall, with a roof enclosed by

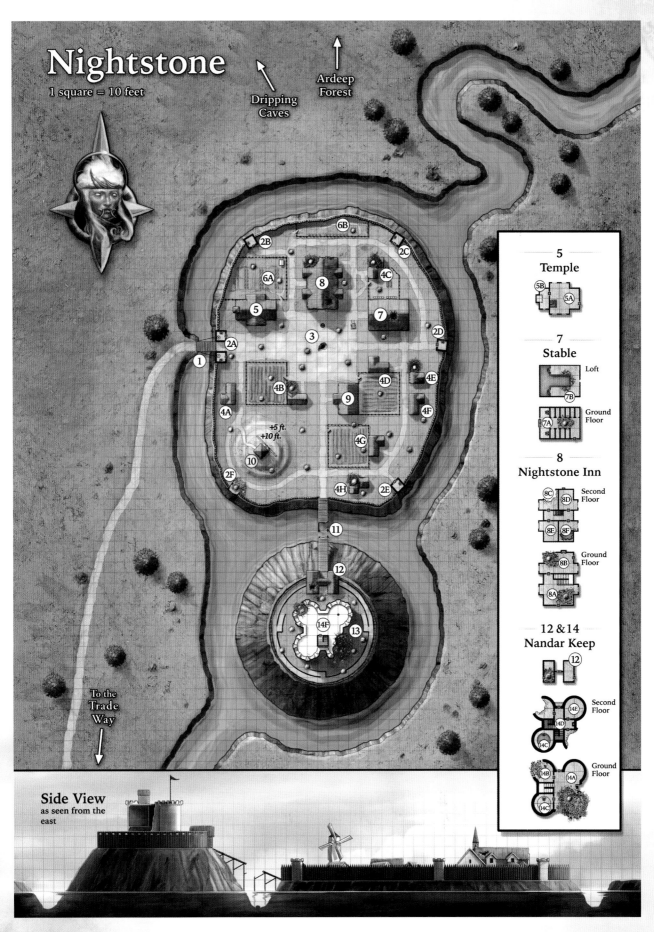

# Nightstone

1 square = 10 feet

Dripping Caves

Ardeep Forest

2B

6B

2C

6A

8

4C

5

7

2A

3

2D

1

4B

4D

4E

4A

9

4F

+5 ft.
+10 ft.

4G

10

2F

4H

2E

11

12

14F

13

To the
Trade
Way

### Side View
as seen from the east

Map 1.1: Nightstone

---

**5**
**Temple**

5B  5A

---

**7**
**Stable**

Loft

7B

7A  Ground Floor

---

**8**
**Nightstone Inn**

8C  8D  Second Floor

8E  8F

8B  Ground Floor

8A

---

**12 & 14**
**Nandar Keep**

12

14E  Second Floor

14D

14C

14B  14A  Ground Floor

14C

crenellated battlements. Inside each tower is a wooden ladder that leads to an unlocked trapdoor in the roof.

### 2A. WEST TOWERS

Two watchtowers flank the entrance to the village, forming a gatehouse of sorts. Each tower contains a winch, and both mechanisms must be turned to extend or retract the chains that raise and lower the drawbridge. If both winches are operated simultaneously, it takes 1 round to raise or lower the drawbridge by 30 degrees. In other words, the fully lowered drawbridge can be fully raised in 3 rounds.

### 2B. NORTHWEST TOWER

This watchtower stands between the village's two graveyards (areas 6a and 6b). It contains nothing of interest.

### 2C. NORTHEAST TOWER

Two pigs are chewing on some grass near the base of this tower. The pigs escaped from their pen (area 4c) and are harmless. The tower is empty.

### 2D. EAST TOWER

The door to this tower is ajar, and a greedy **goblin** named Gwerk lurks within. Gwerk stole a silver locket from a nearby residence (area 4e) and is quietly admiring it. She's afraid the other goblins might try to take it from her.

***Treasure.*** Gwerk's silver locket is shaped like a fish and contains a painted portrait of a rosy-cheeked male halfling named Larlow. The locket belongs to Larlow's widow, Taela Summerhawk, and is worth 25 gp. Taela is in the Dripping Caves (see area 4, map 1.2).

### 2E. SOUTHEAST TOWER

The door to this tower is ajar. Unless they are drawn to area 4g by sounds of combat, two **goblins** named Larv and Snokk are searching the tower for treasure.

***Treasure.*** Larv carries a sack filled with stolen utensils (worthless) and three vials of perfume (worth 5 gp each). Snokk carries a sack containing a stuffed blood hawk (worthless) and a battered copper flagon emblazoned with the grinning visage of a halfling (worth 1 gp).

### 2F. SOUTHWEST TOWER

A falling rock punched through the roof of this tower, collapsing everything but the outermost wall. A search of the debris unearths the broken remains of a ladder and a battered wooden door with broken hinges.

### 3. SQUARE

Two **worgs** slaughtered a dog and are feasting on its remains in the northeast corner of the village square. The worgs move to attack any characters who enter the square. The worgs fight to the death. If combat erupts in the square and the temple bell has been silenced, the goblins in areas 4c and 9 hear the noise and investigate. They stay on the fringes of the battlefield and shoot arrows at the characters.

The square is a muddy open area with a 5-foot-deep hole in the middle of it. The nightstone once stood here, but the cloud giants took the megalith and left the hole behind. North of the hole is a covered well. Other features of the village square include an empty wooden cart and a couple of tethering posts planted firmly in the ground. From the square, characters can see signs identifying the Nightstone Inn (area 8) and the Lionshield Coster trading post (area 9).

## 4. RESIDENCES

The village contains eight cottages, each one belonging to a different local family. Half of the homes were badly damaged during the cloud giants' bombardment.

A typical cottage has a 10-foot-square front room that serves as a kitchen and dining area, and a 10-foot-by-15-foot back room where the residents sleep.

### 4A. DELFRYNDEL RESIDENCE

This cottage belongs to the Delfryndels, a human family that owned and operated the windmill (area 10). The goblins have already rummaged through the residence, taking anything of value and leaving the interior in disarray.

### 4B. OSSTRA FARM

A giant rock destroyed the back room of the Osstra residence, and two more rocks are embedded in the garden where the family grew wheat. Goblins searched the home for treasure and dumped everything they didn't want onto the floor.

### 4C. SOUTHWELL FARM

This residence belonged to a middle-aged human woman named Semile Southwell, who raised pigs and chickens. Semile was killed when a rock fell on her house. Characters searching through the wreckage find Semile's crushed body.

A muddy fenced-in yard next to the Southwell residence contains wooden feeding troughs and chicken coops. Unless they are drawn to the village square by sounds of combat there, two **goblins** named Pojo and Tot are in the yard, chasing after a pair of chickens that escaped from one of the coops. The goblins attack characters on sight. If one is killed, the other flees.

***Treasure.*** Pojo has a pouch containing a gold ring (worth 25 gp), which he pulled from Semile Southwell's dead hand. Tot carries a pouch that holds 5 cp and a sack containing a live chicken.

### 4D. HULVAARN FARM

The Hulvaarns are human farmers, and their cottage backs onto a fenced-in potato and turnip garden. The cottage wasn't damaged during the cloud giants' bombardment, but a rock fell on the garden and killed Nestor Hulvaarn, the family patriarch, on impact. His crushed corpse is visible underneath the rock.

The cottage door hangs open. Goblins have already searched the interior for treasure, finding nothing of value but leaving the place in a shambles.

### 4E. SUMMERHAWK RESIDENCE

The Summerhawks, a family of halflings, lived here. Taela Summerhawk and her husband, Larlow, were apothecaries. They also grew flowers, as evidenced by the small flower gardens and many flowerpots around their home. When a rock fell on the front room of their house, Larlow was killed instantly. Taela managed to escape with their four children.

**Treasure.** Goblins have already searched the cottage, but characters who conduct their own search and succeed on a DC 15 Wisdom (Perception) check find a hidey-hole under a loose floorboard containing an herbalism kit, a vial of antitoxin, and a pouch containing 15 gp.

### 4F. AGGANOR RESIDENCE

This cottage belongs to Destiny Agganor, the village's tiefling midwife, and her adult son, Grin. The cottage has locked shutters over its windows. The door, which is also locked, has row upon row of ornate runes burned into it. Most villagers assume that the ornate runes are purely decorative, but any character who understands Infernal can translate the script as follows: "Let all who enter this home without the consent of its owner burn for ninety-nine years in the depths of Nessus and freeze for a thousand more in the icy wastes of Cania."

The goblins tried to enter the cottage but were thwarted by the locks. A character can use thieves' tools to pick the lock on the door or open a set of window shutters by succeeding on a DC 15 Dexterity check.

**Treasure.** A search of the cottage interior yields an unlocked wooden chest containing a golden holy symbol of Asmodeus (worth 75 gp), a healer's kit, and a *potion of healing*.

### 4G. NESPER FARM

Two **goblins** are dancing in the garden behind this cottage, which belongs to the Nespers, a human family of pumpkin and squash farmers. The goblins, Blik and Flik, are wearing eyeless, hollowed-out pumpkins on their heads and playing a game of blind tag. While wearing the pumpkins, the goblins are effectively blinded.

If combat erupts here, the goblins in area 2e hear the disturbance and investigate.

The goblins have already looted the Nesper cottage, the front door to which hangs open. The cottage, though undamaged, has been thoroughly ransacked.

**Treasure.** Blik carries a pouch that contains 4 cp and 3 sp. Lying in the southwest corner of the garden is Flik's sack of loot, which contains a tinderbox, a smoking pipe, a stuffed teddy bear, and boxed set of Three-Dragon Ante cards (worth 1 gp).

### 4H. XELBRIN RESIDENCE

The Xelbrins were an elderly human couple who moved to Nightstone from Waterdeep four years ago at Lady Nandar's request. Melantha Xelbrin served as the village's notary and record keeper. She and her husband, Lathan, were killed when the roof of their cottage collapsed. Rillix, their pet **tressym** (see appendix C), lurks amid the wreckage. If the characters take the time to explore the cottage, Rillix flies out of the shadows, possibly startling one or more of them, before finding someplace else to hide.

**Treasure.** The goblins haven't yet looted the Xelbrin residence. Characters searching the cottage find the dead bodies of Lathan and Melantha. A search of Melantha's desk also reveals evidence of her profession (wax seals, jars of ink, blank scrolls, quill pens, land owner-ship documents, and tax records), along with a money pouch containing 32 gp and 17 sp.

## 5. TEMPLE

This wooden temple is dedicated to Lathander (god of the dawn) and Mielikki (goddess of forests). It has a slender steeple containing a large bronze bell, and stained glass windows depicting images of birth, the dawning sun, trees, and unicorns. When the characters first arrive here, the front door to the temple is wide open and the bell is ringing incessantly.

### 5A. TEMPLE AND PULPIT

Sunlight or moonlight pours into this high-vaulted chamber through four stained-glass windows set into the north and south walls. Beneath the windows are plain wooden benches for the elderly or infirm to sit on. The room is mostly empty otherwise. Standing against the back wall is a wooden pulpit with steps leading up to it. The floor of the temple is composed of dirt.

Set into the west wall, north of the pulpit, is a half-open door, beyond which lies area 5b.

### 5B. BEDROOM AND STEEPLE

This back room contains a plain wooden bed where Hiral Mystrum, the village's acolyte of Lathander, slept. The mattress has been torn open and its straw pulled out. The floor is strewn with the contents of two wooden chests: priestly vestments and worthless personal effects. The creatures responsible for the disarray are two **goblins** named Beedo and Vark.

The goblins are gleefully swinging on a knotted rope that hangs from the bell in the steeple. The sound of the bell delights the goblins, and they won't stop ringing it until they perceive some threat to their well-being. If the characters enter the room, the goblins drop from the rope, brandish their scimitars, and attack.

**Treasure.** Each goblin has a sack lying on the steeple floor. Beedo's sack contains three blocks of incense (worth 5 gp each), a silver holy symbol of Mielikki shaped like a unicorn's head (worth 25 gp), and some stolen (and worthless) personal effects. Vark's sack holds three empty vials that used to contain holy water (Vark drank them) and an unlocked wooden "poor box" containing 37 cp and 15 sp.

## 6. GRAVEYARDS

Most of the villagers who perished since the founding of Nightstone are interred in these two graveyards. Almost half of them died when wood elves attacked the village five years ago (see "The Nandars of Nightstone" sidebar).

### 6A. NANDAR CRYPT AND GRAVEYARD

Narrow footpaths meander among the graves, most of which are marked with granite headstones. A couple of these markers were destroyed when a giant rock fell on them.

In the northeast corner stands an aboveground crypt with the name Nandar engraved over its sealed entrance. Cracking the door seal requires a crowbar or similar tool and a successful DC 11 Strength (Athletics) check.

The Nandar crypt contains a stone bier, upon which rests a wooden coffin. The coffin can easily be pried open and holds the skeletal remains and tattered burial shroud of Lord Drezlin Nandar, the village's founder, who died one year ago. Neither the coffin nor the crypt contains anything of value. If one or more characters remove any of Lord Nandar's bones from the crypt, a **specter** forms in the crypt and attacks them. The specter can't leave the graveyard and disappears when reduced to 0 hit points or when it has no enemies it can attack.

### 6B. NORTH GRAVEYARD

This graveyard was created when the one next to the temple ran out of space. It contains nothing of interest.

## 7. STABLE HOUSE

The Nandar family (see "The Nandars of Nightstone" sidebar later in the chapter) procured horses for the village and kept them in this stable house. The panicked villagers left the horses behind after a rock punched through the stable house roof. Fortunately, none of the horses were harmed.

### 7A. BARN

The barn has a dirt floor. Five draft horses and five riding horses are confined to the wooden stalls that line the north and south walls. Hanging on the walls are bits, bridles, and leather saddles. Two wooden ladders allow easy access to the hayloft (area 7b).

Characters who enter the barn are attacked by the goblin hiding in the loft.

### 7B. HAYLOFT

The loft is filled with haystacks and sacks of oats. A **goblin** named Derp is searching the loft for treasure. If he detects enemies in the barn, Derp takes cover behind a haystack and shoots arrows at enemies below, drawing his scimitar only when forced into melee combat.

***Treasure.*** Derp carries a coin pouch that holds 1 cp and a sack containing a wooden box engraved with the symbol of the Lionshield Coster (see area 9). Derp stole the box from the store, and packed inside it are ten silvered darts.

## 8. NIGHTSTONE INN

A shield dwarf named Morak Ur'gray owns this establishment. An ornate wrought-iron sign bearing the inn's name hangs above the entrance, facing the town square.

Morak is a natural leader. Realizing that the village couldn't defend itself against the cloud giants' bombardment, he led his fellow villagers to the Dripping Caves. In the confusion and panic, Morak left behind his only guest at the time: Kella Darkhope, a Zhentarim spy posing as a traveling monk. Kella has nefarious plans for Nightstone and has no intention of abandoning the settlement (see area 8f for details).

### 8A. DINING ROOM

This room is strewn with wreckage. A giants' rock punched through the roof and landed here, destroying a dining table and a pair of long benches. The remains of a bed and a wardrobe (from the chamber above) lie among the shattered dining room furnishings. Two smaller round tables and several chairs remain intact, and resting atop each table is an unlit oil lamp. Characters exploring this room can hear someone rummaging through the kitchen (area 8b).

Lying on the floor in the middle of the room is a dead goblin with a crossbow bolt sticking out of its chest. The goblin fell prey to Kella Darkhope, who is spying on the room through the gaping hole in her bedroom floor (see area 8f). A character who inspects the corpse and succeeds on a DC 10 Wisdom (Medicine) check can determine that the wound is fresh, indicating that the goblin has been dead only a few minutes. If the characters linger here, Kella tries to eavesdrop on their conversation and learn more about them without revealing her location. Any character who peers up through the hole in the ceiling can spot Kella lurking in the shadows with a successful Wisdom (Perception) check contested by Kella's Dexterity (Stealth) check.

### 8B. KITCHEN AND PANTRY

A **goblin** named Gum-Gum is searching through the rubble of the inn's pantry and stuffing edibles into a large sack that's almost too heavy for her to drag, let alone carry. The northwest corner of the inn (pantry included) was destroyed by a falling rock. Most of the kitchen, however, was undamaged. Set into the north wall is a stone fireplace, and the floor is covered with broken dishware and scattered utensils.

If one or more characters confront Gum-Gum, she tries to flee with her hard-won loot. While dragging the heavily laden sack behind her, Gum-Gum suffers a 10-foot reduction to her speed.

***Treasure.*** Gum-Gum's sack contains several muffins, a block of cheese, a cooked chicken, a frying pan, an iron pot, a bullseye lantern, two flasks of oil, a set of cook's utensils, a jar of cloves (worth 1 sp), a jar of saffron (worth 1 gp), a dented silver jug (worth 20 gp), and a cracked hourglass (worth 25 gp if repaired).

### 8C. MORAK'S BEDROOM

Most of the furnishings in Morak's room were destroyed when a rock flattened the northwest corner of the inn. Hanging on the east wall is a tapestry depicting a mountain landscape, and tucked under the window in the southeast corner is a locked wooden chest. What remains of the floor is safe to walk on.

***Treasure.*** A character can attempt to unlock the iron chest using thieves' tools, but the built-in lock is tricky and requires a successful DC 20 Dexterity check to open. The chest contains a suit of chain mail sized for a dwarf, a dwarven helm, a leather bag that holds 45 gp and two 100 gp gemstones, and a *potion of heroism*.

### 8D. GUEST BEDROOM

This vacant bedroom contains two beds, an empty wardrobe, a desk, and a matching chair. An oil lamp sits on one corner of the desk, and another rests on a small table tucked between the two beds. A bearskin rug lies on the floor.

### 8e. Guest Bedroom

This room is similar in all respects to area 8d.

### 8f. Kella's Bedroom

Kella Darkhope, a Zhentarim **spy** (NE female human), lurks in the shadows of this room—or what's left of it. A falling rock punched a hole in the roof and tore away most of the floor before coming to rest in the dining room (area 8a). It destroyed two beds and a wardrobe as it passed through the chamber, leaving a desk and chair tucked under the window in the northeast corner of the room unscathed.

Kella infiltrated Nightstone in the guise of a traveling monk and is waiting for Zhentarim reinforcements to arrive (see the "Seven Snakes" section). She had nothing to do with the cloud giant attack, but she intends to take over the village and turn it into a Black Network base. Her original plan was to drive away the Lionshield Coster and bully Lady Velrosa Nandar into subservience, but the cloud giant attack has left the abandoned village ripe for conquest while leaving its defenses more or less intact.

Kella isn't alone. The morning after the cloud giants attacked, a **flying snake** carrying a message from her Zhent associates arrived. The snake belongs to Xolkin Alassandar (see the "Seven Snakes" section), and it now coils around Kella's left arm. Its message is scrawled in Common on a strip of parchment in Kella's possession. The message reads, "On our way."

***Treasure.*** In addition to her weapons and armor, Kella has a pouch containing 8 gp and 5 sp.

***Development.*** Kella tries to remain hidden until the Seven Snakes arrive. If discovered, she pretends to be a guest who was knocked unconscious by falling debris and left behind after the giant attack. She claims that her escape was thwarted by the sudden arrival of the goblins, whom she believes have nothing to do with the giants. Characters can see through her ruse with a successful Wisdom (Insight) check contested by Kella's Charisma (Deception) check. Any character who belongs to the Zhentarim recognizes the flying snake as a symbol of that faction. Kella claims it is merely her pet.

## 9. Trading Post

Mounted above this building's entrance is a circular blue shield emblazoned with a stylized golden lion: the symbol of the Lionshield Coster, a trading company. The door to the trading post hangs open, and characters can hear a ruckus within.

The trading post consists of a 20-foot-square store and a 10-foot-by-20-foot side room containing storage shelves and a cot. The store's proprietor was a Tethyrian human named Darthag Ulgar. He escaped the giant attack but didn't survive long as a prisoner of the goblins (see the "Dripping Caves" section for details).

A **goblin** named Jilk is rummaging through the store's contents and stuffing choice items into a backpack. He fights to the death if cornered here.

KELLA DARKHOPE

***Treasure.*** During their initial search, the goblins pulled almost everything off the shelves and broke many of the store's for-sale items, including bottles, lamps, ink jars, spice jars, and crockery. Nevertheless, many items remain intact. Characters who search the trading post can find anything on the Adventuring Gear table in chapter 5 of the *Player's Handbook* that is worth 10 gp or less. Roll a d4 to determine how many of each available item can be found.

## 10. Windmill

Nightstone's windmill stands atop a 10-foot-high grassy hill. Two sets of goblin tracks are clearly visible in the muddy path that leads up the hill to an open doorway in the northwest side of the windmill.

The windmill's interior is dark, gloomy, and filled with wooden gears and cogs that help turn the millstone. Two **goblins** named Longo and Yek are climbing among the rafters near the roof, roughly 25 feet above the floor. They heckle intruders and shoot arrows at them while enjoying half cover against ranged attacks made from below.

***Treasure.*** Longo and Yek are more interested in having fun than searching for treasure. They each carry a pouch that holds 1d6 cp.

## 11. Bridge

A 70-foot-long, 10-foot-wide sloped bridge used to connect the village bailey to the motte. However, a falling rock struck the bridge and destroyed a 15-foot-long section of it, cutting off Nandar Keep from the village.

A creature with a Strength score of 15 or higher can leap across the broken section of the bridge if it moves at least 10 feet before the jump. The jump is made more difficult by the fact that the bridge is sloped:

- A creature jumping from the lower part of the bridge to the higher part must succeed on a DC 10 Strength (Athletics) check to land on its feet. On a failed check, the creature falls prone at the broken edge of the bridge and takes 2 (1d4) bludgeoning damage from the fall.
- A creature jumping from the higher part of thc bridge to the lower part must succeed on a DC 10 Dexterity (Acrobatics) check to land on its feet. On a failed check, the creature tumbles to the bottom of the bridge, landing prone and taking 5 (2d4) bludgeoning damage from the fall.

## 12. GATE TO THE KEEP

Set into the motte's curtain wall are two windowless stone gatehouses with wood-shingled, high-pitched rooftops. Between them stands a set of oak doors with iron hinges. The doors can be barred shut from within, but they aren't barred when the characters first arrive. Characters can push open the doors to gain access to Nandar Keep and its bailey.

### GATEHOUSES

The gatehouses are set aside as guard barracks. The east building contains six bunk beds (twelve beds in all) and a dozen footlockers containing worthless personal effects. The west building was similarly furnished, but a falling rock destroyed half the building's contents. Characters searching the damaged gatehouse find the bodies of three human guards who died when the roof fell on them.

## 13. INNER BAILEY

The cloud giants heavily bombarded the keep, and the inner bailey is strewn with rocks. Ramps lead up to the 8-foot-high stone parapet that encircles the yard. No guards are currently standing watch on the walls.

---

### THF NANDARS OF NIGHTSTONE

The beauty of Ardeep Forest and the mystique of its elven ruins have long attracted nobles from Waterdeep. The nobles of House Nandar had a hunting lodge in the forest two centuries ago, but elves forced them to abandon it. Ten years ago, members of House Nandar—Lord Drezlin Nandar and Lady Velrosa Nandar—decided it was time to return. They built a new motte-and-bailey settlement south of the Ardeep Forest and began making forays into the woods with friends to hunt and explore. Unknown to the Nandars, wood elves from Evermeet then settled in the forest, determined to protect the remnants of old elf empires from plunder and desecration. As in the past, the interests of the elves and Nandars were at cross purposes. A year ago, the conflict came to a head, and the elves attacked Nightstone. Drezlin was among the many slain—shot and killed by elf arrows while standing on the roof of his keep. His widow, Lady Velrosa Nandar, made peace with the elves and promised to make no further incursions into the Ardeep Forest—a promise she kept for the rest of her life. Velrosa was mortally wounded when the cloud giants bombarded Nightstone, leaving the village without a lord or lady to govern it.

---

A search of the bailey yields the corpses of two dead human guards, both of whom were struck and killed by falling rocks.

Characters can enter the keep through the front door, or they can climb over rubble and enter the keep through one of its shattered walls. Treat rubble-filled areas as difficult terrain.

## 14. NANDAR KEEP

The cloud giant attack left Nandar Keep in a sorry state and also claimed the life of Lady Velrosa Nandar, the High Steward of Nightstone. She was buried under rubble and died from her wounds before the castle guards could reach her. The few guards who remain are demoralized, in shock, and at each other's throats.

### 14A. GREAT HALL

Half of the great hall lies buried under rubble. Four **guards** (NG male and female humans) have placed the body of Lady Velrosa Nandar atop the shattered remains of an oak dining table and are arguing about next steps. The guards' names are Sydiri Haunlar, Torem Breck, Alara Winterspell, and Kaelen Zam. No strong leader stands among them, so they turn to the characters for guidance and leadership. If the characters question the guards about what happened, they share the following information:

- Nightstone was bombarded by rocks dropped from a giant castle in the sky. The keep was cut off from the village when a rock tore away part of the bridge.
- With nowhere to hide, the people in the village lowered the drawbridge and fled north. In the event of an attack, the villagers are supposed to retreat to the keep; with the bridge out, that was no longer an option.
- North of Nightstone, about a mile away, are some bat caves. The villagers probably hid there.
- Several guards stationed in the village fled north with the villagers.
- Once the villagers had fled, four pale-skinned giants descended from the sky, uprooted the nightstone in the village square, and took it back to their castle. The cloud castle left soon thereafter, drifting eastward.
- Lady Nandar was in the great hall when the roof collapsed. She was buried under the rubble and died before anyone could reach her.

The great hall once served as a throne room and a dining room. Doors in the west wall lead to the kitchen (area 14b) and den (area 14c). Between these doors is a wooden staircase leading up to the second floor (area 14d).

***Treasure.*** Lady Nandar wears a gold wedding ring set with tourmalines on the third finger of her left hand. The ring is nonmagical and worth 750 gp. The keep guards strongly object to anyone attempting to take the ring.

### 14B. KITCHEN

This room is buried under rubble.

## 14c. Den and Library

This corner room consists of two levels. The lower level is the den. It is decorated with overstuffed chairs and bearskin rugs, and the walls are adorned with weapons, shields, and the mounted heads of wild animals. A decorative wooden ladder leads to a 20-foot-high circular balcony with a sculpted wooden railing. The upper level is a library, and its walls are lined with bookshelves. Lord Drezlin Nandar and his hunting companions used the den as a place to relax and tell stories, while Lady Velrosa Nandar used the library to store her collection of books on philosophy, nature, and poetry.

While the contents of this room held great sentimental value to the Nandars, there's nothing particularly valuable to be found here.

## 14d. Upstairs Hall

This L-shaped hall is decorated with rich carpets, gilded sconces, and framed paintings of places in Waterdeep. A door at the north end of the hall leads to a stone balcony overlooking the entrance to the keep. Other doors lead to bedchambers, two of which have been destroyed. A wooden staircase in the west wall descends to the main floor. A similar staircase in the south wall climbs to the roof.

## 14e. Master Bedroom

This room is the only one of three bedchambers to survive the cloud giants' attack. Tapestries and oil lamps are mounted on the walls, and wolfskin rugs cover the wooden floor. The room's centerpiece is a large bed, its ornate headboard sculpted with images of roses and foxes. Four wardrobes stand against the walls; each contains a season's worth of women's clothing, all in the latest fashions of Waterdeep. At the foot of the bed is an unlocked wooden chest.

Mounted above the door is a longsword. This weapon is actually a **flying sword** that attacks anyone who opens the chest. (Only Lady Nandar was able to open the chest without causing the sword to attack.) The guards in area 14A try to prevent anyone from looting the contents of the chest.

***Treasure.*** The interior of the wooden chest is divided into small compartments. A thorough search yields a velvet sack containing 180 sp (money used to pay the guards), a silk pouch containing four 100 gp gemstones, and a silver jewelry box (worth 25 gp) containing three beautiful gold necklaces (worth 250 gp each).

## 14f. Roof

Falling rocks caused sections of the roof to collapse, but what remains of the roof is safe to walk on. A flag waves in the breeze atop a 30-foot-high wooden flagpole that rises from the northeast corner. The flag depicts the stylized head of a golden fox with a rose clenched in its teeth, on a purple background.

# SPECIAL EVENTS IN NIGHTSTONE

The following special events can occur while the characters are in Nightstone. Ideally, the characters are 2nd level before either event occurs.

XOLKIN ALASSANDAR

## SEVEN SNAKES

This event takes place after the characters rid Nightstone of its goblin infestation but before they have time to finish a long rest.

Seven Zhentarim mercenaries arrive at the village on horseback. If the drawbridge is lowered, they ride to the square and call out for Kella Darkhope. If the characters raised the drawbridge, the Zhents call out for someone to lower it. If she's still alive, Kella tries to let them in.

The leader of the new arrivals is Xolkin Alassandar (LE male half-elf **bandit captain**), a charming, ruthless man in his mid-thirties. He and his six subordinates (LE male and female human **bandits**) are mounted on seven **riding horses**. Known as the Seven Snakes, Xolkin's band does "dirty work" for the Snail, a Zhent leader based in Daggerford (see the "Daggerford" section in chapter 3). Their current mission is to help Kella Darkhope turn Nightstone into a base for the Black Network. The settlement's defensibility and its proximity to Waterdeep make it ideal for Zhentarim operations. The Seven Snakes had planned to infiltrate the village posing as bounty hunters in search of a wanted criminal (Kella), but they drop the ruse once it becomes apparent that the village is mostly abandoned.

Xolkin is in love with Kella and would do just about anything for her, even though he knows that she doesn't feel the same way about him. If Kella is a prisoner, Xolkin tries to buy her freedom (see "Treasure"). Failing that, he tries to liberate her by force. If Kella wormed her way into the characters' good graces, she reveals her allegiance to the Zhentarim once the Seven Snakes are close enough to protect her. If the party includes one or more characters with strong ties to the Black Network, Kella tries to convince them to help secure the village as a Zhentarim base.

If the characters do nothing to oppose the Zhent mercenaries, Xolkin orders his men to raise the drawbridge while he uses his flying snake to send a message to the Snail, letting him know that the village is under the Black Network's control. If the characters killed Xolkin's flying snake, Xolkin orders one of his mercs to ride to Daggerford and report the news while the others "hold down the fort." If combat erupts, Xolkin drinks his *potion of invulnerability* before leaping into the fray.

The Zhents have no easy way to reach the keep and ignore it for the time being. That said, if the Zhents learn that some of Lady Nandar's guards are holed up in the keep, they urge friendly characters to dispose of the guards. Similarly, if the characters are on friendly terms with the guards in the keep, the guards ask the characters to save the village from Zhentarim occupation.

The characters are under no obligation to rid Nightstone of Kella Darkhope and the Seven Snakes. If they defeat the Zhents or come to terms with them, allow the characters to take a long rest, if they wish, before continuing with the "Ear Seekers" event.

**Treasure.** Xolkin wears a gold ring (worth 25 gp) emblazoned with the symbol of the Zhentarim: a black winged serpent. He also carries a pouch that holds 4 pp, 13 gp, five 100 gp gemstones that he willingly trades for Kella's life, and a *potion of invulnerability*.

Each of the other mercenaries carries a pouch that holds 2d10 gp.

## EAR SEEKERS

The wood elves of the Ardeep Forest are at war with a neighboring band of orcs called the Ear Seekers (so named because they wear necklaces made of elf ears). Gurrash, the orc leader, recently led an attack on the forest. Unfortunately for the orcs, the elves were ready for them. More than half of the orc band perished, and the surviving orcs were forced to flee. Gurrash and several orcs escape out of the forest, make their way south, and stumble upon Nightstone. Knowing that the elves aren't far behind, Gurrash and his orcs try to fight their way into the village and make a stand there.

Gurrash, the **orc war chief**, is bleeding from wounds inflicted by elven arrows and has 60 hit points remaining. He leads a force consisting of twenty uninjured **orcs** and an uninjured **orc Eye of Gruumsh** named Norgra One-Eye. Norgra is Gurrash's lieutenant and assumes command if Gurrash dies.

The orcs have no gear other than their weapons and armor. If the drawbridge is lowered, they rush toward it and try to storm the village. If the drawbridge is raised, the orcs swim across the moat and try to climb the palisade, with no success. After being thwarted by the palisade, Gurrash sends scouts downriver to find another point of entry. It takes these orcs 10 minutes to realize that they can enter the village through the gap in the palisade where the bridge (area 11) leads up to the keep. Once the orcs enter the village, they fight to the death and don't take prisoners. Because the orcs don't know what they're up against, characters can try to hide in the village and pick off a few orcs at a time. They can also retreat to the keep, which the orcs ignore.

If the orcs lose more than half their number without gaining a foothold in the village, the survivors flee into the surrounding hills. Once the orcs are defeated, the characters can advance to 3rd level and head to the Dripping Caves to locate and retrieve the missing villagers. If they're not sure where the villagers went, Kella Darkhope or the guards in the keep can point them in the right direction.

**Strange Bedfellows.** If the characters came to terms with the Black Network in the previous event and the Seven Snakes are still around when the orcs arrive, the Zhents help the party defend Nightstone. Xolkin and Kella aren't heroes and don't place themselves in unnecessary danger, but they are quick to raise the drawbridge or position defenders on the watchtowers as needed. Knowing that orcs are devastating melee combatants, the Zhents favor ranged attacks and try to keep the orcs at a distance.

**Elves to the Rescue!** If the characters are in danger of being overwhelmed by Gurrash's orcs, eight elves of the Ardeep Forest (CN male and female wood elf **scouts**) arrive from the north to assist them. The leader of this band is a daring wood elf named Rond Arrowhome. He and his fellow elves have no love or respect for the residents of Nightstone, but they dislike orcs more. Once the orcs are defeated, Rond yells out, "You're welcome!" before leading the elves back to the Ardeep Forest. The elves aren't looking to pick a fight or mend fences with Nightstone's inhabitants, and they aren't interested in any kind of reward.

# DRIPPING CAVES

The hills around Nightstone are riddled with caves. The villagers hid in the Dripping Caves, located a mile north of Nightstone, after the cloud giant attack. Characters who follow the villagers' tracks or are given directions discover a gaping cave mouth on the south face of a rocky hill topped with pine trees. Characters who use this entrance arrive in area 1 of the Dripping Caves.

If the characters take an hour to circle the hill, they find two other entrances. At the base of the hill, on the west side, is a narrow tunnel into which a stream flows. This tunnel is 40 feet long and leads to area 6. On the east side of the hill is a dry, 100-foot-long tunnel that gently slopes down to area 3a.

If the characters climb to the top of the hill and look around for other possible entrances, they find a natural chimney (a 5-foot-diameter shaft) that descends 50 feet to area 7. The chimney has abundant handholds and can be climbed with a successful DC 10 Strength (Athletics) check. No ability check is required if the characters use a rope or climbing gear.

A goblin clan driven from the Ardeep Forest by wood elves took refuge in the Dripping Caves a little over a month ago. A week later, while scouring the hills for food, they befriended a mated pair of ogres and lured them to the caves for protection. The goblins and ogres captured the Nightstone refugees and have started eating the villagers. Prisoners that the goblins haven't eaten are doomed to meet a similar fate unless the adventurers intervene.

1 square = 5 feet

MAP 1.2: DRIPPING CAVES

Hark, the goblin boss, isn't an unreasonable creature. His instincts for self-preservation outweigh any natural animosity he feels toward his enemies or his prey. Characters can negotiate with Hark and avoid unnecessary bloodshed (see area 9), or they can kill Hark and his followers to win the villagers' freedom—the choice is theirs.

The characters should be 3rd level by the time they set foot in the Dripping Caves. Map 1.2 shows the caves' layout. The sections that follow describe locations on that map.

---

### DRIPPING CAVES: GENERAL FEATURES

The Dripping Caves are naturally formed and have the following features in common.

**Darkness.** The Dripping Caves contain no light sources. The goblins and ogres rely on their darkvision to see.

**Dripping Water.** The caves get their name from the water that constantly drips from the stalactites in the main cavern (area 1). The sound of dripping water echoes throughout the complex but isn't loud enough to drown out other distinctive noises.

**Narrow Tunnels.** The tunnels leading away from the main cavern (area 1) are 7 to 8 feet high and range in width from 2 to 5 feet. Ogres and other Large creatures can squeeze through these passages, but they suffer the normal penalties for doing so (see the "Squeezing into a Smaller Space" section in chapter 9 of the *Player's Handbook*).

**Walls.** The walls are damp and slick, but thanks to an abundance of handholds and footholds, they can be climbed with a successful DC 10 Strength (Athletics) check.

---

## 1. MAIN CAVERN

Characters who follow the villagers' tracks arrive at a yawning cave mouth, 12 feet wide and 20 feet high. Beyond the cave mouth is a vast cavern with a forest of stalagmites in its center and 10-foot-high ledges along its walls. Water drips from the stalactite-covered ceiling, which rises to a height of 30 feet in the middle of the cavern. Six naturally formed tunnels lead from this central cavern to other parts of the cave complex. The floor is littered with broken spears, broken shields, and drops of bat guano.

Characters who peer into the cave can see a male ogre bathing in a pool of mud (see area 1b). Those with darkvision can also see one or more goblin sentries on ledges (see area 1a). If the characters are carrying light sources or making a lot of noise, the creatures in areas 1a, 1b, and 1c detect them and attack.

### 1A. LEDGES

Ten-foot-high ledges of rock have formed along the walls of the cavern. Climbing up to a ledge or safely descending from one requires a successful DC 10 Strength (Athletics) check.

Five **goblins** stand guard on the ledges—one on each ledge marked with a "1a" tag on the map. Their names are Gleek, Lop, Nitch, Pox, and Slibberdabber. When they detect intruders, the goblins cry out "Bree-yark!" and begin shooting arrows. Their cries of alarm put the rest of the cave complex on alert, but no reinforcements arrive.

### 1b. Hot Mud Bath

A male **ogre** named Nob bathes in a 5-foot-deep pool of hot mud near the cave entrance. The pool is heated by a natural vent that keeps the temperature of the mud around 90 degrees Fahrenheit. Nob doesn't carry any javelins but keeps his greatclub in the pool with him. The mud pool is considered difficult terrain.

Nob and his mate (see area 1c) work for Boss Hark, who browbeats them into service with his superior intellect and nasty disposition. Nob tries to crush enemies with his greatclub. If his enemies try to flee, Nob and his mate chase after them.

### 1c. Stalagmite Forest

A cluster of stalagmites has formed in the middle of the cavern. The stalagmites range in height from 3 to 15 feet. In the middle of the stalagmite "forest" is a clear space. The ogres have turned this space into a den, and a female **ogre** named Thog is sleeping here when the characters first arrive. She awakens to sounds of combat or cries of alarm, and either hurls javelins or wades into battle with her greatclub. A search of the ogres' den yields nothing of value.

### 1d. Polluted Pool

A shallow pool has formed against the northeast wall of the cavern, the floor of which is lower here. Runoff from the pool trickles eastward into area 4. The water is polluted with toxic minerals and is unfit for drinking.

## 2. Goblin Warrens

A tunnel that the ogres find uncomfortably narrow leads to a cramped network of caves where the weakest members of the goblin tribe live. These goblins cower in their dens and avoid getting into fights with armed adventurers. If threatened, they cry and beg for mercy. Each has AC 10, 1 hit point, and no effective attacks.

### 2a. Sleeping Caves

Six of these caves are marked on the Dripping Caves map, and each one contains 1d6 goblin noncombatants. The floor in each cave is covered with a grass pallet on which the goblins sleep. Apart from a few rusty pots, odd tools, and goblin toys, the sleeping caves contain nothing of value.

### 2b. Cave of Bones

The goblins discard the bones of the creatures they devour here. The floor of the cave is littered with the bones of small animals (mostly bats) and a few unlucky Humanoids, including some recently eaten villagers. A search of the area yields no treasure.

## 3. East Caves

After a few unfortunate run-ins with the monster in area 3a, the goblins avoid this tunnel. The goblins refer to the monster as the Blob.

### 3a. The Blob

Stalactites and stalagmites crowd this 20-foot-high, 15-foot-wide cave. Rising up from the middle of the floor is a particularly large (10-foot-tall) stalagmite riddled with 4-inch-wide, 12-inch-deep naturally formed holes that bore down into a hollow central cavity. Lying near the base of the stalagmite are the badly corroded remains of two goblin scimitars.

A **black pudding** has taken residence inside the stalagmite's hollow core, and the holes in the stalagmite's "shell" are wide enough that a character can stick an arm, a staff, or a weapon into any one of them. The pudding makes a free pseudopod attack against anything that is inserted into one of the stalagmite's holes.

The pudding has total cover while inside the stalagmite's core. If left undisturbed, the pudding remains inside the stalagmite until the characters make their way toward area 3b, whereupon it quietly emerges and follows them. Once the characters are trapped in area 3b, the pudding attacks.

***East Tunnel.*** This 5-foot-wide, 7-foot-high tunnel slopes gently upward as it travels east. After 100 feet, it breaks through the east side of the hill.

### 3b. Water Supply

A small waterfall pouring from the 8-foot-high ceiling forms a 5-foot-deep pool at the southwest end of the cave. The goblins used to come here to drink fresh water, but they stopped visiting the cave when the black pudding in area 3a started picking them off.

Growing near the southeast wall is a patch of twenty green mushrooms. A character who inspects the mushrooms and succeeds on a DC 10 Intelligence (Nature) check can ascertain that they are poisonous. Any creature that ingests a mushroom must succeed on a DC 10 Constitution saving throw or take 1 poison damage and be poisoned for 1 hour. The effects of eating multiple mushrooms are cumulative.

## 4. Bats and Prisoners

A short tunnel leads to a sunken cavern that echoes with the sound of flapping wings. The sound emanates from a naturally formed pit in the cavern's floor, which is covered with bat guano. Ten-foot-high ledges surround the pit and form raised alcoves to the north, east, and south. Huddled in these alcoves are thirty Nightstone villagers. The villagers are prisoners of the goblins and ogres, and they are trying to remain as quiet as possible for reasons that might not be readily apparent to the characters.

Directly below this cavern is another similarly sized cavern filled with thousands of bats. Any loud noise in either cavern agitates the bats. When the bats become agitated, have the characters roll initiative. On initiative count 10, the bats fly up the pit and flutter about the upper cave, shrieking loudly. The fluttering bats reduce visibility in the upper cavern to 5 feet. A creature takes 1 piercing damage whenever it enters a 5-foot-square area filled with fluttering bats. At the start of each of the bats' turns, roll a d6. On a roll of 1–5, the bats remain agitated. On a roll of 6, the bats return to the lower cavern and are no longer agitated.

The pit descends through 20 feet of solid rock before opening into the lower cavern, which is 30 feet deep.

## Nightstone Villagers

Boss Hark stripped the villagers of their weapons before herding them into this cavern. The villagers fear for their lives but can't escape the Dripping Caves until the monsters in area 1 are defeated. Every few hours, one of the ogres enters the cave, grabs a prisoner, and takes the unfortunate villager away to be eaten (if not by the ogres, then by the goblins in area 2 or the giant rats in area 9).

In the absence of a true leader, Morak Ur'gray (LG male shield dwarf **commoner**), the owner and proprietor of the Nightstone Inn, speaks on behalf of the villagers. Morak is an optimist, and he's counting on Lady Velrosa Nandar coming to the rescue. When he lays eyes on the adventurers, he breathes a sigh of relief and assumes they were hired by Lady Nandar. (He would be dismayed to learn that she didn't survive the attack on Nightstone.)

Other noteworthy prisoners trapped in the cavern include Hiral Mystrum (LG male human **commoner**), the village's cowardly priest of Lathander, and six unarmed guards (LN male and female **guards**). The guards were wounded by the goblins and ogres in the process of being captured; each has only 1d6 hit points remaining.

The other prisoners found here are surviving members of local families. All the adults are unarmed **commoners**, and all the children are noncombatants. They let Morak speak on their behalf. The families are as follows:

**Agganor Family.** Destiny Agganor (age 42) is Nightstone's tiefling midwife. Her son, Grin Agganor (age 27), worked in the village's stable house, feeding the horses and cleaning the stalls for Lady Nandar. Destiny worships Asmodeus but doesn't impose her beliefs on anyone else, including her son.

**Delfryndel Family.** The Delfryndels are humans. They own and operate Nightstone's windmill. The surviving family members are Renarra Delfryndel (age 64), her youngest son Zalf (age 40), his wife Elize (age 37), and their two adolescent children, Darson (age 17) and Hildy (age 14). No family members died in the giant attack, but Renarra's eldest son, Olaf, was killed and eaten by the goblins.

**Hulvaarn Family.** The Hulvaarns are human potato and turnip farmers. The surviving family members are Godrick Hulvaarn (age 32), his wife Prennis (age 30), and their three children: daughter Jehanna (age 12) and twin sons Ellis and Ghalt (age 9). The children lost their grandfather (Godrick's father, Nestor) in the giant attack on Nightstone.

**Nesper Family.** The Nespers are human pumpkin and squash farmers. None of them were killed in the giant attack, but three of them died at the hands of the goblins and ogres in the Dripping Caves. The remaining family members are Yondra (age 15) and her brother Sarvin (age 11). They lost both of their parents and an older sister named Sylda.

**Osstra Family.** The Osstras are human wheat farmers. The surviving family members include Thelbin Osstra (age 52) and his husband, Brynn (age 52), and their good-hearted nephew, Broland (age 23). Brynn lost his elderly mother and younger sister (Broland's mother) to the goblins.

**Summerhawk Family.** The Summerhawks are strongheart halflings. Taela Summerhawk (age 28), an apothecary, comforts her four young children, Barley (age 10), Midge (age 8), Nincy (age 6), and Dollop (age 3). Taela's husband, Larlow, was killed in Nightstone when a rock fell on their house.

## 5. Fissure

An 8-foot-wide, 20-foot-deep fissure splits a tunnel leading north. The goblins won't cross the fissure and haven't explored the tunnel. Where the tunnel leads is up to you. It might break the surface at some point, or it might lead to a monster's lair or the Ardeep Forest. If you don't want the characters wandering too far afield, inform the players that the tunnel collapsed after a few hundred feet, forcing the characters to turn back.

## 6. Underground Stream

An ankle-deep stream of water pours through a narrow tunnel in the west wall and forms a small pool in this otherwise empty cave. The water doesn't taste good because of its high mineral content, but the goblins have been forced to drink it because their supply of fresh water has been cut off (see area 3).

If the characters enter the caves undetected and take refuge here, there's a 50 percent chance each hour that a goblin noncombatant enters the cave, looking for a drink of water. The goblin flees at the sight of intruders, heading north to area 9. The goblin has AC 10, 1 hit point, and no effective attacks.

## 7. Natural Chimney

A chimney has formed in the 7-foot-high ceiling of this small side cave. The chimney is 5 feet wide and has abundant handholds and footholds. A creature can climb up or down the shaft with a successful DC 10 Strength (Athletics) check. No ability check is required if a rope or climbing gear is used.

An unscrupulous and ambitious **goblin** named Snigbat stands guard at the bottom of the shaft. Snigbat's job is to watch for intruders and report what she sees to Boss Hark. Snigbat considers this duty a form of punishment. If she sees one or more well-armed adventurers, Snigbat offers to lead them to Boss Hark if they promise to kill Hark and help Snigbat become the new boss. Snigbat knows where Hark keeps his treasure (area 8) but doesn't share this information with the characters in the hopes that she might get it.

### Development

If the characters form an alliance with Snigbat and dispose of Hark, Snigbat asks them to slay the ogres in the main cavern (area 1), since she has no influence over them. With Hark and the ogres dead, Snigbat can seize the title of boss without being challenged. Once she becomes the new boss, she allows the characters and the villagers of Nightstone to leave the Dripping Caves unharmed.

## 8. HARK'S HOARD

A large round rock fills the low, 4-foot-diameter tunnel leading to this cave. The boulder fits snugly in the tunnel and must be pushed into the cave to clear the passage. Moving the boulder out of the way requires a successful DC 11 Strength (Athletics) check. The sound of the rolling boulder is loud enough to be heard by the creatures in area 9.

The cave has an 8-foot-high ceiling and contains a grass pallet (Hark's bed), next to which rests a battered wooden chest with a rusty lock. The lock is purely for show and falls apart if handled roughly.

### TREASURE

The chest contains the treasure that Boss Hark has amassed in his short lifetime:

- 12 gp, 55 sp, and 87 cp (loose)
- A matching pair of silver salt and pepper shakers (worth 10 gp apiece or 25 gp for the pair)
- A bloodstained leather case containing a complete set of thieves' tools (worth 25 gp)
- A holy symbol of Silvanus carved from wood and inlaid with gold (worth 25 gp)
- One magic item, determined randomly by rolling on Magic Item Table A in chapter 7 of the *Dungeon Master's Guide*

## 9. BOSS HARK'S CAVE

This 10-foot-high cave contains Hark, the **goblin boss**, two female **goblins** (bodyguards) named Ratcha and Zukluk, and seven **giant rats** (Hark's beloved pets). When the characters enter the cave for the first time, Hark and his bodyguards are gleefully watching the rats feed on the corpse of a slain villager (Darthag Ulgar, the proprietor of the Lionshield Coster trading post).

Hark has collected all the weapons and shields belonging to the captured villagers and stashed the equipment in a western alcove behind rocks. Characters who search the cache find nine spears, five clubs, two daggers, and six wooden shields.

### HARK'S LARDER

At the north end of the cave is a smaller cave where Boss Hark keeps prisoners before feeding them to his giant rats. Cowering in the back of this 6-foot-high larder is Lady Velrosa Nandar's terrified lady-in-waiting, Daphne Featherstone (LG female Tethyrian human **commoner**). Daphne was in the village when the cloud giants attacked. Unable to make it back to Nandar Keep, Daphne fled to the Dripping Caves with the other villagers—a decision she has come to regret. If she learns that Lady Nandar is dead, Daphne becomes inconsolable.

### DEALING WITH HARK

Characters can try to negotiate with Hark instead of attacking him. He agrees to release the remaining villagers if the characters do one of the following things (and leave the goblin lair in peace):

- Pay a ransom of 1 gold piece per villager. (The total amount is 31 gp, minus 1 gp for each villager who has died since the characters arrived at the caves.)

- Give Hark a working lock. Hark needs the new lock for his treasure chest in area 8.
- Kill the Blob (see area 3). If the characters provide Hark with proof of the black pudding's demise, he releases all the villagers into their custody.

## MORAK'S QUEST

Characters who survive the perils of the Dripping Caves and return to Nightstone should advance to 4th level.

Once he is safely back in the village, Morak Ur'gray takes stock of the damage, makes arrangements to deliver news of the giants' attack to Waterdeep, and urges the characters to undertake one of the following three quests. If Morak died in the Dripping Caves, another NPC can give the quest in his place. Choose whichever quest you like. Your choice will determine whether the characters visit Bryn Shander, Goldenfields, or Triboar in the next leg of the adventure (see chapter 2).

Whether or not the characters accept Morak's quest, continue with the "Tower of Zephyros" section.

### BRYN SHANDER QUEST

Morak's friend and neighbor, Semile Southwell, was killed in the giant attack. Although she had no family in Nightstone, Semile spoke often about her brother, Markham. Morak knows that Markham is the sheriff of Bryn Shander and asks the characters to travel to Icewind Dale and deliver the sad news of Semile's passing.

### GOLDENFIELDS QUEST

The Xelbrins were killed in their home when the giants bombarded the village (see "Nightstone," area 4h). Morak recalls that the elderly couple had a son, Miros, who lives in Goldenfields. Morak asks the characters to visit Goldenfields and let Miros know what has happened. If the Xelbrins' tressym is still alive, Morak asks the characters to deliver it safely to Miros.

### TRIBOAR QUEST

Morak's friend and neighbor, Darthag Ulgar, was eaten by giant rats. Darthag ran the Lionshield Coster trading post in Nightstone, and his ex-wife runs a similar trading post in Triboar. Morak asks the characters to travel to Triboar and deliver the sad news of Darthag's passing to Alaestra Ulgar.

## TOWER OF ZEPHYROS

The day after the characters accept Morak's quest, they have their first encounter with a giant. Read or paraphrase the following boxed text to the players:

> You see an enormous tower floating on a billowy cloud a thousand feet overhead. The tower must be hundreds of feet tall, and its spire looks strangely like a pointy wizard's hat. As the tower drifts closer, stairs made of clouds begin to form underneath it and descend toward you.

Map 1.3 shows the tower. The stairs are made of firm cloud stuff and spiral downward, stopping just short of the ground. They are sized for humans and safe to climb. After climbing the stairs for 1,000 feet, the characters stand in front of the tower's entrance, on a cloud that feels as firm and safe as solid ground. If the characters enter the first floor of the tower, a cloud giant wizard named Zephyros descends from the second floor (using a *levitate* spell) to greet them.

Zephyros is an eccentric cloud giant with windswept white hair, a wispy white beard, and a billowy purple robe adorned with gold stars. He poses no threat to Nightstone or the characters.

Ever since the ordning shattered, Zephyros has been using *contact other plane* spells to find a way to set things right. Failed castings of the spell have driven him insane on multiple occasions. He has recovered from the insanity, yet it has accentuated his eccentricity. His magical investigations led him to Nightstone. He had nothing to do with the cloud giant attack on the settlement and is horrified to learn of the damage his fellow giants caused.

Zephyros holds "small folk" in higher regard than most giants. If the characters introduce themselves to him, a wide smile settles on the cloud giant's face as he realizes they are the ones mentioned by the mysterious planar entities with which he has spoken. Convinced that the characters can restore the ordning, Zephyros offers to transport them to one destination of their choice in the North. That is the extent of his involvement. The planar entities with whom Zephyros has spoken via the *contact other plane* spell warned him against taking a more direct hand in events. The party's destination should coincide with Morak's quest. After safely delivering the characters to their destination, Zephyros and his tower depart for the Moonshae Isles.

If the characters ask Zephyros to take them somewhere other than Bryn Shander, Goldenfields, or Triboar, Zephyros (eccentric wizard that he is) gets a little befuddled and ends up taking them to one of these places by accident.

Zephyros is a **cloud giant**, with the following changes:

- Zephyros is neutral good.
- He has an Intelligence score of 18 (+4) and the Spellcasting action option described below.
- He carries a giant-sized *staff of the magi* instead of a morningstar. As an action, he can make two melee attacks with the staff. Each attack has a +15 bonus to hit and deals 20 (3d6 + 10) bludgeoning damage on a hit, or 23 (3d8 + 10) bludgeoning damage if used with two hands. This damage is considered magical.
- He has a challenge rating of 13 (10,000 XP).

***Spellcasting.*** Zephyros casts one of the following spells, requiring no material components and using Intelligence as the spellcasting ability (spell save DC 17, +11 to hit with spell attacks):

At will: *message, prestidigitation, ray of frost*
2/day each: *gust of wind, levitate, magic missile*
1/day each: *cone of cold, contact other plane* (cast as 1 action), *greater invisibility, mass suggestion, nondetection, Otiluke's resilient sphere, protection from energy, tongues*

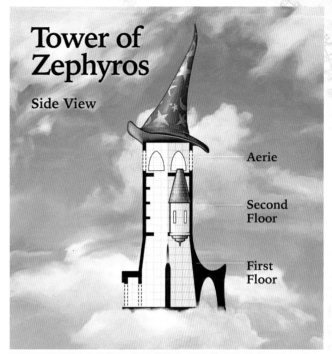

# Tower of Zephyros
## Side View

Aerie

Second Floor

First Floor

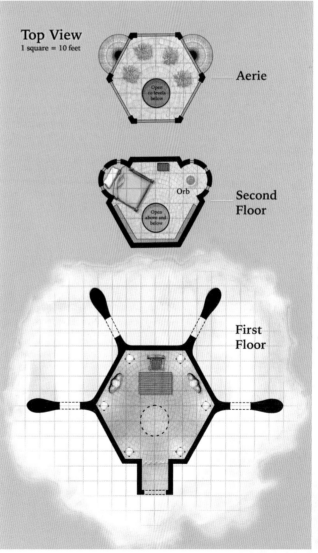

**Top View**
1 square = 10 feet

Open to levels below

Aerie

Orb

Open above and below

Second Floor

First Floor

MAP 1.3: TOWER OF ZEPHYROS

ZEPHYROS

Zephyros's tower has no fitting accommodations for small folk, but the cloud giant wizard allows the party to camp on the first floor. He requests that the characters confine their activities to the first floor and stay away from the second floor and the aerie. Zephyros controls the tower's movements using a *navigation orb* (see appendix B) on the second floor.

The Tower of Zephyros Travel Times table summarizes how long it takes the tower to travel from Nightstone to Bryn Shander, Goldenfields, or Triboar. Regardless of their ultimate destination, the characters have at least one encounter en route (see the "Unfriendly Skies" section for details).

### TOWER OF ZEPHYROS TRAVEL TIMES

| Destination | Travel Time |
| --- | --- |
| Bryn Shander | 624 hours (26 days) |
| Goldenfields | 72 hours (3 days) |
| Triboar | 275 hours (11½ days) |

### FIRST FLOOR

The tower rests atop a cloud that feels solid underfoot. An open archway leads to an empty vestibule, at the back of which hangs a thin, translucent blue curtain that flaps in the breeze. Beyond the curtain lies a 100-foot-high hexagonal chamber containing a giant-sized wooden table and stone chair. Dangling from the ceiling by iron chains are six crystal spheres with *continual flame* spells cast on them. The illuminated spheres keep the room brightly lit.

The tower's second floor can be seen through a 20-foot-wide hole in the soaring ceiling.

### SECOND FLOOR

This level of the tower has an 80-foot-high ceiling and tall, slender windows set with panes of stained glass. Furnishings include a giant-sized bed and an enormous wooden chest sealed by an *arcane lock* spell. Stone shelves protrude from the walls at heights of 20, 40, and 60 feet, and these shelves bear the weight of Zephyros's vast collection of journals (see "Treasure").

Floating 10 feet above the floor is a *navigation orb* (see appendix B) that Zephyros uses to control the movement of the tower.

Zephyros uses magic to move between levels. A 20-foot-diameter hole in the floor allows access to the first level, the floor of which is 100 feet below. A similarly sized hole in the ceiling leads to the aerie.

### TREASURE

The wooden chest is 9 feet long, 5 feet wide, and 5 feet tall. It contains an assortment of giant-sized robes, a giant pair of sandals, a large electrum comb encrusted with moonstones (worth 750 gp and weighing 25 pounds), and Zephyros's spellbook. The spellbook weighs 250 pounds has gilded silver covers. It contains all the spells that Zephyros has prepared plus the following additional spells: *arcane eye*, *continual flame*, *fire shield*, *hypnotic pattern*, *mage armor*, *mirror image*, *misty step*, *modify memory*, *shatter*, and *slow*.

Zephyros's library contains more than five hundred research journals that he wrote himself. For the past fifty years, Zephyros has been drifting around the Moonshae Isles and cataloging its many wonders, both magical and mundane. Each book weighs 100 pounds, consolidates a month's worth of research, and is worth as much as 250 gp.

### AERIE

The highest level of the tower has open archways set into its walls. Four **griffons** have made nests in the aerie, and Zephyros treats them like cats. At any given time, 1d4 of the griffons are present; absent griffons are out hunting and return after 1d4 hours. Griffons that are present attack if they or their nests are disturbed. The griffons' nests contain no treasure.

## UNFRIENDLY SKIES

One or both of the following encounters occur while the characters are traveling with Zephyros. If the characters are making the journey on their own, without the cloud giant's assistance, skip this section and use the Random Wilderness Encounters table in chapter 3 to generate overland encounters.

### DAY 3: THE HOWLING HATRED

On the third day of the party's journey, representatives of an evil elemental cult called the Howling Hatred arrive at Zephyros's tower, hoping to find a powerful cloud giant ally whose goals coincide with those of Yan-C-Bin, the Prince of Evil Air.

The cultists use giant vultures as flying mounts. When they spot the cloud giant's tower, they investigate. The cultists land outside the tower's entrance on the first floor. Zephyros is sleeping on the second floor when they arrive and only becomes aware of visitors if the characters wake him or if combat erupts.

> On the third day of your journey, you spot nine very thin and lightly armored humans riding giant vultures. They land atop the cloud, whereupon the humans dismount. All the riders wear steel helms that cover their eyes and resemble stylized bird heads. One of them is equipped with a shoulder bag adorned with a smiling face.

The visitors include two **cult fanatics** (NE male humans) and seven **cultists** (NE male and female humans). The cultists try to enter the tower while their nine **giant vultures** remain outside. The vultures allow only members of the cult to ride them, and they attack anyone else who approaches within 5 feet of them. A character who dons a cultist's costume can, with a successful DC 12 Charisma (Animal Handling) check, fool a giant vulture into allowing him or her to ride it. The giant vulture attacks the character if the check fails.

The cult fanatics are named Amarath and N'von. They speak for the rest of the group and claim to speak on behalf of Yan-C-Bin as well. Amarath and N'von wish to make contact with a cloud giant and have no interest in dealing with anyone else. If the characters get in the way, the cultists ignore them and call out for master of the tower. If the characters get pushy or turn violent, the cultists attack them.

Amarath carries a magic bag (see "Treasure") with an **invisible stalker** inside it. On his first turn in combat, Amarath releases the invisible stalker and commands it to attack the cult's enemies.

HOWLING HATRED CULTIST
AND GIANT VULTURE

## TREASURE

Amarath's "smiling bag" is actually a *bag of holding*. The bag becomes empty once the invisible stalker leaves it.

N'von carries a pouch containing ten pinches of faerie dust. He offers the pouch to Zephyros as a gift (see "Development").

One pinch of the faerie dust can substitute for the material components of any enchantment spell of 3rd level or lower. The faerie dust has other magical effects as well. If a pinch of faerie dust is sprinkled on a creature, roll percentile dice and consult the Faerie Dust table to determine the effect.

### FAERIE DUST

| d100 | Magical Effect |
|---|---|
| 01–70 | The creature sprinkled with dust gains a flying speed of 30 feet for 10 minutes. |
| 71–80 | The creature sprinkled with dust must succeed on a DC 11 Constitution saving throw or fall unconscious for 1 minute. The creature awakens if it takes damage or if it is shaken or slapped as an action. |
| 81–90 | The creature sprinkled with dust must succeed on a DC 11 Wisdom saving throw or be affected by a *confusion* spell. |
| 91–00 | The creature sprinkled with dust becomes invisible for 1 hour. Any equipment it is wearing or carrying is invisible as long as it is on the creature's person. The effect on the creature ends if it attacks, deals any damage, or casts a spell. |

## DEVELOPMENT

If a battle erupts between the characters and the cultists, Zephyros (eccentric wizard that he is) watches the chaos unfold from a safe distance. Only if the characters are near defeat does the cloud giant cast a *mass suggestion* spell on the cultists and the invisible stalker, urging them to leave at once and never return.

If the characters allow the cultists to speak to Zephyros, they offer him the pouch of faerie dust as a gift and urge him to help Yan-C-Bin "return the world to its primordial state, as it was at the dawn of history." The cultists are hazy on how this can be achieved and more interested in a yes or no from the giant.

Zephyros accepts whatever counsel the characters wish to offer. Unless the characters advise him to send away the cultists, Zephyros accepts the cultists' gift and allows them to remain in his tower while he considers their offer. He then retreats to the second floor and casts *contact other plane* to determine the best course of action. If he fails the spell's Intelligence saving throw, he remains catatonic until he finishes a long rest. If the save is successful, he determines with the aid of the spell that the cult's interests are opposed to his own, and politely asks the cultists to leave. The cultists grudgingly concede to his request and take their leave, but not before Amarath chastises the cloud giant wizard for his "foolish and shortsighted decision."

After his business with the cultists is concluded, Zephyros feels bad about keeping their gift and gives the pouch of faerie dust to the characters, believing they might get more use out of it than he will.

# DAY 10: OPERATION "ORB STRIKE"

This encounter occurs on day 10 of the party's journey and takes place only if the characters are traveling to Bryn Shander or Triboar. The preponderance of giant activity in the North has members of the Lords' Alliance on edge, and their operatives are gathering information while taking steps to curtail the giants' advances.

Any character standing guard outside Zephyros's tower or watching the sky from the tower's aerie spots danger approaching if his or her passive Wisdom (Perception) score is 15 or higher.

> A huge silver dragon glides through the clouds, approaching quickly. As it flies closer, you see a number of armored dwarves clutched in its talons.

A male **adult silver dragon** named Clarion owes a favor to Queen Dagnabbet of Mithral Hall and is transporting a Lords' Alliance strike team to Zephyros's tower at her behest. The dragon clutches three shield dwarves in each foreclaw. The dwarves have orders to disable cloud giant strongholds, and they plan to locate and destroy the tower's *navigation orb*. Neither they nor the dragon know that Zephyros poses no threat to the settlements of the North, nor do they care. They have orders from their queen and a mission to complete, and by Moradin's beard, they intend to succeed!

Characters who spot the silver dragon have 1 minute to prepare for its arrival. Otherwise, all of the tower's inhabitants are startled by the sound of the dragon's flapping wings as he lands on the cloud outside the tower. After dropping off the dwarves, Clarion takes to the air, frightens away the griffons in the tower's aerie, and waits there while the dwarves complete their work.

The shield dwarves are named Daina Ungart, Ildehar Ironfist, Hewen Horn, Voldrik Firehammer, Griswelda Torunn, and Naalt Splintershield. They use the **veteran** stat block, with these changes:

- The dwarves are lawful good.
- Their speed is 25 feet.
- They have darkvision out to a range of 60 feet.
- They speak Common and Dwarvish.
- They have advantage on saving throws against poison, and they have resistance to poison damage.
- They wield battleaxes instead of longswords, and handaxes instead of shortswords (the handaxes deal slashing damage instead of piercing damage).
- Each is equipped with a *potion of gaseous form*.

The dwarves quaff their *potions of gaseous form* upon landing and make their way into the tower, searching for the *navigation orb*. Realizing that the orb isn't on the first floor, they fly up to the second floor. Once the orb is

in sight, the dwarves revert to their true forms and attack it. Zephyros does his best to protect the orb without harming any of the dwarves, using spells such as *charm person*, *Otiluke's resilient sphere*, and *mass suggestion* to trap or divert them. Meanwhile, the dragon watches the battle from the aerie and tries to neutralize the cloud giant wizard with its paralyzing breath.

The dragon and the dwarves avoid armed conflict with the characters. If the characters kill one or more of the dwarves or deal damage to the dragon, they are accused of conspiring with giants to bring about the downfall of dwarven civilization in the North. The strike team turns on the party, attempting to knock the characters unconscious instead of killing them.

## DEVELOPMENT

A character can try to persuade the dragon and the dwarves to end their assault by convincing them that Zephyros means no harm. If the player roleplays well and makes a convincing argument, allow the character to use an action to make a DC 15 Charisma (Persuasion) check, with advantage if the character is a member of the Lords' Alliance, and with disadvantage if one or more members of the strike team are dead. If the check fails, the dwarves say they "can't take any chances" and press forward with their plan, though the character can try again. If the check succeeds, the dragon and the dwarves call off the attack.

If the dwarves destroy the *navigation orb*, the tower is stranded until Zephyros crafts a replacement (which could take months). Rather than strand the characters in his tower, he helps them return to the surface, points them in the right direction, and bids them farewell before returning to his tower to ponder his options.

If the strike team is thwarted or calls off the mission, the dwarves ask Clarion to fly them back to Mithral Hall. If the dwarves are killed, the dragon returns to Mithral Hall alone. Once the Lords' Alliance strike team is gone, Zephyros thanks characters who helped defend the tower, mutters something about dragons under his breath, and carries on as though nothing happened.

---

### CHARACTER ADVANCEMENT

Characters gain levels in this chapter by completing the goals summarized below:

- Characters who explore Nightstone and defeat the goblins in the village advance to 2nd level.
- Characters who deal with the Zhentarim operatives and survive the orc siege (with or without the assistance of the elves of the Ardeep Forest) advance to 3rd level.
- Characters who survive the perils of the Dripping Caves advance to 4th level, regardless of how many villagers they rescue.
- Characters advance to 5th level after their encounters with the air cultists and the Lords' Alliance strike team.

The characters should be 5th level by the time they reach Bryn Shander, Goldenfields, or Triboar, as described in chapter 2.

---

# CHAPTER 2: RUMBLINGS

SETTLEMENT IN THE NORTH COMES UNDER giant attack. You decide which location to use: the walled town of Bryn Shander in the cold heart of Icewind Dale; Goldenfields, a fortified farming settlement and abbey northeast of Waterdeep; or Triboar, a frontier town and caravan rest stop in the Dessarin Valley. This chapter includes a map and a detailed overview of each settlement. The attacking giants have a specific goal. If the characters help defend the location against the giants' onslaught and succeed in defeating or driving off the attackers, the characters are rewarded with quests that lead them deeper into the adventure. Be warned: these encounters are designed to test the party's leadership and tactical skills, and characters who don't exercise some degree of caution will likely perish.

## SPECIAL NPCs

In this chapter, each player runs not only a player character but also an NPC who has ties to the settlement that the characters are defending. Once you've determined where the adventure begins, make photocopies of the six NPCs corresponding to the location you've chosen. These NPCs are gathered in appendix D. Each NPC comes with a brief description, personality traits (a bond, an ideal, and a flaw), and a stat block. When the giant attack begins, give one NPC to each player and tell the player where the NPC is at the start of the encoun-

ter, as noted in the encounter description. If your group has more than six players, one or more of them won't receive an NPC, and that's okay. (Let the players decide who gets one and who doesn't.) If your group has fewer than six players, give one NPC to each player and put the extra NPCs aside. These leftover NPCs don't participate in the battle.

After giving out the NPCs, read the following explanatory text to the players:

> In addition to your character, each of you has received a special nonplayer character with ties to the location where the adventure begins. Take a moment to review your NPC's personality traits and statistics. One of your goals in this part of the adventure is to keep your special NPC alive. For each of these NPCs that survives, your party will receive a special quest that yields a reward upon its successful completion. The details of these special quests won't be revealed until the end of this part of the adventure.

The player-controlled NPCs are intentionally simpler and easier to run than the players' own characters, and the NPCs help bring the location to life. The players will be far more inclined to defend the location knowing that its inhabitants are more than just faceless figures with hit points. These NPCs are predisposed to aid in their settlement's defense, but players might try to keep them out of harm's way instead. Each NPC has an ideal, a bond, and a flaw, and though you should encourage players to roleplay these traits accurately, players can portray the NPCs as they choose.

Rather than have each player roll initiative for a special NPC, assume that the NPC acts on the same initiative count as the player's character, immediately after that character's turn. If an enemy is forced to choose between attacking a player character or an NPC, assume it attacks the NPC unless it has a strong incentive to do otherwise.

At the end of the battle, regardless of the outcome, take back all the special NPCs. For each NPC who survives, give the characters that NPC's corresponding special quest. A special quest is imparted even if the NPC didn't participate in the battle. These special quests shouldn't be revealed to the players until you're ready to move on to the next part of the adventure. Once the dust has settled, the surviving NPCs approach the characters and present their quests (not necessarily all at once). The characters are under no obligation to accept and complete a quest, though doing so usually leads to some kind of reward.

The adventurers don't receive any quest (or the reward gained from completing it) that is tied to an NPC who dies and isn't brought back to life using a *revivify* spell or some other means.

If you are running the adventure for inexperienced players, you can run one or more of the special NPCs yourself and use them to assist or advise the player characters, rather than have the players run the NPCs in addition to their own characters. If the NPCs survive the battle, award one special quest per character in the party.

# Bryn Shander

Bryn Shander is the largest of ten settlements known collectively as Ten-Towns, located in the frigid heart of Icewind Dale. Here, caravans from the south converge with traders from across Icewind Dale to swap goods and rumors. Fishers, trappers, furriers, and sellswords rub elbows in the town's taprooms, and gruff dwarves, wide-eyed travelers, and skulking ne'er-do-wells wander its streets. Merchants from the south trade dyes, hardwood, dried herbs and spices, textiles, fruits, wines, and other commodities for scrimshaw and other items made from the bones of the knucklehead trout that populate the region's rivers and lakes.

The town is situated atop a hill south of the mountain known as Kelvin's Cairn, a major landmark in Icewind Dale. From its windswept perch, Bryn Shander has a commanding view of the surrounding tundra, and an attacking force must climb the barren hillside under fire from archers before it can assault the outer wall. The circular wall that surrounds Bryn Shander stands 30 feet high and is made of tight-fitting stone blocks. Defenders stand atop a planked walkway that hugs interior of the wall. Spaced along the wall are stone watchtowers, wherein guards can take shelter during blizzards and warm their hands and feet by iron stoves.

The buildings of Bryn Shander are plain wooden structures with pitched rooftops to keep snow from settling on them. Clouds of white smoke issue forth day and night from stone chimneys and holes in rooftops.

Each community in Ten-Towns has an elected speaker who leads the residents and represents their interests. The current speaker of Bryn Shander is Duvessa Shane. She has appointed Markham Southwell as her sheriff, making him responsible for training the town's militia and keeping the peace.

## Locations in Bryn Shander

The following locations are identified on map 2.1.

### B1. Outer Gates

The town has three sets of 15-foot-high hinged wooden gates, dubbed the North Gate, the East Gate, and the Southwest Gate. These gates can be barred from the inside with heavy, iron-banded hardwood beams. Barred gates have AC 15, 200 hit points, a damage threshold of 10, and immunity to psychic and poison damage. Forcing open a set of barred gates requires a successful DC 28 Strength check.

Two 30-foot-tall cylindrical stone towers flank each gate and watch over one of the trails that lead to and from the town. The trail from the North Gate travels two miles north to the village of Targos on the frozen shore of a lake called Maer Dualdon. The trail leading east, called the Eastway, stretches roughly thirteen miles to the town of Easthaven on the shore of Lac Dinneshere. The southwest route, known as the Caravan Trail, is called the Ten Trail where it passes through the Spine of the World. This trail is the safest way to the lands south of the mountains, but it is nigh impassable in the winter.

Under normal circumstances, the gates of Bryn Shander stand open, and the guards assigned to the gatehouses say and do nothing as people come and go. When Bryn Shander is threatened, however, the guards close and bar the gates, refusing to open them unless ordered to do so by the sheriff or the speaker. There are four guards at each gate at any given time. Another eight guards are on patrol, moving between the stone watchtowers along the wall. Most of the guards are human, with a sprinkling of shield dwarves, halflings, and other races.

A sheriff's deputy named **Augrek Brighthelm** (see appendix D) often stands watch at the southwest gate. She delights in greeting first-time visitors to town. In fact, she has a well-rehearsed speech that makes some of the other guards at the gate roll their eyes: "Well met, travelers! Keep yer fingers and extremities under wraps, lest Auril bite them off! Mind yer tempers, and you'll be most welcome here! Brought goods to sell? The market lies straight ahead. Craving a warm drink? May I recommend a drop of Firebeard's Firebrandy, sold only at Kelvin's Comfort, located on yer right as you enter the market square!" (If the characters arrive at a different gate, you can relocate Augrek to that gate.)

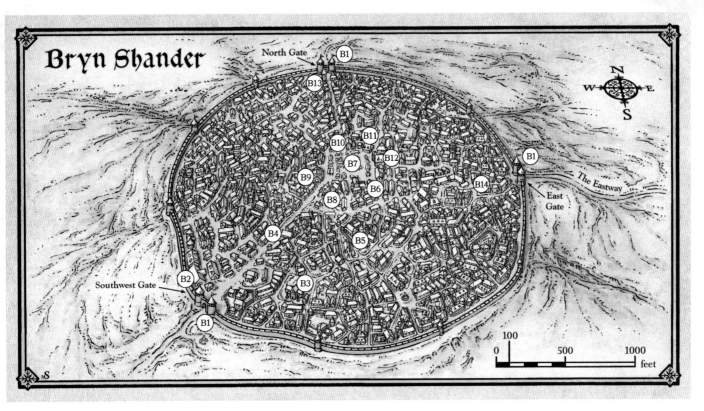

Map 2.1: Bryn Shander

**Bryn Shander**

North Gate

The Eastway

East Gate

Southwest Gate

MAP 2.1: BRYN SHANDER

## B2. STABLES

These stables stand against the outer wall. Any horse, pony, or mule brought into the city can be quartered here and fed for 1 sp per night.

## B3. COUNCIL HALL

Located near the southwest gate, the council hall is a nondescript warehouse where the speakers of Ten-Towns engage in discussions about matters that concern their communities. When no meetings are in session, the building stands empty. In the event of a crisis that affects the other settlements of Ten-Towns, the council hall can be converted into a shelter for refugees.

## B4. HOUSE OF THE TRIAD

Bryn Shander's largest place of worship, the only one that truly deserves to be called a temple, is an impressive stone edifice built by the dwarves of Kelvin's Cairn. The House of the Triad stands about halfway between the southwest gate and the central market. It honors the three gods known as the Triad: Tyr, the god of justice; Torm, the god of courage and self-sacrifice; and Ilmater, the god of endurance in the face of suffering.

The temple is attended and maintained by visiting priests and acolytes from Neverwinter and Waterdeep, who usually stay for no more than two years before returning whence they came. At present, the temple is home to a priest of Torm from Neverwinter named Dellvon Ludwig (LG male human **priest**) and his faithful friend, **Sirac of Suzail** (see appendix D).

Sirac knows that he's a son of the immortal Artus Cimber and thus carries the Cimber bloodline, not that it has ever benefited him. Artus's immortality, it is said, comes from a magic ring—a ring that Sirac has never seen. Sirac's parents gave him up as a baby; he was raised in an orphanage and learned his survival skills as a teenager living on the streets of Suzail. He traveled west with a caravan to Baldur's Gate, then sailed up the Sword Coast to Neverwinter. He came to Icewind Dale three months ago to try his hand at knucklehead trout fishing, and ended up befriending Dellvon Ludwig. Sirac has since come to appreciate Torm's mantra, espousing courage and heroism above all.

## B5. SPEAKER'S PALACE

The Speaker's Palace is the private residence of the town speaker. The "palace" part of its name is an overstatement, compared to such buildings elsewhere in the world. Yet, fashioned by dwarves out of cut stone, with a pitched slate roof and a colonnade in front, the palace is so out of place among the rough wood dwellings in Bryn Shander that it looks as if it had been magically transported here from some other region of Faerûn.

The current elected speaker, **Duvessa Shane** (see appendix D), is the daughter of a trader from Waterdeep who settled in Bryn Shander after she fell in love with a local tavern server. Duvessa inherited her mother's talent for negotiation and her father's charm, and she can argue and debate for hours without tiring. Others might bristle at her temerity, but she usually gets what she wants.

## B6. Town Hall

Bryn Shander's town hall is the largest building that borders the central square. It is reserved for community feasts and gatherings on various holy days and other notable events. The hall can also accommodate refugees from neighboring settlements in times of emergency.

In the back of the hall is a short flight of stone steps that lead down to a sunken cellar with walls of frozen, hard-packed earth. The cellar has been converted into a sheriff's office and an adjoining jail cell. The sheriff, **Markham Southwell** (see appendix D), spends little time here, and the jail cell is usually unoccupied. When troublemakers need to be locked up, two deputies (LN male or female Illuskan human **guards**) are assigned to watch over them. Sheriff Southwell carries the key to the cell door, which can be picked open with thieves' tools and a successful DC 15 Dexterity check. If the guards need to get into the cell for some reason, one of them leaves to fetch the sheriff while the other waits.

## B7. Marketplace

The marketplace is a roughly circular space in the center of town where local and foreign traders sell their wares. Tents and covered wagons provide some shelter against the cold wind, but not much. In a few places, campfires with people huddled around them crackle and smoke.

One heavily bundled figure commonly seen loitering about the market square is a haggard, homeless young woman named **Beldora** (see appendix D). She wears boots that are much too big for her feet, and thick gloves made from walrus hide. She earns coin by helping to tend other folks' campfires, staying warm and overhearing rumors at the same time.

Beldora's secret is that she's a Harper agent. She likes to huddle next to strangers and learn what they know. She conceals a *sending stone* on her person and uses it once a day to pass along information to Thwip Ironbottom, a Harper agent based in Hundelstone.

## B8. Kelvin's Comfort

The most popular tavern in town, owing to its extensive stock of dwarven ales and brandies, is Kelvin's Comfort. The common room is bedecked with dwarven craft of Battlehammer make, but most of the liquors are imported from Mirabar, on the other side of the Spine of the World. The one Ten-Towns specialty of note is a treacly mead from Good Mead, a neighboring settlement. Caravan masters and guards with plenty of coin often come here, as do visiting dwarves from Kelvin's Cairn. The proprietor of Kelvin's Comfort is Ogden Flamebeard (NG male shield dwarf **commoner**), who has a temper as fiery as his signature drink—a Mirabarran rotgut he gets for cheap and rebottles as Flamebeard's Firebrandy (reselling it at a sizable markup). In his youth, Ogden worked in many famous mines, and he has contacts throughout the dwarfholds of the North, including Mithral Hall.

One of the patrons of Kelvin's Comfort is **Sir Baric Nylef** (see appendix D), a knight of Tyr and a member of the Order of the Gauntlet. He's hoping that a few shots of Flamebeard's Firebrandy will keep a nasty cold at bay

while he keeps an eye out for a dwarf named Worvil "the Weevil" Forkbeard, a criminal rumored to be hiding in Ten-Towns. The Weevil led a gang of dwarf brigands that raided summer caravans traveling between Luskan and Mirabar. He also spearheaded several raids on the Mines of Mirabar, stealing food and drink mainly. The Order of the Gauntlet captured most of his gang, but Worvil disappeared into the mountains. Interrogation of the captives led Baric to discover the Weevil's craving for Flamebeard's Firebrandy. So, Baric has adopted the guise of an unemployed caravan guard, and his plan is to hang around Kelvin's Comfort for a few days, on the chance that his quarry will walk right through the door.

## B9. Armory

The town armory is situated just off the central square. Only the town speaker and the sheriff have keys to this building, which stores arms for the militia.

## B10. Blackiron Blades

This small shop and smithy stands just north of the town square and is well known as a one-stop shop for adventurers and other travelers in the region. Rather than attempting to compete with the dwarf-crafted weapons from Kelvin's Cairn, the smith, Garn (N male human **commoner**), makes his living by manufacturing the cheapest blades in Ten-Towns. His sister, Elza (NG female human **commoner**), runs the shop. Elza has expanded the business in recent years by offering a selection of adventuring supplies—rations, fur cloaks, leather gloves and boots, ice picks, snowshoes, and other survival gear. While a Blackiron weapon typically sells for half the price listed in the *Player's Handbook*, Elza marks up other goods by 50 percent to keep the business profitable. Most of the town's veteran sellswords disdain Garn's smithcraft, and jokes told about hapless newcomers to Icewind Dale often end with the line ". . . an' 'e was carryin' a Blackiron blade, to boot!"

## B11. The Hooked Knucklehead

This longstanding inn caters to the scrimshanders and traders who come to Bryn Shander from other towns to conduct business. The innkeeper, Barton (NG male human **commoner**), doesn't meddle in his clients' affairs. The accommodations are meager, and the few private rooms lack hearths and are bitterly cold at night. Most of the clientele sleeps in the spacious common room, near the large stone hearth.

## B12. Rendaril's Emporium

This is the largest trade house in Bryn Shander, on the site of the original cabin around which the town sprang up. The entrance facing the market square serves as the storefront, where visitors can view an assortment of the finest goods for sale in all of Ten-Towns: fishing rods fashioned from elven yew, yeti-skin coats with scrimshaw buttons, mithral fishhooks, axe heads and daggers crafted by the dwarves of Kelvin's Cairn, and more. Around the back of the building is an entrance for wholesalers, where caravan traders offload their stock and local adventurers sell pelts and tusks collected on their travels. The owner, Rendaril (CG male half-elf **commoner**), is a shrewd merchant who learned his trade in the cutthroat markets of Waterdeep. More coin passes through his hands in a week than most other businesses in Bryn Shander see in a season.

## B13. The Northlook

The Northlook is the inn most frequented by mercenaries and adventurers, and as such it's the rowdiest and most dangerous place to stay in Bryn Shander. At the same time, its taproom is the best place in all of Ten-Towns to get the latest news and rumors, including leads on profitable ventures. The proprietor, a retired sellsword who goes by the name Scramsax (N male human **veteran**), takes advantage of the high hopes and good fortunes of his customers by charging the most exorbitant rates in town. (His prices for room and board are double those listed in the *Player's Handbook*.) Scramsax often cuts a break for customers who are between jobs, allowing them to stay on credit and then presenting them with a bill inflated by interest charges after they earn their next payday. Those who don't settle their accounts discover that the former mercenary doesn't take "no money" for an answer, and he still remembers how to handle a blade.

## B14. Geldenstag's Rest

One of the oldest inns in town, Geldenstag's Rest is run by Myrtle (LN female human noncombatant), a gray-haired widow. Myrtle makes it her business to know everyone else's business, asking her guests a lot of questions about what they're up to each day. The inn's accommodations are lackluster—the small rooms are furnished with only a stool, a chamber pot, and two cots with dirty furs thrown over them. It might seem the kind of place that would attract lowlifes and troublemakers, but Myrtle's pestering tends to drive away people who have secrets to keep. The absence of that element from its clientele makes Geldenstag's Rest a popular destination for travelers who aren't looking for too much excitement during their stay in Bryn Shander.

# Attack on Bryn Shander

Twelve **frost giants** come to Bryn Shander looking for Artus Cimber and the *Ring of Winter*. Their leader, Drufi, has two **winter wolves** traveling with her. While nine of her giants encircle the town, Drufi, the wolves, and two other frost giants (Drufi's bodyguards, one male and one female) stride boldly toward the southwest gate, demanding to parlay with whoever's in charge of the town. Sheriff Markham Southwell leads Town Speaker Duvessa Shane to the gatehouse to speak with the angry giant. Augrek Brighthelm is already there.

## Beginning the Encounter

The characters are in Bryn Shander when the attack begins, either together in one place or scattered throughout the town. Read or paraphrase the following boxed text when the attack begins.

> Another dreadfully cold day in Icewind Dale has you bundled up in your warmest furs. Bryn Shander's market square bustles with knucklehead trout fishers selling their finest scrimshaw to traders from the south, while other common folk warm their hands and faces by small campfires. Everywhere across town, people are trudging through snow-covered streets on errands. The town's outer walls block the worst of the wind, but not all of it. A sudden blast occasionally catches everyone by surprise, causing shivers and grumbling all around.
>
> The mood of the town changes abruptly. Something is amiss. Pedestrians are vacating the square with great haste, disappearing into their hovels. As spear-toting guards with grim faces move with purpose toward the southwest gate, you hear a booming voice from that direction as it calls out, "Surrender Artus Cimber or die!"

The frost giants believe that a male human named Artus Cimber is holed up in Bryn Shander, and Drufi demands that the town hand over Artus and all of his possessions to her immediately. Duvessa and Markham know of no such person, and no such person steps forward.

Drufi carries a horn made from a mammoth's tusk and can blow it as an action. The horn can be heard out to a range of one mile. If her demands aren't met immediately, Drufi uses the horn to signal the other frost giants, who advance to within 100 feet of the town and begin hurling rocks over the walls, not targeting anyone or anything specifically but looking to cause widespread panic. As townsfolk take cover, Drufi and her two giant bodyguards try to break down the southwest gate and fight their way inside. While this is happening, a young man named Sirac at the House of the Triad learns what the giants are after and realizes he might be able to save the town.

## Defense of Bryn Shander

The threat of a full-scale frost giant attack throws the town of Bryn Shander into chaos. Many guards abandon their posts, leaving the defense of the southwest gatehouse to the adventurers. The characters can either confront the giants and the winter wolves that are breaking through the southwest gate or deal with the rock-hurling giants as they see fit. Once the characters choose their enemies, assume that Bryn Shander's militia is dealing with the other threats.

Give each player one of the following NPCs to play during this encounter:

**Augrek Brighthelm**, a sheriff's deputy (starts at area B1, southwest gate)
**Sirac of Suzail**, an acolyte of Torm (starts at area B4)
**Duvessa Shane**, the town speaker (starts at area B1, southwest gate)
**Markham Southwell**, the sheriff (starts at area B1, southwest gate)
**Beldora**, a Harper spy (starts at area B7)
**Sir Baric Nylef**, a knight of Tyr (starts at area B8)

Statistics and roleplaying notes for these NPCs appear in appendix D. How the players run their NPCs during the battle is up to them, but encourage the players to review their NPCs' ideals, bonds, and flaws. For more information on how to use and run these NPCs, see the "Special NPCs" section at the start of this chapter.

If the players try to keep the special NPCs out of the fight, you can endanger them by having one or more giants break through the wall, storm the town, and threaten the NPCs directly, thereby requiring the players' NPCs to act.

## TREASURE

Drufi's ivory horn is worth 750 gp intact. The frost giant also has fifteen 100 gp gemstones set into her helm that can be pried loose. Each other frost giant carries a sack that holds 1d6 mundane items, determined by rolling on the Items in a Giant's Bag table in the introduction, as well as 1d4 art objects worth 25 gp each (roll on the appropriate Art Objects table in chapter 7 of the *Dungeon Master's Guide*). The winter wolves have no treasure.

## DEVELOPMENT

If the characters and their allies defeat Drufi, her two frost giant bodyguards, and her two winter wolves, the remaining frost giants abandon their assault on Bryn Shander and retreat westward, toward the Sea of Moving Ice, where a giant longship waits to transport them to Svardborg (see chapter 7, "Berg of the Frost Giants"). They don't remain there long before Jarl Storvald sends them back out in search of Artus Cimber.

Drufi won't leave Bryn Shander until she has either the *Ring of Winter* or knowledge of its exact whereabouts, so characters will probably have to kill her.

Once the characters defeat the frost giants, they gain special quests and rewards based on which NPCs survived the battle.

# BRYN SHANDER QUESTS

For each special NPC who survives the attack on Bryn Shander, the party receives a quest and gains a particular reward for completing that quest. The quests encourage characters to explore other locations throughout the North. Whether the characters travel over land or by sea, use the "Random Wilderness Encounters" section in chapter 3 to stage encounters along the way.

## AUGREK BRIGHTHELM'S QUEST

Hoping to win favor with Sheriff Southwell but unwilling to leave her post, Augrek asks the characters to meet with one or more representatives of the Brighthelm clan in Ironmaster and ask her clanfolk to send reinforcements to Bryn Shander. She warns the characters that the dwarves of Ironmaster don't allow non-dwarves inside their lands. But, she says, if the characters travel toward Ironmaster, stand next to one of its menhirs, and wait, some dwarves will eventually approach them. If the characters announce that they've come on behalf of Augrek, one of her older cousins, Gwert Brighthelm (LN male shield dwarf **noble** armed with a warhammer instead of a rapier), will be summoned to hear what the

characters have to say. Gwert promises to take Augrek's request to the clan elders.

**Treasure.** At the end of the conversation, Gwert gives each character a 100 gp gemstone as payment for delivering Augrek's message.

**Development.** If the characters aren't sure where to go next, Gwert suggests that they visit Dasharra Keldabar, a griffon rider and trainer living in the village of Fireshear, and use the gemstones to pay her to train them to ride griffons. (The gemstones aren't enough to pay for the training, but Gwert doesn't know this.) For more information on Fireshear and Ironmaster, see chapter 3.

## SIRAC OF SUZAIL'S QUEST

Realizing that the frost giants are after the *Ring of Winter*, Sirac confesses to the characters after the battle that he's the son of Artus Cimber, and says that he believes his father has the ring. Although he doesn't know his father's present whereabouts, Sirac recalls that Artus had connections to the Roaringhorns, a noble family in Waterdeep. He urges the characters to visit the Roaringhorn estate in Waterdeep and speak to someone there. Fearing that the frost giants might come after him again, Sirac offers to accompany the characters as far south as Luskan, where he can catch a ship heading south. Guided by Jarl Storvald's *blod stone*, the frost giants continue hunting for Sirac. If the characters allow Sirac to accompany them, assume that any frost giants that appear in a random encounter are searching for him.

If they travel to Waterdeep, the characters learn that the Roaringhorn family has a villa, called the High House of Roaringhorn, in the city's North Ward. Although it's one of the grandest residences in Waterdeep, and currently hosting one of its many infamous parties, this one a welcome celebration for visiting relatives from Cormyr. Upon their arrival, the adventurers are greeted by Lord Zelraun Roaringhorn (LN male human **archmage**). Having quaffed a few *potions of longevity* in his lifetime, he has the appearance and vigor of a thirty-year-old despite his being a couple decades older than that. A **shield guardian** accompanies Zelraun at all times. Zelraun tells the characters (truthfully) that he has no idea where Artus is, and all prior attempts to divine his whereabouts or scry on him with magic have failed. Zelraun hides the fact that both he and Artus are Harpers, although he secretly suspects Artus has "gone rogue." Even if Zelraun knew where Artus was, it would be improper for him to divulge such information and potentially expose another member of the Harpers to harm.

Zelraun asks the characters who sent them in his direction. If they reply truthfully, he engages them in conversation about where they have come from and where they're headed next.

**Treasure.** Once he realizes that the characters have important work ahead of them, Zelraun gives each of them a magic item. To determine each item, roll on Magic Item Table B in chapter 7 of the *Dungeon Master's Guide*, or allow each player to choose one item from that table.

## DUVESSA SHANE'S QUEST

After dispatching scouts to check on the other settlements of Ten-Towns, Duvessa tells the characters that she has an aunt (her father's sister) living in Waterdeep who is the captain of a ship called the *Dancing Wave*. Duvessa writes a letter to her aunt, Inirva Coldwater, asking her to provide passage and accommodations to the characters if they need to travel up or down the Sword Coast.

If the characters seek out information about the *Dancing Wave*, they learn that the ship is missing and several weeks overdue. It was transporting goods from Luskan to Waterdeep when it disappeared. Rumor has it that Neverwinter privateers aboard a ship called the *Moon Maiden* sighted floating debris while traveling south to Waterdeep.

The characters can find Osk Thunderhale (CN male human **bandit captain**), the captain of the *Moon Maiden*, taking it easy at the Hanging Lantern, a festhall near Waterdeep's docks. Thunderhale is a skilled fiddler (Performance +6). In fact, he's playing his fiddle to amuse his crew and other festhall patrons when the characters show up to question him.

If they confront him, Thunderhale takes umbrage and tries to pick a fight. Twelve members of the *Moon Maiden* crew (CN male human **bandits**) stand ready to leap into the fray. If the characters reduce Thunderhale to 32 hit points or fewer, he surrenders, smiles, and offers his hand in friendship while complimenting the characters on their fighting prowess. If the characters defuse the situation by not responding to his initial attack, Thunderhale is just as pleased. He pays for their drinks and covers any damage to the festhall, then claims to be in the employ of Lord Dagult Neverember of Neverwinter.

Thunderhale has no proof that the debris he saw came from the *Dancing Wave*, but he's aware of no other Waterdhavian merchant ships that have gone missing of late. Furthermore, he claims to have seen "a ship as big as a mountain" prowling the northern waters and thinks it might have attacked and destroyed the *Dancing Wave*. If the characters express interest in mounting a search, either for the *Dancing Wave* or the mysterious vessel, Captain Thunderhale commits his ship and crew for 10 gp per day and two-thirds of whatever spoils are found. He can be talked down to an even split of the spoils with a successful DC 15 Charisma (Persuasion) check. Once a deal is reached, Thunderhale agrees to set sail whenever the characters are ready to depart, and he reminds them that they must secure their own provisions.

The *Moon Maiden* is anchored in the bay and can be reached by rowboat. Eight crew members (CN male and female human **bandits**) stand watch on deck while the ship is in port. Use the ship deck plan in appendix C of the *Dungeon Master's Guide* to represent the *Moon Maiden*, if necessary.

***Treasure.*** Captain Thunderhale keeps a wooden treasure chest in his ship's hold. It's locked and rigged with a poison needle trap (see the "Sample Traps" section in chapter 5 of the *Dungeon Master's Guide*). Thunderhale wears the key to the chest on a string around his neck. The chest contains 1,100 cp, 800 sp, 120 gp, nine 50 gp

gemstones, and 1d4 magic items. Determine one magic item by rolling on Magic Item Table B in chapter 7 of the *Dungeon Master's Guide*, and any other magic items by rolling on Magic Item Table A.

## MARKHAM SOUTHWELL'S QUEST

The sheriff asks the characters to patrol Icewind Dale and return at once if they see further evidence of giant activity in the region. If the characters accept the quest, Southwell deputizes them and gives them three weeks' worth of provisions, as well as a signed letter attesting that they are acting on his behalf. Characters can present the letter to the town speaker of any other Ten-Towns settlement and expect to receive free room and board.

You can plan encounters as the characters explore Icewind Dale using the random encounter table in the "Icewind Dale" section in chapter 3. After encountering one or more frost giants, they can return to Bryn Shander and report to the sheriff. If they return with the heads of one or more slain giants, Sheriff Southwell rewards each of them with the title "Defender of Icewind Dale" and spreads news of the party's heroism throughout Ten-Towns. As long as the characters do nothing to sully their reputations, Ten-Towners are friendly toward them and extend them every courtesy.

Shortly after the characters earn their new titles, they are approached by a pair of freelance bounty hunters named Sorelisa Zandra (N female human **spy**) and Naeremos (N male human **thug**). The bounty hunters wear thick cloaks over their armor, and Naeremos is missing his left arm (which was torn off by a troll).

Although they claim to work for the government of Mirabar, Sorelisa and Naeremos are actually working for the Zhentarim. They are searching for a dwarf fugitive known as the Weevil, who is wanted for banditry. Sorelisa shows the characters a crude sketch of the Weevil (a dark-haired dwarf with a wicked gleam in his eyes) and asks them if they know his whereabouts, while failing to mention that the city of Mirabar has placed a 5,000 gp bounty on the Weevil's head.

The Zhentarim wants to protect and recruit the Weevil, not turn him over to the Mirabar authorities. Zhentarim operatives stationed in various cities of the North have seen neither hide nor hair of him, leading Sorelisa to suspect that the Weevil is hiding in one of the smaller settlements. Sorelisa promises that if the characters capture the Weevil and deliver him to her and Naeremos alive, she will match Mirabar's bounty, offering the party a cache of gemstones as payment (see "Treasure").

See the "Xantharl's Keep" section in chapter 3 for more information on the Weevil and his current whereabouts.

***Treasure.*** Sorelisa and Naeremos share a room in Geldenstag's Rest (area B14). A hidden compartment in one wall holds a fat leather pouch containing 10 500 gp gemstones. A thorough search of the room accompanied by a successful DC 17 Wisdom (Perception) check reveals the hidden compartment, which is not trapped.

## BELDORA'S QUEST

Beldora urges the characters to head southwest and take Ten Trail through the mountains to the mining settlement of Hundelstone. She suggests they make contact with a gnome named Thwip Ironbottom, who lives there year-round. If one or more of the party members are Harpers, she tells them that Thwip serves as the organization's eyes and ears in Hundelstone. Beldora uses her *sending stone* to inform Thwip that the characters are coming.

***Treasure.*** Upon the characters' arrival, Thwip gives them a gift: a Tiny clockwork dog made of copper and tin, along with a copper wind-up key. A character must use the key and an action to wind the dog, after which it follows that character for 12 hours. At the end of that duration, the clockwork dog stops until wound again. The dog has AC 5, 1 hit point, and a walking speed of 30 feet.

***Development.*** When the heroes are ready to leave Hundelstone, Thwip urges them to visit Everlund and seek out Krowen Valharrow, a Harper wizard who resides at Moongleam Tower (see the "Inner Circles" section in chapter 3). The gnome describes Krowen as a powerful wizard known to sponsor adventurers.

## SIR BARIC NYLEF'S QUEST

Sir Baric is determined to find the Weevil. At this point, however, he fears that the trail has gone cold. He plans to remain in Bryn Shander only a couple more days before searching elsewhere, and he doesn't want to waste the characters' time in what could end up being a futile hunt for the criminal. Baric believes it's more important to keep the Order of the Gauntlet apprised of his whereabouts and intentions, so he asks the characters to locate another member of the order and report on Sir Baric's status. He suggests that they seek out Sir Lanniver Strayl, a devout follower of Tyr who lives in Neverwinter.

Sir Lanniver (LG male human **knight** wearing a *cloak of protection*) is grooming his **warhorse** when the party arrives. Though he is dismayed to learn about the attack on Bryn Shander, he's relieved to find out that his friend, Sir Baric, is alive and well. Characters who succeed on a DC 10 Wisdom (Insight) check notice that Sir Lanniver is deeply troubled. If they pry into his affairs, Sir Lanniver reveals that he's concerned about another member of the Order of the Gauntlet named Dannika Zarrn, a knight of Helm who has joined a splinter faction of the Order of the Gauntlet called the Order of the Gilded Eye. Sir Lanniver provides the following information about the organization if the characters seem interested in learning more.

- The Gilded Eye has taken root in Helm's Hold, a monastery south of Neverwinter.
- The Gilded Eye believes that demons and their vile worshipers are spreading corruption throughout the North.
- Gilded Eye inquisitors have taken their worship of Helm to extremes and are determined to destroy anyone they believe is under the demons' sway, as well as anyone who challenges the edicts or their beliefs.

Sir Lanniver has no quest for the characters but warns them to be careful when visiting Helm's Hold. See chapter 3 for more information on this location.

***Treasure.*** If the party includes a member of the Order of the Gauntlet (or a character with a strong commitment to stamping out evil), Sir Lanniver gives that party member his *cloak of protection* as a gift.

# GOLDENFIELDS

Goldenfields is a huge, walled temple-farm dedicated to Chauntea, the goddess of agriculture. Called "the Granary of the North," it's the only reason many Northerners ever taste soft-fleshed fruit larger than bush berries. Waterdeep and its neighbors consume the temple's reliable output: carefully husbanded grains and dried, oil-packed, or salted foodstuffs preserved in vast storage cellars, vats, and squat stone grain-towers.

Run by Abbot Ellardin Darovik, Goldenfields is a stronghold of the Emerald Enclave. Members of that faction are as welcome here as clergy of Chauntea; many of them stay for months at a time to help with the work and the vigilant defense of the farm against insects and blights, as well as would-be vandals and plunderers. Hired guards and adventurers patrol the walls and the land immediately around them. Inside the farm, young treants allied with the Emerald Enclave hide within stands of trees, ready to animate trees to repel invaders. More than five thousand people live and work in Goldenfields year round, farming more than twenty square miles of tillage in gangs of hard-working gardeners.

The sprawling temple-farm is built on higher ground than the surrounding fields, and it's enclosed on all sides by a wall of mortared stone. The outer wall is 60 feet high (20 feet high inside the compound) and 30 feet wide. The wall is built out at several points, spaced at least a mile apart, with stone pagodas and barracks at those locations. These watch posts have unobstructed views of the surrounding countryside.

The outer wall is in need of repair in many places. Time and weather have eroded some of the mortar, creating ruts between the stones that can serve as handholds and footholds. Scaling the walls requires a successful DC 15 Strength (Athletics) check.

The entrance to Goldenfields is a large stone gatehouse set into the middle of the south wall. Beyond its gates, dirt roads crisscross the interior of the compound, providing passage between and through its fields and orchards. Roads also run along the inside of the wall, connecting the various watch posts. During the harvest season, wagons make their way between the fields, gathering food and grain and transporting it to cellars beneath the watch posts, where the food is kept under lock and key until caravans from Waterdeep and other settlements arrive to pick it up. In addition to the large grain fields, fruit orchards, and vegetable gardens, smaller gardens hug the outer walls. These gardens grow berries, rhubarb plants, and other such fare.

Most of Goldenfields' workers live in a small town situated near the abbey, where the abbot hosts morning, noon, and evening prayer. North of town is an enormous inn called Northfurrow's End. Visitors planning to spend the night in Goldenfields are directed here.

# Goldenfields

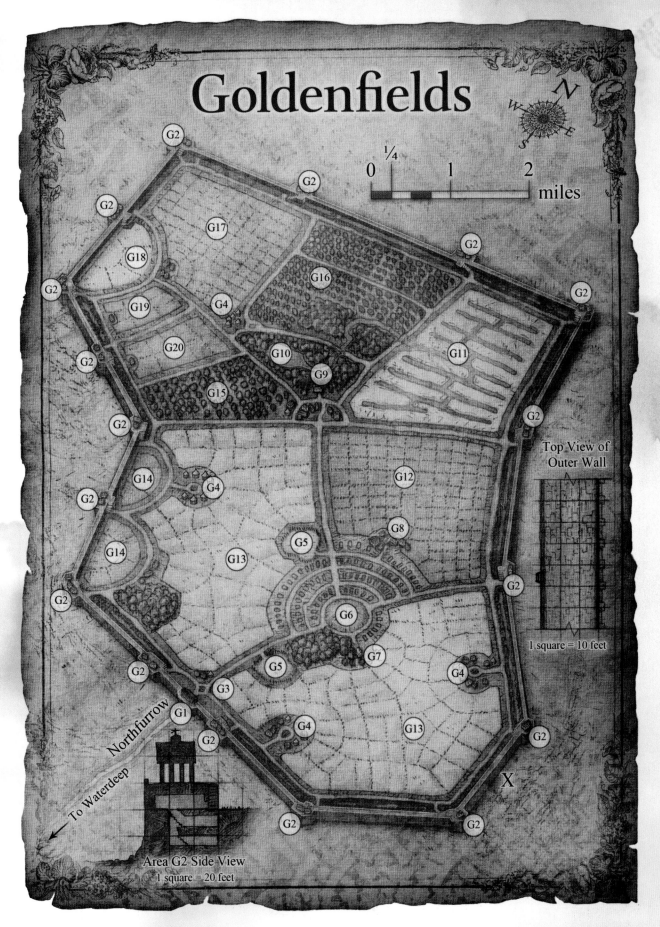

G2
G2
G2
G17
G18
G19
G20
G4
G16
G10
G9
G15
G11
G2
G2
G2
G2
G2
G2
G14
G4
G14
G2
G12
G5
G8
G13
G6
G5
G7
G4
G2
G2
G3
G4
G1
G2
G4
G13
G2
X
G2
G2

1/4    0    1    2    miles

Top View of
Outer Wall

1 square = 10 feet

Northfurrow

To Waterdeep

Area G2 Side View
1 square = 20 feet

# GOLDENFIELDS LOCATIONS

The following locations are identified on map 2.2.

## G1. GATEHOUSE

The Northfurrow trail ends before a magnificent stone gatehouse carved with images of a full-bodied woman (representations of Chauntea) cradling cornucopias. The gatehouse is a fortress in its own right. Above its tall, thick wooden doors are arrow slits that seem to peer down suspiciously on all visitors.

The gatehouse has an inner set and an outer set of double doors. When locked, these doors are too thick to be forced open using brute strength. They can be damaged and broken down, however. Each set of doors has AC 16, 500 hit points, a damage threshold of 10, and immunity to poison and psychic damage.

The gatehouse staff operates in three daily shifts that end at five bells in the morning, one bell in the afternoon, and nine bells at night, respectively. Each shift consists of a **priest** of Chauntea (NG male or female human), four **acolytes** (NG male and female humans), a hired **mage** (N male or female human), ten **scouts** (N male and female humans) hidden behind arrow slits, and thirty well-trained **guards** (N male and female humans). The gatehouse castellan is a Waterdhavian noble who is appointed by the Masked Lords of Waterdeep and holds the post for a year, beginning on the first day of winter. The current castellan, a boorish twit named Hantanus Tarm (LN male human **noble**), is responsible for defending the gates but has no military experience. The gatehouse guards report to him, but his position is seen as mostly political and ceremonial, and he has no influence anywhere but at the gatehouse. The gatehouse is spacious enough to accommodate the members of all three shifts, and any attack on the gates brings the full force of the gatehouse staff to bear.

Merchants and other visitors who come seeking food are rarely turned away, but their wagons and belongings are thoroughly searched in the gatehouse to make sure they contain nothing that could damage crops, such as rodents and vermin. Guests who want to spend the night are directed to Northfurrow's End (area G8).

## G2. WATCH POSTS

At more or less regular intervals around the perimeter of Goldenfields, the outer wall (which is 60 feet high on the outside and 20 feet high on the inside) widens to accommodate broad stone parapets with buildings atop them. Each parapet features a 30-foot-tall stone pagoda topped by a weather vane. A wooden statue of Chauntea stands in the middle of each pagoda, holding a large bronze gong and surrounded by cornucopias. Next to each pagoda are one or two stone outbuildings that serve as barracks. A 10-foot-wide, moss-covered stone staircase leads from the top of the parapet down to the compound. A set of locked, ironbound wooden doors at ground level provide access to storerooms and cellars located underneath each watch post. Picking a door lock requires thieves' tools and a successful DC 15 Dexterity check. The rooms and cellars are packed with harvested fruit and vegetables in the fall and are empty by midwinter.

The watch posts are crucial to the defense of Goldenfields. Stationed at each post are thirty **scouts** (NG males and females of various races) two-thirds of whom are on duty at any given time. The rest are asleep in their bunks. Of the twenty scouts on duty, twelve are stationed on the parapet, spread hundreds of yards apart and looking outward for signs of trouble. The other eight patrol the adjacent walls in pairs.

The watch posts are far enough apart that shouts of alarm are ineffective. If a watch post needs to sound an alarm, a guard runs to the pagoda and strikes the gong with a heavy mallet. The pagodas are designed to amplify sound, allowing the ringing of each gong to be heard as far as two miles away. Any other watch posts within that range ring their gongs as well, putting more of the compound on alert.

The watch posts were designed to warn Goldenfields of approaching armies and dragons. Even though the watch posts and the wall patrols provide a great measure of security, a small group of invaders could scale the outer wall and enter the compound undetected if they were lucky enough to avoid the notice of the guards.

## G3. EARTH MOTHER'S BOUNTY

The first thing visitors to Goldenfields see as they pass through the gatehouse is a 20-foot-tall wooden statue of Chauntea, depicted as a plump, smiling woman standing with her hands on her hips in a garden of golden wheat, surrounded by a dirt roundabout. North of the statue is a stone building with an open front, above which hangs a sign that reads "Earth Mother's Bounty." Visitors can buy seeds and cornucopias here. Tasked by the abbot with overseeing the store and its inventory is Sevembra Tumbleleaf (LN female strongheart halfling **druid**), a member of the Emerald Enclave who sells nothing but the finest seeds. She also gives away lots of free samples.

## G4. GRAIN TOWERS

Grain is stored in these squat stone towers.

## G5. LIVESTOCK FIELDS

On the outskirts of the town are two large fields of roaming oxen and cattle, with cordoned-off pens for sheep, chickens, turkeys, and pigs. Each field is roughly a half-mile in diameter and enclosed by wooden fences with rearing horses carved into their posts. During the day, shepherds as well as workers with milk buckets and wool shears can be seen moving among the herds of cows and sheep.

One of the new shepherds, **Shalvus Martholio** (see appendix D), is a Zhentarim spy—a wolf in sheep's clothing, as it were. His assignment is to determine how easy it would be for the Black Network to gain control of Goldenfields, and report his findings to Nalaskur Thaelond in Bargewright Inn. Shalvus often leaves the livestock pens to hang around Northfurrow's End. He returns to the pens at night to check on the animals.

## G6. Town

The buildings that house most of the residents of Goldenfields are arranged in concentric half-rings around a central square where locals can socialize and gather for picnics after midday prayers. Orderly rows of wooden longhouses, each one large enough to house a hundred people, face inward toward a central plaza, with the abbey of Chauntea off to the southeast. Each longhouse is a work of art, its beams sculpted with images of a particular animal, thereby differentiating it from its neighbors. Most of Goldenfields' workers are human **commoners**. A handful of peaceful Chauntea worshipers (NG male and female **druids** of various races) live and work among them.

Wagons and wheelbarrows are parked just about everywhere, free for anyone to use. The oxen needed to pull the wagons are kept in the livestock fields (area G5).

A grove of trees south of town is home to three young treants. If the town or the abbey comes under attack, their job is to animate nearby trees and aid in the town's defense. The grove is also home to an awakened tree named **Lifferlas** (see appendix D). Created by a long-dead druid, Lifferlas is the oldest living resident of Goldenfields. It speaks Common and has long entertained the children of the workers with harrowing, often humorous tales of heroes and monsters, as well as legends about the gods, Chauntea in particular. The tree allows children to climb it while it walks about cautiously with hosts of them clinging to its boughs and screaming with delight.

## G7. Harvesthome Abbey

The largest and most elaborate building in Goldenfields is the abbey, Harvesthome, a centuries-old stone edifice whose outer walls have statues of Chauntea at every corner, her hands raised to the sky as though casting a spell to summon rain. Well-tended hedges surround the foundation, and a sun-shaped window of stained glass is set above the entrance and the steps leading up to it. Narrow windows of stained glass decorated with images of wheat, fruit, and vegetables light the pillared arcades within. Toward the back of the building, mounted between sturdy roof beams, is a large bronze bell that is rung fifteen minutes before prayers every morning, noon, and evening.

Wandering the abbey halls are two old **black bears** named Darlow and Tilbee. A few months ago, they startled some workers in the south fields. No one could fathom how the two bears crept into the compound unseen, spurring rumors that they were gifts from the Earth Mother. Rather than drive them out, the workers sheltered and fed them. The bears eventually followed workers into the abbey. They try to mooch food from visitors while posing no danger to anyone.

The Abbot of Goldenfields, Ellardin Darovik (NG male human **priest**), is a worshiper of Chauntea and a member of the Emerald Enclave. He's a generous, reserved man who avoids confrontation and doesn't like to ruffle feathers. He leads prayer services at nine bells in the morning, highsun, three bells in the afternoon, and six bells in the evening, and though attendance isn't mandatory, most workers take a break from their chores once a day to hear the abbot's words.

There are no guards in the abbey, just a handful of acolytes. One of them, **Zi Liang** (see appendix D), has scolded Father Darovik many times for putting the defense of Goldenfields in the hands of incompetent military leaders, which has made her somewhat unpopular. When she isn't busy with chores or prayers, Zi takes it upon herself to patrol the outer walls.

## G8. Northfurrow's End

Standing north of the town is a three-story stone edifice with arched windows that offer a view of the surrounding gardens. Thin plumes of smoke issue from its many chimneys on rainy days and cold nights. Life-size statues of rearing horses flank the double doors that lead to the common room. Above these doors hangs a wooden sign that proclaims the name of this grand establishment, Northfurrow's End, in fancy lettering. West of the main building is a stable house that can hold and feed up to fifty horses.

The proprietor of the inn is an elder member of the Fellowship of Innkeepers guild of Waterdeep and, as such, must operate within the strictures of his guild. His name is **Miros Xelbrin** (see appendix D), and he's a retired carnival attraction—dubbed "the Yeti" during his heyday because of his barrel-shaped body and the thick, white hair covering his arms, chest, back, and head.

Miros is a staunch supporter of the Emerald Enclave and offers free room and board to members of the organization and their companions. His rooms are spacious and comfortable, his food plentiful and delicious (made with only the freshest ingredients). He has little tolerance for rabble-rousers and can spot adventurers from a mile away. Miros employs a staff of twenty cleaners and servers. He sells a local brand of beer called Goldengulp, though the first flagon to a new customer is always free.

In the back of Northfurrow's End is a pottery kiln that Miros uses to make the inn's trademark flagons. These large, varnished clay mugs have sheaves of golden wheat painted on their sides. Miros doesn't sell these minor works of art, but the mugs are occasionally stolen and sold elsewhere.

One of the patrons of Northfurrow's End at present is a visitor from Waterdeep. That city's Watchful Order of Magists and Protectors has an agreement with the abbot. Every midwinter, the guild sends one of its members to Goldenfields as a sign of its commitment to protecting Waterdeep's interests. The wizard serves for one year and acts as a liaison between the city and the abbot, while also aiding in the defense of Goldenfields. The guild's current attaché is **Naxene Drathkala** (see appendix D), a quiet and bookish young woman who lives in a lavishly furnished suite above the inn's stable house and spends most of her time writing papers on subjects both arcane and esoteric. In addition to being a member of the Watchful Order, Naxene is an agent of the Lords' Alliance and a loyal spy for Lady Laeral Silverhand of Waterdeep. Miros has tried to court Naxene, but she ignores his halting advances.

Among the other guests of Northfurrow's End are numerous actors, musicians, acrobats, and other performers from Waterdeep and Daggerford. These spirited folk entertain locals during afternoon picnics in the town circle (area G6). A halfling singer and lute player named **Oren Yogilvy** (see appendix D) is the only permanent resident of the inn among them. He has a fondness for Goldengulp and gets free room and board for keeping the residents of Goldenfields entertained. After a few drinks, Oren likes to wander the compound in search of inspiration and often wakes up in a field the morning after.

## G9. Goldengulp Brewery

Goldenfields' brewery is a stately, two-story manse where a beer called Goldengulp is made, using the finest local barley and hops. Visitors aren't allowed in the brewery, which is locked up tight at night. Longhouses in the brewery's front yard are home to the sixty **commoners** who comprise the brewery staff. In the same area is a locked stone warehouse packed to the rafters with casks of Goldengulp. A locked door can be picked open with thieves' tools and a successful DC 15 Dexterity check.

Rising from the back of the brewery is a cylindrical watchtower, known to locals as the Dragon's Spire because a young bronze dragon once perched atop it on a quiet winter afternoon in 1374 DR, the Year of Lightning Storms. The stone tower serves as the headquarters for the Captain of the Guard, who is responsible for Goldenfields' defense. It has its own ground-floor entrance and is four stories tall, with a flat roof enclosed by green marble battlements. Two **guards** (CG male and female humans) stand at the base of the tower, and four more stand watch atop it. The current Captain of the Guard is Strog Thunderblade (NG male orc **veteran**). Boredom and easy access to fine food and beer have made him fat and lackadaisical. He falls asleep early, wakes up late, and leaves the tower once a day around three bells in the afternoon to meet with the abbot and submit a daily report. Strog has a pleasant, easygoing demeanor, and the abbot likes him despite his obvious shortcomings.

## G10. Freshwater Spring

Northwest of the brewery is a natural spring that bubbles up to form a small lake. A river flows gently eastward, then northward, then eastward again, passing under two arching, moss-covered stone bridges before bleeding into the rice paddies. Frogs gather around the edge of the lake at night, filling the night air with a symphony of croaks.

## G11. Rice Paddies

Water-filled furrows nourish the rice paddies of Goldenfields. On warm days, workers in sandals wade through standing water and muck, tending the rice crop.

## G12. Vegetable Gardens

Dirt paths crisscross large tracts of land where carrots, onions, squash, tomatoes, potatoes, radishes, and other vegetables are grown. Workers till the gardens and tend the crops from dawn to dusk.

## G13. Wheat Fields

Nearly half of the tilled earth in Goldenfields is set aside for growing wheat. During the harvest season, the wheat fields are full of workers wielding scythes and carrying bushels of sheared wheat over their shoulders.

## G14. Herb Gardens

The road along the inside of Goldenfields' western wall detours around a pair of semicircular herb gardens. Stone cottages located nearby belong to a dozen **druids** (N male and female humans), who worship Chauntea. The druids not only grow the herbs but also roam the fields and gardens of Goldenfields, tending to sick plants.

## G15. Orange Orchard

Rows of orange trees populate the section of the Goldenfields compound that lies northwest of the wheat fields.

## G16. Apple Orchard

Many a bard has sung songs about Goldenfields' apple orchard; its old yet seemingly ageless trees yield thousands of baskets of tart apples every year. Much of the apple picking is performed by children, who climb the trees and gather the picked fruit in baskets, leaving them to be transported by adult workers. A grove of trees to the southeast of this area harbors a pair of young treants. Their job is to make sure no harm befalls the orchard.

## G17. Corn Field

By the end of summer, the stalks of Goldenfields corn are at least ten feet tall. After the harvest, the field is bare until it is tilled and new crops are planted in the spring.

## G18. Barley Field

About one-sixth of the barley grown in the compound goes into making Goldengulp. The rest of the harvest is shipped out to supply other settlements.

## G19. Hops Field

Hop plants, whose flowers are used in the making of beer, are grown here. The workers who tend the hops and the barley field live in a large house nearby.

## G20. Pumpkin Patch

This field produces some of the largest and firmest pumpkins found anywhere in the North. A large house overlooking the pumpkin patch houses workers who tend both the patch and the berry bushes that grow near the outer wall.

# Attack on Goldenfields

Guh, the self-styled chief of the hill giants, has driven off her female rivals and conquered their husbands. Now, she tasks her mates with collecting food for her voracious appetite. Two of these big dummies, Lob and Ogg, wandered the hills and valleys south of Grudd Haug, the den of Guh's clan. They eventually blundered into the Forlorn Hills and, a few weeks ago, stumbled upon a gang of bugbears and goblins. The goblinoids told Lob and Ogg about a large farm on the far side of the

Dessarin River. It occurred to the hill giants that they should attack it. So, the giants waded across the river and hurled rocks at Goldenfields, pounding its outer wall and alarming its residents. Archers on the wall retaliated with a barrage of arrows. The giants and goblinoids withdrew to nurse their wounds, leaving Goldenfields' defenders to wonder when the next attack would come. The attack hasn't changed the mood among the residents, who place great stock in the strength of their outer defenses and militia.

Lob and Ogg spent the next month lost in the hills, trying to find their way back to Grudd Haug. When they got there, they told Guh about the "big farm." Guh dispatched a horde of hill giants, ogres, bugbears, and goblins to pillage it. With Lob and Ogg leading the way, the horde got lost in the hills and blundered into a copper dragon's territory. Many giants, ogres, bugbears, and goblins died that day. The survivors fled, only to stumble into an Uthgardt ambush. At that point, it became clear to those who remained alive that Lob and Ogg were poor guides and detrimental to the success of the mission. The bugbears took over from there, leading the remnants of the horde to Goldenfields, with Lob and Ogg bringing up the rear and blaming one another for their misadventures.

The following monsters make it to Goldenfields and participate in the attack:

- Six **hill giants**, including Lob and Ogg
- Twelve **ogres**, six of them fitted with goblin huckers
- Twelve **bugbears**
- Sixty **goblins**, split into two groups of thirty

All of the bugbears, and half of the ogres and goblins, climb over the walls in the dead of night. They slip into the wheat fields in search of food to plunder, not realizing that most of the edible food is stored in cellars under the watch posts along the walls. As the intruders quietly prowl Goldenfields in search of food, the six hill giants stand beyond the wall with open sacks, waiting to catch whatever food the goblins and bugbears toss over the wall. Meanwhile, the remaining six ogres and thirty goblins lurk in the darkness outside the wall.

Luckily for the people of Goldenfields, a half-drunk halfling named Oren Yogilvy (see area G8) spots the monstrous trespassers and sounds the alarm.

## Beginning the Encounter

The following boxed text assumes that the characters are staying at Northfurrow's End (area G8).

> A mighty yell shatters the night's silence. "We're under attack!" the voice calls out. "To arms! To arms!" Gathering your wits and weapons, you stumble outside the inn. A low mist blankets the quiet gardens to the north and slinks between the rows of darkened longhouses to the south. A small figure stumbles around the corner of the nearest longhouse, loses his balance, and falls. You have never seen such a clumsy, disheveled halfling.

Not long after the initial attack on Goldenfields, the abbot received reports of giant sightings throughout the Dessarin Valley. He shared these reports with Strog Thunderblade, his Captain of the Guard. Unfortunately, Strog did nothing to prepare for another giant attack. In fact, he never got around to briefing his men or drafting workers or adventurers to help patrol the outer wall, as per the Abbot's instructions.

Thanks to Strog's lackluster handling of the situation, the ogres, bugbears, and goblins are able to scale the eastern wall at the point marked X on the map and enter the wheat fields (area G13) undetected. Once over the wall, they split into three gangs, with two ogres, four bugbears, and ten goblins per gang. The Moon Biters gang reaches the animal pens (area G5) at the same time that the Eye Stabbers reach the town (area G6). The Hill Howlers get lost in the wheat field and emerge near a random cluster of grain towers (area G4). Once they realize their mistake, they head back into the field and make their way toward the abbey (area G7). Oren Yogilvy spots the Eye Stabbers while wandering through town, half-drunk, mulling over lyrics for a new song. Using his powerful set of lungs, he sounds the initial alarm and rushes back toward the inn.

## Defense of Goldenfields

The guards at the gatehouse (area G1), on the wall (area G2), and at the brewery (area G9) are too far away to hear Oren's call to arms, but adventurers in the town, the abbey, or the nearby inn hear him loud and clear, as do various special NPCs. Give each player one of the following NPCs to play during this encounter:

**Shalvus Martholio**, shepherd and Zhentarim spy (starts at area G8, inside the inn)

**Lifferlas**, awakened tree (starts at area G6, in the grove of trees)

**Zi Liang**, acolyte of Chauntea (starts at area G7)

**Miros Xelbrin**, innkeeper (starts at area G8, inside the inn)

**Naxene Drathkala**, resident mage (starts at area G8, inside the stable house)

**Oren Yogilvy**, musician (starts at area G8, outside the inn)

Statistics and roleplaying notes for these NPCs appear in appendix D. How the players run their NPCs during the battle is up to them, but encourage the players to review their NPCs' ideals, bonds, and flaws. All of these NPCs are familiar with Goldenfields' defenses and can run to get help, if that's what the players want them to do. For more information on how to use and run these NPCs, see the "Special NPCs" section at the start of this chapter. If the players try to keep the special NPCs out of the fight, you can endanger them by having one or more groups of monsters threaten the NPCs directly, thereby requiring the player-controlled NPCs to act.

Each gang of monsters is a separate encounter. If the abbey's bell hasn't been rung by the time the second gang of goblinoids is defeated, the abbot rings it. (It takes time for the abbot to realize something is amiss and reach the bell in the dead of night.) The ringing bell can be heard for miles and puts all of Goldenfields' defenses on alert. The bell panics any ogres, bugbears, and goblins that are still inside the compound, and they flee back toward the wall.

During this time, inexplicably, Lob and Ogg decide to climb over the wall and enter the compound rather than flee, while the other four hill giants regroup with the ogres and goblins lurking outside Goldenfields. The giants leave behind their greatclubs, since they can't climb the walls with their clubs in hand. A handful of guards confront the two foolish giants, but they retreat once Lob and Ogg start breaking off and hurling wall battlements (treat as hurled rocks). The two giants eventually make their way toward the abbey (area G7). If either giant is reduced to 15 hit points or fewer, he surrenders (see "Development" below).

If forced into melee combat, an unarmed hill giant can use its action to make two unarmed attacks. Replace the giant's greatclub attack with the following attack option:

***Unarmed Attack.*** *Melee Weapon Attack:* +8 to hit, reach 10 ft., one target. *Hit:* 12 (3d4 + 5) bludgeoning damage.

After the characters deal with the threats inside the walls, townsfolk emerge from their longhouses and begin to scour the fields for stray threats. Characters who join the search find trails that lead back to the wall. By this time, the sky to the east has lightened enough to reveal the presence of giants, ogres, and goblins outside

the wall. The invaders close to within 120 feet of the wall and begin hurling rocks and goblins.

## GOBLIN HUCKERS

The six ogres that remain outside Goldenfields wear hobgoblin inventions called goblin huckers. Each of these contraptions is essentially a portable trebuchet strapped to a leather harness. The contraption rests on an ogre's back and shoulders, and despite its cumbersome appearance, it doesn't inhibit the wearer's mobility or fighting ability. It takes 10 minutes for someone else to attach or remove the elaborate harness, or 1d6 hours if an ogre attempts to do so unassisted. The contraption is built for ogres specifically. A dwarf or similarly built Humanoid that is magically transformed to Large size can don or doff a goblin hucker in 10 minutes.

The sling of the trebuchet is big enough to hurl a rock, a flaming cask of pitch, or a similarly sized projectile— but the contraption was designed to fling goblins. A goblin used as a projectile typically wears a spiked helmet, so that it deals piercing damage to the target on impact. The thirty goblins outside Goldenfields are equipped with helmets. A goblin rarely survives the experience of being hurled through the air in this fashion. The goblins here stand ready to be flung at enemies on the wall, while the ogres position themselves 300 feet away from their targets.

The wearer of a goblin hucker launches its payload in a high arc, so it can hit targets behind cover. Loading the sling is an action that the contraption's wearer can't perform. A goblin willing to serve as a living projectile can load itself, if necessary. The ogre must then use an action to aim the weapon and pull the cord that releases the sling and hurls the projectile through the air.

***Goblin Projectile.*** *Ranged Weapon Attack:* +3 to hit, range 150/600 ft. (can't hit targets within 30 feet of the hucker), one target. *Hit:* 5 (2d4) bludgeoning damage, or 10 (4d4) piercing damage if the projectile is wearing a spiked helmet. *Hit or Miss:* The goblin projectile takes 1d6 bludgeoning damage per 10 feet it travels through the air (maximum 20d6).

## TREASURE

Each hill giant carries a sack that holds 1d4 mundane items, determined by rolling on the Items in a Giant's Bag table in the introduction, and 1d4 − 1 art objects worth 250 gp each (roll on the appropriate Art Objects table in chapter 7 of the *Dungeon Master's Guide*). Each bugbear carries a pouch that holds 1d6 gemstones (worth 10 gp each), and each goblin carries 1d6 cp in a pouch as well as various worthless belongings (necklaces made of woven dwarf beards and strung with halfling ears, bowls made from human skulls, and the like). The ogres have no treasure.

## DEVELOPMENT

The monsters inside the compound are smart enough to realize that they can't survive in Goldenfields for long after an alarm has sounded. Those that escape rejoin their comrades waiting outside the wall. Lob and Ogg are the exceptions; more afraid of Guh than of the Goldenfields defenders, they hate the thought of returning to their chief without a mountain of food. But neither giant wants to die, and each surrenders if reduced to 15 hit points or fewer, falling to the ground and beginning to sob like a big baby. If questioned, Lob or Ogg responds by blubbering incoherently. A successful DC 15 Charisma (Intimidation) check pries the following information out of a defeated but conscious hill giant:

- "Guh want food."
- "Me get food for Guh."
- "Guh big. Real big. Bigger than me."
- "Grudd Haug. Home."

Characters who successfully intimidate one or both giants can command them to lead the way to Grudd Haug. But because neither giant has a good sense of direction, any such expedition is doomed. The hill giants become disoriented while leading the party into the Forlorn Hills east of Goldenfields. Stupid beyond belief, Lob and Ogg are unable to find their way back to Grudd Haug no matter how strongly the characters motivate them.

Captured monsters that are left to the tender mercies of the Goldenfields defenders are put to death, by order of Captain Strog Thunderblade. The captain then takes credit for defeating the monstrous horde that attacked Goldenfields. The abbot, being much more sensible, thanks the adventurers profusely and makes sure they're cited for their heroics and well supplied when the time comes for them to leave. If the characters call for Strog's resignation, the abbot vows to give their recommendation serious thought.

Whether or not the characters thwart the attack on Goldenfields, they gain special quests and rewards based on which NPCs survived the battle.

## GOLDENFIELDS QUESTS

For each special NPC who survives the attack on Goldenfields, the party receives a quest and gains a particular reward for completing that quest. The quests encourage characters to explore other locations throughout the North. Whether the characters travel over land or by sea, use the "Random Wilderness Encounters" section in chapter 3 to stage encounters along the way.

### SHALVUS MARTHOLIO'S QUEST

Shalvus asks the party to escort him overland to Bargewright Inn so that he can report everything that has happened to his boss, Nalaskur Thaelond.

After making his report, Shalvus takes his leave and shacks up with some friends in Bargewright Inn until Nalaskur gives him a new assignment. Grateful for their assistance, Nalaskur offers the characters a warm dinner and clean beds for the night, free of charge. The next morning, he asks the characters to accompany a beer wagon to the Troll in Flames, a tavern in the village of Mornbryn's Shield. Two **draft horses** pull the wagon, which has a pair of drivers named Jostin and Lessilar (N male human **thugs**). They take turns at the reins.

If the delivery is made, the characters pass Nalaskur's test. Unless they do something to turn the Black Network against them, the characters receive an anonymous bundle from the Zhentarim the next time they visit Bargewright Inn, Everlund, Mirabar, Silverymoon, Neverwinter, Waterdeep, or Yartar (all of which have a strong Zhentarim presence). The bundle contains a block of excellent cheese wrapped in silk, a black bottle of "Old Bargewright" wine, and a folded piece of parchment on which are written the following words:

> *Zira*
> *The Happy Cow*
> *Daggerford*

Any character who has spent time in Daggerford can, with a successful DC 10 Intelligence check, recall that the Happy Cow is a halfling-run tavern in town. If the adventurers visit the tavern, a female **adult bronze dragon** in half-elf form buys them a round of drinks. The dragon, Zirazylym ("Zira" for short), is on the Black Network's payroll.

***Treasure.*** If the characters seem nice, Zira grants them a special favor (see the "Marks of Prestige" section in chapter 7 of the *Dungeon Master's Guide*). When they call in the favor, Zira does her best to help them, though she will not cause direct harm to others or violate local laws. She tries to hide the fact that she's a dragon, but if the characters need swift transportation to some far-flung destination, she offers to fly them there. She can also hook them up with a *spell scroll* containing any one spell of 5th level or lower.

### LIFFERLAS'S QUEST

Lifferlas urges the characters to seek out its creator, a moon elf druid named Aerglas. The awakened tree tells them that Aerglas was not only a member of the Emerald Enclave but also an adventurer who slew many giants in his day. Aerglas left Goldenfields thirty years ago on a pilgrimage to Shadowtop Cathedral (see chapter 3). The druid planned to follow the Dessarin River and seek out an old treant named Turlang. Lifferlas suggests that the characters do the same.

Turlang isn't at Shadowtop Cathedral when the characters arrive, but a morose **satyr** named Greenwhistle assures them that the treant "will be along any time now." Greenwhistle is disappointed because a dryad spurned his advances, so he sits by a pool playing sad songs on his panpipes day and night. Between songs, Greenwhistle repeatedly assures the characters that Turlang "will be along any time now." The treant arrives on the third night after the characters arrive, in the company of a friend named Tharra Shyndle (NG female half-elf **druid**), who is a member of the Emerald Enclave.

The treant is initially indifferent toward the heroes and not of a mind to please. If one or more characters approach the treant in a nonthreatening manner and initiates a conversation, Tharra urges the treant not to lose its temper. The treant groans audibly and answers brusquely. It doesn't know Lifferlas but remembers Aerglas fondly. The treant hasn't seen the druid in many years and doesn't know where Aerglas can be found. If the characters reveal their opposition to the giants, Turlang offers them help in the form of two **awakened trees** and one **awakened shrub**. These awakened plants speak Common and heed the party's commands.

***Treasure.*** Tharra offers to guide the party to the Evermoor Way, north of the forest. If they accept, they have no hostile encounters en route. Once they reach the forest's edge, Tharra makes a decision whether to befriend the characters or not. If they seem friendly and show concern for the fate of the natural world, she declares her friendship by giving them a pouch of 1d4 + 4 magical silver berries that she picked near the Lost Peaks. Swallowing a berry has the same effect as imbibing a *potion of invisibility*. If one or more characters are destructive and rude, she bids them farewell upon reaching the forest's edge and heads off on her own.

**Development.** As she guides the characters through the forest, Tharra says she plans to visit an old friend—a ranger named Quinn Nardrosz who lives in Jalanthar. If she's friendly toward the characters, she invites them to join her, saying she could use the company. If the characters accept the invitation, Tharra leads them to Everlund, then east to Jalanthar by way of the Rauvin Road. Quinn is so delighted that the characters took the trouble to accompany Tharra that he gives them three magic items that he "acquired" during his days as an adventurer; roll on Magic Item Table F in chapter 7 of the *Dungeon Master's Guide* for the first item, and on Magic Item Table B for the other two.

### ZI LIANG'S QUEST

In addition to being an acolyte of Chauntea and an Emerald Enclave sympathizer, Zi is the beneficiary of a considerable inheritance from her parents, who traded in silk, whale oil, fine glass, maps, and other commodities. They were based in Baldur's Gate but owned several businesses in Waterdeep.

**Treasure.** Zi gives the characters a black pearl pendant (worth 750 gp) that she keeps hidden among her belongings and tells them to bring it to Cauldar Marskyl (LG male human **commoner**), the head butler of House Thann in Waterdeep, where he will give them a gift in exchange.

House Thann is one of Waterdeep's leading vintners, and although Cauldar is elderly and forgetful, he recalls with perfect clarity that the Thann family and Zi's family are allies. He has been entrusted with some items that once belonged to Zi's parents, and though Zi is now old enough to have them, she has no immediate need of them and prefers an ascetic lifestyle. If the characters show Cauldar the pendant, he understands that Zi has bequeathed her inheritance to them. He sends servants to the attic to retrieve an old wooden trunk and bring it to the characters, then unlocks it with a key and lets them claim the two magic items inside. Roll on Magic Item Table C in chapter 7 of the *Dungeon Master's Guide* to determine each item. Cauldar offers to keep Zi's pendant and see it safely returned to her, but he doesn't protest if the characters insist on keeping it.

### MIROS XELBRIN'S QUEST

Miros suggests that the characters travel to Amphail and "give his regards" to Arleosa Starhenge, the proprietor of a local tavern called the Stag-Horned Flagon. If the characters do so, Arleosa is delighted to hear that Miros is well and offers to buy them a round of drinks. The two performed together in a traveling carnival troupe many years ago.

If the characters make the effort to get to know Arleosa and reveal that they're adventurers, Arleosa playfully recalls that she captivated a few adventurous admirers in her day. One of them, Arleosa says, was so enchanted with her that he gave her a wooden ring adorned with dancing nymphs and told her that it represented a special favor. Should she need anything, all she must do is whisper his name ("Keltar Dardragon") into the ring, and he would appear and provide assistance. She never found the need to do so, but she offers the ring to the character she likes the most (as determined by you). The ring radiates evocation magic under the scrutiny of a *detect magic* spell.

**Development.** If a character whispers Keltar's name into the ring while wearing it, a friendly halfling apparition appears within 5 feet of the ring's wearer. The ring loses its magical property once the apparition appears. Nothing can alter Keltar's cheery demeanor. The dead halfling points them in the direction of an old tower in the wilderness, claiming (in Common) that they'll find useful items hidden inside it. If the characters follow Keltar's directions, run the "Old Tower" encounter in chapter 3. The apparition can't be harmed and provides no other assistance. It vanishes forever once it has imparted its information, waving goodbye as it fades away.

### NAXENE DRATHKALA'S QUEST

Every bone in her body tells Naxene that the attack on Goldenfields is just the beginning. She's heard "rumblings" that other settlements have been impacted by the sudden appearance of giants—and not just hill giants but also stone, frost, fire, and cloud giants. Naxene is convinced that now is not the time for half-measures. She has read books about the ancient conflict between dragons and giants, and she urges the characters to seek out a powerful good dragon, convince it to contact other good dragons, and use them to combat the giants. Naxene is confident that the Lords' Alliance will support this plan, given the gravity of the situation. She couldn't be more wrong.

Naxene is unaware that the Lords' Alliance leaders would rather hurl themselves into the Nine Hells than deal with dragons. She recommends that the party speak to an acquaintance of hers—a "dragon expert" in Waterdeep named Chazlauth Yarghorn (CN male human **mage**). Naxene provides directions to his residence in the city's North Ward: a tall stone house with a tower on one corner.

Chazlauth has a **silver dragon wyrmling** companion named Irizzorl that he keeps hidden in his tower, along with several **cats** that the dragon likes to terrorize. The racket in the tower is constant during the party's visit, during which Chazlauth dismisses Naxene's crazy plan and proposes an even crazier one. He suggests that the characters travel to the Kryptgarden Forest and seek out Old Gnawbone, a powerful and eccentric green dragon rumored to possess a collection of *crystal balls* that she uses to scry on everyone and everything. Based on what Chazlauth knows about green dragons, and Old Gnawbone in particular, he doesn't think the dragon will harm the characters if they seem intent on ending the giant threat, and he's willing to risk their lives to test his theory.

**Treasure.** If the characters agree to seek out Old Gnawbone, Chazlauth plucks a handful of potions from a shelf in his tower and gives one to each character. One of them is a *potion of poison* that has been mislabeled "Potion of Poison Resistance." The others are actual *potions of poison resistance*. All the potions look the same; roll randomly to determine which character receives the poison one.

**Development.** Run the suggested encounter in the "Kryptgarden Forest" section in chapter 3 once the characters enter Old Gnawbone's domain.

## OREN YOGILVY'S QUEST

Oren is spooked by rumors that giants are rampaging throughout the North. He asks the characters if they could check on his sister, Lily, who works at the Happy Cow tavern in Daggerford. He also wants them to deliver a hastily written letter to Lily that tells her he's doing fine, and would she please send him some more money.

Lily (LG female strongheart halfling **commoner**) married into the Hardcheese family, which owns and operates the Happy Cow tavern in Daggerford. The real family business, however, is moneylending. The halflings use the tavern to attract new clients, and while the Happy Cow breaks even, it's not a big moneymaker, and right now the Hardcheese moneylending business is on the ropes. The Black Network has agents in Daggerford handing out interest-free loans (but breaking the arms of anyone who fails to pay up); the Hardcheeses simply can't compete.

If the characters deliver Oren's letter to Lily, her husband Koggin Hardcheese (LG male strongheart halfling **commoner**) asks them to speak with Nelkin "the Snail" Danniker, a Zhentarim operative who is staying at the River Shining Tavern and Inn, and kindly tell him to back off. Koggin would do it himself, but he thinks that the adventurers stand a better chance of persuading the Snail to relent. Nelkin is described in the "Daggerford" section in chapter 3. If the characters agree to his terms, as outlined in that section, Nelkin will stop undermining the Hardcheeses' moneylending business.

**Treasure.** Oren gives the party a cask of Goldengulp (worth 15 gp) as a gift before they leave Goldenfields.

Koggin Hardcheese gives the characters a cornucopia stuffed with fresh fruit and bread if they come to terms with the Snail. If the characters are visibly unhappy with this reward, he throws in a bottle of winterberry wine (worth 10 gp).

# TRIBOAR

The bustling mercantile town of Triboar stands where the Long Road meets the Evermoor Way. Triboar's name is thought to have come from a traveler's tale of slaying three boars here in the same day, over four hundred winters ago. The town is built on flat, fertile land, with a few natural rises here and there. Nearly half of Triboar's population lives outside the town proper, on sprawling ranches and neighboring farmsteads, most of which lie to the north or east.

The current lord protector of Triboar is a good-natured Harper and ex-adventurer named Darathra Shendrel. Darathra enacts and modifies local laws (known as "the Lord's Decree"), which are then enforced by the Twelve—a squad of a dozen mounted warriors drawn from the militia.

Triboar is a market for the horses raised by nearby ranches. Blacksmiths, harness-makers, and wagon-works also flourish in town. In addition, a number of guides operate out of Triboar. They take merchants and other travelers all over the Sword Coast, typically for stiff fees.

## LOCATIONS IN TRIBOAR

The following locations are identified on map 2.3. Out-lying ranches and farmsteads are not described here, since they have little bearing on this part of the adventure. You can develop these outlying areas as you see fit.

### C. COTTAGE

Each of these plain stone cottages is home to 1d4 adult **commoners** and 1d4 − 1 children (noncombatants) of various ethnicities.

### F. FARM

Each of these plots of land contains a modest stone farmhouse, a wooden outhouse, and a tilled garden or pasture. The farm is occupied by 1d6 adult **commoners** and 1d6 − 1 children (noncombatants) of various ethnicities.

### T1. MARKET SQUARE AND TOWER

The center of Triboar, where the Long Road meets the Evermoor Way, is a huge open space used as a market by local farmers and visiting peddlers. Dominating the space is the two-story Tower of the Lord Protector, a simple stone keep that leans decidedly to the east. Hanging above the entrance is the dusty banner of the lord protector, which depicts three black boars running toward the head of the banner on a blood-red field.

The current Lord Protector of Triboar is **Darathra Shendrel** (see appendix D), a Harper agent from Water-deep elected by the people of Triboar to command the town militia, settle disputes, and keep the peace. Her association with the Harpers is not widely known, but she is widely regarded as a fair and clear-headed leader.

The regular militia takes turns serving in the Twelve, a mounted police force (good-aligned male and female human **veterans** on **riding horses**) that patrols the town, the roads that lead between the outlying ranches, and the eastern half of the Triboar Trail. If needed, Darathra can muster a well-armed militia of fifty in the night, and three hundred by highsun the next day. The lord protector also has the authority to draft mercenaries and adventurers, as needed.

### T2. NORTH CARAVAN CAMPGROUND

Caravans passing through Triboar use this fenced-in field as a place to park their wagons and contain their oxen for free. There's also plenty of room to pitch tents and build campfires. Fresh water can be drawn from a 30-foot-deep stone well in the southeast corner of the yard.

A cottage stands in the east corner of the lot. Its elderly occupant, **Darz Helgar** (see appendix D), is paid by the lord protector to keep the town's campgrounds clean by removing the garbage and burying the excrement. Darz has also buried his shady past; he was a member of a thieves' guild in Waterdeep who was caught and imprisoned for his many crimes. After his release from prison, he moved to Triboar to start a new life.

### T3. West Caravan Campground

This campground is similar to area T2. A 30-foot-deep stone well in the middle of the yard provides fresh water for guests.

### T4. Happy Horse Ranch

The Karnveller family raises, trains, sells, and stables horses. Three large buildings stand on their property: a two-story log house with a detached outhouse (the family estate); a stone storehouse full of used saddles, bridles, and reins; and stone stables connected to a fenced-in riding yard and grazing field.

Janele Karnveller (NG female human **commoner**) is the family matriarch, a feisty middle-aged widow who enjoys the company of horses more than people. She has three adult sons named Aldo, Hingo, and Rasko (LG male human **veterans**), all of whom are members of the town militia.

### T5. Wainwright's Wagons

A longtime fixture in Triboar, Wainwright's Wagons has its own horse-driven sawmill and large buildings for lumber storage. The establishment originally catered to the wealthy elite by crafting the finest, most expensive wagons in the Dessarin Valley. The current owner, Tosker Wainwright (N male human **commoner**), is more interested in profit than quality. Lacking the carpentry skills of his ancestors, he relies on underpaid apprentices to assemble wagons that are little better than ordinary, yet they cost five times as much. The Wainwright brand name is the only thing keeping the establishment in business . . . for now.

### T6. The Lion's Share

This building was recently purchased and refurbished by the Lionshield Coster, a merchant company based in the city of Yartar. Above the store's entrance hangs a polished shield emblazoned with the head of a stylized golden lion on a blue background.

Lionshields are not well liked in Triboar, since Triboar and Yartar are bitter rivals, and few locals spend their money in this place. The store caters mostly to caravans and out-of-towners, selling provisions and animal fodder up front, and adventuring gear, armor, and weapons in back. Rooms on the second floor contain accommodations for the store's young proprietors, Alaestra Ulgar (NG female human **commoner**) and **Narth Tezrin** (see appendix D), as well as a hidden vault containing their wealth. Alaestra and Narth run a successful business even in the face of local insults and mild harassment. They have an agreement with the lord protector not to sell weapons to anyone they think might be a threat to the town. In exchange, the lord protector makes sure the store isn't victimized by vandals and local troublemakers.

***Treasure.*** A closet-sized vault on the second floor is hidden behind a secret door that requires a successful DC 15 Wisdom (Perception) check to spot. The vault contains an empty *Heward's handy haversack* and a locked iron strongbox that contains 3d10 × 10 gp in mixed coinage and a gray *bag of tricks*. Alaestra and Narth each carry a key to the strongbox. Its lock can be picked with thieves' tools and a successful DC 20 Dexterity check.

### T7. Ransor's Open Road

This establishment once sold feed and caravan supplies, as well as the services of caravan guards. Its owner passed away many years ago, and the business has been closed ever since. The yard is a riot of weeds, and the buildings have become havens for rats and other vermin. Locals have removed most of the wooden shingles from the rooftops, using them to replace the old shingles on their own roofs.

### T8. The Cart and Coin

This establishment sells and swaps horses and draft animals, and also deals in feed, horseshoes, and gear. The owners are a married couple named Arn and Syreen Widdens (NG human **commoners**). They have four young children (noncombatants) and employ half a dozen workers (N male human **commoners**) to feed and exercise the animals, clean the stables, and replace horseshoes.

### T9. The Triboar Travelers

Merchant sponsors can hire the personnel and the vehicles of the Triboar Travelers to make caravan runs to Waterdeep and back, for 600 gp each way, plus 25 gp for each wagon beyond the tenth. Runs to Everlund and back are 800 gp each way, as monsters from the Evermoors are known to prey on caravans along this route, plus 30 gp for each wagon beyond the tenth. The company hires mercenaries and adventurers to serve as guards, paying each person 4 gp per day plus food and drink. Each guard also receives a bonus of 25 gp if all caravan goods arrive at the destination.

Urlam Stockspool (N male human **spy**), a shrewd, immaculately dressed businessman, runs the caravan company and is a recruiter for the Black Network. He's proud of his affiliation: he lost an eye in combat several years ago and wears a red eye patch emblazoned with the black serpent symbol of the Zhentarim. Urlam is rarely seen without his suave bodyguard, Valken Naspeer (N male half-elf **assassin**). Although Urlam and Valken are good-humored and speak highly of the local authorities, they know that the lord protector keeps a watchful eye on them. They have no idea that Darathra is affiliated with the Harpers, but it wouldn't surprise them to learn as much. At any given time, the bunkhouse next to Urlam's residence holds 2d6 Zhentarim caravan guards (N male and female human **thugs**) waiting for their next job.

Characters might approach Urlam looking for work. He has nothing for them unless one or more characters

# Triboar

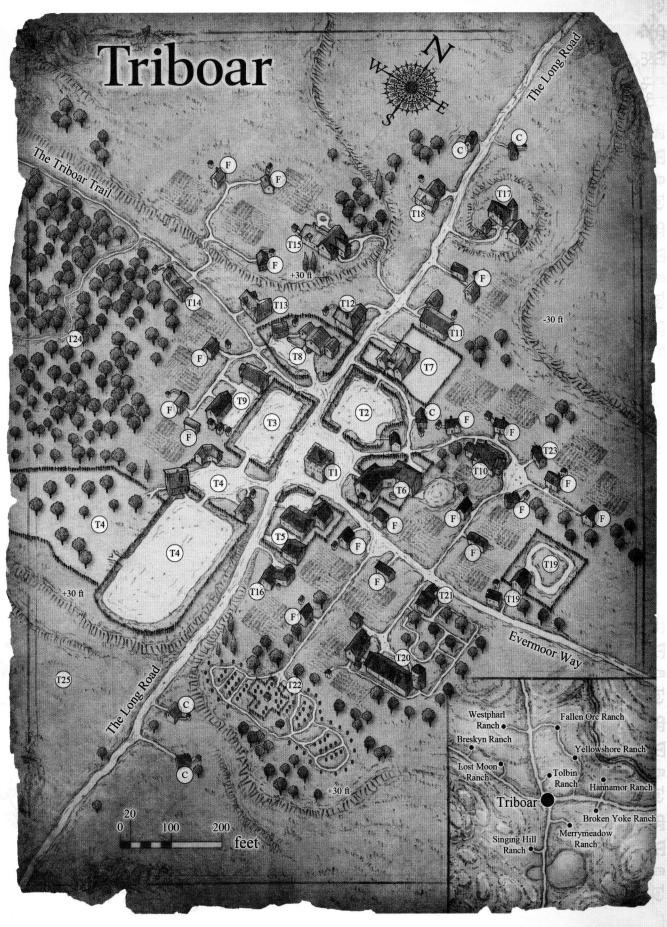

The Triboar Trail

The Long Road

The Long Road

Evermoor Way

+30 ft

-30 ft

+30 ft

+30 ft

F F F F F F F F F F F F F F F F F F F F F F F

C C C C C C

T1 T2 T3 T4 T4 T4 T5 T6 T7 T8 T9 T10 T11 T12 T13 T14 T15 T16 T17 T18 T19 T19 T20 T21 T22 T23 T24 T25

Westpharl Ranch
Breskyn Ranch
Lost Moon Ranch
Fallen Orc Ranch
Yellowshore Ranch
Tolbin Ranch
Hannamor Ranch
Broken Yoke Ranch
Merrymeadow Ranch
Singing Hill Ranch
**Triboar**

20
0    100    200
feet

Map 2.3: Triboar

are members of the Black Network, in which case he gives them a quest. If they complete the quest, he gives them another until they've completed three quests. The three quests are as follows, and every quest the characters complete earns them a 500 gp gemstone as payment:

- Urlam suspects that Othovir (see area T11) is hiding a secret, and he wants to know what it is. To complete this quest, the characters must learn that Othovir has blood ties to House Margaster in Waterdeep. Othovir won't divulge this information willingly, so the characters must either charm or interrogate Othovir to learn the truth.
- Urlam is convinced that Tolmara Hysstryn (see area T14) has a secret, and he wants to know what it is. The characters can complete this quest by finding Tolmara's dead husband in the attic of the Six Windows rooming house.
- Urlam believes that Nemyth (see area T16) has a secret, and he wants to know what it is. In truth, Nemyth has no secrets, and Urlam's belief stems from prejudice toward tieflings. If the characters wish to complete this quest, they must contrive a secret and convince Urlam of its veracity, which can be accomplished with a successful Charisma (Deception) check contested by Urlam's Wisdom (Insight) check.

## T10. Northshield House

Northshield House is a fine local inn—stately, clean, and quiet. The proprietor, **Urgala Meltimer** (see appendix D), is a retired adventurer who bought the inn from the Phorndyl family a little over ten years ago, after her wife (a wizard) vanished in the Underdark on an expedition. She much prefers retirement and warns armed guests to keep their blades sheathed during their stay. Urgala has three **mastiffs** (hunting dogs) that sleep in the ground floor common room, and she employs a staff of six loyal, well-paid **commoners** (LG males and females of various races). Guests sleep in private rooms on the upper floor.

## T11. Othovir's Harness Shop

A skilled harness-maker named **Othovir** (see appendix D) lives and works here, making the finest elk-skin harnesses in the Dessarin Valley. He hunts the elk, keeps their skins, and sells the rest to the Lionshield Coster (area T6). His harnesses have elaborate designs pressed into the leather, and his work is popular among Waterdhavian nobles who enjoy horseback riding. Although he hails from a prominent Waterdeep family (the Margasters), Othovir never speaks of his past or his family, and he has no interest in describing how he ended up a shop owner in Triboar. The truth is, several members of Othovir's family are secret worshipers of Asmodeus, and he wants nothing to do with that.

## T12. The Talking Troll

The Troll is what Waterdhavians would call a dive—a dim, smelly, low-beamed place crammed with mismatched, battered old furniture and drunks. Part of the roof caught fire two summers ago and has yet to be repaired. The holes in the roof have allowed birds to build nests among the beams, and the floor and tables are speckled with bird droppings. The Troll's one redeeming feature is its large, well-stocked cellar. The owner and proprietor of the Troll is a struggling actor named Kaelen Sarssir (LN male human **commoner**). He "inherited" the tavern after the previous owner fled in the wake of a scandal and has done the minimum amount of work necessary to keep it operational. Kaelen has dreams of turning the Troll into a theater, but he lacks the funds and the ambition to do so. He shares his dream with new patrons, hoping one or more of them might make a donation or otherwise sponsor the endeavor. Kaelen might even be persuaded to accept a business partner, provided there's little or no risk to him.

A **priest** of Helm named Silvarren Loomshank (LN male human) sleeps in a drunken stupor in a corner of the common room, barely noticed by the Troll's other patrons. A lifelong resident of Neverwinter, he was "banished" by his superiors to the Allfaiths Shrine in Red Larch. He has yet to arrive there, choosing instead to stop and drown his sorrows in Triboar. He hasn't lost his faith in Helm, merely his faith in himself and his superiors. Consumed by self-pity, he sees himself as a victim of "temple politics." He has spent all of his traveling money and racked up a drinking debt of 5 gp. He won't leave Triboar until the debt is paid off. If the characters settle Silvarren's debt, they can persuade him to attend to his duties in Red Larch with a successful DC 10 Charisma (Persuasion) check.

## T13. The Frost-Touched Frog

This old inn is boarded up and empty. Vandals have carved lewd phrases into the planks covering the doors and windows, and tall weeds have the building surrounded.

## T14. Six Windows

This chilly, creaking, decrepit wooden rooming house is run by Tolmara Hysstryn (CN female human **commoner**), a middle-aged woman. Visitors unable to secure rooms at Everwyvern House or Northshield House might be forced to bunk here, but they rarely stay longer than a night because they quickly discover that Tolmara isn't shy about spying on them through keyholes and listening at doors while chuckling to herself.

Locked in the Six Windows' attic are the bones of Tolmara's dead husband, Mirak, of whom she rarely speaks. Tolmara hides the key to the attic door in her brassiere. The lock can be picked with thieves' tools and a DC 10 Dexterity check. If Mirak's bones are touched, his **skeleton** animates for 1d4 rounds, after which it clatters to the floor. The effect repeats if the bones are touched again, unless the skeleton is reduced to 0 hit points or the bones are destroyed, in which case they can't animate. The skeleton is unarmed and deals 1 bludgeoning damage on a hit.

Any character who casts a *speak with dead* spell on Mirak's skull and asks Mirak's spirit how he died learns that Tolmara drugged him and sealed him in a barrel with a poisonous snake, which killed him with its bite. Mirak has no clue why Tolmara killed him, and

Tolmara is too addled to remember the incident or the circumstances leading up to it. Casting a *greater restoration* spell on Tolmara restores her sanity, whereupon she confesses to murdering her husband for being unfaithful.

If the characters report Tolmara's crime to Darathra Shendrel, the lord protector has Tolmara arrested and imprisoned pending a trial. Darathra also notifies Mirak's two brothers, who work on a nearby ranch. For years, they were led to believe that Mirak had left town with another woman; they are grateful to the characters for unearthing the truth and offer them a *+1 longbow* (a family heirloom) as a reward.

### T15. Boar's Rest

Built on a ridge that overlooks the rest of town, Boar's Rest is the stone mansion of a rich, retired adventurer named Hyuth Kolstaag (NE male human **mage**). Ever since Kolstaag had the place built and moved in five years ago, his unbridled arrogance and sense of self-importance have won him no friends in Triboar. Moreover, he has been targeted by so many enemies and rivals that other townsfolk consider him a magnet for disaster. He lives surrounded by trophies of his past adventures, and rarely emerges from his estate. He never condescends to protect the town or use his wealth to aid the less fortunate.

A few weeks ago, a trio of assassins slipped into town one night and tried to slay the mage in his sleep. The rest of Triboar was awakened by peals of thunder and blasts of lightning coming from Kolstaag's estate, and though the assassins survived, they were forced to steal horses from the Cart and Coin (area T8) and murder a stablehand to make good their escape. Kolstaag never offered to reimburse the Widdens family for their loss and never admitted any responsibility for the event.

Since the latest attack on his person, Kolstaag has enlisted four **gargoyles** to perch on the corners of his rooftop and serve as living sentries. To alleviate their boredom, the malevolent gargoyles swoop down on townsfolk from time to time and terrify them for the sake of amusement, which has led to some tense meetings between the lord protector and the wizard of Boar's Rest, who doesn't see the harm.

***Treasure.*** Kolstaag hides his valuables with the aid of a *Leomund's secret chest* spell. He keeps the tiny replica needed to recall the chest on his person, or on a nearby nightstand while he sleeps. Only Kolstaag can use the replica to recall the chest, which he does before entering combat to gain access to the magic items within. If he's captured, he can be persuaded to recall the chest in exchange for a promise of freedom. The extradimensional chest contains six 500 gp gems, Kolstaag's *bracers of defense*, and a *+1 wand of the war mage*.

### T16. The Triboar Arms

The Triboar Arms has burned to the ground twice and been rebuilt twice. Its owner and proprietor is Nemyth (NG male tiefling **commoner**), a savvy businessman with a wicked smile. He likes to lean against the tap-room doorway, drying and polishing a mug while nodding and smiling at passersby. His prices are reasonable, his staff cordial.

The tavern is a popular hangout for rangers and scouts, most of whom sell their services as wilderness guides. One of Nemyth's "regulars" is a friendly and capable guide named Zindra Winterbow (NG female half-elf **scout**), a member of the Emerald Enclave. She charges 10 gp per day for her services, regardless of the danger. She has noticed more and more hill giants, ogres, and Uthgardt hunters wandering the hills around Triboar recently, and she warns adventurers leaving town to be wary of them.

### T17. Uldinath's Arms

This hilltop smithy across the road from Foehammer's Forge (area T18) is run by Harriet Uldinath (LG female human **commoner**), the great-granddaughter of the establishment's founder. Harriet has known Ghelryn Foehammer since she was a child, and the two are friendly rivals. Harriet sells fine weapons stamped with the Uldinath family glyph, which generally increases their value by 25 percent.

### T18. Foehammer's Forge

**Ghelryn Foehammer** (see appendix D) makes fine weapons, armor, and other metalworks. Ghelryn is getting a bit long in the tooth for the daily grind of metalsmithing, so he's looking for a skilled apprentice, but no one has met with his approval so far. A year ago, Ghelryn made splendid suits of ceremonial armor for King Morinn and Queen Tithmel of Citadel Felbarr, and the royals were so impressed that they bestowed upon Ghelryn the honorary title of Royal Armorer. For that and other reasons, the Foehammer name is synonymous with top-quality goods throughout the Dessarin Valley, and Ghelryn intends to keep it that way.

Ghelryn hates orcs and giants. During the War of the Silver Marches, he obtained reports of orcs and giants attacking dwarfholds throughout the North. Many times he wanted to take up arms and travel north to join the war, yet he restrained himself because he had a business to run. But when giants attack Triboar, he refuses to stand back and idly watch.

### T19. Merivold Pony Park

North of the Evermoor Way, a quaint cottage stands near a brightly painted barn topped with a pony-shaped weather vane. A white picket fence encloses a small field behind the barn. Set among flowers on the front lawn is a sign that reads "Merivold Pony Park." Two spinster-sisters named Janna and Leera Merivold (LN female human **commoners**) raise and train ponies here, including riding ponies for halflings. At any given time, the Merivolds have 2d4 ponies for sale.

### T20. Everwyvern House

This expensive inn caters to Waterdhavian nobility and other well-to-do folk who wouldn't be caught dead in a more modest establishment. The property is situated behind the Pleasing Platter (area T21) on a beautifully landscaped patch of land with private stables, private gardens, and a meandering path through a small orchard. The inn itself is a beautiful stone building with lamps hanging from its eaves and a turret in one corner.

The snobbery of Everwyvern House is equaled by its elegant foppery. The atmosphere in the place is like a parody of the grandest Waterdhavian noble parties. Folk come here to be awed by it, to be amused by it, or to feel at home in it. Minstrels play quiet background music among floating plants and many-hued driftglobes, while startlingly gowned women and dashingly sashed and ruffled men chat, stroll, dance, and sneer at each other. Several of these well-dressed fops are actually escorts (N male and female human **commoners**) employed by the inn's proprietor to enhance the mood. They are coached to speak and parade about like nobles, but they are nothing more than low-paid actors.

The Everwyvern's condescending peacock of a proprietor, Draven Millovyr (NE male human **mage**), tried and failed to gain membership in the Arcane Brotherhood. When that career path didn't pan out, he used his inherited wealth to buy Everwyvern House. The Everwyvern's beds are comfortable but horribly overpriced (15 gp per night), though the fee includes room service and companionship, if desired. The meals on the menu are prepared just as they are in Waterdeep's finest restaurants, but nonetheless they are extraordinarily expensive (25 gp per plate). Draven employs spies to keep him apprised of the latest dining and fashion trends.

Draven doesn't allow "nobodies" to stay at his inn, and he employs six bouncers (NE male human **thugs**) to throw out the trash. Adventurers of noble blood and their servants are welcome; others are not.

Draven keeps his wealth in his locked quarters, located on the top floor of the Everwyvern's turret. He carries the only key to the door. Its lock can be picked with thieves' tools and a successful DC 15 Dexterity check. A *glyph of warding* spell cast on the door is triggered when someone other than Draven opens it. When triggered, the glyph casts a *conjure animals* spell that summons a pair of **death dogs**. They attack anyone not accompanied by Draven.

***Treasure.*** A locked chest in Draven's quarters contains 540 gp in mixed coinage—funds that Draven uses to pay his staff and maintain his "modest" lifestyle. A secret compartment in the chest's lid holds three bejeweled necklaces (stolen from visiting Waterdhavian noblewomen) worth 750 gp each. The compartment can be found with a successful DC 15 Wisdom (Perception) check. Draven carries the key to the chest, which can otherwise be opened with thieves' tools and a successful DC 20 Dexterity check.

## T21. The Pleasing Platter

This fine restaurant is next door to the grandiose Everwyvern House, and it has adopted similar pretensions. Its tables are far apart. Each is screened from the others by strategically placed plants, statues, or pillars. Minstrels play soft and soothing music in the background. Service is fast, polite, and deft, with special requests honored swiftly and obligingly to meet a guest's culinary preferences. House specialties include smoked quail, rothé steak cooked in wine and nuts, and grilled silvertail fish. Prices are comparable to those at Everwyvern

House, and free flasks of sweet water (see area T23) are served with dinner. The owners and chefs are Heltzer and Pentavasta Duncask (LG male and female human **commoners**), a cheerful and randy older couple.

## T22. Graveyard

Perched atop a ridge at the south end of town is an old cemetery where many of Triboar's first settlers are buried under weatherworn headstones. The oldest graves are located on a plot of land enclosed by an old, unpainted picket fence.

## T23. Apothecary

Across the road from Northshield House (area T10) is the town apothecary, a slouched wooden cottage with ivy-covered walls. Tarmock Felaskur (CN male human **commoner**) sells herbal medicines and salves of questionable efficacy. Parked outside the apothecary's front door is a ramshackle wheelbarrow, hanging above which is a wooden sign shaped like a potion bottle. In addition to herbs and salves, Tarmock sells "sweet water" for 1 gp a flask. The sweet, naturally carbonated water bubbles up from a tiny spring in the shed behind Tarmock's cottage. Tarmock makes most of his money selling the water to the proprietors of The Pleasing Platter.

## T24. Gwaeron's Slumber

Gwaeron Windstrom, the god of tracking, is said to visit this mystical forest. Rangers who venerate Gwaeron or Mielikki, the goddess of forests, come here for inspiration. Some claim to have seen Gwaeron walking among the trees, appearing as a tall, muscular man whose long, white hair and beard whip and billow as if in an endless breeze, even when there is no wind. It is also said that worshipers of Gwaeron or Mielikki who sleep in this wood will receive prophetic dreams. In truth, Gwaeron never visits those who come seeking him, though he appears unexpectedly in the grove on rare occasions.

To avoid angering Gwaeron, the law in Triboar forbids cutting any wood from these trees or hunting any creature in the woods. Many of the trees in Gwaeron's Slumber are trapped in a perpetual autumnal state, with leaves in dazzling shades of yellow, orange, and red.

An **oni** that lives in a hillside cave west of Triboar occasionally visits this grove to feast on unsuspecting rangers as they sleep among the trees, appearing before them as Gwaeron Windstrom. The oni cleans up after itself, leaving little evidence of its victims behind. This "tidiness" has led others to believe that sometimes Gwaeron, rather than sending prophetic dreams, appears and spirits a worthy supplicant away to his divine domain.

## T25. Marshaling Field

An old, partially ruined wooden fence encloses a large, muddy field south of town. In years past, armies gathered and camped here before marching off to war. The field has seen little use in recent years.

## ATTACK ON TRIBOAR

Thousands of years ago, giants and dragons fought a great battle here, during which the giants unleashed an enormous dragon-slaying construct called the Vonindod. Part of the construct broke off and was embedded in the ground. Over time, this fragment became buried deep in the earth. Today, it lies under a campground in the heart of town (area T2).

Fire giants loyal to Duke Zalto have been using *rods of the Vonindod* (see appendix B) to locate fragments of the construct. One such rod has led a mated pair of **fire giants** named Okssort and Ildmane to Triboar. Their entourage includes five **orogs**, six **orcs** mounted on **axebeaks**, and twelve **magmins** split into two gangs of six.

### BEGINNING THE ENCOUNTER

Around highsun, the town is shaken from its peacefulness by the screams of women and children, followed by a man yelling, "Giants! Run!" Perplexed residents and shopkeepers emerge from their domiciles in time to see a large rock fall from the sky and crash onto an old cart, splintering it. As a cloud of dust erupts from the wreckage, a second rock hits the ground, tumbles through a fence, and slams against the wall of a building, startling a pair of mules tethered to a post nearby. All around you, people begin to shriek and scatter.

Okssort and Ildmane's plan is to barge into town, dig up the Vonindod fragment, and haul it back to Ironslag (see chapter 8, "Forge of the Fire Giants"), destroying anything that gets in their way. As they approach the center of Triboar, they hurl boulders into the town to strike fear into the hearts of the townsfolk, hoping to frighten most of them away. The magmins run alongside the giants, eager to please. Whenever a fire giant points to a building or other flammable structure, a gang of magmins runs toward the target and tries to set it ablaze.

The orogs, clad in heavy plate mail, march ahead of the fire giants, knocking down fences and clearing the way of rabble. Anything the orogs don't knock down is crushed underfoot by the advancing fire giants. The orogs spread through town, attacking civilians who cross their path and drawing attention away from the fire giants.

The orcs ride their axebeaks into town after the initial volley of boulders. Their job is to distract the town's defenders and engage enemy archers in melee combat. The axebeaks act on the orcs' initiative count. Rules for mounted combat can be found in chapter 9 of the *Player's Handbook*.

The fire giants and their entourage approach from the northeast, damaging Othovir's Harness Shop (area T11) and destroying Ransor's Open Road (area T7) as they make their way toward the north campground (area T2). The fire giants are so intimidating that most townsfolk stop what they're doing and flee, heading south along the Long Road. Others hunker down in their homes and businesses.

If either fire giant is reduced to 81 hit points or fewer, the giants realize that they have underestimated Triboar's defenses. They quickly leave the way they came while commanding their underlings to cover their retreat.

## DEFENSE OF TRIBOAR

After receiving reports of orcs attacking ranches to the southeast, Lord Protector Darathra Shendrel sends the Twelve to Merrymeadow Ranch and Broken Yoke Ranch to ascertain the extent of the danger and aid the ranchers. These attacks are merely distractions. While the Twelve are away, the fire giants attack from the northeast, leaving the adventurers and a handful of determined townsfolk to defend the town. Give each player one of the following NPCs to play during this encounter:

**Darathra Shendrel**, Lord Protector of Triboar (starts at area T1)
**Darz Helgar**, campground caretaker (starts at area T2)
**Narth Tezrin**, Lionshield Coster representative (starts at area T6)
**Urgala Meltimer**, innkeeper and retired adventurer (starts at area T10)
**Othovir**, harness-maker (starts at area T11)
**Ghelryn Foehammer**, blacksmith (starts at area T18)

Statistics and roleplaying notes for these NPCs appear in appendix D. How the players run their NPCs during the battle is up to them, but encourage the players to review their NPCs' ideals, bonds, and flaws. For more information on how to use and run these NPCs, see the "Special NPCs" section at the start of this chapter.

If the players try to keep the special NPCs out of the fight, you can endanger them by having stray orogs or magmins threaten the NPCs directly, thereby requiring the player-controlled NPCs to act.

## VONINDOD FRAGMENT

Ildmane clutches a *rod of the Vonindod*, which guides her to area T2. When the fire giants arrive there, they use their greatswords like shovels, digging up the ground to reach the Vonindod fragment—a bent and broken band of 2-inch-thick adamantine roughly 11 feet long and weighing 1,000 pounds. It takes ten actions by the giants to unearth the C-shaped fragment, and another action for one of them to pull it free. One fire giant can carry the fragment using both hands or drag it using one hand.

Any character who inspects the broken adamantine ring can, with a successful DC 15 Intelligence (Arcana) check, determine that it was once part of some kind of enormous construct. Casting a *detect magic* spell on the fragment reveals a faint, lingering magical aura, though the school of magic can't be ascertained. If the characters obtain the fragment, Alaestra Ulgar (see area T6) and Urlam Stockspool (see area T9) each offers to buy it for 5,000 gp (paid in 500 gp gemstones), though its actual value is three times as much.

## TREASURE

Ildmane carries no treasure other than a *rod of the Vonindod* (see appendix B). Okssort carries a sack holding 1d6 mundane items, determined by rolling on the Items in a Giant's Bag table in the introduction, and a ruby pendant (worth 750 gp). The magmins and the orcs have no treasure. Each orog carries a pouch that holds 1d20 gp in mixed coinage.

## DEVELOPMENT

If the fire giants obtain the Vonindod fragment and leave town, they make the long trek back to Ironslag with their prize, avoiding roads and settlements. If the fire giants are forced to leave without the Vonindod fragment, they retreat to the Surbrin Hills and roust four hill giants, returning to Triboar 2d4 + 2 days after their initial attack. This time, they fight to the death to claim the fragment for their lord and master, Duke Zalto. The adventurers need not feel obliged to stay and defend the town from this second attack, because the local militia has been assembled and placed on alert.

Whether or not the characters thwart the fire giants, they gain special quests and rewards based on which NPCs survived the initial battle.

# TRIBOAR QUESTS

For each special NPC who survives the attack on Triboar, the party receives a quest and gains a particular award for completing that quest. The quests encourage characters to explore other locations throughout the North. Whether the characters travel over land or by sea, use the "Random Wilderness Encounters" section in chapter 3 to stage encounters along the way.

## DARATHRA SHENDREL'S QUEST

Darathra doesn't have much contact with her fellow Harpers, but it strikes her as odd that fire giants would make it this far into the Dessarin Valley without her receiving some kind of warning. She wants to make sure her organization is aware of the gravity of the situation. She gives the characters a platinum badge (worth 50 gp) bearing the Triboar insignia (three boars charging forward) and urges the characters to travel east along the Evermoor Way, visit Danivarr's House in Everlund, and give the badge to Dral Thelev, the one-eyed orc proprietor.

If the characters follow Darathra's instructions, Dral pockets the badge, uncorks a flask of elven wine that he claims is Silverymoon's finest, and pours its contents into small wooden cups—one per character. Characters who take even the smallest drink of the wine are teleported to a parlor in the heart of Moongleam Tower, the Harpers' stronghold in Everlund (see the "Everlund" section in chapter 3). Dral explains how the magic of the elixir works after one party member takes a sip and disappears, expecting that the others will want to follow.

The parlor in Moongleam Tower contains austere furnishings and a dozen harmless, domesticated **tressym** (see appendix C) behaving like house cats. A silent *alarm* spell notifies Krowen Valharrow, the tower's resident archmage, of the party's arrival. The dotty old wizard enters the parlor shortly after the characters appear, greets them warmly, and grants them free access to a secret network of teleportation circles until, as he puts it, "the Harpers decide otherwise" (see the "Inner Circles" section in chapter 3).

**Treasure.** After showing them the teleportation circle in Moongleam Tower, Krowen gives the adventurers a small wooden coffer that Darathra sent him for his birthday a few years back. The coffer's interior space is divided into six compartments, each of which contains a rolled-up *spell scroll*. The spells written on the scrolls are *dispel magic*, *fly*, *magic weapon*, *sending*, *tongues*, and *water breathing*. (If the characters meet Krowen in Everlund but are not engaged in Darathra's quest, Krowen does not provide the scrolls.)

## Darz Helgar's Quest

Darz relates to the characters that he was recently visited by an old acquaintance, a merchant from Mirabar, with an interesting tale to tell. The merchant saw a dwarf cleaning stables in Xantharl's Keep, a fortified village on the Long Road, and later recognized him from a wanted poster he saw while traveling south through Longsaddle. The merchant is sure that the dwarf he saw is a wanted brigand known as the Weevil; according to the wanted poster, whoever delivers him alive to the authorities in Mirabar can collect a reward of 5,000 gp.

Darz briefly entertained the idea of going after the Weevil himself, but then admitted to himself that he's too old for such things. Passing this information along to the characters is his way of thanking them for their help during the attack.

**Development.** If the characters head to Xantharl's Keep, they can catch the Weevil and turn him over to the Axe of Mirabar. See the "Xantharl's Keep" section in chapter 3 for more information.

## Narth Tezrin's Quest

A few months ago, the Lionshield Coster received a payment from one Amrath Mulnobar, castellan of Noanar's Hold, for five horse harnesses made by none other than Triboar's finest harness-maker, Othovir. Othovir recently finished the last of the harnesses, and Narth needs to arrange for their delivery to Noanar's Hold. Since the recent giant attack, he has become worried about the safe arrival of the shipment. Narth has never been to Noanar's Hold, but he describes it as a village near the High Forest that once attracted wealthy hunters.

Narth packs the harnesses in a large crate with the Lionshield Coster emblem painted on its sides and asks the characters to make the delivery for him. If they accept the quest, he tells them how to get to Noanar's Hold by following the Evermoor Way. When they're ready to leave, assuming they haven't made provisions to transport the shipment by other means, Narth has a cart waiting for them with the crate loaded on it, pulled by a draft horse named Boris.

**Treasure.** Narth offers them 100 gp up front to make the delivery. Narth also lets the characters keep Boris and the cart once they complete the delivery.

**Development.** When the characters arrive at Noanar's Hold, they are told that they can find Amrath Mulnobar in the keep overlooking the village. Amrath takes the harnesses off their hands without so much as a thank-you. Thus ends the quest.

With no other settlements nearby, the characters might be inclined to spend the night in the White Hart Inn, where they meet three middle-aged brothers from Neverwinter (LE male human **nobles**) who are gearing up for a hunt. Their names are Rantharl, Marthun, and Lezryk Daerivoss, and they tell the characters that they've come to Noanar's Hold to hunt hill giants. The brothers don't want company. They quietly saddle their horses, strap on their rapiers, and ride out at dawn. The younger brothers return before dusk, but Rantharl is not with them, and Marthun has a laceration on his right shoulder that a successful DC 11 Wisdom (Medicine) check confirms is a rapier wound.

If pressed, the brothers claim that a hill giant killed Rantharl. Marthun claims that he was struck by the giant's spiked greatclub and denies any assertion that his wound was caused by a rapier. A successful DC 15 Wisdom (Insight) check confirms that Marthun and Lezryk are lying, though Marthun welcomes any healing that the characters can provide.

The brothers are playing a murderous game with their inheritances at stake. The agreement was simple: the brother who first deals the killing blow to a hill giant would gain the inheritances of the other two. Rantharl won the contest, but Marthun and Lezryk turned against him. A fight ensued, Marthun was wounded, and Rantharl died. With Rantharl gone and no clear winner, Marthun and Lezryk have agreed to track down another hill giant.

If the characters follow the brothers on their hunt and are spotted, the brothers attack them. If the characters do nothing, Marthun and Lezryk begin another hunt the following day, but they encounter no hill giants. Lezryk betrays and kills Marthun, then returns to the inn to rest before making the long trip back to Neverwinter to deliver the sad news of his brothers' untimely deaths at the hands of "rampaging hill giants." Characters can blackmail Lezryk for a cut of the brothers' inheritance (worth 10,000 gp total), or deal with the treacherous cad in some other manner as they see fit.

## Urgala Meltimer's Quest

In the aftermath of the battle, Urgala relates to the characters that one of her former adventuring companions, a wealthy knight named Harthos Zymorven, had a *giant slayer* greatsword. (Change the weapon to a *giant slayer* greataxe if that would be more desirable to a party member.) The last time Urgala spoke with him, Harthos was living in Zymorven Hall, his ancestral keep on the Rauvin Road northwest of Silverymoon. Urgala thinks Harthos might be willing to part with the weapon if the characters mention her name to him and explain their reason for needing it.

If the characters journey to Zymorven Hall, they find Lord Harthos Zymorven, but he is sad to report that his son Harthal has stolen the *giant slayer*. Harthal committed this act after Lord Zymorven disowned him for marrying a common thief from Yartar (whose name he doesn't recall). What Harthal did with the sword, Lord Zymorven can only imagine.

The characters can travel to Yartar and search for Harthal there. After a few polite inquiries, it becomes apparent that the local thieves' guild, the Hand of Yartar, might be their best hope of finding Harthal. A character can bribe a tavern server at the Wink and Kiss (5 gp is sufficient) to learn the identity and whereabouts of a known Hand of Yartar member. They're as common as rats. If the characters obtained a letter of recommendation from Tamalin Zoar (see the "Calling Horns" section in chapter 3), they can show it to the Hand of Yartar member, who promises to have the information they need in a few hours. Otherwise, the thief demands a 500 gp payment up front. When the thief returns 1d6 hours later, she tells the characters that Harthal was arrested and imprisoned for murdering a man, and the greatsword found its way into the hands of a corrupt watch captain named Tholzar Brenner (LE male human **knight**).

The characters can try to relieve Brenner of the weapon by force. The man has many enemies, so he usually travels with eight **guards** (LE male and female humans). He refuses to relinquish the weapon willingly. Under normal circumstances, the death or disappearance of a watch member would trigger an investigation, but in Captain Brenner's case, Waterbaron Nestra Ruthiol is happy to be rid of him and doesn't order one.

Any character who belongs to the Harpers or the Zhentarim can approach his or her faction for help. If the character succeeds on a DC 15 Intelligence (Investigation) check, he or she locates a faction safe house and gains entry. A failed check can be rerolled after another day spent searching, until a check succeeds or the character gives up the search. Inside the safe house, the character meets a faction representative, who sets a few wheels in motion. A few hours later, the stolen weapon is delivered to the safe house.

A character who belongs to the Lords' Alliance can petition the Waterbaron for help. The character must succeed on a DC 15 Charisma (Deception or Persuasion) check to gain an audience. Deception is appropriate if the character makes false claims to gain an audience; otherwise, use Persuasion. A failed check can be rerolled the next day, but each failed check increases the DC by 1. If a character succeeds on this check, the Waterbaron wrests the sword from Captain Brenner's clutches and sees it delivered safely to that individual.

***Treasure.*** Lord Zymorven's weapon is indeed a *giant slayer* greatsword (or greataxe).

## OTHOVIR'S QUEST

After his close call during the giants' attack, Othovir expresses his gratitude to the characters by sharing a secret with them: he knows the location of a stash of magic items that the Margaster family, his kin, keeps locked away for emergencies. If the characters ask him how he came by this information, Othovir tells them that he has a history with the Margaster family, which he despises for reasons he'd rather not discuss. The family owns a three-story tower in Silverymoon that has a detached carriage house on the property, and it is here that the characters must travel. He provides the following details:

- The carriage house is a 30-foot-square stone building with two floors. The windowless ground floor that holds the carriage has a big wooden sliding door in the front. The upper floor is an apartment with a floor made of wooden planks and a barred window set into each wall. An open wooden staircase in one corner of the building connects the floors.
- Two human guards with spears are stationed in the upstairs apartment.
- An *arcane lock* spell protects the sliding wooden door.
- The carriage has two **draft horses** harnessed to it, ready to leave at a moment's notice. The carriage is protected by an *alarm* spell, set to go off when a carriage door is opened.
- The magic items are hidden in a compartment under the passenger seat inside the carriage.

Othovir doesn't know what magic items are included in the stash. He also doesn't know that the human guards are actually two **cambions** using *alter self* spells to conceal their true forms. The cambions are loyal to House Margaster and attack anyone they catch infiltrating the carriage house.

The *alarm* spell not only attracts the cambions but also alerts Xamlyn Margaster (LE female human **mage**), who lives in the nearby tower. She emerges from the tower on the third round and casts spells at anyone trying to make off with the magic items or the carriage.

***Treasure.*** The compartment has four magic items. Determine two of them by rolling on Magic Item Table C in chapter 7 of the *Dungeon Master's Guide*, and the other two by rolling on Magic Item Table B.

## GHELRYN FOEHAMMER'S QUEST

As a reward for their efforts, Ghelryn writes the characters a letter of recommendation (see the "Marks of Prestige" section in chapter 7 of the *Dungeon Master's Guide*) and suggests they present it to King Morinn or Queen Tithmel should they find themselves in Citadel Felbarr. See the "Citadel Felbarr" section in chapter 3 for more information on the king and queen.

***Treasure.*** If the characters pay a visit to Citadel Felbarr and show Ghelryn's letter to King Morinn and Queen Tithmel, the royal couple ask about Ghelryn's well-being, commend the party's devotion to ending the giant threat, and award the characters a special gift to help them in their war on giants: two *figurines of wondrous power* (golden lions).

> ### CHARACTER ADVANCEMENT
> If the characters help defend Bryn Shander, Goldenfields, or Triboar, they should advance to 6th level before setting out to explore other locations or beginning any of the special quests in this chapter.

# CHAPTER 3: THE SAVAGE FRONTIER

VAST FRONTIER SERVES AS THE BACKDROP for this story. As it turns out, giants are everywhere and wreaking all sorts of havoc, from the Sword Coast to the desert of Anauroch. This chapter describes this setting, beginning with an overview of the Savage Frontier and some of its key inhabitants, then presenting descriptions of specific locations. The chapter concludes with three encounters that help propel the story forward:

- In the "Old Tower" section, adventurers meet a lonely hill giant with an axe to grind;
- The "Inner Circles" section describes a series of teleportation circles that the adventurers can use to expedite travel;
- The "Harshnag" section introduces adventurers to a frost giant who means to help them.

Until the characters find a more expeditious means of transportation, they will be doing a lot of overland traveling. Chapter 5 of the *Dungeon Master's Guide* provides advice and tools to help make wilderness travel fun for you and the players, as well as rules for foraging and becoming lost. You can use the travel-montage approach or the hour-by-hour approach, or you can experiment with both to see which approach works best for you. That chapter also includes a table to randomly determine the weather and a table of random urban encounters (useful when the adventurers arrive at a city).

## PEOPLES OF THE NORTH

The Savage Frontier, or the North, is a harsh and untamed wilderness dotted with fortified settlements and the lairs of terrible monsters. In hundreds of bloodcurdling tales of danger and hardship, the North is portrayed as a vast, cold, and lawless domain that defies all attempts to civilize it. Grim dwarfholds, clans of fierce nomads, and half-legendary elf realms might stand for a short time, but none are destined to last. An orc horde or a flight of dragons could sweep them all away tomorrow, leaving nothing but mile upon unmapped mile of wilderness.

The Savage Frontier lies between the Sword Coast and the desert of Anauroch, extending as far north as Icewind Dale and as far south as the city of Waterdeep. The denizens of the North are accustomed to cool, mild summers and fierce, bitter winters. Beacons of civilization hug the Sword Coast and dot the fertile river valleys, yet despite the abundant natural resources and scenic beauty, survival is a day-to-day concern for the people who live here.

The North is a land of great mineral wealth and seemingly limitless stands of timber. Here, too, can be found the wealth of history—the plunder of lost civilizations such as Illefarn and Eaerlann, the ancient kingdoms of the gold elves; Delzoun, a long-buried nation of dungeon-dwelling dwarves; and Netheril, a fallen empire of human spellcasters. Throughout the Savage Frontier lie the ruins and dungeons of these and other "forgotten realms." Cities such as Waterdeep, Mirabar, and Neverwinter would like to claim this wealth and knowledge for themselves, but enforcing such claims is next to impossible. The cities have a hard enough time protecting their farmlands and roads from brigands and monsters.

## Settlements

Humans are the most widespread folk of the North, but no unified human nation exists in the North—only individual cities, towns, villages, fiefdoms, farmsteads, fortresses, and outposts connected to one another by long, mostly unprotected rivers and roads. Human settlements rely on various industries for survival. For example, most of the humans of Ten-Towns and Port Llast are fishers, the humans of Mirabar and Leilon are primarily miners, and the humans who live in Beliard, Triboar, and other settlements of the central Dessarin Valley are mostly farmers. Coastal cities such as Waterdeep, Luskan, and Neverwinter—as well as riverside cities such as Yartar, Everlund, and Silverymoon—are home to human traders, shipbuilders, and artisans.

Although each city of the North enjoys and maintains its independence, all these communities are at risk of being overrun by the monstrous threats that live outside their walls. Fear of the wilderness and its many terrors led to the formation of the Lords' Alliance, a loose confederacy of human-dominated settlements built on mutually beneficial trade agreements and a willingness to seek out and destroy threats to civilization. Members of the Lords' Alliance include the cities of Waterdeep, Neverwinter, Mirabar, Yartar, and Silverymoon, as well as the towns of Amphail, Daggerford, and Longsaddle and the dwarfhold of Mithral Hall. Baldur's Gate, a city hundreds of miles to the south, is also a member.

Within the settlements of the North, one can find humans, dwarves, elves, and other folk commingling more or less peacefully. Waterdeep, in particular, is a melting pot of races from all over Faerûn. Outside these communities, however, people have much less tolerance for strangers, as folk tend to feel safer among their own kind. Small towns and villages dominated by humans tend to have few if any nonhumans, with most dwarves, elves, and halflings preferring to live in their own settlements, far from human-claimed lands. In generations past, most human settlers of the North were light-haired and light-skinned. Since then, the riches and promise of the Savage Frontier have attracted distant foreigners, and several generations of cultural intermingling have given the humans of the North much more diversity in their appearance (see "Human Names and Ethnicities" in chapter 2 of the *Player's Handbook*).

## Northlanders

The terms Northlander, Northfolk, and Northmen are interchangeable. They refer to one of several tall, fair-haired, seagoing peoples that ply the cold northern waters and dwell on the islands of the west, including Tuern, Gundarlun, Ruathym, the Purple Rocks, and the Korinn Archipelago. Northfolk ancestors built small villages along the Sword Coast that have since become cities, including fabled Illusk (now Luskan), Eigersstor (now Neverwinter), and Nimoar's Hold (now Waterdeep). These early Northlanders farmed the rocky coastlines, fished coastal waters, and hunted seals and whales on the open sea. A few clans of Northlanders explored the monster-infested interior of the Savage Frontier, and they became the ancestors of the Uthgardt tribes and the present-day denizens of Icewind Dale.

Northlanders farm, fish, and mine their rugged lands, then shrewdly trade their goods with foreign buyers. Many once-feared tribes have become merchants whose bartering skills are equal to or better than the warlike talents of their ancestors, such that many a Northlander merchant is wealthier than their raiding neighbors.

## Reghed Nomads

The frozen tundra of Icewind Dale is home to the Reghed nomads. They are named after the Reghed Glacier that forms a towering ice wall along the eastern boundary of their domain. Markedly taller than most southerners, with some men approaching seven feet in height, Reghed nomads have blue eyes and hair of blond, red, or light brown. Their skin is bronzed from the sun and cracked by the wind, giving their faces the look of tough leather set in an expressionless mask. They dress in leather and furs. At one time, scores of Reghed tribes roamed the frozen north. Now, due to wars with other creatures and battles against their own kind, only four Reghed tribes remain. They follow herds of reindeer on the animals' annual migrations, moving southwest in the winter and northeast in the summer. The nomads live in large, round tents made of deerskin and supported by beams of wood or whalebone.

In the past, the Reghed tribes were known to raid the settlements of Ten-Towns for supplies, but now the Tribe of the Elk is learning to live in peace with the people of Ten-Towns. The other three Reghed tribes—the Tribe of the Tiger, the Tribe of the Wolf, and the Tribe of the Bear—are more likely to attack one another than to threaten Ten-Towns, fighting over sustenance at the risk of their own extinction.

A single Reghed tribe is made up of small clans scattered throughout Icewind Dale, each with its own chieftain. The chieftains choose the most powerful among them to be their king or queen—the one around whom others rally in times of crisis. When a monarch dies, the tribe's chieftains gather to choose a new one. Disputes over who should be named king or queen are resolved through trials by nonlethal combat. Without a unifying leader, a Reghed tribe is more fractured and vulnerable to its enemies. Thus, chieftains are motivated to name one among them who rules above all. A chieftain who becomes king or queen wears that mantle for life.

Most Rheged nomads will set aside tribal rivalries to unite against white dragons and frost giants, since those creatures threaten Icewind Dale's food supply. The Tribe of the Wolf and its king, Isarr Kronenstrom, don't ally with the other tribes—they are so vicious and bloodthirsty as to be unapproachable. The kings and queens of the other tribes would see the Tribe of the Wolf obliterated, but the Wolf King and his followers are adept at avoiding the traps set for them by their rivals.

## TRIBE OF THE BEAR

One of the Bear tribe's two remaining chieftains, Wolvig Barrundson, recently fell under the sway of evil and formed an alliance with a supernatural entity known as the Ice Witch. Her demise also spelled Wolvig's doom, allowing the sole remaining chieftain, Günvald Halraggson, to declare himself the Bear King. He tries to be honorable, but he is without mercy and doesn't change his mind easily. He has trouble relating to Ten-Towners and other settled folk, so he tries to avoid them.

## TRIBE OF THE ELK

For the most part, the Tribe of the Elk lives in peace with the Ten-Towners. King Jarund Elkhardt, a towering figure, rules his people with wisdom and care. He has seen other kings rise and fall, has made war with his friends and peace with his enemies, and has led warriors he knew as babes to their deaths in battle. The strain of his long years is written on his face.

## TRIBE OF THE TIGER

It is unusual for a woman to lead a Reghed tribe, but Bjornhild Solvigsdottir is no ordinary woman. The fearless wife of King Korold, she fought alongside him in many battles. After a frost giant slew Korold, the formidable Bjornhild took his place. Bjornhild worships Auril the Frostmaiden and is so ruthless that

her enemies believe she has actual ice flowing through her veins.

## TRIBE OF THE WOLF

Weakened by conflict, the Tribe of the Wolf was without a king or queen for three winters. Its most powerful chieftain, Isarr Kronenstrom, is a bloodthirsty tyrant who worships Malar the Beast-Lord. He hunts Ten-Towners for sport and strikes fear into the hearts of his enemies, many of whom believe he's the Chosen of Malar. Several members of Isarr's clan have deserted him or been killed off by rival tribes, but the few that remain are fiercely loyal, Though Isarr's clan has dwindled in recent years, the other Wolf chieftains fear Isarr and are too weak to challenge him. They are also afraid to ally with the other Reghed tribes against Isarr. Although Isarr calls himself the Wolf King, few others in the Wolf tribe support him in that claim.

## UTHGARDT

The Uthgardt are a black-haired and blue-eyed people—large, hale, territorial folk who don't trust outsiders. Few Uthgardt are willing to trade with non-Uthgardt settlements. Many are raiders who pillage and destroy any caravan or homestead they come across.

The Uthgardt take their name from Uthgar Gardolfsson, a great hero-chief who battled giants and conquered much of the North before ascending to godhood.

In addition to revering Uthgar, each tribe venerates a totem animal spirit after which the tribe is named.

Numerous Uthgardt tribes have been vanquished over the years, and at least one tribe previously thought to be extinct has returned in force. There are currently eleven known Uthgardt tribes scattered throughout the North. Each one claims a vast tract of wilderness as its hunting grounds—territory that often overlaps with the hunting grounds of other Uthgardt tribes as well as land claimed by orcs, dragons, goblinoids, and other creatures. Encounters with the Uthgardt can occur almost anywhere in the Savage Frontier.

The Uthgardt speak their own language (called Bothii), which has no alphabet. Each tribe is made up of several widely scattered clans, each with its own chieftain and shaman. The chieftains of a particular tribe choose one among them to become the great chief of the tribe, with power comparable to a monarch.

The Uthgardt typically bury their dead under cairns and earthen mounds. These burial sites are scattered throughout the North in out-of-the-way places. Each Uthgardt tribe also has a single spirit mound that is sacred to its people. A spirit mound is where members of the tribe gather to revere Uthgar, honor their ancestors, make sacrifices to their totem animal spirit, and choose a new great chief when the old one dies. The Uthgardt believe that their ancestors trapped their totem spirits under these mounds so that they and their descendants could commune with the spirits and gain their power.

The Uthgardt fear magic so much that they will attempt to kill and dismember spellcasters they meet. Tribal shamans are not attacked because their power comes from the spirits of their dead ancestors. (See appendix C for more information on Uthgardt shamans.)

The Uthgardt hunt and forage for food. With one exception among the tribes, they don't build houses or permanent settlements, preferring a nomadic lifestyle.

Uthgardt tribes will unite against a common enemy. The Uthgardt hate giants most of all—Uthgardt legends are replete with tales of how evil giants slew their ancestors and threatened Uthgar's rise to godhood.

## BLACK LION TRIBE

The Black Lion tribe prowls the northern Silver Marches and the Druarwood, protecting its spirit mound at Beorunna's Well (which it shares with the Red Tiger tribe). The Black Lions have been known to raid poorly defended homesteads for food and supplies during harsh winters. The great chief of the Black Lion tribe, Stellok Kolraavi, wears armor made from orc hide and has a fearsome reputation. His younger sister, Tysis Kolraavi, is a shaman and Stellok's only trusted advisor. The siblings venerate Uthgar, and they have no tolerance for diplomacy or for the trappings of civilization.

## BLACK RAVEN TRIBE

The Black Ravens claim the icy foothills west of Mirabar, as well as the Ice Lakes and the land west to the Frozenfar. They like to prey on caravans that travel the Northern Means and the Blackford Road. Black Raven warriors often ride giant ravens (use the **giant vulture** stat block) into battle. The Black Ravens share their

spirit mound at Raven Rock with the Gray Wolf tribe. The great chief of the Black Raven tribe is Ojin Voninsdottir, a cold, heartless woman with an orc-skull helm.

## BLUE BEAR TRIBE

The easternmost of the Uthgardt tribes, the Blue Bear tribe was thought destroyed more than a century ago. Recently, clans haunting the High Forest have emerged and begun to spread throughout Delimbiyr Vale, from the Nether Mountains to the northern edge of the High Moor—territory unclaimed by their Uthgardt rivals. The Blue Bears are careful to stay hidden when traveling to and from their spirit mound at Stone Stand, preserving the myth that they are extinct. The tribe's great chief is a canny old woman named Kriga Moonmusk, who travels in a fur-draped chair carried by four tribal warriors.

## ELK TRIBE

The Elk tribe (no relation to the Reghed nomads' Tribe of the Elk) wanders the Evermoors and the land north of the Dessarin River, between Yartar and Noanar's Hold. The Elk tribe's spirit mound is a rocky tor in the southeastern Surbrin Hills called Flint Rock. The tribe's great chief is Rond Vaarson, an old, battle-hardened warrior who has spilled so much blood that he no longer craves it. Younger chieftains are waiting for him to die so that they can vie for the honor of being his successor, but Rond doesn't plan on leaving this world anytime soon.

## GRAY WOLF TRIBE

The Gray Wolf tribe is made up of werewolves, which roam in packs with ordinary wolves. They hunt down and kill those who survive their attacks to prevent the spread of lycanthropy among non-tribe members. Gray Wolf packs (as the clans call themselves) can be found throughout the North, as far west as the Sword Coast and as far east as the Delimbiyr Vale. Adventurers from Neverwinter recently slew the last great chief of the Gray Wolves, Syken Nightblaze. Envir Sykensdottir has taken over her father's pack and plans to attack Neverwinter to prove that she should be named the next great chief of the tribe.

## GREAT WORM TRIBE

The Great Worm tribe has fallen under the sway of a brutal chieftain known as Wormblod. The tribe's spirit mound is located inside Great Worm Cavern, in the Spine of the World. Wormblod and his tribe strike out from this cavern only occasionally to defend their territory, which includes the surrounding mountains, the Fell Pass, the Frost Hills, the Lurkwood, and the northern reaches of the Silver Marches. The Great Worms also venture into the Crags and the plains west of the Surbrin Hills when food is scarce. Wherever he goes, Wormblod wages war and hoards any treasure he finds.

## GRIFFON TRIBE

The great chief of the Griffon tribe, Halric Bonesnapper, is the great-grandson of Kralgar Bonesnapper, who was killed by orcs many years ago. Like his ancestor, Halric longs to wipe out the cities of the North, but his tribe has made too many enemies of late, and its numbers are dwindling. The tribe still maintains a permanent walled settlement in the Surbrin Hills called Griffon's Nest, but it's more of a guarded encampment than the welcoming trading post it once was. The tribe's spirit mound, Shining White, is northeast of the settlement, near an artery of the Surbrin River. Some of the more jaded tribesfolk believe that the Bonesnapper clan has lost Uthgar's divine favor. Halric refutes such claims by staging bold raids. Griffon warriors venture as far west as the Sword Coast and as far east as the Silver Marches, and they are known to raid homesteads and ranches in the Dessarin Valley north of Triboar and Yartar.

### RED TIGER TRIBE

The Red Tiger tribe shares the spirit mound at Beorunna's Well with the Black Lion tribe. Whereas the Black Lions tend to avoid settlements in the Silver Marches, the Red Tigers attack them often. They also prey on caravans traveling along the roads while avoiding the heavily fortified keeps built to watch over them. The tribe even attacks boats on the Rauvin River from time to time. Recently, Red Tiger hunters have moved into the forests that surround the Silver Marches and begun making forays into elf-controlled regions of the High Forest in an effort to find the Grandfather Tree and lay claim to it. Seriska Hungermaw is the tribe's great chief.

### SKY PONY TRIBE

During the War of the Silver Marches, Sky Pony warriors harried and attacked orcs that spilled out of the mountains. Great Chief Arnzan Vashk was badly wounded in one such altercation, leaving him with an orc spearhead embedded in his chest. He refuses to have it removed and tries to hide the pain it causes, not realizing that the tip of the weapon is close to piercing his heart and killing him. The great chief's rivals are circling and preparing to unseat him. The tribe's spirit mound, One Stone, lies in the Moonwood.

### THUNDERBEAST TRIBE

The spirit mound of the Thunderbeast tribe, a bone-strewn hill called Morgur's Mound, lies in the Crags. Members of the tribe have not visited the site in years, and there have been no encounters with Thunderbeast tribesfolk in what used to be their favored hunting grounds in and around the Crags. Great Chief Harthulk Hornspear is a towering man with a terrible scowl and skin as cracked and tough as dinosaur leather. He has convinced all of the Thunderbeast clans to hide in the depths of the Lurkwood and is arming them for a "stampede" through the Surbrin Hills and the Dessarin Valley to the south—a bold thrust that won't end until his people or their enemies are all dead.

### TREE GHOST TRIBE

After years of conflict with other Uthgardt tribes and the elves of the High Forest, the Tree Ghosts have declared themselves to be the protectors of the Grandfather Tree. Rarely seen, these Uthgardt share the High Forest with the region's native elves. Great Chief Boorvald Orcbane, true to his name, hunts orcs and frequently launches attacks against the Iceshield orc-holds along the western edge of the forest. Boorvald has six sons and three daughters, each of whom was given an *oathbow* from

the tribe's elf neighbors as a gift of friendship. Living among the Tree Ghosts are members of various other Uthgardt tribes who found their way to the Grandfather Tree and gained some measure of enlightenment, such that they have forsaken their tribal allegiances and pledged to help the Tree Ghosts protect the tree.

## ORCS

The history of the North is replete with tales of orc hordes spilling out of the mountains to attack the mines, ranches, farmsteads, and settlements of other folk. These orcs hear the call of Gruumsh, the one-eyed god of slaughter, and must satisfy his hunger for carnage lest he visit ruin upon them. When a particularly strong orc chieftain unites multiple clans under one banner, the resulting horde typically rampages across the land, laying waste to strongholds and slaughtering other creatures in its path. Reghed and Uthgardt clans usually put aside their territorial rivalries to oppose and destroy a rampaging orc horde. Settlements throughout the North form their own coalitions to combat rampaging orcs, with mixed results. The War of the Silver Marches (1484–1485 DR), the latest such conflict, saw orcs fighting alongside white dragons and frost giants. Though the orcs and their mighty allies were defeated and sent scurrying back to their mountain lairs, numerous settlements throughout the Silver Marches were left in ruins, among them the fortress-city of Sundabar.

Not all orc chieftains are bent on destruction: King Obould Many-Arrows forged a tenuous alliance with his dwarf neighbors and helped maintain peace in the Silver Marches during his tumultuous reign.

## SHIELD DWARVES

Shield dwarves (also known as mountain dwarves) have a number of strongholds in the North, including Citadel Adbar and Citadel Felbarr in the northern mountains, Sundabar in the Silver Marches, Mithral Hall in the Frost Hills, Ironmaster on the Sword Coast, and Gauntlgrym under the mountains northeast of Neverwinter. Few non-dwarves live in these bastions of dwarvenkind. Outside their walls, clans of shield dwarves are spread thinly throughout the North, to the extent that it's hard to find a settlement that doesn't include at least a handful of dwarven residents. The dwarves' affinity for trade brings them in contact with other races; beyond that, there's also a sense among shield dwarves that all of the North is their land, as evidenced by the ruins of long-lost dwarven kingdoms scattered throughout.

## ELVES

Sun elves and moon elves, like dwarves, live among humans in settlements throughout the North, particularly in Silverymoon. The elven kingdoms of old are distant memories even to elves, and only a few ancient ruins and relics of these kingdoms survive. Wood elves are known to haunt the forests of the North, the High Forest in particular, but they are dangerous and xenophobic.

## HALFLINGS

Small populations of lightfoot halflings can be found in most human-dominated settlements of the North. Scattered throughout the fertile valleys of the North are small clusters of strongheart halfling homesteads. Halfling homesteads tend to be off the beaten path and fairly well hidden, thus minimizing the halflings' contact with bandits and marauders. It's not unusual to see a quaint hamlet of halfling homesteads nestled in a grassy ravine or along the shore of a river.

# RANDOM WILDERNESS ENCOUNTERS

Characters exploring the North are likely to encounter wandering monsters. Such encounters can occur as often as you like—but keep in mind that too many random encounters can bog down the adventure and cause players to lose interest in the story. You can roll on the Random Wilderness Encounters table or choose an appropriate encounter. Each encounter is described in more detail after the table. For guidelines on how to use random encounters effectively, see "Random Encounters" in chapter 3 of the *Dungeon Master's Guide*.

If the characters are crossing terrain not represented in the table, such as a swamp, you can create terrain-appropriate encounters by choosing creatures from the monster lists in appendix B of the *Dungeon Master's Guide*. Chapter 5 of that book also contains a Random Urban Encounters table, in case the characters find themselves exploring a town or city.

### BANDITS

A marauding gang of bandits confronts the party. The gang consists of a **bandit captain** and 3d6 + 2 **bandits**, all wearing cloaks and mounted on **riding horses**. There is a 25 percent chance that the bandits attack without provocation. Otherwise, the captain promises not to attack in exchange for a toll (no less than 100 gp worth of treasure). If the characters pay up, the captain bids them a safe journey before departing peacefully.

***Sea.*** If this encounter occurs at sea, the characters encounter a pirate captain (use the **bandit captain** stat block) and twenty pirates (use the **bandit** stat block) on a longship. Longships have a speed of 3 miles per hour. If the vessel the characters are in moves at least as fast, they can successfully flee from the pirates. Otherwise, the pirates overtake the characters' vessel and board it, threatening to kill everyone aboard unless the characters surrender the contents of their ship's hold. If the characters comply with the pirates' demands, the pirates transfer the cargo and flee with their booty.

***Treasure.*** Each bandit carries a pouch containing 1d10 gp. The bandit captain's pouch holds 2d10 gp and 1d6 gems worth 100 gp each.

### BATTLEFIELD

The characters discover the corpses of 3d10 Uthgardt and 1d4 frost giants. The humans and giants appear to have killed one another within the past week. Carrion birds and one or two **wolves** pick at the corpses and flee if they are startled or attacked.

## CLOUD CASTLE

The characters spot a giant castle in the clouds. The castle is drifting a mile above the ground and poses no imminent threat. If this encounter occurs anywhere near the Evermoors, the castle belongs to an evil cloud giant named Countess Sansuri (see chapter 9, "Castle of the Cloud Giants"). Otherwise, the castle is home to 1d6 + 4 neutral good **cloud giants** who are searching for ancient ruins built by their ancestors. By finding and rebuilding these ancient sites, the giants hope to please their gods and help cloud giants rise to the top of the ordning. These aloof giants have no interest in helping small folk and prefer to be left alone.

## CRAG CATS

A group of 1d4 + 1 adult **crag cats** (see appendix C) hides and attempts to surprise the party. Due to their natural camouflage, the cats have advantage on their Dexterity (Stealth) checks.

## DIG SITE

A **fire giant** equipped with a *rod of the Vonindod* (see appendix B) has located a particularly large fragment of the Vonindod and has tasked its minions with digging it up. The giant oversees 1d4 + 1 **ogres**, 2d6 + 2 **hobgoblins**, and 2d6 + 10 **goblins**. The ogres are using ropes to pull the 2,000-pound fragment out of a 50-foot-wide, 30-foot-deep crater. The hobgoblins scream at the ogres to put their backs into it. The goblins lie around the outskirts of the crater, picks and shovels scattered between them. The goblins have spent the past several days digging the crater and are suffering from five levels of exhaustion (see appendix A in the *Player's Handbook*).

*Treasure.* The ogres and goblinoids carry no treasure. The fire giant has a sack containing 3d6 × 100 cp, 2d6 × 100 sp, 1d6 × 100 gp, and one mundane item, determined by rolling on the Items in a Giant's Bag table in the introduction.

## DRAGON

The characters spot a **young copper dragon** flying lazy circles over its domain. Adventurers who get the dragon's attention might be able to bribe it in exchange for a small favor. A sample copper dragon is described below.

Vexilanthus doesn't consider the party a threat unless they attack him. If the characters mention that they're on the lookout for giants, Vexilanthus says that he spotted a hill giant prowling around an old tower in the hills. The dragon steers the adventurers in that direction, hoping that they'll dispose of the giant. If the characters take the bait, see the "Old Tower" section at the end of this chapter. For a payment of 500 gp or more, Vexilanthus will provide safe escort to the nearest settlement.

## ELK

The characters come across 2d10 **elk** (or reindeer). The elk aren't hostile and flee if attacked.

*Treasure.* There is a 1 percent chance per elk present that one of them has antlers of pure gold. Each of its antlers is worth 250 gp.

## ELVES

A band of 3d6 wood elves offers to escort the party through the forest, steering the characters around the elves' hidden settlements. If they accept the offer, the characters have no hostile encounters while passing through the forest. If the characters refuse, the elves of-

## RANDOM WILDERNESS ENCOUNTERS

| Encounter | Forest | Grassland | Hills/Moors | Mountains | Road/Trail | Sea | Tundra |
|---|---|---|---|---|---|---|---|
| Bandits | 01–08 | 01–07 | 01–04 | — | 01–08 | 01–20 | — |
| Battlefield | 09–11 | 08–13 | 05–08 | — | — | — | 01–04 |
| Cloud castle | — | 14–15 | 09–10 | 01–05 | — | — | 05–07 |
| Crag cats | — | — | 11–15 | 06–22 | 09–13 | — | 08–20 |
| Dig site | 12–19 | 16–22 | 16–18 | 23–25 | — | — | 21–25 |
| Dragon | — | — | 19–21 | — | 14–20 | — | — |
| Elk | 20–27 | 23–29 | 22–30 | 26–33 | — | — | 26–38 |
| Elves | 28–43 | — | — | — | — | 21–30 | — |
| Fire giant | 44–45 | 30–31 | 31–33 | 34–39 | 21–28 | — | 39–40 |
| Food hunters | 46–52 | 32–38 | 34–39 | 40–42 | 29–37 | — | 41–42 |
| Frost giants | 53–57 | 39–41 | 40–41 | 43–50 | 38–41 | 31–50 | 43–54 |
| Hill giants | 58–60 | 42–43 | 42–46 | 51–52 | 42–46 | — | 55–58 |
| Horse-drawn wagon | 61–65 | 44–50 | — | — | 47–55 | — | — |
| Knight | 66–70 | 51–53 | 47–50 | 53–54 | 56–64 | — | — |
| Ogres | 71–72 | 54–59 | 51–55 | 55–56 | 65–69 | 51–60 | 59–60 |
| Orcs | 73–80 | 60–66 | 56–60 | 57–69 | 70–73 | — | 61–71 |
| Ranger | 81–85 | 67–69 | 61–64 | 70–73 | 74–78 | — | 72–78 |
| Stone giants | — | — | 65–67 | 74–75 | 79–80 | — | 79–80 |
| Travelers | 86–90 | 70–73 | 68–70 | 76–80 | 81–00 | 61–80 | 81–85 |
| Uthgardt marauders | 91–00 | 74–00 | 71–00 | 81–00 | — | 81–00 | 86–00 |

fer no further assistance and disappear into the woods. The elves use the **scout** stat block, with these changes:

- The elves are chaotic good.
- Their speed is 35 feet, and they can attempt to hide even when they are in an area only lightly obscured by foliage, heavy rain, falling snow, mist, and other natural phenomena.
- They have advantage on saving throws against being charmed, and magic can't put them to sleep.
- They have darkvision out to a range of 60 feet.
- They speak Common and Elvish.

**Sea.** If this encounter occurs at sea, the characters encounter 3d6 friendly sea elves. These elves know the location of Maelstrom (see chapter 10, "Hold of the Storm Giants") and can lead characters there upon request; they also warn characters about Maelstrom's whirlpool if they're headed in that direction. Sea elves use the **merfolk** stat block, with these changes:

- The sea elves have the elf subtype and are chaotic good.
- They have advantage on saving throws against being charmed, and magic can't put them to sleep.
- They have darkvision out to a range of 60 feet.
- They speak Common and Elvish.

### FIRE GIANT

A **fire giant** is searching for lost fragments of the Vonindod. The giant carries a *rod of the Vonindod* (see appendix B), and 1d4 + 2 **smoke mephits** are fluttering around it. The giant is frustrated because weeks of searching have yielded nothing of value. If it spots the adventurers, it puts away the rod and begins hurling rocks at them to alleviate its boredom and frustration. The mephits follow the giants' commands to the best of their ability, though they loathe melee combat. On subsequent occurrences of this encounter, you can replace the mephits with 1d2 **hell hounds**, 1d2 **fire elementals**, or 1d4 + 2 **magmins**.

**Treasure.** The fire giant has a sack containing 3d6 × 100 cp, 2d6 × 100 sp, 1d6 × 100 gp, and one mundane item, determined by rolling on the Items in a Giant's Bag table in the introduction.

### FOOD HUNTERS

A male **hill giant** is looking for food, stuffing anything that looks even remotely edible into a big sack that he drags behind him. Lagging a few hundred feet behind the giant are 1d4 bored **ogres** and 1d6 **bugbears**. Characters spot the giant from far enough away that they can plan an ambush. For an ambush to succeed, the characters must catch the monsters by surprise by succeeding on a group DC 10 Dexterity (Stealth) check. The ogres and bugbears carry no treasure. The hill giant's sack contains 1d4 mundane items, determined by rolling on the Items in a Giant's Bag table in the introduction.

### FROST GIANTS

The characters come upon 1d3 **frost giants**. If a single giant is encountered, it has a **winter wolf** companion. The giants are marauders looking for homesteads or caravans to wreck and plunder.

**Sea.** If this encounter occurs at sea, the party encounters a frost giant greatship (see chapter 7, "Berg of the Frost Giants") with twenty hostile **frost giants** aboard. If the characters are traveling aboard a vessel that has a speed of at least 3 miles per hour, their ship can outpace the frost giants' greatship. Otherwise, the greatship overtakes them.

**Treasure.** Each frost giant has a sack containing 3d6 × 100 cp, 2d6 × 100 sp, 1d6 × 100 gp, and one mundane item, determined by rolling on the Items in a Giant's Bag table in the introduction.

### HILL GIANTS

A band of 1d2 + 1 male **hill giants** is searching for homesteads to pillage. The giants hurl rocks at any small folk they see. If the giants are anywhere near Grudd Haug (see chapter 5, "Den of the Hill Giants"), the characters might be able to convince a defeated, captured giant to lead them there. Each giant carries a sack holding 1d3 mundane items; roll on the Items in a Giant's Bag table in the introduction to determine the contents of each one.

### HORSE-DRAWN WAGON

The characters encounter a **draft horse** pulling a battered old wagon. Accompanying the wagon are 1d6 − 1 people (use the **commoner** stat block unless otherwise noted below). If the die result indicates that no commoners are present, that means the drivers are either missing or dead, leaving the horse and wagon unattended. If one or more people are present, assume that they are guiding the wagon toward the nearest settlement. The encounter might be one of the following:

- Friendly furriers transporting 2d4 bundles of animal pelts worth 50 gp per bundle
- Friendly peddlers transporting 3d6 ten-gallon kegs of dwarven ale worth 5 gp each
- Friendly, dirt-poor musicians looking for a tavern or an inn; the wagon holds their instruments, food, and traveling gear
- Hostile **bandits** (NE male and female humans) posing as friendly traders, transporting a stolen wagon laden with foodstuffs to their encampment
- A family fleeing their homestead in the wake of rumors of giant sightings; the wagon contains their food and their mundane belongings
- A friendly merchant transporting 2d4 pigs worth 3 gp each; any other persons present are Zhentarim **guards** (N male and female humans) hired to ward off bandits and other threats
- Friendly Zhentarim mercenaries (NG male and female human **veterans**) transporting thirty longswords (worth 15 gp each) and fifty shortswords (worth 10 gp each) to a Zhent merchant waiting for them in the nearest settlement

### KNIGHT

The Order of the Gauntlet is taking strides to deal with the giant threat. The characters encounter a **knight** of the order mounted on a **warhorse** clad in chain mail barding (AC 16). There is a 50 percent chance that the knight has a squire—a **guard** mounted on an unarmored

**warhorse**. Two sample knights (one with a squire, one without) are presented below.

Lady Harriana Hawkwinter (LG female knight of Helm) is a Waterdhavian noble and a champion of the god of watchfulness. She and her squire recently rescued a couple of children trapped under the wreckage of a barn that had been demolished by stone giants. Lady Hawkwinter asks the characters to take the orphans to the nearest settlement while she continues to follow the giants' path and search for other survivors.

Sir Jordeth Tavilson (LN male knight of Tyr), a believer in swift justice, has a gash in his armor and a broken lute strapped to his back. The lute belonged to his squire, who perished in a recent battle against two frost giants. Jordeth managed to kill one giant, but the other got away. He wants justice and asks the characters to join him on his quest to slay the wounded giant.

## Ogres

The characters hear loud, deep voices and spot 1d4 + 1 **ogres** from a safe distance away. The big dummies are lost and trying to find their way home, whether that is Grudd Haug (see chapter 5, "Den of the Hill Giants") or some other location. The characters catch them in the middle of a loud argument about which direction they should go, and can easily avoid the ogres or take them by surprise. The ogres have no treasure.

**Sea.** If this encounter occurs at sea, the party encounters 1d4 + 1 **merrow**. The merrow try to harpoon characters and pull them into the water.

## Orcs

The characters come across 2d6 + 2 **orcs**. There is a 75 percent chance that the orcs are friendly and looking for a suitable place to build a homestead. Otherwise, the orcs are hostile and have prisoners in tow. A sample group of prisoners is presented here, but you can create others.

The prisoners are 1d4 + 2 strongheart halfling **commoners** belonging to the Woodhew clan. The oldest among them is a feisty old gardener named Ollie Woodhew. The orcs set fire to the Woodhew homestead and captured these family members as they tried to flee. One of the orcs even broke Ollie's favorite walking stick.

**Treasure.** If the characters escort the Woodhews back to their torched homestead, the halflings are reunited with the members of their family who avoided capture. One of them rewards the party with a family heirloom (a magic item) hidden in the burnt remains of the family home. Roll on Magic Item Table F in chapter 7 of the *Dungeon Master's Guide* to determine the item.

## Ranger

The characters encounter a helpful ranger, who might be a member of the Emerald Enclave or simply a wanderer of the wilderness. Either way, the ranger is happy to serve as a guide or a source of information. There is a 50 percent chance that the ranger has a **riding horse**, one or more Beast companions, or both. A ranger with neither travels alone on foot. Two sample rangers are presented below, but you can create others.

Vordana Jezral (NG female lightfoot halfling **scout**) has the psionic ability to cast the *misty step* spell once per day. She is familiar with the roads and trails of the North and the settlements along them. She knows every innkeeper from Neverwinter to Deadsnows, and she has two traveling companions: a **tressym** (see appendix C) named Flycatcher and an old **mule** named Tod, which she freed from an abusive owner.

Saarvin (CN male dragonborn **scout**) travels on foot and carries his own gear. He was born in Fireshear and is the self-proclaimed King of the Frozenfar. He claims to have climbed the tallest peak in the Spine of the World and plucked coins from the hoard of a white dragon sleeping less than 10 feet away. Each night, while sitting by the campfire, he carves a tiny wooden figurine depicting one of the characters and gives it to that individual as a gift the next morning.

## Stone Giants

A group of 1d3 + 1 **stone giants** is searching for settlements to destroy and ruins to dismantle. The giants might already be in the midst of dismantling a ruin, intent on wiping its existence from the face of the world. They hurl rocks at any "small folk" they see.

**Treasure.** Each giant has a sack containing 2d6 × 100 gp, 1d6 100 gp gems, and one mundane item, determined by rolling on the Items in a Giant's Bag table in the introduction.

## Travelers

The characters encounter one or more travelers (use the **commoner** stat block) with a tale to tell:

**Forest:** 1d6 hunters or trappers who heard something big moving through the forest and ran

**Grassland:** 1d6 farmers whose homestead was attacked by hill giants, or 1d4 ranchers on **riding horses** who are heading to a nearby settlement to warn it about giants in the area

**Hills/Moors:** 1d4 shepherds guiding the remnants of their flock to safety after a harrowing hill giant encounter

**Mountains:** 1d4 prospectors or miners who had a close call with some frost giants or stone giants and were forced to leave behind their mining gear, supplies, and treasure

**Road/Trail:** Either 3d6 peasants fleeing their homes after a frost giant, hill giant, or stone giant attack; an angry mob of 6d6 peasants looking to reclaim their land or avenge dead loved ones; or a lone merchant or minstrel in a horse-drawn wagon who is relocating to a safer settlement

**Sea:** Either a friendly vessel carrying 6d6 crew and passengers who saw a cloud giant castle or a frost giant greatship, or 1d4 survivors floating on debris after their ship was sunk by a frost giant greatship

**Tundra:** 1d4 hunters or trappers who narrowly escaped from a fire giant or a frost giant but were forced to leave a companion behind

## Uthgardt Marauders

The characters encounter a hostile group of Uthgardt consisting of 4d6 **tribal warriors** and an **Uthgardt shaman** (see appendix C). If the group has twenty or more tribal warriors, add 1d3 **berserkers** and a chieftain (a **berserker** with 90 hit points) to the group. If the encounter occurs during the day, the Uthgardt are prowling the countryside while hunting wild game; if the encounter occurs at night, they are camped.

Use the information in the "Uthgardt" section to choose an appropriate tribe based on the location where the encounter takes place. If these Uthgardt belong to the Gray Wolf tribe, use the **werewolf** stat block for the chieftain and the berserkers, and give the chieftain 90 hit points. Also give the Gray Wolf chieftain 1d4 **wolves** as animal companions.

The Uthgardt carry no treasure.

***Sea.*** If this encounter occurs at sea, the characters encounter 1d3 longships, each with ten **berserkers** and thirty **tribal warriors** aboard. One of the berserkers serves as the captain. These hostile, bloodthirsty North-folk raiders hail from Gundarlun, the Korinn Archipelago, Tuern, or the Whalebones. The longships have a speed of 3 miles per hour. If the vessel the characters are in moves at least as fast, the characters can flee from the raiders and avoid an altercation.

# LOCATIONS OF THE NORTH

The locations described in this section appear on the wilderness maps in this chapter. Additional information on several of these places can be found in the *Sword Coast Adventurer's Guide*. Not depicted on the maps are scores of tiny hamlets and hundreds of isolated homesteads scattered throughout the North. These places are too small to be of consequence. Even so, adventurers traveling along a road or a trail might come across a tiny settlement consisting of a handful of homesteads built around an inn or tavern where locals gather. (If you need a tavern name, use the Tavern Name Generator table in chapter 5 of the *Dungeon Master's Guide*.)

Some location entries include a suggested encounter that occurs when the characters first arrive or shortly thereafter. You can ignore the encounter and create your own activity based on the information given in a location's description; for example, the "Arn Forest" section mentions rock gnomes who inhabit the woods, which might make for a fun encounter of your own creation.

## AMPHAIL

Amphail lies north of Waterdeep on the Long Road. The town is named after one of Waterdeep's early warlords, who is said to haunt the surrounding hills in spirit form, frightening away monsters. Horses are bred and trained here, rich Waterdhavians maintain secluded estates in the hills, and farmland is plentiful. Stands of dark dusk-wood and spruce trees are everywhere.

In one corner of the town square stands the Great Shalarn, a black stone statue of a famous war stallion bred in Amphail long ago. Gelded by a prankster, the rearing stone horse is often painted in bright colors by high-spirited locals. Children are allowed to hurl stones at birds perched on the statue, to help keep it free of droppings. The children often climb it themselves and cling precariously to the high, tilted saddle, waving their arms and commanding imaginary armies into battle. Within spitting distance of the statue is the Stag-Horned

Flagon, a cozy tavern run by an gray-haired, middle-aged woman with a wry sense of humor named Arleosa Starhenge (NG female human **commoner**). Born in a wild magic zone, Arleosa has the innate magical ability to cast the *alter self* spell three times per day. In her youth, she was a member of a traveling carnival and used this power to entertain folks. She no longer cares about using the ability, and no one in Amphail knows she even has it.

The three Waterdhavian families with the most influence in Amphail are Houses Amcathra, Ilzimmer, and Roaringhorn. These houses rule the town, with the controlling family changing each Shieldmeet. The current Lord Warder of Amphail is Dauner Ilzimmer (LN male human **noble**), a bombastic family man who loves horses more than he does most people. Thanks largely to the influence of its nobles, Amphail is a member of the Lords' Alliance and enjoys the protection of Waterdeep's city guard. The lord warder also hires adventurers from time to time to take care of pesky bandits and monsters.

### SUGGESTED ENCOUNTER

It's Tylandar Roaringhorn's sixty-third birthday, and the noble wants all of Amphail to know it. He has imported the finest food and ale from Waterdeep for an outdoor banquet, and everyone in town is invited. Pavilion tents and tables have been set up in the town square. In the middle of the square is a platform where Tylandar plans to thank the crowd. Some cynical Amphailians view Tylandar's birthday banquet as a blatant attempt by the noble to warm hearts before he takes over as lord warder when Lord Ilzimmer's tenure is concluded.

If the characters stick around for the banquet, three male **hill giants**, drawn by the scents of roasted hog and grilled corn, barge into town. Some townsfolk hurl food at the giants, slowing them down long enough for other citizens to clear the square of children and elderly. If the characters do nothing, the town guards help get people to safety while the giants storm the tents and grab armfuls of food before fleeing north along the Long Road. It's clear that the giants mean no harm to the townsfolk.

If the characters defeat the giants or drive them off before they can grab food, Tylandar Roaringhorn (NG male human **noble**) takes notice of their heroism. He tells them afterward that he has received reports of giants of various kinds attacking settlements throughout the Dessarin Valley.

## ANAUROCH

This once-verdant land is now a desert. Northernmost Anauroch is a cold land of frost-rimed rock and the black glacier known as the High Ice. Farther south lies the waterless Plain of Standing Stones, where winds scour jagged rocks amid a sea of gravel. Anauroch's most southerly part is the Sword—a hot, sandy desert. Use the Desert Monsters table in appendix B of the *Dungeon Master's Guide* to inspire encounter ideas.

# ARDEEP FOREST

This forest east of Waterdeep and the Dessarin River was once part of the long-lost elven kingdom of Illefarn. Now it's home to a small clan of wood elves recently arrived from Evermeet. They refuse to leave their woods, guarding relics and ruins of ages past, and they want nothing to do with the world beyond their borders.

# ARN FOREST

This stretch of pine trees and muskeg bogs lies on the northeast flank of the Nether Mountains, near the western edge of Anauroch. Little is known about this forest except that rock gnomes dwell in the eastern portion. They emerge occasionally to trade furs and pelts in Deadsnows or Citadel Adbar.

# ASCORE

As one travels east away from the Silver Marches, the old road passes between the Vordrorn Forest to the north and the Arn Forest to the south. Before reaching the edge of Anauroch, the road ends at a great set of stone doors set into a high ridge. Statues of dwarves once stood in rows on either side of these doors, but all that remains of them now are the marble plinths upon which they once stood. The doors open to reveal a passageway that goes underground for nearly a mile before emerging at the desert's edge. Standing outside the yawning exit are two gigantic stone statues of crouching griffons, and beyond them lies one of the great wonders and mysteries of the North: Ascore. This ruined dwarven city once overlooked a sea. Now it lies half-buried in the cold northern sands of Anauroch, its mighty stone docks still thrusting eastward, pointing toward the empty hulks of colossal stone ships lying half-buried in the sand. Dwarven magic once enabled these ships to float on water, but that magic has long since faded.

## SUGGESTED ENCOUNTER

The ancient blue dragon Iymrith claims Ascore as part of her domain. Though she's not here to watch over it, two of her offspring have made separate lairs for themselves inside a couple of the great stone ships. These **adult blue dragons**, Anaxaster and Chezzaran, frequently accost each other in the sky, playfully jousting and breathing lightning as they zoom around. They are flying over Ascore when the characters first lay eyes on the ruined city. After an hour of fun, the dragons return to their lairs to rest. If the characters take no steps to conceal themselves and enter the city while the dragons are in the sky, the dragons spot the party and attack.

The ships that the dragons have turned into their lairs are hollow, sand-filled hulks surrounded by open desert. Each ship has 1d6 + 4 **gargoyles** perched on it, watching the sands for treasure-seekers. If the characters make their way past the gargoyles into a dragon's lair and defeat the dragon within, they find the dragon's hoard hidden under the sand. Roll on the Treasure Hoard: Challenge 11–16 table in chapter 7 of the *Dungeon Master's Guide* to determine the contents of each dragon's trove.

# AURILSSBARG

See the "Ice Peak" section.

# BARGEWRIGHT INN

Once a hilltop wayside inn, this site has become a walled community of ramshackle, frequently rebuilt wooden towers and buildings. Its structures now entirely cloak a hill that overlooks the village of Womford across the Dessarin River. A long wooden bridge, wide enough for a single wagon to cross, spans the river between these two settlements. Known as the Ironford Bridge, it has stood for centuries but is showing its age.

Bargewright Inn reeks of manure and filthy mud. It houses dealers who buy and sell horses, mules, and oxen, blacksmiths, wheelwrights, coopers, and wagon-makers. It has inns, stables, and warehouses, and two concentric rings of high walls with gates that are barred at night. (From sunset until dawn, someone who wants to enter or leave can pay a stiff fee to be raised and lowered on a rope-slung chair, but nothing can be taken along beyond what the customer can carry.)

Bargewright Inn fell under Zhentarim influence a few years ago. Any member or ally of that faction can find a discreet welcome (and few or low fees) within its walls. Bargewright Inn is ruled by a plutocracy of business owners, most of whom are in the pockets of the Black Network. The unofficial leader is Chalaska Muruin (LN female human **veteran**), the terse, cold-eyed "Senior Sword" and master of the militia.

The largest inn, the Old Bargewright, was recently rebuilt as a substantial stone structure with thick walls and private chambers hidden behind secret doors. Innkeeper Nalaskur Thaelond (N male half-elf **spy**) keeps watch over who comes and goes, for this is where Zhentarim operatives meet to broker deals involving smuggled goods, poisons, dangerous magic, and the like. Nalaskur is a member of the Black Network.

One of the inn's few permanent residents is Arik Stillmarsh, a well-dressed, young-looking man with a sallow complexion who lives like a hermit in a corner room on the uppermost floor of the old inn. Rumor among the rabble has it that Stillmarsh swindled one or more prominent Waterdhavian families, and that the Black Network is sheltering him. In truth, Stillmarsh is a neutral evil, human **vampire** whom Nalaskur occasionally calls upon to dispose of unwanted guests. Stillmarsh has an agreement with Nalaskur not to feed on locals or other guests without the Black Network's approval. To sate his appetite at other times, he preys on rural encampments, night travelers on the Long Road, and the poor people of Womford. In Womford, the vampire is spoken of in whispers as the "Womford Bat."

Stillmarsh's earth-filled coffin is hidden in the attic above his room at the Old Bargewright, accessible through a secret door in the ceiling of a closet. Spotting that door requires a successful DC 15 Wisdom (Perception) check.

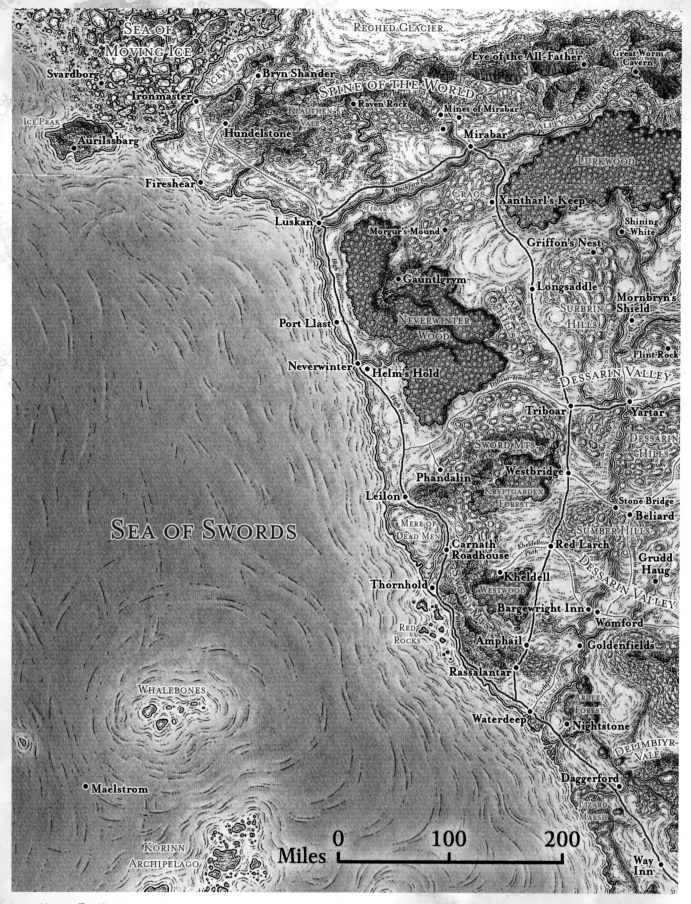

MAP 3.1: THE NORTH

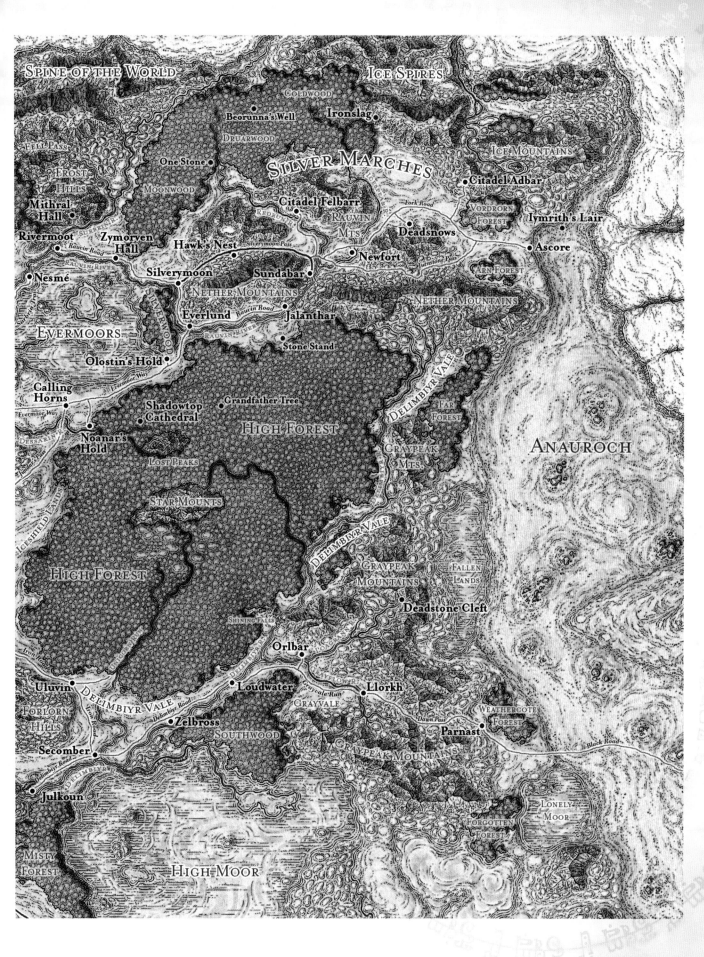

MAP 3.2: BEORUNNA'S WELL

## BELIARD

Beliard is a market-moot for local cattle drovers. It surrounds the intersection of the dusty Dessarin Road and the Stone Trail.

Beliard is home to many cattle ranchers whose herds roam the hills around the village, particularly to the east. The community has a public well, as well as a pond where harnessed horses or oxen can be driven through the water to bathe them, drive off flies, and let them drink. It also boasts a tanner, a smith, some horse dealers and trainers who keep extensive stables, and an inn: the venerable, popular, and several-times-expanded Watchful Knight. The inn was named for an inoperative helmed horror that once stood in the common room. The creature mysteriously vanished years ago, and the innkeeper went missing shortly thereafter.

### SUGGESTED ENCOUNTER

Hill giants have attacked many of the cattle ranches around Beliard. Every attack is the same: the giants ignore the ranchers and instead raid the animal pens, making off with pigs, sheep, chicken coops, and cattle. The ranch owners have pooled their resources and posted "Adventurers Wanted!" signs that promise a payment of 500 gp to anyone who finds out where the hill giants' lair is located. Characters who visit the Watchful Knight and question its patrons learn that most of the giants fled southward with their loot. Characters who explore the hills south of Beliard might find an old tower containing a female hill giant who recently lost her mate (see the "Old Tower" section at the end of this chapter).

## BEORUNNA'S WELL

The spirit mound of the Black Lion and Red Tiger tribes of Uthgardt rests in the heart of the Druarwood. It's not a mound per se, but an ice-cold cavern whose ceiling is partially open to the sky. Characters are likely to come upon at least one Black Lion or Red Tiger hunting party as they make their way toward the site.

According to legend, Beorunna, an Uthgardt hero, died fighting a demon in these woods. In the final moments of the battle, the ground beneath Beorunna's feet crumbled, plunging him into a cavern. The triangular cavern contains, among other things, a heated pool with a steady geyser. This pool came to be known as Beorunna's Well. Uthgardt exploring the cavern for the first time found what they thought were Beorunna's bones, which actually belonged to a half-ogre.

Uthgar's followers buried the half-ogre's bones alongside a relic stolen from their enemies, the giants, and built an altar upon the burial site. When the Uthgardt call upon Uthgar for guidance or seek to appease their totem spirits, they slaughter a woodland animal and place its carcass atop the altar, where it slowly rots. Today, the tribes maintain a tenuous truce and take turns protecting their spirit mound. Each tribe has erected its own totem pole near the altar. The Black Lion totem pole is covered with dried pitch and has a lion's skull atop it. The Red Tiger totem pole is stained with blood and has a tiger's skull surmounting it.

A small stand of pine trees called the Sunken Grove grows in the middle of the cavern. Outside the perimeter of the grove, the cavern is hooded by a ceiling lined with stalactites and pierced with tree roots. The floor around the outside of the Sunken Grove beneath the ceiling is dotted with stalagmites.

The distance from the top of the pit to the cavern floor is 250 feet. The Uthgardt have tied a long, knotted rope to a tree stump and left it dangling in the cavern. They use this rope (and others like it) to climb into and out of Beorunna's Well, and characters can climb the rope (no ability check required). In the northeast corner, surrounding a campfire, are three tents inhabited by members of the Black Lion tribe (see "Suggested Encounter").

## ANCIENT RELIC

The altar is a blood-spattered stone block, 9 feet long by 6 feet wide by 3 feet tall, weighing several tons. A creature as big and strong as a stone giant can move it, as can multiple Small or Medium creatures if at least five of them succeed on a DC 20 Strength (Athletics) check. The altar can also be broken in half to get underneath it; it has AC 17, 100 hit points, a damage threshold of 10, and immunity to poison and psychic damage. Beneath the altar is a rough-hewn niche containing the skeletal remains of a half-ogre and a relic of giantkind: a fossilized horn made from the tusk of a mammoth and engraved with images of giants battling dragons. The cracked horn weighs 250 pounds and has lost its magical powers, but it's worth 750 gp nevertheless.

## SUGGESTED ENCOUNTER

Ten members of the Black Lion tribe (CE male and female Uthgardt humans) guard the cavern. They include three **berserkers**, six **tribal warriors**, and an **Uthgardt shaman** (see appendix C). The berserkers and three of the tribal warriors huddle around the campfire in the northeast corner and are visible in the firelight. The remaining warriors are asleep in their tents. The shaman sleeps under a blanket of snow in the Sunken Grove and can be spotted by any character with a passive Wisdom (Perception) score of 20 or higher. The shaman and the warriors awaken to the sound of any loud disturbance. All the tribe members are hostile toward interlopers.

A **manticore** also calls the cavern home. Having formed a tenuous alliance with the Black Lion tribe, it lairs in the western corner of the room, on a rocky shore next to the spring. The shore is strewn with humanoid and animal bones—the remains of the manticore's kills. The manticore joins any battle that unfolds in the cavern, eager for its fair share of meat.

## BLACK ROAD

Long ago, the Zhentarim built this trade route to connect its established footholds in the east with its lucrative ventures along the Sword Coast. For some time it was lost to the Zhentarim when the Netherese reappeared and reclaimed Anauroch, but with the second fall of Netheril and the magical return of the desert, the Zhentarim have been able to reclaim the route.

The Black Road stretches eastward from the village of Parnast across Anauroch's sandy wasteland for hundreds of miles. Black Network caravans using the road are heavily guarded because of desert bandits.

## BLACKFORD ROAD

This trade trail runs east from Luskan to Mirabar. The road is named for a little-used ford across the River Mirar that allows travelers to avoid Luskan should they wish. Caravan masters have many other names for the road, none of them flattering: Auril's Ride, the Stygian Road, Ol' Frozenfinger, and the Dead Yeti Highway, to name a few. Where the road spans the Black Raven River, south of Raven Rock, stands a stone bridge with broken statues of rearing horses at each end.

## BRYN SHANDER

Bryn Shander is the largest of ten permanent settlements in Icewind Dale collectively known as Ten-Towns. See chapter 2 for more information on this location, and the "Icewind Dale" section in this chapter for more information on the other Ten-Towns settlements.

## SUGGESTED ENCOUNTER

If the adventure didn't begin in Bryn Shander, you can run the "Attack on Bryn Shander" encounter (see chapter 2) whenever the characters visit the town.

## CAIRN ROAD

The Cairn Road is a well-worn wagon trail that crosses the Dessarin Valley between the village of Red Larch and the Bargewright Inn trading post.

## CALLING HORNS

Calling Horns was nothing more than a trailside inn until a few years ago, when Tamalin Zoar (N female human **noble**) bought the establishment and retired here. Using her hard-won wealth and influence, she attracted settlers to the region, giving rise to a small village whose citizens pay monthly "tithes" for Tamalin's protection. Still spry at sixty, Tamalin is "the law" in Calling Horns—an irony that never ceases to amuse her. She employs nine deputies (N male and female **veterans** of various races) who live in the village proper to help keep the peace. Tamalin also gives free room and board to adventurers who help solve local problems. Given the village's proximity to the Evermoors, few villagers have cause to complain about Tamalin's protection racket. She keeps them safe from orcs, trolls, and other monsters, and that's good enough for them.

Calling Horns stands where Jundar's Pass meets up with the Evermoor Way. The intersection is marked by a cairn of weathered and lichen-covered orc skulls that commemorates the long-ago slaughter of a horde here. The village proper is made up of rows of small log cottages with bark-shingled rooftops. The Calling Horns Inn, a large fieldstone structure with adjoining stables, stands atop a ridge that overlooks the intersection, surrounded by tall, old trees. The inn's cellar contains an impressive selection of ales and wines, as well as a secret tunnel that leads to a hidden exit in the hillside.

## Suggested Encounter

As fire giants scour the Evermoors for fragments of the Vonindod, trolls native to the area are fleeing to avoid becoming enslaved by the giants. If the characters stay at the Calling Horns Inn for a night, they and Tamalin are awakened in the wee hours by a strange racket. Two **trolls** are trying to claw their way into the inn's stable to feast on the horses inside. The trolls are hungry and fight to the death. Once the trolls are dealt with, Tamalin reveals to the characters that troll attacks are becoming more common, and she offers to give the adventurers a letter of recommendation (see the "Marks of Prestige" section in chapter 7 of the *Dungeon Master's Guide*) if they find the root cause. Tamalin tells them that her letter can win them a powerful friend in Everlund if they show it to the orc innkeeper at Danivarr's House (see the "Everlund" section), or it can be given to a member of the Hand of Yartar (Yartar's thieves' guild) in exchange for a special favor.

If the characters take up Tamalin's quest and they spend at least two nights in the Evermoors, they witness a female **fire giant** slapping around a **troll** shortly before highsun on the third day. The fire giant, Zaastrid, carries a *rod of the Vonindod* (see appendix B). Zaastrid is hungry and upset that her enslaved troll has found nothing to eat. The characters can choose to keep their distance and avoid conflict, or they can engage the ravenous fire giant and her troll in battle. Zaastrid and the troll fight to the death. If the characters return to Calling Horns and report their fire giant sighting to Tamalin, she is satisfied and gives them her letter.

## Carnath Roadhouse

This walled compound served as a hostelry on the High Road between Waterdeep and Neverwinter in the days when trade between the two cities flourished. It fell into disuse when that trade stopped after the eruption of Mount Hotenow (see the "Neverwinter" section). Now that Neverwinter has recovered and commerce has resumed, the road has been rebuilt and the roadhouse repaired and put to use as a supply depot and wagon park. It stands on the west side of the road, a stone's throw from the edge of the Mere of Dead Men. Fog drifting off the mere engulfs the roadhouse at night and lingers well into the following afternoon. The sounds of the marsh, from croaking frogs to buzzing insects, are only somewhat dampened by the roadhouse's walls and doors.

The superintendent of the Carnath Roadhouse is a brusque but well-educated half-orc named Bog Luck (N male half-orc **veteran**). Accustomed to doing business with shady traders and contraband, he doesn't trouble his clients with too many questions. He simply takes their money while assuring them that the gates and walls of the roadhouse are strong enough to hold back any threat. Bog Luck employs four stable boys and a cook named Gristle Pete (N male human **commoners**), though he doesn't pay them much.

The Carnath Roadhouse figures prominently in *Tyranny of Dragons*. That adventure also includes a map of the roadhouse. Bandits and monsters lurk near the road both north and south of the roadhouse.

## Citadel Adbar

Citadel Adbar has stood in the bitter cold of the Ice Mountains for almost eighteen centuries, impregnable and defiant. The fortress, carved out of a mountain spur, consists of two great towers ringed with spikes to keep large flying creatures from landing to attack the structures directly. The great chimney of the citadel's central foundry stands between the towers, belching smoke like a volcano about to erupt. Ringing the citadel is a host of platforms, battlements, and arrow slits from where defenders can fire crossbows at foolish attackers. A great drawbridge allows no one to enter the dwarven enclave except patrols and honored guests. Cleverly hidden traps await those who storm the halls uninvited, and beneath the citadel is an expansive network of tunnels and caverns designed to confuse would-be invaders. If Adbar's defenses should ever prove inadequate, the dwarves have created a secret evacuation tunnel that stretches for hundreds of miles, connecting to passages that lie under Citadel Felbarr to the west. Adbar's garrison offers a reward of 10 gp for each orc head brought to the city gates, or 100 gp for each giant head.

The population of Citadel Adbar was severely depleted by the War of the Silver Marches, which drew away many of Adbar's greatest warriors, including its long-ruling king, Harbromm. King Harbromm led his knights into battle against the orc hordes invading the Marches and died on the field. Harbromm's twin sons, Bromm and Harnoth, inherited the throne and, like their father, left Citadel Adbar to join the war. Bromm later perished, leaving the crown to Harnoth. Harnoth and his followers fought many battles during the war, but the new king made some poor decisions that winnowed the once-great Knights of the Mithral Shield down to a handful of members. Fortunately for Harnoth, the Iron Guard—Citadel Adbar's defending army—remains strong.

What's not generally known is that Harnoth, too, was killed by orcs toward the end of the war. To prevent political turmoil in Citadel Adbar, the elders of Adbar's dwarven clans hired a **doppelganger** to impersonate King Harnoth. True power in Citadel Adbar now lies with the clan elders, who meet in secret and tell their "king" what to do and say before every one of his public appearances. The doppelganger is so smitten with its role that it sometimes forgets itself and makes decisions that the elders haven't approved, behavior that is a growing cause of concern for some.

### Suggested Encounter

Adventurers are welcome in Citadel Adbar, and news of their arrival is quickly brought to the doppelganger-king's attention. After meeting with the clan elders, "Harnoth" demands a private audience with the adventurers in his throne hall. In the presence of three elders (LG male shield dwarf **nobles** armed with warhammers instead of rapiers) and four bodyguards (LG male and female shield dwarf **guards** armed with warhammers instead of spears), the king asks the characters to attack Ironslag, a fire giant forge in the mountains to the northwest. Dwarven patrols have seen fire giants hauling large fragments of adamantine to the underground forge, which had until recently stood abandoned.

"Harnoth" wants the adventurers to find out what the giants are doing and thwart them if possible.

"Harnoth" promises that if the characters agree to explore Ironslag and return with evidence of a successful mission, such as Duke Zalto's head or a group of freed dwarven prisoners, he will reward each character with a rare magic item of that individual's choice. He secures the desired items while the characters are off completing their quest. If the characters have already cleared out Ironslag, the king expresses his surprise and gratitude and urges them to rest in Adbar while he gathers their rewards. For more information on Ironslag, see chapter 8, "Forge of the Fire Giants."

As the doppelganger-king is trying to persuade the adventurers to undertake his quest, or in the wake of their foray to Ironslag, seven **yakfolk warriors** (see appendix C) barge into the throne hall to kill the king and the adventurers. The yakfolk have used their Wind Ghost power to possess six Knights of the Mithral Shield. These individuals use the **knight** stat block, with these changes:

- The knights are lawful good shield dwarves that speak Common and Dwarvish. While they are possessed by yakfolk, their alignment is lawful evil and they also speak Yikaria (the yakfolk tongue).
- Each knight carries a shield and has AC 20.
- Each knight wields a warhammer (instead of a greatsword) that deals 7 (1d8 + 3) bludgeoning damage on a hit, or 8 (1d10 + 3) bludgeoning damage if used with two hands.
- Each knight has a walking speed of 25 feet and darkvision out to a range of 60 feet.
- Each knight has advantage on saving throws against poison, and resistance to poison damage.

The king, curiously, seems reluctant to enter the fray. "Harnoth" calls for the treacherous knights to stand down, but they ignore his commands. As combat ensues, the elders withdraw from the audience chamber to summon reinforcements, which arrive after the battle ends. As the characters battle the knights, the king's bodyguards surround and protect their lord. They join the fray only if the characters are on the verge of defeat.

If the adventurers defeat the possessed dwarves, "Harnoth" urges them to stay in Citadel Adbar for a couple of days while he arranges for suitable rewards. He commissions jewelers to craft mithral medals (one per character) shaped like shields, and he also drafts a signed letter of recommendation and presents it to the party. The bearer of the letter gains advantage on Charisma checks made to influence shield dwarves throughout the North. For more information on medals and letters of recommendation, see the "Marks of Prestige" section in chapter 7 of the *Dungeon Master's Guide*.

## CITADEL FELBARR

This formidable dwarven fortress-city lies beneath the Rauvin Mountains. To enter the place, one must traverse an elevated road, with 100-foot-high cliffs on both sides, and pass through two enormous gates called the Hammer and the Anvil. Two wide parapets with crenellated battlements called North Vigil and South Vigil stand outside these gates on the nearby mountainsides, ready to rain ballista bolts and catapult stones down on would-be invaders. The road ends at the Runegate, the main entrance to the underground city. Deep beneath the mountains are tunnels connecting to Felbarr's mines, the Underdark, and the distant dwarven bastions of Mithral Hall and Citadel Adbar.

Citadel Felbarr has fallen to orcs twice in its long history, only to be reclaimed and rebuilt by the dwarves each time. Felbarr's great hero-king, Emerus Warcrown, who restored Felbarr to its former glory during the War of the Silver Marches, died shortly after the war while helping his fellow dwarves reclaim the lost city of Gauntlgrym. Since Emerus's death, leadership of the Felbarren dwarves has fallen to Emerus's distant kin, King Morinn and Queen Tithmel. The two monarchs rule wisely as equals.

### SUGGESTED ENCOUNTER

The king and the queen have received disturbing reports of fire giant sightings in the hills to the northwest. They fear that the giants might be in the process of reigniting the ancient underground forge known as Ironslag. If the adventurers visit Citadel Felbarr, the sovereigns learn of their arrival and summon them to their throne hall for an audience. King Morinn and Queen Tithmel tell the characters about their suspicions concerning Ironslag and ask them to investigate. In return, they offer to build the heroes a fortified tower. It would be erected on a large estate in the Silver Marches (exact location determined by you). The tower takes one hundred days to build, and the dwarf sovereigns vow to cover the construction costs. To earn this reward, the characters must go to Ironslag and return to Felbarr with proof that the fire giants are no longer a threat. (Duke Zalto's head or the word of freed dwarven prisoners will do.)

If the characters take care of Duke Zalto (see chapter 8, "Forge of the Fire Giants"), King Morinn and Queen Tithmel honor their pledge to build the party a tower stronghold. On top of that, they offer to supply a garrison of ten stalwart, unfailingly loyal Felbarren dwarves. Use the **guard** stat block, with these changes:

- The shield dwarves are lawful good.
- They have a walking speed of 25 feet.
- They have darkvision out to a range of 60 feet.
- They have advantage on saving throws against poison and resistance to poison damage.
- They speak Common and Dwarvish.

## COLDWOOD

See the "Glimmerwood" section.

## CRAGS

The hills south of Mirabar are strewn with abandoned mines that have become infested with goblins, hobgoblins, and bugbears. Uthgardt are known to prowl the Crags, hunting wild game and occasionally preying on caravans that travel the Long Road.

# Daggerford

Built on a hillside in the floodplain of the Delimbiyr River, the walled town of Daggerford is dominated by a three-story keep that belongs to its duchess, Morwen Daggerford. From atop Daggerford's walls, dozens of farms and a scattering of hamlets are visible, all under the protection of the duchess and the Lords' Alliance.

Unknown to Daggerford's citizens, a **succubus** named Pencheska has usurped Morwen's identity and now governs in her stead. The succubus has imprisoned the real duchess in Cromm's Hold, a keep on the edge of the Lizard Marsh (see the "Lizard Marsh" entry for details). Pencheska is using her position to infiltrate the Lords' Alliance. She rules Daggerford much as Lady Morwen did, sternly but fairly, and does little to arouse suspicion.

Recently, hill giants ranging south of the Forlorn Hills have begun to encroach upon the farmlands and noble estates around Daggerford. The succubus, hoping to appear benevolent, is readying the town to accommodate farmers looking for sanctuary, and the town's outer walls bristle with lookouts. The "duchess" has also raised taxes to pay for Zhentarim mercenaries to patrol the lands north of Daggerford. Pencheska has forged a promising alliance with the Black Network, and her primary Zhentarim contact in town is a plump halfling weasel named Nelkin Danniker (N male lightfoot halfling **spy**), known to his associates as the Snail because of his slow, deliberate way of talking. The Snail relaxes at the River Shining Tavern and Inn, watched over by 1d6 **thugs** (N male and female humans) posing as nondescript inn patrons.

Another popular tavern in town, the Happy Cow, is run by Koggin and Lily Hardcheese (LG male and female strongheart halfling **commoners**). Koggin also operates a money-lending enterprise out of the tavern and employs several other family members to help run both businesses, including three brothers and three sisters, a dozen nieces and nephews, and several distant relations. One of the Happy Cow's regular patrons is a female half-elf named Zira, who is actually an **adult bronze dragon** named Zirazylym in polymorphed form. Zira is fond of the Hardcheese family and doesn't meddle in their business. She avoids contact with the characters unless events involving the Black Network bring them together (see the "Shalvus Martholio's Quest" section in chapter 2).

## Suggested Encounter

If the adventurers hang around town or pay a visit to the Happy Cow, the Snail hears about them and sends one of his thugs to request a meeting. The Snail is happy to meet the characters in a public or private place, whichever they prefer. He opens the meeting by putting his offer on the table. If all members of the party sign a written agreement stating that they won't interfere in the Black Network's Daggerford operation or accept any quests or special commissions from Duchess Morwen Daggerford, Nelkin offers them the following benefits:

- Free room and board at the River Shining Tavern and Inn, paid for by the Zhentarim

- One free riding horse or pony for each party member, with stable fees in Daggerford paid for by the Zhentarim
- Ownership of a fortified tower in "fair condition" that overlooks the Delimbiyr River west of Orlbar (recently abandoned by the Zhentarim after a stone giant attack)

If the Snail can't get the entire party to agree to his terms, he ends the meeting politely, but thereafter he keeps close track of their activities in town while doing nothing to antagonize them. He does, however, inform the duchess that the adventurers are in town and recommends that she avoid them. Because of her arrangement with the Zhentarim and her fear of being exposed, the succubus posing as Duchess Morwen distances herself from adventurers and denies them an audience.

If the characters check out the fortified tower west of Orlbar, they arrive to find six **stone giants** dismantling it stone by stone. If the characters kill three or more giants, the rest flee east along the Loagrann River to their lair in Deadstone Cleft (see chapter 6, "Canyon of the Stone Giants"). Repairing the damage to the tower costs 1,000 gp and takes 10 days.

# Dawn Pass

This stretch of road is the only wagon-friendly route through the Graypeak Mountains. At dawn, the rising sun shines brightly through the pass, hence its name.

Halfway between Llorkh and Parnast, just east of the mountains, the Zhentarim have built a stone gatehouse over the road, with cliffs to both sides. Two heavy iron portcullises drop down to trap travelers so that a well-armed garrison of twenty Zhentarim **veterans** (N male and female humans) can extort money from them. Those who pay the toll of 1 gp per head (including the heads of horses, ponies, and mules) are sent on their way. Those who can't pay the toll or refuse to do so are turned back. Characters who can prove that they are members of the Black Network are allowed through without question, along with any traveling companions. While conversing with other members of the Black Network, the guards report seeing stone giants spying on them from a distance, but so far the gatehouse has not been attacked.

# Deadsnows

The Nether Mountains throw cold shadows over the town of Deadsnows, nestled in the alpine bosom of two foothills. Sheep graze on the lower slopes, guarded by crossbow-toting shepherds, as they nibble at the coarse grass that grows between rocky outcroppings. Beyond the grazing fields, the land rises to crags covered sparsely with fir trees, and then to the mist-shrouded and snow-covered mountains that rear into the sky.

The main feature of Deadsnows is the Hospice of Marthammor, a fortified abbey in the middle of town. Surrounding it are several wood-frame buildings that make up the town, and all is contained within a crumbling wall that's in desperate need of repair. Winter roses along the wall blossom throughout the year. Just inside the wall, overlooking the road that leads to the town, is a stone watchtower. A banner flies from its topmost turret, depicting the golden sunrise of Lathander. A dozen worshipers of the Morninglord (LG male and female **priests** and **acolytes** of various races) staff the watchtower.

The abbey is a dwarf-made fortress dedicated to Marthammor Duin, the dwarven god of wanderers. The abbey's venerable leader, Kerrilla Gemstar (NG female shield dwarf **priest** of Marthammor Duin), oversees a staff of **commoners** who have taken vows of service. The abbey offers assistance to anyone in need, while the clerics of the Watchtower are devoted to protecting the town and insuring the well-being of its residents.

The Icespear noble family held much influence in Deadsnows for many generations, until Lord Delvon Icespear was killed in the War of the Silver Marches. He left no heirs, and the family estate has been locked up ever since. Halfhearted attempts to locate other members of the Icespear family have proven fruitless. The town has survived for several seasons without a governor—no one in town wants the power or the burden.

Visitors who would rather not endure the bland food and drafty halls of the Hospice can find a cozy tavern, the Blazon, and a decent inn, the Rose and Hammer, within the town.

## DEADSTONE CLEFT

A misty canyon in the Graypeak Mountains called Deadstone Cleft is home to a clan of stone giants under the influence of Thane Kayalithica, a devout but misguided worshiper of Skoraeus Stonebones. See chapter 6, "Canyon of the Stone Giants," for more information on this location.

## DELIMBIYR ROAD

Also called the Shining Trail, the Delimbiyr Road is a trade road that follows the north shore of the Delimbiyr River. Terrified refugees heading west along the road warn adventurers of rampaging stone giants to the east. They claim that the giants have destroyed homesteads and settlements throughout Grayvale, and that Loudwater is doomed to fall as well.

## DELIMBIYR VALE

Delimbiyr Vale is the seemingly endless valley through which the Delimbiyr River flows. It begins at the foothills of the Nether Mountains and stretches southwest for hundreds of miles toward the sea. The least settled part of the valley stands between the High Forest and the Graypeak Mountains. As the valley sweeps south of the great forest, more and more settlements begin to appear along the river. The largest settlement along the vale is Daggerford, near the coast, but even that is but a town. With its easy access to water and ample resources, the Delimbiyr Vale seems ripe for settlers—but the valley's resources also attract monsters from the nearby forests, hills, and mountains.

## DESSARIN HILLS

The rugged, scruffy hills south of Yartar provide a safe haven for orcs, ogres, hill giants, manticores, and Uthgardt. Scattered throughout the Dessarin Hills are ancient dwarven ruins, crumbling towers, lost mines, and abandoned hunting lodges, any of which might contain monsters and other perils.

## DESSARIN ROAD

The Dessarin "Road" is no more than a glorified wagon trail that meanders across the eastern Dessarin Valley, connecting the rural settlement of Beliard to the Iron Road near Womford.

## DESSARIN VALLEY

The lowlands on either side of the Dessarin River constitute the Dessarin Valley, a vast tract of fertile land stretching north from Waterdeep to the Surbrin Hills. The Long Road hugs the west border of the valley, which is hemmed in on the east by the High Forest and the Forlorn Hills. The valley is dotted with settlements, farms, and isolated homesteads, yet most of it is unsettled. The valley's primary trade route is the river itself.

## DRUARWOOD

See the "Glimmerwood" section.

## EVERLUND

Situated on the banks of the Rauvin River, Everlund is one of the North's most active mercantile communities. A thick stone wall encloses the city, pierced in five places by gates. Like the spokes of a wheel, broad, straight avenues lead from each gate to the Bell Market at the city's center. The streets are clean and wide enough to accommodate large caravan vehicles. Soldiers of the city's army make a show of patrolling the walls, to reassure citizens and visitors as well as to discourage attackers. The buildings of Everlund are stately and well maintained, with steeply pitched rooftops and tall spires that sport colorful banners. Two bridges span the river, which has parks and trees along its shores.

Until recently, Everlund was a member of the Lords' Alliance. The five leaders who currently comprise the city's Council of Elders voted three to two in favor of separation and, in a symbolic show of support for Sundabar (see the "Sundabar" section), condemned the alliance for its failure to come to Sundabar's aid during the War of the Silver Marches. The decision was touted as an opportunity for Everlund to chart its own course, but more educated citizens believe the vote was orchestrated by the Zoar family, a group of influential nobles that moved to Everlund from Waterdeep over a century ago amid some scandal. The Zoars have gained considerable political influence in Everlund, to the extent that they now have a representative on the Council of Elders.

The Hall of the Elders is where the council meets to discuss issues affecting the city. Only the councilors know who voted which way concerning the decision to leave the Lords' Alliance. The members of the Council of Elders are as follows:

- High Captain Horix Zoar (LN male human **noble**), commander of Everlund's army and a windbag
- High Sorcerer Vaeril Rhuidhen (NG male sun elf **archmage**), a quiet voice of moderation and reason

# Everlund

1. Silverymoon Gate
2. Downriver Gate
3. Bridge Gate
4. Upriver Gate
5. Mountain Gate
6. Evermoor Way
7. Moongleam Tower
8. Bell Market
9. Hall of the Elders
10. Knightbridge
11. Dwarfbridge
12. Barracks and Armory
13. Danivarr's House

Map 3.3: Everlund

who keeps the peace between the council's more fractious members (and who formerly served as liaison to the Lords' Alliance)

- The Keeper of the Bridges, Kythora Shen (LN female human **veteran**), a retired soldier and skilled bureaucrat charged with overseeing the city watch and the conduct of commerce in the city
- The Master of Guilds, Boldor Steelshield (N male shield dwarf **noble**), representing the merchants of Everlund, who is prone to hyperbole and rumored to accept bribes
- The Speaker of the Town, a citizen elected every seven years to represent the common folk in the city; currently the post is held by Vatrice Stormwright (CG female human **commoner**), an easily flustered woman who owns a modestly successful chimney-sweeping business in the city

The most prominent edifice in Everlund is Moongleam Tower, a keep of black stone that serves as a Harper stronghold in the North. It rises from one of the higher knolls in the city and consists of four narrow, cylindrical towers joined together, surrounded by a dry moat that can be quickly flooded through a system of cisterns and pumps. Crowning the roof is an open turret, where a signaling mirror shaped like a crescent moon stands.

At any time, from five to fifteen Harpers are in residence, attended by a loyal staff and a private garrison of twenty veterans. Moonlord Daviana Yalrannis (CG female human **knight**) is the master of the tower, charged with its defense and upkeep. A powerful Harper wizard named Krowen Valharrow (CG male human **archmage** with a *robe of useful items* and a *staff of fire*) also resides in the tower, along with dozens of domesticated **tressym** (see appendix C) and a handful of apprentice **mages**. Apart from their ability to fly, the tressym behave like normal house cats. If one or more characters show an interest in the tressym, Krowen offers to bequeath one (but no more than one) to the party. The tressym bonds with the first character to earn its trust, which requires some obvious sign of affection accompanied by a successful DC 17 Charisma check. A character with proficiency in the Animal Handling skill has advantage on the check. The bonded tressym obeys that character's commands and no one else's.

Near the top of Moongleam Tower is a circular, windowless room that contains a permanent *teleportation circle*, which high-ranking Harpers use to enter and leave the tower unseen (see the "Inner Circles" section at the end of this chapter).

The city boasts many temples, the most prominent of which are dedicated to Helm, Mielikki, and Corellon Larethian. Everlund also has many fine places to eat and rest, the oldest and largest being Danivarr's House. Once a noble's mansion, this rambling inn is a favorite haunt for adventurers. The Zoar family bought the establishment a few years ago, but leaves the running of Danivarr's House to a one-eyed orc named Dral Thelev (LG male orc **commoner**). Both the Harpers and the Zhentarim keep a close eye on this place.

## DEVELOPMENT

If the characters received a letter of recommendation from Tamalin Zoar (see the "Calling Horns" section) and they show it to Dral Thelev, the orc tells them that the Zoar family has power in the city and that the characters can give the letter of recommendation to Dral in exchange for one favor from the Zoars (see the "Marks of Prestige" section in chapter 7 of the *Dungeon Master's Guide*). When the characters decide to call in the favor, Dral contacts his employers, and High Captain Horix Zoar does everything in his power to give the characters what they want, provided it's within his power and isn't likely to burden him or the Zoar family. Examples of what he might provide include a meeting with one or more members of the Council of Elders, an arranged meeting with a Lords' Alliance representative from another city, and a *spell scroll* of *raise dead*.

## EVERMOOR WAY

The Evermoor Way has long been a vital trade route, connecting the settlements of the Dessarin Valley with those of the Silver Marches. The section between Triboar and Yartar is an ancient road, relatively flat and composed of tight-fitting stones. East of Yartar, the road becomes a gravel and dirt wagon trail that passes a little too close to the Evermoors for most merchants' comfort. Between Olostin's Hold and Everlund, the trail passes through an area that used to be forest and is now full of tree stumps. Efforts to turn this long stretch into a proper road have long been thwarted by disagreements between the leaders of Yartar and Everlund, and Everlund's exit from the Lords' Alliance has dashed all hope.

## EVERMOORS

The Evermoors is a vast, unsettled area of fog-shrouded hills, cold bogs, rocky ridges, and small peaks. Adventurers crossing this expanse might spot the occasional castle ruin or crumbled tower—a remnant of a bygone realm. Although the region attracts many prospectors, no kingdom or civilization in recent history has been able to tame it. Hill giants, ettins, ogres, orcs, and trolls dwell here in great numbers. Settlements that stand on the edge of the Evermoors face constant threats from these and other monsters.

Floating a mile above the Evermoors is Lyn Armaal, Countess Sansuri's cloud castle (see chapter 9, "Castle of the Cloud Giants"). The view of the castle from the ground is fleeting as it disappears behind overcast skies.

## EYE OF THE ALL-FATHER

Built by giants long ago, this temple dedicated to Annam the All-Father lies hidden under the Spine of the World. A snow-covered pass that begins in the Valley of Khedrun leads to the temple. See chapter 4, "The Chosen Path," for more information on this location.

## FALLEN LANDS

Countless ruins dot this rugged, barren land, where ancient cities once stood and great battles once raged. Strange witchlights float around the ruins at night—the lingering vestiges of ancient spells, some say.

## FAR FOREST

Named for its remoteness, the woodland expanse between Anauroch and Delimbiyr Vale is home to families of sprites, lonely dryads, irksome satyrs, and territorial centaurs. Owlbears also prowl the Far Forest in alarming numbers, while the darkest depths are home to frightful ettercaps and their giant spider pets.

## FELL PASS

Between the northernmost rampart of the Frost Hills and the Spine of the World lies a high, cold pass that links the Lurkwood to the Surbrin River. Tribes of Uthgardt hunt the Fell Pass, occasionally clashing with other Uthgardt over contested territory.

## FIRESHEAR

Long ago, a meteor strike blasted a crater in the frozen tundra near the coast of the Trackless Sea, shearing away tons of rock and exposing rich veins of copper and silver ore. In the years that followed, miners settled nearby, giving rise to the town of Fireshear. The miners work for a consortium of three allied merchant companies: Hammaver House (based in Mirabar), the Silver Triangle (based in Neverwinter), and the Delvers of Brokenstone (based in Waterdeep). The settlement is made up of squat stone structures that resemble igloos, their domes good at supporting the weight of snow and deflecting the cold wind. Most homes are dug out of the rock and include deep cellars laden with preserves.

The miners of Fireshear dwell here all year. Ramps carved into the cliffs lead down to the shore, where stone docks protrude into a shallow bay that freezes by late fall and doesn't thaw until early summer. Fireshear imports most of its food, clothing, and other necessities. Ice fishing is a popular pastime among children, but all able-bodied adults are expected to toil in the mines.

The town has three leaders, who form a ruling triumvirate that handles trade negotiations with representatives of other settlements and disperses supplies among the townsfolk. Each member is a representative of one of the town's founding companies. Triumvirate members serve for life or until they resign, and they are known to take bribes, rewarding families who pay them in coin or precious ore with supplies of higher quality or in greater quantity. The current members are Tharkus Gromm (NE male shield dwarf **thug**) of Hammaver House; Darva (NG female dragonborn **mage**) of the Silver Triangle; and Zalaron Daska (N male human **veteran**) of the Delvers of Brokenstone.

Fireshear is also home to a retired civilar (captain) of Waterdeep's Griffon Cavalry and a member of the Emerald Enclave named Dasharra Keldabar (LG female shield dwarf **veteran**). She lives north of town, in a mostly underground hovel on a ridge that overlooks the sea. Locals know that Dasharra raises griffons, trains them as mounts, and teaches people how to ride them. The griffons are kept in a low, sturdy wooden shelter next to her home. At any time, Dasharra has 1d4 + 6 adult **griffons** and 1d4 griffon eggs in her care. Dasharra employs six Zhentarim mercenaries (N male and female human **veterans**) as guards, three of whom

**Map 3.4: Flint Rock**

ice or wading through frigid waist-deep water toward the docks, eager to raid and pillage. The remaining eight frost giants remain aboard the ship.

As townsfolk retreat to the mines or flee across the open tundra, the raiding giants fan out, allowing characters to take on two or three of them at a time. Dasharra provides aerial support, attacking giants at range with her heavy crossbow while mounted atop her griffon. If six or more frost giants fall in battle, the rest retreat to their ship. Left alone, the surviving frost giants (including those that didn't participate in the initial assault) regroup and launch a second attack 1d4 + 1 hours later, this time leaving no giant behind.

The frost giant raid occurs whether the characters remain in town or not. If the characters aren't present to defend the town, the frost giant raiders force hundreds of townsfolk to take refuge in the mines. The giants pile boulders in front of the mine entrances to trap the townsfolk inside, then loot the town. Townsfolk who fled into the tundra rather than hide in the mines return 2d6 hours later to find their homes reduced to rubble and their supplies gone. The giants pay no mind to Dasharra's hovel north of town.

## Treasure

Each giant carries a sack containing 1d4 mundane items (roll on the Items in a Giant's Bag table in the introduction). Aboard the greatship is an unlocked wooden chest, its lid frozen shut. Dealing 5 damage or more to the lid forces it open. The chest contains 1,500 sp, 450 gp, and 1d3 magic items, determined by rolling on Magic Item Table C in chapter 7 of the *Dungeon Master's Guide*.

# Flint Rock

The spirit mound of the Elk tribe (see the "Uthgardt" section earlier in this chapter) is situated in the midst of the Evermoors atop a gnarly knob of flinty stone that's perpetually shrouded in fog. Its rings, cairns, and altar mound are created from piles of heaped rock, barren of plant growth. The altar is a rectangular slab of stone 10 feet long, 6 feet wide, and 3 feet tall, its surfaces worn smooth by time. The enormous basin surrounding the altar mound is shaped like the silhouette of a leaping elk stag, although this image isn't readily apparent when the area is seen from ground level. Buried under the cairns are the bones of the Elk tribe's greatest warriors.

On the higher ground of the ring outside the basin, placed outward from the altar along the cardinal directions, are four menhirs of solid gray stone that the Elk tribe's shamans use to track the passage of time, the changing of the seasons, and the movement of the stars.

## Ancient Relic

Casting *detect magic* on the altar reveals a faint aura of divination magic originating from underneath it. The slab weighs several tons and is too large to be lifted or moved by any creature smaller and weaker than a stone giant, but multiple Small or Medium creatures lifting in tandem can move the stone if at least five of them succeed on a DC 20 Strength (Athletics) check. The altar

stand watch outside the griffon pens while the others rest in a cramped loft above the griffons' stalls.

If one or more characters are members of the Emerald Enclave, the adventurers can easily convince Dasharra to help them fly to Svardborg, Lyn Armaal, or some other destination within a few hundred miles of Fireshear. Otherwise, they must pay for her services. She charges 250 gp per person for training and another 25 gp per person per day of travel. Characters who want to be trained must undergo three days of intense lessons, after which they know enough about griffon riding to control their mounts. Each griffon is able to carry one Medium rider or two Small riders (along with their armor and portable gear), and Dasharra has saddles and reins sized for both Small and Medium riders. Dasharra's "alpha griffon," Screecher, allows no one but her to ride it. Dasharra's other griffons are trained to follow Screecher wherever it goes and can't be coaxed into veering off course unless they are magically charmed.

## Suggested Encounter

Three days after the characters arrive in Fireshear, a frost giant greatship with white dragon wings for sails and mammoth tusks lashed to its bow emerges from the thick fog shrouding the coastline. The greatship (see the "Svardborg: General Features" sidebar in chapter 7, "Berg of the Frost Giants") cuts a swath through the icy crust over the shallow bay as it approaches and slowly grinds to a dead stop. The ship carries twenty **frost giants**. Twelve of them leap over the sides, walking across can be broken in half to get at the ground underneath; it has AC 17, 100 hit points, a damage threshold of 10, and immunity to poison and psychic damage.

Uthgar's early followers who founded the Elk tribe buried a relic of giantkind under the altar to empower it: a 5-foot-long mithral spear tip weighing 75 pounds. The spear tip is the source of the faint aura of divination magic, though it no longer has the powers it once held.

### SUGGESTED ENCOUNTER

The first time the characters arrive here, the only creatures present are two **elks**—a mated pair—foraging for moss. The elks observe the party but pose no threat, fleeing if they are attacked or if they detect one or more party members within 60 feet of either one. Any creature that wounds or kills an elk on Flint Rock must succeed on a DC 16 Wisdom saving throw or be cursed. For as long as the curse lasts, members of the Elk tribe recognize the cursed creature as a hated enemy and are hostile toward it. In addition, the creature can't benefit from natural healing until the curse is removed with a *remove curse* spell or similar magic.

## FORGOTTEN FOREST

The Forgotten Forest has long been the domain of fey creatures and belligerently protective treants. Thus, it is best "forgotten." An immortal druid named Pheszeltan dwells deep in the woods and is willing to offer advice to those with the skill to reach him.

## FORK ROAD

The Fork Road is the only well-traveled trail between Sundabar and Citadel Adbar. At a point commonly known as "the Fork," the trail splits. One path heads north to Citadel Adbar (becoming the Adbar Road), while the other continues down a little-used path east toward Ascore.

## FORLORN HILLS

A great forest claimed by elven kingdoms once covered the Forlorn Hills. When the elves left, the forest was cleared to make room for a dwarven empire, which also faded from memory. The area is home to scores of hill giants and ettins, while the mountains in its center are claimed by copper dragons who have invaded ancient dwarven vaults and throne halls and turned these chambers into their lairs.

## FROST HILLS

The southernmost spur of the Spine of the World, the Frost Hills combine with the Evermoors to form the west border of the Silver Marches. Mithral Hall, one of the strongest dwarfholds of the North, lies deep within the Frost Hills, as do various Uthgardt encampments.

## GAUNTLGRYM

Once a great city and a bastion of the empire of Delzoun, this dwarven stronghold stood abandoned for centuries beneath the mountains. Recently, an army of shield dwarves led by Bruenor Battlehammer reclaimed it, ousting drow squatters and sending them scurrying back into the Underdark. Bruenor now sits on Gauntlgrym's throne as king.

The "heart" of Gauntlgrym is its legendary forge, within which is trapped a fire primordial known as Maegera the Dawn Titan. For more information on Gauntlgrym and its inhabitants, see the *Sword Coast Adventurer's Guide* and the adventure *Out of the Abyss*.

### SUGGESTED ENCOUNTER

Drow of House Xorlarrin infiltrate Gauntlgrym through secret passageways of which not even the dwarves are aware. Bearing an *iron flask* given to them by the great fire giant chief Duke Zalto, they slip into the forge, murder a few guards, trap the fire primordial in the flask, and try to flee with their prize. If the characters are in Gauntlgrym prior to visiting Ironslag (see chapter 8, "Forge of the Fire Giants"), they can attempt to thwart the theft and keep the primordial out of Zalto's hands. In this encounter, the characters confront the drow as they try to escape. The encounter begins in one of two ways:

- The characters are making their way down a hallway in Gauntlgrym when they face the drow interlopers.
- The characters are with Bruenor Battlehammer when news of the theft of the primordial reaches the king's ear, in which case the characters are asked to help find those responsible.

In either case, the characters encounter the drow in a dusty, 20-foot-wide, 30-foot-high hall lined with 10-foot-tall dwarven statues. Assume the two groups are 60 feet apart when they see each other. The dark elves are making their way toward a secret door set into the wall behind one of the statues, beyond which is a 5-foot-wide, 7-foot-high, mile-long tunnel that the drow intend to use as their escape route. The secret door is between the two groups—20 feet from the drow party and 40 feet from the adventuring party at the start of the encounter—and the characters have no prior knowledge of it. So masterfully crafted is the secret door that spotting it requires a careful search of the wall and a successful DC 25 Wisdom (Perception) check. The drow are already aware of the secret door, having used it to creep into Gauntlgrym undetected.

The leader of the all-male party is a slippery, never-say-die dark elf named Draac Xorlarrin. Taal, his younger cousin, accompanies him. Both are **drow mages**. Their escort consists of six male **drow elite warriors** and two **shadow demons** (one summoned by Draac, the other by Taal).

Draac and Taal have both used their Summon Demon ability, as well as all of their 5th-level spell slots. They know that they can't afford to spar with adventurers or risk getting caught. On their first turns in combat, Draac and Taal cast *Evard's black tentacles* spells. The tentacles erupt from the floor in front of the characters, filling the two 20-foot squares between them and the secret door. Confident that the tentacles will hold their enemies at bay, the drow mages then head toward the secret door and try to escape. The drow elite warriors and the shadow demons follow the mages, serving as personal bodyguards. Once inside the secret tunnel, the mages use *web* spells to obstruct the passageway behind their party, hoping to ensnare or slow down their pursuers.

### TREASURE

Draac Xorlarrin carries the *iron flask* that has **Maegera the Dawn Titan** (see appendix C) trapped inside it. He also carries a staff topped with web patterns on the haft and a sculpted obsidian spider with small diamonds for eyes at the top (worth 1,500 gp). The staff is ornate but nonmagical. Taal carries a pouch with four 100 gp gems inside it, and he wears a fine black cloak embroidered with webs made of platinum thread (worth 750 gp).

### DEVELOPMENT

If the drow escape, the characters might encounter them again in Ironslag (see the "Special Delivery" section at the end of chapter 8). Maegera the Dawn Titan can be safely released from the flask in one of two locations. If it is released inside Gauntlgrym's forge, Maegera becomes trapped there once more. If it is released inside the adamantine forge in Ironslag (see chapter 8, "Forge of the Fire Giants," area 29), the fire primordial is trapped within that forge and likewise contained. If the primordial is released anywhere else, it goes on a rampage, attacking any creature it sees, until it is again trapped inside an *iron flask* or some other receptacle.

## GLIMMERWOOD

Three forests grew together to form the Glimmerwood: the Moonwood to the west, the Coldwood to the east, and the Druarwood between them. The Glimmerwood's pine, fir, and spruce trees grow atop the rocky foothills and escarpments of two converging mountain ranges: the Spine of the World and the Ice Spires. The trees are more stunted and sparse as the altitude increases to the north.

### MOONWOOD

This dense coniferous forest north of the Evermoors seems very quiet and still. The southern fringes of the Moonwood are home to small bands of moon elves and wood elves, as well as the rustic homes of a few wood-cutters and trappers. Uthgardt and lycanthropes prowl its northern depths.

### DRUARWOOD

Uthgardt of the Black Lion and Red Tiger tribes live and hunt here. The two tribes share a spirit mound in the forest's icy northern reaches (see the "Beorunna's Well" section).

### COLDWOOD

Branches of the Icespear River emerge from the heart of the Coldwood, trickling south toward the Silver Marches. The Glimmerwood is so frigid that the ground is covered with several inches of snow even during the height of summer. In winter, the trees are bent under several feet of snow and ice, while the ground remains navigable because of the shelter that the dense foliage overhead provides. Fire giants have used fire and their greatswords to clear wide swaths through the eastern woods, to expedite overland travel to and from Ironslag.

In these areas, the stench of burned wood hangs in the air above rows of incinerated trees.

## GOLDENFIELDS

Goldenfields is a walled farming complex dedicated to Chauntea, the goddess of agriculture. It also serves as a base for the Emerald Enclave. Its harvests are crucial to cities throughout the North, Waterdeep in particular. See chapter 2 for more information on this location.

### SUGGESTED ENCOUNTER

If the adventure didn't begin in Goldenfields, you can run the "Attack on Goldenfields" encounter (see chapter 2) when the characters visit the location.

## GRANDFATHER TREE

Deep within the High Forest is an oak tree of immense size, with a base measuring 50 feet in diameter and a crown soaring to a height of over 350 feet. Around this ancient tree are two rings of raised earth. The innermost ring has four normal-sized oak trees (healthy and mature ones) growing out of it. Buried beneath the outermost ring are the moldy bones of long-dead Uthgardt, most of them from the Tree Ghost tribe.

Tree Ghosts patrol the woods surrounding Grandfather Tree. Characters who venture into the forest on foot in search of the tree should encounter one or more patrols, each consisting of 3d6 Tree Ghost **tribal warriors** and an **Uthgardt shaman** (see appendix C). There is a 25 percent chance that the group includes one of Great Chief Boorvald Orcbane's adult children, who leads the patrol. This Uthgardt leader is a **berserker**, with the following changes:

- The leader is chaotic neutral.
- He or she has a Dexterity score of 15 (+2) and AC 14.
- He or she speaks Bothii (the Uthgardt language), Common, and Elvish.
- The leader carries an *oathbow* and has a +5 bonus to hit with the weapon, which deals 7 (1d8 + 3) piercing damage on a hit, plus an extra 10 (3d6) piercing damage against a sworn enemy. (See chapter 7 of the *Dungeon Master's Guide* for other properties of the *oathbow*.)

Characters who travel by air have an easy time spotting the tree and can reach the perimeter of this area without encountering any ground patrols.

Grandfather Tree has AC 15, 500 hit points, a damage threshold of 15, and immunity to fire and psychic damage. As long as it has 1 hit point remaining, it regenerates 50 hit points on initiative count 0. Although it's a living creature like any plant, Grandfather Tree isn't self-aware and can neither move nor take actions. Creatures tasked with protecting the tree gain the effect of a *bless* spell while they are beneath its great boughs. In addition, any creature that finishes a long rest under the boughs gains the benefit of the *greater restoration* spell.

### ANCIENT RELIC

Many small chambers are hidden between the exposed roots of Grandfather Tree. A Medium or smaller creature can reach these chambers by crawling among the roots. Half buried in the root network's innermost chamber is a relic of giantkind left here long ago by a Tree Ghost shaman: a nonmagical electrum torc etched with Giant runes. Formerly the nose-ring of a powerful hill giant chief, this U-shaped piece of jewelry is worth 250 gp as an art object and weighs 25 pounds. It can be worn around the neck by a Medium Humanoid; though cumbersome, it doesn't hinder its wearer in any way.

## Suggested Encounter

Seven **centaurs** have come to Grandfather Tree for its restorative powers. The centaurs fell victim to a curse as they explored some ancient ruins in the High Forest. Until the curse is lifted, the centaurs exude a charnel stench, can't regain hit points, and can't eat or drink anything without making themselves sick. The centaurs are not spoiling for a fight and prefer to be left alone.

Four **dryads** live in the smaller oak trees that encircle Grandfather Tree. They emerge from their trees when one or more characters approach within 50 feet of Grandfather Tree's base, demanding in Elvish that the characters leave at once. The dryads know nothing of the giant relic hidden among Grandfather Tree's roots and have no attachment to it. With a successful DC 14 Charisma (Intimidation or Persuasion) check, a character can convince the dryads to let the party search for the relic and take it away. The check is made with disadvantage if the dryads can't understand the character's words. If the party conducts a search without the dryads' consent, the dryads attempt to charm the characters and command them to return whence they came. The dryads attack intruders who resist their charms

or refuse to leave, calling on the centaurs to aid them (which the centaurs are more than happy to do).

Whenever a dryad is killed, one or more conjured animals rise up out of the ground within 30 feet of her and join the fray, acting on the dryad's initiative count. Roll on the Avenging Animals table to determine what appears. A conjured animal can distinguish enemies from allies, and it gains the benefit of Grandfather Tree's *bless* spell. It disappears after 1 hour, or when it drops to 0 hit points, or when it is dispelled (DC 15).

### Avenging Animals

| d4 | Animal(s) |
|----|-----------|
| 1 | 2 brown bears |
| 2 | 2 dire wolves |
| 3 | 1 giant boar |
| 4 | 1 giant elk |

## Graypeak Mountains

An intermittent range of mountains running north and south separates Delimbiyr Vale from the Fallen Lands and the desert of Anauroch. The Graypeak Mountains are named for the clans of gray-skinned stone giants who dwell here. The expanse is riddled with abandoned mines of both dwarven and Netherese origin.

## Grayvale

Nestled in the southern part of the Graypeak Mountains, a beautiful and fertile valley stands between the settlements of Loudwater and Llorkh. The Grayflow

Map 3.5: Grandfather Tree

River flows through the middle of Grayvale, which is dotted with farmsteads, hunting lodges, old dwarven mines, and the ruins of bygone elven kingdoms. Now, many of Grayvale's homesteads and hamlets lie in ruins, after recently being flattened by rampaging stone giants. The vale has been mostly evacuated, except for a few scattered farms whose inhabitants refuse to leave.

## Suggested Encounter

As the characters explore Grayvale, a **young brass dragon** named Silixia spots them from a nearby hilltop. The friendly dragon offers greetings and warns the party that stone giants are laying waste to farms, homesteads, and ruins throughout Grayvale. She has spent the past few weeks helping farmers and other locals flee the vale. She doesn't know why the normally reclusive giants are suddenly out to destroy everything. If the characters ask Silixia where the stone giants live, she offers to lead them to Deadstone Cleft and warns them that the giants have a roc "pet" that guards the entrance to their canyon lair. Silixia has no interest in battling the giants, but she can be bribed into luring away the roc or providing some other form of assistance. A rare magic item or a collection of gems worth at least 5,000 gp is enough to satisfy her. A character who barters with the dragon can, with a successful DC 17 Charisma (Persuasion) check, convince Silixia to accept an uncommon magic item or 2,500 gp as payment.

# Grayvale Run

The trail known as Grayvale Run extends from Loudwater and eastward, following the Grayflow River, to Llorkh and beyond. The trail's name changes to the Dawn Pass where it cuts through the Graypeak Mountains. All along Grayvale Run are wagons, fences, and cottages that the stone giants of Deadstone Cleft have wrecked and flattened with rocks.

## Suggested Encounter

The characters observe three **stone giants** quietly, almost reverently, dismantling an old stone cottage. One giant gathers the stones while a second one rearranges them into decorative pillars. The third giant digs holes with its hands and buries the cottage's other contents. Characters who succeed on a DC 10 Intelligence check realize that the giants are erasing all evidence of the cottage and using its stones to create something artistic and timeless in its place. Once they finish, the giants move on to the next ruined homestead they find. The giants are too distracted to notice anyone watching them from a distance. If the characters confront the giants or antagonize them, the giants hurl rocks at them. If the characters flee, the giants don't pursue, opting instead to continue their work. The giants carry no treasure.

# Great Worm Cavern

The spirit mound of the Great Worm tribe is inside a spacious cavern at the northeast end of the Valley of Khedrun, deep in the Spine of the World. Thick ice hangs above the pillared entrance to Great Worm Cavern, and the interior walls of the place are covered with an icy glaze and lined with massive icicles that gleam and glitter in reflected light. The walls are too slippery to be climbed without gear or magic.

The cavern floor is a sheet of slippery ice (see the "Wilderness Hazards" section in chapter 5 of the *Dungeon Master's Guide*) flanked by 70-foot-high ledges of rock, atop which stand two totem poles of chiseled ice with carvings that resemble winged snakes. The walls of these ledges are riddled with caves in which the Great Worm tribe members live. Natural steam vents in the rock keep the caves warm throughout the year. Above the ledges, dug into the cavern walls, are narrow crypts where the honored dead are placed, their frozen corpses propped up in a standing position.

## Altar

Rising from the back of the cavern is a triangular promontory of ice-covered rock, 120 feet above the cavern floor at its peak. Thereupon stands an altar of frost-covered stone, carved in the shape of a coiled serpent with great wings. The altar represents Elrem, the Great Worm. Here, the tribal warriors make sacrifices to the Great Worm in honor of Uthgar. Doing so, they believe, ensures that Elrem doesn't return to devour them.

Bound inside the altar is a **couatl**. It can phase into and out of the altar at will. While inside the altar, the couatl is undetectable and can sense creatures within 120 feet of it. The first time a good-hearted character approaches within 20 feet of the altar, the couatl telepathically reaches out to that character without divulging its location or identity. Communicating in a language that the character understands, the couatl warns the character that the Great Worm tribe has fallen under the sway of an evil chieftain named Wormblod. It asks the character to hunt down and slay Womblod, promising a reward for this good deed. The couatl knows that Wormblod is away, searching for a missing concubine named If the characters present proof of Wormblod's death as an offering to the altar, see "Development."

If anyone damages the altar, the couatl emerges and tries to frighten them off, attacking only as a last resort.

## Ancient Relic

At the back of the cave hangs a relic of giantkind: a crescent-shaped gong in a stone frame. The gong, a circular disk 13 feet in diameter, was once the shield of a frost giant champion, but it was broken in combat and is now missing a large piece. What remains of it weighs 250 pounds. The shield is made of red dragon scales bolted to a beaten copper frame. Its leather arm straps are long gone. The ropes holding up the gong can be cut with two swings of a sword.

If the gong is struck inside the cavern, its deep tone echoes throughout the cavern and causes a few large icicles to break away from the ceiling and crash down onto the icy floor. The crashing ice awakens three **young remorhazes** hibernating in a cyst beneath the ice. The remorhazes burst up through the ice and attack any creatures they see. The Great Worm tribesfolk are unaware of the remorhazes and have no way to control them once they burst forth.

MAP 3.6: GREAT WORM CAVERN

## SUGGESTED ENCOUNTER

Most Great Worm tribe members are nomads who hunt and forage in the wilderness. Those who dwell here are typically the elderly, mothers, and children. Each small cave at the base of the cavern holds 1d4 + 4 non-combatants, and standing atop the ledges, watching the entrance, are four **tribal warriors** (two per ledge). They have a stack of spears to hurl down at intruders.

## TREASURE

The remorhaz lair can be explored and plundered if the creatures are killed. The area is a 20-foot-diameter oval chamber with walls of glazed ice. Scattered on the floor are three 500 gp gemstones, fifteen 100 gp gemstones, and one magic item determined by rolling on Magic Item Table C in chapter 7 of the *Dungeon Master's Guide*.

If the characters slay Wormblod and bring proof of his demise, the couatl emerges from the altar and bestows on each of them a *charm of restoration* (see the "Supernatural Gifts" section in chapter 7 of the *Dungeon Master's Guide*). The couatl then returns to the altar and makes no further attempt to communicate with them.

## GRIFFON'S NEST

A wooden palisade topped with the rotting heads of dead orcs encircles a hilltop village of huts and longhouses in the northern part of the Surbrin Hills. Roughly three hundred Uthgardt of the Griffon tribe dwell here. Perched atop the rocky crest of Griffon's Nest is the longhouse of the great chief, Halric Bonesnapper. This building is where Halric meets with the other tribal chieftains to settle important matters and plan for the tribe's future. While Halric enjoys the comforts of a king, the rest of the tribe lives in squalor.

At various times in the past, visitors were welcome to meet and trade with the chieftains, but the Griffon tribe no longer opens its gates to strangers and in fact actively tries to slaughter them. Most of the residents of Griffon's Nest are **tribal warriors**, with a few dozen **berserkers**. An **Uthgardt shaman** (see appendix C) wanders the settlement, making sure no one speaks ill of the great chief. If the characters approach Griffon's Nest, the settlement opens its gates to them, inviting them to enter. This is a ploy. If the characters enter the settlement, the Uthgardt try to slaughter them and feast on their remains.

Great Chief Halric Bonesnapper is a **berserker**, with the following changes:

- Halric is chaotic evil and speaks Bothii (the Uthgardt language) and Common.
- He has 99 hit points and wields a *+1 greataxe*. He has a +6 bonus to hit with this weapon and deals 10 (1d12 + 4) slashing damage on a hit.

## GRUDD HAUG

Built on a branch of the Dessarin River, Grudd Haug is the den of Chief Guh and her hill giant brood. See chapter 5, "Den of the Hill Giants," for more information on this location.

# GUNDARLUN

The island nation of Gundarlun (see map 3.10) is a string of barren mountains rising up out of the Trackless Sea. Mighty waves crash against its rocky shores. Clinging to the mountainsides above the water are stone keeps with fishing villages huddled around them, each one ruled by a ruthless jarl who answers to the King of Gundarlun, Olgrave Redaxe (CN male human **berserker** with 90 hit points). The king lives in a crumbling fortress that overlooks Gundbarg, the island's only port.

# GUNDBARG

A city of dour Northfolk, Gundbarg tolerates visitors only because it depends on trade for its survival. What the Northfolk can't buy, they plunder. Visitors typically stay at the Dragon Turtle Inn, a salt-encrusted stone edifice near the docks. High rock walls enclose Gundbarg's harbor, which contains the King's Fleet, consisting of nearly two hundred longships.

# HAWK'S NEST

Hawk's Nest is a fortified settlement that overlooks Silverymoon Pass, built to defend the pass against orc hordes and other threats, thus protecting Silverymoon's eastern flank. Perched atop a rocky crag and surrounded by high battlements, Hawk's Nest is under the protection of the Order of the Gauntlet. High stone walls enclose a keep and a densely packed village that includes three small temples (dedicated to Helm, Torm, and Tyr), a blacksmith, a leatherworker, a caravan supplier, a rough-and-tumble tavern (the Spiked Gauntlet), and two cozy yet spacious inns (the Hawk's Roost and the Inn of the Silver Sword).

The Lord of Hawk's Nest is Arthus Cavilos (LG male human **knight** of Tyr), a member of the Order of the Gauntlet. His wife, Lady Fenris Agathonn (LG female human **mage**), is the great grand niece of Lord Taern Hornblade of Silverymoon. Arthun and Fenris have two spirited daughters, Lavencia and Eryl; one is training to be a wizard, the other a knight of Tyr like her father.

Lord Cavilos raises **hippogriffs**, which the knights of Hawk's Nest train as mounts and use to patrol the trade road between Silverymoon and Sundabar. Characters who are looking for an expeditious means of travel can petition Lord Cavilos to ferry them to their destination on the backs of hippogriffs. If the characters impress upon him the urgency of their mission, Lord Cavilos commands his fellow knights to fly the characters where they need to go, then return to Hawk's Nest with the hippogriffs. A hippogriff carrying a knight and one other rider must rest for 1 hour for every 3 hours it flies, and can travel about 54 miles per day.

## SUGGESTED ENCOUNTER

When fire giants attack an armored wagon heading east to Sundabar, knights on hippogriffs are forced to swoop down, rescue the survivors, and deliver them back to Hawk's Nest. The characters learn about the attack when the knights return with the survivors. They also find out that the armored wagon was transporting wages to workers who are rebuilding Sundabar's defenses, which were destroyed during the War of the Silver Marches. Characters can show their valor by undertaking a quest to retrieve the stolen wages, which were kept in two locked iron strongboxes. While traveling east along the trade road, the characters come upon the wreckage of the armored wagon. From there they can follow fire giant tracks heading north into the mountains. Several hours later, they come upon two **fire giants** and two **hell hounds**. Each giant carries a sack that contains one of the iron strongboxes. The giants have broken the locks off them, leaving them unlocked.

If the characters return the strongboxes to Hawk's Nest or deliver them to Sundabar, Lord Cavilos is impressed. If the party includes a paladin or a cleric of good alignment who isn't already a member of the Order of the Gauntlet, Lord Cavilos offers that character membership in the order. If the party already includes any members of the order, Lord Cavilos offers each of them a knighthood and a hippogriff mount. He also invites all party members to attend a dinner with his family, during which Lord Cavilos regales his honored guests with unexaggerated tales of victorious battles he fought during the War of the Silver Marches.

## TREASURE

Each strongbox contains 500 gp. Each giant's sack also holds 1d4 mundane items, determined by rolling on the Items in a Giant's Bag table in the introduction.

# HELM'S HOLD

Located a short distance southeast of Neverwinter, Helm's Hold is a fortified monastery enclosed on all sides by stone walls patrolled day and night by members of the Order of the Gilded Eye, a splinter sect of the Order of the Gauntlet. Helm's Hold is firmly under the Gilded Eye's control, and its members have taken Helm's doctrine of protection to extremes. The high-minded inquisitors of the Gilded Eye are convinced that evil is rampant. They are determined to root out those under "demonic influence" and are quick to persecute anyone who doesn't act in accordance with their beliefs.

Within the walls of Helm's Hold are numerous residences surrounding a central district called the Heartward, wherein the characters can find a roomy tavern (called the Old Dirty Dwarf), several quiet hostels, and a bustling marketplace. A wooden hangman's scaffold stands in the center of the marketplace, and on certain nights, when clouds obscure the waning moon, luminous ghosts wander around it, going about the business of the living. Phantom vendors sell ephemeral apples at empty stands, ghost children play in the streets, and spirits hang one another on the scaffold. Some of the scenes appear to be reenactments of past events, whereas others have not occurred—at least, not yet. The ghosts speak mostly nonsense, but some of what they say might offer clues to past or future happenings.

Dominating the skyline is the Cathedral of Helm, a towering and inspiring edifice of pale gray stone that's visible for miles around. As much a fortress as a temple, the cathedral contains an orphanage, a hospital, an asylum, and training grounds for Gilded Eye initiates.

Holy Watcher Qerria (LG female human **priest** of Helm), who presides over the cathedral, is determined to root out corruption wherever she finds it. Few doubt that her words carry the weight of Helm's divine wisdom. She is served by dozens of Gilded Eye inquisitors (male and female **cult fanatics** of various alignments) who employ a host of **acolytes**, **assassins**, **guards**, **knights**, **spies**, and **veterans**. Evildoers and enemies of the Gilded Eye are rounded up and brought to Helm's Hold to face judgment. Those deemed to be under "demonic influence" or those who threaten the Gilded Eye are hanged, their bodies burned to ashes to prevent them from being raised from the dead.

## Suggested Encounter

Adventurers who enter Helm's Hold are watched closely by the Gilded Eye. However, as long as they don't stir up trouble, they have little to fear from the order, which prides itself on making visitors feel safe and protected. The Gilded Eye relies on trade to finance its activities, and adventurers are usually good for the settlement's economy. The Gilded Eye is also known to use adventurers to do its dirty work.

The leaders of the Gilded Eye have received reports of giant marauders in the region. Trained to deal with demonic threats, the order is less keen to face giants in battle. Zara Dalkor (LG female **knight** of Helm) and her squire, Thora Tamlarrin (LN female half-elf **guard**), approach the characters and offer them the opportunity to help the Gilded Eye and the people of Helm's Hold, promising nothing in return except the Gilded Eye's gratitude. If the characters decline to help, Zara apologizes for taking up their time and reports back to her superiors.

If the characters express any interest in helping the Gilded Eye, Zara shares the following information:

- Scouts from Helm's Hold have spotted frost giants wandering the lands to the south.
- The frost giants have attacked and plundered several homesteads and caravans along the High Road.
- The Gilded Eye wants the characters to find out where the giants are coming from.

Characters who accept the quest and head south for 10 miles spot a **frost giant** walking toward the coast. The giant recently attacked a caravan traveling north along the High Road and has 88 hit points remaining. He carries a sack stuffed with pillaged food as well as 1d4 mundane items (roll on the Items in a Giant's Bag table in the introduction). The giant fights to the death if he is attacked. If the characters follow the giant while keeping their distance, he leads them to a miles-long stretch of 100-foot-high cliffs. Anchored a half mile off the coast is a greatship (see the "Svardborg: General Features" sidebar in chapter 7, "Berg of the Frost Giants") with two giant-sized punts tethered to it. Three **frost giants** are aboard the ship. When the giant carrying the sack of food waves from the top of the cliffs, one of the giants aboard the ship climbs into a punt and rows it to shore, while the first giant climbs down the cliff to meet it. Most of the ship's crew is still plundering the mainland, so the ship isn't leaving anytime soon.

Sixteen frost giants have yet to return to the ship from their inland raids. If the characters hide aboard the ship or remain within sight of it, roll a d20 at the end of each hour that passes. On a roll of 17 or higher, 1d4 **frost giants** return and signal the ship to send a punt to shore. If no punt is available, the giants swim to the ship to find out what happened.

### Treasure

Characters who board the ship and defeat the giants find a ton of stolen foodstuffs, along with a dozen barrels of cheap ale of little value, twelve casks of expensive brandy (worth 300 gp each), 10,000 gp in mixed coinage, and 2d4 stolen art objects worth 750 gp each (roll on the appropriate table in chapter 7 of the *Dungeon Master's Guide* to determine each art object).

Each returning giant carries a sack stuffed with pillaged supplies as well as one mundane item, determined by rolling on the Items in a Giant's Bag table in the introduction. There is also a 25 percent chance of a sack containing 1d10 × 100 gp in mixed coinage.

# High Forest

Although much less expansive than in ancient times, the High Forest is still vast and mysterious. Larger than most kingdoms, it encompasses mountains. The High Forest is home to treants of enormous size, stags with antlers as wide across as a wagon, brown bears bigger than large sheds, owlbears, wolves, unicorns, and many other creatures, including fiercely territorial wood elves and Uthgardt of the Tree Ghost tribe. The forest holds many hidden settlements, haunted ruins, fey crossings, and ancient magical wards.

In the outermost fringes of the forest, woodcutters ply their trade, and outlaws on the run might find refuge. But as everyone knows, those who venture too deep into the High Forest are often not seen again.

# High Moor

The High Moor isn't part of the North per se. A great cataclysm occurred here long ago, wiping out an entire elven kingdom, but little evidence of this event now remains except for some haunted ruins, tombs, and dungeons shrouded in thick fog. Many adventurers have perished in search of these ancient sites, for the High Moor is home to many monsters.

# High Road

This well-traveled highway follows the coast from Luskan to Waterdeep, connecting with Neverwinter along the way. For years, the stretch of the High Road between Neverwinter and Waterdeep fell into disuse and disrepair because of frequent monster attacks. When he was both the Lord Protector of Neverwinter and the Open Lord of Waterdeep, Lord Dagult Neverember hired adventurers to make the old road safe and spent considerable coin to repair it. Many now consider the High Road a safer means of travel than a sea voyage.

## HUNDELSTONE

At the highest elevations along Ten Trail, only a few shrubs cling to life amid patches of moss-covered rock. Travelers on this route eventually come to Hundelstone, perching on the mountain slopes much like the surrounding flora. The town's buildings are low, with most of their rooms cut out of the hard soil and rock below ground level, and their roofs steeply pitched to better shed the snows that blanket the mountains in the winter. The shield dwarves and rock gnomes in Hundelstone get a chuckle out of warning visitors to stoop low as they walk about town, lest they be blown away by the wind.

For most people, Hundelstone is either the last outpost of civilization before taking the pass north to Icewind Dale or the first welcome sign of refuge after making the wearying trip back. Many of the dwarves and gnomes here spend their days excavating tunnels, mining ore, or smelting and smithing the local iron and tin. (Adventurers who venture down into these tunnels might be surprised to find that some of them descend for miles, in some cases all the way to the Underdark.) Hundelstone's few score human residents are mostly sellswords or would-be adventurers who earn a living as caravan guards or beast hunters in the crags.

One notable resident of Hundelstone is an inventor named Thwip Ironbottom (CG male rock gnome **commoner**). A spy for the Harpers, Thwip keeps an eye on strangers passing through town and uses a *sending stone* to stay in touch with Beldora, a Harper spy in Icewind Dale (see the "Beldora's Quest" section in chapter 2 for more information about Thwip).

## ICE PEAK

The frozen island that lies southeast of the Sea of Moving Ice is named for the snow-capped promontory that dominates its northern half. Most of the inhabitants live in a few settlements clustered around the twin bays on the southern shore. Caves in the mountain's peak serve as a lair for Arveiaturace, the white wyrm known to sailors as Iceclaws because of her habit of diving on hapless vessels and tearing them apart with her talons.

Longships crowd the docks of Aurilssbarg, the island's largest community. Typical of the settlements on Ice Peak, the streets of Aurilssbarg are paved with logs laid side by side, and its buildings are low wooden structures whose pitched roofs are covered in sod. The heart of Aurilssbarg is Green Hall, a spacious tavern with a lengthy firepit that can spit six goats at a time to feed the cold and hungry crews that arrive after unloading their ships at the docks. Locals come here as well to hear the latest news from the mainland, although by the time it reaches Ice Peak, such news is often out of date and wildly exaggerated, little better than idle rumor. Still, the isolated inhabitants of Aurilssbarg eat it up all the same.

The island's smaller coastal settlements include the fishing and trapping villages of Bjorn's Hold and Icewolf. The natives of Ice Peak survive by catching fish and hunting goats, seals, and whales. The island boasts a large yeti population. They feed on mountain goats, avoiding Northlanders unless food is scarce.

## ICE MOUNTAINS AND ICE SPIRES

The Ice Mountains and the Ice Spires are reckoned by some to be the easternmost extent of the Spine of the World, rather than being mountain ranges in their own right. The difference is academic, since all three areas have soaring peaks, permanent snowpack at all but the lowest elevations, and monster infestations. White dragons commonly vie for dominion in this region.

## ICESHIELD LANDS

Where a branch of the Dessarin Valley meets the western High Forest are rolling grass-covered hills recently claimed by the orcs of the Iceshield clan. They dwell in lodges made from timber cut from the forest. Elves and centaurs regularly emerge from the High Forest to attack and set fire to these lodges, but the orcs keep cutting down trees and rebuilding them.

## ICEWIND DALE

Icewind Dale has snow, ice, and freezing temperatures in abundance. The sun never rises far above the horizon even at the height of summer—and the height of summer is a fleeting thing. Winter here is long and ruthless.

Icewind Dale is surrounded by perilous terrain. The ice cliffs of the Reghed Glacier rise up in the east like prison walls. The towering, snow-capped peaks of the Spine of the World loom to the south. To the north and west, the Sea of Moving Ice churns bergs and floes in an endless tumult, like winter grinding its teeth in anticipation of its next freezing assault. Between these formidable obstacles lies windswept tundra dotted with settlements and the occasional small forest or stand of trees.

A singular mountain called Kelvin's Cairn rises from the heart of Icewind Dale. During the summer, snow from Kelvin's Cairn flows into three mineral-rich lakes: Maer Dualdon, Lac Dinneshere, and Redwaters. By midsummer, Icewind Dale shakes off the torpor of winter and comes forth in full flower. Grasses grow two or three feet high in the span of weeks. Birds flock to the marshes formed by the thawing soil, and reindeer calves fill out the herds that diminished in the winter.

Reghed nomads follow the reindeer herds as they migrate across Icewind Dale, and dwarf miners haunt the caves and tunnels under Kelvin's Cairn, rarely emerging except to trade ore for food. Most of Icewind Dale's inhabitants, however, live in ten permanent settlements collectively known as Ten-Towns:

- The walled town of Bryn Shander, which lies at the northern end of the Ten Trail, is the first stop for most visiting merchants and traders and by far the largest of the ten communities.
- The hunting and fishing villages of Bremen, Targos, Termalaine, and Lonelywood line the shores of Maer Dualdon, which feeds into the Shaengarne River and holds seemingly countless numbers of knuckle-head trout.
- The villages of Dougan's Hole and Good Mead stand a few miles apart on the north shore of Redwaters which, contrary to its name, sparkles emerald green during the day and silver in the evening.

- The town of Easthaven and, nestled among the foothills of Kelvin's Cairn, the villages of Caer-Dineval and Caer-Konig hug the shores of Lac Dinneshere, which freezes in winter.

The population of Ten-Towns is composed mostly of humans and dwarves, with the humans outnumbering the dwarves roughly twenty to one. In times of great peril, the leaders of Ten-Towns, known as town speakers, meet at Bryn Shander to discuss solutions to their problems. If one of the smaller settlements comes under attack by a threat too great to overcome, its inhabitants are trained to flee to Bryn Shander and take shelter behind its walls.

## RANDOM ENCOUNTERS

When in this region, use the Random Encounters in Icewind Dale table instead of the Random Wilderness Encounters table earlier in this chapter.

### RANDOM ENCOUNTERS IN ICEWIND DALE

| d20 | Encounter |
| --- | --- |
| 1 | 1 ancient white dragon |
| 2–5 | 1d4 + 2 crag cats (see appendix C) |
| 6–8 | 1d3 frost giants |
| 9–12 | Reghed nomads |
| 13–15 | 3d8 reindeer |
| 16–17 | Ten-Towners |
| 18–19 | 1d6 yeti |
| 20 | 1 young remorhaz |

**Ancient White Dragon.** Arveiaturace, better known to Northfolk as Iceclaws, claims Icewind Dale as part of her domain. The characters catch sight of her in the sky overhead. Rarely does she condescend to meddle in the affairs of land dwellers; however, if one or more characters neglect to take cover, she swoops down for a closer look at them (and they at her).

The dragon is quite insane, and she wears a saddle to which is strapped the dead, withered corpse of a wizard she once regarded as a great friend. Arveiaturace occasionally calls out to the corpse in Draconic, as though the wizard were still alive. The dragon isn't hungry or spoiling for a fight. But if one or more characters refuse to cower before her, Arveiaturace might strafe them once with her breath weapon or try to snatch up one of them with her claws, grappling the victim instead of dealing damage on a hit, only to drop the poor fool from a perilous height several rounds later.

**Crag Cats.** The crag cats hide in the snow and attempt to surprise the party.

**Frost Giants.** If a lone giant is encountered, it has a **winter wolf** companion. The frost giants are hunting for food. They have no treasure to speak of, though each carries a sack containing 1d4 mundane items, determined by rolling on the Items in a Giant's Bag table in the introduction.

**Reghed Nomads.** The characters come upon a Reghed **berserker** leading a band of 2d4 + 2 **tribal warriors**, or their encampment. Determine their tribe randomly by rolling a d4: 1, Bear; 2, Elk; 3, Tiger; 4,

Wolf. If the nomads belong to the Bear tribe or the Elk tribe, they give the party a wide berth and attack only if threatened. (Anyone who approaches them with weapons drawn is considered a threat.) Nomads belonging to the Tiger tribe or the Wolf tribe attack the party on sight. The Tiger nomads want the party's rations, and the hungry Wolf nomads want to murder the characters, skin them, and eat them.

**Reindeer.** Use the **elk** stat block to represent the reindeer. The reindeer are nonthreatening.

**Ten-Towners.** The characters chance upon 1d4 + 1 **scouts** (trappers) from one of the small settlements of Ten-Towns. There is a 50 percent chance that they're heading home with 2d6 animal pelts worth 5 gp each. They know the wilderness well and can direct or guide characters to the nearest settlement. If the characters ask them about giant sightings, there is a 25 percent chance that the scouts have come across frost giant tracks in the past twelve hours, in which case they can steer the characters toward them.

**Yeti.** If the characters encounter only one yeti, it's an **abominable yeti.** Yetis use the howling wind and the blowing snow to conceal their approach, giving them advantage on their Dexterity (Stealth) checks.

**Young Remorhaz.** The cracking of ice and a faint tremor presage the arrival of this hungry monster. Characters who have a passive Wisdom (Perception) score of 11 or higher aren't surprised when the young remorhaz bursts out of the snow and ice nearby.

## IRON ROAD

Once a prominent thoroughfare built by the dwarves of Besilmer, the Iron Road remains one of the few visible relics of that bygone kingdom. Most of its stones have been stolen or buried under grass, weeds, and earth. Today, the Iron Road is nothing more than a wagon trail with small patches of interlocking stones here and there. The route begins a few miles east of Womford and hugs the northern edge of the Forlorn Hills as it travels southeast through Uluvin, crosses the Delimbiyr Vale, and ends at the town of Secomber. Dwarves in Secomber claim that their ancestors used the Iron Road to transport iron ore from the Forlorn Hills to forges in various outlying settlements—hence the road's name.

## IRON TRAIL

An overland route called the Iron Trail connects Ironmaster to the Ten Trail, but it virtually disappears in the winter, buried under snow. It crosses wind-blasted hills and tundra, offering precious little shelter. Characters traveling the Iron Trail in wintertime are subject to extreme cold temperatures (see the "Wilderness Survival" section in chapter 5 of the *Dungeon Master's Guide*).

## IRONMASTER

The dwarven city of Ironmaster is perched at the western edge of Icewind Dale, where the Shaengarne River flows into the Sea of Moving Ice. The city is nestled in a great cleft where the Shaengarne rushes to the sea. Its stone towers rise like spikes from the valley floor, and the rooms and passages of Ironmaster weave in and out

of never-melting ice and the stone of the valley walls. Mining tunnels extend from the valley walls far below the tundra, providing the dwarves with an apparently limitless supply of iron.

Ironmaster is populated exclusively by dwarves. Members of other races are forbidden to set foot in Ironmaster Vale. Great stone menhirs marked with the city's arms—a red anvil on a gray diamond standing on end—are arranged in a perimeter around the vale to warn away travelers who stray too close.

## Ironslag

Millennia ago, the giants of Ostoria used this great forge to craft weapons and armor. When the giants' empire fell, Ironslag was abandoned. A fire giant chief named Duke Zalto has recently reoccupied Ironslag and seeks to reignite its adamantine forge. See chapter 8, "Forge of the Fire Giants," for more information on this location.

## Iymrith's Lair

The blue dragon Iymrith has claimed a Netherese ruin in Anauroch as her lair. The ruin lies half-buried in the desert northeast of Ascore. See chapter 12, "Doom of the Desert," for more information on this location.

## Jalanthar

The village of Jalanthar is a riverbank waystop for barges traveling up and down the Rauvin River. The hardy residents, who call themselves Jalantharren, live in stone cottages with mud-sealed timber roofs that are covered with turf to resist burning. The homes are half-buried in the ground and from a distance can be easily mistaken for small grassy knolls. The hills north of Jalanthar are riddled with caves, wherein the natives take refuge should the village come under attack. The caves are furnished and well-stocked with preserves.

Jalanthar boasts just one amenity for travelers. The Crowing Cockatrice inn is a low-walled, poorly built oval stone keep in the heart of the village. It features a central yard covered by a rickety roof made of old shields and bits of rusted armor, pounded flat and held up with a profusion of props and cross-braced poles to form a stable. The innkeeper, Myles Heldruin (LG male human **commoner**), is a friendly, talkative young man eager to please those with coin to spend.

Village law is whatever the local Council of Elders says it is. The current head of the council is a retired ranger and active member of the Emerald Enclave named Quinn Nardrosz (NG male human **scout**). Many years ago, an Uthgardt of the Red Tiger tribe bit off Quinn's left ear, but Quinn prefers to talk about the part of the story where he cracked open the Uthgardt's skull with a rock.

## Julkoun

A motte-and-bailey village called Julkoun marks the west end of the old Delimbiyr Road and rests on the north shore of the Delimbiyr River (which locals call "the River Shining"). A moat surrounds the village, which is further enclosed by wooden palisades. A few burned cottages stand outside, their blackened remains a testament to the bandits and other perils that haunt the nearby wilderness. Visitors are welcome at the Jester's Pride tavern, which serves robust dwarven ale.

## Jundar's Pass

This wagon trail threads through the Dessarin Hills between Beliard and Calling Horns, crossing over the Dessarin River at a place known as Dead Horse Ford.

## Kheldell

Kheldell is a fortified logging village on the north edge of Westwood, in the shadow of the Sword Mountains. The people here are beholden to the mysterious Dusk Circle, a group of druids who reside in hermitages in the surrounding mountains and forest. Folk in Kheldell log, hunt, plant, and harvest when and where they are told.

## Kheldell Path

Ox-drawn carts laden with cut timber from Kheldell use a well-worn trail called Kheldell Path to reach Red Larch, and from there the communities north and south along the Long Road.

## Klauthen Vale

Klauthen Vale is a narrow, winding valley in the mountains west of Mirabar. Thanks to ancient and powerful magic, the valley is warm throughout of the year—an oasis in the cold, cold north. Roaming this expanse are hundreds of sheep, goats, and cattle plucked from other regions of the North by the vale's dread overlord, the red wyrm Klauth. Scattered here and there are the crushed or charred bones of powerful adventurers and entire orc hordes that dared to enter the valley.

"Old Snarl," as Klauth is also known, likes to lie on a ledge high on one of the valley walls and survey his domain, descending occasionally to snatch up an animal or intruder. The walls around the valley contain numerous caves, two of them large enough for Klauth to shelter in. He keeps his legendary hoard in tunnels beneath one cavern, which can be entered only by lifting or pushing aside a massive slab of stone—a task impossible for anyone not as large and strong as an ancient dragon.

Klauth is one of the largest and most fearsome red dragons ever known in Faerûn. Huge but graceful, he's as supple as a cat. His body is covered in old, wicked-looking scars where scales have been torn away and never grown back. He brutally attacks other dragons, seeking to slay any wyrm that might rival him in power, in a fighting style marked by sudden attacks and just as sudden disappearances.

Klauth spends many waking hours scrying Faerûn with his spells, and he probably knows more about the deeds and whereabouts of surface-world creatures in the North and along the Sword Coast than any other being alive today. Old Snarl obeys strange whims that prompt him to perform acts of kindness for creatures he doesn't think can harm him. Such a whim leads him to give the adventurers a gift to expedite their travels across the North (see the "Airship of a Cult" section in chapter 4, "The Chosen Path").

### Suggested Encounter

Klauth spies on trespassers from afar. If the characters harm his animals or get too nosy, a sudden rage overcomes him, and he launches a series of hit-and-run attacks. Jets of fire and bolts of lightning spring forth as he swoops down on foes—the discharges of wands he has learned to control. All of Klauthen Vale is considered his lair, and he can use his lair actions anywhere within it.

Klauth is an **ancient red dragon**, with the Dual Wand Wielder trait, Special Equipment trait, and Spellcasting action option described below, all of which increase his challenge rating to 25 (75,000 XP):

***Dual Wand Wielder.*** If Klauth is carrying two wands, he can use an action to expend 1 charge from each wand, triggering the effects of both wands simultaneously.

***Special Equipment.*** Klauth carries a fully charged *wand of fireballs* and a fully charged *wand of lightning bolts*, and he wears a *ring of cold resistance*.

***Spellcasting.*** Klauth casts one of the following spells, requiring no material components and using Charisma as the spellcasting ability (spell save DC 22):

At will: *comprehend languages, detect magic, mage hand, minor illusion, prestidigitation*
2/day each: *darkness, detect thoughts, ice storm*
1/day each: *banishment, cloudkill, disintegrate, etherealness, find the path* (cast as 1 action), *greater invisibility, haste, locate object, nondetection, mass suggestion, mirage arcane* (cast as 1 action), *prismatic spray*

## Korinn Archipelago

Hundreds of rocky islands form this archipelago north of the larger Moonshae Isles. Dragon turtles and seafaring human marauders prowl the waters around these islands, which are home to griffons, harpies, wyverns, dragons, goblinoids, and old ruins haunted by evil wizards, gargoyles, and other forsaken creatures.

## Kryptgarden Forest

A small wooded region near Westbridge hides many old dwarven ruins and the extensive underground city known as Southkrypt. For centuries, Kryptgarden Forest has been the home and hunting ground of the ancient female green dragon Claugiyliamatar, better known to many as Old Gnawbone. She earned her nickname from her habit of gnawing on old kills, and is often seen with a mangled corpse hanging from her mouth. Other dragons rarely remain in Kryptgarden Forest for long, because Claugiyliamatar drives them out.

### Suggested Encounter

Claugiyliamatar rarely meddles in the affairs of small folk. Even so, her collection of *crystal balls* allows her to stay abreast of events happening in the world. She is aware that giants have become nuisances once more, and that adventurers have their work cut out for them. As the characters travel through her forest, Old Gnawbone's woodland spies (birds, rodents, and other harmless forest critters) warn her of their presence. She decides on a whim to leave her lair and confront them. The characters hear something enormous approaching them through the dark woods and tangled underbrush, and they might be startled when a great green dragon's head bursts into view with the tenderized corpse of an Uthgardt dangling from its mouth.

If the characters attack Claugiyliamatar, she breathes poison gas at them, takes to the air, and returns to her hidden lair. If the characters restrain themselves, she tells them (in Common) to travel north to the Valley of Khedrun and search for a giant temple called the Eye of the All-Father. "Therein," she says, "you'll learn what must be done to end the giant menace." She also tells them to keep an eye out for a frost giant wearing a helm made from a white dragon's skull, as he can help them. (See the "Harshnag" section later in this chapter.) Once she has imparted this information, Old Gnawbone takes flight and returns to her lair to finish her meal.

Claugiyliamatar is an **ancient green dragon**, with the following additional action option:

*Spellcasting.* Claugiyliamatar casts one of the following spells, requiring no material components and using Charisma as the spellcasting ability (spell save DC 19):

At will: *detect magic, druidcraft, speak with animals*
2/day each: *animal messenger, cure wounds, dispel magic, entangle, invisibility*
1/day each: *blight, legend lore* (cast as 1 action), *locate creature, pass without trace, protection from energy, true seeing*

## LEILON

Leilon was a small town near the High Road, straddling the distance between mines in the mountains and the mudflats on the coast from which its people would send out barges of ore to waiting ships. For many years, the town stood abandoned because the protective magic around a wizard's tower called the House of Thalivar went awry, causing any who looked at it to be paralyzed. The few travelers still taking the High Road and braving the expansion of the Mere of Dead Men had to travel for miles around Leilon or pass by it at night to avoid the tower's mysterious power. When Lord Neverember decided to reopen the High Road to travel, tearing down the tower became a top priority. It is now safe to pass through Leilon, and it is once again a working town, but all who live there owe allegiance to Lord Neverember.

## LIZARD MARSH

Instead of flowing freely into the sea, the Delimbiyr River dissolves into a morass of waterways threading around and beneath trees festooned with moss, forming a vast swamp. Lizard Marsh is known for two things: bloodthirsty insects and dangerous monsters. In the event the characters find themselves here, use the Swamp Monsters table in appendix B of the *Dungeon Master's Guide* to inspire encounter ideas.

Near the northeastern edge of the Lizard Marsh stands Cromm's Hold, a squat stone keep surrounded by a wall. Baroness Wynne Cromm (LE female human **noble**) and her garrison of eighteen soldiers (male and female human **veterans**) watch the Lizard Marsh for signs of lizardfolk aggression. Wynne also harbors a dark secret: she has the Duchess of Daggerford, Lady Morwen (LN female human **veteran**), locked in her dungeon. A succubus named Pencheska has usurped Morwen's identity, and once her work is done, she plans to install Wynne as her successor. The baroness grows impatient waiting for that day to come.

## LLORKH

Human and dwarf prospectors founded the mining town of Llorkh on the eastern shore of the Grayflow River. When the Zhents first began running trade along the Black Road through Anauroch, they conquered Llorkh, using it as a foothold in the North. The Zhentarim also laid claim to the gold and silver mines in the nearby hills and utterly depleted them, all the while fighting off Grayvale militias attempting to recapture the town.

After the mines were tapped out, the Zhents packed up and left the town in ruins. Llorkh later became a bandit lord's stronghold until that villain was finally dispatched. Most recently, an attempt to rebuild Llorkh had just gotten under way when the stone giants of Deadstone Cleft attacked. The residents were driven out, and the giants have begun dismantling the town stone by stone in an effort to erase it from the surface world.

### SUGGESTED ENCOUNTER

Six **stone giants** are combing through the ruins of Llorkh, separating rocks, tombstones, clay roof tiles, and other bits of stonework from blackened timbers, smashed furnishings, wood-and-iron tools, and other detritus. They toss the stone and clay into the river while burying the other wreckage under earth. The giants hurl rocks and tombstones at any "small folk" they see. The giants are spread out such that the characters can fight them in three groups, each group consisting of two stone giants. The adventurers can also keep their distance and leave the giants alone.

### TREASURE

Each stone giant carries a sack containing 1d6 × 100 gp in mixed coinage, 1d6 100 gp gemstones, and one mundane item, determined by rolling on the Items in a Giant's Bag table in the introduction.

## LONELY MOOR

The aptly named Lonely Moor is a desolate, dusty waste of scrub and rock that stretches from the desert of Anauroch to the Forgotten Forest and the foothills of the Graypeak Mountains.

## LONG ROAD

The Long Road, one of the North's busiest trade routes, begins at the gates of Mirabar and continues for hundreds of miles southward through the Dessarin Valley, meeting the High Road just north of Waterdeep. Many towns and villages lie along the route and depend on the relative safety that the Long Road provides for caravans and other travelers. Unfortunately for those travelers, the road is far too long to be defended properly along its entire length, and attacks by bandits and monsters are all too frequent in some areas.

# LONGSADDLE

This sleepy little frontier village and member of the Lords' Alliance straddles the Long Road, with rows of homes and businesses on either side of the trade route. Noteworthy establishments include a rustic inn called the Gilded Horseshoe and a friendly festhall called the Gambling Golem, where card games and a local marbles game known as scattershields are popular. Off in the distance, one can see horses and herds of cattle on sprawling ranches.

Monsters or brigands sometimes mistake Longsaddle for easy pickings—unaware that a family of powerful human wizards, the Harpells, lives nearby. Their grand house, Ivy Mansion, lies west of Longsaddle at the end of a long, winding path. The Harpells founded the village but take no part in its government, preferring to live quietly on their estate. Magical wards placed throughout Longsaddle and the Ivy Mansion warn the Harpells when trouble's afoot.

As the characters pass through Longsaddle, they see a wanted poster bearing a charcoal sketch of a dwarf with dark hair and a wild gaze, under which are written words in Common: "Let justice be done! The Marchion of Mirabar hereby offers 5,000 gold pieces for the capture of the brigand Worvil Forkbeard, known from Luskan to Mirabar as the Weevil. Last seen around the Mines of Mirabar, the Weevil is wanted for theft and murder. He is armed and dangerous. Deliver him to the Axe of Mirabar to receive payment." Characters who make inquiries in Longsaddle find no leads, but they might find the brigand in Xantharl's Keep to the north if they visit it (see the "Xantharl's Keep" section).

# LOST PEAKS

These forested mountains rise up in the northwest part of the High Forest. Many fey creatures dwell around these peaks, as well as a large tribe of centaurs that keep a careful eye on human hunters and woodcutters operating out of Olostin's Hold.

# LOUDWATER

With Zelbross, Orlbar, and Llorkh in ruins, Loudwater is the last bastion of civilization in the Delimbiyr Vale east of Secomber. If the town is worried, it doesn't show it. Loudwater provides a welcome respite for weary caravan and riverboat drivers, not to mention adventurers. It lies on both sides of the Delimbiyr River, the two halves linked by an arching stone overpass built by dwarves to honor the elves. Ancient wards placed on the overpass to preserve it had an unintended magical side effect: river trout attempting to swim under the bridge are propelled over it instead, which is why locals refer to it as the Flying Fish Bridge. People crossing the bridge are occasionally struck by these fish, which deal no damage. Whenever a fish hits a traveler and flops onto the bridge, it's a local custom (and considered good luck) to toss the fish back into the river.

Once a home to elves, Loudwater is a human town today. Its grand wood-and-stone buildings are overgrown by vines and hung with flowering plants. Streets curl and meander. Huge, old trees line the riverbanks, and gardens and bowers are everywhere. The town replaced its earthen rampart with a wall years ago, but the wall has flowers growing along its foundations both inside and outside the settlement. The river is unusually wide here, providing the town with space for a modest harbor.

The High Lord's Hall is a mansion on the north side of the river. The town's current high lord is Telbor Zazrek (N male human **mage**), a retired adventurer and well-paid puppet of the Zhentarim who enjoys the power that has been handed to him. Through Zazrek, the Black Network maintains an invisible stranglehold on the town. All goods that aren't supplied by the Zhentarim are heavily taxed, and the cost of living in Loudwater is so high that all of its establishments are forced to charge exorbitant prices.

Adding to Loudwater's problems are the stone giants of the Graypeak Mountains (see chapter 6, "Canyon of the Stone Giants"), who have begun laying waste to Llorkh, Orlbar, and the hamlets of Grayvale. Refugees are pouring into Loudwater, and those who can't afford to stay at the local inns are being herded like cows into warehouses overlooking the harbor. As if that weren't bad enough, stone giants have been seen spying on the town from afar, no doubt trying to determine its defensive capabilities. Since the Black Network keeps its forces well hidden in Loudwater and the town militia is a small force, Loudwater might seem like an easy target.

# LURKWOOD

The southern verge of the Lurkwood is safe enough to attract woodcutters, trappers, and hunters from Mirabar, Xantharl's Keep, and Longsaddle, but there's really no corner safe from the Uthgardt tribes that hunt here (primarily Black Raven and Thunderbeast). Goblinoids, wolves, and dire wolves also prowl these woods.

# LUSKAN

The City of Sails often conjures romantic images of a magnificent port metropolis, majestic merchant galleons with bright sails, and dashing swashbucklers who greet their enemies with a playful wink and a tip of the hat.

In reality, Luskan is anything but that. It's a dirty dive with filthy streets, squat buildings, ramshackle docks, creaky old longships, and crass pirates thinly disguised as sea traders. Rising above the fog and the stench is the Hosttower of the Arcane, home of a league of greedy, power-hungry wizards called the Arcane Brotherhood. Their ghastly tower branches into multiple thinner spires at the top. From a distance, the Hosttower might be mistaken for a giant, leafless tree. To those who have the misfortune of seeing it up close, it looks like a clawed hand bursting out of the ground, each of its fingers a tower with many peering windows.

Five High Captains rule the city. Each one is a glorified pirate lord who controls a fleet of longships. The five fleets serve many purposes: they defend Luskan against seafaring enemies, they conduct legitimate sea trade up and down the Sword Coast, and they raid and plunder the island kingdoms to the west (and the occasional settlement on the Sword Coast). The High Captains have no influence over the actions of the Arcane Brotherhood, nor is it apparent that the wizards have any allegiance to Luskan.

Luskan's best-kept secret is that the High Captains are under the sway of Jarlaxle Baenre, the leader of a clandestine brotherhood of drow mercenaries and rogues called Bregan D'aerthe. Jarlaxle is a master schemer (and a master of disguise) who would like to bring Luskan into the Lords' Alliance, but the City of Sails has such an unsavory reputation and so little to offer that most alliance members won't allow it. That doesn't stop Jarlaxle from trying, especially now that the alliance has lost two members: Everlund and Sundabar.

Characters approaching Luskan for the first time see a thick black cloud of smoke rising from the harbor. The smoke billows out of a frost giant greatship (see the "Svardborg: General Features" sidebar in chapter 7, "Berg of the Frost Giants") that blew into port and rammed several longships, sinking them before a group of wizards emerged from the Hosttower of the Arcane and set the ship ablaze with a flurry of *fireball* spells. The wizards have since returned to their monstrous tower, and the High Captains are waiting for the ship to stop burning before they board and search it. (Given the size of the ship, that could take a while.) Several charred frost giant corpses float facedown in the frigid water around the burning wreck, and the greatship's deck is strewn with other dead giants.

For a map of Luskan and more information about it, see the *Sword Coast Adventurer's Guide*.

## MAELSTROM

The daughters of King Hekaton reside in this undersea fortress, which stands amid reefs and barnacle-covered shipwrecks in the depths of the Trackless Sea. See chapter 10, "Hold of the Storm Giants," for more information on this location.

## MERE OF DEAD MEN

A kingdom that stood here long ago was washed away when a lich named Iniarv caused the sea to flow inland. The swamp gets its name from the thousands who died in the flood. Travelers on the High Road, which skirts the Mere to the east, must resist the urge to be lured into the swamp by bobbing will-o'-wisps. Countless adventurers have perished in the Mere, drawn by true tales of ruined castles half-sunk in the mire. These once noble estates are now home to lizardfolk, undead, and worse. The greatest threats to would-be treasure hunters are the ancient black dragon twins Voaraghamanthar and Waervaerendor. While the former is considered the undisputed lord of the Mere, the latter is hardly known at all—and the two dragons like it that way.

If the characters explore the Mere, use the Swamp Monsters table in appendix B of the *Dungeon Master's Guide* to inspire encounter ideas.

## MINES OF MIRABAR

The rugged land around Mirabar is littered with mine heads, open quarries, and heaps of slag and rubble. The mines of Mirabar yield up vast quantities of most known metals and gemstones. Working mines of any significance are heavily fortified. All miners who enter—dwarf and human—are searched both before and after shifts, ensuring security. It is an inconvenience the miners accept because, unlike many other places in the North, Mirabar pays well and cares for the workers.

## MIRABAR

Mirabar is the richest city of the North by far. It sits atop a knoll on the north side of the Mirar River like an unassailable fortress, enclosed on all sides by sloped outer walls as wide at the base as many city blocks in Waterdeep. Defenders can fire arrows down from atop the walls, or, in winter, pour water down them to make ice slides. There is no shortage of stone and weaponry. Even the docks have battlements and fortifications.

Visitors to Mirabar often wonder why they don't see more dwarves, as humans make up the majority of the city's surface dwellers. Another city lies just below the surface, and that place is dominated by dwarves. Underground, Mirabar is a city of lit residential caverns, superheated forges, foundries that operate day and night, and tunnels leading to the mines.

Mirabar's marchion, Selin Ramur (LN male human **noble**), meets with the other members of the Lords' Alliance to ensure that Mirabar's interests aren't ignored. While the marchion handles foreign policy, true power within the city rests with the Council of Sparkling Stones, a group of dwarf elders that manages the city's security and decides where the output of Mirabar's mines are sold. The city's defense falls to the Axe of Mirabar, a well-armed garrison. All members of the Axe of Mirabar are shield dwarves. A typical member is a **veteran**, with the following changes:

- A member of the Axe of Mirabar has AC 18 (plate), 67 (9d8 + 27) hit points, and a speed of 25 feet.
- He or she has a Constitution score of 16 (+3) and darkvision out to a range of 60 feet.
- He or she speaks Common and Dwarvish.
- He or she has advantage on saving throws against poison and resistance to poison damage.
- He or she wields a battleaxe instead of a longsword, and a handaxe instead of a shortsword.

## MISTY FOREST

This evergreen forest gets its name from the fog that creeps down from the High Moor and enshrouds it, making navigation difficult on even the best of days. The forest is patrolled by wood elves, who defend the woods from poachers. Visitors who leave the inhabitants of the Misty Forest alone, and who build their campfires small and solely of fallen branches, are usually not disturbed.

## MITHRAL HALL

The ancestral home of the Battlehammer clan of shield dwarves is a nigh-impregnable vault beneath the Frost Hills, with massive granite doors sealing its entrance and a host of battle-hardened defenders waiting beyond. Despite its almost mythic reputation, Mithral Hall is more of a stronghold than a city, with tunnels to other dwarfholds hidden deep below its mines.

Bruenor Battlehammer gave up the title of King of Mithral Hall for the third and final time when he set out to reclaim the lost dwarven city of Gauntlgrym. His handpicked successor, Dagnabbet Waybeard, now rules Mithral Hall as queen. A bold leader and a fierce warrior, Queen Dagnabbet firmly supports Mithral Hall's membership in the Lords' Alliance.

## Moonwood

See the "Glimmerwood" section.

## Morgur's Mound

The spirit mound of the lost Thunderbeast tribe (see the "Uthgardt" section earlier in this chapter), Morgur's Mound stands in the Crags and is named after Uthgar's brother. The mound (see map 3.7) is shaped like a long-necked, wingless dragon—the Uthgardt impression of a thunderbeast. A ridge of dragon bones juts from the head, neck, back, and tail of the mound. Enormous cairns encircle the mound out to a range of a quarter mile. Beneath them lie the bones of revered Thunderbeast tribal warriors.

The Thunderbeast tribe has not visited its spirit mound in years, leaving it ripe for plunderers. Several dig sites left by previous expeditions attest to the mound's popularity among treasure hunters.

### Treasure

Superstitious members of the Thunderbeast tribe buried many magic items in their spirit mound so that they could be watched over by the dead. Looters have unearthed nearly all of these items, leaving little else for intrepid adventurers to find. If the characters mount their own archaeological dig, they might turn up something if they're patient. They can either dig deeper at an existing excavation or start their own hole.

A party member who spends 8 hours excavating beneath Morgur's Mound can make a DC 20 Intelligence (Investigation) check. On each successful check, roll once on Magic Item Table B in chapter 7 of the *Dungeon Master's Guide* to determine what is found. Only two such treasures can be unearthed. The next party member to succeed on the check finds a giant-sized tooth (see "Ancient Relic"). Once the party finds the relic, further excavations yield nothing of consequence or value.

### Ancient Relic

The character unearths a gold-plated fire giant's tooth, which is an ancient relic of giantkind. The tooth is non-magical and small enough to fit in the hand of a human.

### Suggested Encounter

When the tooth is lifted from the hole, the ground trembles as four animated thunderbeast skeletons erupt from the mound and fight until turned or destroyed. They focus their attacks on whoever has the fire giant's tooth. Each one uses the **ankylosaurus** stat block, with these changes:

- A thunderbeast skeleton can attack with its bite instead of its tail. Its bite attack has a +7 bonus to hit, has a reach of 5 feet, and deals 18 (4d6 + 4) piercing

Map 3.7: Morgur's Mound

damage on a hit. Unlike its tail attack, its bite attack can't knock a target prone.
- It has vulnerability to bludgeoning damage.
- It is Undead and has immunity to poison damage, the poisoned condition, and exhaustion.
- It has darkvision out to a range of 60 feet.

## Mornbryn's Shield

Mornbryn's Shield, a village on the western fringe of the Evermoors, takes its name from the rocky, horseshoe ridge that forms a natural rampart along the west and south sides of the settlement, protecting it against flooding when the Surbrin River swells in the spring. At the northeast end of Mornbryn's Shield is a small stone keep with fire-hurling catapults aimed toward the Evermoors. Mornbryn was a ranger of some fame in the North centuries ago, and legend has it that his treasure-filled tomb is hidden somewhere close by.

The villagers are accustomed to facing threats from the Evermoors, but nothing as formidable as fire giants. Three weeks ago, a quartet of fire giants strode through the village, climbed over the ridge west of town, waded across the river, and disappeared into the Surbrin Hills without so much as a sideward glance. The villagers were left untouched, and property damage was minimal. It was clear to the Shield's residents that the giants had no interest in the village. It merely stood in their path.

## Suggested Encounter

After hearing of the fire giants' "attack" on Mornbryn's Shield, Zhentarim operatives in Yartar dispatched mercenaries to the village, offering protection. The mercenaries rode into town on **warhorses**, acting like shining knights. The villagers welcomed them at first, but the mercenaries are proving to be more trouble than they're worth. They seem more interested in finding the lost tomb of Mornbryn than in guarding the village. The mercenary leader, Oboth Thornsteel (NE male human **veteran** with 90 hit points), has turned the Troll in Flames—the local inn—into his personal headquarters, with six mercenaries (NE male and female **veterans** of various races) posted outside and six more inside. During the day, the remaining twelve mercenaries round up villagers from time to time and bring them to the inn for questioning, while Oboth takes notes in a large book clad in black leather with the Zhentarim symbol imprinted on the front. Oboth suspects that someone in town knows where the tomb is hidden, or knows some bit of lore hinting at its location.

Not long after the characters arrive, the mercenaries alert Oboth, who insists on speaking with the newcomers. If Oboth thinks the characters are troublemakers, he insists that they look for shelter elsewhere. If they challenge his authority, he promises them quiet accommodations in the local graveyard unless they do as he commands. Oboth likes to intimidate others, but doesn't like to be intimidated. He has little respect for adventurers, but he tolerates their presence if one or more of them are members or allies of the Black Network.

## Treasure

Each mercenary carries 2d10 gp in a pouch. Oboth also wears an electrum signet ring (worth 50 gp) bearing the symbol of the Zhentarim: a black, winged snake.

# Nesmé

Despite a heroic effort to save the town, Nesmé fell during the War of the Silver Marches to a horde of orcs aided by an ancient white dragon named Arauthator. It was then conquered by drow until they too were forced to abandon it. Today, Nesmé lies in ruins, and monsters from the Evermoors thwart efforts to rebuild it.

The town stood on the east side of the Surbrin River, enclosed within a circular wall festooned with ballistae and catapults, and connected by a fortified bridge to a formidable castle on the west side of the river. This western bastion enclosed the docks, paddocks, and stock pens, and also gave the townsfolk and the militia a place to fall back to in the event the town was breached. Although the militia put up a good fight against the orcs, the town couldn't withstand the dragon's attacks. The castle on the western shore has partially collapsed, the bridge has been destroyed, and the town's defenses have been torn down. Within the town walls, now breached in several places, are piles of debris that were once shops, taverns, inns, and festhalls. Skulls, bones, rusted armor, and broken weapons are all that remain of those killed by orc axes and the dragon's icy breath.

## Suggested Encounter

Eight Zhentarim **thugs** (LE male and female humans) mounted on **riding horses** are watching the Surbrin Trail. They intercept characters walking or riding north toward Nesmé, threatening to kill them unless they turn back immediately. If the characters defeat or circumvent these guards, they arrive at Nesmé to find Zhentarim representatives awaiting the arrival of a female fire giant representing Duke Zalto (see chapter 8, "Forge of the Fire Giants"). Characters can eavesdrop on this event about to unfold by hiding behind some rubble. They must each succeed on a DC 10 Dexterity (Stealth) check to go unnoticed.

The Zhentarim force consists of a negotiator named Fylo Krevius Nelgorn (LE male **priest** of Bane with a **flying snake** curled around his left arm) and twenty Zhentarim **thugs** (LE male and female humans). The Zhents' **riding horses** are tethered to some ruins across town. The **fire giant**, Gundahella, and her retinue of twenty **hobgoblins** approach from the north and enter the meeting area through a gash in the outer wall. The negotiation lasts only a few minutes.

Fylo pledges the assistance of the Zhentarim to keep the Lords' Alliance and other groups from interfering in the fire giants' search for the Vonindod fragments, on the condition that the adamantine colossus not be used to attack settlements or parts thereof without the Black Network's consent. Fylo mentions Moongleam Tower in Everlund as a likely target to illustrate his point.

Gundahella agrees to Fylo's terms and tells him that Duke Zalto is going to release a Zhentarim prisoner currently being held in Ironslag as a token of good faith; she doesn't know the Zhent by name, only that he's a dwarf.

If the characters do nothing but observe, the meeting concludes with Gundahella and her force leaving the way they came and Fylo dispatching his flying snake with a scroll to his superiors in Yartar, informing them that the meeting went as well as could be expected. He and his thugs set up camp amid the ruins and wait for the flying snake to return with further instructions.

If the characters interrupt the negotiations, both evil forces attack them. Regardless of the outcome of the conflict, Gundahella is furious that the Zhentarim failed to ensure the safety of the meeting site. She ends the negotiation with no agreement reached.

# Nether Mountains

The dark, brooding peaks of the Nether Mountains are the source of many legends about lost Netherese magic, as well as a repository of tangible riches such as granite. The mountains are also full of orcs, while the eastern peaks are home to several blue dragons that were chased out of the northern Anauroch desert by Iymrith and her brood (see the "Anauroch" section).

# Neverwinter

Once known as the Jewel of the North, the city of Neverwinter was badly damaged when nearby Mount Hotenow (see the "Neverwinter Wood" section) erupted about fifty years ago. Now, the City of Skilled Hands works furiously to rebuild itself. Neverwinter's reconstruction is far from complete, however. Some of its outer walls still lie in ruins, and several of its neighborhoods remain abandoned. Even so, the great chasm to the Underdark that opened within the city has been magically sealed (at great expense), and that achievement bodes well for Neverwinter's future.

Dagult Neverember is the Lord Protector of Neverwinter, ruling in the absence of a true heir to Neverwinter's crown. At present, no legitimate heirs are known to exist, and many believe that the royal line is dead. Lord Neverember is taking no chances, though. He quietly pays off or disposes of anyone who claims to be a member of the Alagondar bloodline.

Neverember was formerly the Open Lord of Waterdeep as well, maintaining residences and offices in both cities. In the wake of several political scandals, Neverember was deposed as Open Lord and forced to flee Waterdeep. Now he lives in Neverwinter all year round and strives to see Neverwinter eclipse Waterdeep in wealth and prosperity. Neverember, who was courted and ultimately betrayed by sycophantic nobles and guildmasters in Waterdeep, doesn't want a repeat of those events in Neverwinter. Thus, he levies heavy taxes against the wealthy, preventing noble families from gaining a political foothold in the city, and has enacted harsh laws that prevent guilds from being formed.

Neverwinter is a member of the Lords' Alliance, and Neverember supports the efforts of the organization to spread civilization throughout the North and hires adventurers to help protect the city and its interests. Still, his main concern is to rebuild Neverwinter and its economy while keeping a tight hold on the reins of power.

The Order of the Gauntlet has a strong presence in Neverwinter. Most of its resident members are clerics and knights of Helm, Torm, and Tyr, along with their acolytes and squires.

For a map of Neverwinter and more information about it, see the *Sword Coast Adventurer's Guide*.

# NEVERWINTER WOOD

The forest east of Neverwinter seems to have a magical quality about it, or at least an air of mystical secrecy. Neverwinter Wood holds countless ruins and more than a few crumbling castles. The always-warm Neverwinter River, which flows out of the wood, has its source deep beneath Mount Hotenow, an active volcano in the northern reaches of the forest. The volcano last erupted some fifty years ago. Lava pouring down from the mountain burned a wide swath through Neverwinter Wood, destroying everything it touched. New trees have begun to grow where the ancient ones once stood, though the effect of the catastrophe is still plain for all to see.

# NEWFORT

Newfort is a motte-and-bailey stockade on the south side of the Fork Road, east of Sundabar in the foothills of the Rauvin Mountains. A few dozen wood-frame cottages stand outside the stockade, as does a cozy tavern called the Hero's Reward, run by an amiable and talkative young half-elf named Delf Dereldar (LG male half-elf **commoner**). Delf spends his idle time gazing at

a chessboard on the bar; he plays regular games with the village constable, Jorok Narm (N male orc **veteran**), who drops in after work hours for a drink or two before retiring for the evening.

Two retired members of the Zhentarim founded Newport. They are long dead, and over the years the settlement has become less of a Black Network stronghold and more of a way station open to anyone in need of a safe place to spend the night. Constable Narm and his militia of twenty **guards** (N male and female humans) keep the peace.

# NIGHTSTONE

This motte-and-bailey settlement lies south of the Ardeep Forest, between Waterdeep and Daggerford. See chapter 1, "A Great Upheaval," for more information on Nightstone.

# NOANAR'S HOLD

This village on the edge of the High Forest grew up around a famous hunting lodge built over two hundred years ago. In its heyday, Noanar's Hold hosted wild hunts that attracted the wealthiest nobles and merchants of the North. Some who ventured to Noanar's Hold never returned, spurring dark rumors that the five Hunt Lords who ruled Noanar's Hold were arranging wanton slaughters to amuse their guests and even allowing their guests to hunt one another. The place was shunned, and the village fell on hard times. Any character who has proficiency in the History skill can recall these dark rumors with a successful DC 15 Intelligence (History) check. A successful check also confirms that the Hunt Lords were human.

As it happens, the rumors are true. The Hunt Lords played all sorts of terrible games at the expense of their wealthy employers. A century and a half ago, to escape their inevitable deaths, the Hunt Lords forged a pact with Orcus, who transformed them into five **wights**. Necromancers in the demon lord's service helped the Hunt Lords turn the inanimate bones of their long-dead horses into five animated **warhorse skeletons**. Every night, after sunset, the Hunt Lords ride out on their skeletal steeds to patrol the lands around Noanar's Hold, looking for worthy prey to hunt. They always return to their keep before sunrise the following morning. They have no interest in harming the local villagers, whom they view as their subjects. The villagers are well aware of the Hunt Lords' escapades, but Noanar's Hold is so isolated that few others know that the Hunt Lords still exist. A handful of villagers have moved away from Noanar's Hold over the years, but most are too frightened to flee, believing the rumors (although they are false) that the Hunt Lords track down and kill villagers who try to leave. Today, residents of Noanar's Hold rarely stray far from their homes. They don't speak of the Hunt Lords, nor do they warn visitors away. Fearing the Hunt Lords' wrath, they keep to themselves and say little or nothing about their undead masters.

The village's once-famous hunting lodge, the White Hart Inn, stands amid low stone cottages and stables. The creaky building is well maintained on the inside, offering a bit of grandeur in an otherwise rustic setting. The innkeeper is a courteous little man named Avgar Filroy (N male human **commoner**), who has permanent unseen servants to help with cleaning. He is a little delusional and speaks of the Hunt Lords as if they are still alive, even though he has seen evidence to the contrary. He says the Hunt Lords are retired and don't wish to be disturbed, and he warns guests to stay in the lodge at night, claiming the land around Noanar's Hold is haunted by the spirits of dead hunters.

Characters who seek an audience with the Hunt Lords must first speak to Amrath Mulnobar (NE male shield dwarf **veteran**), the castellan of the Hunt Lords' keep. Amrath has served the Hunt Lords for more than two centuries, dating back to when they were still alive. Now he's a gray-bearded curmudgeon who hangs about the dark halls of the keep like a bad smell. The keep had a small garrison once, but only Amrath remains.

The keep is nestled among old pine trees on a hilltop overlooking the sleepy village. The building has three stories, corner turrets, and rooftop battlements. One of the turret rooftops has collapsed, leaving a gaping hole through which birds and other creatures can enter. All the windows are bricked up, and the heavy oaken doors on the ground floor are barred from within. Forcing them open requires a successful DC 27 Strength check. If the characters knock on these doors, Amrath arrives a minute later, opens an iron slit in the door at dwarf's-eye level, and demands to know what they want. The dwarf doesn't open the doors unless the characters are delivering new saddles for his masters' steeds (see the "Narth Tezrin's Quest" section in chapter 2). Amrath allows the characters to place the saddles in the entrance foyer, then quickly tries to usher them out.

The Hunt Lords lurk in a dusty ground-floor banquet hall, slumped in chairs around a cobweb-draped dining table. They spend their days reminiscing about the "good old times" and attack any creature other than Amrath who disturbs them. Behind their chairs are piles of horse bones. As a bonus action on its turn, a Hunt Lord can command the nearest pile of bones to rise up and become a warhorse skeleton under its command.

### TREASURE

At the back of the Hunt Lords' banquet hall is a locked treasure chest. Amrath wears the key to it around his neck, but a character can pick the lock using thieves' tools with a successful DC 20 Dexterity check. The chest contains 600 gp in a gray sack made of stitched orc skin, a leather pouch that holds six 50 gp gems, and 1d3 magic items, determined by rolling on Magic Item Table B in chapter 7 of the *Dungeon Master's Guide*.

## NORTHERN MEANS

The Northern Means is a snowy, windswept trail that connects the city of Luskan to the frozen lands of the high north. The trail all but disappears during the winter, buried under deep snow. Moreover, the area has few trees or hills to provide shelter.

## NORTHFURROW

The Northfurrow extends from Waterdeep to the fortified farming compound of Goldenfields. Wagons laden with food make their way south under heavy guard to the city, while empty wagons head north to fetch more bounty. The traffic is heaviest after the harvest. Human and halfling cottages and farmsteads have sprung up on both sides of the trail, and the humble rural folk who live here refer to themselves as Northfurrowers.

## OLOSTIN'S HOLD

A fortified keep stands on the northern side of the Evermoor Way between Yartar and Everlund. Enclosed within the high walls of Olostin's Hold is a small village with a market, a smithy, a caravan supplier, an inn called the Headless Troll, and a tavern known as the Flaming Flagon. The inn gets its name from an incident involving a beheaded troll that wandered into village, caught fire, and nearly burned down the establishment. The tavern is the namesake of an ordinary flagon that was ensorcelled during a wizards' duel long ago and now floats and sheds light in the middle of the taproom.

## ONE STONE

The spirit mound of the Sky Pony tribe lies in a grove of oak trees surrounded by the tall pines of the Moonwood, west of the Redrun River. The Sky Ponies' spirit mound is a two-tiered plateau. On the lower tier, cairns cover the buried remains of the tribe's honored dead. The upper tier is shaped like a sky pony (a pegasus), though the form of this feature is readily apparent only from the air. A round, 15-foot-diameter boulder planted firmly in the ground in the northeastern part of the area represents the eye of the sky pony. The boulder is covered with line engravings chiseled by an unknown hand, and it's this stone that the spirit mound's name refers to. The Sky Ponies use the stone as an altar, and Sky Pony shamans believe they can commune with Uthgar simply by touching the boulder while its surface is bathed in the light of the full moon.

A swift but shallow stream of sparkling, fresh water encircles the spirit mound like a moat, although it is by no means defensive in nature. Overlooking the stream at the northeast and southwest ends of the plateau are unpainted totem poles, the tops of which are carved to look like sky ponies with spread wings. The withered and moldering corpses of trespassers are lashed to these poles as warnings to others.

Sky Pony warriors patrol the woods surrounding the spirit mound. Adventurers are likely to encounter one or more of them as they traverse the forest (see the "Moonwood" section).

### ANCIENT RELIC

Casting a *detect magic* spell on the boulder reveals an aura of transmutation magic emanating from it. The boulder itself is a relic of giantkind that was shaped, carved, and abandoned long ago by a stone giant earth shaman. Uthgar and his followers found it in its shrunken form and brought it here. Any character who succeeds on a DC 15 Intelligence (Arcana) check can tell that the engraved lines adorning its outer surface are carefully designed to channel magical energy. Casting an *identify* spell on the boulder allows one to learn its magical properties, each of which is activated by tracing specific lines on its surface:

- A creature can use an action to cast the *control weather* spell or the *divination* spell from the stone. Once either spell is cast, this property can't be used again for 7 days.
- A creature can use an action to shrink the stone to the size of a 6-inch-diameter orb weighing 25 pounds, or enlarge the boulder to its normal size (15-foot diameter) and weight (12 tons). Anything the enlarged boulder falls on takes 55 (10d10) bludgeoning damage. A creature can avoid taking this damage by tumbling out of the way with a successful DC 15 Dexterity saving throw. Once the reducing or enlarging effect is used, this property can't be used again for 24 hours.

## SUGGESTED ENCOUNTER

When the characters reach the uppermost tier of the plateau, the ground beneath their feet begins to tremble. Seconds later, a **bulette** erupts from the ground 50 feet away from them. Mounted on its back is a member of the Cult of the Black Earth named Tau (NE male human). He knows the properties of the One Stone and seeks to claim the relic in the name of Ogrémoch, the Prince of Elemental Earth. He doesn't want any witnesses and attacks the characters on sight. Two rounds later, on the bulette's initiative count, a second **bulette** mounted by a Black Earth cultist named Sharda (NE female human) erupts from the earth and joins the fray. Tau and Sharda use the **cult fanatic** stat block, with these changes:

- These cult fanatics are neutral evil.
- They speak Common and Terran.
- They wear stone breastplates instead of leather armor, giving them AC 16.
- They wield stone clubs instead of daggers that deal 4 (1d4 + 2) bludgeoning damage on a hit.

The cultists aren't easily frightened or intimidated, but characters who capture one can attempt an interrogation. Any character who succeeds on a DC 15 Charisma (Intimidation) check convinces a captured cultist to reveal that the individual is a member of the Cult of the Black Earth, which operates in and around the Sumber Hills, and that the cult worships Ogrémoch. These cultists have no connection to the giants; their leaders are described in *Princes of the Apocalypse* (see that adventure for more information).

As the battle winds down, before the characters have time to take a short rest, twenty **tribal warriors** and an **Uthgardt shaman** (see appendix C) of the Sky Pony tribe emerge from the northwest edge of the woods, having been drawn here by sounds of combat. They rush forward and attack.

## TREASURE

The cultists' stone breastplates are treated with magical oil and weigh the same as metal breastplates. They are worth 250 gp each.

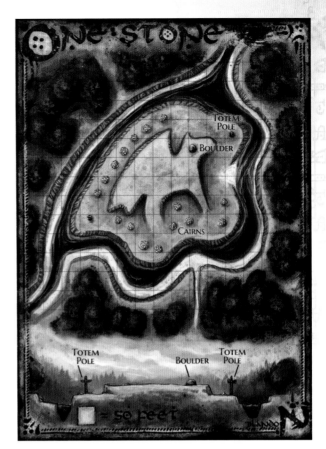

MAP 3.8: ONE STONE

## ORLBAR

Far removed from civilization, the old village of Orlbar overlooks the confluence of the Loagrann and Grayflow rivers and attracts only those with an adventurous spirit. The place is all but abandoned now, its few remaining shepherds driven off by the stone giants of Deadstone Cleft (see chapter 6, "Canyon of the Stone Giants").

## SUGGESTED ENCOUNTER

Thane Kayalithica's stone giants have flattened every building in Orlbar, buried the scrap iron and lumber, and left behind piles of stones. In their wake, a mute **stone giant** named Zorkh has begun stacking the stones in pleasing ways, creating a veritable forest of piled-up stones, some as much as 20 feet tall, on the slopes where Orlbar once stood. Six **goats** follow Zorkh around wherever he goes, eating the grass around him as he sorts through stones and stacks them. Zorkh, who lives like a hermit in the Graypeak Mountains, understands Giant but can't speak. If the characters ask him how to get to Deadstone Cleft, he leads them to the shore of the Loagrann River, then points in the direction of Deadstone Cleft. Any character who succeeds on a DC 15 Wisdom (Insight) check realizes that the giant is suggesting that the party follow the river. Zorkh won't accompany the characters, for he believes that Deadstone Cleft is cursed. Zorkh has no treasure but carries a sack that holds 2d4 mundane items, determined by rolling on the Items in a Giant's Bag table in the introduction.

## PARNAST

Parnast is an unremarkable village nestled between the foothills of the Graypeak Mountains and the Weathercote Forest. A map and description of Parnast appear in the adventure *Tyranny of Dragons*.

## PHANDALIN

In the northern foothills of the Sword Mountains lies the nondescript mining settlement of Phandalin. Although the village might not look like much, it provides a safe haven for adventurers eager to explore the surrounding wilderness, which is home to many old ruins and abandoned dwarven mines.

A map of Phandalin appears in the *Lost Mine of Phandelver* adventure in the D&D *Starter Set*.

## PORT LLAST

This coastal town has been, at various points in its violent history, plundered by pirates, enslaved by evil cults, set ablaze, overrun by sahuagin, and even raided by drow—yet it weathered every storm and until recently showed glimmers of renewed prosperity once more. It's the only port between Luskan and Neverwinter, and the only place between the two cities where tall cliffs give way to sandy shores. Port Llast's harbor is strewn with shipwrecks—the tombs of seafarers who fought for the town's spoils and lost.

### SUGGESTED ENCOUNTER

Port Llast has fallen once more, this time to marauding frost giants whose greatship has run aground on two smaller wrecked ships in the harbor roughly 60 feet from shore. Frost giants have already attacked the town once in the past month; this is their second raid. Twenty **frost giants** have descended upon the fog-shrouded town and are plundering it for food, ale, and other supplies. The streets are littered with the crushed and cloven remains of townsfolk who stood their ground.

The heavy fog makes dealing with the frost giants a bit easier, allowing characters to pick them off one or two at a time. A creature can see out to a range of 60 feet in the fog. The area beyond that is heavily obscured.

The giants left two **winter wolves** aboard the greatship to guard it (see the "Svardborg: General Features" sidebar in chapter 7, "Berg of the Frost Giants"). The wolves attack any characters who board the vessel. If one wolf dies, the other wolf uses its next action to howl a warning to the frost giants. If there are any frost giants still alive in town, they quickly return to the ship. Half of the giants take 5 rounds to reach the ship; the remaining giants take 10 rounds.

### TREASURE

Characters who defeat the winter wolves and search the greatship find six crates of plundered foodstuffs, fifteen empty ale barrels, a lidless wooden chest containing 3,000 sp, a sleigh laden with animal pelts (worth 300 gp for the lot), and twenty giant sacks, each containing 1d6 × 100 gp and one mundane item. You can roll on the Items in a Giant's Bag table in the introduction for each mundane item, or forgo the rolls and choose twenty items from the table. The fattest sack also contains one magic item, determined by rolling on Magic Item Table F in chapter 7 of the *Dungeon Master's Guide*.

## PURPLE ROCKS

A cluster of rocky islands far to the west in the Trackless Sea is named for the dark purple hue that they take on under stormy skies. The two largest islands among the Purple Rocks (see map 3.13) have one settlement apiece: the town of Vilkstead on the eastern island of Utheraal, and the slightly smaller town called Ulf of Thuger on the island of Trisk to the west. Each island also has its own king: Sea-King Frannis of Utheraal and Sea-King Krulk of Trisk (CN male human **gladiators**).

The Northlanders of Utheraal and Trisk are under the sway of the kraken Slarkrethel. They show their devotion, among other ways, by tossing their newborn children into the sea. The islanders wear tattoos of krakens made with squid ink and build longships that boast kraken-shaped figureheads. They greet visitors with food and shelter, but don't speak of Slarkrethel or the absence of children from their communities.

Visitors who try to investigate the mysteries of the Purple Rocks are asked to leave. Those who refuse to do so are captured and sacrificed to the sea.

## RASSALANTAR

Many a traveler has come upon the quiet village of Rassalantar and taken comfort in the soft beds and rich ale of the Sleeping Dragon, a cozy roadside inn. Few pay much attention to the walled farms and grazing sheep around the town, and fewer still take notice of the ruined keep hidden among the stand of trees west of the village. Yet Waterdeep has long maintained a large contingent of its City Guard here, using a nearby barracks as the base for outriders who infrequently patrol the road north as far as Amphail and south to Waterdeep.

Yondral Horn (N male shield dwarf **spy**), a retired adventurer on the Black Network's payroll, runs the Sleeping Dragon and keeps an eye on the activities of the City Guard and any Lords' Alliance members that come through. Anyone who is a member of the Lords' Alliance receives the finest quarters, which happen to have thin walls so that Yondral can spy on his guests.

Rassalantar's keep has largely been robbed of its stone to build other structures in the village, and its cellars and dungeons are waterlogged. A hidden chamber in the dungeon holds a permanent teleportation circle used by the Blackstaff (Waterdeep's highest-ranking wizard) to send messages and aid to Rassalantar.

## RAUVIN MOUNTAINS

This purple-hued mountain range has peaks rising to heights of seven and eight thousand feet. Orcs live here in seemingly infinite numbers, boiling forth every few decades to raid the lands around.

# Rauvin Road

The lightly patrolled Rauvin Road follows the Rauvin River from Rivermoot to Jalanthar, passing through Silverymoon, Everlund, and numerous smaller settlements along the way.

# Raven Rock

On the icy slopes of the Spine of the World stands the spirit mound of the Black Raven and Gray Wolf tribes. Raven Rock gets its name from a 100-foot-tall stone carved in the likeness of a perching raven, sitting in the center of the highest plateau of the mound and facing west. The Black Ravens leave carcasses by the stone raven's feet as offerings. At dusk, giant ravens gather to feast on the remains. After devouring the carrion, the giant ravens perch on timber roosts and squawk at one another until nightfall, when they fly off. Warriors of the Black Raven tribe sometimes ride these giant ravens into battle.

Surrounding Raven Rock are four 50-foot-tall menhirs that the Uthgardt shamans use to track the changing of the seasons and the movement of the stars.

The Gray Wolves aren't allowed atop the high plateau. Instead, they gather around an altar mound in the heart of a wolf-shaped depression southwest of Raven Rock. Their altar is a rectangular slab of stone with the phases of the moon carved into its sides.

In winter, everything is under a foot or more of snow.

## Ancient Relics

Two ancient giant relics are buried here—one in the ground before the giant stone raven, and another under the Gray Wolves' altar. Uthgar's early followers planted these objects here to empower and ward their spirit mound. A *detect magic* spell reveals an aura of conjuration magic emanating from the ground in front of the giant stone raven, and an aura of transmutation magic from underneath the altar. The ground in both locations is frozen solid year-round.

Without the aid of magic, it takes 5 hours for one character to dig up the relic hidden in the ground by the giant stone raven; reduce the amount of time proportionately if other party members help. The relic is a ring of hardened magma sized for a fire giant's finger. When a creature attunes to the ring, it magically shrinks to fit that creature's index finger, and warm orange light spills from minuscule cracks that form on its outer surface. The ring has 6 charges left. While attuned to the ring, a creature can expend 1 charge to cast *conjure minor elementals* (summoning either four **magma mephits** or four **magmins**, as the wearer wishes) or *fire shield* (warm shield version only) from the ring. Once all of its charges are spent, the ring loses its spellcasting properties but retains its resizing property.

To reach the relic buried under the Gray Wolves' altar, the characters must smash through the altar or burrow underneath it. One character can accomplish either task in 10 hours; reduce the amount of time proportionately if other party members help. The buried relic is a 14-foot-long, 250-pound red dragon's thighbone. Part of the bone is wrapped in old leather, suggesting that

MAP 3.9: RAVEN ROCK

it was once used as a giant's greatclub. If a creature attunes to the greatclub, it magically shrinks to a size that the creature can wield effectively. The greatclub is considered a magic weapon that deals an extra 2d8 bludgeoning damage whenever it hits any creature of the Dragon type.

## Suggested Encounter (Day)

If the characters arrive at Raven Rock in the morning or the afternoon, they see 2d4 giant ravens (use the **giant vulture** stat block) flying lazy circles at a height of 300 feet above the spirit mound. If the characters arrive in the evening, the giant ravens are perched quietly on their wooden roosts. The ravens aren't present at night. The giant ravens don't attack intruders or squawk at them, but they remember with perfect clarity any trespassers they see and describe them to the next group of Black Ravens they meet.

If the giant ravens see the characters take the magma ring, the Black Ravens learn about the theft 1d4 days later. After that time, there is a cumulative 5 percent chance per day that the Black Ravens locate the characters (or a subset of them, if the party splits up). Alternatively, you can have them catch up to the party at a dramatic moment of your choice. Wherever the characters happen to be, an **Uthgardt shaman** (see appendix C) and six **tribal warriors**, each mounted on a giant raven, attack the characters. Rules for mounted combat appear in chapter 9 of the *Player's Handbook*.

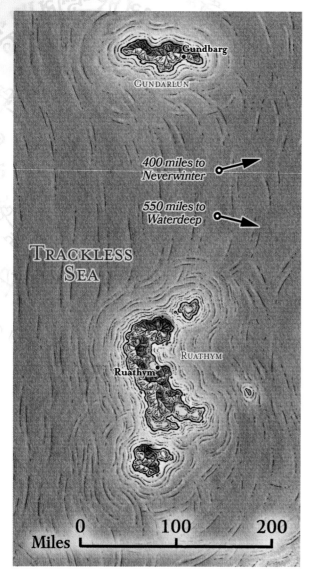

MAP 3.10: GUNDARLUN AND RUATHYM

## SUGGESTED ENCOUNTER (NIGHT)

Characters who explore Raven Rock in the dead of night encounter 2d4 **wolves** and 1d4 + 1 **werewolves** in wolf form. The werewolves are members of the Gray Wolf tribe.

## RED LARCH

Named for a distinctive stand of red larch trees that were cut down when the village was founded, Red Larch is situated on a fertile patch of land on the western outskirts of the Sumber Hills, at a place where the Kheldell Path and the Cairn Road meet the Long Road. Despite its small size, Red Larch offers many fine amenities, including the Allfaiths Shrine, a place of worship that caters to multiple faiths; the Swinging Sword, a respectable three-story stone inn with a high-pitched roof; and the Helm at Highsun, a ramshackle yet lively tavern.

A map of Red Larch and a detailed description of the village and its inhabitants can be found in the adventure *Princes of the Apocalypse*.

## RED ROCKS

Off the coast lies a collection of tiny islets known collectively as the Red Rocks. Most of these landforms are sea stacks carved by the waves of the Sea of Swords, but some are little more than boulders peeking up above the waves. The Red Rocks have sunk countless ships over the centuries, so sailors tend to give the area a wide berth. Fishers in small vessels frequent these waters, however, since the area is home to a huge variety of fish and shellfish, many of which are prized in Waterdeep.

## REGHED GLACIER

The cold winds that give Icewind Dale its name blow down off this high, frozen landscape. Few dare to venture near the high walls of its easternmost edge, and little is known of what might live on or within the glacier.

## RIVERMOOT

This small village stands at the west end of the Rauvin Road, where the Rauvin and Surbrin rivers meet. Rivermoot's wood-frame dwellings are built on stilts because the rivers swell during the spring and flood the ground around them. The villagers tether canoes to their cottages so that they can move about during the river's rise.

## RUATHYM

The human clans of Ruathym (see map 3.10) are at war with Luskan and have been for as long as any of them can remember. Luskanite raiders have plundered and razed the island's settlements more than once, but the natives keep rebuilding their villages and their ships while singing songs of bloody vengeance.

The reigning king of Ruathym is First Axe Vok Dorrg (CE male human **priest**), a blind and vindictive old man who worships Valkur, a lesser god of the sea. The king rules from the Hall of Black Waves, a temple in the seaside town of Ruathym. Although he's too old to take up arms himself, Vok Dorrg has many fierce sons, daughters, and grandchildren to captain his ships and terrorize his enemies.

## SEA OF MOVING ICE

The sea west of Icewind Dale is a maze of shifting ice sheets and icebergs. A few frozen islands are inhabited by Ice Hunters, a group of humans the Northlanders pushed toward the pole long ago. An armada of frost giant greatships under the command of Jarl Storvald hunts whales, walruses, and seals in these waters.

The Sea of Moving Ice is also the domain of several white dragons, the largest and most powerful of which are two **ancient white dragons** named Arauthator and Arveiaturace. Each dragon makes its lair inside a hollowed-out iceberg. Arauthator's iceberg, Oyaviggaton, has Northfolk living on it and is described in the adventure *Tyranny of Dragons*. Arveiaturace is known to hunt in Icewind Dale and might be encountered there (see the "Icewind Dale" section).

Characters who explore the Sea of Moving Ice in wintertime are subject to extreme cold temperatures (see the "Wilderness Survival" section in chapter 5 of the *Dungeon Master's Guide*).

## SECOMBER

This town of farmers, fishers, brewers, and stonecutters is perched on three hills located near the confluence of the Unicorn Run and the Delimbiyr River. Beneath these hills lie ruins that were once part of Athalantar, a bygone kingdom. The townsfolk have turned the buried ruins into cellars, larders, and shelters.

Secomber is under the heel of the Urshani hobgoblins, who dwell in the High Moor and demand tribute several times a year. Secomber has no defense against the Urshani. Its residents give the hobgoblins food, homemade ale, and ore to retain their freedom. The hobgoblins' demands have left the community impoverished.

### SUGGESTED ENCOUNTER

The characters arrive to find two **cloud giants** named Nirva and Jaral sitting in the middle of town, listening to townsfolk talk about the founding of Secomber and the ancient kingdom of Athalantar, on whose bones the town was built. Despite their intimidating size, the giants (who are neutral good in alignment) mean no harm. They recently found an artifact—half of a giant-sized vase—in the High Moor, and they're widening their search for other evidence of a cloud giant castle that crashed in this area thousands of years ago. Nirva and Jaral are siblings on a quest. They want to elevate cloud giants (and themselves) to the top of the ordning by finding maps to ancient Ostorian ruins and long-buried treasure vaults. The castle they seek is rumored to hold maps that could prove useful in their search.

Nirva and Jaral try not to overstay their welcome. After listening quietly to the locals' stories, they bid the townsfolk farewell and fly back to their castle, which has landed in the High Moor (and is obscured by fog). The castle has another ten **cloud giants** aboard—guards loyal to Nirva and Jaral. If the characters question the cloud giants about their motives, they summarize the information in "The Ordning" and "King Hekaton and His Daughters" sections in the introduction. They also tell characters to beware of Countess Sansuri, an evil cloud giant lord who equates "small folk" with vermin. They don't know the location of her castle, however.

## SHADOWTOP CATHEDRAL

A closely packed stand of towering shadowtop trees lies in the High Forest. The dark canopies of the trees form a high roof that permits only hints of sunlight to touch the ground beneath. Shadowtop Cathedral is an important meeting place for the Emerald Enclave. The forest within 50 miles of the site is seeded with **awakened trees** and **awakened shrubs** that are loyal to the enclave. These plants hide the trails that lead to Shadowtop Cathedral. If the awakened plants spot a creature openly wearing or carrying the symbol of the Emerald Enclave, the plants move aside to reveal hidden trails. Other creatures searching the forest for trails have disadvantage on ability checks made to find them and to avoid becoming lost.

When the characters first arrive at Shadowtop Cathedral, no one else is present, and there are no tracks on the ground. Each day at dawn, highsun, and dusk, there is a cumulative 10 percent chance that a friendly **druid** (NG male or female moon elf) visits the site. The druid doesn't stay long but urges characters seeking assistance to wait for the cathedral's caretaker to return. If they heed the druid's advice, assume that the caretaker returns at the next dawn.

The primary caretaker of Shadowtop Cathedral is a xenophobic, moss-covered treant named Turlang. He visits the site only occasionally. When he's not at the cathedral, Turlang wanders the forest, frightening off interlopers. He uses the **treant** stat block, has 200 hit points, and has the following additional action option:

***Spellcasting.*** Turlang casts one of the following spells, requiring no material spell components and using Wisdom as the spellcasting ability (spell save DC 15):

At will: *druidcraft, guidance, resistance, speak with plants*
2/day each: *animal messenger, detect magic, entangle, goodberry, gust of wind, pass without trace, speak with animals*
1/day each: *commune with nature* (cast as 1 action), *conjure woodland beings, hallucinatory terrain* (cast as 1 action)

## SHINING FALLS

Traffic on the Delimbiyr River comes to a halt at a spectacularly beautiful waterfall where the river flows through a mountain pass. The ancient elf kingdom of Eaerlann once had an outpost at the Shining Falls, but no trace of it remains. Even a once-busy portage road around the falls is little more than a deer trail now.

## SHINING WHITE

The spirit mound of the Griffon tribe sits atop a rocky hill overlooking a tributary of the Surbrin River, south of the Lurkwood. During the winter, most of Shining White is buried under snow. During the summer, the grass atop the mound grows tall.

Two raised rings of grass-covered earth form Shining White, which gets its name from a 280-foot-tall spire of white chalk that rises atop the hill. This landmark is visible for miles. The menhirs and altar that once stood atop the spirit mound were carved from opalescent marble. Three stone giants recently desecrated the mound, knocking over all the menhirs and cairns. They also dug up and pulverized the central altar. The Uthgardt who claim this mound have not yet learned of the desecration (but see "Suggested Encounter").

### ANCIENT RELIC

In the middle of Shining White is an altar mound surrounded by a griffon-shaped indentation in the earth, the form of which isn't readily apparent until one takes to the air or climbs to the top of the rocky spire. The stone giants smashed the marble altar to rubble, but they didn't dig underneath it. There, the followers of Uthgar buried both halves of a giant relic: a colorfully painted porcelain mask crafted long ago for a cloud giant. The mask is nonmagical, and each half weighs 20 pounds. If the halves are brought together, they display the image

MAP 3.11: SHINING WHITE

of a face that bears a fearsome scowl. The mask is too large to be repaired with a *mending* spell.

## SUGGESTED ENCOUNTER

If the characters linger here for an hour or more, four **griffons** descend from the sky and attack. The griffons target horses and ponies first, then mules, then humanoids. They are hungry and fight to the death. Any creature that kills a griffon at Shining White is cursed. The cursed creature gains the following flaw: "I have an insatiable craving for horse flesh." In addition, Beasts with a challenge rating of 2 or lower treat the cursed creature as hostile and do everything they can to avoid it. A *remove curse* spell or similar magic lifts the curse.

## SILVER MARCHES

Also known as Luruar, this region of the North is hemmed in by the Ice Spires to the north, the Rauvin River to the south, the Frost Hills to the west, and the desert of Anauroch to the east. Mineral-rich mountain ranges, beautiful alpine slopes and valleys, and fertile farmland make the Silver Marches a tempting place to live. At the same time, monsters abound here. Orcs and giants inhabit the mountains, Uthgardt haunt the northern forests, and the drow city of Menzoberranzan lies in the Underdark below. Dragons also assault farms and settlements from time to time.

The War of the Silver Marches exacted such a heavy toll—including the destruction and occupation of Sundabar—that the final victory over the orcs felt hollow.

One can't help but notice the corpse-strewn battlefields, ravaged homesteads, and maimed soldiers and citizens that are lasting reminders of the war's brutality.

## SILVERWOOD

Growing atop the rugged, hilly terrain between the Evermoors and the Nether Mountains, the Silverwood was once part of the High Forest, but over centuries, loggers working the woodlands on either side of the Evermoor Way have carved a great wound through the terrain. Bare hillsides littered with stumps line this gap.

## SILVERYMOON

The Gem of the North is a fitting epithet for Silverymoon: a beautiful, tranquil city where trees and gardens live in harmony with buildings, bridges, and sculptures. Silverymoon is an enlightened place, with a great library, breathtaking temples and shrines, and respected schools of magic, art, and music. Its beauty awes visitors and is the subject of many bardic songs and tales.

High Marshal Methrammar Aerasumé, the city's lord, resides in a tall, slender palace on the east side of the city and commands Silverymoon's knight-defenders. The city's magical defenses are even more formidable than the knights and have served the city well for years. Silverymoon is also a haven for Harpers—not surprising, given that many Harpers are wizards and bards.

Grand and enlightened though the city may be, Silverymoon's reputation was tarnished by its halfhearted efforts in aid of Sundabar during the War of the Silver Marches. The city remains a powerful and influential member of the Lords' Alliance, however.

For more information on Silverymoon, see the *Sword Coast Adventurer's Guide*.

## SILVERYMOON PASS

A road traverses the hills northeast of Silverymoon, providing passage between two mountain ranges and then southward to Sundabar. Silverymoon Pass has seen little traffic since Sundabar was overrun during the War of the Silver Marches. The rotted corpses of hundreds of orcs lie strewn on either side of the road—grisly evidence of how close Silverymoon came to suffering the same fate as Sundabar.

## SOUTHWOOD

Hemmed in by the Delimbiyr Vale to the north and west, the High Moor to the south, and the Graypeak Mountains to the east, the Southwood has the same variety of trees found in the High Forest, without the High Forest's mysterious reputation. Hunters and rangers from Grayvale like to travel these woods.

## SPINE OF THE WORLD

Mountains of ice and black rock form a sky-scraping wall of frigid peaks across the far north, which few creatures have the ability to surmount. Brutally cold winds, avalanches, and icy rifts are the least of a traveler's problems in the Spine of the World. Clans of giants, goblinoids, and orcs dwell there, holding every cavern or abandoned dwarven delve but those claimed by dragons.

## STAR MOUNTS

Cloaked in clouds and vaguely menacing, these mountains rise from the heart of the High Forest and are tall enough to be seen from any edge of the forest. The Star Mounts are the site of strange, gleaming lights on clear nights, and dragons are sometimes seen flying to and from the peaks. Fierce winds swirl through and around the mountains, forcing flying creatures away or causing them to veer suddenly and crash against the rocks.

## STARMETAL HILLS

The Starmetal Hills are a range of rocky knolls between Neverwinter Wood and the Long Road. They are so named because the area has been the target of several meteor showers over the millennia. The hills are haunted by various tribes of Uthgardt, giving few others reason to visit the area.

Deep in the Starmetal Hills, a group of dwarves devoted to Marthammor Duin (the dwarven god of explorers, travelers, and outcasts) established the village of Twilight Tor, on the shores of a cold, crystal-clear lake known as Lake Glorfindar. Few but the dwarves know of this place. Travelers of good will are welcome, and the stargazing is excellent.

## STONE BRIDGE

A gigantic stone archway, two miles from end to end and four hundred feet tall at its apex, comfortably spans the Dessarin River and the plain around it, remaining high and dry during even the worst springtime floods. The Stone Bridge is a sacred site of pilgrimage for many dwarves. Long ago, the dwarf god Moradin appeared atop the bridge to rally dwarves of the Ironstar clan against a horde of orcs, and the founder of the ancient dwarven kingdom of Besilmer, Torhild Flametongue, died fighting a hill giant in the same location.

The Stone Bridge is made of smooth, fused granite. It is only 15 feet wide and lacks railings or barriers, so anyone traversing it is at the mercy of the wind.

### SUGGESTED ENCOUNTER

The first time the adventurers approach the midpoint of the bridge, they see a **fire giant** and a **hell hound** approaching from the opposite direction. The fire giant, Stolvor, isn't carrying any rocks or valuables, but he clutches an enormous greatsword and has a *rod of the Vonindod* (see appendix B) tucked in his belt. He and his hound have been searching for fragments of the Vonindod (with no luck) and are spoiling for a fight. They charge into battle, the hell hound advancing in front. If their enemies flee, they pursue.

A creature can try to push another creature off the bridge by shoving it, using the rules for "Shoving a Creature" in chapter 9 of the *Player's Handbook*. Any creature that is successfully shoved in this way must succeed on DC 15 Dexterity saving throw or fall into the river below, taking 70 (20d6) bludgeoning damage.

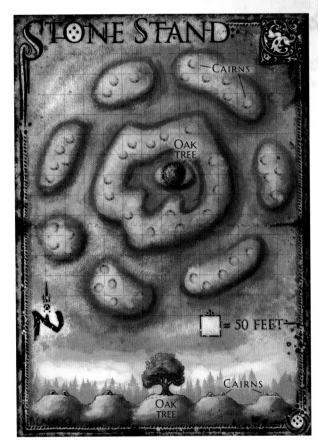

MAP 3.12: STONE STAND

## STONE STAND

The Blue Bear tribe is thought to be extinct, its spirit mound a haunted place best avoided. In truth, the Blue Bears prowl the High Forest and the eastern Delimbiyr Vale, doing their best to remain hidden. Their members visit Stone Stand infrequently, and only under the cover of night.

Stone Stand (see map 3.12) is situated upon a lonely hill north of the High Forest. Atop this hill, the Blue Bears built a mound upon which they planted a branch of the Grandfather Tree. This branch grew into a towering oak tree, which today is surrounded by a raised inner ring of cairns and a broken outer ring of mounds with more cairns atop them. Beneath these cairns lie the moldy bones of the tribe's ancient dead.

### ANCIENT RELIC

Early followers of Uthgar buried a relic of giantkind under the central mound, believing that its magic would empower and protect the oak tree. The tree's roots wrap around the ancient relic, which is actually a source of unrest for the Uthgardt ghosts that languish here (see "Suggested Encounter"). A *detect magic* spell cast within range of the tree reveals an aura of necromancy magic emanating from underneath it. To reach the relic, characters must dig under the tree and hack away at its roots. This exercise takes a single character 40 hours to accomplish; multiple party members working together can reduce the amount of time accordingly. The buried relic is the skull of Gurt, Lord of the Pale Giants, a frost giant that Uthgar defeated in single combat at the site of Morgur's Mound. The skull weighs 100 pounds. If it is taken from Stone Stand, the ghosts that haunt the spirit mound are finally laid to rest.

## Suggested Encounter

The presence of a living creature within 30 feet of the oak tree causes the **ghost** of an Uthgardt chieftain to appear next to the tree. It enters the world from the Border Ethereal and attacks any trespassers that it sees, first using its Horrifying Visage action, and then its Possession and Withering Touch. If it succeeds in possessing a creature, the ghost uses the host body to attack other trespassers. If the ghost drops to 0 hit points, it vanishes with a furious scream.

In the round after the ghost is defeated, on what would be its initiative count, the **ghost** of another chieftain appears next to the tree. This process continues until four Uthgardt ghosts have been defeated.

The ghosts don't attack members of the Blue Bear tribe. Any character dressed as a Blue Bear warrior or shaman can fool a ghost with a successful DC 12 Charisma (Deception) check. Although they can speak Bothii (the Uthgardt language), the dead Uthgardt chieftains have no inclination to communicate with trespassers, and they don't know why they've been denied a place at Uthgar's side in the afterlife. Any ghosts that are defeated re-form at midnight and can reappear thereafter. If the frost giant skull is removed from its resting place under the tree, the Uthgardt spirits are laid to rest and the ghosts don't reappear.

The oak tree has AC 15, 100 hit points, a damage threshold of 10, and immunity to psychic damage. Attacking or destroying it has no effect on a ghost that has already manifested. Even if the tree is reduced to 0 hit points, it grows back over years, unless it is uprooted.

## Stone Trail

This dirt road runs north of the Sumber Hills and connects Westbridge to Beliard. A major landmark, the Stone Bridge, lies along this route.

## Sumber Hills

The Sumber Hills are an area of windswept badlands sparsely covered in dry grass. Much of the terrain features exposed rock faces or steep escarpments. Although the earth of the hills is arid, countless tiny streams rise from hidden springs (usually clean and drinkable water), then flow down through crevices in the slopes to join the Dessarin River, which bisects the hills.

Most locals think only of the larger, higher hills west of the river when they hear "Sumber Hills," because that area once boasted rich quarries and good hunting. Some hunting lodges and keeps owned by wealthy Waterdhavians and adventurers remain—and in recent years have become homes to bandits and monsters. Those who excavate the Sumber Hills for building stone and gravel often talk of finding gemstones and rich veins of ore in the hills—but for the most part, these persistent tales have never been anything but fiction.

For a map of the Sumber Hills and descriptions of various locations in and around the area, see the adventure *Princes of the Apocalypse.*

## Sundabar

Mirabar's sister-city is a shattered ruin. An orc horde destroyed this once-mighty fortress city during the War of the Silver Marches, wiped out its human population, drove the dwarven population deep underground, slew the city's dwarf king, and, perhaps worst of all, dealt a fatal blow to Sundabar's longstanding alliance with its human and elf neighbors.

The remaining dwarves of Sundabar have turned their backs on those who offered little or no aid in the city's time of need. They no longer consider themselves part of the Lords' Alliance. The dwarves have turned their attention to rebuilding what they can. Now, although the surface city remains a hollowed-out ruin, its outer walls mostly intact but its inner buildings reduced to piles of debris, the underground smithies and foundries are operational once more. The city is currently off limits to non-dwarves.

## Surbrin Hills

Wise folk steer clear of the Surbrin Hills east of Longsaddle, for they are the Uthgardt hunting grounds of the Griffon tribe. Hill giants, trolls, and other monsters also prowl this area.

## Surbrin Trail

A trail extends north from the city of Yartar, through farmland patrolled by Yartarran soldiers on horseback. Once the Surbrin Trail reaches the hills on the other side of the Dessarin Valley, the farms peter out, along with the patrols, and the trail hugs the eastern shore of the Surbrin River as though shying away from the Evermoors. At the north end of the trail, beyond Mornbryn's Shield, is Nesmé.

## Svardborg

Deep within the Sea of Moving Ice floats Svardborg, the iceberg fortress of Jarl Storvald and his frost giants. See chapter 7, "Berg of the Frost Giants," for more information on this location.

## Sword Mountains

The steep, craggy mountains north of Waterdeep are home to a few scattered clans of orcs and goblinoids. The hills around the Sword Mountains are strewn with the ruins of bygone kingdoms and more than a few half-forgotten dungeons and tombs.

## Ten Trail

A pass leads through the western mountains into the Spine of the World, though the route is nigh impassable in winter because of the snow and ice. Well-armed caravans use the Ten Trail to move goods to and from the settlements of Icewind Dale. Although it's the safest route between Icewind Dale and the lands to the south, travelers are still at risk of attacks from crag cats, yetis, orcs, brigands, and even the occasional white dragon.

The trail extends as far south as Fireshear. Characters traveling the Ten Trail in wintertime are subject to extreme cold temperatures (see the "Wilderness Survival" section in chapter 5 of the *Dungeon Master's Guide*).

## THORNHOLD

Thornhold is a coastal fortress, a castle of gray stone with a thick, curved wall and a two-towered central keep on the southern tip of the Mere of Dead Men. The cliff facing the sea is so sheer and smooth that no wall need be built on the side of the hill where Thornhold sits. The castle is without adornment; only crenellations and arrow slits break its solid face of stone. Inside the walls, surrounding the bailey, are small buildings of wood and plaster that house animals and are used for smithwork, candlemaking, gemcutting, repairing wooden items (including wagons and the like), and brewing beer.

Thornhold was once the property of the Margaster family of Waterdeep and has been held by the Knights of Samular (paladins of Tyr) and the Zhentarim in the past. Its current occupants are the shield dwarves of the Stoneshaft clan. They refer to the castle as Stoneshaft Hold. The Stoneshaft dwarves are reclusive and secretive, yet they are interested to hear what's afoot in Waterdeep, for they suspect the Margaster family is plotting to attack the fortress and reclaim its ancestral holding.

Travelers are free to visit Thornhold, up to a point. The Stoneshaft dwarves allow adventurers and caravans to make camp within their walls, but they forbid access to the keep and the extensive caves below. Thornhold is rumored to contain a passage to the Underdark—a claim that the dwarves neither confirm nor deny.

For more information on Thornhold, see the *Sword Coast Adventurer's Guide*.

## TRADE WAY

The Trade Way begins at Waterdeep and heads southward, though only the stretch between Waterdeep and Daggerford is well traveled. Merchants who can't afford to transport their goods by ship use the Trade Way, hiring guards to fend off the brigands and monsters that live in the surrounding wilderness.

## TRIBOAR

Triboar, a frontier town in the fertile Dessarin Valley, sits at the crossroads of two major trade routes: the Long Road and Evermoor Way. It's a popular way station for caravans and rangers. See chapter 2 for more information on this location.

If the adventure didn't begin in Triboar, you can run the "Attack on Triboar" encounter (see chapter 2) when the characters visit the town.

## TRIBOAR TRAIL

This path meanders south of Neverwinter Wood, connecting the High Road to the Long Road. It's the safest overland route between the Dessarin Valley and Neverwinter. Orcs and goblinoids prey on travelers from time

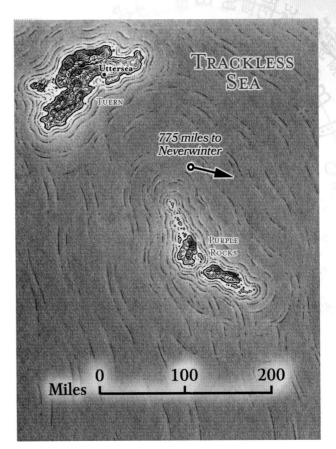

MAP 3.13: TUERN AND PURPLE ROCKS

to time, but copper dragons in the northern foothills of the Sword Mountains help thin out the monsters' ranks.

## TUERN

The merciless Northfolk of Tuern (see map 3.13) pay tribute to three adult red dragons that live inside and beneath the island's active volcanoes—a chain of black, grumbling, lava-filled cauldrons that belch smoke and ash into the sky. Five Northfolk clans live on the island, each with its own settlement, king, and fleet of dragon-headed longships. Four of the kings recognize the fifth, High King Ossul Haarn of Uttersea (CE male human **gladiator** with 90 hit points and a *ring of fire resistance*), as their liege. Uttersea is the largest town on the island and has a port for the High King's armada of longships. The island is also home to small families of fire giants who strive to unseat the island's draconic overlords and enslave the Northfolk.

## TURNSTONE PASS

A harrowing trail threads through the cold, windswept Nether Mountains. Hill giants, orcs, wyverns, griffons, gargoyles, and other creatures make travel through Turnstone Pass perilous. Only heavily armed travelers have any hope of making it from one end to the other.

## ULUVIN

This dry, dusty village is located south of the High Forest, on the old Iron Road between Womford and Secomber. A branch of the road turns northeast and heads toward Unicorn Run, a gently flowing river that pours out of the High Forest.

## SUGGESTED ENCOUNTER

Two teenage cattle ranchers named Albie Grizlow and Leshonna Daar (CE male and female human **commoners**) mounted on **riding horses** intercept the characters as they approach within five miles of Uluvin. The teenagers tell the party that the village has fallen to hill giants and goblins and that many villagers have taken refuge in the nearby forest.

Characters can give the village a wide berth, or they can deal with the threat. If they get within three miles of the village, they start to see scattered farmsteads surrounded by dry fields. At each farmstead are 3d6 **goblins**; they either are searching the cottage and barn for treasure, chasing chickens and swine in the field, or dancing around 1d4 tied-up prisoners (**commoners**). The goblins have covered their captives' heads with old buckets, flowerpots, and feedbags so that they can't see. There is a 50 percent chance that an **ogre** is also present, trying to catch a pig or lift a cow and take it back to Grudd Haug (see chapter 5, "Den of the Hill Giants"). The goblins and the ogre are too distracted to notice the adventurers if they stick to the road. The ogre and most of the goblins have no treasure, but the goblin leader at each farmstead carries a trinket (roll on the Trinkets table in chapter 5 of the *Player's Handbook*).

If the characters enter the village, they see dusty wood-frame buildings with tall facades lining the Iron Road. Three **hill giants** are outside in plain view, overturning wagons, smashing through clay-tiled rooftops with their greatclubs, and stuffing into their sacks anything that catches their eye. Characters can easily take these hill giants by surprise. An inn and saloon called the Black Bull's Tail stands at the intersection where the road branches. Two more **hill giants** have ripped through the inn's facade and destroyed most of the furnishings, including the stairs leading up to the second floor, and are in the midst of gorging themselves on food and ale. If they hear sounds of combat outside, they investigate, hurling benches, rain barrels, and whatever else they can find in lieu of rocks.

## TREASURE

Each hill giant has a sack containing 2d6 × 100 cp and 1d4 mundane items, determined by rolling on the Items in a Giant's Bag table in the introduction.

Once the monsters are driven out, the characters can travel north to the edge of the High Forest and let the villagers know that it's safe to return. If they do so, a grateful old widow named Zoranda Heller (LG female **commoner**) gives them a *ring of protection* that her late husband, a rancher, found in a field.

## UTTERSEA

See the "Tuern" section.

## VALLEY OF KHEDRUN

The frozen vale on the southern fringe of the Spine of the World is named for a legendary dwarf hero who used his axe to carve out the homeland of the dwarves in the North from lands watched over by wolves, orcs, and goblinoids. The Valley of Khedrun is haunted by the Great Worm clan of the Uthgardt.

## VORDRORN FOREST

The pine forest south of Citadel Adbar is sometimes called the Ghostwood for two reasons. First, its proximity to the Ice Mountains leaves it constantly shrouded in cold mists. Second, undead are known to haunt the Vordrorn Forest, particularly incorporeal types such as wraiths, specters, and ghosts. These restless spirits seem content to remain in the forest and rarely trouble travelers who stay away from their territory.

## WATERDEEP

The City of Splendors is a bustling, walled city on the Sword Coast. Some merchants have dubbed Waterdeep the best supply center in the world, with the largest collection of superb craft workers, experts, useful contacts, and potential hirelings to be found anywhere. Others caution that the city houses a veritable army of potential enemies for those who aren't careful—and everyone agrees that its wide, crowded streets are full of spies.

Waterdhavian noble families and guilds hold tremendous political and economic sway up and down the Sword Coast, but within the city itself, true power lies with the Masked Lords of Waterdeep—rulers who convene in secret and whose identities are largely unknown. The public face of this ruling body is the Open Lord of Waterdeep. The current Open Lord, Lady Laeral Silverhand, has held the position for only a few months. Many of the city's nobles and guildmasters are vying for her attention while conspiring to wrest power away from her office. There's also trouble brewing between the Zhentarim, which has gained an economic foothold in the city, and the Xanathar Thieves' Guild, which controls much of the city's criminal underworld.

Characters who belong to the Harpers, the Order of the Gauntlet, the Lords' Alliance, or the Zhentarim can find faction representatives in Waterdeep. For a map of Waterdeep and more information about its features and inhabitants, see the *Sword Coast Adventurer's Guide*.

## SUGGESTED ENCOUNTER

Shortly after the characters arrive in Waterdeep, a cloud giant castle emerges from the clouds overhead and looms above the city, its ominous shadow causing widespread panic. Lady Laeral Silverhand dispatches heralds to calm the people and assure them that no harm will befall the city. If the adventurers decide to investigate, they must devise a method of reaching the giant castle, which hangs 1,000 feet in the air. The castle has a configuration similar to that of Lyn Armaal (see chapter 9, "Castle of the Cloud Giants") and is home to a neutral good clan made up of four adult **cloud giants**, three young cloud giants, four pet **griffons**, and eight **stone giants** that serve as guards. The young cloud giants use the **hill giant** stat block, with these changes:

- The young cloud giants have an Intelligence score of 10 (+0) and Wisdom and Charisma scores of 12 (+1).

- They have the following skills: Insight +4, Perception +4. They have a passive Wisdom (Perception) score of 14.
- They speak Common and Giant.

These cloud giants are cartographers engaged in remapping the Sword Coast while searching for ancient battlegrounds and long-lost relics of Ostoria. They mean no harm to Waterdeep, but the city intrigues them, for they believe it was built on an old giant settlement that was destroyed by dragons tens of thousands of years ago. The cloud giants plan to meet with the city's leaders to learn more about Waterdeep's history and determine whether any remnants of Ostoria survive today. The family's noble patriarch is a scholarly and cautious cloud giant named Count Nimbolo. His wife, Countess Mulara, is distrusting of "small folk" and doesn't allow the characters to move about her home unescorted.

Although these giants pose no threat to Waterdeep, they know of at least one evil cloud giant who is bent on conquering the lands of the small folk once the ordning is recast in her favor: Countess Sansuri. They tell the characters that Sansuri is looking for a lost trove of dragon magic, but they don't know where her cloud castle is located.

## Treasure

If the characters defeat the giants, they can plunder the giants' possessions. Countess Mulara wears two bejeweled necklaces (each worth 7,500 gp and weighing 125 pounds). Both she and the count own a collection of twenty ornate masks made of painted gold (each worth 750 gp and weighing 50 pounds). Among the furnishings in their bedchamber is an alabaster chest containing 800 pp and 1d3 magic items, determined by rolling on Magic Item Table F in chapter 7 of the *Dungeon Master's Guide*. The chest weighs 500 pounds and has an *arcane lock* spell cast on it.

## Way Inn

Southeast of Daggerford, the Trade Way runs right through the middle of Way Inn, a small village enclosed by a 20-foot-tall wall of mortared granite with wooden gates to the north and south along the road. A large two-story inn, also called the Way Inn, dominates the village and has long been a popular stop for weary travelers. Wealthy merchants and nobles stay here while making hunting forays into the Misty Forest. The innkeeper, Cross Wheeler (NG male human **scout**), is a retired ranger who knows the forest pretty well and has friends among the wood elves who live there.

## Weathercote Forest

For reasons unknown, no divination spell or scrying sensor can penetrate the dry patch of greenery on the edge of the Anauroch desert. Woodcutters from Parnast warn adventurers not to enter too deeply into Weathercote Forest, as ancient elven magic has a way of making people disappear forever.

## Westbridge

A village strung out along the Long Road between Red Larch and Triboar, Westbridge (so named because it lies to the west of the Stone Bridge) is home to the Harvest Inn, on the west side of the Long Road facing the Stone Trail. The inn's proprietor is the affable Herivin

Dardragon (CG male strongheart halfling **commoner**), a curly-haired collector and reseller of paintings and statuettes of questionable taste.

## WESTWOOD

A tangled forest cloaking the eastern foothills of the Sword Mountains, the Westwood is home to a shrine of Mielikki, several woodcutters' camps that are often taken over forcibly for a season or a few months at a time by bandits or Uthgardt, and a few overgrown remnants of the ancient elven kingdom of Rilithar.

## WHALEBONES

Petty, warmongering kings rule over the small islands known as the Whalebones, so called because of the whale skeletons that litter the islands' beaches. Several of the larger islands are home to rocs that the storm giants of Maelstrom use as mounts. The islanders leave treasure for the giants and food for the birds as tribute.

## WOMFORD

A tiny village along the Iron Road was known as Ironford until shortly after a dragon was slain nearby. Passersby began to call the settlement Wyrm Ford—a name subsequently corrupted, thanks to the thick local accent, into Womford. The village has a dock on the Dessarin River for shipping grain from its gristmill. It's also the market and the source of supplies for the surrounding farms from which the grain comes. Aside from the mill, the village has a handful of granaries and a larger handful of cottages, several of which house tiny shops. West of the village is the Ironford Bridge, a long, narrow, ramshackle wooden bridge that spans the Dessarin River and leads to Bargewright Inn, which looms atop a hill.

Womforders lock and bar their doors and shutter their windows at night, for fear of the so-called Womford Bat, a nocturnal predator that snatches folk it can catch outside after dark; see the "Bargewright Inn" section for more information on this creature.

## XANTHARL'S KEEP

Xantharl was a well-known ranger and explorer of the North. The fortified village that bears his name stands in the middle of nowhere, on the west side of a notoriously dangerous and rugged stretch of the Long Road. An outer wall with heavy crossbows mounted to its battlements encloses a keep sheltered by a steep roof to shed snow. Surrounding the keep are dozens of narrow stone houses with heavy shutters and steep roofs of their own. The Falling Orc inn and tavern, a wood-frame structure built on the remains of an older stone building that caught fire and burned down, stands near the main gates next to the stables. The hulking yet friendly proprietor, Arzastra (LG female **half-ogre**), recently took pity on a coinless shield dwarf adventurer named Larg and is paying him a few coppers to clean the stables.

"Larg" told Arzastra that he and his adventuring companions were caught in an avalanche while hunting a red dragon in the Valley of Khedrun, and only he survived. The story is a fabrication, but Arzastra bought it. The shifty dwarf is actually a wanted criminal named Worvil "the Weevil" Forkbeard. The characters might know of him from talking to certain NPCs (such as Sir Baric Nylef in Bryn Shander or Darz Helgar in Triboar), or from a wanted poster in Longsaddle. The Weevil can be found cleaning the inn's stables during the day or drinking in a private, plainly furnished guest bedroom on the upper floor of the inn at night. The Weevil avoids making eye contact with strangers. He use the **bandit captain** stat block, with these changes:

- The Weevil is neutral evil.
- His speed is 25 feet.
- He has advantage on saving throws against poison and resistance to poison damage.
- He has darkvision out to a range of 60 feet, and he speaks Common, Draconic, and Dwarvish.
- Instead of a scimitar and a dagger, he wields a pair of *+1 handaxes* (+5 to hit with each). As an action, he can make three melee attacks, two attacks with one handaxe and one attack with the other handaxe. Each handaxe deals 6 (1d6 + 3) slashing damage on a hit.

The Lord of Xantharl's Keep is Narbeck Horn (N male shield dwarf **knight** armed with a greataxe instead of a greatsword), who reports to the marchion of Mirabar. Narbeck has a *sending stone* that allows him to speak to the marchion directly, ensuring that news of any threat to Mirabar from the south is quickly relayed. Narbeck commands a garrison of one hundred fifty veterans, which is over twice the population of the village itself.

### SUGGESTED ENCOUNTER

Guards on the rooftop of the keep spot a **frost giant** approaching from the west with a small army of fifty **goblins** and ten **hobgoblins**, plus five **ogres** equipped with goblin huckers (see the "Goblin Huckers" section in chapter 2). The hobgoblins form a phalanx in the front of the group, with the frost giant behind them and the unruly mob of ogres and goblins bringing up the rear.

Even without the characters' help, the keep can turn back the attackers with few casualties. (Many goblins are killed as their bodies are flung against the keep by the huckers.) During the uproar, any character who succeeds on a DC 20 Wisdom (Insight) check realizes that the siege is a ruse to draw attention away from the village's east gate, where the real attack is taking place.

A while back, Worvil Forkbeard told a few friends that he needed a place to hide and planned to lie low in Xantharl's Keep. One of his friends betrayed that confidence to the frost giant now attacking the keep, who is named Kaltivar. The giant intends to collect on the 5,000 gp reward being offered for the dwarf's capture and is using the goblinoids and ogres as a distraction to help him bag the dwarf. While the garrison is occupied on the west side of town, ten stealthy **bugbears** climb over the eastern wall and attempt to capture Worvil. If the characters already have the dwarf in custody, the bugbears try to take Worvil from them. If Worvil is dead and the bugbears see his corpse, they immediately try to flee the keep and report back to Kaltivar. Characters who are unaware of the Weevil's presence or his true identity can hear the dwarf and bugbears fighting in the stables with a successful DC 15 Wisdom (Perception) check, and the Weevil manages to kill a couple of bugbears before he's dragged off in a sack.

## TREASURE

Kaltivar the frost giant carries a sack containing 2d6 × 100 gp, 1d4 mundane items (determined by rolling on the Items in a Giant's Bag table in the introduction), and one magic item, determined by rolling on Magic Item Table C in chapter 7 of the *Dungeon Master's Guide*. The goblinoids have no treasure.

## YARTAR

The fortified city of Yartar stands on the east bank of the Dessarin River. On the west bank is a walled citadel under the city's control. Between them stretches a wide stone bridge. Travelers must move through the citadel and pass inspection before continuing west to Triboar or crossing the bridge to the city's west gate. The Evermoor Way cuts through the heart of Yartar, connecting the city's western and eastern gates. East of the city, the trade road becomes a gravel trail.

Yartar is prosperous and becoming increasingly crowded. Some of its old buildings have been torn down and taller ones built—four stories high, in some cases.

Because the city is a major river port, Yartar's elected leader is called a Waterbaron. The current Waterbaron is Nestra Ruthiol (LE female human **noble**), a shrewd, vindictive woman in her late fifties. Yartar is a member of the Lords' Alliance, and Ruthiol considers that relationship vital to her city's survival and prosperity. She knows that the Harpers and the Zhentarim are well established in the city, but her path crosses with theirs only when the well-being of Yartarrans is threatened. Both factions have infiltrated the local thieves' guild, the all-female Hand of Yartar.

Characters who obtain Tamalin Zoar's letter of recommendation (see the "Calling Horns" section) can present it to a member of the Hand of Yartar and gain the guild's assistance in any of the following ways:

- If the characters are looking for an individual in the city whose location isn't well known, the Hand of Yartar can reliably track down that person in 4d6 hours.
- If the characters need to sell loot, the Hand of Yartar can find (not necessarily honest) buyers for them.
- If the characters come to Yartar seeking an expeditious means of travel, the Hand of Yartar tells them about a not-so-secret *teleportation circle* guarded by a wizard named Kolbaz (see the "Inner Circles" section at the end of this chapter).

The greatest threat facing Yartar is the Kraken Society (see the "Factions in the North" section in the introduction), which is trying to seize control of the city from within and turn it into a stronghold. One of Yartar's nobles is a Kraken Society member named Khaspere Drylund. Lord Drylund is eager to displace Ruthiol as the city's Waterbaron. He can't have Ruthiol eliminated, however, until he has gathered enough support to guarantee victory in the election to determine her successor. He hopes to win votes by identifying and bribing

(or blackmailing) Yartar's most corruptible officials, and by hosting extravagant parties aboard his private, splendidly decorated riverboat. For more information on Lord Drylund and his boat, see chapter 11.

## ZELBROSS

Halfway between Secomber and Loudwater, on the old Delimbiyr Road, are the charred wooden remains and the crumbled stone chimney of an inn that was burned down by brigands many years ago. A scorched wooden sign cut in the shape of a fox's head still hangs above a blackened doorframe, with the inn's name—the Sly Fox—all but obliterated by fire. An overgrown dirt road branches southward from the inn.

Characters who follow the dirt road discover the razed ruins of a farming village on the north shore of the Delimbiyr River. Only some rickety wooden docks remain to mark what used to be the village of Zelbross. The abandoned site has a lovely view of the Southwood across the river, so it's easy to imagine why settlers chose this spot, but there's no evidence of what became of the villagers or whatever attacked them. Zelbross has been abandoned for more than ten years.

### SUGGESTED ENCOUNTER

If the characters search the ruins of the Sly Fox, they encounter a runaway child from the Blue Bear tribe (see the "Uthgardt" section earlier in this chapter). He is hiding in the inn's hearth, and characters who have a passive Wisdom (Perception) score of 12 or higher spot him as they search the ruin. Orok is a nine-year-old human boy armed with a rusty dagger and a homemade sling. He is covered head to toe with soot and grime, and he has sticks woven into his flea-ridden mane of black hair. He is smart enough not to attack well-armed adventurers but has no qualms about trying to harm anyone who antagonizes him. Orok uses the **kobold** stat block, with these changes:

- Orok is chaotic neutral.
- He doesn't have darkvision.
- He speaks Bothii (the Uthgardt language) and broken Common.
- He lacks the kobold's Sunlight Sensitivity feature (but retains the Pack Tactics feature).

Orok's siblings bullied him mercilessly, so he ran away from his tribe. Although he's clearly an Uthgardt child, he carries nothing that identifies him as a member of the Blue Bear tribe, nor does he disclose his tribal affiliation for fear of being delivered back to the tribe. If the characters offer Orok food, he takes it and scuttles back to his "den" to devour it. He also retreats to the hearth if he sees any magic. Like most Uthgardt, he is fearful of magic and distrustful of spellcasters.

Orok is drawn to rough-looking wilderness types, such as barbarians and rangers. If such a character is friendly toward him, he bonds with that character and becomes that character's follower. Orok doesn't willingly accompany the party otherwise, preferring to remain in his lair and live by catching fish in the nearby river.

# ZYMORVEN HALL

Perched atop a crag overlooking the Rauvin Road, with a clear view of the Evermoors to the south and the Moonwood to the north, is a keep of mortared stone with a high-pitched roof that has wooden statues of baying wolves rising from its peaks. A branch in the road winds up to the keep's gatehouse and bailey. From the keep, the Zymorven family of Silverymoon has watched over the surrounding lands for four generations.

Lord Harthos Zymorven (CG male human **knight**) commands Zymorven Hall, which appears to have no guards to defend it. Many of the hallways and rooms, however, have suits of armor standing in dark corners, swords mounted on oak-paneled walls, and dusty carpets spread across stone floors. These are actually suits of **animated armor**, **flying swords**, and **rugs of smothering** that obey Lord Zymorven's commands. Lord Zymorven retains the services of a scribe, a stablehand, a cook, and a musician (all **commoners**), as well as an old witch (use the **druid** stat block) who is skilled at making herbal remedies and poultices.

Lord Zymorven's duty is to be vigilant and watch for trouble, which could come from any direction. Soldiers patrolling the Rauvin Road on horseback are welcome to use the keep as a place where they can rest as well as obtain food, drink, and lodging for their horses. Characters who take up Urgala Meltimer's quest (see chapter 2) might have cause to pay a visit to Zymorven Hall.

# FEATURED ENCOUNTERS

The following encounters work best if they occur before the characters are ready to move on to chapter 4, "The Chosen Path." Some of the special quests given out in chapter 2 might blaze a trail that leads to one of these encounters; the same can be said for a few of the suggested encounters presented earlier in this chapter.

## OLD TOWER

You can use this encounter any time the characters are traveling overland. The location isn't important, but somewhere in the Dessarin Valley would be ideal.

> You spot a crumbling tower atop a hill less than a quarter mile away. Parts of its conical roof and outer shell have fallen inward, leaving a gaping hole above which four hawks circle.

If the characters approach within a few hundred feet of the tower (see map 3.14), add:

> A large boulder blocks the tower's ground-floor entrance, and a horrible noise comes from within—a deep, guttural, dirge pouring from the lips of something big and awful.

A female **hill giant** named Moog has barricaded herself in this lonely tower so that she can wallow in self-pity

undisturbed. Chief Guh has taken Moog's husband, Hruk, as her own, leaving Moog with no one to abuse on a daily basis. Moog is singing a mournful tune, which is amplified by the acoustics of the tower.

Moog sits on the upper level of the tower (area 2), her calves and bare feet dangling through a hole in the floor. From this position, she can see anyone that enters the tower through the front door, the hole in the upstairs wall, or the window above the doorway. She has her back to the upstairs window that faces east, and can't see anyone approaching from that direction. Her incessant singing is so loud that she can't hear anything but the loudest noises outside the tower.

The hawks circling above the tower are four **blood hawks**. Any character who pays attention to the hawks can discern their crimson feathers with a successful DC 10 Wisdom (Perception) check or recall their aggressive nature with a successful DC 10 Intelligence (Nature) check. The blood hawks attack any creature that tries to enter the tower through the broken wall or the roof, but otherwise they keep their distance. Once the hawks attack, Moog can't be surprised.

## 1. LOWER LEVEL

Moog has parked a large boulder in front of the doorway. A Small character can squeeze through a narrow opening to enter the tower. Otherwise, the boulder can be rolled aside with a successful DC 25 Strength (Athletics) check. A stone staircase hugs the inside wall, spiraling upward in a clockwise direction and forming landings at various points. Situated next to each landing is a 9-foot-tall arrow slit that tapers to a width of 5 inches. Much of the tower floor and the staircase is strewn with rubble—stone from the crumbling walls and wood from the partially collapsed roof. The rubble counts as difficult terrain.

***Treasure.*** Any character who searches through the rubble finds a cracked floor tile with what appears to be a compartment underneath it. Years ago, a halfling adventurer named Keltar Dardragon buried a treasure chest under the floor here, and he never had a chance to reclaim it before he died. Moog hasn't noticed the chest, which is locked but in poor condition. A character can easily break or pick the lock (no ability check required). The chest holds 300 sp and two magic items, determined by rolling on Magic Item Table B in chapter 7 of the *Dungeon Master's Guide*.

## 2. UPPER LEVEL

Nothing of value is to be found on this level of the tower except a large sack lying on the floor. Determine its contents by rolling three times on the Items in a Giant's Bag table in the introduction.

Moog is here unless she has been lured elsewhere. If the characters wait her out, Moog gets hungry and stops her mournful singing after 2d20 minutes. The hungry giant leaps down to the ground floor, pushes the boulder aside, and exits the tower in search of food. If the characters hide and let her go, she returns to the tower 3d10 hours later with a squealing boar tucked under one arm.

Moog has had some bad experiences with small folk in the past. Her inclination is to attack if confronted.

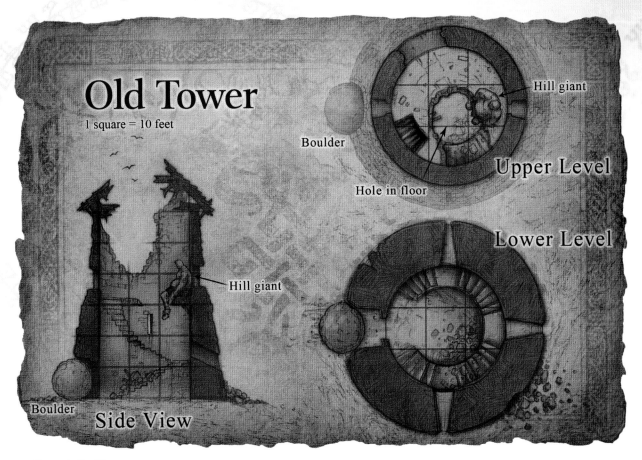

**Old Tower**

1 square = 10 feet

Boulder

Upper Level

Hill giant

Hole in floor

Lower Level

Hill giant

Boulder

Side View

MAP 3.14: OLD TOWER

Her tower contains enough rubble that she won't run out of rocks to throw anytime soon. Any character who tries to allay Moog's concerns by speaking to her calmly and soothingly in Giant can make a DC 12 Charisma (Persuasion) check. If Moog is also bribed with food or treasure, this check is made with advantage.

If the check succeeds, Moog stops attacking long enough to hear what the character has to say. She also reveals why she's so unhappy. If the characters promise to reunite Moog with her husband, she is delighted and tries her best to help them in return. Moog knows where Chief Guh lives and can lead the party to Grudd Haug (see chapter 5, "Den of the Hill Giants"). She also knows that Grudd Haug is full of orcs, goblins, hobgoblins, and ogres. Moog is more frightened of Chief Guh than she is of the characters and won't voluntarily help them attack Grudd Haug. She prefers to remain a safe distance away from the hill giant den (at least half a mile), but characters can convince Moog to accompany them by claiming that they need her help to identify Hruk and rescue him from the hill giant chief. Even when coaxed into joining the assault on Grudd Haug, Moog won't attack other hill giants. If she comes across her husband, she grabs him by the hair and leads him far away from Grudd Haug.

Moog is chaotic evil, and thus prone to abrupt mood swings. She loses patience with the characters and attacks them if they don't continually renew their promise to help her and give her food. Whenever Moog awakens after a long rest, she forgets who the characters are and attacks them, whereupon a character must repeat the Charisma (Persuasion) check to regain her trust.

## INNER CIRCLES

Various special quests in chapter 2 can lead adventurers to Moongleam Tower in the city of Everlund. If the characters receive none of these quests, you can still use this encounter by having an agent of the Harpers approach the party and suggest that they visit Moongleam Tower, particularly if they're looking for a faster mode of travel.

Moongleam Tower is described in more detail in the "Everlund" section earlier in this chapter. Its resident archmage, Krowen Valharrow, is well aware of "the giant problem." If the characters approach him, Krowen warns them that the giants' upheaval poses a grave threat to the balance of power in the North. He has it on good authority that the Harpers, the Lords' Alliance, the Emerald Enclave, the Order of the Gauntlet, and the Zhentarim are all taking steps to protect civilization against the giants' depredations. Krowen knows that giants and dragons have a long history of conflict, and he suspects that the dragons might somehow be responsible (directly or indirectly) for the giants' uprising.

Krowen isn't very adventurous himself, but he's fond of adventurers and uses them to do his dirty work. If the characters explain that they're trying to thwart the giants, Krowen grants the party free access to a secret network of *teleportation circles* that he and his fellow Harper wizards use for travel. He also gives the characters a sheet of parchment that shows all six circles and their sigil addresses (show the players figure 3.1). The circles are located in Everlund, Loudwater, Mirabar, Neverwinter, Waterdeep, and Yartar. The specific locations of these circles are briefly described below, and a Harper spellcaster stands ready at each site to cast the *teleportation circle* spell should the party require it. Each spellcaster uses the **mage** stat block, with these changes:

- Each spellcaster speaks Common, Draconic, Dwarvish, and Elvish.
- Each spellcaster has the *teleportation circle* spell prepared instead of *cone of cold*.

## EVERLUND CIRCLE

The *teleportation circle* in Everlund is located inside a circular chamber in Moongleam Tower. An *arcane lock* spell has been cast on the chamber door, though tower mages can bypass it. Krowen has assigned a brusque but reliable apprentice named Nespril Menk (LG male human **mage**) to watch over this circle during the day, and a lazy, sleep-deprived apprentice named Flewen Aldhark (NG male human **mage**) to mind the circle at night. If the characters arrive while Flewen is on duty, there is a 90 percent chance he's propped up in a chair, sound asleep.

## LOUDWATER CIRCLE

The *teleportation circle* in Loudwater is located in a 30-foot-square cellar under a tavern called the Smiling Satyr. Tucked underneath a wooden staircase is an unmade bed where the circle's attending mage sleeps. His name is Revil Slombarr (CG male human **mage**). He's a heavyset young man who shirks his duties from time to time to visit nearby festhalls. There is a 50 percent chance that Revil is absent when the characters arrive, in which case he returns after 1d4 hours.

The stairs leads up to a secret door that opens inside a large wooden trunk bolted to the floor above. Characters who climb out of the trunk find themselves in a curtained cloakroom near the taproom. A Harper sympathizer named Gharwin Umbryl (LG male human **commoner**) runs the Smiling Satyr and does his best to cover for Revil.

## MIRABAR CIRCLE

The Mirabarran authorities would be angry to learn that the Harpers have compromised the city's security by constructing a permanent *teleportation circle* within Mirabar's walls. The circle is inscribed in a stable house loft and can be quickly hidden under hay. The circle's attendant, Zazspar Bronzefire (LG male shield dwarf **mage**), poses as a stablehand, complete with leather overalls and straw in his beard.

## NEVERWINTER CIRCLE

The circle in Neverwinter is drawn on the floor of an attic, in a creaky old three-story rowhouse that the Harpers use as a meeting place. Minding the circle is a confident but socially awkward young woman named Sandyse Thunderquill (NG female human **mage**), whom the Harpers are training to infiltrate the Arcane Brotherhood. Stairs lead from the attic down to a study, where Sandyse surrounds herself with lit candles and piles of open books.

## WATERDEEP CIRCLE

The Waterdeep circle is located inside a raised crypt in Waterdeep's walled cemetery, the City of the Dead. The crypt has two levels, and the name MYRNA is inscribed above its entrance (which is sealed with an *arcane lock* spell). The topmost level is the crypt itself, which contains a stone sarcophagus watched over by a **shield guardian** that is trained to lift the lid whenever someone speaks the name Myrna aloud. The sarcophagus contains a stone staircase leading down to a magically lit room. The circle is on the floor of this chamber, which also includes a small study alcove and a cot for its attending mage, a pale wisp of a girl named Thestryl Mellardin (LG female human **mage**). She wears the shield guardian's control amulet around her neck.

## YARTAR CIRCLE

The Harpers purchased a villa in the heart of Yartar that was about to be torn down. Behind the dilapidated building is a 40-foot-square garden patio enclosed by an 8-foot-high wall of ivy-covered stone. A *hallucinatory terrain* spell conceals not only the *teleportation circle* inscribed in the middle of the patio but also the broken benches, weed-infested flowerbeds, and shattered statuary that surround the circle. While the *hallucinatory terrain* spell is in effect, the garden looks as it did in its heyday, with statues of frolicking dryads and satyrs situated among the flowers and stone benches. A cantankerous old Harper named Kolbaz (NG male human **mage**) dwells in the villa and renews the *hallucinatory terrain* spell every day at highsun (he has that spell prepared instead of *ice storm*). He uses his cantrips to frighten away squatters and other unwanted intruders.

# HARSHNAG

This encounter can occur anywhere in the North and is designed to lead characters toward chapter 4 of the adventure, "The Chosen Path." After romping around the North for a while, the characters might reach a point where they can't decide where to go next. That's the best time to use this encounter.

Fate brings the characters into contact with Harshnag the Grim, a legendary good-aligned frost giant. In taverns throughout the North, he is known as a monster to some and a hero to others. In Waterdeep, he's remembered as the largest member of Force Grey, a notoriously destructive adventuring company that came to the city's defense on more than one occasion. Believed to be hundreds of years old, Harshnag wanders the wilderness with greataxe in hand, seeking to lay low his evil giant brethren.

Harshnag's history isn't important to this adventure, and he doesn't like to talk about his past. What's important is that he knows that the ordning has been broken, that the storm giants no longer have the power to keep the smaller giants in check, and that King Hekaton has gone missing. He aims to protect the North from the depredations of evil giants while seeking out adventurers who share this goal. By the time the characters meet him, he has already slaughtered a few giants.

Figure 3.1: Harper Teleportation Circles

Harshnag looks like a typical frost giant except that he's clad in plate armor and wears the skull of a white dragon as a helm. His jagged axe also looks quite formidable. He's a giant of few words who prefers to let his actions do his talking. When he does speak outside of combat, he comes across as surprisingly calm and soft-spoken. While swinging his axe in battle, however, he bellows and laughs like a berserker. In the company of small adventurers, he tries not to dominate social situations or make too many decisions for them, because he knows how fragile and inflated their egos can be.

Harshnag knows the North well and has no chance of becoming lost in its wilderness. He's sensitive to the fact that many small folk have a freshly rekindled fear of giants striding into their settlements. As a result, if the characters visit a settlement while Harshnag is with them, he prefers to remain unseen on the outskirts. The exception is Waterdeep; he considers that city his home and has no qualms about entering it, gently brushing aside guards who stand in his way.

Harshnag is a **frost giant**, with the following changes:

- His alignment is chaotic good.
- He has 204 hit points and wears a suit of *+3 plate armor* that resizes to fit its wearer. This armor gives him AC 21.
- He speaks Common and Giant.
- Harshnag has legendary resistance. Once per day, when he fails a saving throw, he can choose to succeed instead.
- He wields *Gurt's greataxe*, which has a long history as well as some cold-related properties (see appendix B). He has a +11 bonus to hit with the axe, which deals 26 (3d12 + 7) slashing damage on a hit, or 39 (5d12 + 7) slashing damage if the target is human.
- His challenge rating is 9 (5,000 XP).

## Harshnag's Idea

Although he has been happy to wander the North, slaughtering his fellow giants at every turn, Harshnag now thinks it might be time to consult with a higher authority. He knows the location of a mountain temple built by his ancient ancestors under the Spine of the World. He calls it the Eye of the All-Father. According to giant legend, the temple contains a divine oracle. Harshnag offers to lead the characters to the temple so that they can consult with this oracle and learn how best to end the giants' threat to the North.

If the characters agree to follow Harshnag, he leads them from their present location to the Valley of Khedrun. From there, he guides them along a snowy path that climbs up the frozen mountains to the temple's entrance (see the "Journey to the Eye" section at the start of chapter 4). Depending on where the characters are when Harshnag meets them, the journey to the temple might be long and perilous; use the Random Wilderness Encounters table to make the trip a memorable one.

## Harshnag in Play

Harshnag tries not to dominate combat if it means making his smaller compatriots feel inferior. He doesn't want to be seen as a showoff. He can reduce his combat effectiveness in the following ways:

- He makes one attack on his turn instead of two.
- He uses the Help action to aid a character's next attack against a foe (see the action's description in chapter 9 of the *Player's Handbook*).
- He does nothing on his turn except taunt an enemy who might otherwise attack a character. Assume the effort is successful and the target switches its attention to Harshnag, unless the character insists on being the target of that threat.

# CHAPTER 4: THE CHOSEN PATH

UIDED BY HARSHNAG THE FROST GIANT, the adventurers travel to the Spine of the World, scaling icy mountains to reach a temple built by the giant lords of Ostoria. Within this complex, they find the Eye of the All-Father, a chamber that the ancient giants used as an oracle. Here, the characters eventually choose a path that leads them to the storm giants of Maelstrom, who hold the key to restoring order among giants.

After receiving direction from the oracle, the characters embark on the next leg of their quest, but a surprise encounter with Iymrith threatens to end their effort before it begins. Realizing that the adventurers are no match for the ancient blue dragon, Harshnag challenges Iymrith, distracting her so that the characters can flee. The temple's stones tremble and fall as the frost giant and the blue dragon clash, trapping them under the mountain while the characters make good their escape.

## JOURNEY TO THE EYE

Harshnag offers to lead the characters to the Eye of the All-Father. He isn't shy about using roads and trails, nor does he blanch at traversing the uncharted wilderness or crossing cold rivers. He expects the characters to keep up but travels at a normal pace so that they don't suffer the effects of exhaustion.

The Eye of the All-Father is hidden under the icy peaks of the Spine of the World and can be reached by way of a mountain pass that starts in the Valley of Khedrun. After two days traversing the desolate valley, Harshnag finds the pass. Characters should be 7th level when they're ready to explore the Eye of the All-Father.

An overland journey to the Eye might include one or more random encounters, at your discretion. See the "Random Wilderness Encounters" section in chapter 3 for more information. Characters are also subject to extreme cold temperatures (see the "Wilderness Survival" section in chapter 5 of the *Dungeon Master's Guide*).

## EYE OF THE ALL-FATHER

The Eye of the All-Father is an underground complex built by giants (see map 4.1), which has survived for tens of thousands of years. The giant lords of Ostoria came here for divine wisdom and also for refuge. Harshnag is one of only a handful of giants who know about the temple. A few ancient dragons—including Iymrith, Claugiyliamatar, and Klauth—also know of its location.

Everything within the dungeon is built to giant scale. Harshnag is familiar with the general features and layout of the complex (except for area 9), but not its traps or current denizens.

### 1. DOMED ENTRANCE

A 40-foot-wide, naturally formed stone causeway leads to the entrance of the Eye of the All-Father. Sheer cliffs plunge hundreds of feet on both sides of the route. The causeway is covered with a foot of snow, in which the characters can see fresh tracks heading toward the mountainside. With a successful DC 15 Wisdom (Survival) check, a character can determine that the tracks are those of eight humans. These tracks were made by the Uthgardt in area 4.

The causeway ends before a stone dome carved from the mountainside. Six 30-foot-tall stone pillars support the dome, which is in no danger of collapse, even if the pillars were to be toppled. Each pillar is carved with a wraparound bas-relief. From north to south, the pillars depict the following scenes:

- A hill giant lifting a rock above its head
- A frost giant chopping down a great pine
- A cloud giant flying among birds in the sky
- A flying storm giant hurling lightning bolts at a ship
- A stone giant climbing a mountain
- A fire giant with chained dwarf prisoners in a cavern

At the back of the dome, a 40-foot-wide, 40-foot-high hallway heads into the mountain. Wind has blown the snow far into the hallway. The snow thins out and disappears after about 100 feet. The tracks of the humans continue east into the dungeon complex.

## 2. STONE BLOCKS

If the characters haven't confronted the Uthgardt in area 4, they hear the Uthgardts' grunts when they reach this point. The tunnel is 40 feet wide, 40 feet tall, and level. Characters who have a passive Wisdom (Perception) score of 14 or higher notice gaps in the ceiling, suggesting the presence of two hanging blocks of stone.

---

### EYE OF THE ALL-FATHER: GENERAL FEATURES

The following features are common throughout the temple.

**Ceilings.** Interiors have 60-foot-high ceilings.

**Doors.** The double doors located throughout the complex are made of granite adorned with bas-reliefs that depict regal giants fighting and slaying dragons. Door hinges and handles are made of wrought iron, and the handles are 12 feet off the floor. A Huge giant has no trouble opening doors that aren't frozen shut. A smaller creature can try to open a door if that creature can reach the door's handle and unlatch it. While the handle is unlatched, a creature must use an action to push or pull on the heavy door, opening it with a successful DC 12 Strength (Athletics) check. See area 6 for rules on dealing with giant doors that are frozen shut.

**Frost.** Frost covers the floors, walls, ceilings, and furnishings everywhere except for area 7. The frost makes climbing the walls impossible without climbing gear or magic.

**Illumination.** Interior areas are unlit except for areas 6, 7, and 11 (see those areas for details).

**Oversized Furnishings and Objects.** The furnishings and other items in the temple are sized for Huge giants. Exceptions are noted in the text. Tables, benches, and other room fixtures are typically three times as high as their human-sized equivalents and roughly twenty-seven times the weight. Small and Medium creatures can scuttle under and clamber over giant-sized furniture, treating them as difficult terrain.

**Stairs.** Staircases within the temple are sized for giants. Each step is 5 feet tall and 5 feet wide. Creatures of Large size and smaller treat the staircases as difficult terrain.

---

Characters who search for traps and succeed on a DC 14 Wisdom (Perception) check also notice these blocks, which constitute the temple's outer defenses.

Each block is a 40-foot-tall, 40-foot-wide, 20-foot-thick slab held up by mechanisms buried in the mountainside. When the lever in area 2A is moved to the down position, the block of stone closer to the entrance (area 1) falls, sealing off the tunnel. When the lever in area 2B is moved to the down position, the inner block does the same thing. Each block takes about 6 seconds to drop to the floor, allowing time for creatures to get out of the way. Any creature that doesn't get out of the way takes 132 (24d10) bludgeoning damage and is knocked prone and pinned underneath the block, or crushed to a pulp if the damage reduces its hit points to 0. A creature pinned under a block is restrained until the block is lifted (by raising the appropriate lever). *Knock* spells and similar magic have no effect on these gigantic barricades.

### 2A. NORTHWEST GUARD ROOM

This 60-foot-square room is featureless except for a large iron lever in the south wall. The lever is 12 feet off the ground and frozen in the up position. Pulling it down requires a successful DC 24 Strength (Athletics) check. Medium and smaller creatures have disadvantage on the check because they can't put much weight behind their efforts, although they can offset the disadvantage by helping one another (using the Help action). Using a torch or other open flame to thaw the ice around the lever (which takes at least 1 minute) reduces the DC to 20.

Moving the lever down causes the outer block of stone in area 2 to lower, sealing off the temple entrance.

### 2B. SOUTHWEST GUARD ROOM

This room is like area 2A, but the lever is in the north wall and controls the inner block of stone in area 2.

## 3. BOULDERFALL HALL

The ceiling in this hall is 60 feet high, sloping down to 40 feet as it moves toward area 2. Although the ceiling remains level heading eastward, its distance from the floor decreases to 40 feet on the landing in front of area 4 because of the staircase leading up to that location.

Overlooking the hall to the north and south are unguarded 20-foot-high ledges that have no railings or battlements. Giants once stood atop these ledges, ready to hurl rocks at interlopers that passed below.

Five niches are carved into the back wall of each ledge. Each one holds an iron sconce that radiates a faint aura of conjuration magic under the scrutiny of a *detect magic* spell. Touching a sconce with an open flame causes a spectral fire to materialize above the sconce. This flame sheds light and heat like a normal torch, and it burns until smothered. If a sconce is taken from its niche, it loses its magic forever. Lighting a sconce in this hall alerts the berserkers in area 4, who investigate.

### UTHGARRDTS AT THE GATE

As the characters cross this hall from west to east, they see the flickering light of a single torch and can hear human grunts and groans ahead. Characters carrying

# Eye of the All-Father

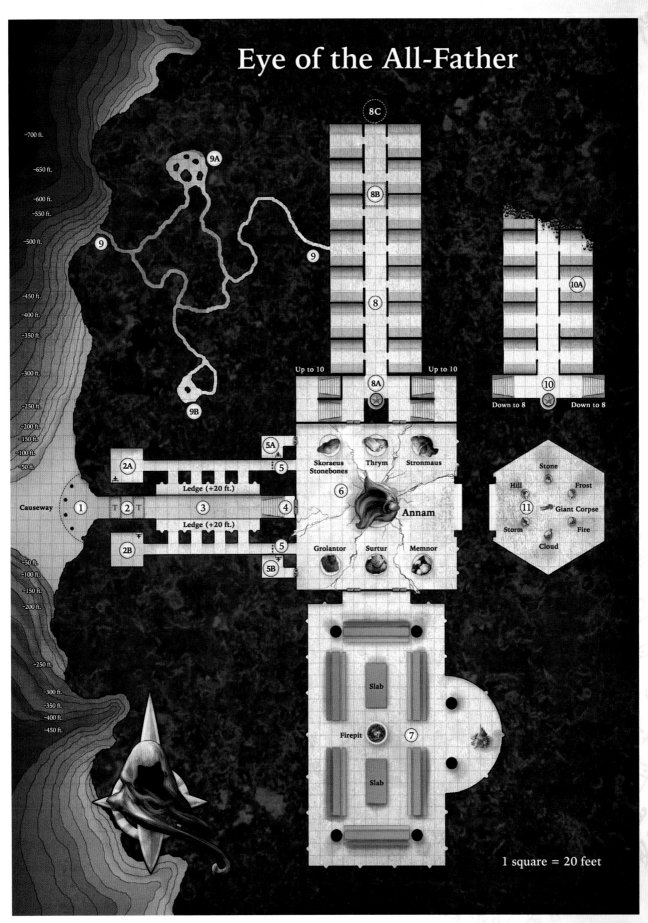

Map 4.1: Eye of the All-Father

light sources can't surprise the Uthgardt in area 4. If the party advances quietly without light sources, the characters can surprise the Uthgardt with a successful group DC 14 Dexterity (Stealth) check.

## 4. GIANT DOORS

A 40-foot-long flight of steps leading east ascends 20 feet to a landing, next to which stands a pair of 30-foot-tall granite doors carved with images of giant gods locked in battle with dragons. The doors are impervious to all types of damage and coated with ice on the inside. Any Huge or larger creature with a Strength of 23 or higher can throw its weight against the doors and force them open. If Harshnag is with the party, he does exactly that if given the chance. Smaller creatures can't open the doors until the ice on the other side is chipped away or melted (see area 6). *Knock* spells and similar magic are likewise ineffective until the ice is removed.

Pushing on the doors are six **berserkers** (CE male and female Uthgardt humans) of the Great Worm tribe. Overseeing them is Wormblod, a bloodthirsty **berserker** (CE male Uthgardt human with 90 hit points) who is also the Great Chief of the Great Worm tribe. He keeps a **white dragon wyrmling** for a pet and a female **Uthgardt shaman** (see appendix C) of the Great Worm tribe as an advisor. She carries a lit torch in one hand and has a sacred bundle slung over her back.

Wormblod and his warriors have come to the Eye of the All-Father to find a missing member of their tribe (see area 9A). The chieftain is secretly hoping to use this opportunity as an excuse to plunder the temple of its treasures, but his berserkers have been unable to get through these doors. The Uthgardt and their leader are hostile toward anyone who isn't a member of their tribe, and they fight to the death. This is true even if the characters open the doors or offer to do so.

### TREASURE

Wormblod wears an *amulet of proof against detection and location*. Tied to his belt is a sack containing seven 100 gp gemstones.

### DEVELOPMENT

If the characters kill Wormblod, they can use his severed head or one of his possessions (such as his magic amulet or his greataxe) to affect future dealings with the Great Worm tribe. Other Great Worm tribe members are horrified to learn that their chieftain is dead. Until a new great chief is chosen, they either flee from the characters or allow them to pass through their territory unmolested. They will even allow the characters to take the giant relic from their spirit mound. Killing Wormblod also allows the characters to gain a supernatural gift from the couatl in Great Worm Cavern (see the "Great Worm Cavern" section in chapter 3 for details).

## 5. PORTCULLISES

A heavy iron portcullis 20 feet wide by 30 feet tall, with a 30-foot-high wall above it, blocks this 60-foot-high passage. The portcullis can be lifted with a successful DC 25 Strength (Athletics) check. It can also be raised with a *knock* spell or by moving an iron lever hidden in one

of two secret rooms (area 5A or 5B, whichever is closer). The bars of the portcullis are ice cold to the touch and spaced far enough apart that a Small creature can squeeze between them.

### 5A. NORTHEAST GUARD ROOM

This square room is hidden behind a secret door (see area 6 for details) and featureless except for an iron lever set into the south wall. The lever is 12 feet off the ground and frozen in the down position. Pushing it up requires a successful DC 24 Strength (Athletics) check. Medium and smaller creatures have disadvantage on the check because they can't put much weight behind the effort, although they can offset the disadvantage by helping one another (using the Help action). Using a torch or other open flame to thaw the ice around the lever (which takes at least 1 minute) reduces the DC to 20.

Moving the lever to the up position causes the portcullis in area 5 to rise into the ceiling, leaving an open doorway 30 feet high. Pushing the lever down causes the portcullis to lower back into place. It takes about 6 seconds to fall, allowing creatures underneath it time to get away. If a creature is unable to move out of the way, it is knocked prone and restrained under the portcullis.

### 5B. SOUTHEAST GUARD ROOM

This room is similar to area 5A, except that the lever is located in the north wall.

## 6. ANNAM'S TEMPLE

When the characters enter or peer into this temple, read:

> Thick frost clings to every surface of this 100-foot-high vaulted chamber. Seven enormous statues dominate the room. The largest of them is an 80-foot-tall robed giant, his arms outstretched and his face hidden beneath a stony cowl, facing a glowing archway in the east wall. Kneeling in rows to each side of this statue are six statues half its size, each impressive in its own right and depicting a paragon of a type of giant: hill, stone, frost, fire, cloud, and storm. These smaller statues face the bigger one in the room's center. In their outstretched arms, five of the giants hold weapons—gifts for their All-Father. Only the frost giant statue is unarmed.

The archway can be further described as follows:

> The archway is 40 feet wide and 40 feet tall. Six different runes are carved into it, each one inlaid with mithral, and a glowing mist fills the arch. Niches in the walls on either side of it contain empty, ice-covered sconces made of iron.

The double doors that lead to this chamber are 30 feet tall and open into the room. The double doors leading to areas 4 and 7 are covered with a 4-inch-thick layer of ice that must be chipped away or melted before the doors

## Giant Statues and Their Weapons

| Son of Annam | God of ... | Weapon | Weight | Matching Rune |
|---|---|---|---|---|
| Grolantor | Hill giants | Bone greatclub | 500 lb. | Haug |
| Skoraeus Stonebones | Stone giants | Stone boulder | 750 lb. | Stein |
| Thrym | Frost giants | Steel greataxe (missing) | 750 lb. | Ise |
| Surtur | Fire giants | Iron greatsword | 800 lb. | Ild |
| Memnor | Cloud giants | Mithral spear | 600 lb. | Skye |
| Stronmaus | Storm giants | Adamantine trident | 800 lb. | Uvar |

can be pulled open from this side (either physically or with the aid of knock spells or a chime of opening). A *fireball* spell produces enough heat to melt the ice on one set of doors. Otherwise, it takes a character using a weapon, a pick, or a similar tool 1 hour to chip away the ice covering one set of doors, or 1 hour to melt the ice with a torch. Multiple characters working together to remove the ice shorten the time proportionately.

Characters who search the temple for secret doors and succeed on a DC 20 Wisdom (Perception) check find two secret doors behind the frost that covers the west wall. These slabs of stone are 40 feet tall by 20 feet wide, and each pushes open to reveal a chamber beyond (area 5A or 5B). Each secret door requires a successful DC 20 Strength (Athletics) check to open or close.

The iron sconces are bolted to their niches and radiate faint auras of conjuration magic under the scrutiny of a *detect magic* spell. Touching a sconce with an open flame causes a spectral fire to appear above the sconce. This flame sheds light and heat like a normal torch, and it burns until smothered. If a sconce is taken from its niche, it loses its magic forever.

### Statues

The big statue in the middle of the temple depicts Annam the All-Father. The statue's face is a mask of bare rock, bereft of facial features. The giants who carved the statue had no clue what Annam looked like, and they dared not misrepresent him.

The six smaller statues depict the sons of Annam, who are listed in the table Giant Statues and Their Weapons. Five of these statues grasp giant-sized weapons that can be removed. Thrym's weapon is missing and can be found in area 7. Removing any of these weapons from the dungeon causes it to vanish and reappear in the appropriate statue's grasp. If the statue is destroyed, the weapon has nowhere to return to and disappears. The table shows which statue holds which weapon, as well as the weight of each weapon and the archway rune associated with each weapon (see "Archway and Runes").

Each statue has AC 20, a damage threshold of 10, and immunity to poison and psychic damage. The statue of Annam has 750 hit points; the others have 250 hit points each. Dealing 50 damage or more to the statue of Annam desecrates it and triggers a ceiling collapse, as described in the "Encounter with Iymrith" section later in this chapter.

### Archway and Runes

Six mithral-inlaid runes empower the archway. Prying out the mithral or defacing the runes causes the archway's mist to fade away and renders the archway

inoperable. The runes are arranged in an arc around the opening, as shown in figure 4.1.

The six runes include a haug (hill) rune, a stein (stone) rune, an ise (frost) rune, an ild (fire) rune, a skye (cloud) rune, and an uvar (storm) rune. The characters have to figure out which rune is which through trial and error, or with the aid of magic such as the *divination* spell. A character who has proficiency in the Arcana skill can tell that the runes are magical, but not what the runes mean. Harshnag is familiar with the ise rune and can identify it; the other runes are unknown to him. Iymrith, Klauth, Claugiyliamatar, and most other ancient dragons know all of these runes by name and appearance.

The mist in the archway dimly illuminates the temple. A *detect magic* spell reveals an aura of conjuration magic around the archway, but nothing happens when something enters the mist While the archway is inactive, cold rock wall can be felt beyond the churning mist.

The archway is a portal that connects the temple to the divine oracle (area 11), allowing instantaneous two-way travel once it is activated. To activate the portal, a giant of the hill, stone, frost, fire, cloud, or storm variety (or a creature polymorphed into one of these forms) must take a weapon from one of the statues of the six lesser giant gods and touch it to the appropriate rune on the archway. The wielder must use the weapon belonging to the god that corresponds to the wielder's physical form; for example, Harshnag (a frost giant) can activate the portal only by using Thrym's steel greataxe, and only by touching it to the ise (frost) rune. As soon as the archway activates, the weapon vanishes and reappears in the

FIGURE 4.1: ARCHWAY RUNES

## RUNE TRAPS

| Rune | Giant Type | Spell Effect |
|------|-----------|--------------|
| Haug | Hill | Multiple *confusion* spells activate (save DC 15), such that each creature in the room is targeted once. |
| Stein | Stone | Four *conjure elemental* spells activate, causing four **earth elementals** to rise up from the floor—one in each quadrant of the room. They attack any other creatures they detect, but can't leave the temple's confines. They disappear when destroyed or after 1 hour. |
| Ise | Frost | Every creature in the room is within the area of one *ice storm* spell (save DC 15). |
| Ild | Fire | A *meteor swarm* spell activates. Every creature in the room is subject to the spell's effect (save DC 15). |
| Skye | Cloud | A *reverse gravity* spell activates (save DC 15), affecting the entire room. Creatures and objects that aren't anchored fall upward. The spell remains in effect for 1 minute, after which time creatures and objects on the ceiling fall back down to the floor. The giant statues and their weapons are considered anchored. |
| Uvar | Storm | A *storm of vengeance* spell activates, affecting the entire room (save DC 15). No other area is affected. The storm lasts for 10 rounds. |

hands of the statue it came from, unless that statue has been destroyed, in which case the weapon disappears.

Touching a rune with the wrong weapon triggers a spell effect, as described in the Rune Traps table. The effect also occurs when a non-giant touches a rune.

When the portal activates, the glowing mist transforms into churning thunderclouds lit by flashing but harmless lightning, and creatures can see another room (area 11) beyond the clouds. The sound of rolling thunder fills the temple, loud enough to be heard throughout the complex. Any creature that steps into the archway appears in area 11. The archway remains active for 1 hour. Any creature still in area 11 when the archway becomes inactive again is trapped there unless it has some means of escape (such as a *teleport* spell). If the portal closes, it can be reopened from the temple side.

### DEVELOPMENT

Iymrith the blue dragon arrives at the temple just as the characters return from the divine oracle after choosing which giant lord they intend to fight (see area 11). See the "Encounter with Iymrith" section later in this chapter for more information.

## 7. FEAST HALL

The double doors that lead to this room are coated with ice and can't be pulled open until the ice is chipped away or melted (see area 6 for details). The room is 240 feet wide by 440 feet deep, with a 200-foot-wide alcove in the center of the east wall. Six pillars, each 20 feet in diameter and 60 feet tall, support the vaulted ceiling. The walls are lined with niches and sconces identical to the ones in areas 3 and 6.

A hungry **remorhaz** is curled up in the alcove until one or more party members enter the room, at which point it uncoils and rushes forward to attack.

The room is warm, dry, and brightly lit. The source of the light and the heat is a raging fire contained within a bowl-shaped basin in the center of the chamber. Natural gas escaping through holes in the basin feeds the fire, sustaining it indefinitely. Any creature that enters the fire or starts its turn there takes 10 (3d6) fire damage.

Arranged about the fire pit are six tables carved out of granite, with matching benches, and two 9-foot-tall stone slabs stained with blood and grease. Atop the southernmost slab are neat stacks of plates and goblets made of beaten copper, all green and black with age.

The stacks of plates and goblets on the northernmost slab have been knocked over, creating a mess.

### THRYM'S AXE

Leaning against the southernmost slab is a 750-pound steel greataxe sized for a frost giant. An absentminded giant removed it from the temple (area 6) and left it here. Like the other weapons in area 6, it can be used to activate the portal leading to the divine oracle (area 11).

## 8. TRAPPED HALL

This part of the temple contains quarters where visiting giants used to rest, with two sets of stairs leading to an upper level (area 10).

A 60-foot-high hall stretches northward. The hall is inclined at a slight angle, so that the floor in the north end of the hall is higher than in the south end. The slope isn't so great that the frost on the floor presents a hazard. Fourteen 30-foot-tall archways spaced along the west and east walls lead to 60-foot-square chambers furnished with frost-covered stone couches that serve as beds. Some of these beds have tattered furs atop them. A fissure in the back wall of the center room on the west side leads to a network of natural tunnels (area 9).

This hallway contains a magical trap, and a *detect magic* spell can reveal certain clues, as described in areas 8A and 8B. The trap triggers when one or more creatures that aren't giants enter area 8B, a 40-foot-square section of the hallway. It triggers even if they fly over or move invisibly through that area. Harshnag is unaware of this trap and can't warn the party about it.

When the trap activates, walls of stone (created by *wall of stone* spells) seal off the archways along the west and east walls. When that happens, all creatures in the hallway or the adjacent rooms must roll initiative. On initiative count 15, a 40-foot-diameter sphere of solid granite phases out of the north wall at area 8C and rolls southward down the corridor. It rolls 200 feet on each of its turns until it reaches the end of the hall. The sphere can move through creatures' spaces, and creatures can move through its space, treating it as difficult terrain. Whenever the sphere enters a creature's space or a creature enters its space while it's rolling, that creature must succeed on a DC 12 Dexterity saving throw or take 55 (10d10) bludgeoning damage and be knocked prone. The sphere can't harm creatures above it.

When the sphere reaches the south end of the hallway, the stone giant statue (area 8A) animates and uses its outstretched arms to stop the sphere before it slams into the wall around the alcove. Each round thereafter on initiative count 15, the statue moves 20 feet northward, rolling the sphere ahead of it. The statue and sphere move slowly enough that creatures can easily get out of the way. When the statue reaches the north end of the hallway, it pushes the sphere back into the wall (the sphere melds with the stone as it comes into contact with it). The statue then lumbers back toward its alcove, moving 60 feet on each of its turns. While the giant is out of its alcove, the magic trap is disabled. The trap resets when the statue returns to its alcove. The walls of stone disappear when the trap resets.

## 8A. Stone Giant Statue

Standing in an alcove at the eastern end of the hall is a life-size statue of a stone giant that radiates an aura of transmutation magic under the scrutiny of a *detect magic* spell. Its arms are lifted up with hands outstretched and palms facing the west end of the hall.

The statue is immobile until activated and uses the **stone golem** stat block, with these changes:

- It is Huge and has 195 (17d12 + 85) hit points.
- It knows no languages and ignores communication.
- It lacks the Multiattack, Slam, and Slow actions.
- It has a challenge rating of 0 (0 XP).

## 8B. Magical Trap

A *detect magic* spell reveals conjuration magic filling this 40-foot section of hallway. Successfully casting *dispel magic* (DC 18) on the area disables the trap.

## 8C. Stone Sphere

When it is fully within the wall, this 40-foot-diameter stone sphere is undetectable, even with the aid of magic.

# 9. Ice Spider Tunnels

Harshnag doesn't know about these tunnels and caves, which were formed by earth tremors and aren't part of the dungeon's original construction. In recent years, they have become a haunt for ice spiders. Ice spiders have red eyes and white fur covering their bodies, and they weave liquid webs that crystallize quickly, forming frosty sheets and icy cocoons.

The tunnels are 10-foot-high, 5-foot-wide cracks in the mountain rock (too narrow for Harshnag). Due to the icy and uneven floors, the tunnels are difficult terrain. Creatures that have the Spider Climb trait (or that are under the effect of a *spider climb* spell) can move through the tunnels at a normal pace. A thin layer of frost coats the walls, floor, and ceiling throughout.

The westernmost tunnel branch opens high upon the mountainside. The slope is so steep that a creature falling from this height would tumble almost 400 feet down the mountainside before landing on any sort of ledge. Although there are abundant handholds, the slope is icy and treacherous, requiring a successful DC 15 Strength (Athletics) check to climb without gear. There is no view of the entrance (area 1) from this tunnel exit.

The easternmost tunnel branch opens into the back wall of a giant dormitory (area 8).

***Tunnel Intersections.*** The first time one or more party members reach a tunnel intersection, four ice spiders come crawling out of the darkness and attack. Use the **giant spider** stat block, with these changes:

- Ice spiders have resistance to cold damage.
- While restrained in an ice spider's web, a creature takes 1 cold damage at the start of each of its turns.
- The web lacks immunity to bludgeoning damage.

## 9A. Larder

This natural cave has a 30-foot-high ceiling supported by five rocky columns. The floor is flat and is normal terrain. The cavern is filled with translucent ice spider webs that block line of sight. Characters who succeed on a DC 15 Wisdom (Perception) check can spot a cluster of cocoons on the floor at the back of the cave.

Although they're made of ice, the webs are sticky (like frozen metal). They use the same rules as normal webs (see the "Dungeon Hazards" section in chapter 5 of the *Dungeon Master's Guide*) except that they are brittle and thus lack immunity to bludgeoning damage.

Characters who smash or burn their way through the webs can reach the cocoons, of which there are three. The first one contains the exsanguinated corpse of a mountain goat. The second one holds a dead shield dwarf prospector wearing a tattered fur cloak and clutching a miner's pick close to his chest. The third one contains a living Uthgardt of the Great Worm tribe named Noori, a **berserker** with the following changes:

- Her alignment is chaotic evil.
- She has 0 hit points and is unconscious but stable.
- She has the following skills: Stealth +3, Survival +2.
- She speaks Bothii (the Uthgardt language) and Common.
- She is unarmed, having lost her greataxe. If she obtains a nonmagical weapon, Noori has a +5 bonus to attack rolls made with it and adds her Strength bonus (+3) to the weapon's damage on a hit.

If Noori is revived, she is startled and confused by her surroundings. Like most Uthgardt, she is suspicious of magic and resentful of spellcasters. If the characters killed Wormblod (see area 4) and Noori learns of this, she attacks them with whatever weapon she has in hand, fighting to the death. Otherwise, she remains with the party until an opportunity to escape from the complex and return to Great Worm Cavern presents itself.

If Noori rejoins her tribe, she shares the tale of her ordeal. The characters' act of heroism could affect their dealings with the Great Worm tribe, to the extent that the tribe thinks twice about attacking them. If Wormblod learns of their deed, he gives them his magic amulet as a token of respect, then warns them to leave Great Worm territory or face his wrath. He has no interest in forging an alliance with "civilized folk."

## 9B. Nest

This egg-shaped chamber has a flat floor, which is normal terrain. A single column supports a domed ceiling 20 feet overhead. Curtains of icy webbing stretch from the column to the walls, creating an enclosure that holds an ice spider queen, a **giant spider** with the following changes:

- It has 44 hit points and a challenge rating of 2 (450 XP).
- It has resistance to cold damage.
- Any creature that starts its turn within 5 feet of the queen takes 5 (2d4) cold damage.
- While restrained in the ice spider queen's web, a creature takes 2 (1d4) cold damage at the start of each of its turns. Ice spider webbing doesn't have immunity to bludgeoning damage.

The queen sits atop a cluster of thirty-two ice spider eggs, each one as big as a grapefruit. If the queen dies, the eggs immediately hatch, and the newborn spiders form a **swarm of insects (spiders)** that acts on the queen's initiative count. The swarm has resistance to cold damage. If there are no foes for the swarm to attack, it begins devouring the corpse of its mother.

*Treasure.* Lying next to the ice spider eggs is a frozen *potion of climbing* and a warhammer with a sapphire (worth 1,000 gp) set into the end of its haft. The potion must be thawed before it can be quaffed. It takes 1 minute to thaw the potion over a torch or campfire. A character can forgo the thawing process by breaking the potion flask and eating the potion in ice form.

## 10. Upstairs Quarters

This upstairs hallway is structurally similar to area 8, except that much of it has collapsed, leaving a few rooms to the east and west for the characters to explore. Standing in an alcove at the south end of the hall is a life-size statue of a female cloud giant wearing an angry mask, her arms positioned in a way that suggests she's casting a spell. The statue is inanimate and harmless.

### 10A. Giant Sack

This room contains a pair of sculpted stone couches that double as beds. Frost covers everything.

*Treasure.* Characters who search this room find a stitched leather sack on one of the beds. The sack has been here for months, left behind by an old and forgetful frost giant. It contains 1d4 mundane items determined by rolling on the Items in a Giant's Bag table in the introduction. The sack also contains a *shard of the ise rune* (see appendix B) and three severed, frozen dwarf heads (two male and one female). One of the heads has ten gold teeth (worth 1 gp each).

## 11. Eye of Annam

This room lies deep within the mountain, farther from the temple than the map suggests. The contents of this room—including any creatures within it—are hidden from divination magic. They can't be targeted by such magic or perceived through magical scrying sensors. No doors or passages lead to or from the room. The characters arrive here by way of the teleportation archway in the temple. They can leave the same way, as long as the archway is still active (see area 6). Otherwise, they are stranded here unless they have some way to teleport out.

When the characters pass through the archway, read:

> Beyond the thundering archway lies a hexagonal chamber whose walls rise 50 feet before tapering to a 90-foot-high apex. Standing in each corner of the room is a life-size statue of a giant holding up a heavy, iron lantern with one raised arm. Each type of giant is represented: hill, stone, frost, fire, cloud, and storm. A cold, magical light radiates from each lantern, illuminating a giant corpse lying on the floor beneath a shroud of frost in the middle of the room. The corpse looks like it has been here for some time, preserved by the cold. Next to the body rests a giant, frost-covered morningstar.

This chamber allows communion with a divine proxy of Annam the All-Father. It's called the Eye of Annam because ancient giants thought the chamber enabled them to gain wisdom from him directly. Casting *detect magic* reveals an aura of divination magic in the room.

The corpse belongs to a young cloud giant named Eigeron, whose father, Blagothkus, betrayed and murdered him. If the characters disturb Eigeron's body or come within 10 feet of it, the giant's ghost rises up from the corpse (see "Eigeron's Ghost").

The dead giant wears a golden breastplate (see "Treasure"). His morningstar is nonmagical and made for a Huge creature. Characters close enough to touch the cloud giant's corpse or the morningstar notice a rune-inscribed circle carved into the floor, obscured by frost (see the "Words of the Divine Oracle" section).

The teleportation archway looks much the same as it does when viewed from area 6, except it bears no runes, and it can't be activated from this side. Characters who study the arch and succeed on a DC 17 Intelligence (Arcana) check can sense that the archway will remain open for a short time only, perhaps as long as an hour.

The statues are impressive and harmless. The lights in their lanterns are created by *continual flame* spells.

### Eigeron's Ghost

Like many giants before them, Eigeron and his father, Blagothkus, came to the Eye of Annam seeking wisdom. The divine oracle told them that a great upheaval would upset the balance of power in the world, giving all giants the opportunity to win the respect of their gods and bring glory to their race. The oracle told Blagothkus outright that he could never impress the gods enough to earn their favor, then urged Eigeron to step out from beneath his father's "dark shadow." Blagothkus was overcome with despair and envy. A terrible fight between father and son ensued, in which Blagothkus slew Eigeron. Blagothkus then retired to his castle to mourn.

Eigeron manifests as the spirit of a cloud giant. He wants to know why the characters have come and tries to be helpful. He knows how the oracle works and can explain what the characters must say to contact it (see "Words of the Divine Oracle"). After he gives this information, he asks the characters to avenge his death by killing his evil father, Blagothkus (see "Development").

If the party attacks the ghost, it fights back. Eigeron's spirit is a **ghost**, with the following changes:

- It is neutral good.
- It is Huge and has 65 (10d12) hit points.
- It speaks Common and Giant.
- It lacks the Horrifying Visage action option.
- It can possess Giants as well as Humanoids, though its ability is limited; it can't leave this chamber. If a creature possessed by the ghost is forcibly removed from the Eye of Annam, the ghost is expelled from its host and re-forms in the middle of this room.
- If it is destroyed, it re-forms after 24 hours. To truly destroy the ghost, characters must lay Eigeron's spirit to rest by killing Blagothkus.

### TREASURE

The dead cloud giant wears a *+2 breastplate* that resizes to fit its wearer and has an *opal of the ild rune* (see appendix B) clutched in its frozen right hand. The ghost doesn't object if one of the characters takes the armor or the opal.

### DEVELOPMENT

If the characters want to try to help Eigeron by slaying Blagothkus, they must first learn where Blagothkus is located. They can ask the oracle, but its answer is vague (see "Words of the Divine Oracle"). Neither Harshnag nor Eigeron's spirit knows what "Parnast" is, though characters might surmise that it's a place.

Parnast is a village that appears on few maps, and few folk know of it. Characters who consult with a member of the Surveyors', Map & Chartmakers' Guild in Waterdeep or any learned sage in Everlund or Silverymoon can procure a map for 100 gp that shows Parnast's location. The village lies between the Graypeak Mountains and the Weathercote Forest, near the western edge of the desert of Anauroch. If they travel to Parnast, the characters see Blagothkus's flying castle hovering nearby, its towers casting long shadows over the village.

What happens if the characters decide to pursue Blagothkus is beyond the scope of this adventure. Statistics for the evil cloud giant and detailed plans of his flying castle are provided in the *Tyranny of Dragons* adventure. If the characters are intent on confronting Blagothkus, you can run the final chapter of that adventure, which is an appropriate challenge for a party of 7th-level adventurers. Also see the information about Blagothkus presented in the "Tyranny of Dragons" section in appendix A of this book.

## WORDS OF THE ORACLE

Etched into the floor of area 11 and hidden under a thin layer of frost is a 20-foot-diameter, mithral-inlaid circle inscribed with the kong (king) rune (see appendix E) and the words "Ask Your Question and Know Truth" in Dethek, the Dwarvish script. The kong rune, which is nearly as big as the circle enclosing it, is often associated with Annam the All-Father. Characters spot the circle and the rune as soon as they come within 5 feet of either. Otherwise, the frost must be cleared away to reveal the presence of the circle and its rune.

The oracle has 6 charges. Any creature in the circle that asks a question receives a truthful, thundering answer in the Giant tongue (even if the question was asked in another language). Each answer the oracle gives expends 1 charge and causes one of the six lanterns in the room to go out. The oracle regains all expended charges at dawn, whereupon the lanterns relight. If a question is asked and the oracle lacks charges, it gives no answer.

The oracle's power is similar to a *divination* spell. If creatures ask different questions simultaneously, the oracle chooses one of them at random to answer.

Answers to several likely questions are presented here, although you can tweak these answers to make them more clear or cryptic, as you see fit.

**Why are the giants threatening the North?** "The ordning between them has been broken."

**Who broke the ordning?** "Annam the All-Father, the greatest of the gods."

**Why did Annam break the ordning?** "To rouse his children from their complacency."

**What must be done to stop the giants?** "Find a magic conch of the storm giant king, Hekaton. Use it to visit Hekaton's court. Root out the evil therein." If the characters already have a *conch of teleportation* in their possession, the oracle says, "Use the conch to visit Hekaton's court. Root out the evil therein."

**Where is the conch?** "In the clutches of a giant lord." If the oracle is asked for the name of the giant, it gives a special quest (see "Quest for the Giant Relics").

**What do the evil giants want?** "Power, glory, and the favor of their gods, so that when the ordning is remade, they are elevated to the top."

**What is Guh's plan?** "To become the biggest giant the world has ever seen."

**What is Kayalithica's plan?** "To obliterate the works of the surface-worlders."

**What is Storvald's plan?** "To bring about the Age of Everlasting Ice."

**What is Zalto's plan?** "To rebuild a dragon-slaying colossus."

**What is Sansuri's plan?** "To find a lost trove of dragon magic."

**Where is [giant lord's name]?** The oracle answers with a special quest (see "Quest for the Giant Relics").

**Where is Blagothkus?** "His shadow falls on Parnast."

**Can Klauth be trusted?** "No ancient dragon can be trusted, especially not him."

**What's up with the storm giants?** "The storm giant court is in chaos following the disappearance of King Hekaton."

**Where is King Hekaton?** "Unknown." (The storm giant king is being held in a place impervious to divination magic; see chapter 11, "Caught in the Tentacles.")

**How can we find Hekaton?** "Speak to Serissa, his youngest daughter. She has a clue to her father's whereabouts, and she needs your help."

**Who rules in Hekaton's stead?** "His daughter, Serissa."

**What befell Hekaton?** "He was misled by his eldest daughters, Mirran and Nym, who covet his throne."

**Are Mirran and Nym acting alone?** "No. They are pawns of a much greater evil named Iymrith—a blue dragon in the guise of a storm giant."

**Where is Iymrith now?** "Maelstrom." (The oracle's answer changes to "Nearby" if Iymrith has left Maelstrom to consult with the oracle; see the "Encounter with Iymrith" section later in this chapter.)

**How do we reach Maelstrom?** "King Hekaton's conch will take you there. The path you choose here will lead you to it." If the characters already have a *conch of teleportation* in their possession, the oracle says, "Use the conch to visit Hekaton's court."

## QUEST FOR THE GIANT RELICS

The first time Harshnag or a party member asks the oracle to divulge the location of Hekaton's conch or of any of the evil giant lords, the oracle replies as follows:

> "First, you must prove yourself! When human warriors came to these lands, they fought our kind and stole our relics, burying them in the ground. The humans built altars to Uthgar, their god-king, atop these relics and surrounded their altars with burial mounds. Go to these mounds, retrieve one or more of our lost relics, and bring them here as tribute. Do this, and your path will be made clear. There are many paths you can take. The more relics you deliver, the more paths you will have to choose from. Several evil giant lords stand ready to oppose you. You can ruin all of their plans by defeating just one of them. Which one that is remains to be seen."

The characters are under no obligation to complete the oracle's quest if they already have a *conch of teleportation* or a means of determining the whereabouts of one.

The Lost Giant Relics table summarizes which relics are buried where, and which enemy the characters can choose to defeat if a certain relic is offered up as tribute to the oracle. The Uthgardt spirit mounds are described in chapter 3, and their locations are marked on the maps of the North in that chapter.

### LOST GIANT RELICS

| Spirit Mound | Relic | Giant Lord |
| --- | --- | --- |
| Beorunna's Well | Cracked horn | Kayalithica |
| Flint Rock | Mithral spear tip | Sansuri |
| Grandfather Tree | Electrum nose-ring | Guh |
| Great Worm Cavern | Broken shield | Storvald |
| Morgur's Mound | Gold-plated tooth | Zalto |
| One Stone | Magic boulder | Kayalithica |
| Raven Rock | Magma ring | Zalto |
| | Bone greatclub | Guh |
| Shining White | Porcelain mask | Sansuri |
| Stone Stand | Frost giant skull | Storvald |

## HEKATON'S CONCHS

King Hekaton crafted magic conch shells and gave them to various giant lords so that they could appear before him at his imperial summons. When he wanted to summon the lords to his stronghold, he would transmit through the conchs the sound of crashing waves. The lords would then be expected to use the teleportation power of their conchs to travel to Maelstrom. Each lord that appears in this adventure has a *conch of teleportation* (see appendix B). The characters need only one of them to reach Maelstrom.

## HARSHNAG'S MAP

Harshnag knows the names and locations of all nine spirit mounds. He can take an hour to draw a crude map that shows where the spirit mounds are located relative to key landmarks and terrain features. He doesn't know what relics are buried at each mound or which giant lord is associated with each relic. If the characters take Harshnag's map, give the players a copy of map 4.2 for reference.

Harshnag declines to accompany the characters on their quest to retrieve the giant relics, opting instead to wait for them in Annam's temple (area 6) and guard the portal. Before the characters leave, he cautions them that defiling the Uthgardt spirit mounds will likely bring the party into conflict with one or more Uthgardt tribes.

## RETURNING WITH THE RELICS

To offer a relic as tribute, it must be placed inside the mithral circle on the floor of the oracle chamber. Eigeron's ghost knows this, and Harshnag can figure it out if the characters are stumped. When this is done, the relic disappears forever. As a relic disappears, the oracle says in a booming voice, "You have done a great deed for all giants! A new path lies before you!" For each relic that the characters offer as tribute, a stony bas-relief depicting the giant lord associated with that relic (see the Lost Giant Relics table) protrudes from one of the chamber's five bare walls. For example, if the characters offer up the cracked horn found under the altar at Beorunna's Well and the mithral spear tip found under the altar at Flint Rock, bas-reliefs of Thane Kayalithica and Countess Sansuri appear, leaving three walls bare. The giant bas-reliefs remain until one or more characters stand inside the mithral circle in the middle of area 11 and declare which giant lord they want to face. The majority vote wins. If the characters make no such declaration before leaving the oracle chamber, the bas-reliefs disappear and reappear when one or more characters return. After making their choice, characters in the oracle chamber gain the magical ability to know the shortest, most direct physical route to the lair of the chosen giant lord. This ability lasts until they reach their destination.

If the characters have a *conch of teleportation* in their possession, no bas-reliefs form when they pay tribute to the oracle. Upon receiving one or more giant relics, the oracle says, in Giant, "Your path is clear. Use the conch to reach the court of King Hekaton!"

## THE CHOSEN FOE

The oracle utters something based on the chosen foe:

## CHIEF GUH

"Travel south over tree, hill, and vale. Let the great river be your guide. There, on one of its eastern arms, you'll find Grudd Haug—the den of the hill giant chief. The conch you seek is close to her."

"The great river" refers to the Dessarin River. The hill giant den lies along one of its eastern tributaries. When the characters are ready to head there, continue with chapter 5, "Den of the Hill Giants."

## THANE KAYALITHICA

"Travel southeast, o'er lands high and low. Cross the great forest to the gray peaks, and search for Deadstone Cleft, canyon of the stone giant thane. The conch you seek is in her possession."

"The great forest" refers to the High Forest, "the gray peaks" to the Graypeak Mountains. When the characters are ready to head there, continue with chapter 6, "Canyon of the Stone Giants."

## JARL STORVALD

"Travel west, o'er mountains, to the Sea of Moving Ice. There, among the glaciers, you'll find Svardborg—the berg of the frost giant jarl. The conch you seek rests on his icy throne."

When the characters are ready to head there, continue with chapter 7, "Berg of the Frost Giants."

## DUKE ZALTO

"Travel east, o'er mountains and snow, to distant spires. There, on a cold mountainside, you'll find a village of yak-folk and below that, Ironslag—the forge of the fire giant duke. The conch you seek is in his quarters."

"Distant spires" refers to the Ice Spires mountain range. When the characters are ready to head there, continue with chapter 8, "Forge of the Fire Giants."

## COUNTESS SANSURI

"Travel southeast to the untamed moors, and look to the sky for Lyn Armaal—the castle of the cloud giant countess. The conch you seek is in a secret chest. Search the highest spire!"

Sansuri's castle currently floats above the Evermoors. When the characters are ready to head there, continue with chapter 9, "Castle of the Cloud Giants."

MAP 4.2: HARSHNAG'S MAP

# AIRSHIP OF A CULT

This encounter introduces the characters to an unlikely band of allies and occurs as the party leaves the Eye of the All-Father in search of Uthgardt spirit mounds to plunder (see the "Quest for the Giant Relics" section).

Klauth, one of the largest and most terrifying red dragons in Faerûn, has been scrying on the giants. It amuses him to watch his old enemies fumble about at the whims of their gods. "Old Snarl" knows that the civilizations of the North won't abide the giants' depredations for long. The dragon fully expects adventurers to mobilize and take the fight to the giant lords. Not surprisingly, Klauth has been keeping an eye on Harshnag and, more recently, the player characters.

Klauth has brought members of the Cult of the Dragon to his vale. (For more information on Klauth's lair, see the "Klauthen Vale" entry in chapter 3.) The cultists are in awe of the great dragon and follow his orders without question. On this occasion, Klauth has ordered the cultists to deliver a special gift to the characters: an airship to help expedite their travels.

## NEED A LIFT?

The dragon cultists' airship flies from Klauthen Vale to the Eye of the All-Father, arriving just as the characters emerge from the giant temple. Read or paraphrase the following text to the players when the airship appears.

> A strange vehicle hangs in the sky overhead, slowly drift-ing closer. It looks like a small ship with sleigh runners, held aloft by a giant red balloon.

The airship drops two 50-foot-long rope ladders over the sides of the ship so that the characters can climb aboard without the vehicle landing. Characters can fly up to the ship if they have the means to do so. If they decline to board the vessel, the crew signals for them to come aboard. If they still decline, the airship lands so that the dragon cultists can reveal who sent them and why.

The ship's crew consists of eight members of the Cult of the Dragon (NE male and female human **cultists**), all wearing black leather armor and black leather masks. The cultists are a humorless but resolute bunch. Their names are Delsephine, Nyzroth, Brassik, Laz, Oriskus, Perella, Tralt, and Zalthia. Delsephine is their leader. Four are on duty at any time (two to crew the ship and two standing watch) while the others rest. A party member who observes one or more cultists operating the airship for an entire day can, with a successful DC 15 Intelligence check, learn enough about the ship's operation to take the place of a cultist on the crew. For their part, the cultists are willing to crew the vessel so that the characters can focus on navigation, as well as loading, aiming, and firing the onboard weapons.

The cultists' orders are to steer the ship as the characters direct and help the characters defend it. They don't assist the characters otherwise and avoid putting themselves in harm's way. Characters can leave the cultists behind if they wish, but the cultists are quick to point out that the characters will find it impossible to operate the ship on their own. Klauth doesn't care what becomes of the cultists once the airship is delivered to the party, nor does he care exactly what the characters do with the airship once it comes into their possession. He does, however, expect the cultists to relay the following message to the characters when the two groups first meet.

> "We come to you on behalf of Klauth, the Great Dragon of the North! Klauth offers you this vessel and our services as a gift, so that you may cross his vast dominion while avoiding the many perils of the land below. War against the giants is inevitable, but the Great Dragon commands you forge ahead and face your destiny! The ordning of the giants is broken, and they are not united. Slay their leaders, and you may yet prevail. If you succeed in quelling the giant threat, Klauth bids you come to his hidden vale, so that he can reward your bravery."

The cultists have never visited the Eye of the All-Father before and know nothing about its layout or its contents. They do know a few things about the ordning, however:

- The ordning dictated the hierarchy of giant society, but the giant gods have apparently dissolved it.
- Before the ordning's dissolution, storm giants were at the top of it, hill giants at the bottom.
- The disappearance of Hekaton, a storm giant king, has prompted a number of other giants to misbehave. These giants' efforts to rise to the top of a new ordning bode ill for the budding empires of the North.

The cultists know the way to Klauthen Vale, but they won't lead the characters there willingly until after King Hekaton is set free. Although the cultists don't know it, Klauth's promise of a reward is disingenuous. If the characters accept his offer and visit him at the appointed time, he attacks them as they enter Klauthen Vale, seeing no further use for them. Old Snarl has no intention of giving the them even one coin from his vast hoard.

## AIRSHIP DESCRIPTION

The airship's enormous balloon is made from dragon hide that has been dyed bright red. Atop the balloon is a crow's nest that is reached by crawling up the ropes on the outside of the balloon. Crawling up the ropes requires a DC 10 Strength (Athletics) or Dexterity (Acrobatics) check. If the check fails, no progress is made; if the check fails by 5 or more, the creature falls.

The balloon is roped to a gondola that has been fitted with steel runners. The airship has a speed of 8 miles per hour while skiing across ice or snow or flying in the air. A strong headwind reduces the ship's speed to 4 mph, while a strong tailwind increases its speed to 12 mph. By changing altitude, the ship can use air currents to move in a particular direction. A propeller aft of the gondola thrusts the ship forward and can also be pivoted. The hull of the gondola is watertight and buoyant in water, and the propeller can push it across water.

The airship can hold up to 1 ton of cargo and requires a crew of two, one to operate the propeller and one to operate the furnace. If the ship has fewer than two crew members on duty, its speed can't be controlled, and it moves in a random direction, carried by the wind, until control is regained or until it collides with something.

The gondola and the balloon are separate targets. The gondola has AC 13, 250 hit points, and a damage threshold of 10. The balloon has AC 11 and 50 hit points. Both have immunity to poison and psychic damage. If the balloon drops to 0 hit points, it bursts, and the ship loses the ability to fly. While the balloon or gondola has at least 1 hit point, it can be repaired. Repairing 1 hit point of damage to either the balloon or the gondola requires 1 day and costs 20 gp. (*Mending* spells can repair superficial damage but can't restore hit points.)

## AIRSHIP LOCATIONS

The following locations are identified on map 4.3.

### 1. FURNACE

In the middle of the upper deck is a 10-foot-tall, cylindrical bronze furnace with a **fire elemental** magically trapped inside it. A narrow hatch in the front of the furnace has a small grill through which the elemental can be seen, and the heat pouring out through the grill helps keep the deck crew warm on cold days and nights. An iron wheel on the starboard side of the furnace opens and closes a bronze valve at the top of the cylinder, which has the effect of increasing or reducing the size of the fire spilling out of the furnace. The more heat that is allowed to fill the balloon, the higher the ship can rise.

Opening the hatch or the valve doesn't release the fire elemental, but destroying the furnace does, as does successfully casting *dispel magic* (DC 19) on it. The furnace has AC 15, 30 hit points, a damage threshold of 10, and immunity to fire, poison, and psychic damage. The fire elemental goes berserk if released, attacking all other creatures it sees. Inside or outside the furnace, it can be banished using a *banishment* spell or similar magic, or trapped inside an *iron flask* or a similar device. If the furnace is destroyed or the elemental released from within it, the air inside the balloon cools, causing the airship to descend at a rate of 10 feet per round.

While the furnace chamber is intact, a fire elemental under the control of another creature can be trapped in the furnace, until it is released as described above. The furnace can contain only one fire elemental at a time.

### 2. HARPOON GUN

A spring-loaded harpoon gun, fashioned from burnished bronze with iron fittings, is bolted to the forward upper deck. It has a 90-degree arc of fire (side to side, as well as up and down). The gun comes with a winch, a 500-foot coil of rope, and ten steel-tipped harpoons. Although it fires harpoons instead of bolts, the gun is considered a ballista (see the "Siege Equipment" section in chapter 8 of the *Dungeon Master's Guide*).

Tying a rope to a harpoon, if desired, takes an action. In addition to dealing 16 (3d10) piercing damage on a hit, a harpoon impales its target. While impaled, the target can't take any action on its turn other than trying to free itself from the harpoon, which requires a successful DC 15 Strength check. If the check succeeds, the target takes 5 (1d10) piercing damage as the harpoon is pulled free and is no longer impaled. If a harpoon is attached to the gun by a rope, a creature impaled on that harpoon can't move farther away from the gun or increase its altitude until it frees itself. A creature within reach of the gun's winch can use its action to reel in a **harpooned** creature, pulling it up to 20 feet closer to the gun.

### 3. Ballista

A wooden ballista is mounted on an iron swivel on the aft castle. It has a 90-degree arc of fire (side to side, and up and down). Behind it rests a crate that holds a dozen bolts. For ballista rules, see the "Siege Equipment" section in chapter 8 of the *Dungeon Master's Guide*.

### 4. Propeller Hatch

A wooden door behind the furnace (area 1) on the upper deck pushes open to reveal stairs leading down to the lower deck. Portholes on the landings look out to port and starboard. The porthole windows are latched shut from the inside, and each porthole is wide enough for a Medium creature to squeeze through.

At the foot of the stairs is a steel hatch bolted shut from the outside, with two horizontal-sliding iron levers in the adjacent wall. One lever is labeled Thrust, the other Direction (in Common). Behind the hatch is a steel-walled compartment that holds a magically bound **air elemental**. The air elemental powers the aft propeller. Moving the Thrust lever to the left opens valves that allow wind from the elemental to spin the propeller. Moving the lever to the right closes the valves, and the propeller stops turning. Moving the Direction lever to the left or right causes the propeller to pivot in that direction, allowing the ship to turn while the propeller is operating. When the Direction lever is centered, the propeller moves the vessel straight ahead. Opening the hatch frees the elemental, whereupon it attacks any creature it sees. Without the air elemental to propel it, the ship can't push itself across ice or snow and, if aloft, it moves in accordance with the prevailing wind.

Any air elemental under the control of another creature can be commanded to enter the compartment. If the compartment's hatch is then closed and locked, the elemental becomes trapped inside.

### 5. Crew Quarters

Each of these cabins has a door that can be bolted shut from the inside, though none of the doors is locked normally. A door can be broken open with a successful DC 13 Strength (Athletics) check. Each cabin contains two hammocks (one above the other), a writing desk, a chair, a footlocker, and a porthole. The portholes' windows are latched shut from the inside, each set in a frame wide enough for a Medium creature to squeeze through.

Each footlocker has a partition that divides its interior space in half, with room on each side for one person's clothing and personal effects. Atop each desk are a sturdy lamp, a dragonchess set, and playing cards.

### 6. Storeroom

This room is packed to the ceiling with crates of rations, barrels of fresh water, and casks of dwarven ale and fine elven wine—enough food to feed ten people for 100 days. Nets secured to iron rings bolted into the walls prevent the containers from moving around.

Klauth plundered these goods from various caravans, and many of the containers bear the names and emblems of their previous owners.

## Airship Travel

The Travel Distances in Miles table shows the distances between the various Uthgardt spirit mounds as the crow flies. Use it to track the party's airship travel, remembering that the vessel's speed is 8 miles per hour, not accounting for strong headwinds or tailwinds (see the "Airship Description" section).

Although the characters have no planned encounters in the air, you can add an encounter whenever it suits you. Roll a d20 and consult the Random Aerial Encounters table. You can also use the Weather table in chapter 5 of the *Dungeon Master's Guide* to determine the prevailing weather conditions. Under clear skies, characters on deck or in the crow's nest spot approaching creatures automatically, giving the crew time to load and aim the ship's weapons before the creatures get close.

A downside of traveling by airship is that the vessel is easily spotted. Characters can't surprise hostile creatures while traveling in the airship unless they are guiding the vessel through thick fog or heavy falling snow.

### Random Aerial Encounters

| d20 | Encounter |
|---|---|
| 1–5 | 2d6 **aarakocra** |
| 6–9 | 1d4 + 1 **manticores** |
| 10–11 | Mounted **storm giant** |
| 12–13 | Mounted Uthgardt |
| 14–17 | Strong winds |
| 18–19 | 1 **young green dragon** |
| 20 | 1 **young silver dragon** |

### Travel Distances in Miles

| From/To | Eye | BW | FR | GT | GW | MM | OS | RR | SS | SW |
|---|---|---|---|---|---|---|---|---|---|---|
| Eye of the All-Father | — | 300 | 260 | 385 | 45 | 190 | 270 | 210 | 390 | 150 |
| Beorunna's Well (BW) | 300 | — | 325 | 260 | 250 | 450 | 60 | 510 | 200 | 300 |
| Flint Rock (FR) | 260 | 325 | — | 200 | 240 | 225 | 260 | 350 | 250 | 110 |
| Grandfather Tree (GT) | 385 | 260 | 200 | — | 350 | 415 | 210 | 530 | 80 | 270 |
| Great Worm Cavern (GW) | 45 | 250 | 240 | 350 | — | 220 | 225 | 250 | 350 | 140 |
| Morgur's Mound (MM) | 190 | 450 | 225 | 415 | 220 | — | 400 | 140 | 460 | 160 |
| One Stone (OS) | 270 | 60 | 260 | 210 | 225 | 400 | — | 475 | 165 | 245 |
| Raven Rock (RR) | 210 | 510 | 350 | 530 | 250 | 140 | 475 | — | 560 | 265 |
| Stone Stand (SS) | 390 | 200 | 250 | 80 | 350 | 460 | 165 | 560 | — | 300 |
| Shining White (SW) | 150 | 300 | 110 | 270 | 140 | 160 | 245 | 265 | 300 | — |

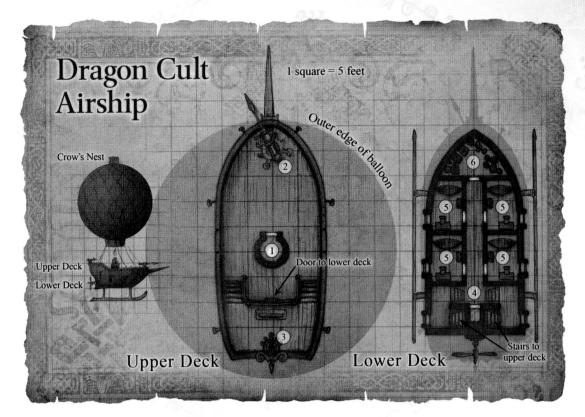

MAP 4.3: DRAGON CULT AIRSHIP

## AARAKOCRA

These intelligent avians fly close to the airship to get a better look. They have had several deadly run-ins with the Cult of the Dragon and recognize the cultists from their attire. If they spot one or more uniformed cultists on the deck of the airship or in the crow's nest, they attack. Otherwise, the aarakocra fight only in self-defense. If at least five aarakocra are present, they try to perform an aerial dance to summon an **air elemental** for assistance. Characters can negotiate a truce with the aarakocra by succeeding on a DC 15 Charisma (Persuasion) check, but only if they refrain from attacking and communicate in a language that the aarakocra understand.

## MANTICORES

A manticore flings its tail spikes at creatures on deck or in the crow's nest. If it sees no one, it flings its tail spikes at the balloon, hoping to bring down the ship.

## MOUNTED STORM GIANT

The characters spot a **storm giant** riding a **roc**. The two are looking for clues to King Hekaton's whereabouts. The giant concludes that the ship contains nothing of interest and steers the roc away, staying at least a quarter of a mile away. The giant has no interest in involving "small folk" in its investigation. It avoids combat and ignores signals from the airship.

## MOUNTED UTHGARDT

Characters on the upper deck or in the crow's nest spot 1d4 + 2 **berserkers** (CE male and female humans) who belong to either the Black Raven tribe or the Griffon tribe of Uthgardt. Each berserker rides a trained giant raven (use the **giant vulture** stat block) or a **griffon**, as appropriate.

The Uthgardt guide their mounts next to the airship, then leap onto the deck and attack all aboard. Riderless mounts withdraw from the battlefield immediately.

## STRONG WINDS

The ship is at the mercy of strong winds for 1d4 hours. At the end of that time, it has been blown off course far enough to add 2d4 × 10 miles to the current journey.

## YOUNG GREEN DRAGON

This dragon wants the airship. It circles the vessel and strafes the deck with its gaseous breath while staying out of melee range, hoping to slay the crew. If reduced to half of its hit points or fewer, it flees. The dragon doesn't give up its prize easily, however. If it withdraws and this encounter occurs again, the same dragon has returned, having regained its hit points and tracked down the ship.

## YOUNG SILVER DRAGON

Dalanyrr, a female silver dragon barely twenty years old, is flitting among the clouds when she spots the airship. Her curiosity piqued, she tries to land on deck and speak to the crew. Though friendly, Dalanyrr has no useful information to impart and has no interest in joining the party. If the characters ask her to perform a task for them, she agrees to do so for payment, provided the task isn't too hard or dangerous. She won't help them plunder Uthgardt spirit mounds or attack giant strongholds, but she can be persuaded to scout ahead or escort the airship for a day or two.

The silver dragon encounter occurs once. If you roll it again, choose a different encounter.

# Encounter with Iymrith

This encounter takes place after the adventurers return to area 6 from area 11, having delivered one or more giant relics and chosen a giant lord to defeat. Iymrith appears as they prepare to exit the temple for the last time.

The blue dragon has come to the Eye of the All-Father to consult with the oracle and learn how far along the giant lords' plots are. She arrives in dragon form and enters the temple through the giant doors (area 4). If the characters have an airship outside, she ignores it and makes her way inside, expecting to run into trouble. If the airship's crew deals damage to her, she destroys the airship's balloon with her breath weapon and casts *ice storm* on the crew. The dragon cultists, if they're still aboard the airship, recognize her and stay out of her way. They know the following information about her:

- Iymrith lives in the desert of Anauroch and is known as the Doom of the Desert.
- The dragon is a spellcaster and a shapechanger.
- She and Klauth know each other, but rarely meet. Her presence in Klauth's domain is provocative.

## The Blue Wyrm

When Iymrith confronts the characters in area 6, read:

> You hear the crunch of frost under heavy feet as an enormous blue dragon bursts through the main doors of the temple. The great wyrm pays no mind to the statues here. Instead, it fixes its hateful gaze on you.

Iymrith is an **ancient blue dragon** (see appendix C). If the characters aren't with Harshnag when she appears, they must confront the dragon by themselves. Her initial assessment of them is that they pose no threat. If they negotiate for safe passage, she lets them leave if they do so immediately. If they antagonize her or deal any damage to her, she tries to kill them, ignoring those who slip away and any who take refuge in the narrow ice spider tunnels (area 9). To reach the Eye of Annam, she assumes the form of a storm giant and uses Stronmaus's trident to activate the temple's portal (see area 6).

If Harshnag is with the party, he attacks the dragon. He hopes to distract her long enough for the characters to escape. Ideally, this scene unfolds in area 6.

## Harshnag's Sacrifice

If Harshnag encounters Iymrith in area 6, he charges the dragon and yells for the characters to flee while he keeps her distracted. If the characters heed the frost giant, they can escape. If they join the battle instead, Iymrith uses her frightful rage. If one or more characters continue to harass her, she focuses her attention on Harshnag while using her legendary actions (specifically her tail attack and wing attack) against the characters.

Harshnag quickly becomes annoyed with the adventurers' refusal to leave. If they linger in area 6 for more than 2 rounds, Harshnag resorts to extreme measures on his next turn to scare them off. Read:

> Seeing his warnings fall on deaf ears, Harshnag swings his greataxe at the statue of Annam the All-Father and chips it. The entire temple shudders. The frost giant scowls, dodges the dragon, and strikes the statue once more, this time breaking off a large chunk. This act of desecration causes cracks to form in the ceiling, and the mountain begins to fall down around you. "Flee!" yells Harshnag. "Your fate lies elsewhere!"

Harshnag's desecration of the statue of Annam dooms the temple. On initiative count 0, each creature in area 6 must make a DC 20 Dexterity saving throw, taking 21 (6d6) bludgeoning damage from falling debris on a failed save, or half as much damage on a successful one.

Harshnag refuses to leave and does his utmost to keep Iymrith from fleeing by attempting to grapple her on later turns. After falling debris deals damage for 2 rounds, the ceiling collapses the next time initiative reaches 0, killing and burying anyone inside the temple.

Iymrith escapes the cave-in with the aid of her *teleport* spell. Harshnag's fate is uncertain. Either he is killed in the collapse, or he manages to retreat to a safe location (such as area 11) at the last possible moment. In either case, the characters are unlikely to encounter him again unless he makes a surprise reappearance (see the "Harshnag Returns!" sidebar in chapter 12).

Whether or not Iymrith's efforts to reach the oracle succeed, the adventurers meet her again at Maelstrom (see chapter 10, "Hold of the Storm Giants").

# Troubleshooting

If all goes according to plan, the characters will visit the Eye of the All-Father twice. During the characters' first visit, the oracle urges them to retrieve one or more giant relics buried under Uthgardt spirit mounds. Harshnag remains at the temple until they return, and Klauth sends them an airship to expedite their travels. During their second visit, the oracle reveals the whereabouts of a giant lord with a *conch of teleportation*. As the characters prepare to leave the temple for the second time, Iymrith appears and triggers an altercation with Harshnag that forces the characters to press on without him.

Things don't always go according to plan, however. The characters might ignore the oracle's quest and take the adventure in a different direction. If they don't return to the Eye of the All-Father, their encounter with Iymrith doesn't occur (and that's okay). If the characters try to persuade Harshnag to stay with them, he politely declines, preferring to walk his own path.

> ## Character Advancement
>
> By the end of this chapter, the characters should know the location of one of five evil giant lords. Continue with chapter 5, 6, 7, 8, or 9, depending on which giant lord they choose. Allow the characters to advance to 8th level before they arrive at the giant lord's stronghold.

# CHAPTER 5: DEN OF THE HILL GIANTS

IN THIS CHAPTER, ADVENTURERS MATCH WITS with Guh, a monstrously fat hill giant chief whose den lies on a branch of the Dessarin River in the hills northeast of Goldenfields. If the characters defeat Guh and obtain her *conch of teleportation*, they can use it to teleport to Maelstrom, King Hekaton's undersea citadel (see chapter 10, "Hold of the Storm Giants"). Obtaining the conch is their main goal here. They must be careful not to put the den on alert before eliminating key threats, lest they become overwhelmed by all of Grudd Haug's denizens.

## HILL GIANTS

Before running this part of the adventure, review the information on hill giants in the *Monster Manual*. It will help you roleplay the giants in this chapter.

## GUH'S GLUTTONY

Chief Guh would like hill giants elevated above their traditional betters. But she's no brighter than a typical hill giant, so her plan is anything but inspired. She plans to eat until she grows so enormous that the gods take notice and show her favor. To her, the biggest giant rules.

Guh's gluttony knows no bounds. She has been feasting for several months and has grown to such a size that she can no longer walk on her own. She spends her time slumped in a wagon with broken axles, surrounded by heaps of stolen loot and crying out for more food.

## THE HUNT FOR FOOD

Chief Guh has driven away all the other female hill giants in her clan and taken their husbands as her own. She tasks her many husbands with bringing her food, and she doesn't care how they go about it. Some of her mates form marauding gangs. Others set out on their own, pillaging the countryside for anything edible.

Farmers who live downriver from Grudd Haug have suffered the most from the giants' depredations. The first inkling of trouble was a sudden drop in the river's water level, caused by the dam-like structure of the hill giant den. Not long thereafter, Guh's husbands and their followers began plundering livestock from riverside farms, stealing trees from orchards, knocking down cottages, and snatching up folk who didn't run fast enough.

So far, most of the hill giants' activities have been confined to the region of the Dessarin Valley closest to their den, but as food becomes scarce, Guh's husbands are forced to expand their efforts outward. The villages of Beliard, Womford, and Uluvin, as well as caravans traveling the Iron Road between Womford and Uluvin, are all within the hill giants' threat radius. Meanwhile, the female hill giants exiled by Guh have taken to the hills. They crave the return of their husbands, but they are neither strong enough nor shrewd enough to unseat Guh. They might be convinced to help adventurers overthrow her if it means they get to beat their husbands into submission once more. See the "Old Tower" section in chapter 3 for an example of a female hill giant outcast.

# GRUDD HAUG

The hill giants' den is called Grudd Haug, which means "river mound" in Giant. Resembling a beaver dam, it straddles a river. The lower level of the den is lodged between two rocky outcroppings and made of piled timber packed with clay and mud, with hollow cavities that resemble caves. Above this piled timber foundation is a mud steading (a house made to giant scale) with a log roof. The structure is an impressive feat of engineering, well beyond the ability of hill giants to fabricate on their own. In fact, Grudd Haug's design is the work of hobgoblin and goblin engineers, assembled with the might of hill giant and ogre laborers. East of the steading is a yard enclosed by a 20-foot-high palisade wall made of logs lashed together with thick twine.

## REACHING GRUDD HAUG

The characters can travel to Grudd Haug (shown on map 5.1) on foot or horseback. They can also guide a raft upstream or downriver to the hill giant den. In either case, you can make the journey more interesting by adding one or more wilderness encounters appropriate for hill terrain (see the Random Wilderness Encounters table in chapter 3). If Moog the hill giant is with the party, see the "Old Tower" section in chapter 3 for tips on how to roleplay her once she arrives at Grudd Haug.

If the characters have an airship (see the "Airship of a Cult" section in chapter 4), they can land it pretty much anywhere outside Grudd Haug. The hobgoblins in the gong tower (see "Approaching the Den") spot the airship if it approaches within 1 mile of the stronghold and sound the alarm, putting the entire den on alert (see "Denizens"). If the characters use the airship's weaponry to attack Grudd Haug, the den's defenders

---

**GRUDD HAUG: GENERAL FEATURES**

The following features are common throughout the hill giant den, which reeks of filth.

**Ceilings.** Unless otherwise noted, interior chambers have 30-foot-high ceilings, with 20-foot-high passages and doorways connecting them.

**Climbing.** Walls of piled timber have many handholds and footholds and can be climbed with a successful DC 10 Strength (Athletics) check. Other sloped and vertical surfaces in Grudd Haug, including mud walls and log roofs, require a successful DC 15 Strength (Athletics) check to climb.

**Curtains.** Hanging in several doorways are curtains of stitched animal hides, held in place with iron spikes. The curtains are thick enough to intercept arrows and crossbow bolts fired through them. A curtain can be pulled down with a successful DC 13 Strength (Athletics) check.

**Illumination.** The gong tower (area 8) and the stockyard (area 9) get plenty of natural light. Oil lamps dimly illuminate rooms and caves that have no windows.

**Oversized Furnishings and Objects.** Most of the furnishings and other items in Grudd Haug are sized for hill giants. Exceptions are noted in the text. Tables, benches, and other room fixtures are typically twice as high, long, and wide as their human-sized equivalents and roughly eight times the weight. Small and Medium creatures can scuttle under and clamber over giant-sized furniture, treating the spaces they occupy as difficult terrain.

---

are smart enough to take cover behind walls. Defenders armed with weapons that deal piercing damage target the balloon; those that hurl rocks and use weapons that deal bludgeoning damage target the crew.

The characters might instead approach on a flying mount. They can obtain griffon mounts in Fireshear or hippogriff mounts in Hawk's Nest. Neither settlement is close to Grudd Haug, requiring the characters and their mounts to rest between flights. Characters mounted on hippogriffs can travel 54 miles per day (three 3-hour flights with 1-hour rests in between). Those mounted on griffons can travel 72 miles in the same amount of time. The hobgoblins in the gong tower (see "Approaching the Den") spot flying mounts that approach within a quarter mile of the stronghold and sound the alarm, putting the entire den on alert (see "Denizens").

## APPROACHING THE DEN

Adventurers can approach Grudd Haug from any direction. Those who come near the den without taking efforts to conceal themselves are spotted by the hobgoblins in the gong tower (area 8), who ring the gong to sound the alarm. Characters stand a better chance of infiltrating the den if they approach cautiously, taking advantage of the terrain and using darkness, fog, camouflage, or magic to conceal their movement. Regardless of how the characters approach the den, have them make a group Dexterity (Stealth) check contested by the hobgoblins' Wisdom (Perception) check. (Roll once for all the hobgoblins in the tower.) If the characters take precautions, give them advantage on their checks. If they take none, impose disadvantage on their checks.

## DENIZENS

The Grudd Haug Roster table summarizes the locations of the den's inhabitants and indicates how those creatures react when intruders are detected.

As soon as trespassers are spotted or combat erupts, the entire den goes on alert. As a consequence, adventurers might find themselves fighting several encounters' worth of creatures at once. Grudd Haug's defenders lack a cohesive defense strategy, but they are many.

If Guh dies, the morale of Grudd Haug's other denizens breaks, and they flee into the wilderness.

All the hill giants in Grudd Haug, with the exception of Guh, are enslaved males. The ogres serve Guh because they are impressed by her size and her determination to rise to the top of the ordning (and, they hope, bring them along with her). The goblinoids have been promised shares of the spoils. The Iceshield orcs haunt the hills and grasslands north of Grudd Haug, near the western edge of the High Forest, and have forged a tenuous alliance with Guh. They are the least loyal of her supporters and don't get along with the goblinoids.

## REINFORCEMENTS

Adventurers can use hit-and-run tactics to weaken Grudd Haug's defenses. Depending on how much time passes between the adventurers' forays, the hill giant den might gain reinforcements from the nearby hills.

## Grudd Haug Roster

| Area | Creature(s) | Notes |
|---|---|---|
| 1 | 1 male **hill giant** | On Guh's command, the giant moves the boulder into the doorway and stands guard outside. |
| 2 | Chief Guh, 5 male **hill giants**, 4 ogres, 6 goblins | Guh doesn't move. The giants and ogres defend her, while the goblins shoot from their ledge. |
| 3 | 4 **wolves** | A wooden gate confines the wolves to their pen. |
| 4 | 5 Iceshield **orcs** | The orcs join their kin in area 9 by way of area 2. |
| 5 | 6 goblins | The goblins retreat to area 14 by way of area 6. |
| 7 | 1 hobgoblin | The hobgoblin investigates loud noises in area 5. Otherwise, it guards the north docks. |
| 8 | 4 hobgoblins | The hobgoblins remain in the tower until intruders reach the den, then head to area 2 by way of area 5. |
| 9 | 10 Iceshield **orcs** | The orcs stay here to guard the animals. |
| 10 | 2 male **hill giants** | One giant moves the boulder outside area 9 to seal off the stockyard, stopping to fight enemies in its path. The other giant bolsters the orcs in area 9. |
| 12 | 1 ettin, 7 bugbears | The ettin and the bugbears remain here. |
| 13 | 2 bugbears | The bugbears stay here until they hear combat in area 12. They then investigate that area. |
| 14 | 1 male **hill giant**, 1 otyugh | The hill giant and otyugh remain here. |
| 16 | 1 hobgoblin, 2 goblins | The hobgoblin climbs the ladders behind the smithy and heads to area 7. The goblins stay here and attempt to hide. |

## Grudd Haug Reinforcements

| d100 | Creature(s) |
|---|---|
| 01–50 | None |
| 51–60 | 1 male **hill giant** carrying a live pig, sheep, goat, cow, pony, or mule |
| 61–70 | 2d4 **bugbears**, each carrying a basket of apples, carrots, or potatoes |
| 71–80 | 1 **hobgoblin warlord** mounted on a **wyvern**, which lands on the rocky outcropping by area 1 |
| 81–90 | 3d6 Iceshield **orcs** and 1 Iceshield **orc war chief**, who travel downriver on two rafts |
| 91–00 | 1d4 + 1 male **hill giants**, each carrying a basket of dead fish, a barrel of pickles, or a block of sugar |

At the end of each hour, roll percentile dice and consult the Grudd Haug Reinforcements table to determine what creatures, if any, appear. Unless otherwise noted, such creatures enter through the stockyard (area 9) and go to the feasting hall (area 2), to pay homage or deliver food to Chief Guh. There is a 25 percent chance that the creatures have 1d4 prisoners (unarmed **commoners**) in tow. If Guh commands the reinforcements to stay, they take up defensive positions in and around the stockyard after confining their prisoners in area 13. Otherwise, they leave by the route they came after 20 minutes or so.

## 1. Main Entrance

A muddy trail leads up to a 40-foot-wide open doorway, parked outside of which is a 30-foot-diameter boulder. North of the boulder is a 60-foot-tall outcropping of rock with a flat, lopped-off peak. This outcropping can be climbed with a successful DC 15 Strength (Athletics) check. Standing in the shadows inside the doorway is Hruk, a male **hill giant** who reeks of dung. A swarm of flies buzzes around him. Hruk carries a sack that contains 1d4 + 1 mundane items, determined by rolling on the Items in a Giant's Bag table in the introduction.

When Guh feels threatened, she yells at Hruk to move the boulder to block the doorway. The boulder, however, is smaller than the doorway. Small and Medium creatures can move around it unimpeded, while a Large creature can squeeze past the boulder with a successful

DC 10 Dexterity (Acrobatics) check. A character can push the boulder 10 feet on flat ground by using an action and succeeding on a DC 22 Strength (Athletics) check. A hill giant can do it without the check.

### Development

Hruk is Moog's mate (see the "Old Tower" section in chapter 3). He longs to be reunited with Moog, but dares not defy the mighty Guh. The orcs in area 4 investigate any disturbance here if they aren't elsewhere.

## 2. Feasting Hall

Chief Guh is found here, along with five male **hill giants**, four **ogres**, and six **goblins**. Oil lamps in iron sconces are mounted to thick wooden pillars that support rafters 30 feet from the floor and the roof, which peaks 65 feet overhead. Protruding from the north, west, and south walls is a 10-foot-wide, 20-foot-high wooden ledge that the goblins use to get around the room. (The ledge was added after several goblins were crushed underfoot by careless hill giants and ogres.) A wooden ladder climbs up to the ledge, and windows a couple of feet above the ledge let shafts of natural light into the hall.

Eight sturdy but battered wooden tables covered with globs of grease, gnawed bones, empty casks, and scraps of food stand near the north and south walls, while empty ale barrels lie around and underneath them. Refuse covers the dried mud floor, in the middle of which are two 20-foot-diameter circular holes topped with crisscrossing wooden beams held in place by mud cement. The beams are far enough apart that a Medium or smaller creature can slip between them without having to squeeze. A horrible stench rises from the holes, accompanied by the squealing of pigs (see area 12).

Chief Guh lies at the west end of the hall, slumped atop a four-wheeled, flatbed wagon that bends and creaks under her great bulk. The wagon's axles are cracked and bowed, its wheels canted inward. Piled around the wagon are bones and other refuse from Guh's recent meals, as well as the treasures she has amassed (see "Treasure"). Guh weighs more than 20,000 pounds. She can't move, so she keeps her great-club close by so that she can bop creatures on the noggin. She is a **hill giant** with the following changes:

- She has 160 hit points and a speed of 0 feet.
- Her Dexterity is 1 (−5), giving her AC 9.
- She speaks Common, Giant, and Goblin, though her vocabulary is limited to monosyllabic words.

An unarmed **goblin**, Snert, is stuck in the folds of Guh's flesh. While stuck, the goblin is restrained and unable to speak, and it has total cover. When Guh drops to 0 hit points, Snert is no longer restrained and tumbles into an unoccupied space next to her, gasping for air. He isn't one of the six goblins guarding the room.

If the characters get this far without raising the alarm and present themselves to Guh, she initially doesn't know what to make of them. Are they servants sent by one of her allies? Are they food? Unless the characters convince Guh that they are more valuable alive than dead, she assumes the latter and orders her mates and minions to beat them to death so that she can feast on their flesh and gnaw on their bones.

If the characters tell Guh a story that explains why they need her *conch of teleportation*, she wiggles uncomfortably but refuses to give up the item, instead ordering her servants to attack. If her underlings are defeated, she trades the conch for her life.

The male hill giants are slumped against the tables and walls, tired from having scoured the countryside for food to bring to Guh. The ogres stand ready to serve meals to Guh as they are brought before her. While the ogres and the giants engage in melee combat, the goblins spread out atop the wooden ledge and pepper intruders with arrows. Meanwhile, the wolves in area 3 begin barking and howling, which puts the rest of the den on alert. If the characters flee, Guh orders her hill giant mates to stay and protect her while any surviving ogres chase after the fleeing characters.

### Guh's Wagon-Throne

Any character who studies Guh's "throne" can, with a successful DC 10 Intelligence check, figure out how to sever a wagon axle with a single hit, causing the wagon bed to fall and spilling Guh onto the floor. Hitting the axle just right requires a successful melee or ranged attack against AC 15 that deals 7 or more damage. Not only does this send Guh tumbling to the floor, but on her next turn she tries to stand up and instead rolls into the nearest pit, breaking through the wooden crossbeams.

She falls 30 feet to the floor of area 12, taking 10 (3d6) bludgeoning damage. She also lands prone and can't get up without assistance. Any creature unfortunate enough to be underneath Guh when she falls must succeed on a DC 10 Dexterity saving throw or take 21 (6d6) bludgeoning damage; the creature is also knocked prone, trapped underneath her, and restrained while trapped in this way. A creature can use an action to attempt a DC 15 Strength (Athletics) check on its turn, pulling itself or another creature out from under Guh on a success.

Once Guh is toppled from her "throne," characters can spot the valuables hidden therein (see "Treasure").

### Treasure

Guh's *conch of teleportation* (see appendix B) is in the wagon, hidden under her bulk, along with 1d4 + 1 magic items. Roll on Magic Item Table F in chapter 7 of the *Dungeon Master's Guide* to determine the first item, and on Table B for any other items. Characters can't see or reach these items until Guh is toppled from her throne.

The rest of Guh's treasure lies amid the refuse of her past meals and consists of 5,600 cp, 2,200 sp, 630 ep, and 150 gp; a wooden rocking horse with silver inlay and blue quartz eyes (worth 25 gp); a small wooden chest containing a disguise kit (worth 25 gp); a wooden coffer containing six vials of holy water (worth 25 gp each); a life-size wooden statue of a grinning halfling smoking a golden pipe (worth 25 gp); a battered hat with five carnelians sewn into it (worth 50 gp each); a gold flute (worth 250 gp); a flowerpot carved from jade with images of green dragons (worth 750 gp); and a wooden puppet theater with gold trim, along with gold-stringed puppets wearing bejeweled costumes (worth 2,500 gp).

### Development

Combat and other loud disturbances in this room can be heard throughout Grudd Haug, putting the entire den on alert; see the Grudd Haug Roster table for notes on how the den's occupants react.

With the conch, the characters might try to escape the den. The surviving denizens of Grudd Haug pursue fleeing characters until they're out of sight.

A character must attune to the conch before its property can be used, and doing so requires a short rest. Instead of fleeing, the characters can barricade themselves inside the den, using heavy furniture or magic to seal off entrances until a character attunes to the conch.

## 3. Wolf Pen

A wooden portcullis bars this room. The portcullis can be lifted with a successful DC 16 Strength (Athletics) check. Small creatures can squeeze between its bars with a successful DC 10 Dexterity (Athletics) check.

The room is empty except for a pair of latched wooden gates in the north wall. Beyond the gates are two wolf pens strewn with gnawed bones. Opening or closing a gate requires an action. Two vicious, hungry **wolves** are locked in each pen. The goblins use them as mounts.

## 4. Guard Room

This room is tucked behind a mud-splattered curtain. Five **orcs** of the Iceshield clan sleep on filthy pallets

# Grudd Haug

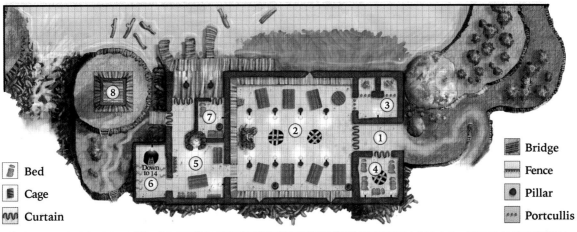

**Bed**

**Cage**

**Curtain**

**Bridge**

**Fence**

**Pillar**

**Portcullis**

Down to 14

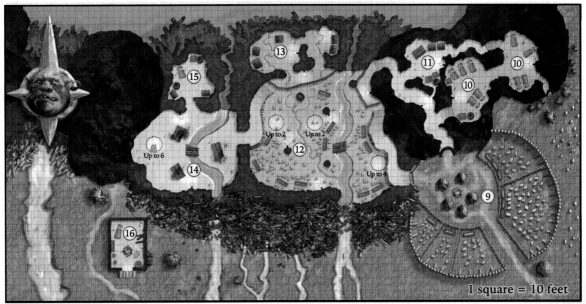

Up to 6

Up to 2

Up to 2

Up to 4

1 square = 10 feet

MAP 5.1: GRUDD HAUG

strewn around a large hole in the floor. They awaken to sounds of combat and calls of alarm, and they head to area 9 if there are no hostile creatures in sight. The hole in the floor is 20 feet in diameter and is topped with crisscrossing wooden beams held in place by mud cement, forming a grate of sorts. The beams are far enough apart that a Medium or smaller creature can slip between them without having to squeeze. A horrible stench rises from the holes, accompanied by the squealing of pigs (see area 12).

The orcs have no treasure.

## 5. KITCHEN

The floor of this filthy kitchen is covered with mud, dirty pots, and leftover food crawling with maggots. In the center of the room, a crackling fire rages in a dome-shaped fireplace. Six **goblins** are tying a halfling to a wooden spit and stoking the fire. They plan to roast the halfling alive and serve it up to Chief Guh. The goblins panic at the sight of interlopers, drop the halfling, and flee to area 14 by way of the larder (area 6).

More dirty pots are piled atop two wooden tables, one of which has a handaxe embedded in one of its legs. Shelves packed with clay dishes and wooden utensils line the walls. A curtained doorway at the end of the north passage leads to the docks. To its left, another curtained doorway leads outside, to the area east area 8.

### DEVELOPMENT

If the characters attack the goblins or otherwise make a lot of noise in this area, the hobgoblin in area 7 investigates. The hobgoblin is accustomed to ignoring the squeals, shouts and arguments of the goblins, so only out-of-place noises draw its attention.

The tied-up entrée is Roderik Hilltopple (LG male strongheart halfling **commoner**), an unarmed shepherd who was captured by a hill giant. Though he's grateful to be rescued, he refuses to leave without taking some sheep for his trouble. He asks his liberators to help him free the sheep in the pens (area 9). If they oblige, Roderik leads the sheep back to his farm thirty miles away.

## 6. LARDER

Hooks protrude from the walls of this room, the floor of which is stained with pools of blood—some dry, others still moist. Hungry flies buzz about.

Beast and Humanoid carcasses are often hung here to dry, though the larder is currently empty. A wooden ladder descends through a 20-foot-diameter hole in the floor, leading down 30 feet to area 14. The rungs of the ladder are spaced 3 feet apart. Small and Medium creatures find the ladder a bit awkward to climb, such that every 3 feet traveled costs an extra 1 foot of movement.

## 7. WATERMASTER

This room faces the docks and contains a bedroll, a barrel of fish, and two crates of rations. A fishing pole leans in the corner near the bedroll.

A male **hobgoblin** calling himself the Watermaster lives here. His job is to catch fish from the river, guard and repair the dam, and guard the den's supply of rations (and keep it out of Guh's hungry hands). He has an inflated sense of his own might and authority, and isn't afraid of facing off against multiple enemies.

### TREASURE

The Watermaster hides his treasure in an unlocked wooden coffer at the bottom of the fish barrel. The coffer contains 80 sp, 45 gp, and a nonmagical platinum ring of elven design worth 100 gp.

## 8. GONG TOWER

Central to the den's defense is this 60-foot-tall log tower perched atop an 80-foot-high bluff overlooking the river. A wooden ladder sized for Medium Humanoids is lashed to the south side of the tower. Hanging from the tower's rafters is a brass gong with a wooden mallet.

Four **hobgoblins** stand guard in the tower, facing north, south, east, and west. They have a fairly unobstructed view of the countryside out to a range of 1 mile, though there are hillocks and trees behind which creatures can hide. If the guards spot any unusual creatures approaching the den, or if they come under attack, one of the hobgoblins strikes the gong. The ringing of the gong is loud enough to put the entire den on alert (see the Grudd Haug Roster table for notes on how the den inhabitants react). The ringing of the gong also causes Chief Guh to bellow, "Lunch time! Me want food!"

### TREASURE

Each hobgoblin carries 1d10 gp in a pouch.

## 9. STOCKYARD

Five tents stand in the middle of this muddy yard, surrounding a campfire. Ten **orcs** of the Iceshield clan are gathered here, five around the fire and another five resting in the tents. The orcs have no treasure. Their job is to watch over the one hundred sheep that are penned in the yard, and they remain here when an alarm sounds. The 4-foot-tall wooden fences that enclose the sheep pens have simple gates built into them. Each pen contains one or more wooden food troughs.

Use the **goat** stat block for the sheep, with these changes:

- It is a Small Beast with 3 (1d6) hit points.
- Its speed is 30 feet.
- It lacks the Charge feature and any effective attacks.
- Its challenge rating is 0 (0 XP).

A palisade of 20-foot-tall sharpened logs encloses the stockyard, except for an opening to the southeast with a giant boulder outside. The boulder, if rolled into place, is just big enough to fill the opening. A character can push the boulder 10 feet across flat ground by using an action and succeeding on a DC 22 Strength (Athletics) check. A hill giant can do it without needing to make the check.

North of the stockyard, a mud trail climbs a ramp and curves back toward area 1. At the bottom of the ramp, at the base of a 60-foot-tall stone bluff, is the entrance of a tunnel that leads north to areas 10 and 11. To the west, a wide opening in the log dam leads to area 12.

## 10. Giants' Caves

Guh's hill giant mates are housed in two adjoining underground chambers on filthy, flea-ridden pallets. The only other furnishings are two empty ale barrels and a half-smashed crate that once contained foodstuffs.

Two **hill giants** sleep here at any given time, snoring loudly. One sleeps in the westernmost chamber, the other in the easternmost chamber. They awaken to the booming thunder of Guh's voice or the ringing of the gong in area 8. They also awaken if attacked. They don't wake up to the sound of other creatures talking in the room or moving about. If awakened by the gong, both hill giants head to area 9. One takes up a position among the orcs while the other seals off the stockyard using the boulder outside the palisade. Enemies who get between the giants and their destinations are attacked.

### Treasure

The caves hold a total of ten sleeping pallets. Each hill giant pallet has a stuffed sack that doubles as a pillow. Each sack contains 3d6 × 100 cp, 2d6 × 100 sp, and 1d6 × 100 gp plus 1d3 mundane items, determined by rolling on the Items in a Giant's Bag table in the introduction.

## 11. Pigkeeper's Den

This cave belongs to the ettin in area 12. It contains a bloodstained wooden table of giant size, two crates of pig entrails, a barrel of filth, and two iron cages, each containing a boar with a hankering for pig entrails. Each cage has a door on one side with a simple bolt latch.

## 12. Pigpen

The walls of this filthy room are made of packed mud with logs jutting out of them. The river seeps through a gash in the north wall and forms a stream that cuts across the eastern half of the area before spilling out through a hole in the south wall, tumbling down logs as it goes. A creaky wooden bridge spans the stream at one point. Smaller rivulets also seep into the room and connect to the wider stream, but they are narrow enough to step over. Timber pillars caked in mud support the 30-foot-high ceiling, which has three circular holes cut into it (leading up to areas 2 and 4). Crisscrossing wooden beams cover these holes, though the beams are far enough apart that a Small or Medium creature can fit through them without having to squeeze.

Two 10-foot-high earthen ramps lead down to the chamber's sunken floor, with fences erected around lower tunnels that lead to areas 11 and 14. Scores of fat pigs snort, waddle about, wallow in the mud, and gorge themselves at wooden troughs overflowing with slop. A pig uses the **boar** stat block, with these changes:

- A pig has AC 10 and 5 (1d8 + 1) hit points.
- Its speed is 30 feet.
- It lacks the Charge and Relentless features, and it has no effective attacks.
- Its challenge rating is 0 (0 XP).

Tending the pigs are seven mud-covered **bugbears** and an **ettin**. The bugbears push the pigs around to make sure the stronger ones don't hoard all the food for themselves. They also shovel pig waste into the stream. The ettin fills the food troughs and fattens up the pigs before they're served to Guh. The ettin chooses which pigs get slaughtered. Doomed pigs are picked up and taken to area 14 to die.

The ettin and the bugbears prefer melee combat to ranged combat. If the bugbears are subjected to ranged attacks, they use the pigs as cover. If the ettin is taking damage and has no enemies to attack, it retreats to its den (area 11) and releases the boars there.

## 13. Prison

In the area north of the pigpen, rivulets of water trickle down the north wall and carve shallow ruts in the floor as they snake their way across the room and through openings in the opposite wall. Five wooden cages are arranged about the room. Their doors are situated on top, with heavy rocks placed on them. A creature can use an action to attempt a DC 15 Strength (Athletics) check to knock off a rock or open a cage door that has a rock pressing down on it. The sound of a rock hitting the cave floor alerts the guards in this area.

Three of the five cages contain prisoners destined for Guh's gullet. Two **bugbears** guard the prisoners. These bugbears can't be surprised once the alarm sounds or if they hear combat in area 12.

### Prisoners

Unless otherwise noted, all the adult prisoners are **commoners**. Child prisoners are unarmed noncombatants.

One cage contains human farmers: a father, a mother, and their three children (a teenage girl and two boys).

A second cage holds an unarmed **tribal warrior** of the Elk tribe, Gryhark (CN male Uthgardt human). He fights alongside his liberators. If he makes it out of Grudd Haug, he bites into the palm of his hand and tries to smear his blood on the faces of those who freed him. Anyone who succeeds on a DC 13 Intelligence (Religion) check realizes that this gesture is a sign of gratitude. Gryhark leaves to return to his tribe whether the characters accept his gratitude or not.

A third cage holds an unarmed prisoner: Emerald Enclave member Ghalvin Dragonmoor (CG male half-elf **scout**). If freed, he asks the characters to escort him to Goldenfields, so that he can report to the Abbot what he has seen.

## 14. Abattoir

Pigs are slaughtered here, as are unwanted trespassers. The river has punched a hole in the north wall, creating a stream that runs through the place. A crude log bridge spans the waterway, which flows out of a gash in the south wall and tumbles down a wall of logs outside. Flies buzz around three blood-spattered wooden tables spaced about the room. A 30-foot-long wooden ladder climbs to a 20-foot-wide hole in the ceiling (leading up to area 6). The rungs of the ladder are spaced 3 feet apart. For Medium and smaller creatures, every 3 feet climbed on it costs 1 extra foot of movement.

Lying atop the easternmost table is the carcass of a slaughtered pig, and looming behind it is Slub, a male **hill giant** covered head to toe in pig's blood and clutching a handaxe. Before fighting, Slub embeds his axe in the tabletop and picks up his greatclub from the floor.

Slub has a pet **otyugh** that follows him around like a faithful dog, eating bones and carrion. The otyugh fights to the death to protect the hill giant.

A tunnel in the north wall leads to area 15.

### Treasure

Slub wears a *gavel of the venn rune* (see appendix B) on a cord around his neck, like a pendant.

## 15. Slub's Den

This damp cave belongs to Slub the hill giant (see area 14). It contains a sleeping pallet, a half-empty barrel of pig snouts, a half-empty barrel of vinegar, an old wooden crate, and two empty iron cages with rusty iron doors. Flies buzz around the crate, which contains the half-eaten corpse of an orc as well as Slub's treasure.

### Treasure

Lying next to the half-eaten orc is a bloodstained sack containing 3d6 × 100 cp, 2d6 × 100 sp, and 1d6 × 100 gp plus 1d4 mundane items, determined by rolling on the Items in a Giant's Bag table in the introduction.

## 16. Smithy

This freestanding building has mud walls and a 50-foot-high ceiling beneath an arching straw roof that is sturdy enough for a Medium or smaller creature to stand on without falling through. The warm interior contains a fire pit heaped with hot coals, with red-hot pieces of metal sticking out of it. Leaning against the walls are blacksmithing tools, including tongs and hammers. A barrel of water stands in one corner by the open door-way, and a sleeping pallet rests in the northwest corner.

Grudd Haug's blacksmith is a female **hobgoblin** who doesn't mind fighting enemies one at a time but retreats or surrenders when faced with overwhelming opposition. When the gong is rung (see area 8), she leaves her smithy and heads to the Watermaster's quarters (area 7). Assisting the hobgoblin are two **goblins**, who hide behind the barrel when an alarm sounds. If intruders enter the smithy, the hidden goblins make Dexterity (Stealth) checks to slip out through the open doorway. Their checks are contested by the Wisdom (Perception) scores of creatures within sight of the doorway. If they are cornered, the goblins surrender in the hope that their lives will be spared. They know the layout and defenses of Grudd Haug, and they share that information if they think it will improve their chances of survival.

### Treasure

The hobgoblin carries a pouch containing 1d10 gp. Each goblin carries a pouch containing 1d10 cp.

> ## Character Advancement
>
> If Guh has the *conch of teleportation* and the characters obtain it, they can use it to teleport to Maelstrom once a character attunes to the item. The characters might have a few issues to resolve before using the conch, such as escorting Ghalvin Dragonmoor to Goldenfields. The characters should advance to 9th level before moving on to chapter 10, "Hold of the Storm Giants.".

# CHAPTER 6: CANYON OF THE STONE GIANTS

EADSTONE CLEFT IS THE REMOTE CANYON
lair of a xenophobic clan of stone giants
who worship Skoraeus Stonebones. If the
characters defeat the zealous stone giant
thane Kayalithica and obtain her *conch of
teleportation*, they can use it to teleport to
Maelstrom, King Hekaton's undersea cita-
del (see chapter 10, "Hold of the Storm Giants"). Obtaining the conch is the adventurers' primary goal in this
part of their mission. Whether they kill the stone giant
thane or not is up to them.

Stone giants aren't the only antagonists the characters
must face. Thane Kayalithica has won the allegiance
of the Blue Bear tribe of Uthgardt, many of whom are
camped in Deadstone Cleft. See chapter 3 for more information on this tribe.

## STONE GIANTS

Before running this part of the adventure, review the information on stone giants in the *Monster Manual*.

### A POX ON THE LAND

Unlike most stone giants, Thane Kayalithica is a neutral evil extremist. She is using the dissolution of the
ordning as an excuse to destroy what she has come to
fear and abhor—the rapidly spreading civilizations of humans and their ilk. Kayalithica's followers, who are pre-
dominantly neutral, believe that violence against small

folk is justified, because their thane has assured them
that she is heeding the will of Skoraeus Stonebones.

Kayalithica believes that the works of the small folk
are a pox on the land. They desecrate the very stone
upon which they are built. By obliterating them, she
hopes to impress the gods and elevate her people to the
top of the ordning. By the time the adventurers set a
course for her canyon, Kayalithica has already led major
assaults against the nearby settlements of Orlbar and
Llorkh. The stone giant thane now has her sights set
on Loudwater or Parnast, and she has asked Skoraeus
Stonebones to send her divine guidance about which
community to attack next.

Not all members of Kayalithica's clan support the
thane. A few have fled into the nearby mountains and
foothills, fearing that Deadstone Cleft has become a
cursed place. These stone giants won't easily be turned
against their thane, but they might be persuaded to help
adventurers survive the perils of Deadstone Cleft by providing information about the canyon and its defenses.
They can also shed light on Kayalithica's evil intentions.

### THE GREAT STILLNESS

A stone giant of Deadstone Cleft can enter a meditative
state that leaves it petrified for a time. When the petri-
fication ends, the giant awakens with tremorsense (see
the *Monster Manual*) and the ability to cast a handful of
spells for a limited time. Stone giants refer to the petrified state as Olach Morrah, which translates as "the

Great Stillness." The giants of Deadstone Cleft gain the following feature.

***Olach Morrah.*** The giant meditates for 1 hour, during which time it can do nothing else. At the end of the hour, provided the giant's meditation has been uninterrupted, it becomes petrified for 8 hours. At the end of this time, the giant is no longer petrified and gains tremorsense out to a range of 30 feet, as well as a measure of innate spellcasting ability based on Wisdom. For the next 24 hours, it can innately cast the following spells, requiring no material components:

3/day: *meld into stone, stone shape*
1/day: *stoneskin, time stop*

The adventure notes which giants have recently completed the meditation and emerged from their petrified state with tremorsense and the ability to cast spells.

# DEADSTONE CLEFT

In the desolate, fog-shrouded foothills of the Graypeak Mountains is a dead-end canyon with the petrified bodies of stone giants embedded in its hundred-foot-tall gray walls. The corpses create a sense of unease and dread, warning visitors that Deadstone Cleft is a place of death. As cold wind passes through the canyon, it produces a moan that seems to issue from the gaping mouths of the bodies, adding to the eerie atmosphere. Dotting the canyon walls are several openings that lead to stone-carved tombs and other chambers, some open to the sky and others beneath hundreds of feet of stone. Carved stone bridges also span the canyon.

Deadstone Cleft is sacred to the stone giants of the Graypeak Mountains, for it contains an ancient temple dedicated to their god, Skoraeus Stonebones, and a magical stalactite, the Steinfang, into which the giants carve questions. The carvings fade on nights of the new moon and are replaced with answers. The giants believe that these replies come from Skoraeus Stonebones himself, though in truth they are produced by an ancient, evil earth primordial trapped under the Graypeak Mountains since the dawn of time. Human and dwarven miners have long avoided the canyon for fear of antagonizing the stone giants known to dwell at Deadstone Cleft. The stone giants don't tolerate uninvited guests in their hallowed halls, attacking them on sight.

Adventurers can find the canyon by traveling upstream along an arm of the Loagrann River. This great flow once carved the canyon out of the rock that now surrounds it. Time has reduced it to a stream that tumbles along the canyon floor before widening and continuing its long journey southwest, where it merges with the Delimbiyr River on its way to the sea.

## REACHING DEADSTONE CLEFT

No roads lead to Deadstone Cleft (shown on map 6.1), but characters can traverse the foothills of the Graypeak Mountains and cross shallow rivers to reach the canyon, with or without horses. They can also take a boat up the Loagrann River. Use the Random Wilderness Encounters table in chapter 3 to generate encounters, as desired. The characters can also reach Deadstone Cleft by air, using the methods discussed in the sections that

follow. See the "Approaching the Canyon" section for more information on where they can land and the likelihood of them being spotted.

### AIRSHIP

If the characters have an airship (see the "Airship of a Cult" section in chapter 4), they can use it to reach Deadstone Cleft and avoid both the rugged terrain and any land-based random encounters.

### FLYING MOUNTS

Characters can obtain griffon mounts in Fireshear or hippogriff mounts in Hawk's Nest. Neither settlement is close to Deadstone Cleft, requiring the characters and their mounts to rest between flights. Characters mounted on hippogriffs can travel 54 miles per day (three 3-hour flights with 1-hour rests in between). Griffon riders can travel 72 miles in the same amount of time. Any NPCs who accompany the characters on this excursion remain with the mounts, protecting them while the characters explore Deadstone Cleft.

## APPROACHING THE CANYON

Billowing clouds of mist lightly obscure Deadstone Cleft, the location of which is ultimately betrayed by the moaning wind that passes through it—a haunting dirge that can be heard up to a quarter mile away. Guarding the mouth of the canyon is a roc that the stone giants have tamed (see area 2). Characters who see the mouth of the canyon can also see the roc's nest nearby.

The canyon is easily spotted from the air, as are three nearby caves that are open to the sky (areas 5, 7, and 12). Characters who have an airship or flying mounts can land above or inside the canyon, or in one of these open caves. If the characters approach Deadstone Cleft in an airship and move into the roc's line of sight, the roc takes to the sky and attacks it. The airship can't outrun or outmaneuver the roc, which is too big to land on the deck or reach creatures on the deck with its claws. The roc can bite creatures on deck, but it prefers to attack the balloon itself (see the "Airship of a Cult" section in chapter 4 for the balloon's statistics). If it successfully brings down the airship, the roc spends a few rounds picking through the wreckage in search of food before returning to its nest. If the characters approach on flying mounts, the roc attacks them only if they approach within 120 feet of its nest and it can see them.

Characters above the canyon have the option of climbing down into the jagged rift at a point of their choosing. The sounds of their descent are muffled by the wind.

## DENIZENS

Ten stone giants reside in Deadstone Cleft when the adventurers arrive, including Thane Kayalithica. With the exception of the giant in area 6, who checks on the roc, the giants remain in their caves and wait for enemies to come to them. Once they enter combat, the giants pursue enemies that attempt to flee.

The Blue Bear tribe shares Kayalithica's belief that civilization is a blight on the land. The Uthgardt stalk the foothills of the Graypeaks and hunt wild game in Delimbiyr Vale. They also occupy several caves within

## Deadstone Cleft Roster

| Area | Creature(s) | Notes |
|---|---|---|
| 2 | 1 **roc** | The roc takes to the air and attacks anything it perceives as a threat. |
| 3 | Hydia Moonmusk, 2 adult cave bears, 1 young cave bear | Hydia gathers her tribemates (see areas 15A–15D) and forms a hunting party, The adult bears chase down fleeing prey. The young bear remains in the cave. |
| 4 | 1 **stone giant** | The giant pursues fleeing enemies but otherwise remains here. |
| 5 | 2 **stone giants** | The giants pursue fleeing enemies but otherwise remain here. |
| 6 | 1 **stone giant** | If the giant hears the roc screeching in area 2, it investigates. Otherwise it remains here. |
| 9 | 2 **stone giants**, 16 mountain **goats** | The giants pursue fleeing enemies but otherwise remain here. The goats remain here. |
| 10 | 1 **stone giant**, 10 **piercers** | The giant pursues fleeing enemies but otherwise remains here. The piercers remain here, dropping onto creatures only when the giant commands them to do so. |
| 11 | 2 **black puddings** | The puddings remain here. |
| 12 | 1 **roper** | The roper remains here. |
| 13 | 2 **stone giants** | The giants pursue fleeing enemies but otherwise remain here. |
| 14 | Thane Kayalithica, 1 **stone golem** | Kayalithica remains here and orders the stone golem to pursue fleeing enemies. |
| 15A | 5 **tribal warriors** | The warriors remain here until Hydia Moonmusk (area 3) gathers them or until they hear a disturbance coming from an adjoining area. |
| 15B | 10 **tribal warriors** | Same as area 15A. |
| 15C | 3 **berserkers**, 1 **Uthgardt shaman** | Same as area 15A. |
| 15D | 6 **tribal warriors**, 2 **rust monsters** | Same as area 15A. The warriors release the rust monsters before they leave. The rust monsters remain here. |

## Deadstone Cleft Reinforcements

| d100 | Creature(s) |
|---|---|
| 01–50 | None |
| 51–60 | 1 **stone giant** carrying 1d4 captured shield dwarf **commoners** (prospectors) in a net |
| 61–65 | 1 **stone giant** and its animal companion, which is either a cave bear (**polar bear**) or a **giant goat** |
| 66–70 | 1 **stone giant** shepherding 2d6 mountain **goats** |
| 71–75 | 2d6 Blue Bear **tribal warriors** returning from an unsuccessful hunt |
| 76–80 | 2d6 Blue Bear **tribal warriors** returning from a successful hunt with a dead elk or mountain lion |
| 81–85 | 1d4 Blue Bear **berserkers** returning from a raid carrying the severed heads of 2d6 humans or 2d6 shield dwarves |
| 86–90 | 1d4 Blue Bear **scouts** and 1 **Uthgardt shaman** (see appendix C) bearing news from other Blue Bear clans |
| 91–95 | 1 **stone giant** carrying a sack of nonmagical, human-sized weapons and armor collected from a distant battlefield |
| 96–00 | 1d4 + 1 **stone giants**, each carrying a handful of 2d6 + 10 gemstones (worth 100 gp each) |

Deadstone Cleft and look after the stone giants' cave bear pets. Hydia Moonmusk, the fearless daughter of the Blue Bear tribe's great chief, has made a den for herself in the bear cave near the mouth of the canyon (area 3).

Characters who allow Hydia enough time to gather her tribemates might face all of the Uthgardt in Deadstone Cleft at once. The stone giants prefer to wait for enemies to come to them.

The Deadstone Cleft Roster table summarizes the locations of the canyon's inhabitants when the characters approach and indicates how those creatures react when intruders are detected.

## REINFORCEMENTS

Many stone giants and Uthgardt haunt the Graypeak Mountains and its foothills. For every hour that passes during the characters' exploration, there is a chance that other creatures pay a visit to Deadstone Cleft. At the end of each hour, roll d100 and consult the Deadstone Cleft Reinforcements table to determine what comes knocking. Reinforcements enter through area 1. How these creatures behave is up to you and should depend on the state of affairs at Deadstone Cleft when they arrive. If the newcomers spot corpses lying about, they might explore Deadstone Cleft expecting to find trouble within. If all seems normal and quiet, they might stick around only briefly.

At your discretion, one or more stone giants among the reinforcements might be neutral or neutral good, with strong misgivings about what Thane Kayalithica is doing to shake up the ordning. Any such giant can, with a successful DC 15 Charisma (Persuasion) check, be convinced to turn against Kayalithica and help the characters in some fashion, provided the characters are able to communicate with it. For an example of how non-evil stone giants might behave, see area 13.

# 1. CANYON ENTRANCE

The mouth of the canyon is a grassy ravine with a shallow but swift-flowing river at the bottom. A moss-covered log spans the river at one point. As one heads north into the canyon, the grass gives way to barren gray rock.

Through the mist and fog, characters can see petrified stone giants along the canyon walls (see the "Deadstone Cleft: General Features" sidebar). They can also see a giant bird's nest atop a 60-foot-tall promontory (area 2) and three cave mouths, one on the west side of the river (leading to area 6) and two on the east side (leading to areas 3 and 15A). Unless the characters take steps to remain hidden, they are spotted by the roc in area 2.

# 2. ROC'S NEST

The stone giants refer to the **roc** of Deadstone Cleft as the Jotunglang (meaning "the giant above"). To sneak past the gargantuan bird, the party must succeed on a DC 14 group Dexterity (Stealth) check. If the group check fails, the roc detects one or more trespassers and screeches. The inhabitants of areas 3 and 6 investigate the disturbance, emerging from their caves 2 rounds later.

## TREASURE

The roc's nest is 30 feet across and consists of felled trees, wagon wreckage, crushed bales of hay, and the occasional bent shield or rusty helm. Characters who search the roc's nest find a scratched-up wooden chest containing 4,500 sp as well as 1d3 magic items. Roll on Magic Item Table H in chapter 7 of the *Dungeon Master's Guide* for the first item, and on Table B for any other items.

# 3. BEAR CAVE

This dry cave is tucked under a grassy bulge in the mountainside. The main cave is home to a mated pair of cave bears (use the **polar bear** stat block) and one cave bear cub (use the **black bear** stat block). Hydia Moonmusk, the leader of the Blue Bear tribe in Deadstone Cleft, rests in a chamber at the back of the main cave. She is the daughter of the Blue Bear tribe's great chief. She is a **gladiator**, with the following changes:

- Hydia's alignment is chaotic evil.
- She speaks Bothii (the Uthgardt language) and Common.
- She carries three spears.

The cave bear cub fights only in self-defense and follows characters around if they feed it. Characters who search the cave find nothing but a few gnawed bones.

## TREASURE

Hydia carries a hide pouch containing seven 50 gp gemstones. She gives the roper in area 12 a gemstone every time she passes through its lair.

## DEVELOPMENT

Hydia and the adult cave bears investigate any disturbances outside. If they detect intruders, Hydia commands the bears to attack while she gathers the other members of her tribe, beginning with the warriors in area 15A. Avoiding high ledges, she heads north through areas 4, 5, and 9, to the camp in area 15B. Then she heads to area 15C, passing through areas 9 and 10 on the way. Next she moves through area 12 to reach area 15D, bribing the roper in area 12 with a gemstone. Gathering all of her tribemates takes about 10 minutes. With them in tow, she doubles back through area 12 and makes her way south through the central canyon.

# 4. GORGON MUD POOL

Three fossilized stone giants stand in alcoves along the south wall of this cave, the floor of which gently slopes down to a 70-foot-wide, 20-foot-deep pool of gorgon mud (see below). Natural light illuminates a rising tunnel to the northwest that leads to a high ledge overlooking the canyon.

This cave contains a stone giant that has gained the benefits of the Olach Morrah feature (see "The Great Stillness" section earlier in this chapter) and cast a *meld into stone* spell on itself. It hides in the eastern wall, between the tunnels that lead to areas 5 and 15A. It uses its tremorsense to detect intruders. As soon as a character passes by, the giant emerges from the wall and tries to shove that character into the pool of gorgon

mud on its first turn in combat. It does so if it succeeds on a Strength (Athletics) check contested by the target's Strength (Athletics) or Dexterity (Acrobatics) check (the target chooses the ability to use).

When the giant appears, it surprises characters who have a passive Wisdom (Perception) score lower than 12. After attempting to shove a character into the mud, the giant attacks the party with its greatclub.

### Gorgon Mud

This pool of thick, magical mud is treated as quicksand (see the "Wilderness Hazards" section in chapter 5 of the *Dungeon Master's Guide*), and it also can petrify creatures that become immersed in it. A creature that ends its turn in an area of gorgon mud must succeed on a DC 12 Constitution saving throw or be petrified. Gorgon mud removed from its pool becomes ordinary mud. The pool radiates an aura of transmutation magic under the scrutiny of a *detect magic* spell.

A petrified creature can be pulled out of the mud. For simplicity's sake, assume that a petrified Small character weighs 250 pounds and a petrified Medium character weighs 600 pounds.

## 5. Thanes' Tomb

This cave, open to the sky, has 100-foot-high walls. The cave floor is bowl-shaped, with a 10-foot-deep pool of rainwater in the middle. Five fossilized stone giants wearing stone regalia—the remains of long-dead thanes—stand in alcoves, their eyes wide and mouths agape. Set into the walls are three pairs of carved stone doors with simple stone hinges. The doors are 25 feet tall and weigh several tons, but are well balanced on their hinges; a character can pull one open with a successful DC 18 Strength (Athletics) check.

This room contains two **stone giants** that have gained the benefits of the Olach Morrah feature (see "The Great Stillness" section earlier in this chapter). They have

used *meld into stone* spells to sink into the floor near the tunnels that lead into this area. They rise up and attack intruders, surprising those who have a passive Wisdom (Perception) score lower than 12.

Behind each door is a rough-hewn chamber with a 50-foot-high ceiling. The southwest chamber appears empty but contains a nasty surprise (see "Trap"). The giants store their valuables in the rooms to the east and northeast (see "Treasure").

### Trap

The floor in the middle of the southwest chamber is illusory and conceals a circular pit that's wide enough for a giant to fall through (marked on the map with a dotted circle). Any creature that treads on this section of floor falls through the illusion into a chute that slants toward the south and plunges the creature into the pool of gorgon mud in area 4. Prodding the floor reveals the illusion, which can be dispelled (DC 16).

### Treasure

Lying on the floor of the northeast chamber are four giant-sized sacks. Each sack contains 3d10 × 100 cp, 2d10 × 100 sp, and 1d10 × 100 gp, plus 1d3 mundane items, determined by rolling on the Items in a Giant's Bag table in the introduction.

On the floor of the east chamber is an old rowboat big enough to hold six Small or Medium characters and their gear. The stone giants use it as a storage container. It contains five more sacks of treasure, their contents determined as above. In addition, one randomly determined sack in the rowboat also contains a magic item, determined by rolling on Magic Item Table G in chapter 7 of the *Dungeon Master's Guide*.

## 6. Roc Handler

This cave is unfurnished. A **stone giant** stands guard here and passes the time by chiseling pictograms into a wall and then using its *stone shape* spell to wipe the wall clean and start over. This giant has gained the benefits of the Olach Morrah feature (see "The Great Stillness" section earlier in this chapter). When it spots intruders, it tilts its head and gives them a quizzical look before casting *stoneskin* on itself and advancing to attack.

### DEVELOPMENT

If the stone giant hears the roc screeching in area 2, the giant casts *stoneskin* on itself and then investigates. It takes 2 rounds for the giant to reach the end of the south tunnel.

## 7. TOMB OF THE SKODKONG

Here lies the tomb of the Skodkong ("Fog King"), the first of Deadstone Cleft's thanes. Unlike most stone giants, the Skodkong had pale gray skin—hence its moniker. The chamber is open to the sky and has 100-foot-high walls. Pools of rainwater have formed on the floor to each side of a giant slab of pale gray stone. Three dead, fossilized stone giants in alcoves loom above the Skodkong, posing no threat to intruders.

The stone slab is actually the Skodkong's reshaped body, which has giant hand-shaped indentations all over it. Any creature that presses its hands to the stone leaves shallow indentations in its surface, as though the slab was made of soft clay. Nothing else can reshape or penetrate the stone.

The first character who attempts to reach into the slab is irresistibly pulled into it, after which the stone instantly hardens. While trapped in the stone, the character is restrained, can't hear or see anything, and has total cover. The character hears a deep, rumbling voice say, "Ask!" in Common. The character can now ask the Skodkong three questions, and it provides truthful, all-knowing answers that only the character can hear. (You can take the character's player aside if you wish, because the other characters can't overhear what's being said.) Once it has answered three questions, the Skodkong releases the character, who is pushed out of the slab. The Skodkong can't be contacted more than once during this adventure. If the character drawn into the slab asks no questions, the Skodkong expels the character after 1 minute. Once that character is expelled, another character can attempt to contact the Skodkong as described above. Only one character at a time can be pulled into the slab.

## 8. STONECARVER'S CAVE

Characters must scale a 10-foot-high ledge to reach this cave, regardless of the direction from which they approach. Light from a single torch reflects off gem deposits in the walls. Two stone tables rise naturally out of the floor. Resting on them are several giant-sized awls and chisels.

### TREASURE

Characters who have time on their hands can chip gemstones from the walls using picks and similar tools. A character who spends 1 hour doing so excavates 100 gp worth of uncut gems. The cave holds 15,000 gp worth of uncut gemstones. The walls are bare once all of the gemstones are removed.

## 9. GOAT CAVE

A large campfire burns in the middle of this cave. The fire illuminates wall carvings that depict stone giants heaving boulders over their heads.

Sitting around the campfire are two **stone giants**. They are meditating in order to gain the benefits of the Olach Morrah feature (see "The Great Stillness" section earlier in this chapter). If they remain undisturbed for another 30 minutes, they turn to stone and remain petrified for the next 8 hours. If they detect intruders before then, they rise to their feet and hoist their stony greatclubs. Enraged at the interruption, they attack the intruders and pursue those who flee.

Ten-foot-high ledges form wide steps that curl up the south wall to a tunnel that leads to area 15B. A tunnel in the northeast wall leads to a naturally lit, 30-foot-high ledge overlooking the canyon. To the northwest is a sunken side-cave containing sixteen mountain **goats**, which the stone giants occasionally eat. A 10-foot-high ledge traps the goats inside the cave. The goats are non-threatening.

## 10. MUSHROOM FARM

This damp cave contains a large, shallow pool, around which colorful beds of moss grow. Sprouting from these mossy beds are scores of mushrooms that range in height from a few inches to 5 feet tall. The stone giants consider the mushrooms a delicacy and eat them raw. A narrow stream originating from a fissure in the northeast tunnel feeds the pool before snaking westward and spilling into the canyon.

A **stone giant** bathes in the pool. It has gained the benefits of the Olach Morrah feature (see "The Great Stillness" section earlier in this chapter). If it hears intruders approaching, it uses its *meld into stone* spell to sink into the stone at the bottom of the pool. If the characters disturb the pool or attempt to cross the room, the giant rises up and attacks with its greatclub. Characters with a passive Wisdom (Perception) score lower than 16 are surprised by the giant as it rises from the pool.

Clinging to the 50-foot-high ceiling are ten **piercers**. As a bonus action on its turn, the giant can hum a tone and cause one of the piercers to drop on another creature in the cavern. The piercers don't attack otherwise.

## 11. OVERGROWN TUNNEL

The fungi in area 10 have spread throughout this tunnel. A forest of sticky mushrooms ranging in height from a few inches to 3 feet tall covers the floor, and the fossilized stone giants standing in alcoves along the walls are covered with blue, gold, and scarlet moss.

When one or more characters reach the middle of this area, have all the characters in the tunnel make a DC 13 Wisdom (Perception) check. Those who fail the check are surprised when two **black puddings** boil out of crevices in the floor and attack.

# Deadstone Cleft

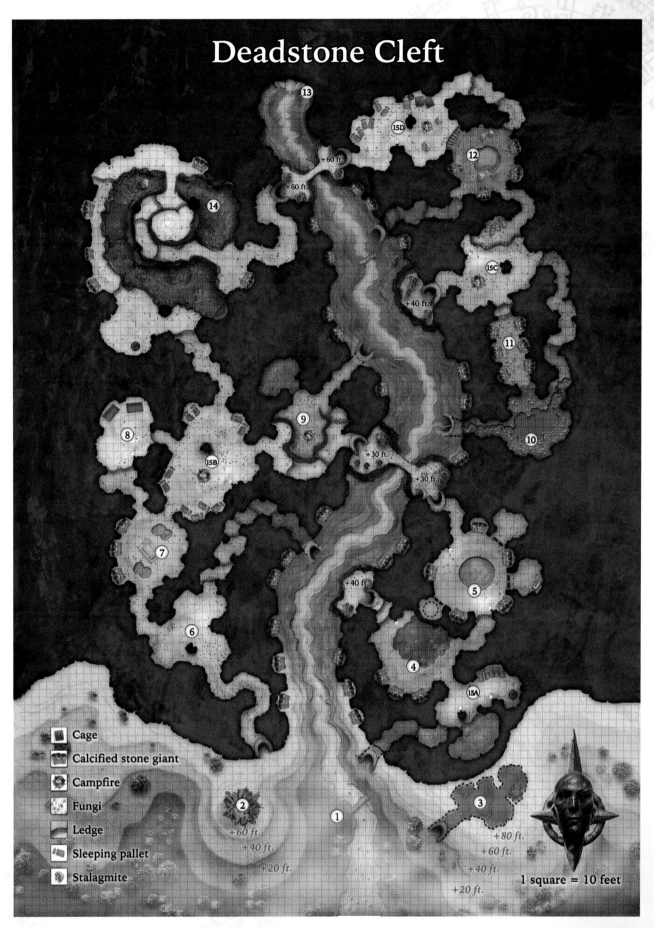

Cage

Calcified stone giant

Campfire

Fungi

Ledge

Sleeping pallet

Stalagmite

1 square = 10 feet

MAP 6.1: DEADSTONE CLEFT

## 12. WARRIORS' TOMB

This cave, open to the sky, has 150-foot-high walls with scores of natural, moss-covered ledges and overhangs. Firelight spills from an opening at the top of a 30-foot-high ledge in the northwest wall. Beyond this ledge is another cave (area 15D) that can be reached by ascending through a tunnel in the northeast wall.

A 5-foot-deep pool of rainwater stands in the middle of the floor between three stalagmites, and the fossilized remains of four stone giants fill alcoves carved into the walls. Harmless **bats** nest in their gaping mouths during the day and flutter around the cave at night.

The southernmost stalagmite is actually a **roper** that feeds on the bats but craves more succulent prey. It attacks characters as they move through the room. The stone giants and the Uthgardt appease the roper by offering it gemstones. If the roper is offered a gemstone worth 50 gp or more, it swallows the gem and lets intruders pass unmolested. The roper must be bribed every time one or more creatures want to cross the room safely, and it costs one gemstone regardless of how many creatures are trying to pass.

### TREASURE

The roper has twelve 50 gp gemstones, four 100 gp gemstones, and one 500 gp gemstone in its gizzard, which can be retrieved once the creature is dead.

### DEVELOPMENT

The Uthgardt in area 15D can hear sounds of combat here. They respond by hurling spears at intruders from the top of the 30-foot-high ledge overlooking the cave.

## 13. SKORAEUS STONEBONES

The stone giants have carved the back wall of the canyon into a 150-foot-tall statue of their god, Skoraeus Stonebones, who looks like a powerfully built stone giant with spikes protruding from his head and shoulders. The monument is an astonishing bit of stonecraft in terms of its sheer size. Rivulets of water pour down from the mountain onto the statue, which channels the water into a stream that flows out through the canyon. The sound of falling water is quite loud here, and a thick mist drifts over everything. Characters who inspect the statue and succeed on a DC 20 Wisdom (Perception) check spot a *crystal ball*-sized orb embedded in its right eye (see "Treasure").

Two **stone giants** kneel before the statue, their heads bowed, their stone greatclubs lying on the ground beside them. They haven't performed the meditation ritual and thus don't gain the benefits of the Olach Morrah feature (see "The Great Stillness" section earlier in this chapter). Characters who attack surprise them. These giants are neutral, however, not evil. They have begun to question Kayalithica's sanity and are praying to Skoraeus Stonebones for wisdom. If the characters attack them, the giants become enraged and retaliate in kind. If the characters get their attention in a nonthreatening manner, the giants rise to their feet and look at them quizzically, but don't immediately reach for their greatclubs. The giants speak and understand Giant only. If the characters ask them about Kayalithica or her *conch of teleportation* in that language, the giants share the following information:

- Kayalithica is in the temple. (The giants can point the way to area 14, but they also warn the characters that only stone giant thanes are permitted in the temple.)

- She carries a *conch of teleportation* given to her by King Hekaton.
- She is carving questions into the Steinfang, a giant stalactite. The answers to her questions will come to her during the next new moon.
- Kayalithica believes that she can please her gods and elevate stone giants to the top of the ordning by wiping out the blasphemous works of the surface dwellers.

These giants aren't brave enough to stand against Kayalithica at this time, but they won't hold a grudge if the characters attempt to eliminate her.

### TREASURE

Embedded in the statue's right eye is an *orb of the stein rune* (see appendix B). Any character within reach of the orb can pry it free with a blade or similar tool. Stone giants who witness the theft do their utmost to kill the thief and recover the orb.

## 14. TEMPLE

Only stone giant thanes are allowed inside this hallowed cave. All other stone giants must remain outside or face certain punishment, by order of Thane Kayalithica and the others who have come before her. The Uthgardt are likewise forbidden to enter, as are the characters.

The fossilized remains of three long-dead thanes stand in alcoves carved into the west wall, their eyes fixed on a rocky island surrounded by gorgon mud (see area 4). The mud, which Kayalithica refers to as the Fjellblod ("blood of the mountain"), oozes into the cave through stone grates in the northeast and southeast walls. The mud is 20 feet deep. Two sturdy stone bridges span the mud pool, connecting the island to nearby ledges. Overlooking these bridges are two more fossilized stone giant thanes.

The room's most prominent feature is the Steinfang, a 40-foot-long stalactite that hangs from the ceiling above the island. From a base 20 feet in diameter, it tapers to a rough point a few feet above the surface of the island. The Steinfang is etched with questions written by Kayalithica in Dethek, the Dwarvish script. The stone giant thane is carving new questions into the stalactite when the characters arrive. By entering the cave, the characters have committed a blasphemy that Kayalithica can't forgive. She is a **stone giant**, with the following changes:

- Kayalithica is neutral evil and has 170 hit points.
- She has a Charisma of 14 (+2).
- She has gained the benefits of the Olach Morrah feature (see "The Great Stillness" section earlier in this chapter).
- She wields an *adamantine greatclub*. This magic weapon has no bonus to attack or damage rolls. A creature can attune to it, and the weapon enlarges or reduces to be an appropriate size for that creature.

Once during this adventure, as an action, Kayalithica can point to one of the fossilized stone giants in this cave and cause it to animate as a Huge **stone golem** with 195 (17d12 + 85) hit points. Its statistics are otherwise those of a stone golem. She animates the giant that stands closest to the character or characters she considers the most threatening, then orders the construct to attack them. The golem obeys Kayalithica's commands; it crumbles and is destroyed instantly if she dies.

If the characters make ranged attacks against her, Kayalithica casts *meld into stone* and hides within the stalactite. She waits until they are close before emerging to attack them with her *adamantine greatclub*. The Steinfang is impervious to all spells of 3rd level or lower, but has vulnerability to bludgeoning, slashing, and piercing damage from adamantine weapons. It has AC 15, a damage threshold of 10, and 100 hit points. When the Steinfang drops to 0 hit points, it explodes, and each creature on or above the island must make a DC 15 Dexterity saving throw, taking 70 (20d6) bludgeoning damage from flying debris on a failed save, or half as much damage on a successful one. A creature melded with the Steinfang when it explodes takes no damage and appears out of the midst of the explosion.

### KAYALITHICA'S QUESTIONS

Like her ancestors before her, Kayalithica believes that the stalactite allows her to commune with Skoraeus Stonebones, the god of stone giants. In truth, the Steinfang is part of a malevolent earth primordial named Draunn, which lies trapped somewhere deep beneath the Graypeak Mountains. The primordial sleeps most of the time, waking only on nights of the new moon. Other thanes who earlier allowed themselves to be corrupted by the Steinfang were held in check by King Hekaton, but with him out of the way, Kayalithica is free to cause the harm that her "god" demands.

Any creature can carve questions onto the stalactite. These questions (along with anything else carved into the stone) remain until the next new moon, when the carvings are replaced by answers written in Dethek, the Dwarvish script. Any carving that isn't a question simply vanishes, with nothing appearing in its place. Questions that Kayalithica has carved into the Steinfang include:

*What must I do next to please you, noble father?*
*Do the dream-creatures pose any danger to us?*
*Are there any traitors in my clan?*
*Can these puny Uthgardt be trusted?*
*Is the gnome lying about Loudwater's defenses?*

The primordial isn't an all-knowing entity—quite the contrary. Its answers are motivated by a desire to sow discord, and it has no knowledge of anything happening in the world. If the characters wait around to see what answers appear, roll a d20 and assume that the next new moon occurs in that many nights. Its answers to the above questions are as follows: "Destroy the works of the surface dwellers," "Yes," "Yes," "No," and "Yes."

### TREASURE

Thane Kayalithica has three pouches (the equivalent of normal-sized sacks) tied to a mithral belt (worth 750 gp) around her waist. One of the pouches contains 500 pp. Another contains her *conch of teleportation* (see appendix B) and seven 500 gp gemstones. The third holds a rock gnome clockmaker named Elister Noggins. Although he isn't treasure per se, the affable rock gnome promises them "a hefty reward" if the characters see him safely to his shop in Loudwater.

## Development

Elister the rock gnome was captured by a stone giant and brought to Kayalithica because he claimed to have useful information about Loudwater's defenses. When Kayalithica questioned the gnome, he tried to discourage her from attacking the town by inflating his description of its defensive capabilities. Kayalithica is waiting for the Steinfang to confirm whether the gnome spoke truthfully. In the meantime, she keeps Elister tucked away. He has survived by using his magic to create food and water. He claims there was no point in trying to escape Deadstone Cleft on his own, since the stone giants would probably kill him for trying. Elister uses the **priest** stat block, with these changes:

- He is Small and chaotic neutral.
- He has a speed of 25 feet.
- He has darkvision out to a range of 60 feet.
- He has advantage on all Intelligence, Wisdom, and Charisma saving throws against magic.
- He has the *create food and water* spell prepared instead of *spirit guardians*.
- He speaks Common and Gnomish.

A devout worshiper of Gond, god of inventors, Elister gives the party a small clock (worth 1,500 gp) from his shop as a reward for saving his life and getting him home safely. The clock contains a tiny bell that rings at the top of each hour and can be heard out to a range of 60 feet. After ringing at highsun, the clock must be wound or it stops working. Winding the clock requires a tiny key (which Elister provides) and takes an action. The clock keeps excellent time.

Characters who visit Elister's shop in Loudwater discover that he has a gnome-sized clockwork companion. The construct, Tick Tock, uses the **animated armor** stat block except that its size is Small and it has 27 (6d6 + 6) hit points. It follows Elister's commands only.

If the characters have an airship, Elister takes a shine to it and asks to remain aboard, offering to oversee repairs and serve as an emergency medic. The first time he and Tick Tock are left aboard the airship by themselves, they try to steal it and fly away.

## 15. Uthgardt Camps

Each of these caves has walls engraved with mazelike patterns and whorls. The ceiling has numerous stalactites hanging from it. Several Uthgardt of the Blue Bear tribe inhabit each cave. Some are resting; others are eating, sharpening weapons, or standing watch. Each member of the tribe has a bedroll. The Uthgardt investigate loud noises in adjacent areas.

### 15A. Beer Barrel

This cave reeks of strong beer. The odor originates from a 10-foot-diameter barrel that stands against the eastern wall. It radiates an aura of conjuration magic and magically refills itself with beer each day at dawn. The stone giants found the barrel in the cellar of a destroyed tavern in Llorkh and kept it. An engraved stone mug sized for stone giants is set into a niche above the barrel.

Five Blue Bear **tribal warriors** (CE male and female Uthgardt humans) lair here. If they aren't drawn elsewhere, two are sleeping in their bedrolls, one is sharpening a spear, and two others are standing guard by the stone column in the western part of the cave. A 10-foot-high ledge to the southeast overlooks an empty side cave.

### 15B. Gathering Cave

Thane Kayalithica holds clan meetings here. As an action, she can command a stone throne to rise from the floor or melt back into it. At this time, however, ten Blue Bear **tribal warriors** (CE male and female Uthgardt humans) are using the cave as a lair. If they haven't been disturbed, half of the warriors sleep in their bedrolls while the rest dine on roasted goat and sharpen their weapons around a large campfire that burns in the middle of the cave.

### 15C. Shaman's Cave

Characters hear chanting as they approach this cave unless its occupants have been drawn elsewhere.

The northern area of the cave is 10 feet lower than the rest of the cave floor. It contains four bedrolls that belong to three **berserkers** (CE male and female Uthgardt humans) and one **Uthgardt shaman** (see appendix C) of the Blue Bear tribe. The berserkers are gathered around a campfire in the main area, chanting a prayer to Uthgar while the shaman dances in a counterclockwise circle around them with his sacred bundle clutched tightly to his chest. Roasting on a wooden spit above the flames is a dead goat.

### 15D. Rust Monsters' Cave

Six Blue Bear **tribal warriors** (CE male and female Uthgardt humans) dwell here. Three sleep in their bedrolls while three hunker down next to a campfire that burns between a rocky pillar and two tall stalagmites. Southeast of the campfire is a 30-foot-wide hole in the southeast wall that looks out into a naturally lit grotto (area 12), the floor of which lies 30 feet below.

Two large wooden cages are tucked under a natural overhang along the north wall. The cage doors have simple sliding bolt locks, and opening a cage door requires an action. One cage is empty; the other holds two captured **rust monsters**. The rust monsters can't harm anyone while they are confined to their cage, although their antennae are long enough to touch metal objects brought to within 1 foot of the cage bars.

## Development

If the tribal warriors are drawn elsewhere, they release the rust monsters and leave them to guard the cave. They don't release the rust monsters otherwise.

---

**CHARACTER ADVANCEMENT**

If Kayalithica has the *conch of teleportation* and the characters obtain it, they can use it to teleport to Maelstrom once a character attunes to the item. The characters might have a few issues to resolve before using the conch, such as seeing Elister safely returned to Loudwater. The characters should advance to 9th level before moving on to chapter 10, "Hold of the Storm Giants."

---

# Chapter 7: Berg of the Frost Giants

ROM THEIR ICY FORTRESS OF SVARDBORG, Jarl Storvald and his frost giants strike out in their ships in search of the *Ring of Winter*, an artifact they can use to bring about the Age of Everlasting Ice. Although they're far from reaching that goal, the frost giants pose a terrible threat to the North. In this part of their mission, the characters confront this threat head-on.

If the characters obtain Storvald's *conch of teleportation*, they can use it to travel to Maelstrom, King Hekaton's undersea citadel (see chapter 10, "Hold of the Storm Giants"). In the course of accomplishing that goal, the characters must elude or overcome the many ruthless denizens of the fortress.

The good news is that things could be worse. The bad news is that they soon will be. When the adventurers first arrive at Svardborg, Jarl Storvald isn't there. He's aboard the *Krigvind*, his flagship, hunting whales in the Sea of Moving Ice. As the characters search for his conch, the *Krigvind* and its giants are on their way back.

## Frost Giants

Review the information on frost giants in the *Monster Manual*. It'll help you roleplay the giants in this chapter.

### Reclaiming Svardborg

When Annam the All-Father shattered the ordning, Jarl Storvald and his frost giants set sail in an enormous ship called the *Krigvind* to reclaim Svardborg, a circle of immense lodges built atop an iceberg in the Sea of Moving Ice. In Svardborg's temple of Thrym, the giants found seven white dragon eggs. Shortly after the giants seized the eggs, a mated pair of adult white dragons, Cryovain and Isendraug, returned from a hunt and demanded that the giants relinquish their offspring. Storvald threatened to destroy the unhatched wyrmlings unless Cryovain and Isendraug submitted to his will. The dimwitted white dragons conceded and were subdued. The giants confined Isendraug to her lair in the temple, and Cryovain was chained to the deck of the *Krigvind*.

After enslaving the dragons, the giants stumbled upon a clan of Northlanders living on ice floes in the Sea of Moving Ice and conquered them as well. The Northfolk were transported to Svardborg and tasked with repairing the frost giants' lodges and freeing several greatships (giant-sized longships) entombed in the ice. These humans respect the might of the frost giants and, being evil themselves, serve the giants without protest. The Northfolk speak Yeti as well as Giant, and have several yetis working among them. The frost giants and the yetis don't share a language, so the giants rely on the Northlanders to command the yetis.

### The Ring of Winter

After reclaiming Svardborg, Jarl Storvald used rune magic to divine how best to find the *Ring of Winter*—what the frost giants call the Ice That Never Melts. The runes told Storvald that help would come to him after he staged a series of raids on coastal communities. He sent ships to attack sites along the Sword Coast, and during a raid on Port Llast, the giants captured a Zhentarim mage, Nilraun Dhaerlost. Nilraun was dragged before Storvald and came to realize that the frost giants were searching for the *Ring of Winter*. As the runes had foretold, Nilraun was also searching for the ring and knew about its recent history. He suggested the formation of an alliance between Jarl Storvald and the Black Network, sweetening the deal by offering the frost giant jarl exactly what he needed: information on the ring's current wearer, Artus Cimber, and a drop of Cimber's blood (which the Black Network had in its possession). Nilraun is now waiting for the frost giants to track down the ring, so that he can steal it and claim it for himself. Storvald also wants the ring, and each villain is secretly plotting to betray the other once the ring is found.

Storvald used Artus Cimber's drop of blood in a rune magic ritual to turn a giant diamond into a *blod stone* (see appendix B). Unfortunately for the jarl, the item can't find Artus Cimber specifically; instead, it identifies the location of the nearest creature that has Artus's blood flowing through its veins. Artus has many living relatives, and a few of those reside in the North. The *blod stone* has pointed Storvald toward the town of Bryn Shander in Icewind Dale, where one of Artus's children dwells (see chapter 2). The jarl has sent a band of frost giants there to find Artus Cimber and obtain the ring.

The *Ring of Winter* is an elusive artifact, and neither it nor its bearer can be found in the course of this adventure. Characters who set out to find the ring for themselves will quickly hit one dead end after another. Even divination won't reveal the ring's current whereabouts. Over the years, various Harpers have dedicated resources toward finding Artus Cimber and the ring, to no avail. If the Harpers catch wind of the characters' attempts to locate Artus and the ring, they try to discourage any such pursuit. Artus Cimber and the *Ring of Winter* have roles to play in another adventure.

# SVARDBORG

In the age when giants ruled the North, Svardborg was a remote village where frost giants came to hunt whales and giant walruses. It was abandoned after the empire of Ostoria fell and, over time, drifted northward and became entombed in ice. Today, Svardborg floats amid hundreds of other icebergs in the Sea of Moving Ice. Three of the lodges are still entombed in ice, while the others have been chipped out of the ice and rendered habitable. The expansion and contraction of the ice over the centuries damaged the lodges, and repairs to them are under way. Jarl Storvald has sent ships to the mainland to gather the wood needed to make repairs.

The lodges are perched on sheer cliffs of ice that plunge 50 feet into the sea. The cliffs are only 10 feet high near the Drydock Lodge (area 3), where the giants have built a wooden pier for docking their punts.

A wide cleft in the iceberg offers access to Svardborg's hollow heart—a water-filled chamber open to the sky where the giants moor their greatships. Stretched across the passage is a gate in the form of a net of thick iron chains. The giants lower the chains into the water to let their ships pass through. A small vessel, such as a rowboat sized for humans, can slip through the net even while the gate is raised. Ships bigger than a rowboat are too large to pass through the gate when it is raised.

## REACHING SVARDBORG

Unless they have the means to get there by air, the characters must secure passage on a ship and travel across the Sea of Moving Ice to reach Svardborg (shown on maps 7.1 and 7.2).

### AIRSHIP

If the characters have an airship (see the "Airship of a Cult" section in chapter 4), they can use it to reach Svardborg and avoid a long, icy sea voyage.

### FLYING MOUNTS

The coastal village of Fireshear is home to a griffon rider and trainer, Dasharra Keldabar. Characters seeking flying mounts in Waterdeep, Neverwinter, or Luskan are directed to Dasharra. They can pay her for griffon-riding lessons and then use the griffons to fly to Svardborg. When the characters are ready to leave, Dasharra leads the way on Screecher, her personal griffon mount. Dasharra's griffons fly at a speed of 8 miles per hour and can travel roughly 64 miles per day when flying against the wind. The flight to Svardborg takes five days, with strong, cold headwinds the entire way. Thanks to a stiff tailwind, the return trip is shorter, with the griffons able to cover roughly 80 miles a day. Dasharra expects characters to provide their own cold weather survival gear, supplies, and rations.

When the group reaches Svardborg, Dasharra recommends that the characters land their griffons on the docks south of area 3 (see the "Approaching Svardborg" section for other possible places to land). Dasharra remains with the griffons while the characters explore the frost giant fortress, and the characters can count on her to stick around for the return trip.

Characters can secure flying mounts of a different sort at Hawk's Nest, where knights of the Order of the Gauntlet breed hippogriffs. The journey from Hawk's Nest to Svardborg is long. Flying west against headwinds, the hippogriffs can travel 45 miles per day (three 3-hour flights with 1-hour rests in between). An eastward journey benefits from tailwinds, allowing the hippogriffs to travel 60 miles per day.

### SEAFARING VESSEL

Characters who need to make the trip by ship can find a seafaring vessel in Luskan, Neverwinter, or Waterdeep.

**Luskan.** The characters can approach one of the city's High Captains. For a bribe of no less than 1,500 gp (half up front, half upon safe return), a High Captain provides a longship with a crew of forty pirates (CN male and female human **bandits**) and an arrogant but green captain, Vaalrik Redreef (CN male human **bandit captain**). Once Svardborg is sighted, the ship drops anchor behind a nearby iceberg. The characters can lower rowboats into the sea and use them to reach Svardborg in 30 minutes. Captain Redreef agrees to wait up to 24 hours before raising anchor and setting sail for Luskan. If Svardborg's warning horn (area 2C) is sounded, the inexperienced captain panics and abandons the party, ordering the crew to return home.

Characters who want to buy a ship can pay 10,000 gp for a leaky old longship that belongs to one of the High Captains. The characters must hire a crew of at least forty. A common sailor (use the **commoner** stat block) costs 2 sp per day, while a skilled sailor (use the **bandit** stat block) demands 2 gp per day. The characters can also try to hire a captain (use the **bandit captain** stat block) who normally charges 10 gp per day. One of the characters can serve as captain to avoid this expense, but that leaves no one with command experience aboard the ship after the characters disembark.

***Neverwinter.*** If one or more characters are members of the Lords' Alliance, they can arrange a brief meeting with Lord Dagult Neverember and try to convince him to sponsor a voyage to Svardborg. Neverember knows that the Sea of Moving Ice is patrolled by white dragons and seafaring marauders, so a character must make a successful DC 17 Charisma (Persuasion) check to convince him of the mission's importance. If he decides to help, Neverember arranges for a galley called the *Seabreaker* to transport the characters.

The *Seabreaker*'s captain is an uptight albino wizard, Draevyn Thornbolt (N male human **mage**). He dresses impeccably and looks thin and stern. He commands a crew of twenty trained sailors (male and female human **bandits** of various alignments and ethnicities) and sixty raw recruits (**commoners**). Draevyn's first mate is an affable brute, Kodd (NG male orc **bandit captain**), whose main tasks are to supervise the crew and keep everyone in good spirits.

Upon sighting Svardborg, the *Seabreaker* goes behind a smaller iceberg and drops anchor. Captain Thornbolt promises to wait up to 24 hours for the adventurers to return. The characters are given rowboats and can use them to reach Svardborg in 30 minutes.

There are no other crews in Neverwinter that are daring or foolhardy enough to venture into the Sea of Moving Ice, for any price, and there are no ships to buy.

***Waterdeep.*** If one or more characters are members of the Harpers, they can arrange to meet with the Open Lord of Waterdeep, Lady Laeral Silverhand. During the meeting, Laeral explains that ships are hard to come by in Waterdeep these days; the City of Splendors is in the midst of building a new navy after its fleet was scuttled by Dagult Neverember. Saying it's the best she can do, Laeral offers to give the characters a damaged longship that was recently captured by privateers. What the adventurers choose to do with it is up to them. The ship has 150 hit points and is worth 5,000 gp in its present condition. (For rules on ship repair, see the "Owning a Ship" section in chapter 5 of the *Dungeon Master's Guide*.) The longship's bow is carved and painted to look like the head and neck of a red dragon. The crew costs in Waterdeep are the same as those in Luskan.

If the characters are unable to meet with Laeral Silverhand, they can find a Tethyrian captain willing to take them north into the Sea of Moving Ice for 5,000 gp. The captain, Lady Taska Sonadora (CG female human

noble), is, by all accounts, insane. She likes to spend her inherited wealth on bold (some would say foolish) ventures, and dreams of killing a white dragon and draping its hide over the wooden throne she keeps in her spacious cabin. She can be talked down to 2,500 gp if the characters promise to help her slay a dragon and let her keep its hide as a trophy.

Captain Sonadora's sailing ship is called the *Bobbin' Flagon*, and she stocks its hold with the finest Waterdhavian food and brandy for her crew of twenty sailors (CG male and female human **bandits**). Her manservant is the overworked, underpaid, mean Finn (CN male lightfoot halfling **commoner**).

The *Bobbin' Flagon* has four rowboats. Sonadora won't risk her ship in an assault of Svardborg, but she can easily be persuaded to accompany the adventurers as they explore the frost giant fortress if she thinks there's a white dragon to be had. In that case, she orders Finn and six armed sailors to join her. Two rowboats are needed to transport Captain Sonadora and her away team, leaving two rowboats for the adventurers.

## APPROACHING SVARDBORG

Svardborg is so isolated that the frost giants don't bother posting lookouts. Their lack of vigilance makes it easy to approach the iceberg unseen.

### BY WATER

Characters who approach Svardborg by water can tether their vessels to the 10-foot-high wooden docks south of the Drydock Lodge (area 3). Or they can avoid the docks and scale one of Svardborg's 50-foot-tall icy cliffs, tying their boats to a spike hammered into the cliff face. Neither of these methods of approach attracts attention.

If the characters enter the hollow interior of the iceberg, they risk being spotted by the creatures on the greatships (areas 7 and 9). The gate is up, but the characters can maneuver their rowboats through the gaps between its thick chains.

### BY AIR

Characters who approach Svardborg on flying mounts can land on the outer docks (near area 3) without attracting attention. Although the iceberg's central grotto is open to the sky and it's possible to land griffons on the decks of the greatships within, doing so without being noticed by the creatures on the greatships is impossible.

Characters arriving by airship can land the vessel in the water by the docks. There are also a few landing zones on the iceberg itself, each marked with stars on the map. These areas include two flat patches of ice and snow between areas 1 and 2, as well as a pillar of ice west of area 2 that's connected to the main iceberg by a natural ice bridge. Other places on the iceberg are ill equipped for landings, because the terrain is sloped. Characters can also land their vessel on the water inside the central grotto, but the creatures on the greatships (areas 7 and 9) automatically spot them.

## DENIZENS

When the characters first arrive, most of Svardborg's frost giants are out hunting whales aboard Storvald's

## SVARDBORG ROSTER

| Area | Creature(s) | Behavior |
|------|-------------|----------|
| 1A | 8 ice mephits | The mephits remain in this area. |
| 1E | Nilraun Dhaerlost | Nilraun retreats to area 1G. |
| 1G | 2 frost giants, 2 winter wolves | These creatures fight to the death to guard the dragon eggs. |
| 1H | 1 giant owl | The owl is caged until released. If released, it flies off to find the *Krigvind*. |
| 2A | 3 frost giants | One giant climbs the stairs and tries to blow the warning horn (area 2C). |
| 4D | 2 frost giants | The giants watch over the dragon (area 4E) at all times. |
| 4E | Isendraug (adult white dragon) | The dragon can be persuaded not to attack the characters in exchange for the safe return of its eggs. If the characters return her eggs, the dragon attacks them anyway. |
| 5 | 8 yetis | The yetis pursue intruders but otherwise remain in this area. |
| 7 | 1 frost giant, 18 tribal warriors, 3 yetis | If the horn in area 2C sounds, the creatures use the nearby punts to reach the far side of the lagoon. The giant and half of the warriors go to the jarl's lodge (area 1). The other creatures go to the drydock lodge (area 3). |
| 9 | 2 frost giants (one per ship) | The giants head to area 2A if the warning horn in area 2C sounds. |

flagship (see "The *Krigvind*" section at the end of this chapter). A few giants stayed behind to guard the white dragon eggs and watch over the Northlanders and yetis. Also present in Svardborg are Isendraug, a female adult white dragon who desperately wants her eggs back, and Nilraun Dhaerlost, the evil Zhentarim mage who is plotting with Jarl Storvald to find the *Ring of Winter*. Characters who interrogate Nilraun can learn where Storvald is and what the frost giant jarl is up to.

The giants' lodge has a warning horn on the upper floor (in area 2C). If it is blown, the sound puts all of Svardborg on alert. Some giants remain at their posts and can't be surprised. Others gather the Northlanders and the yetis and search Svardborg for intruders to kill.

The Svardborg Roster table specifies the locations of the occupants and indicates how those creatures behave when the horn sounds or when intruders are detected.

# 1. JARL'S LODGE

This three-story lodge is partially buried under ice but has numerous entrances. Steps ascend to the main doors (leading to area 1A), and a tunnel cuts through the ice to a door set into the north wall of the lodge (leading to area 1D). Flying or climbing characters can reach a balcony on the second floor (leading to area 1G) or a gaping window on the third floor (leading to area 1H).

## 1A. FEAST HALL

The frost giants have tracked snow into this great hall, which is illuminated by *continual flame* spells cast on torches that are mounted to the walls and wooden pillars. These cold fires bathe the hall in a bluish light.

Six massive wooden tables, each one 5 feet tall, are arranged about the room. The frost giants sit around them to eat. Wooden goblets and scraps of frozen meat lie strewn upon the tables as well as underneath them. In the center of the hall is the thawing carcass of a mammoth suspended on a giant wooden spit. Three large, empty ale barrels also stand about the room.

Perched on the frozen rafters 30 feet overhead are eight **ice mephits**. They watch intruders closely but don't attack unless one or more of them are harmed.

## 1B. HUNTING RACKS

Wooden racks and hooks on the western wall hold fishing equipment: dozens of harpoons, nets, and coils of rope. Curtains made of stitched walrus hide hang over doorways at the north and south ends of the east wall.

## 1C. STORES

These rooms contain supplies that the frost giants have plundered from ships along the Sword Coast, including crates of foodstuffs and barrels of salt, wine, and ale.

## 1D. OAR STORAGE

Giant oars hang from the walls of this room, which has snowy giant tracks on the floor. A door in the north wall opens to a tunnel through the ice. It leads to a ledge overlooking a greatship (area 9). A wooden staircase leads up along the western wall. The stairs creak if anyone climbs them, alerting the villain in area 1E.

## 1E. STEWARD'S OFFICE

This room contains a wooden table, two large empty barrels, and a crate filled with packing straw. Standing against the north wall is a cabinet without doors, in which hang three cloaks made of walrus hide.

Also present is a fur-clad Zhentarim wizard, Nilraun Dhaerlost (NE male human **mage** with a *wand of fireballs*), who believes that the frost giants are his best shot at obtaining the *Ring of Winter*. He tries to remain close to Storvald, but the frost giant jarl won't allow Nilraun to accompany him on his whale-hunting expeditions. Nilraun spends his idle hours contemplating how to steal the ring while reminding the giants that the Zhentarim can be a powerful ally. Nilraun knows the command word to free Cryovain ("uvenfetter"), and he trades this information for his life if he is subdued or cornered. For more information about the captured white dragon, see "The *Krigvind*" later in this chapter.

Nilraun has blond hair, piercing blue eyes, and a perpetual scowl. He's pacing the room, trying to stay warm. If he hears trouble below or the sound of someone climbing the stairs, he retreats to Storvald's throne room (area 1G). Two closed doors stand between him and that room. Since he isn't a giant, Nilraun must use

## SVARDBORG: GENERAL FEATURES

Svardborg is an iceberg with several giant-sized lodges situated in a ring on it. Three of the lodges are entombed in ice, while the remainder are partially exposed. All the lodges have a thick layer of ice on them, indicated by the pale blue ring on the map. The hollow heart of Svardborg is a flooded ice cavern that is open to the sky and where the frost giants moor their enormous ships.

**Ceilings.** Unless otherwise noted, ceilings inside the lodges are 40 feet high with 30-foot-high rafters.

**Climbing.** A creature can scale the icy cliffs of Svardborg and the ice-glazed walls of the lodges with a successful DC 20 Strength (Athletics) check. The cliffs that form the outer edge of the iceberg are 50 feet high, except for the wall that adjoins the docks (near area 3), which is 10 feet high.

**Cold Weather.** The temperature throughout Svardborg is well below 0 degrees Fahrenheit. The rules for extreme cold and frigid water apply (see the "Wilderness Survival" section in chapter 5 of the *Dungeon Master's Guide*).

**Doors.** Svardborg's doors are 25 feet tall and made of thick wood, with handles positioned 11 feet above the floor. A Huge giant has no trouble opening one. A smaller creature can attempt to open a door, provided that creature or some other helpful creature can reach the door's handle and unlatch it. While the handle is unlatched, a creature must use an action to push or pull on the heavy door, opening it with a successful DC 13 Strength (Athletics) check.

**Illumination.** *Continual flame* spells cast on torch sconces cast a pale bluish light that illuminates some areas.

**Oversized Furnishings and Objects.** Most of the furnishings and other items in Svardborg are sized for frost giants. Exceptions are noted in the text. Tables, benches, and other room fixtures are typically twice as high, long, and wide as their human-sized equivalents and roughly eight times the weight. Small and Medium creatures can scuttle under and clamber over giant-sized furniture, treating the spaces the furniture occupies as difficult terrain.

**Stairs.** Staircases within Svardborg are sized for frost giants. Each step is 3 feet tall by 3 feet deep. Medium and smaller creatures treat the staircases as difficult terrain.

**Vessels.** The frost giants use two types of ships: greatships and punts. These vehicles are made of frost-covered wood and have sails made from dragon wings. When not in use, the ships are anchored and their sails are lowered.

- Greatships are longships sized for frost giants. A typical greatship measures 240 feet from bow to stern and requires a crew of at least ten creatures that are Large or bigger. A greatship has a speed of 6 mph, AC 15, a damage threshold of 20, and 3,000 hit points. It can hold up to twenty giants plus 200 tons of cargo.
- Punts are keelboats sized for frost giants. Each is roughly the same size as a human-scale longship. A single giant can steer a punt, and a crew of eight Small or Medium Humanoids can operate one as well. A punt typically holds two giants and up to 10 tons of cargo. It has a speed of 2 mph, AC 15, a damage threshold of 15, and 300 hit points.

an action to try to open each door. If he succeeds in opening the doors, he leaves them open behind him.

**Treasure.** Nilraun wears a wolf fur cloak (worth 25 gp), wields a *wand of fireballs*, and has a *spell scroll* of *sending* in a wooden scroll tube fastened to his belt. He also carries a spellbook in which are written the spells he has prepared (see the **mage** in the *Monster Manual*).

## 1F. WINTER WOLVES' DEN

The floor of this room is strewn with gnawed mammoth bones. A frost-covered barrel in the southwest corner contains dead fish. The winter wolves that normally sleep here are encountered in area 1G.

## 1G. THRONE ROOM

Icicles hang from the rafters of this ice-glazed hall, which is illuminated by bluish *continual flame* spells. An ivory drinking horn rests atop a frozen table in the middle of the room. South of the table are a rug made from the hide of a white saber-toothed tiger and a throne carved from ice. Lying on the seat of the throne is a large conch (see "Treasure"). Against the walls stand three shelving units heaped with furs and packed with bottles of wine, stoppered jugs, and casks of mead.

Snowy wind blows in through a pillared opening in the south wall that leads to a balcony with no railing.

Jarl Storvald retires here when he's not plying the northern waters. He isn't here when the characters first arrive at Svardborg. Instead, two **frost giants** and two **winter wolves** stand guard here, watching over seven frost-covered white dragon eggs in the northeast corner of the room. Each egg is 4 feet tall, weighs 300 pounds, and is covered with an icy glaze. An egg has AC 14 and 20 hit points. When an egg is broken, there is a 50 percent chance that the **white dragon wyrmling** inside hatches and is able to attack; otherwise, it is dead.

A wooden ladder ascends 40 feet to area 1H; the rungs of the ladder are 5 feet apart.

The giants and the wolves fight to the death. If Nilraun is here, he casts spells from behind the throne until his life is at risk, then he flees (see "Development").

**Treasure.** Storvald's *conch of teleportation* (see appendix B) rests on the ice throne. The ivory drinking horn on the table is made from the tusk of a mammoth; it's worth 750 gp and weighs 75 pounds. A crate in the southeast corner of the room holds one hundred pieces of scrimshaw (worth 10 gp each) packed in sawdust.

**Development.** Nilraun hasn't placed his fate entirely in the hands of the frost giants. Hiding on a nearby iceberg are two Zhentarim **scouts** (NE female humans) and three **manticores**. If Nilraun ever thinks his life is in jeopardy, he uses his *spell scroll* of *sending* to contact the scouts and waits for them on the balcony. Each scout rides a manticore and provides aerial support while Nilraun mounts the third manticore and uses it to escape. Nilraun and his escorts return to the mainland and report what they've seen to their superiors.

Nothing about Nilraun's appearance suggests that he's a member of the Zhentarim. If Nilraun learns that one or more characters work for the Black Network, he reveals his allegiance to the faction but advises the characters to leave Svardborg before the *Krigvind* returns. Nilraun isn't looking out for anyone's interests but his own; he wants the *Ring of Winter* for himself and doesn't trust other Zhents to help him get it.

Unless you decide otherwise, the *Krigvind* returns after the characters obtain the conch but before they have time to attune to it. The bellows of the *Krigvind*'s crew can be heard in the throne room as the ship approaches (see "The *Krigvind*" section at the end of this chapter).

# Svardborg

+50 ft.

Ice

+50 ft.

4

+30 ft.

7

5

Tunnel

Submerged
Tunnel

8

Ice

9

Ice

+40 ft.

9

+30 ft.

6

2

Tunnel

Tunnel

3

Ice

+50 ft.

Docks

+50 ft.

1

Gate

⭐ = Airship landing zone

1 square = 20 feet

Map 7.1: Svardborg

# Svardborg Lodges

Level 3

Level 2

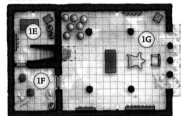

## Jarl's Lodge
(Area 1)

Level 1

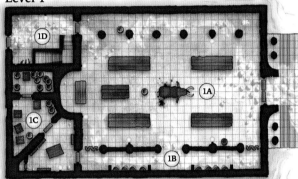

## Drydock Lodge
(Area 3)

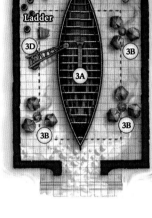

Level 2

## Giants' Lodge
(Area 2)

Open to level 1 below

Level 1

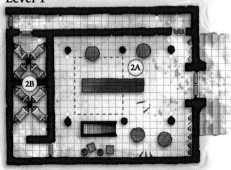

1 square = 10 feet

## Temple of Thrym
(Area 4)

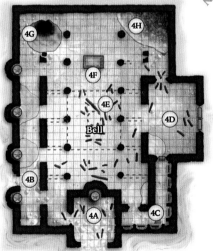

**Altar**

**Barrel**  |  **Door**  |  **Horn**

**Bearskin rug**  |  **Double door**  |  **Pillar**

**Cage**  |  **Furs**  |  **Statue**

**Curtain**  |  **Hammock**  |  **Tent**

## 1H. Treasury

This room on the top floor of the lodge has a pitched roof. A wide triangular opening in the west wall allows wind and snow to enter. Near this opening, hanging from a chain bolted to a rafter, is a 20-foot-tall wooden cage that holds a **giant owl**. Jarl Storvald uses the owl to deliver messages to his fleet. A wooden latch keeps the cage shut. If the owl is released, it flies off, locates the *Krigvind*, and reports to Storvald what it has seen.

***Treasure.*** Characters who search the room find several wooden barrels, crates, and chests. Crates measure 10 feet on a side. Barrels stand 8 feet tall and weigh 500 pounds each. Chests are 10 feet long, 6 feet wide, and 7 feet tall with frozen lids. A lid must be thawed to remove it, or one can be pried open with a successful DC 12 Strength (Athletics) check. (Using a crowbar or a similar tool grants advantage on the check.) Applying an open flame to a lid for 1 minute thaws the ice that binds it. The containers and their contents are as follows:

- A barrel of pitch and two barrels of oil
- A crate packed with sixty flasks of alchemist's fire
- A crate containing a dismantled clockwork mule, along with a scroll of instructional diagrams labeled in Dethek, the Dwarvish script (see "Development")
- A crate packed with a gold-inlaid wooden harp (worth 250 gp, weighs 100 pounds), two drums (worth 6 gp each), and six flutes (worth 2 gp each)
- A chest containing four 50-foot lengths of chain
- Four chests, each one holding 3d6 × 100 cp, 3d6 × 100 sp, and 3d6 × 100 gp
- A chest containing a dead, frozen shield dwarf (female) clad in *adamantine plate armor*, clutching a warhammer and carrying 1d3 magic items, each determined by rolling on Magic Item Table C in chapter 7 of the *Dungeon Master's Guide*.

***Development.*** Characters who cast a *speak with dead* spell on the frozen shield dwarf can learn that she was named Mordana Ur'gray and stowed away aboard a frost giant greatship by hiding in a chest. Unfortunately for her, the chest lid froze shut, and she couldn't get it open.

It takes 8 hours for one character to assemble the clockwork mule. At the end of that time, the character can make a DC 20 Intelligence check. The check is made with advantage if the character has the assembly instructions and can read Dethek (or has someone who can translate). If the check succeeds, the clockwork mule is assembled correctly. If the check fails, the character ends up with one or more leftover parts that the mule needs to function; the character must spend another 1d4 hours working on the mule, and can then make a new Intelligence check to get it working.

The clockwork mule uses the **mule** stat block, with these changes.

- It is a Construct. It follows the orders of its assembler.
- It is immune to poison and psychic damage; the charmed, frightened, paralyzed, petrified, and poisoned conditions; and exhaustion.
- Repairing 1 hit point of damage to the clockwork mule takes 1 hour and requires replacement parts, which can be bought in a large city for 20 gp. If the mule drops to 0 hit points, it is destroyed and unrepairable.

# 2. Giants' Lodge

This two-story lodge is partially buried in the ice. It has three possible entrances: the main entrance on the ground floor (leading to area 2A), an ice tunnel that leads to a door in the back wall of the lodge, and a large window on the second floor that has a great horn sticking out of it (area 2C).

## 2A. Gathering Hall

Three **frost giants** (one male and two females) are engaged in a drinking contest in this area and are so inebriated that they are considered poisoned (see appendix A in the *Player's Handbook*). Despite their present condition, they are spoiling for a fight and hoist their greataxes when intruders appear. After the first round of combat, it occurs to one of the giants that she should sound the warning horn. She staggers up a flight of wooden stairs to blow the horn (area 2C) while the other giants keep fighting. If the characters react quickly enough, they can prevent her from reaching the horn. If they keep the giant from sounding the horn, the other inhabitants of Svardborg aren't placed on alert.

The frost giants have tracked a lot of snow through the main doors. Torch sconces mounted to wooden pillars have *continual flame* spells cast on them, shedding cold blue light. Mounted on the walls of the lodge are the severed heads of polar bears, giant walruses, young white dragons, and remorhazes. A long wooden table and four smaller round tables take up much of the floor space, their tops strewn with wooden mugs and scraps of leftover food. A few empty barrels and crates sit near a wall.

***Treasure.*** Each frost giant carries a sealskin sack containing 3d6 × 100 cp plus 1d6 mundane items, determined by rolling on the Items in a Giant's Bag table in the introduction. A careful search of the room accompanied by a successful DC 15 Wisdom (Perception) check reveals a small pouch hanging from the tooth of a white dragon head mounted on the wall above the empty crates. The pouch contains six 100 gp gemstones.

## 2B. Sleeping Quarters

Each of these two rooms is lit by a *continual flame* spell cast on a sconce and contains four hammocks. Each hammock is suspended between a hook on a central pillar and another hook on one of the surrounding walls.

## 2C. Warning Horn

A wide, covered balcony without a railing overlooks the gathering hall (area 2A) 40 feet below. A few empty crates and barrels are stacked in the corners.

An alcove with a window looking toward the southeast contains a wooden brace supporting an ancient red dragon's horn that the frost giants have etched with runes and made into a musical instrument. The horn weighs 450 pounds. Only a frost giant or similarly sized creature can wrap its mouth around the narrow end of the horn and muster the breath needed to blow it. Sounding the horn requires an action.

***Development.*** If the horn is sounded, the creatures in areas 7 and 9 act as described in the Svardborg Roster table.

## 2D. Jarl's Mess

This room contains a 10-foot-tall wooden table. Resting atop it is a golden platter nearly 8 feet across, a wooden fork as big as a pitchfork, and a mug of bronze as large as a barrel, with handles shaped like a dragon's wings. The platter is worth 750 gp and weighs 75 pounds. The mug is worth 250 gp and weighs 50 pounds.

## 2E. Armory

This room is in shambles. Weapon racks lie broken on the floor, while others cling precariously to the walls, still clutching old spears and javelins. The giants of Ostoria crafted these weapons, which fall apart if handled.

## 3. Drydock Lodge

This lodge is unoccupied when the characters first arrive, but anyone who enters can hear the sound of the Northfolk chipping at the ice in area 7 and the back-and-forth bickering of the frost giant brothers in area 9. Both ends of the lodge are exposed to the air, and its roof is intact despite the amount of ice on it. The lodge's interior is one big, open space with a ceiling that stretches 80 feet above the ground floor and a 40-foot-high balcony with no railing that runs around the perimeter. A decrepit-looking wooden ladder with rungs spaced 5 feet apart offers access to the balcony, but the ladder crumbles under the weight of 500 pounds or more.

Stacked in the corners of the ground floor nearest the grotto are dozens of ale barrels that the frost giants have plundered from merchant vessels.

### 3A. Old Ship Construction

The hull of a greatship takes up most of the interior space. Giant wooden braces hold the ship upright. The giants of Ostoria built the ship, which isn't seaworthy. Any character who inspects the ship and succeeds on a DC 13 Intelligence (Investigation) check can tell that the wood is too brittle to withstand rough seas or collisions.

### 3B. Northfolk Tents

Three camps are set up inside the lodge, each one consisting of three sealskin tents around a smoldering campfire. Each tent contains two bedrolls and a few scattered fish bones. The Northfolk sleep here when they're not working in area 7. The camps are unoccupied when the characters first arrive.

### 3C. Barrel Chute

A barrel chute made of walrus skin pulled over a wooden frame is mounted so that barrels can be rolled down it into the icy lagoon. The barrels are then floated across the lagoon to other locations, as needed. A wooden dock with human-sized steps leads to the water.

### 3D. Crane

A giant wooden crane stands atop the balcony. Used by ancient giants to hoist heavy timbers, its wooden winch, swing-arm, and pulleys still work, though its ropes have rotted and can't support more than 500 pounds.

## 4. Temple of Thrym

Of all the north-facing lodges, this is the only one that has survived more or less intact. Once a temple dedicated to Thrym, the god of frost giants, it was recently taken over by a mated pair of white dragons who turned it into a nursery. Now the frost giants have reclaimed the place and trapped one of the dragons inside.

### 4A. Statue of Thrym

The wind has carried a great deal of snow into this open room, set into the back of which is an alcove that holds a 25-foot-tall statue of Thrym carved from glacial ice. The image looks like a powerfully built male frost giant with clenched fists. Timber from broken rafters and smashed doors lies strewn across the floor.

The ice statue is harmless. Nevertheless, anyone who damages the statue is cursed. Until the curse is lifted with a *remove curse* spell or similar magic, the afflicted creature has vulnerability to cold damage. This curse negates any resistance or immunity to cold damage the creature might otherwise possess.

### 4B. Hall of Jarls

Ice has broken through the walls and ceiling of this hall, and a 12-foot-wide, 15-foot high gash in the outer wall leads outside. Set into alcoves along the corridor are four stone statues that once depicted frost giant jarls—Storvald's ancestors. When the white dragons took over the temple, they broke off the statues' heads and dropped them in the sea. Patches of ice (see the "Wilderness Hazards" section in chapter 5 of the *Dungeon Master's Guide*) have formed around two of the statues.

### 4C. Hall of Heroes

The dragons investigated this area but otherwise left it untouched. The door has been torn from its frame and is nowhere to be seen, though twisted iron hinges offer evidence that the door put up a fight.

Standing in alcoves along the outer wall are seven granite tablets measuring 16 feet tall, 10 feet wide, and 2 feet thick, each one etched (in Dethek, the Dwarvish script) with the name of a frost giant jarl and a florid summary of that chief's legendary deeds. Storvald isn't among the giants honored here.

### 4D. Narthex

The roof of this chamber sports numerous holes above which ice can be seen. The outer double doors have tons of ice pressed against them, and they can't be opened.

Two female **frost giants** stand guard here and watch over the dragon in area 4E. They are eager to spill blood and attack intruders on sight. They have instructions not to harm the dragon unless it harms them first.

***Treasure.*** Each frost giant carries a sealskin sack containing 3d6 × 100 sp, 1d6 × 100 gp, and 1d3 mundane items, determined by rolling on the Items in a Giant's Bag table in the introduction.

### 4E. Bell Tower

Wooden pillars rise to meet the rafters 30 feet overhead, with the pitched roof rising higher, forming an 80-foot-tall bell tower with rafters of its own. Dangling from these rafters is an enormous iron bell weighing 50 tons, with a rim 20 feet in diameter. The bell is missing its clapper and rope; there appears to be no way to ring it.

Curled up inside the bell is Isendraug, a female **adult white dragon**. She is tormented by the theft of her eggs (which the giants keep in area 1G) and is wracking her brain for a plan to get them back and make the giants pay. If she spots any party members, she crawls out of the bell's cold confines and rushes forth to destroy them, thinking they have come to plunder her hoard (area 4H). She prefers to lurk among the rafters and remain out of melee weapon range while attacking with her breath weapon or waiting for it to recharge, but she isn't reluctant to drop down on ranged attackers. If the characters attempt to parley with the dragon, she agrees to let them live in exchange for returning her eggs to her.

Isendraug doesn't gain lair actions and can't cause regional effects in the vicinity of her lair.

**Development.** Isendraug wants her mate, Cryovain, and all seven of her eggs returned to her. She is unwilling to negotiate for anything less. She doesn't know where the frost giants are keeping her eggs, but she knows that they keep Cryovain chained aboard their biggest ship (she doesn't know its name or whereabouts). Like most white dragons, Isendraug is not to be trusted. She has no intention of sparing the characters once they have done what she asks. Clever characters can hold her at bay by threatening one or more of her eggs (or wyrmlings). Isendraug flies into a murderous rage if she witnesses one of her eggs or wyrmlings being harmed.

If Isendraug is reduced to fewer than half her hit points, she tries to escape through the submerged passage (area 4G), smashing through the thin ice that covers it. Once she swims to the surface of the lagoon, she takes flight and looks for a place to roost, such as a greatship or the top of the iceberg. Even if her eggs are destroyed, she won't leave Svardborg until her mate is freed (see "The *Krigvind*" section later in this chapter).

### 1F. ALTAR

This 9-foot-tall block of ice has dwarf skulls and bones within it, and its top is covered with frozen blood.

A character who studies the altar and succeeds on a DC 13 Intelligence (Religion) check can deduce the significance of the bones and the blood. Before a dangerous hunt or voyage, frost giants come here and spill their own blood on the altar to gain Thrym's favor. The bones are meant to consecrate the altar, which is nonmagical.

### 4G. SUBMERGED PASSAGE

The dragons clawed their way through the floor of the lodge to reach the ice underneath, creating a 50-foot-diameter, water-filled tunnel. Thin ice covers the hole. For more information on thin ice and swimming in frigid water, see the "Wilderness Hazards" section in chapter 5 of the *Dungeon Master's Guide*.

The submerged tunnel descends toward the southwest, eventually emerging 300 feet later at the bottom of the lagoon, 80 feet below the water's surface.

### 4H. FROZEN HOARD

A great mound of ice covers the hoard of Cryovain and Isendraug. The ice is transparent enough to see that the bulk of the hoard consists of copper and silver coins, with gold coins strewn among them. Among the coins is a sealed wooden chest buried under 3 feet of ice. A character using a pick or the like can dig out the chest in 1 hour. Each hour a character spends digging for coins yields 100 coins of each type (copper, silver, and gold). It takes 60 hours to retrieve all the gold coins in this way.

**Treasure.** The dragons' hoard consists of 90,000 cp, 41,000 sp, 6,000 gp, and the aforementioned chest, which is unlocked. It contains five hundred wooden coins (worthless), thirty pieces of costume jewelry (worth 5 gp each), a pouch holding twenty silvered sling stones, a silver tinderbox (worth 25 gp), and wooden scroll tube containing a crude treasure map drawn on a piece of walrus hide (see "Development"). Resting atop these items is a wooden pipe with a strip of parchment stuffed inside it that reads (in Common), "Here lies the treasure of Captain Silbarr Snake-Eyes, legendary pirate of the Sword Coast. A hex upon any who plunder this trove." Any character who succeeds on a DC 20 Intelligence (History) check dimly recalls a halfling pirate of no great repute who went by that name.

**Development.** A character who studies the treasure map and succeeds on a DC 10 Intelligence (History) check realizes that it depicts a stretch of the Sword Coast encompassing the islands of Red Rocks, midway between Leilon and Waterdeep. An "X" marks a cove on one island, and a riddle scrawled in Common on the back of the map reads as follows:

*High tide it hides,*
*The moon doth make it rise;*
*The mast points to the prize,*
*Watched by feathered brides.*

If the characters arrive at low tide at the location marked on the map, they see the barnacle-covered, broken mast of a shipwreck poking out of the murky water, pointing toward one of several caves in the cliffs. (The mast is submerged at high tide.) The cave is roughly 30 feet in diameter with a 20-foot-high ceiling. In the cave is the wreckage of a rowboat that two **harpies** have made into a nest. The nest is littered with Humanoid bones and also contains a rotted wooden chest with a black serpent formed in the shape of an "S" burned into its lid. It contains 1d4 magic items. Roll on Magic Item Table G in chapter 7 of the *Dungeon Master's Guide* for the first item and on Table C for any other items.

## 5. YETI CAVE

This cave was carved out of the ice that covers the wreckage of an old frost giant lodge. Frozen shards of timber jut out of the cave walls and floor. Eight **yetis** lurking at the back of the cave rush forth and attack intruders, feeding on anything they kill.

## 6. OUTHOUSE

Half embedded in the ice is an empty wooden building with an open doorway. A 5-foot-wide hole in the middle of the wooden floor leads into a 40-foot-deep, 30-foot diameter cistern carved out of the ice, its floor covered with frozen waste.

## 7. Entombed Greatship

Two punts are anchored next to a frost-covered greatship half-embedded in a wall of ice. The hull of the ship leans at a precarious angle.

Relaxing in one of the punts is a lazy male **frost giant**, who barks orders at eighteen Northfolk (CE male and female human **tribal warriors**). The Northfolk are tethered to the icy wall by ropes tied to iron spikes and are using their spears to chip away at the ice around the greatship. Meanwhile, three **yetis** clamber across the deck and dig at the ice with their claws. The Northfolk won't throw away their spears, so only the giant has a ranged attack. The two punts contain chunks of ice that the giant can hurl at foes.

Fighting on the ship is tricky. Its sloped, icy deck is difficult terrain, and a creature that isn't secured by a rope or braced in some other way must make a DC 10 Dexterity saving throw when it tries to move on its turn or whenever it takes damage. On a failed save, the creature tumbles into the frigid water next to the ship. A creature can climb out of the water and onto a nearby vessel with a successful DC 10 Strength (Athletics) check.

### Treasure

The frost giant carries a sealskin sack containing 3d6 × 100 gp, 1d6 × 100 gp, and 1d3 mundane items, determined by rolling on the Items in a Giant's Bag table in the introduction.

## 8. Underwater Passage

Eighty feet below the water's surface is a tunnel that leads up through the iceberg to area 4G. The white dragons use this tunnel to access their lair. Anyone with a passive Wisdom (Perception) score of 14 or higher spot the submerged tunnel as they cross or fly over the lagoon. From above, it looks like an opening where the side of the iceberg meets the floor of the lagoon.

## 9. Greatships

Two seaworthy greatships (see the "Svardborg: General Features" sidebar) are anchored in the lagoon, each one tied by a thick rope to a massive iron spike pounded into the ice. A 15-foot-wide wooden gangplank allows creatures to board and disembark safely.

One **frost giant** guards each ship. If the horn hasn't sounded, the brothers are throwing ice at each other (the frost giant equivalent of a snowball fight) when the characters approach. If they detect intruders, they hurl chunks of ice at them instead.

### Treasure

Each greatship holds treasure that has been piled up and concealed under a net, waiting to be sorted and divvied up.

Under the net in the easternmost ship is a crate of soap (worth 1 gp), a barrel of salted fish (worth 10 gp), a wooden case inlaid with mother-of-pearl (worth 25 gp) containing 20 crossbow bolts, a leather satchel of alchemist's supplies (worth 50 gp), a crate containing ten fine dresses (worth 25 gp each), and a velvet-lined wooden case containing a spyglass (worth 1,000 gp).

The southernmost ship holds five casks of wine (worth 1 gp each), a wooden mannequin clad in a fur shawl (worth 10 gp), bagpipes (worth 30 gp), a wax-sealed wooden tube containing five nautical charts (worth 25 gp each), and a waterlogged spellbook containing 1d4 + 6 spells (of your choice) of 6th level or lower.

# The Krigvind

The *Krigvind* returns when the characters obtain the *conch of teleportation* in Storvald's throne room (area 1G), but before a character has time to attune to it, or at another time of your choosing. Too big to fit in Svardborg's lagoon, the ship drops anchor next to the iceberg, south of the Jarl's Lodge (area 1) and within view of the docks south of the Drydock Lodge (area 3).

The *Krigvind* requires a crew of at least twenty giants and can hold up to forty giants, plus a thousand tons of cargo. The *Krigvind* has Jarl Storvald plus a crew of twenty **frost giants** (eight males and twelve females). Four operate the ballistae, one trims the sails, one controls the rudder, and fourteen pull the oars. Chained to the deck is Cryovain, a male **adult white dragon**. Behind the dragon are two empty holds where prisoners, slain whales, and stolen goods are kept.

Storvald is returning angry from not having caught a single whale, and that anger intensifies when he realizes that Svardborg has been invaded. If the giant owl in area 1H escaped, it accompanies Storvald and has warned him of intruders in Svardborg. Otherwise, the jarl and his crew become aware of intruders only after finding evidence of such or hearing the sound of the horn in area 2C. If there are obvious targets in sight, such as an airship parked on the iceberg or characters standing in the open, the frost giants use the ship's ballistae to attack them (see the "Features of the *Krigvind*" section).

Whether the frost giants are aware of intruders or not, they split up as follows:

- Five frost giants accompany Storvald as he makes his way to the jarl's lodge (area 1). Storvald heads to his throne room while the others wait in the feast hall.
- Five frost giants head to the giants' lodge (area 2).
- Five frost giants go around the iceberg to check on Cryovain's mate in the temple of Thrym (area 4).
- Five frost giants remain aboard the *Krigvind*—four to man the ballistae and one to guard Cryovain (see the "Dragon in Chains" section).

## The Frost Giant Jarl

Jarl Storvald is a **frost giant**, with the following changes:

- He has 189 hit points.
- He has a *blod stone* (see appendix B) bolted to a 50-pound iron chain that he wears around his neck.
- He speaks Common, Giant, and Giant Owl.
- He has Wisdom and Charisma scores of 16 (+3) and gains the Spellcasting action option described below.

***Spellcasting.*** Storvald casts one of the following spells, requiring no material components and using Wisdom as the spellcasting ability:

1/day each: *jump, locate animals or plants, locate object, water breathing, water walk*

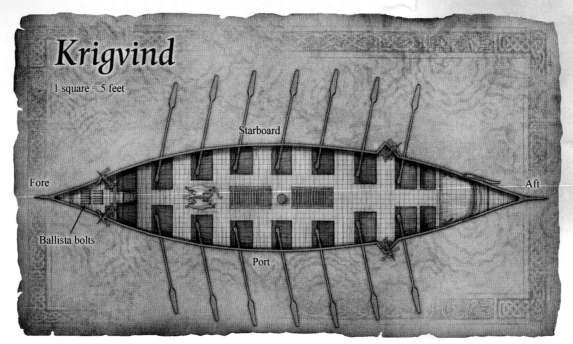

# Krigvind

1 square = 5 feet

Fore

Starboard

Ballista bolts

Port

Aft

MAP 7.3: THE KRIGVIND

## TREASURE

Storvald wears the Helm of Svardborg, a copper helm fitted with red dragon horns. The helm weighs 250 pounds, has no magical properties, and is worth 2,500 gp as an art object.

## DRAGON IN CHAINS

While Cryovain is chained to the deck, he is restrained. Two chains are secured to an iron collar around his neck. Two more chains secure his back legs. A creature can use a bonus action on its turn to magically release the four chains by speaking a command word ("uvenfetter") while within 60 feet of the dragon. Only Storvald and Nilraun know the command word. A *knock* spell or a similar effect can unlock a single collar, and a creature can break a single chain by using an action and succeeding on a DC 27 Strength (Athletics) check, or by reducing the chain to 0 hit points. Each chain has AC 20, 20 hit points, a damage threshold of 20, and immunity to cold, fire, psychic, poison, and thunder damage.

Storvald frees the dragon if the *Krigvind* is boarded or if the ship is attacked from the air. The jarl commands the dragon to fight as his ally. While Storvald has the dragon's mate and eggs as prisoners, Cryovain does as the jarl commands. If Cryovain's mate and young are liberated, the dragon turns on Storvald and his giants.

Cryovain is a mean creature who doesn't make deals with puny humanoids or show mercy toward creatures that are kind to him (including those who try to free him). Once he is freed, he reunites with his mate, and the two of them try to reclaim Svardborg as their lair.

Cryovain doesn't gain lair actions and can't cause regional effects in the vicinity of his lair.

## FEATURES OF THE KRIGVIND

The *Krigvind* is over 500 feet long with a 200-foot-tall mast. It has the fortitude of a floating castle, ignoring all damage except that dealt by the mightiest of siege engines. It has a few other noteworthy aspects.

## GIANT BALLISTAE

Only giant-sized creatures can operate the *Krigvind*'s ballistae. These weapons are mounted on swiveling bases and can fire in any direction. They follow the rules for ballistae (see the "Siege Equipment" section in chapter 8 of the *Dungeon Master's Guide*), except that they deal 44 (8d10) piercing damage on a hit.

## HOLDS

Forward and aft of the ship's mast are two empty holds with hinged doors made from logs lashed together with thick rope. There are no locks on these doors, since their weight alone prevents all but the strongest creatures from lifting them. It takes two frost giants or creatures of similar strength and size to lift one of the doors. Narrow gaps between the logs are wide enough for a Small creature to squeeze through.

The floors of the holds are 12 feet below deck level. The holds' thick wooden walls are sealed with pitch, and small holes at floor level keep the holds from flooding.

## TREASURE

Flying atop the ship's mast, doubling as a flag, is a *pennant of the vind rune* (see appendix B).

Each frost giant crew member with the exception of Storvald carries a sack containing 3d6 × 100 sp, 1d6 × 100 gp, and one mundane item, determined by rolling on the Items in a Giant's Bag table in the introduction.

> ### CHARACTER ADVANCEMENT
>
> Once the characters retrieve Jarl Storvald's *conch of teleportation*, a character can attune to it and use it to transport the party to Maelstrom. The characters might decide not to use the conch right away, perhaps because they want to attack the *Krigvind*, plunder the white dragons' trove, or take care of some other business. Make sure the characters advance to 9th level before moving on to chapter 10, "Hold of the Storm Giants." The characters need not confront Storvald or the white dragons to advance in level.

# CHAPTER 8: FORGE OF THE FIRE GIANTS

ALTO'S FOLLOWERS ARE SPREAD THROUGH-out the North, searching for pieces of an adamantine colossus called the Vonin-dod. The fire giant duke has also struck an alliance with the drow of House Xor-larrin: he promises to help them destroy their enemies if the drow help him steal Maegera, the fire primordial trapped within the under-ground dwarven city of Gauntlgrym. House Xorlarrin once held Gauntlgrym, but King Bruenor Battlehammer and his dwarves recently drove out the dark elves. They know its layout well, however. Duke Zalto has given the drow an *iron flask* (see chapter 7 of the *Dungeon Master's Guide*) in which to trap Maegera. While the drow creep back into Gauntlgrym to perpetrate this great theft (see the "Gauntlgrym" section in chapter 3), Zalto readies his family's ancestral forge for the arrival of Maegera and the Vonindod fragments.

In this part of their mission, the characters journey to Ironslag, Zalto's fortress in the icy mountains north of the Silver Marches. Duke Zalto and his fire giants unlocked and reclaimed the forge several months ago. Since then, the giants have captured prisoners and put them to work in the forges. The dwarves of Citadel Ad-bar and Citadel Felbarr are aware that fire giants have returned to Ironslag; however, the dwarves are still re-covering from the War of the Silver Marches and aren't prepared to mount an attack on the giant fortress.

Characters who visit Ironslag must contend not only with the fire giant duke, his family, and his most loyal

followers but also with a village of sinister yakfolk. If the characters obtain Zalto's *conch of teleportation*, they can use it to travel to Maelstrom, Hekaton's undersea citadel (see chapter 10, "Hold of the Storm Giants") and advance to the next stage of the adventure.

## FIRE GIANTS

Before running this part of the adventure, review the information on fire giants in the *Monster Manual*. It will help you roleplay the giants in this chapter.

### WARMONGER

Fire giants love to fight on a large scale, and Duke Zalto is one of the greatest warmongers of his age. For years, more powerful giants have curtailed Zalto's violent predilections, but with King Hekaton out of the picture and the storm giant court in disarray, Zalto has set into motion a plot to wage war on dragonkind for the glory of Surtur and the divine favor of Annam the All-Father. It begins with the reconstruction of the Vonindod, a drag-on-slaying colossus built by his ancient ancestors.

Duke Zalto has a choleric wife, Brimskarda, and two ill-tempered children—a belligerent daughter named Cinderhild and a sadistic son named Zaltember. The children distract him from his enterprise while his wife chastises him for not acting quickly enough. Brimskarda fears that one of the other giant lords will win the gods' favor first. Zalto is feeling the pressure, given that his success hinges on his ability to reignite Ironslag's adamantine forge and his minions' ability to retrieve all the missing fragments of the Vonindod. Unfortunately for Zalto, those are the least of his problems. The arrogant fire giant duke has failed to account for the interference of puny adventurers and a certain ancient red dragon (see the "Klauthen Vale" section in chapter 3 and the "Airship of a Cult" section in chapter 4).

## THE XORLARRIN ALLIANCE

Duke Zalto's alliance with House Xorlarrin is built on his firm promise that, once he climbs to the top of the ordning, he will use his forge and his newfound might to help House Xorlarrin destroy its enemies, starting with the dwarves who cast the drow out of Gauntlgrym. For their part, the drow are more interested in supporting Zalto's plan to wage war on dragonkind, for such a war would spell certain doom for the human, dwarven, and elven civilizations of the North—something the Xorlarrin drow desire above all else.

By the time the characters begin their journey to Ironslag, the drow have already managed to infiltrate Gauntlgrym (using their extensive knowledge of the dwarven city's layout). If the drow capture Maegera and deliver the *iron flask* to Ironslag, the characters might encounter them in the fire giant fortress. Unless the characters defeat Duke Zalto or otherwise prevent the *iron flask* from falling into his possession, he traps Maegera in the adamantine forge (area 29). The fire generated by Maegera is sufficiently hot for Zalto and his fire giants to begin reforging the Vonindod.

## YAKFOLK NEIGHBORS

Zalto has come to terms with the yakfolk that live on the mountainside above Ironslag. These malevolent creatures watch over the topmost entrance to the giants' fortress and also tend crops for the giants. In exchange, the giants leave them alone. The two kinds of yakfolk, warriors and priests, are described in appendix C. Also present in the village are Humanoid prisoners whom the yakfolk use for manual labor.

The yakfolk feign benevolence, offering food and shelter to wayward visitors, only to shed their guise of friendly hosts when their guests are most vulnerable. While their visitors sleep, the yakfolk beat them unconscious, strip them of their gear and weapons, and consign them to a life of menial labor. Deprived of food and warmth, prisoners rarely survive more than a week.

To untrained eyes, the yakfolk village looks like a peaceful, idyllic hideaway perched atop a mountain cliff, with granite walls to keep the howling wind at bay. The dwarves of Citadel Adbar know better than to trust the yakfolk, and they occasionally send patrols north to spy on the village. One of those patrols was ambushed by yakfolk and the survivors taken prisoner. The yakfolk used their magic to possess the bodies of their dwarven captives and, in the guise of these dwarves, yakfolk spies have infiltrated Citadel Adbar. These agents do everything in their power to discourage the dwarves from attacking Ironslag, mostly by assuring the citadel's leaders that the yakfolk pose no immediate threat. They also stand ready to assassinate Adbar's ruler, King Harnoth, if he tries to mount an attack on the village.

# IRONSLAG

North of the Silver Marches is a range of towering, snow-covered mountains known as the Ice Spires. The great dungeon-forge of Ironslag is under the one known to dwarves of the Silver Marches as Mount Hamarhaast ("hammer of ashes"). Carved into the base of a 500-foot-high mountainside cliff is a pair of 50-foot-tall adamantine doors—airtight valves sealed by ancient magic. Adventurers hoping to gain access to the forge must figure out a way through these doors or find an alternate route. One such route is a staircase carved into the mountainside (see area 1). Another involves the use of flying mounts or an airship.

## REACHING IRONSLAG BY LAND

Characters who travel to Ironslag on foot or by horse must cross a cold, rugged hinterland to reach their destination. They are likely to experience one or more random encounters (use the Random Wilderness Encounter table in chapter 3).

The main benefit of an overland approach is stealth; characters can reach the foot of the mountain and make their way up toward the yakfolk village undetected.

## REACHING IRONSLAG BY AIR

If the characters have an airship (see the "Airship of a Cult" section in chapter 4) or flying mounts (see the "Fireshear" and "Hawk's Nest" sections in chapter 3), they can travel to Ironslag by air and avoid land-based encounters. Characters mounted on hippogriffs can travel 54 miles per day (three 3-hour flights with 1-hour rests in between). Those mounted on griffons can travel 72 miles in the same amount of time.

Flying characters who approach the south side of Mount Hamarhaast see the staircase carved into the mountain (area 1), the yakfolk village perched on the mountainside (areas 2–10), and the great adamantine doors at the foot of the mountain (area 28).

The chimera that lives on the mountain poses a threat to characters who travel by air. If the chimera is home when the party first arrives, it might notice the approaching airship or flying mounts and attack. The chimera is particularly fond of hippogriff flesh; if it sees one or more hippogriffs approaching the mountain, it attacks the nearest one and doesn't break off its attack until it or the hippogriff is dead, or until its prey escapes.

There are plenty of safe places on the mountain for flying mounts to land. Once the chimera is dealt with, they can roost in its cave and use it as shelter. Flying mounts can also land safely on the staircase leading up the mountain or inside the yakfolk village. The airship can safely set down at the base of the mountain or in any level 30-foot-square space within the village. Landing an airship, griffons, or hippogriffs in the yakfolk village triggers a village-wide alarm.

## ZONES AND DENIZENS

Ironslag has two distinct zones: the yakfolk village on the mountainside, and the fire giant forge beneath it (all shown on maps 8.1 and 8.2). These zones are described below in more detail, with additional information

## Yakfolk Village Roster (Day)

| Area | Creature(s) | Notes |
|------|-------------|-------|
| 3 | 2 **yakfolk warriors** | When an alarm sounds, the yakfolk kill their prisoners and then head toward area 8, attacking intruders they encounter along the way. |
| 4A–4C | 1 **yakfolk warrior**, 2d4 **boars**, 2d4 yaks | When an alarm sounds, the yakfolk kills its prisoners and then heads toward area 8, attacking intruders it encounters along the way. If fought in the barn, the yakfolk frees two boars, which attack and pursue intruders. |
| 5B | 1 **yakfolk warrior** | The yakfolk remains here. |
| 5C, 5D | 2 **yakfolk warriors** | The yakfolk remain here. |
| 5E | 1 **yakfolk warrior** | The yakfolk remains here. |
| 6 | 1 **yakfolk warrior** | When an alarm sounds, the yakfolk kills its prisoners, then heads to area 8, attacking intruders it encounters along the way. |
| 7 | 1 **yakfolk warrior** | If the yakfolk spots intruders, it abandons its prisoners and heads to area 8 to warn the chief. If it hears the sound of the gong, the yakfolk kills the prisoners before heading to area 8. |
| 8 | Chief Kartha-Kaya, 2 **yakfolk priests** | If intruders are detected, one yakfolk strikes the gong to raise the alarm throughout the village while the others confront the interlopers. |

## Yakfolk Village Roster (Night)

| Area | Creature(s) | Notes |
|------|-------------|-------|
| 4A–4C | 2d4 **boars**, 2d4 yaks | The animals are trapped in their pens. |
| 5A | 2 **yakfolk warriors** | When an alarm sounds, the yakfolk kill their prisoners and then head toward area 8, attacking any intruders they encounter along the way. |
| 5B–5E | 2 **yakfolk warriors** | The yakfolk remain here. |
| 5F | 2 **yakfolk warriors** | As area 5A. |
| 6 | 1 **yakfolk warrior** | When an alarm sounds, the yakfolk kills its prisoners, then heads to area 8, attacking any intruders it encounters along the way. |
| 8 | Chief Kartha-Kaya, 2 **yakfolk priests** | If intruders are detected, one yakfolk strikes the gong to raise the alarm throughout the village while the others confront the interlopers. |

contained in the "Ironslag: General Features" sidebar. The Yakfolk Village Roster tables and the Forge Roster table summarize the hostile inhabitants of these two zones. An alarm raised in one zone has no effect on the alert status of the other zone.

During the day, some of the yakfolk oversee workers in the mill (area 3), the barns (areas 4A–4C), and the crop fields (area 7). At night, the workers are locked in cages, and the yakfolk retire to their huts (areas 5A–5F). Use the suitable Yakfolk Village Roster table (day or night) based on when the characters arrive.

### Yakfolk Village

Thick, gray clouds and howling wind make it easy for adventurers to approach the yakfolk village unseen and unheard. The doors to the village are barred from within, so the characters must either announce their arrival or find a way to circumvent the walls.

The yakfolk don't post guards and rarely leave their huts. The only yakfolk that has a chance of spotting adventurers who invade the village by climbing or flying over the walls is the one watching over the workers in area 7 during the day. Characters who enter the village within sight of this yakfolk must succeed on a DC 12 Dexterity (Stealth) check to avoid being spotted immediately. If this yakfolk spots any invaders, it heads to area 8 to warn Chief Kartha-Kaya.

The yakfolk chief has a large bronze gong in his hut (area 8). If he or his wives become aware of invaders, one of them strikes the gong. It is loud enough to be heard throughout the village, prompting the other yakfolk to come running. Yakfolk are vile in their pragmatism. Before setting out to confront invaders, they murder their prisoners to prevent them from being freed or turned against them. To conquer the village, the adventurers must defeat all adult yakfolk that live here.

If the adventurers approach the village in a nonthreatening manner, Chief Kartha-Kaya welcomes them with open arms and plays the part of a benevolent host, offering them fresh bread, cheese, jugs of warmed ale, and bowls of hot vegetable and barley soup. He allows them to smoke from his pipe and sleep in his hut. Characters who partake of the chief's hospitality must, after 1 hour of indulgence, succeed on a DC 15 Constitution saving throw or fall unconscious, as a result of either eating soup or smoking pipeweed that has been laced with a poison to which the yakfolk are immune. Elves and half-elves are immune to the sleep-inducing effect of the poison, and dwarves have advantage on the saving throw. A creature rendered unconscious in this way awakens if it takes any amount of damage; otherwise, the unconsciousness lasts for 3d6 hours. If the whole party is rendered unconscious, the yakfolk strip the adventurers of their belongings (including their armor), then bind their wrists and ankles in shackles. The party's belongings are piled in the chief's hut, and the prisoners are set to work harvesting crops in area 7, milking goats in area 6, or cleaning up animal waste in area 4. If the chief can't put the whole party to sleep, he waits to see what effect (if any) the poison has before sounding the gong.

| Area | Creature(s) | Notes |
|---|---|---|
| 10 | 2 **salamanders** | If the salamanders die, the prisoners try to escape from the mines. |
| 12 | 1 **fire giant**, 8 **orcs** | The giant and the orcs remain here. |
| 15 | 2 **fire giants**, 3 **ogres** | The giants head to area 20 if the bucket chain stops moving, while the ogres remain here. Both the giants and the ogres investigate loud noises in area 14. |
| 17 | 1 **salamander** | The salamander remains here to watch over the prisoners. |
| 18 | Zaltember (young **fire giant**), 4 **ogres** | Zaltember and the ogres investigate work stoppages in area 17. If wounded, Zaltember flees to area 31. |
| 20 | 2 armored **ogres** | The ogres remain here to watch over the prisoners. |
| 21 | 1 **fire giant** | The fire giant heads to area 20 if the wheel stops turning and raises the portcullis to area 22 if it needs reinforcements. |
| 22 | 7 **hell hounds** | The hell hounds remain here until they are set free. |
| 23 | 6 **hobgoblins**, 6 imprisoned **orcs** | The hobgoblins remain here to guard the prisoners, which include the orcs. If released, the orcs attack intruders. |
| 25 | 30 **goblins** | The goblins retreat to area 31 if they spot intruders. |
| 26B | Cinderhild (young **fire giant**), 2 **hobgoblins** | Cinderhild and the hobgoblins remain here. |
| 28 | Duke Zalto, 2 **hell hounds** | Duke Zalto and his hell hounds go to area 20 if the bucket chain stops moving. |
| 30 | 1 **iron golem** | The golem remains here until activated. |
| 31 | Brimskarda (**fire giant**), 2 **ogres**, 20 **goblins**, 5 **smoke mephits** | Brimskarda remains here to oversee the goblin and ogre workers. |
| 34 | 4 **fire giants** | The giants head to area 20 if the bucket chain stops moving. |
| 35A–35C | 1 **fire giant** | The giant responds to trouble in area 34 but otherwise remains here. |

As all the other adult yakfolk converge on the chief's hut, Kartha-Kaya and his wives attack conscious party members. The goals of the yakfolk are to beat the characters unconscious, strip them of their possessions, and force them to perform menial labor.

## Fire Giants' Forge

The fire giants' forge is a sprawling, two-level dungeon complex located beneath the yakfolk village and the mines. Raw iron ore from the mines are brought by cart to area 17 and loaded into iron buckets hanging from a carousel-like apparatus called a bucket chain. This bucket chain is turned by a wheel (area 20) and moves clockwise through the upper level of the fortress, transporting the iron ore to the dressing mill (area 12) to be broken up. Iron ore is then loaded into buckets and transported to the foundry, where ogres on the gantries (area 18) use long, hooked poles to tip the buckets, causing the ore to fall into the smelters below (area 34). Enormous bellows raise the temperature inside the smelters, melting the iron. The molten iron spills into a huge stone trough (area 35), where it is channeled into molds and used to forge giant-sized swords and armor.

The iron buckets are spaced 10 feet apart. Each one is 10 feet long, 6 feet wide, and 6 feet deep. A bucket can hold one Large creature or up to four Medium creatures. Two Small creatures can take the place of one Medium creature. While the wheel is turning, the buckets move at a speed of 10 feet per round; it takes a bucket roughly 15 minutes to complete one circuit.

Although the adamantine forge (area 29) isn't lit, the main foundry (area 34) is operational, and the racket from the weapon forges and the slowly revolving bucket chain echoes throughout the complex. The noise is so loud that activity in one area usually doesn't draw the attention of creatures in adjacent areas, making it possible for adventurers to eliminate foes a few at a time.

If the wheel stops turning, the bucket chain stops; this is a sign to the fire giants that something is amiss. Unless the buckets start moving again, all adult fire giants that haven't been killed or incapacitated head toward the wheel to find out what the problem is unless the Ironslag Roster table says otherwise.

## Reinforcements

Check to see if reinforcements arrive once during the day and once at night by rolling d100 and consulting the Ironslag Reinforcements table. If reinforcements are indicated, the fire giant leading them utters a command phrase in the Giant tongue that unlocks and opens the adamantine doors to the Vonindod assembly hall (see area 28). These reinforcements remain in the assembly hall until Duke Zalto commands them to go elsewhere. If Duke Zalto isn't around and there's evidence that the foundry has been attacked, the reinforcements begin searching the complex for intruders and survivors.

### IRONSLAG REINFORCEMENTS

| d100 | Creature(s) |
|---|---|
| 01–60 | None |
| 61–85 | 1 **fire giant** carrying a *rod of the Vonindod* and a Small fragment of the Vonindod that weighs 150 pounds |
| 86–00 | 1 **fire giant** carrying a *rod of the Vonindod* and accompanied by 1 **hobgoblin captain** and 3d6 **hobgoblins** dragging a Huge fragment of the Vonindod that weighs 2,500 pounds |

A set of enormous, airtight, magically locked stone doors seal Ironslag's main vault (area 28). Adventurers hoping to breach the fortress are more likely to succeed by climbing a 500-foot-high staircase carved into the cliffs (area 1) and either attacking or infiltrating the yakfolk village (areas 3–8).

**Yakfolk Village.** The yakfolk village is built on the mountainside and enclosed by 20-foot-high walls of mortared stone. The walls require a successful DC 15 Strength (Athletics) to climb. Double doors made of thick, ironbound oak are set into the walls. The doors are barred shut from within and are too strong to be broken down without the aid of a ram or a siege engine. The village's buildings are single-story huts with thatch roofs and walls made of piled stones held together with clay. The inside walls are made of smooth clay painted with colorful murals of breathtaking landscapes.

The yakfolk imprison their workers in iron cages at night. Each cage is fitted with an iron padlock that can be picked with thieves' tools and a successful DC 15 Dexterity check. Each adult yakfolk carries a key that opens all the cages.

**Ceilings.** The mines have 20-foot-high ceilings. The upper level of Ironslag has 30-foot-high ceilings, and the lower level has 50-foot-high ceilings.

**Doors.** Unless otherwise noted, Ironslag's doors are 20 feet tall and made of riveted iron plates, with handles 9 feet above the floor. A Huge giant has no trouble opening these doors. A smaller creature can attempt to open a door, provided that creature or some other helpful creature can reach the door's handle and unlatch it. While the handle is unlatched, a creature must use an action to push or pull on the heavy door, opening it with a successful DC 13 Strength (Athletics) check. On a failed check, the door doesn't open.

**Fireplaces.** Ironslag's fireplaces are hewn out of the rock and have basalt mantelpieces ornately carved with images of hell hounds and fire elementals. These openings are wide and tall enough for a party of adventurers to stand in. The fire in each one burns constantly, fed by natural gas that spews from 1d4 + 4 holes in the floor. A fireplace's flame can be extinguished by plugging the holes, each of which is 4 inches in diameter. Any creature that enters a fire or starts its turn there takes 10 (3d6) fire damage and catches fire; until someone takes an action to douse the fire, the creature takes 10 (3d6) fire damage at the start of each of its turns. A creature can extinguish the flames by using a quart or more of water, a thick blanket, or some other means.

**Gantries.** The upper level of Ironslag features iron walkways that are bolted to the walls and stabilized with taut chains bolted to the ceiling. Iron cranes, pulleys, and swing-arms are attached to some of these gantries. The gantry floors are iron grills with holes large enough for a human fist to pass through. A gantry grants three-quarters cover against any ranged attack that must pass through it to hit its target.

**Illumination.** The yakfolk village and other outdoor locations rely on natural light. The mines are unlit. Rooms and corridors in Ironslag that are equipped with fireplaces or iron braziers are dimly lit.

**Oversized Furnishings and Objects.** Most of the furnishings and other items in Ironslag are sized for fire giants. Exceptions are noted in the text. Furniture is typically twice as high, long, and wide as its human-sized equivalent and roughly eight times the weight. Small and Medium creatures can scuttle under and clamber over giant-sized furniture, treating the spaces they occupy as difficult terrain.

**Portcullises.** None of the portcullises in Ironslag have mechanical winches or other lifting mechanisms. They must be lifted manually. Any creature as big and strong as a fire giant can use an action to lift a portcullis. Any other creature must succeed on a DC 22 Strength (Athletics) check to lift a gate above its head. Although these gates are giant-sized, their iron bars are close enough together that even Small creatures can't squirm through.

**Stairs.** All staircases in the foundry are sized for fire giants. Each step is 3 feet tall by 3 feet deep. Medium and smaller creatures treat the staircases as difficult terrain.

# 1. THOUSAND STEPS

Thousands of years after Ironslag was abandoned, a clan of yakfolk used Humanoid workers to carve a staircase into the mountain cliff. At the top of these stairs, the yakfolk built a village. In the centuries that followed, clans of dwarves eager to plunder the mines made numerous failed attempts to conquer the yakfolk village before concluding that Ironslag's spoils weren't worth the effort. The rough-hewn steps—all one thousand of them—are proportioned for Medium Humanoids and ascend a total of 500 feet. The staircase, which averages 15 feet in width and has no railing, climbs in a straight line, passing above the sealed adamantine doors of the forge (area 28) and never once doubling back on itself until it reaches the outer walls of the yakfolk village.

Normal horses and ponies are reticent to climb the staircase. Coaxing such a creature to climb the stairs requires a DC 15 Wisdom (Animal Handling) check. Magically summoned mounts can be made to climb the stairs without an ability check. Mules, being surefooted, can climb the steps with ease and don't need to be coaxed.

## CHIMERA LAIR

After climbing 350 feet, the staircase is interrupted by a naturally formed, 50-foot-wide, 50-foot-deep chamber that a **chimera** has made into a lair. The ledge that leads across this area is covered with the bones of the chimera's kills (animals mostly, with a few orc and dwarf bones). The staircase resumes on the opposite side of the ledge, climbing another 150 feet to area 2. In the back of its lair, the chimera has a nest of bones, bits of tattered cloth, and clumps of earth and dead vegetation.

When the characters first arrive, there is a 50 percent chance that the chimera is present, in which case it attacks interlopers on sight. Otherwise, the chimera is out hunting and returns here at a time of your choosing.

**Treasure.** Characters who search the chimera's nest find several items taken from prey: 120 cp, 45 sp, six 100 gp gemstones, a torn-up suit of gnome-sized leather armor with a tiny electrum music box (worth 50 gp) tucked inside one of its many pockets, a dagger with an obsidian blade (worth 75 gp), a gold-plated helm studded with gems and topped with a tiny golden anvil (worth 750 gp), and 1d3 magic items (roll on Magic Item Table B in chapter 7 of the *Dungeon Master's Guide*).

# 2. BRIDGE

A cleft in the mountainside splits the yakfolk village in two. A wooden bridge spanned the gap until it rotted away. The yakfolk later built a safe bridge out of ropes and planks, lashed to four sturdy wooden posts.

## 3. MILL

An enormous wooden water wheel is attached to an iron axle and mounted above a swift-flowing river that spills down the mountainside. As the current turns the wheel, it not only powers the elevator in area 9 but also turns a large millstone located inside a hut next to the wheel, which has a beaded curtain entrance on the south wall. Grain harvested from area 7 is brought here and made into flour. The grinding of the millstone, the cranking of the water wheel, and the rush of water pouring down the mountainside drown out most other noises in this area.

During the day, two **yakfolk warriors** (see appendix C) are here, quietly overseeing a pair of shield dwarves (**commoners**) who shovel flour into burlap sacks, which are then taken to the bread ovens in area 5. The yakfolk sit on stools and either smoke pipes or sew blankets to pass the time as they watch the dwarves work. At night, the mill is unoccupied; the yakfolk retire to their hut (area 5A) while the dwarves sleep in a cage behind it. If the dwarves are rescued, they behave and act as described in the "Prisoners of the Yakfolk" sidebar.

### WATER WHEEL

Characters can try to reach area 9 by climbing through the openings in the frame of the water wheel and crawling along its iron axle. This is a dangerous act, and getting from one side to the other requires a successful DC 15 Strength (Athletics) or Dexterity (Acrobatics) check. A character who fails the check doesn't make it across and must make a DC 10 Dexterity saving throw. On a failed save, the character is swept down the river and tumbles down the mountainside, taking 70 (20d6) bludgeoning damage from the fall. On a successful save, the character manages to hang onto the wheel or the axle and avoid a fall, but is stuck between the spokes of the wheel and must repeat the check on his or her next turn to reach one end of the axle or the other.

Characters might try to make this route safer by preventing the water wheel from turning. Jamming a fence post or similar object between the spokes of the water wheel disables it, as does a successful DC 20 Strength

---

check made to grab the wheel and stop it from turning. When the wheel is stopped, the force of the current puts tremendous strain on it. At the end of each turn, the wheel has a 25 percent chance of breaking apart and tumbling down the waterfall. If that happens, the millstone and the elevator (area 9) cease to function. Any creature on the wheel when it breaks is swept over the cliff with the wreckage and takes 70 (20d6) bludgeoning damage from the fall. The breaking of the wheel puts the yakfolk village on alert. Meanwhile, Zalto orders one of the fire giants in area 34 to go to area 9, find out what has caused the elevator to stop working, and report back. Unless it encounters trouble along the way, the giant arrives in area 9 roughly 20 minutes after the elevator stops working. If the giant finds evidence of foul play, it reports back to Zalto (taking 20 minutes to reach him). Zalto then places the foundry on alert, meaning that its defenders can't be surprised.

## 4. BARN

The village has three barns (areas 4A, 4B, and 4C). Each contains a large chicken coop as well as muddy stalls that hold 2d4 **boars** and 2d4 yaks (use the **elk** stat block). The boars devour food waste and provide meat, while the yaks provide wool and serve as beasts of burden. Shovels, pitchforks, hoes, wooden buckets, yokes, and plows hang from the walls. Shelves hold sacks of seeds waiting to be planted the following spring.

During the day, a **yakfolk warrior** (see appendix C) is inside each barn, overseeing two humans (**commoners**) as they gather eggs, feed the animals, and clean up the stalls. If intruders confront the yakfolk in the barn, it uses an action to open a stall containing two boars. On their next turn, the boars rush out of the stall and attack intruders while the yakfolk kills the humans and then flees to the chief's hut (area 8) to warn Kartha-Kaya. The boars pursue characters who flee from the barn. At night, the yakfolk retires to a nearby hut while its workers are locked in an iron cage next to the barn. If the prisoners are rescued, they behave and act as described in the "Prisoners of the Yakfolk" sidebar.

The yakfolk in area 4A sleeps in area 5B at night. The yakfolk in area 4B sleeps in area 5E at night. The yakfolk in area 4C sleeps in area 5F at night.

## 5. HUT

The village has six huts set aside as homes for yakfolk warriors. Workers rescued from the yakfolk act as described in the "Prisoners of the Yakfolk" sidebar.

Each hut contains a pallet for each yakfolk resident, a stone oven for baking bread and heating soup, and baskets used for storing food and other supplies.

### 5A. MILLKEEPERS' HUT

This hut is unoccupied during the day. At night, the two **yakfolk warriors** (see appendix C) who oversee the mill (area 3) sleep here, while two shield dwarves (**commoners**) are locked in a cage outside.

***Treasure.*** Characters who search the hut find, amid the clutter, a basket containing 250 gp in mixed coinage, four pieces of fancy bead jewelry (worth 25 gp each), and

---

**PRISONERS OF THE YAKFOLK**

Most of the prisoners in the yakfolk village aren't given identities. You can assign names and genders to them as needed. Prisoners of the yakfolk who are set free try to return to their homelands. Prisoners can impart the following information:

- The yakfolk chief is named Kartha-Kaya. He has two wives.
- The yakfolk can't be trusted.
- A giant water wheel turns the millstone (area 3) and also raises and lowers an elevator (area 9) that leads down to the heart of the fire giant forge.
- Many more prisoners have been put to work in the mines. Next to the elevator is a spiral staircase (area 10) that leads down into the mines. One can reach the fire giant forge by traveling through the mines, but the elevator route is faster.
- A flying, three-headed monster (the chimera in area 1) is often seen circling high above the yakfolk village.

172   CHAPTER 8 | FORGE OF THE FIRE GIANTS

one magic item, determined by rolling on Magic Item Table A in chapter 7 of the *Dungeon Master's Guide*.

## 5B. Barnkeepers' Hut

During the day, one **yakfolk warrior** (see appendix C) and one yakfolk child are here. At night, the **yakfolk warrior** who oversees the nearby barn (area 4A) is also present. One moon elf (**commoner**) cleans the hut during the day and is confined in a cage outside at night.

***Treasure.*** Characters who search the hut for treasure find a basket containing 150 gp in mixed coinage and six pieces of fancy bead jewelry (worth 25 gp each).

## 5C. Family Hut

This hut contains two **yakfolk warriors** (see appendix C), day and night. One moon elf (**commoner**) cleans the hut during the day and is confined in an iron cage outside at night.

***Treasure.*** Hanging on the walls between colorfully painted murals of landscapes are four wooden ritual masks carved from wood and decorated with semiprecious gemstones. The masks are worth 250 gp each.

## 5D. Family Hut

This hut contains two **yakfolk warriors** (see appendix C), day and night. One moon elf (**commoner**) cleans the hut during the day and is confined in a cage outside at night.

***Treasure.*** Hanging from the ceiling is a gold censer (worth 250 gp). Four blocks of incense (worth 25 gp each) are kept in a basket next to the bread oven.

## 5E. Barnkeepers' Hut

During the day, one **yakfolk warrior** (see appendix C) is here. At night, the yakfolk warrior who oversees the nearby barn (area 4B) is also present. Two rock gnomes (**commoners**) clean the hut during the day and are confined in an iron cage outside at night.

***Treasure.*** Characters who search the hut find, amid the clutter, a basket containing ten pieces of bead jewelry (worth 25 gp each). One of the gnomes also hides a 500 gp gemstone on her person. She gives it to the characters as a reward if they free her from captivity.

## 5F. Farmers' Hut

At night, two **yakfolk warriors** (see appendix C) sleep here. During the day, the hut is unoccupied. One yakfolk oversees the workers in the nearby barn (area 4C). The other watches over workers tending the crops (area 7). All the workers are confined in one iron cage at night.

***Treasure.*** Characters who search the hut find a basket of miscellaneous nonmagical weapons confiscated from prisoners, including three daggers, a sling, a pouch containing thirteen sling stones, a hand crossbow, and four hand crossbow bolts. Another basket contains three small leather pouches, each containing 2d6 gemstones (worth 10 gp each). These gems were confiscated from prisoners who were later sent to the mines.

## 6. Dairy

This structure is composed of a residential hut attached to a barn and a dairy. An elderly **yakfolk warrior** (see appendix C) oversees the place and has two workers:

a human who cares for twelve goats in the barn and an orc who makes cheese in the dairy (both **commoners**). At night, these workers are locked inside an iron cage in a yard around back; if rescued, they act as described in the "Prisoners of the Yakfolk" sidebar.

### Treasure

Characters who search the yakfolk's hut find a basket containing 800 gp in mixed coinage, and a carved lapis lazuli pipe (worth 25 gp) resting atop a small table next to one magic item, determined by rolling on Magic Item Table B in chapter 7 of the *Dungeon Master's Guide*.

## 7. Crop Fields

Cut into the sloping mountainside are several tiers of tilled earth where the yakfolk grow barley, wheat, corn, flowers, and vegetables. Yaks fitted with yokes and plows till the fields. During the harvest season, crops are picked and stored in baskets.

Four lightfoot halflings (**commoners**) work the crop fields during the day. Watching them closely is a male **yakfolk warrior** smoking a wooden pipe. This yakfolk stands on ground high enough to look out over the entire village. If the halflings are rescued, they behave and act as described in the "Prisoners of the Yakfolk" sidebar.

At night, the fields are unguarded. At sundown, the yakfolk locks the workers in their cage (between areas 4C and 5F) before retiring to its hut (area 5F) until morning. Its mate looks after the north barn (area 4C).

## 8. Hall of the Yakfolk Chief

Built on high ground in the middle of the yakfolk village is a 60-foot-diameter hut with a beaded curtain entrance in the northeast wall, facing an outdoor campfire. The interior of the hut is one large chamber dominated by a shallow, 10-foot-diameter, circular pit around which yakfolk gather to hear the words of their chief. This pit is also where the yakfolk bring workers to fight one another and where they execute prisoners. The rest of the time, the pit contains a campfire that keeps the hut warm. Toward the back of the hut are piles of cushions, baskets laden with foodstuffs, and painted clay vessels filled with water, wine, and broth. Between the fire pit and the south wall is an engraved bronze gong and a wooden mallet that has a head padded with yak hide. The gong and the mallet hang from a wooden frame.

The hut is home to Chief Kartha-Kaya and his two wives, Imberu and Nahala (two **yakfolk priests**). These three spend their day arguing, eating, and smoking pipes. Their outward friendliness masks their cruelty.

Kartha-Kaya is a **yakfolk warrior** with the following changes:

- He has 70 hit points and a challenge rating of 4 (1,100 XP).
- He wields a *flame tongue greatsword*. While the sword is ablaze, it deals an extra 7 (2d6) fire damage on a hit.

Attending the chief are three moon elves: two male **commoners** and a female **noble**. They are unarmed and are searched for weapons each time they enter the hall. The noble is a moon elf princess, Halani Meliamne. The yakfolk infiltrated her clan by possessing several moon

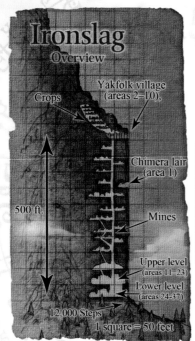

# Ironslag
### Overview

Crops

Yakfolk village
(areas 2–10)

Chimera lair
(area 1)

500 ft.

Mines

Upper level
(areas 11–23)

Lower level
(areas 24-37)

12,000 Steps

1 square = 50 feet

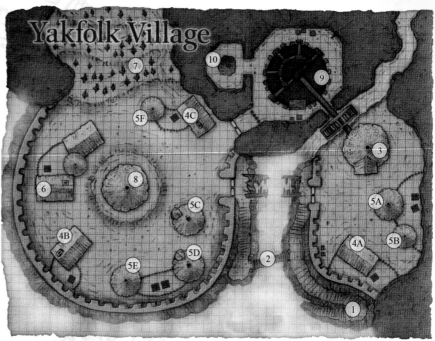

# Yakfolk Village

7

10

9

5F 4C

3

8 5C

6 5A

4B 5D 5B

2

5E 4A

1

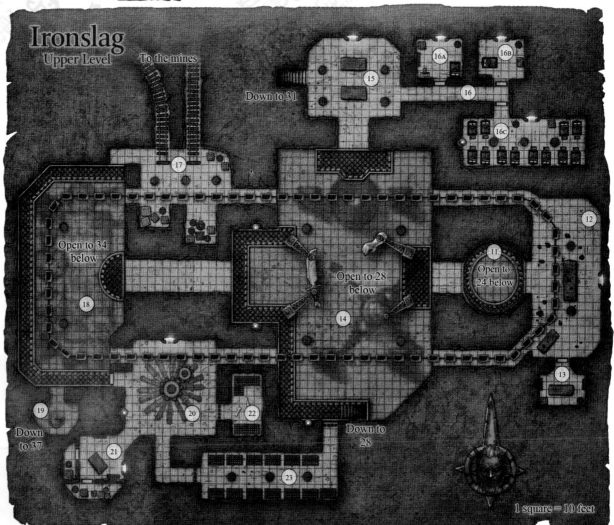

# Ironslag
### Upper Level

To the mines

Down to 31

16A 16B

15

16

16C

17

12

Open to 34
below

11
Open to
24 below

18

Open to 28
below

14

13

19

Down
to 37

20 22

Down to
28

21

23

1 square = 10 feet

MAP 8.1: IRONSLAG

elf hunters. One night, they murdered her brothers and kidnapped her. She longs to return to the Moonwood and offers the characters the gratitude of her clan if they take her home (see "Development" below).

## TREASURE

Hidden under a pile of empty baskets are four locked wooden chests, the keys for which are worn around Chief Kartha-Kaya's neck. Each lock can be picked with thieves' tools and a successful DC 15 Dexterity check.

The first chest contains 420 ep and 270 gp.

The second chest contains a clay jug painted with images of flying djinn (worth 25 gp), packed in straw.

The third chest contains weapons (three shortswords, four daggers, two battleaxes, three shortbows, and three quivers with 2d10 arrows in each) taken from prisoners.

The fourth chest contains a pair of electrum bracers with embossed dwarf faces on them (worth 250 gp for the pair), as well as 1d4 magic items. Roll on Magic Item Table C in chapter 7 of the *Dungeon Master's Guide* for the first item, and on Table A for any others.

## DEVELOPMENT

The moon elves know all the information in the "Prisoners of the Yakfolk" sidebar, as well as the following additional information:

- The elves' names are Halani (female), Jevin (male), and Vandar (male).
- Kartha-Kaya's wives are named Imberu and Nahala, and they serve as his advisors.
- Yakfolk can perform a ritual that lets them possess Humanoids by "crawling under their skin." (The elves have seen the ritual performed in Kartha-Kaya's hut.)
- The yakfolk ambushed a patrol of dwarves from Citadel Adbar, captured several members, and used their possession ritual to inhabit the dwarves. The chief then sent these assassins to kill Citadel Adbar's king. (The elves saw the ritual being performed.)

If the characters agree to escort Halani back to her clan in the Moonwood, she leads them to an icy waterfall in the heart of the forest where they can rest for the night. A group of six moon elf **scouts** wander by a short time later and offer to take Halani home. She has nothing to give the characters in gratitude, but the characters' kindness doesn't go unnoticed by the forest's ancient spirits. After finishing a long rest in the forest, each character who aided in Halani's safe return gains a *charm of the slayer* (see the "Supernatural Gifts" section in chapter 7 of the *Dungeon Master's Guide*).

Characters can follow up on the elves' claim that yakfolk are planning to assassinate the king of Citadel Adbar, either immediately or once they have concluded their business in Ironslag. If they visit the dwarven stronghold and seek an audience with King Harnoth, run the suggested encounter in the "Citadel Adbar" section in chapter 3. If they later return to Ironslag, the yakfolk village remains as they left it.

## 9. ELEVATOR SHAFT

Twenty-foot-tall iron doors in the mountainside northeast of area 8 swing open to reveal a rough-hewn passageway blocked by an iron portcullis (see the "Ironslag: General Features" sidebar for rules on opening doors and lifting portcullises). From the room beyond comes the sound of rushing water from the nearby river.

The passage leads to a cold, dark, and vast chamber with a 50-foot-high ceiling and an 80-foot-diameter, 500-foot-deep shaft in the middle of the floor. An iron rig is bolted to the pit's circular rim. Suspended from this rig by iron chains is a 60-foot-diameter, circular platform made from oak beams held together by iron bands and rivets. The platform ascends and descends the shaft constantly, powered by a wooden water wheel located behind an opening in the southeast wall. Characters who stand on a gantry bolted to the southern lip of the shaft and look down can see the platform as it rises up.

The elevator platform makes a programmed series of fifteen stops on its way up and down the shaft, each delay lasting 30 seconds. One of the stops is here, at the top of the shaft. As the platform descends, it stops at twelve mine levels (see the "Mines" section in area 10) and also pauses at the upper level of Ironslag (area 11) and the lower level (area 24). Accounting for all of its stops, it takes the elevator platform 15 minutes to move from the top of the shaft to the bottom, or vice versa. Between stops, it moves at a constant speed.

Bolted to the northeast wall of the room is a rectangular metal plate with a 3-foot-long iron lever protruding from it. The lever is mounted 10 feet above the floor and is in the up position. Pulling it down triggers a mechanism in the elevator's suspension rig that disengages the elevator from the water wheel axle, which immediately causes the elevator platform to stop. Moving the lever back up reconnects the elevator to the axle, causing the platform to move again. A creature that can reach the lever can use its action to make a DC 17 Strength (Athletics) check, raising or lowering the lever on a success.

The chains supporting the platform are rusty but large and secure. The platform can support tens of thousands of pounds without so much as a groan of protest.

## 10. STAIRS TO THE MINES

In the middle of this otherwise featureless room is a spiral staircase with 10-foot-wide stone steps descending into darkness—to the topmost level of Ironslag's mines.

### MINES

The mines form a multilevel labyrinth of 20-foot-diameter, rough-hewn tunnels—just tall and wide enough for a fire giant to navigate. Spiked to the tunnel floors are rail tracks built for iron carts. To get from one mine level to the next, one must traverse a series of ramps or use the elevator that connects areas 9, 11, and 24.

No map of the mine tunnels is provided. If the characters find themselves here, simply describe the maze of rough-hewn tunnels as having occasional upward- and downward-sloping passages. The upper levels of the mines are abandoned. Characters who explore that area find a few broken picks and shovels, plus the occasional empty cart resting on the tracks. As they make their way down, they begin to hear distant sounds of a mining operation: picks striking stone and the sound of rocks being shoveled into metal carts.

Two **salamanders** in the service of Zalto patrol the deepest levels of the mine, watching over eleven shield dwarves and seventeen rock gnomes (all **commoners**). The prisoners are split into groups of two or three. Some use picks or shovels, while others push carts down ramps toward area 17. All wear ankle shackles, reducing their speed from 25 feet to 5 feet. The shackles' keys are missing, but a lock can be picked with thieves' tools and a successful DC 10 Dexterity check.

## DEVELOPMENT

The dwarves and gnomes dare not try to escape while the salamanders are about. If the characters dispose of the salamanders and clear a path to freedom, the prisoners head to the yakfolk village. Assuming no yakfolk are left there to oppose them, they descend the thousand steps to the foot of the mountain (possibly risking attack from the chimera in area 1). Before they flee, the prisoners tell their liberators that more prisoners have been put to work in other areas of Ironslag. The dwarves and gnomes are familiar with areas 17, 18, 20, 23, and 34. If the characters request a guide, a thankful rock gnome volunteers to join them. Her name is Wiri Fleagol. Wiri is a **commoner**, with the following changes:

- She is chaotic good.
- She has a speed of 25 feet and darkvision out to a range of 60 feet.
- She speaks Common and Gnomish.
- She has advantage on all Intelligence, Wisdom, and Charisma saving throws against magic.
- She has a clockwork mouse in a hidden pocket. When she sets it on the ground, it moves 5 feet in a random direction on each of her turns, squeaking as it goes.

## 11. ELEVATOR, UPPER LEVEL

A ring-shaped gantry is bolted to the wall of the elevator shaft, 50 feet above the floor of the lower level (area 24). When the elevator stops here, the platform is level with the gantry. The circular space that the gantry surrounds is just wide enough for the platform to pass through it.

No guards are stationed here. Characters can hear the rattling of chains all around them.

## 12. DRESSING MILL

Eight **orcs** work here under the watch of a **fire giant**. The bucket chain moves from north to south through this room, the iron buckets dangling a few feet above the floor. As buckets of iron ore pass by, two orcs with hooked poles tip the buckets and dump their contents onto the floor. Two more orcs place the ore atop stone slabs, and two more orcs pick out impurities. The last two orcs load the ore back into the buckets and shovel the impurities into piles. (Once a week, production stops so that the impurities can be loaded into the buckets and transported back to area 17, to be carted away by workers and deposited in cleared sections of the mines.) A fire burns in a hearth in the middle of the east wall.

The orcs are prisoners but fight alongside the fire giant. If the giant dies, the orcs can be persuaded to halt their attack and flee to the elevator (area 11) by a character who makes a successful DC 16 Charisma

(Intimidation or Persuasion) check. The giant carries a 2-foot-long iron key that unlocks the iron trunk in area 16B.

## 13. OVERSEER'S OFFICE

The room to the south of the dressing mill contains a basalt table, a barrel of polluted water with iron pokers sticking out of it, an iron crate filled with manacles, and two racks of hooked poles. Hanging on the south wall is a set of rusty manacles. Prisoners who misbehave are hung up and tortured here. None are here now.

## 14. ASSEMBLY HALL, UPPER LEVEL

Wide iron gantries extend a short distance into a vast chamber. Two lit braziers illuminate the western gantry, which has iron stairs leading down to the floor of area 28. The steps are iron grills with holes large enough for a human fist to pass through. The steps provide three-quarters cover against any ranged attack that must pass through them to hit its target. The northern and eastern gantries are unlit. The ceiling is 40 feet above the gantries, the floor 50 feet below. The rattling of the bucket chain fills the room. Four cable towers support the bucket chain as it moves through this area.

Hanging in midair, held in place by chains bolted to the floor and ceiling, is the helmed head and upper torso of the Vonindod. Cranes extending out from the western and eastern gantries have two other fragments of the colossus hanging from them: an enormous greatsword and a giant gauntlet-like hand and forearm. These fragments are hanging at the same level as the gantries. They are too heavy for the characters to unhitch, but each crane has a winch that can be released, causing the fragment to fall to the floor with a crash that can be heard throughout Ironslag. If they haven't already been defeated or lured elsewhere, the creatures in areas 12 and 15 investigate the sound, arriving on the northern and eastern gantries in 2 and 3 rounds, respectively. Releasing the catch on a winch requires a *knock* spell. A creature can also use its action to make a DC 15 Strength (Athletics) check, releasing the catch on a success. Any creature under the greatsword or the gauntlet when it falls must succeed on a DC 15 Dexterity saving throw or take 55 (10d10) bludgeoning damage and be knocked prone and restrained under the fragment. A creature in this predicament can use its action to make a DC 20 Strength (Athletics) or Dexterity (Acrobatics) check, extricating itself on a success.

Set into the south wall at the top of the stairs, close to another lit brazier, is an iron portcullis. Beyond the portcullis is a dark hallway that leads to area 23.

## DEVELOPMENT

Characters can move quietly onto or along the gantries without being heard or seen by Duke Zalto and his hell hounds in area 28 below. To reach the western gantry, Zalto and his hounds climb the iron stairs. To reach the northern gantry, they must move to area 31, climb the staircase there, and pass through area 15. To reach the eastern gantry, they must take the elevator platform from area 24 to area 11. Loud noises on the north gantry attract the creatures in area 15.

## 15. Mustering Hall

The walls of this room bear frescoes that depict fire giants forging armor and weapons, marching to war, and binding red dragons in chains. Four basalt pillars support the 40-foot-high ceiling, and iron chandeliers bereft of candles hang above a pair of basalt tables. A fireplace in the north wall provides the only warmth and light.

Unless trouble has been detected inside the forge, three **ogres** stand around the northernmost table, where two **fire giants** are locked in an arm-wrestling contest. The ogres are cheering on the giants and paying close attention to the contest. Characters who stay in the shadows and try to cross the room quietly gain advantage on their Dexterity (Stealth) checks.

The fire giants and the ogres investigate any loud disturbance in area 14. If the bucket chain stops moving, the giants head to area 20 to learn why, leaving the ogres, who brawl among themselves.

A staircase in the west wall descends to area 31.

## 16. Giants' Quarters

A long, dark hallway has three doors set into it. The rooms to the north are the living space of Duke Zalto's prisoner overseers (see areas 12 and 21), and the larger room to the south serves as quarters for the general fire giant population. No giants are in these rooms now.

### 16A. Northwest Room

This room contains an iron-framed bed, a cabinet filled with manacles and instruments of torture, a large cask of dwarven ale, a barrel of fresh water, and a wooden trunk bound in iron and fitted with an iron padlock. The trunk is 9 feet tall, 12 feet long, and 8 feet wide, and it weighs 750 pounds. Wooden poles stacked against the wall can be slipped through iron rings on the sides of the chest, making it easy for workers to transport it.

The fire giant in area 21 carries the key to the padlock, which is too big to be picked with thieves' tools. A Small or Medium character can reach into it and open it with a successful DC 20 Dexterity check.

**Treasure.** The wooden trunk holds 2d4 mundane items, determined by rolling on the Items in a Giant's Bag table in the introduction. Among this junk are 11,000 cp, 3,500 sp, 220 gp, and the bronze-plated skull of a slain adult red dragon (worth 750 gp and weighing 750 pounds).

### 16B. Northeast Room

This room holds an iron-framed bed, two cabinets (one containing manacles, the other containing instruments of torture), a barrel of water, a barrel of dwarven ale, two empty ironbound wooden crates, and an iron trunk with a lock built into it. The trunk is 7 feet tall, 13 feet long, and 8 feet wide, and it weighs 1,000 pounds. The fire giant in area 12 carries the key to the lock, which is too big to be picked with thieves' tools. A Small or Medium character can reach into it and open it with a successful DC 20 Dexterity check.

**Treasure.** The trunk contains 15,000 cp, 6,200 sp, 700 gp, a drinking horn made from a gorgon's horn and bearing flame-like patterns (worth 2,500 gp and weigh-

ing 50 pounds), and a sack containing 2d4 mundane items, determined by rolling on the Items in a Giant's Bag table in the introduction.

### 16C. South Room

Twelve iron-framed beds line the walls of this chamber. At the foot of each bed is an unlocked, footlocker made of beaten iron. Three basalt pillars support the ceiling.

**Treasure.** Each footlocker contains a sack holding 1d10 × 100 gp plus 1d4 mundane items, determined by rolling on the Items in a Giant's Bag table in the introduction.

## 17. Ore Depository

Characters who descend through the mines (see area 10) eventually end up here, emerging through one of two tunnels in the north wall. Rail tracks running through these tunnels end at a pair of wooden barriers. Three pillars of black basalt support the ceiling. The bucket chain passes through gaps in the western and eastern walls, its iron buckets dangling a few inches above the floor. A tunnel leading west connects to an iron gantry (area 18) that overlooks the foundry (area 34).

A **salamander** stands guard in the middle of the room, watching over four shield dwarves (**commoners**). The dwarves have ankle manacles that reduce their speed from 25 feet to 5 feet. When a cart of iron ore arrives, the dwarves transfer it to the bucket chain, to be carried east to area 12. The bucket chain moves constantly, even if new ore isn't being transferred, as long as the wheel in area 20 turns.

Empty wooden barrels and crates are piled in the northeast corner of the room and in alcoves to the south. These containers once held food and water for miners, but they are ancient and fall apart if disturbed.

### Development

When they aren't working here, the dwarves are imprisoned in the prisoner pens (area 23). If the salamander dies and the dwarves are released from their shackles, they offer to lead the characters to the wheel (area 20) and the prisoners pens (area 23), in hopes of freeing the human, dwarf, and gnome prisoners in those areas. Their path takes them through area 18.

A few minutes after the workers in this room stop working, other creatures along the bucket chain (in areas 12, 18, and 34) begin receiving empty buckets. The empty buckets don't immediately cause concern, for shift changes and work breaks are common. But if 15 minutes pass and no ore arrives, Zaltember and the ogres in area 18 investigate, entering from the west. If he finds intruders or evidence thereof, Zaltember heads to area 19, descends the staircase to the lower level, and heads to areas 31 and 28 to warn his parents. The ogres remain behind, covering his retreat if necessary.

## 18. Foundry, Upper Level

This area is incredibly hot, and characters who linger here are susceptible to the effects of extreme heat (see the "Wilderness Survival" section in chapter 5 of the *Dungeon Master's Guide*). A rusted iron gantry clings to the north, west, and south walls 50 feet above the floor

ADVENTURERS INCUR THE WRATH OF
DUKE ZALTO AND HIS HELL HOUNDS.

of the main foundry, which echoes with the sound of clanging metal, rattling chains, whooshing bellows, and bubbling molten iron. The ceiling looms 40 feet above the gantry. Cable towers support the bucket chain that runs near the path of the gantry.

Unless they have been drawn to area 17, four **ogres** armed with 15-foot-long hooked poles stand on the gantry above the smelters in area 34. They use the poles to tip buckets of iron ore into the smelters. Overseeing them is Duke Zalto's fat and lazy son, Zaltember. When the characters first arrive, Zaltember is dangling a shield dwarf **commoner** by his ankles over the southernmost smelter and threatening to drop him into it unless the dwarf pleads for his life. (Zaltember plucked the dwarf from the wheel and accused him of slacking off.) The dwarf refuses to give the sadistic young fire giant any satisfaction, which infuriates Zaltember. The ogres merely stand and watch with idiotic glee.

Zaltember is fifteen years old and stands 9 feet tall. He uses the **half-ogre** stat block, with these changes:

- He is lawful evil.
- He wears a chain shirt (AC 13).
- He has Intelligence and Wisdom scores of 10 (+0), and has a passive Perception score of 10.
- He lacks darkvision but is immune to fire damage.

Zaltember is a bully and coward. If wounded, he flees to area 31 (by way of areas 19, 37, 34, and 33) to be with his mother. If he is captured or cornered, he declares that he is the son of Duke Zalto, hoping to cow his captors into letting him go. Zaltember doesn't know where his father keeps his *conch of teleportation* but assumes it's locked in his father's iron chest (see area 26A).

### TREASURE
Zaltember wears a black opal pendant on a golden chain (worth 2,500 gp and weighing 25 pounds).

### DEVELOPMENT
If battle erupts here, the four fire giants working in the foundry below begin hurling globs of molten iron at enemies they can see. (See area 34 for details.)

If the characters take Zaltember prisoner, they can use him as leverage when dealing with either of his parents. Duke Zalto and Duchess Brimskarda don't want any harm to befall their son and will accede to any reasonable demand to have him released. (The duchess speaks for her husband in all respects if she's the one the characters negotiate with.) Before conceding to any demands, the duke and the duchess try to convince Zaltember's captors to release him as a show of good faith. This is a trick; the duke and the duchess will freely renege on their promises if they have nothing to lose.

If the characters refuse to release Zaltember until they have obtained Duke Zalto's *conch of teleportation*, the duke or the duchess gives it to them in exchange for the promise of Zaltember's safe return. Zalto and Brimskarda also allow the characters to leave Ironslag with the conch and whatever other treasure they have amassed, provided the characters agree to release Zaltember once they have made their escape.

If Zalto has Maegera in his custody (see the "Special Delivery" section later in this chapter), the characters can demand that he surrender the fire primordial. This he won't do, for the loss of Maegera would thwart his plan to rise to the top of the ordning. If he must choose between his son and his destiny, Zalto chooses the latter. Not even his wife can convince him otherwise.

## 19. STAIRS DOWN

The floor here is at the same level as the gantry in area 18. A wrought iron spiral staircase descends 50 feet to area 37. The steps are iron grills with holes large enough for a human fist to pass through. The steps provide three-quarters cover against any ranged attack that must pass through them to hit its target.

## 20. WHEEL

A fireplace in the middle of the north wall keeps this area warm and lit. An enormous wheel made of iron gears and wooden spokes dominates the room. The wheel is rigged to the bucket chain that travels throughout the forge. Turning the great wheel are ten shield dwarves and ten humans (all **commoners**) with iron manacles around their ankles. These prisoners all suffer from 4 levels of exhaustion (see appendix A in the *Player's Handbook*). Every 2 hours spent turning the wheel increases their level of exhaustion by 1.

Watching over the prisoners are two **ogres** clad head to toe in spiked iron armor (AC 18). When the prisoners reach level 5 exhaustion, they collapse, and the ogres bellow for the hobgoblins in area 23 to bring replacements. At the end of the shift change, the hobgoblins drag the exhausted prisoners back to their cells to rest.

The prisoners stop turning the wheel if combat breaks out between the characters and the ogres. When this happens, the fire giant overseer in area 21 investigates, joining the battle in the following round. If the overseer can't bring the situation under control quickly, he raises the portcullis to area 22 and frees the hell hounds to join the battle. Once the characters have dealt with the ogres, the fire giant, and the hell hounds, they can try freeing the prisoners from their manacles, either by breaking them or picking the locks. Unless they dispose of the enemies quickly, freeing the prisoners has to wait until Duke Zalto and the others have been dealt with.

### DEVELOPMENT
When the wheel stops turning unexpectedly, the bucket chain stops moving. The entire forge falls quiet, and all adult fire giants in the complex converge on this room to find out what has happened. The first to arrive (after the overseer from area 21) is Duke Zalto with his hell hounds. Zalto climbs the stairs of the western gantry in area 14 and passes through area 23 to reach this chamber, arriving 1 minute after the bucket chain stops.

The prisoners know that there are more prisoners in cages nearby (area 23). They help their liberators but are too exhausted to be of any use in combat.

## 21. Overseer's Office

A fireplace heats and illuminates this chamber. An obsidian mug sized for a fire giant rests atop a basalt table, lying beneath which are several empty casks of ale. Marble shelves on the north and south walls stand bare. Iron doors in the western and southern walls lead to storage rooms that contain stolen crates of rations and barrels of water to nourish the prisoners.

A **fire giant** dwells here. This overseer is tasked with herding and feeding the prisoners, as well as feeding and exercising the hell hounds in area 22. The giant carries an iron key that unlocks the trunk in area 16A.

### Treasure

The obsidian mug on the table is worth 500 gp and weighs 100 pounds.

## 22. Hell Hound Pen

An iron portcullis blocks the tunnel leading to this room. Gnawed, blackened humanoid bones lie strewn upon the chamber floor amid loose sets of rusty manacles.

Seven **hell hounds** howl and growl from within two spacious iron cages. Four hounds are confined in the north cage, three in the south cage. Each cage door is held shut with a simple latch; a creature can use an action to unhook it and open the cage. The hounds are trained to obey fire giants and no one else.

## 23. Prisoner Pens

Iron portcullises seal off this long, foul-smelling hall. Three black basalt pillars support the ceiling, and thirteen 10-foot-tall iron cages line the walls. A padlock hangs from each cage door. A Small or Medium character outside the cage can, with a successful DC 20 Dexterity check, open a lock using thieves' tools.

Six **hobgoblins** guard this hall, two standing next to each pillar. One of the hobgoblins carries a ring of keys; these keys open the locks to the cages in this room.

### Prisoners

Only four of the cages are occupied when the characters first arrive. The first contains five shield dwarves (three male and two female **commoners**), the second holds seven rock gnomes (three male and four female **commoners**), the third contains three humans (one male and two female **commoners**), and the last one holds six **orcs**. Only the orcs wear armor and carry weapons, and they attack anyone who frees them that isn't a fire giant. These orcs replace the ones in area 12 whenever there's a shift change.

The non-orc prisoners wear manacles on their ankles that reduce their speed by 20 feet. These manacles must be broken or picked, since there are no keys to unlock them. The prisoners follow the instructions of their liberators and want nothing more than to escape the fire giant stronghold. They are particularly afraid of Duke Zalto's son, who likes to visit the pens and torment the prisoners from time to time.

## 24. Elevator, Lower Level

The 500-foot-tall elevator shaft that penetrates the fire giant stronghold ends here. Iron pillars support a ring-shaped iron gantry 50 feet overhead (area 11). Wide tunnels lead north and west to areas 25 and 28. A flurry of goblin voices can be heard to the north.

## 25. Feasting Hall

Thirty **goblins** are in the midst of cleaning the feasting hall when the characters first arrive. Fearing the wrath of Duchess Brimskarda, they frantically tidy up giant-sized plates and mugs while fighting over table scraps. If the goblins are attacked, they flee west through the hallway and beat on the doors to area 31 until they are let inside. If the western tunnel is blocked off, they make their stand here.

Iron braziers in alcoves dimly illuminate the hall. Pillars and basalt partition-walls support the 50-foot-high, vaulted ceiling, from which hang heavy iron chandeliers, their candles draped in cobwebs. The chains used to raise and lower the chandeliers are fastened to iron hooks mounted on the walls. Set into the north wall is a fireplace, and arranged about the room are basalt tables covered with bronze dishware. An iron spit is mounted above a fire pit fueled by natural gas.

### Development

Any goblin that is captured and interrogated claims to be in the service of Duke Zalto and Duchess Brimskarda. The goblins are familiar with the layout of the fire giant stronghold and can be bullied into acting as guides or providing directions. Goblin captives always act in their own self-interest, and goblins forced to serve the characters are quick to betray them when the characters no longer have the upper hand.

## 26. Ducal Quarters

This T-shaped hallway has doors to the north and south. Each door opens into a bedchamber.

### 26A. North Bedchamber

Duke Zalto and Duchess Brimskarda sleep here, in an enormous bed with a frame made from crisscrossing iron sword blades welded together. Dangling above the bed are large chains and manacles, the purpose of which is known only to the duke and the duchess. A 15-foot-diameter shield made from adult black dragon scales is displayed on the north wall behind the bed. An iron chandelier hangs from the ceiling over the center of the room, near the foot of the bed. A chain connected to the chandelier is snagged on an iron hook mounted to the east wall above a 10-foot-tall basalt table with some valuable items resting on it and a large iron chest tucked underneath it (see "Treasure"). Two wardrobes of fire-scorched wood stand against the west wall. A giant barrel in the southeast corner serves as a stool and rests in front of a burnished, full-length mirror mounted in the south corner of the east wall. An iron brazier hangs from a hook mounted on the south wall near the door.

***Treasure.*** The duke's wardrobe contains a cloak (worth 2,500 gp and weighing 250 pounds) made from

# Ironslag
### Lower Level

MAP 8.2: IRONSLAG, LOWER LEVEL

a red dragon's scaly hide and wings, with a necklace of engraved gold plates draped over its broad shoulders. The duchess's wardrobe contains a gown made of gold ingots and rings (worth 7,500 gp and weighing 750 pounds). The items atop the basalt table include a bejeweled obsidian hair brush with wire bristles (worth 750 gp and weighing 75 pounds), a tinderbox made of ebony inlaid with flames of melted gold (worth 750 gp and weighing 75 pounds), a hand mirror with a gilded iron handle and frame (worth 250 gp and weighing 125 pounds), and a bronze jewelry chest (worth 250 gp and weighing 250 pounds) that contains six giant-sized gold rings with gemstones set into them (each worth 2,500 gp and weighing 25 pounds).

The iron chest under the table is 9 feet long, 6 feet tall, and 6 feet wide, and it weighs 600 pounds. A crude combination lock is built into it. The lock has three tumblers, each one displaying the ten Dwarvish (Dethek) glyphs for the numbers from 0 to 9. The lock's combination is 7-2-7. Duke Zalto and Duchess Brimskarda are the only ones who know it. The lock can be picked with thieves' tools and a successful DC 21 Dexterity check, or it can be opened with a *knock* spell or similar magic.

If the chest is opened without using the combination, the act releases a cloud of incendiary gas that ignites on contact with the air and fills a 20-foot-radius sphere centered on the chest. Any creature in the area must succeed on a DC 15 Dexterity saving throw, taking 45 (10d8) fire damage on a failed saving throw, or half as much damage on a successful one. The trap can't be disabled from outside the chest and is triggered only once.

Inside the chest, resting on a bed of ashes, is a giant-sized adamantine crown set with six black opals (worth 7,500 gp and weighing 150 pounds). Under the ashes are 6,300 gp, Duke Zalto's *conch of teleportation* (see appendix B), and 1d4 magic items. Roll on Magic Item Table F in chapter 7 of the *Dungeon Master's Guide* for the first item and on Table D for any others.

## 26B. SOUTH BEDCHAMBER

The duke's teenage son and daughter share this room, but only the daughter is here when the characters arrive. Cinderhild feels like a prisoner in Ironslag. She wants to explore the world, which her father has described as a boundless realm full of wonders, but her parents refuse to let her leave, and she's furious at them. She has a low opinion of her younger brother, Zaltember.

Eighteen-year-old Cinderhild stands 11 feet tall. She is big-boned with thick, orange hair and a mean temper. She wields a greatclub and uses the **ogre** stat block, with these changes:

- Cinderhild's alignment is lawful evil.
- Cinderhild is unarmored (AC 9).
- She has Intelligence and Wisdom scores of 12 (+1), and has a passive Perception score of 11.
- She doesn't have darkvision, but has immunity to fire damage.
- Cinderhild hides a 2-foot-long golden pin (see "Treasure") in her hair, and she can use an action to make a melee weapon attack with it. The attack has a +6 bonus to hit, has a reach of 5 feet, targets one creature, and deals 9 (2d4 + 4) piercing damage on a hit.

When the characters first arrive, Cinderhild is lying face down on her bed, weeping and wallowing in self-pity. Two female **hobgoblins** serve as her handmaidens, though they do nothing to comfort her. They are armed with longswords but don't carry longbows.

If the characters try to parley with Cinderhild, she demonstrates the impertinence and mood swings of a spoiled princess. She quickly realizes that she can use the characters to keep her parents distracted while she sneaks out of the fortress. She tells them that her father spends most of his time with the "dragon slayer" (the Vonindod in area 28), while her mother likes to oversee activity in the kitchen (area 31).

It might occur to the characters that they could benefit from capturing Cinderhild and then ransoming her back to her parents. If ordered to surrender, she tells the characters that she's willing to pretend to be their prisoner until her father gives them what they want. If they accept her counterproposal, she allows them to dispose of her handmaidens before surrendering, on the condition that they keep her as their prisoner until they have escaped from Ironslag. Once she is far enough away from her parents, Cinderhild demands to be released, vowing never to trouble the characters again (a promise she aims to keep). She gives them her fire opal pendant (see "Treasure"), which was a gift from her parents, to seal the bargain. Cinderhild doesn't know where her father keeps his *conch of teleportation* but assumes it's locked in his iron chest (see area 26A).

Cinderhild and Zaltember sleep in iron-framed beds. North of Cinderhild's bed is an empty barrel that she uses as a stool when she's sitting in front of a full-length mirror mounted on the north corner of the western wall.

An alcove to the south holds two large, empty crates and a third crate filled with half-burned dolls and broken toys that Cinderhild and Zaltember once cherished.

**Treasure.** Cinderhild wears a fire opal pendant on a gold chain around her neck (worth 2,500 gp and weighing 25 pounds) and has a 2-foot-long golden pin (worth 250 gp and weighing 5 pounds) hidden in her hair.

**Development.** Duke Zalto and Duchess Brimskarda treat Cinderhild's capture the same way they treat the capture of their son (see area 18 for details).

## 27. War Room

A basalt table, its base sculpted to look like a fountain of black fire, stands in the middle of this well-lit room. Bare marble shelves jut from the walls at heights of 10 and 15 feet. Standing against the northwest wall is an **iron golem** with a rune-carved iron ingot embedded in its forehead (see "Treasure"). Although golems normally have elemental spirits of earth trapped within them, this golem holds an elemental spirit of fire. The golem is deactivated and incapacitated, although that fact isn't readily apparent.

Activating the iron golem requires one to speak the proper command word. Not even Duke Zalto knows it. Casting an *identify* spell on the golem reveals the long-lost command word, which is "ildstryke."

When the golem is activated, fires burn in its eyes, and sulfurous smoke billows from vents in its shoulder pauldrons. Any creature that activates the golem can issue commands to it. The elemental spirit that animates it is compelled to obey the commands of fire giants; as a result, a command issued by a fire giant supersedes any other commands the golem has received. The golem is magically programmed to shut down after 1 hour. Once it shuts down, the golem can't be reactivated for 1 hour.

### Treasure

The ingot embedded in the iron golem's forehead is an *ingot of the skold rune* (see appendix B). It can be removed only while the golem is deactivated or when it is destroyed.

## 28. Assembly Hall, Lower Level

Pools of light huddle around lit braziers in niches along the walls, and iron cable towers rise to support the bucket chain that rattles overhead. Basalt pillars support the 90-foot-high ceiling, and iron gantries are bolted to the walls 50 feet above the floor. An iron staircase along the south wall climbs to the western gantry.

### The Vonindod

Suspended and steadied by huge chains near the middle of the room are the helmed head and upper torso of the Vonindod, which have survived more or less intact. The adamantine colossus will stand 80 feet tall once it is fully reassembled; until then, it's nothing more than a dangling, lifeless hulk. One of its eyes has a giant ruby (worth 25,000 gp and weighing 250 pounds) set into it, 40 feet above the floor. The other eye contains a socket for a similar-sized (but missing) gemstone. Climbing the colossus to reach the ruby eye requires a DC 20 Strength (Athletics) check, since the surface has few handholds or footholds. Prying the ruby eye from its socket requires a crowbar, a sword blade, or a similar tool and a successful DC 15 Strength (Athletics) check.

### Adamantine Doors

Set into the southeast wall is a pair of 50-foot-tall adamantine doors sealed by ancient magic. The doors are airtight and soundproof. They open only when a fire giant standing within 50 feet of them speaks, in Giant, the phrase "By Surtur's flame, I command these doors to open!" The doors remain open until a fire giant standing within 50 feet of them speaks, in Giant, the phrase "By Surtur's flame, I command these doors to close!" in Giant. The doors can also be closed manually with a DC 25 Strength (Athletics) check. *Knock* spells and similar magic have no effect on these doors, though a *legend lore* spell or similar magic reveals how the doors can be opened and closed. A clever character can fool the magic on the doors by creating an illusory fire giant and having it speak the pass phrase. Characters can also try to hide and wait for a fire giant to open the doors (see the "Reinforcements" section earlier in this chapter).

### The Fire Giant Duke

Unless he has been lured elsewhere, Duke Zalto is in the assembly hall playing with his two favorite **hell hounds**, Narthor and Zerebor. Zalto has a hollow iron ball, about 4 feet across, riddled with holes and containing the roasted corpse of a rock gnome. Whenever he rolls the ball across the floor, the hounds chase after it, fight over it, blast it with their fiery breath, and otherwise knock it around, much to Zalto's delight.

Duke Zalto is a **fire giant**, with these changes:

- He has 221 hit points.
- He wears a *ring of lightning resistance*.
- He has an Intelligence score of 14 (+2) and speaks Common, Elvish, and Giant.
- He wields a giant iron maul, the head of which doubles as a cage (see "Zalto's Prisoner"). He has a +11 bonus to hit with the maul, which has a reach of 10 feet and deals 28 (6d6 + 7) bludgeoning damage on a hit. He can make two attacks with the maul as an action.

### Zalto's Prisoner

The rectangular head of Zalto's iron maul contains a hollow cell just large enough to confine a Medium creature (or two Small creatures). One wall of the cell is fitted with a door made of vertical iron bars 3 inches thick and spaced 4 inches apart. The cell door has a built-in lock, and Zalto carries the only key. Wrenching open the door requires a successful DC 25 Strength (Athletics) check, while picking the lock requires thieves' tools and a successful DC 20 Dexterity check. Neither of these tasks can be attempted while Zalto is wielding the weapon. Zalto has imprisoned a shield dwarf in the maul. Each time Zalto hits something with the weapon, any creature imprisoned in the head of the maul takes 5 (2d4) bludgeoning damage as it's jostled and knocked about.

Zalto's prisoner is a member of the Zhentarim named Jasper Dimmerchasm. Jasper tried to negotiate with one of Zalto's underlings and was brought to Ironslag to meet with the duke. Zalto decided that he didn't need the Black Network's help to find the missing fragments of the Vonindod, so he locked Jasper inside his maul, weapons and all. Jasper uses the **veteran** stat block, with these changes:

- Jasper is a neutral evil shield dwarf.
- He speaks Common and Dwarvish.
- He has advantage on saving throws against poison, and he has resistance to poison damage.
- He has darkvision out to a range of 60 feet.
- He wields a battleaxe and a handaxe instead of a longsword and a shortsword. As an action, he can make two battleaxe attacks, plus one handaxe attack if he has his handaxe drawn. The battleaxe deals 7 (1d8 + 3) slashing damage on a hit, or 8 (1d10 + 3) slashing damage if used with two hands. The handaxe deals 6 (1d6 + 3) slashing damage on a hit and can be thrown (range 20/60 ft.).

While locked inside Zalto's maul, Jasper can't attack anything outside of his cell and has three-quarters cover against ranged attacks that pass through the cell door. (He has total cover against all other ranged attacks that originate outside of his cell.) If Jasper is rescued, he asks to remain with the characters until they return to civilization. He tries to befriend characters who are members of the Black Network, hoping to conspire with them to seize all of Ironslag's riches for themselves.

## 29. Adamantine Forge

This cold forge looks like a giant adamantine igloo with a chimney on top and a hatch in the south side. The hatch has a sliding bolt lock, and its opening is wide enough for a fire giant to pass through. Inscribed on the floor of the forge is the ild (fire) rune (see appendix E). The forge is an artifact and thus impervious to damage. Trapping an ice primordial inside it for 1 hour, however, causes the forge to crack, whereupon it ceases to function.

Flanking the forge are two cable towers that support the bucket chain 50 feet overhead.

### Development

Duke Zalto needs the incredible heat produced by the adamantine forge to repair his colossus, since normal fires aren't hot enough. If Zalto gets his hands on the *iron flask* containing Maegera the Dawn Titan (see the "Special Delivery" section at the end of this chapter), he goes inside the adamantine forge and opens the *iron flask*, releasing the fire primordial from the flask and trapping it in the forge. Zalto then exits the forge, which begins to put out tremendous heat. The temperature in the room rises immediately, such that any creature that ends its turn in the room takes 5 (1d10) fire damage, or 11 (2d10) fire damage if it's wearing metal armor. A creature that comes into direct contact with the superheated shell of the forge for the first time on a turn takes 33 (6d10) fire damage. A creature that enters the superheated forge for the first time on a turn or starts its turn inside the forge takes 132 (24d10) fire damage.

The ancient rune magic that protects the forge also prevents Maegera from escaping, even while the hatch and the vents are open. Maegera can still be trapped inside an *iron flask* or a similar magical prison, however, and it voluntarily fails any saving throw if doing so enables it to escape from the adamantine forge.

## 30. Overseer's Office

The small room west of the Vonindod is currently unoccupied. It contains a 10-foot-tall wooden table with an iron dagger stuck in its top. The dagger is as big as a human-sized greatsword and twice as heavy; in the hands of a Small or Medium creature, it's considered an improvised weapon that deals 3d4 piercing damage on a hit. The iron dagger is nonmagical and can be pried loose with a successful DC 11 Strength (Athletics) check.

## 31. Kitchen

Standing between black basalt pillars are two 10-foot-tall basalt tables used for food preparation. Underneath the tables are ten empty iron cauldrons weighing 100 pounds each, and above them are dozens of utensils hanging from iron hooks and chains. Brimskarda, the fire giant duchess, stands in front of a fireplace holding an iron spoon to her lips, sampling soup from a fat cauldron suspended above the flames. Five **smoke mephits** dance around the cauldron, cackling with glee. Two **ogres** wearing grease-stained leather aprons stand next to the tables, and twenty **goblins** scurry about, performing menial chores.

Brimskarda attacks intruders on sight and commands her minions to do the same. If the duchess drops to 0 hit points, the mephits retreat to the fireplace and the goblins cower under the tables. The ogres are too stupid to surrender or flee; they fight to the death, wielding giant rolling pins that are treated as greatclubs.

Archways in the north wall lead to storerooms with wooden shelves lined with pots and pans. The eastern storeroom also holds two 500-pound barrels of grease.

### The Fire Giant Duchess

Brimskarda wears a gown made from a young black dragon's scaly hide and wings, and she has wrapped her luxurious orange hair around a black dragon's horn, giving her a coiffure that looks like a curving pillar of flame. She is a **fire giant**, with these changes:

- Brimskarda's dragon-scale dress gives her AC 16.
- Brimskarda has an Intelligence score of 14 (+2) and speaks Common, Giant, and Goblin.
- She wears a crystal flask around her neck like a pendant. The flask contains a *potion of invulnerability*, which Brimskarda quaffs on her first turn in combat.
- She can hurl iron cauldrons instead of rocks (her attack bonus, range, and damage remain the same).

### Treasure

In addition to her *potion of invulnerability*, Brimskarda carries a large wind fan of painted gold (worth 2,500 gp and weighing 50 pounds).

### Development

Characters who capture Brimskarda can use her to gain leverage in any negotiation with Duke Zalto. The duke treats his wife's capture the same way he treats the capture of his son (see area 18 for details).

## 32. Storeroom

One basalt pillar supports the ceiling of this room, which contains wooden crates and barrels that the fire giants brought with them to Ironslag. The crates contain food, and the barrels contain water, rock salt, and ale.

Resting against the east wall is a wooden chest, 10 feet long by 6 feet tall by 8 feet wide. The chest feels cold to the touch, and a *detect magic* spell reveals an aura of transmutation magic around the chest. Its interior stays as cold as an icebox regardless of the temperature outside, and it currently holds the frozen carcasses of an elk and a wolf.

## 33. Cistern

Ice water running off the mountain is channeled through pipes that lead to the room west of the kitchen. Three iron nozzles protrude from the 50-foot-high ceiling, spilling water into three bowl-shaped basins carved into the floor. A 3-foot-high, circular and hollow wall of stone encloses each basin, and drainage holes carved into the rim of each retaining wall prevent the water from spilling over the edge. The shut-off valves for the nozzles are mounted on the north wall, 10 feet above the floor. Each shut-off valve is a rusty iron wheel roughly 5 feet across that must be turned a full rotation to stop the flow of water into the cistern south of it; turning the wheel requires an action and a successful DC 15 Strength (Athletics) check.

Barrels of potable water stand in the rooms' corners.

## 34. Foundry, Lower Level

Characters can hear the clanging of metal and see ripples of heat throughout this brightly lit area. Those who linger here are susceptible to the effects of extreme heat (see the "Wilderness Survival" section in chapter 5 of the *Dungeon Master's Guide*). A 60-foot-wide, 160-foot-long, and 5-foot-deep stone trough filled with molten iron dominates the room. The molten iron spills from four cone-shaped smelters carved out of black basalt. The smelters are fueled by natural gas. Four **fire giants** pump huge bellows to fan the flames within. Any creature that enters the molten iron for the first time on a turn or starts its turn in molten iron takes 44 (8d10) fire damage.

The fire giants hurl globs of molten iron instead of rocks. A giant must be within reach of the trough to make this ranged weapon attack, which has a +11 bonus to hit, has a range of 30/120 ft., and deals 17 (3d6 + 7) bludgeoning damage plus 22 (4d10) fire damage on a hit.

The fire giants in area 35 investigate sounds of combat here.

## 35. Forges

Streams of molten iron flow from the foundry (area 34) into sword-shaped molds carved out of black basalt that sit inside three identical forges (areas 35A, 35B, and 35C), each one tended by a **fire giant** weaponsmith. The heat in these rooms is almost unbearable, and characters who linger here are susceptible to the effects of extreme heat (see the "Wilderness Survival" section in chapter 5 of the *Dungeon Master's Guide*).

The three fire giants are busy hammering and bending iron to make blades and hilts, but they draw their greatswords and attack if they see any intruders.

In addition to the molds, each forge contains a fireplace, a pair of massive anvils, and shelves that hold weaponsmithing tools.

## 36. Armory

Behind a pair of doors south and east of the foundry are two unoccupied rooms. They contain iron weapon racks bristling with greatswords, iron mannequins draped in plate armor, marble shelves that hold iron helms, and hooks with iron shields hanging from them. There's enough equipment here to arm a legion of fire giants, though none of it is magical.

## 37. Stairs Up

A wrought iron spiral staircase climbs 50 feet to area 19. The steps are iron grills with holes large enough for a human fist to pass through. The steps provide three-quarters cover against any ranged attack that must pass through them to hit its target.

# Special Delivery

Draac and Taal Xorlarrin, a pair of **drow mages**, arrive at Ironslag with six **drow elite warriors**. If the characters encountered these drow previously in Gauntlgrym, there might be fewer drow in their party, since they have had no opportunity to replace lost members. If his mission in Gauntlgrym was successful, Draac carries an *iron flask* that he aims to return to Duke Zalto.

The drow quietly make their way up the mountainside, into the yakfolk village, and down into the fire giant forge by way of the elevator (area 9). The yakfolk have been warned that the drow are coming and leave them alone. If the elevator is nonfunctional and they can't get it working, the drow resort to descending through the mines (see area 10). Exactly when they arrive is up to you, but here are some suggestions:

- If the characters slay Duke Zalto, the drow might arrive shortly thereafter and attack.

- If the characters are having an easy time in Ironslag, the drow might be with Zalto when the party finally confronts him. Draac doesn't give Zalto the *iron flask* until the characters are defeated or forced to retreat.
- If the characters leave Ironslag without confronting Duke Zalto, the drow arrive after the party leaves and give Zalto the *iron flask*.

On their first turns in combat, both Draac and Taal attempt to summon a **shadow demon**. If defeat seems likely, Draac orders the remainder of his force to cover his escape while he flees with the *iron flask*.

### Treasure

In addition to the *iron flask*, Draac carries a nonmagical staff topped with web patterns on the haft and a sculpted obsidian spider with small diamonds for eyes at the top (worth 1,500 gp). Taal carries a pouch with four 100 gp gems inside it, and he wears a fine black cloak embroidered with webs made of platinum thread (worth 750 gp). The elite drow warriors carry no treasure.

## Zalto's Iron Flask

Tied to Draac's belt is an *iron flask* that contains **Maegera the Dawn Titan** (see appendix C), a mighty fire primordial that the drow stole from Gauntlgrym. Removing the *iron flask*'s stopper frees Maegera from captivity, whereupon the primordial is compelled to obey the commands of whoever freed it for 1 hour. Once that hour has elapsed, the primordial goes berserk and attacks nearby creatures indiscriminately while incinerating its surroundings.

Duke Zalto and the drow know that Maegera can't be controlled for long, so they won't release the fire primordial anywhere but inside Ironslag's adamantine forge (area 29). If Draac is unable to give the flask to Zalto and is forced to flee, he keeps the flask with him and returns to the Underdark with it, determined to keep it out of the hands of the dwarves of Gauntlgrym.

### Development

The characters might obtain the *iron flask* and try to trap Maegera inside the magic furnace aboard their airship (see the "Airship of a Cult" section in chapter 4). The airship's furnace can hold Maegera, but only briefly. After each hour of confinement, Maegera can make a DC 15 Strength saving throw to escape confinement. If it fails the saving throw, Maegera remains trapped for another hour. If the saving throw succeeds, Maegera breaks free and goes berserk, destroying the furnace in the process.

---

**CHARACTER ADVANCEMENT**

After obtaining Duke Zalto's *conch of teleportation*, the characters might want to hole up somewhere so that one of them can attune to the conch and use it to teleport the party to Maelstrom. The characters might also delay using the conch because they want to continue exploring Ironslag or because they have some loose ends to tie up, such as coming to terms with Jasper Dimmerchasm, helping Cinderhild escape the clutches of her parents, or returning Maegera to Gauntlgrym. In any event, allow the characters to advance to 9th level before moving on to chapter 10, "Hold of the Storm Giants."

# Chapter 9: Castle of the Cloud Giants

OR AS LONG AS GIANTS HAVE WALKED THE world, cloud giants have been one step below storm giants in power and influence. Now, with the ordning dissolved, a few cloud giant nobles have seized the opportunity to rise above the storm giants and thereby fulfill their lifelong dream of becoming the true, undisputed aristocrats among giants.

One such noble is Countess Sansuri, who believes that her destiny lies buried in the past, waiting for her to unearth it. Sansuri's ancient ancestors, anticipating the fall of their great empire, reportedly hid their magical knowledge and wealth in vaults and left markers for future generations to find them. The greatest of these troves was a cache of "dragon magic"—spells and artifacts plundered from the lairs of powerful wyrms. Sansuri wants to find this cache and use her newfound power to destroy her ambitious rivals and convince the rest of giantkind to kneel before her. Sansuri believes the gods will reward her appropriately for doing so. When that day comes, all other cloud giants will thank her for doing what they could only dream of.

After using telescopes to scour the land below for clues, Sansuri has come to the realization that her maps are woefully out of date. She hasn't found a single marker pointing the way to the trove she seeks. When a curious and danger-prone bronze dragon named Felgolos paid her a visit some weeks ago, Sansuri played the role of benevolent host. She tricked the dragon into helping her and, when its guard was down, captured and imprisoned it. When the adventurers come knocking, Sansuri is in the midst of torturing the bronze dragon for information, hoping it knows where one of the ancient Ostorian markers might be. The dragon's roars of pain can be heard for miles.

In this part of their mission, the characters travel to Lyn Armaal, Sansuri's cloud castle, and meet the countess and her family. The countess shares the place with her castellan and consort, Cressaro; her younger brother, Count Thullen; and her twin children, Alastrah and Kaaltar. The castle can be anywhere you want it to be. If you have no particular location in mind, assume that it's hovering one mile above the Evermoors (its default location).

The characters' primary goal is to find the *conch of teleportation* that King Hekaton gave to Sansuri, so that they can use it to travel to Maelstrom, Hekaton's undersea citadel (see chapter 10, "Hold of the Storm Giants"). There's a catch: the conch is hidden inside a *Leomund's secret chest* created by the countess, and only she can summon it.

## Cloud Giants

Before running this part of the adventure, review the information on cloud giants in the *Monster Manual*. It will help you roleplay the cloud giants in this chapter. One important point to remember is that some cloud giants are good, and some are evil.

# LADY OF MASKS

Countess Sansuri is a greedy and vainglorious giant who lives in the clouds, untethered from reality, convinced that she is the victim of a great injustice and surrounded by jealous enemies who yearn to topple her.

As a powerful wizard and noble, Sansuri believes it is her duty to rule over others and command their respect. Even so, she has been forced to bow to the will of King Hekaton and the storm giants her whole life. She resents Hekaton for stifling her ambitions, and she lives for the day when the gods finally elevate her kind above storm giants. Internally, Sansuri is fraught with envy and scorn, but she tries to hide those feelings behind a calm, unassuming facade.

Like many cloud giant nobles, Sansuri keeps a collection of masks. She dons whichever mask best reflects her current mood and switches masks as her mood changes. Her inability to pry useful information out of the bronze dragon has made her very unhappy, so she's wearing her sad mask when the characters arrive.

Sansuri has little regard for "puny folk" and doesn't consider them a threat. How she reacts to the characters depends on the manner in which they approach her castle:

- If the characters attack her castle without provocation or are caught trying to sneak into her home, Sansuri brings her castle's defenses to bear and tries to crush them, capturing those who surrender.
- If the characters approach her castle in a nonthreatening manner, Sansuri instructs her castellan, Cressaro, to escort them to her audience chamber (area 1), where she greets them formally.

In a noncombat situation, Sansuri plays the part of the proud hostess but can't quite hide her impatience. She has no time to entertain unexpected visitors and would prefer to see them quickly on their way. If the characters ask to borrow or use her *conch of teleportation*, she demands to know why but ultimately refuses to help them, even if they offer to buy it or trade for it. Simply put, she doesn't trust "puny folk" and won't lower herself to negotiate with them, nor will she give them the means to reach Maelstrom.

If the characters pry into her business, she tells them that she's conducting an extensive survey to update her maps of the lands below. If the characters ask about the dragon, Sansuri replies coldly, "It's not your concern." Clever characters might claim to possess knowledge useful to Sansuri, such as the locations of ancient Ostorian way-markers that point the way to long-lost treasures. Sansuri regards any such claims with great suspicion, and ability checks made to deceive her have disadvantage.

Sansuri attacks characters who are clearly being disrespectful or deceptive. She also turns on those who seem intent on robbing her. If she loses more than half her hit points, Sansuri casts a *fly* spell on herself, retreats to her tower (areas 31–33), and leaves the castle's other denizens to fend for themselves. If her defeat seems inevitable, Sansuri bargains for her life

and, under such circumstances, is willing to relinquish her *conch of teleportation* (see area 33). She also gives up the conch to protect the lives of her children (see areas 22–23).

If the characters are defeated in combat, Sansuri has them stripped of their armor, weapons, and other equipment. Such items are stored in area 2 until Sansuri has the time and wherewithal to inspect them more thoroughly with the aid of *detect magic* spells. Dead characters are unceremoniously dropped through the hole in the audience chamber floor. Living captives are confined to cages in the dungeon (area 8) and left unguarded. Unless the prisoners manage to escape, Sansuri feeds them to her griffons in area 7 the next day.

## AARAKOCRA SIMULACRA

Years ago, a wounded aarakocra named Jakka landed on Sansuri's cloud castle. Sansuri was struck by the beauty and color of the noble creature, but rather than befriend Jakka, she locked him in a cage and imprisoned him for months while she used *simulacrum* spells to create effigies of him out of ice and snow. (Sansuri's version of the spell allows her to have multiple simulacra of the same creature.) After creating a host of Jakka simulacra, she killed the original, then (in typical noble fashion) had his body stuffed and mounted above the fireplace in her lounge.

The countess uses the simulacra as guards and castle decorations. Their poise and striking plumage are the envy of the cloud giant nobility, and they obey their mistress's commands without question. An aarakocra simulacrum uses the **aarakocra** stat block, with these changes:

- Each simulacrum has 6 hit points and a challenge rating of 1/8 (25 XP).
- When a simulacrum drops to 0 hit points or is subjected to a successful *dispel magic* spell (DC 17), it reverts to ice and snow and is destroyed.

## FELGOLOS'S TORMENT

Sansuri knows that Felgolos has roamed the North for decades. She is torturing him for information that might point her in the direction of the treasure she seeks. Unfortunately for both of them, Felgolos knows nothing that can help her, other than the names and likely whereabouts of other dragons much older and wiser than he.

Felgolos's intermittent roars of pain can be heard for miles, and characters who approach Lyn Armaal can't help but hear them.

# LYN ARMAAL

Countess Sansuri's castle consists of three conjoined towers with a protruding gatehouse, all made of smoothly mortared stone. The central tower constitutes the main keep and has a more slender tower rising from its top that serves as Sansuri's personal quarters. See the "Lyn Armaal: General Features" sidebar for more information on the castle's features.

## LYN ARMAAL: GENERAL FEATURES

A magical cloud supports the tremendous weight of Sansuri's castle, the altitude and movement of which is controlled using a *navigation orb* (see appendix B) located in area 30. The general features of the castle and the cloud are summarized here.

**Ceilings and Floors.** Ceilings throughout the castle are 40 feet high. The floors on level 1 are made of tightly fitted stone, while the interior floors on levels 2–6 are made of thick, varnished wooden planks supported underneath with heavy crossbeams. The grass lawns on the tower rooftops (areas 26, 27, and 29) grow atop 2 feet of packed earth, beneath which are stone floors.

**Cloud.** The cloud upon which the castle rests is opaque, buoyant, and semisolid, with the consistency and coldness of slush. One can sculpt the cloud to form stairs and other features, and a creature that falls onto the cloud sinks into it without taking damage. Any creature that tries to pass through the cloud can do so, treating it as difficult terrain. Inside the cloud, visibility is reduced to zero. The cloud doesn't block sound, however.

**Defenses.** The castle's crenellated battlements are 10 feet tall and 5 feet wide. Arrow slits are 10 feet tall, 10 feet above the floor, and 5 feet wide, narrowing to 2 feet wide on the outside of the wall. Wooden ballistae (see the "Siege Equipment" section in chapter 8 of the *Dungeon Master's Guide*) are positioned behind several of the arrow slits, angled to fire bolts at flying creatures outside. A giant can aim and fire a ballista with a single action.

**Doors.** Each of Lyn Armaal's doors is 27 feet high and made of ornately carved, 6-inch-thick wood with polished bronze fittings. Door handles are 12 feet above the floor. A Huge giant has no trouble opening a door. A smaller creature can attempt to open a door, provided that creature or some other helpful creature can reach the door's handle and unlatch it. While the handle is unlatched, a creature must use an action to push or pull on the heavy door, opening it with a successful DC 14 Strength (Athletics) check. On a failed check, the door doesn't open.

**Illumination.** All indoor areas are brightly lit, either by sunlight filtered through windows or arrow slits, or by magical flames (created by *continual flame* spells) that blaze in golden sconces along the walls. A golden sconce is worth 250 gp and weighs 25 pounds. Outdoor areas have natural lighting.

**Oversized Furnishings and Objects.** Most of the furnishings and other items in Lyn Armaal are sized for cloud giants. Exceptions are noted in the text. Tables, beds, and other room fixtures are typically three times as high, long, and wide as their human-sized equivalents and roughly twenty-seven times the weight. Small and Medium creatures can scuttle under and clamber over giant-sized furniture, treating the spaces they occupy as difficult terrain.

**Stairs.** Staircases within the castle are sized for cloud giants. Each step is 4 feet tall by 4 feet deep. Large and smaller creatures treat the staircases as difficult terrain.

**Telescopes.** Bolted to the battlements are several telescopes that the cloud giants use to spy on the lands below. Each telescope weighs 750 pounds and consists of a 20-foot-long bronze body fitted with transparent crystal magnifying lenses. The telescopes are mounted on steel braces and can be turned and angled to look in different directions, including up or down at a 60-degree angle. The eyepiece of a horizontally level telescope is 20 feet above the floor. Characters who are flying or standing on the shoulders of other characters can use the telescopes to clearly see prominent terrain features and objects hundreds of miles away.

# REACHING LYN ARMAAL

Lyn Armaal (shown on maps 9.1 and 9.2) hangs in the sky, rarely coming within a mile of the ground. To reach it, characters need an airship, flying mounts, or spells and magic items that grant flight. They can also ask one or more helpful metallic dragons to fly them to Sansuri's castle, although there's rarely a dragon around when they need one (see "Metallic Dragons").

If the characters attempt to conceal their aerial approach, either by hiding among the neighboring clouds or traveling under the cloak of night, they can reach the castle undetected without having to make any sort of check. If they don't take such simple precautions, the giants and the aarakocra spot them and sound the alarm.

## AIRSHIP

Characters can approach the castle in the dragon cultists' airship (see the "Airship of a Cult" section in chapter 4), but given the airship's size, there are only a few places on Lyn Armaal that can accommodate the vessel and bear its weight:

- The courtyard of the aft battery (area 6)
- The cloud by the stairs leading up to the gatehouse (area 9)
- The gatehouse's arrival platform (area 10)
- Any of the tower rooftop lawns (area 26, 27, or 29)

## FLYING MOUNTS

Characters can secure griffon mounts in Fireshear or hippogriff mounts in Hawk's Nest. Those mounted on hippogriffs can travel 54 miles per day (three 3-hour flights with 1-hour rests in between), while those mounted on griffons can travel 72 miles in the same amount of time. Hippogriffs and griffons are capable of landing in any outdoor area. They can also fly through the openings in the wall of the griffon aviary (area 7). Any NPCs who accompany the characters on this excursion remain with the mounts, protecting them while waiting for the characters to return.

## METALLIC DRAGONS

Characters who befriended a metallic dragon earlier in the adventure might be able to bribe it or persuade it to transport them to Sansuri's castle. Dragons of the North don't like serving as mounts, however, so characters who aren't extremely persuasive or flattering will need to offer a dragon treasure before it commits to helping them. A young dragon can transport one Medium character, while an adult dragon can transport four Medium characters. Two Small characters can take the place of one Medium character. The dragon can be further bribed into joining the assault on Lyn Armaal, though it expects to receive as its reward the castle itself and all the treasure in it (not counting the *conch of teleportation* that the characters need to continue their mission).

# DENIZENS

Despite its grandeur and immense proportions, the castle is fairly self-contained, and loud sounds in one area can easily be heard in other locations. Any adult giant who yells really loud can be heard throughout the castle.

## Lyn Armaal Roster

| Area | Creature(s) | Notes |
|---|---|---|
| 1 | 4 aarakocra simulacra | The simulacra remain here. |
| 5 | 5 **cloud giants** | The giants muster in area 6. One remains there while the other four head upstairs to operate the ballistae (two in area 16, two in area 18). |
| 7 | 5 **griffons** | If set free by Sansuri, the griffons fly outside and circle the castle, attacking intruders they see on the rooftops or parapets. |
| 8 | Countess Sansuri, Felgolos (**adult bronze dragon**) | If an alarm sounds, Sansuri releases the griffons in area 7 and goes looking for Cressaro, meeting him in area 6 if nothing waylays either of them. The dragon remains imprisoned here. |
| 10 | 2 **air elementals** | The elementals remain here at all times. |
| 11 | 2 aarakocra simulacra | These simulacra assist the elementals in area 10. |
| 13 | 3 **ogres** | The ogres remain here at all times. |
| 14 | Cressaro (**cloud giant castellan**) | If an alarm sounds, Cressaro goes looking for Sansuri, meeting her in area 6 if nothing waylays either of them. |
| 16 | 1 **cloud giant** | The giant remains here, along with reinforcements from area 5. |
| 17 | 2 **cloud giants** | The giants remain here. |
| 18 | 1 **cloud giant** | As area 16. |
| 22/23 | 2 cloud giant children | The children remain in area 22 at night, or area 23 during the day. |
| 24 | 1 **cloud giant** | The giant remains here. |
| 26 | 6 aarakocra simulacra, 1 **water elemental** | If these simulacra are drawn to area 29 by sounds of battle, they aren't encountered here. The water elemental hides in its pool. |
| 27 | 2 **helmed horrors**, 30 suits of **animated armor** | The constructs remain here unless Sansuri or Thullen commands them to move elsewhere. |
| 28 | Count Thullen, 7 **awakened shrubs** | If an alarm sounds, Thullen heads to area 23 to protect the children. The shrubs guard the greenhouse and leave only if Thullen commands them to. |
| 29 | 6 aarakocra simulacra | The simulacra remain here to guard areas 30–33. If battle erupts here, the aarakocra simulacra in area 26 arrive here 2 rounds later. |
| 32 | 2 **invisible stalkers** | The stalkers remains here. |

The Lyn Armaal Roster table summarizes the locations of the inhabitants when the characters approach and indicates how those creatures react when intruders are detected.

Any cloud giant or aarakocra simulacrum can place the castle on alert. A cloud giant does this by bellowing "To arms!" at the end of its first turn in combat. An aarakocra simulacrum does it by shrieking loudly at the end of its first turn. Other creatures in the castle have no means to sound an alarm or don't bother doing so.

When the alarm sounds, the screams of the bronze dragon cease as Countess Sansuri is drawn away from her interrogation of Felgolos. Sansuri moves to a place where she can use a telescope to get a closer look at those who might threaten her. "Puny folk" pique her curiosity. Sansuri permits them to land unmolested and instructs Cressaro to escort her "guests" to the audience chamber (area 1), where she can greet them formally and determine their true intentions. If the characters turn hostile before this meeting can occur, Sansuri dispenses with the formal greeting and helps defend her castle until such time as it's no longer in her best interest to do so (see the "Lady of Masks" section near the start of this chapter for more information on Sansuri's tactics).

## 1. Audience Chamber

This opulent hall features lapis lazuli tile work and murals depicting castles in the clouds as well as cloud giants chasing silver dragons while riding rocs and golden sky-chariots drawn by griffons. Marble bleachers hug the walls near the entrance, across from which stands an ornate alabaster throne inlaid with gemstones (see "Treasure"). "Guarding" the throne on either side are two life-size statues of cloud giants—one male, one female—standing at attention, wearing tall helmets with feather plumage, and clutching mithral-tipped spears. The statues are harmless sculptures.

Set into the floor in front of the throne is a 10-foot-diameter circular hole surrounded by decorative tiles of gold marble, white alabaster, and blue lapis lazuli. Standing at attention with their backs to the hole are four **aarakocra simulacra** (see the "Aarakocra Simulacra" section earlier in this chapter). The aarakocra are alert but remain perfectly still; they do nothing other than defend themselves and obey Sansuri's commands. Any creature that jumps or falls into the hole plummets to the ground far below unless it can fly.

### Treasure
Seventy-two gemstones decorate Sansuri's throne. There are thirty 50 gp gemstones, twenty 100 gp

gemstones, fifteen 500 gp gemstones, and six 1,000 gp gemstones, plus a black sapphire (worth 5,000 gp) set into the top of the throne, in the middle of a sun-shaped marble fitting engraved with runes. A character can use an action to pry loose a gemstone. Removing the black sapphire triggers a *glyph of warding* (explosive runes) spell placed on the throne. The effect deals 36 (8d8) cold damage to all creatures in the spell's area.

## 2. Workshop and Meeting Room

Sansuri uses this room as a magical workshop and private meeting room. A stone table dominates the room, and tall wooden cabinets stand against opposite walls. Other decor includes potted plants (one on the floor and others hanging from the ceiling above the table) and a large wooden waste barrel (currently empty). Next to the door, hanging from a stone hook mounted to the wall 20 feet above the floor, is a 2-foot-long iron key that weighs 25 pounds. This key unlocks the cages in area 8.

The cabinets contain all manner of spell components and trinkets accumulated by Sansuri over the years. Characters can find the material component for any wizard spell of 6th level or lower that has no cost in gold pieces associated with it. To determine what trinkets are here, roll twelve times on the Trinkets table in chapter 5 of the *Player's Handbook*, or simply choose twelve different trinkets from the table.

### Development

If the characters are captured, their equipment is placed atop the table in this room, where it remains until Sansuri finds time to examine it with the aid of her *detect magic* spell. Any magic items found in the party's gear are stored in one of the cabinets, which Sansuri then secures with an *arcane lock* spell.

## 3. Guest Room

The furniture in this room is scaled for giant-sized guests and includes two soft beds, a handsomely carved wooden table, and an empty wooden chest. A spacious closet at the back of the room has some giant-sized cloaks and sleeping garments hanging from bronze hooks on the wall, as well as a giant barrel of wine.

### Treasure

Atop the wooden table are a 5-foot-tall brass decanter (worth 250 gp and weighing 75 pounds) and two 3-foot-tall matching goblets with inlaid gemstones and platinum filigree (each worth 750 gp and weighing 50 pounds).

## 4. Armory

Stored in wooden racks along the walls are dozens of spears and javelins, each one exquisitely crafted and well balanced, as well as tools for repairing armor and weaponry. Two full suits of cloud giant-sized plate armor hang from giant bronze mannequins that stand at attention, their backs against the outer wall. A wooden table rests between two doors, and a rug embroidered with an image of the night sky lies on the floor.

## 5. Barracks

This room is set aside for Sansuri's cloud giant guards. Five beds are spaced along the outer wall, with a barrel of wine and a crate of food stashed in one corner. Three cloaks hang from bronze hooks on one wall, and resting by the door is a large chest (see "Treasure").

Five **cloud giants** sleep here, their morningstars lying on the floor by their bedsides. On a typical day, these guards and the ones on active duty operate on alternating shifts. When the castellan decides that a shift is done, he rouses these guards from their slumber and orders them to replace the guards in areas 16, 17, 18, and 24. Relieved guards return here to rest. When an alarm sounds, the sleeping giants awaken, grab their morningstars, and move to area 6. If there are no enemies to fight in that area, four of them head upstairs to operate ballistae; two head to area 16, and two to area 18. The fifth one remains on guard in area 6.

### Treasure

The large chest near the door is unlocked and contains ten fat sacks, no two exactly alike in appearance but each one containing loot belonging to a particular cloud giant. Each sack holds 3d6 × 100 sp, 2d6 × 100 gp, and 1d4 mundane items, determined by rolling on the Items in a Giant's Bag table in the introduction. If the characters seize all this treasure, don't bother rolling to determine the exact contents of each sack; instead, assume that the entire hoard consists of 10,000 sp, 7,000 gp, and twenty items selected from the table.

## 6. Aft Battery

A 30-foot-high curtain wall with an overhanging rampart (area 17) encloses this stone-tiled courtyard, which contains a few puddles of rainwater here and there. The cloud giants standing watch atop the rampart can see and hear anyone entering the courtyard who isn't trying to stay hidden.

Three ballistae face arrow slits in the outer wall, and two iron grates cover 10-foot-square holes in the floor. The grates are held in place with stone and cement. A Small character can fit through the gaps between the crisscrossing iron bars, and a Medium character can squeeze through. Any creatures that slip or fall through a grate plummet to the ground below unless they can fly.

## 7. Griffon Aviary

Haphazardly arranged about this untidy room are five tall wooden cages. Five **griffons** are kept here, one locked in each cage. The griffons peck and scratch at their cages, and the floor around them is littered with bits of broken wood. The griffons can't attack creatures outside of their cages, but they make a ruckus when intruders enter—so loud that Countess Sansuri can hear them in area 8. She investigates any such disturbance.

The griffons are trained to obey Sansuri and no one else. If an alarm sounds, Sansuri emerges from area 8, uses an action to unlock each cage, and commands the griffons to take flight and circle the castle, attacking intruders on sight and returning here when she calls them off. A simple clasp mechanism, 10 feet above the floor, secures each door. The griffons come and go through wide windows in the outer wall.

A few barrels and crates stashed in one corner of the room contain dried horse and mule meat (griffon treats).

## 8. Dungeon

Felgolos, an **adult bronze dragon**, is chained to the back wall and floor of this spacious, windowless cell. Two locked manacles bind the dragon's hind legs, preventing him from moving more than a few feet in any direction. He has a locked collar around his neck and a locked iron muzzle covering his snout. The muzzle, the collar, and the manacles are all designed to hold a dragon of his size and aren't useful on creatures of other shapes and sizes. The bonds are strengthened by magic, and as such they can't be broken by physical force. The magic on Felgolos's collar prevents him from using his Change Shape ability, and he can't use his Frightful Presence ability while chained up. While he is muzzled, Felgolos can speak with some difficulty, but the range of his breath weapons is reduced to 5 feet. The dragon is bleeding from multiple wounds and has 160 hit points when the characters find him.

A *knock* spell can unlock the shackles around one of the dragon's legs or unlock the dragon's muzzle or collar. Any of these locks can be picked open using thieves' tools, though it requires an action to do so and a successful DC 20 Dexterity check.

Across from the dragon, stashed in a corner of the room, are three empty iron cages sized for Humanoid prisoners. The cages have bars that are 1 inch thick with 4-inch gaps between them. Any party members captured by the cloud giants are stripped of their gear and locked in the cages. The oversized padlock on each cage door is too big to be picked using thieves' tools, but a character outside a cage can use an action to reach into the locking mechanism of the cage's padlock and manually pick the lock, doing so with a successful DC 20 Dexterity check. Sansuri keeps the key to the padlocks in her workshop (area 2).

### The Countess

Sansuri carries a large ring of keys that unlock the dragon's bonds. She uses a mithral-tipped spear to torture the dragon during her interrogation, thrusting the spear's tip between the dragon's scales at various "soft points" to cause maximum pain. If an alarm sounds in another part of the castle, Sansuri ends the interrogation, frees the griffons from their cages in area 7, and makes her way to area 6. Unless he is delayed for some reason, Cressaro (see area 14) meets her there. See the "Lady of Masks" section earlier in this chapter for more information on how Sansuri interacts with unexpected guests.

Countess Sansuri wears a mask (see "Treasure") and is a **cloud giant**, with the following changes:

- Sansuri's alignment is neutral evil.
- She speaks Auran, Common, and Giant.
- She wields a spear instead of a morningstar. In melee, she uses the weapon with both hands, dealing the same damage as a morningstar.

- She has an Intelligence score of 16 (+3) and gains the Spellcasting action option described below.
- She has a challenge rating of 11 (7,200 XP).

***Spellcasting.*** Sansuri casts one of the following spells, requiring no material components and using Intelligence as the spellcasting ability (spell save DC 15; +7 to hit with spell attacks):

At will: *mage hand, message, prestidigitation, ray of frost*
2/day each: *arcane lock, gust of wind, invisibility, magic missile, unseen servant*
1/day each: *globe of invulnerability, haste, hypnotic pattern, ice storm, lightning bolt, Mordenkainen's sword, wall of force*

### Treasure

Sansuri's mask bears an unhappy expression and is worth 250 gp as an art object.

### Development

If the characters free Felgolos, they earn a friend for life. Known to his friends as "The Flying Misfortune," Felgolos has an uncanny and seemingly effortless ability to imperil himself and others around him with his recklessness. He's also quite clumsy and a bit awkward socially. He means well, however. When he uses his Change Shape ability, he prefers to assume the form of a ruddy-skinned halfling with curly, bronze-colored hair or a young human lad with blond hair and sun-bronzed skin.

Felgolos is no friend of the Black Network. Any party member affiliated with the Zhentarim can, with a successful DC 10 Intelligence (History) check, recall tales of a dragon that matches Felgolos's description attacking Zhentarim caravans and snatching their wagons, beasts of burden and all. In fact, Felgolos has a large collection of Zhentarim wagons and isn't afraid to admit it. He won't part with any of them, however, because he considers the wagons and their cargo as his treasure. He targets Zhentarim caravans specifically because he knows the Black Network's sinister reputation and delights in frustrating the Zhents' plans.

Once he is freed, Felgolos offers to remain with the party for the remainder of this part of the adventure but chooses not to accompany them to Maelstrom (see chapter 10, "Hold of the Storm Giants"), saying that he doesn't want to rile up any more giants for a while. Instead, he returns to one of his many dens—a cave overlooking a river that cuts through the western Starmetal Hills. If the characters require the dragon's assistance at some later time, they can search for him there. But, considering his personality, Felgolos might be away when the characters come looking for him, swept up in yet another of his misadventures.

## 9. Cloud Stair

This staircase has been sculpted from the clouds, with steps that are 3 feet high and 6 feet deep. At the top of the staircase is a door in the wall of the gatehouse (area 10). This door is similar to others found throughout Lyn Armaal (see the "Lyn Armaal: General Features" sidebar).

## 10. Gatehouse

Built atop a separate cloud and connected to the main keep by a stone bridge, the gatehouse is where Sansuri's castellan customarily greets visitors before leading them to the countess's audience chamber (area 1). Battlements surround the gatehouse's arrival platform and the bridge. On either side of the door, a short flight of steps leads up to a stone enclosure that contains an unmanned ballista.

Two **air elementals** guard the gatehouse at all times, attacking creatures that attempt to move unescorted across the bridge. The elementals are visible as swirling masses of air with dark areas resembling eyespots. They try to fling enemies off the bridge using their Whirlwind action. A creature flung from atop the bridge must make a successful DC 10 Dexterity saving throw to stop its fall by grabbing hold of the battlements.

### Development

The aarakocra simulacra standing guard in area 11 come to the elementals' aid if a battle erupts here.

## 11. Main Gate

The door at the end of the bridge is the main entrance to the keep, through which all guests are expected to pass. The door is decorated in a cloud motif and guarded by two regal-looking **aarakocra simulacra** (see the "Aarakocra Simulacra" section earlier in this chapter) that stand aside as visitors approach. They attack only if Countess Sansuri commands them to do so or if a fight breaks out in area 10.

Opening the door triggers a permanent *alarm* spell that alerts the castellan in area 14 and the cloud giant guard in area 24. If he's not already aware of visitors, the castellan confronts them in the hall beyond the doors, demands to know their business, and escorts them to area 1 if he deems them worthy of a meeting with Countess Sansuri. If the visitors are threatening or insulting, the castellan attacks them and sounds the alarm. Murder holes in the ceiling above the door allow the giant in area 24 to rain acid down upon intruders who try to breach the castle by this route.

The door can be barred shut from the inside, though the giants do this only when expecting a major attack. A wooden bar hangs on the wall next to the door. The bar weighs 800 pounds, and the braces that hold it in place are mounted 15 feet above the floor. While the door is barred, it can't be opened from the outside without the aid of a battering ram or a siege engine. A Huge or larger creature acting in such a capacity can break down the door with a successful DC 30 Strength check.

## 12. Servants' Quarters

The front room of this area contains a spiral staircase made of decorative wrought iron that climbs to area 19. Three large beds are crammed into a plainly furnished side room. A closet contains an empty crate and a couple of moth-eaten cloaks sized for ogres.

## 13. Kitchen

The kitchen smells of pumpkin. Three **ogres** named Drat, Drek, and Krob work here, and a permanent *unseen servant* cleans on a regular basis. The ogres are docile and shun combat, fighting only in self-defense. Each one is trained to prepare a specific kind of meal: one handles appetizers, another entrées, and the third desserts. Evidence of the *unseen servant*'s presence is obvious from time to time: a broom seemingly sweeping the floor of its own accord, plates and mugs drifting through the air, and utensils being hung on hooks above the center worktable.

Cabinets and cupboards hold dishware and utensils. A fireplace built into the wall across from the door usually has a large pot of stew bubbling above a fire in it. A pantry holds the ingredients the ogres need to prepare meals for the cloud giants. On the table in the middle of the kitchen are a half dozen freshly baked pumpkin pies that the countess eats the way a human might eat cupcakes.

## 14. Castellan's Quarters

Sansuri employs a cloud giant castellan named Cressaro to oversee the guards and see to the castle's defense. He is resting here when the characters first arrive at Lyn Armaal, doing his best to ignore the tiresome roars of the bronze dragon. Cressaro is blindly loyal to Sansuri and follows her orders to the letter. He responds to an alarm by seeking out the countess to make sure she is safe. He heads downstairs to area 6 and meets Sansuri there, assuming that neither of them is waylaid by intruders. Cressaro is a **cloud giant**, with the following changes:

- Cressaro's alignment is neutral evil.
- Cressaro wears *bracers of defense*, giving him AC 16.

Cressaro is a fit young cloud giant in his prime, and, not surprisingly, he also serves the countess as a consort and personal bodyguard. His magical bracers were a gift from the countess, and his private bedchamber is handsomely appointed. A fine cloak hangs from a bronze hook high on one wall, near a shelf that holds a dozen books about dragons, warfare, and the history of the conflict between giants and dragons that led to the fall of the empire of Ostoria. Other furnishings include a handsome rug and a small palm tree growing out of an alabaster vase in one corner of the room. The vase is 7 feet tall, weighs 750 pounds, and has images of armored cloud giant warriors carved into it.

### Treasure

Cressaro's *bracers of defense* magically resize to fit whoever attunes to them.

Each book in Cressaro's collection is worth 500 gp to an interested buyer and weighs 100 pounds. Many historians and sages in Waterdeep would pay for them.

Close inspection of the vase accompanied by a successful DC 10 Wisdom (Perception) check reveals a seam, suggesting that the top half of the vase can be separated from the bottom half. The top half of the vase holds the palm tree and the earth around it. Cressaro

# Lyn Armaal

## Level 1

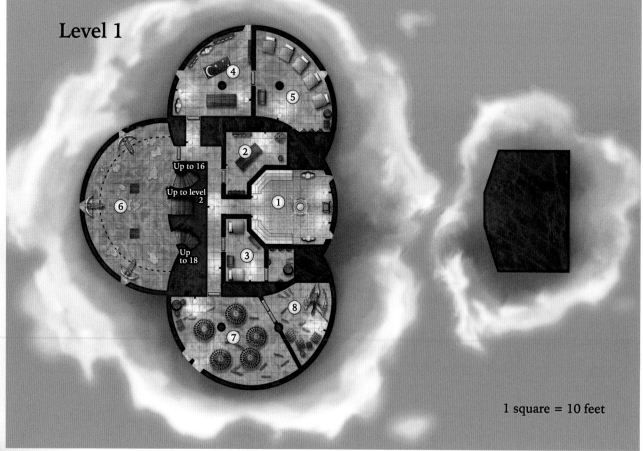

Up to 16

Up to level 2

Up to 18

1 square = 10 feet

MAP 9.1: LYN ARMAAL, LEVEL 1

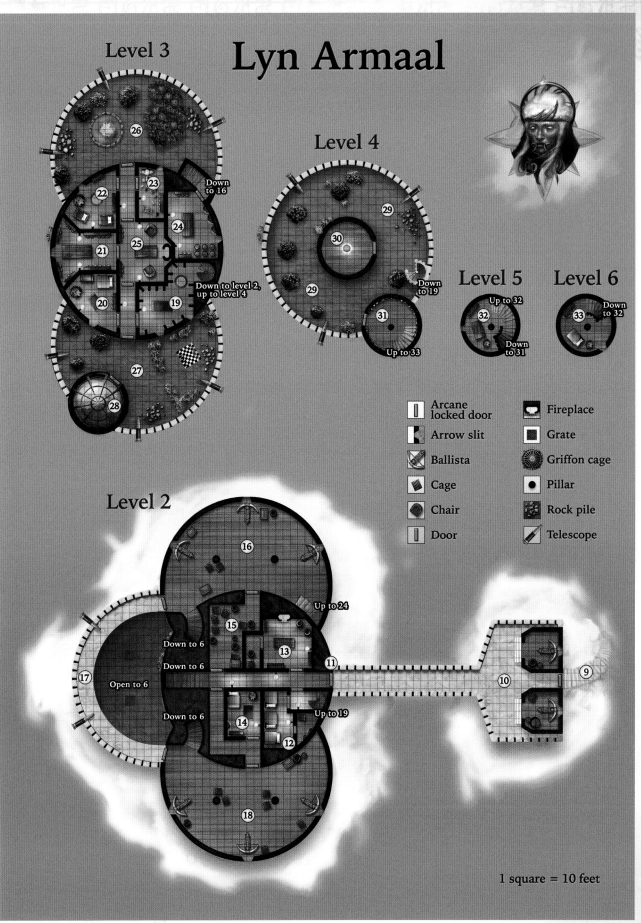

# Lyn Armaal

## Level 3

26

23
22
24
21
25
20
19
27
28

Down to 16

Down to level 2,
up to level 4

## Level 4

29
30
29
31

Down
to 19

Up to 33

## Level 5

32

Up to 32

Down
to 31

## Level 6

33

Down
to 32

### Legend

| | | | |
|---|---|---|---|
| Arcane locked door | | Fireplace | |
| Arrow slit | | Grate | |
| Ballista | | Griffon cage | |
| Cage | | Pillar | |
| Chair | | Rock pile | |
| Door | | Telescope | |

## Level 2

16
15
13
11
17
Open to 6
Down to 6
Down to 6
Down to 6
14
12
18

Up to 24

Up to 19

10
9

1 square = 10 feet

conceals his treasure in the bottom half of the vase. The top half can be lifted away or knocked off with a successful DC 18 Strength check, or characters can smash a hole in the bottom of the vase. Either act exposes a hollow compartment containing 1,200 ep, 3,500 gp, seven 500 gp gems, and a *figurine of wondrous power* (serpentine owl).

## 15. STORES

This room is packed with oversized crates of bread, dried meat and fish, fruits, and vegetables as well as oversized barrels of water and wine.

## 16. PORT BATTERY

Three ballistae face arrow slits in the outer wall, with a few tall crates of ammunition here and there. Two stone pillars support the ceiling. One staircase climbs to a landing outside area 24, and another curls down to area 6.

A **cloud giant** armed with a morningstar stands guard in this room. Five rounds after an alarm has sounded, two more cloud giants from area 5 arrive here, assuming nothing delays them. The three giants load and fire the ballistae as needed. Characters who enter this area and aren't traveling with a cloud giant escort are attacked on sight.

## 17. RAMPART

Two **cloud giants** stand guard atop this rampart, which is equipped with two large telescopes. Each giant keeps a sack nearby that holds a dozen rocks, which the giants hurl at enemies beyond their reach. Characters who enter this area and aren't traveling with a cloud giant escort are attacked on sight.

## 18. STARBOARD BATTERY

Three ballistae face arrow slits in the outer wall, with a few tall crates of ammunition here and there. Two stone pillars support the ceiling. A staircase curls down to area 6.

A **cloud giant** armed with a morningstar stands guard in this room. Six rounds after an alarm has sounded, two more cloud giants from area 5 arrive here, assuming that nothing delays them. The three giants load and fire the ballistae as needed. Characters who enter this area and aren't traveling with a cloud giant escort are attacked on sight.

## 19. GALLERY

A decorative, wrought iron staircase in one corner of this room leads down to the servants' quarters (area 12) and up to the castle roof (area 29). Colorful rugs decorate the floor, while the walls are festooned with partitions forming niches that display all the objets d'art that the countess has collected over the years. The centerpiece of her collection is a stuffed young silver dragon suspended by chains from the ceiling. It isn't valuable, but many other items on display are.

### TREASURE

The countess's collection of art objects includes paintings, statues, ceremonial weapons and costumes, human-sized sarcophagi, vases and other pottery from ancient Ostoria, and well-preserved (nonmagical) scrolls with imperial decrees and divine edicts written in Dethek, the Dwarvish script. Ten of the art objects are nonmagical treasures worth 750 gp each. Use the Art Objects table in chapter 7 of the *Dungeon Master's Guide* to determine what each treasure looks like. Two magic items are displayed here as well.

***Anstruth Harp.*** An exquisitely crafted harp sized for a human rests on a shelf. This *instrument of the bards* was acquired from a human bard who counseled Sansuri for a few months. She had him hurled from the battlements for joking about her quick temper and kept his harp as a memento.

***Banner of the Krig Rune.*** This magical war banner (see appendix B) hangs from a varnished wooden rod bolted to the door. The rod is mounted 20 feet above the floor, and the banner is 9 feet long.

## 20. THULLEN'S BEDROOM

Sansuri's younger brother, Count Thullen, sleeps in his bedroom at odd hours and spends much of his waking time in the greenhouse (area 28). When he isn't tending to his plants, he sometimes looks after Sansuri's two children in his room. Some of their toys lie strewn on the floor, including a chariot big enough for a halfling to ride in and a stuffed, silk-skinned doll as big as a human. Thullen keeps his quarters tidy otherwise. Furnishings include a soft bed, a rug, a bookshelf, and a large, compartmentalized chest containing folded clothing and ordinary personal effects.

## 21. LIBRARY

Like most wizards, Sansuri has acquired books covering a broad range of subjects. Six of the tomes in her library are of considerable worth (see "Treasure"). These valuable tomes are kept on the highest shelves, 25 feet above floor level, and are enormous, with metal covers that are 5 feet tall, 4 feet wide, and 1 inch thick. Each book weighs 150 pounds.

A large wooden table, its legs carved to look like rearing pegasi, dominates the room. An ornate bronze lantern hanging above the table has a *continual flame* spell cast within it.

### TREASURE

Among Sansuri's collection of books are four historical texts chronicling the rise and fall of Ostoria (worth 500 gp each and weighing 50 pounds each) and a one-of-a-kind book of original plays written in Dethek, the Dwarvish script, with Common translations, by a legendary and long-deceased cloud giant poet named Delevarius (worth 750 gp and weighing 50 pounds).

A thorough search of the library yields Sansuri's enormous spellbook, which is 5 feet tall, 4 feet wide, and 2 feet thick. It has bronze covers inlaid with sixty gemstones worth 10 gp each and weighs 250 pounds. The book contains the following spells:

1st level: *alarm, identify, magic missile, shield, thunderwave, unseen servant*
2nd level: *arcane lock, continual flame, gust of wind, invisibility, knock, mirror image*
3rd level: *dispel magic, glyph of warding, haste, hypnotic pattern, lightning bolt, sending*
4th level: *fabricate, ice storm, Leomund's secret chest, Mordenkainen's faithful hound, stoneskin*
5th level: *Bigby's hand, cloudkill, geas, wall of force*
6th level: *globe of invulnerability, guards and wards, true seeing*
7th level: *Mordenkainen's sword, reverse gravity, Sansuri's simulacrum* (see below)

Sansuri's version of the *simulacrum* spell allows her to create multiple duplicates of the same creature—but it requires powdered diamond worth 5,000 gp as an additional material component. The powdered diamond, like the powdered ruby also needed to cast the spell, must be sprinkled over the duplicate and is consumed by the spell.

## 22. NURSERY

This room contains two cribs and a couple of wall shelves with large stuffed toys perched precariously atop them. At night, Sansuri's children (see area 23) sleep here.

## 23. PLAYROOM

Sansuri has twin children who play here unsupervised during the day. Characters who listen at the door can hear the children's laughter beyond. The boy is named Kaaltar, the girl Alastrah. Standing 6½ feet tall and weighing 250 pounds, each is as big as a powerfully built male human. They use the **commoner** stat block, with these changes:

- The children are Medium Giants of neutral alignment.
- Each child has a Strength score of 14 (+2).
- They speak Giant, though their vocabulary is limited.
- They wield wooden toys as clubs, gaining a +4 bonus to hit on their melee weapon attack rolls and dealing 4 (1d4 + 2) bludgeoning damage on a hit.

Their uncle, Thullen (see area 28), checks on them occasionally, but they receive little attention from their mother, since they are too young to be schooled. Emotionally, each child is the giant equivalent of a four-year-old human.

The floor of this room is covered with toys, balls, blocks, dolls, and stuffed animals. A stuffed yeti mounted on a wooden base stands in a corner by the door; it is part of the room's decor, not a toy.

### DEVELOPMENT

If the characters capture one or both children and use them as leverage to obtain Sansuri's *conch of teleportation*, she gives them what they want, even though bowing to their demands infuriates her. She must retrieve the conch from the *Leomund's secret chest* in her bedchamber (area 33). If the characters get greedy and ask for more than the conch, Sansuri is willing to part with just about anything else except her spellbook (see area 21), her castle, and the *navigation orb* (see area 30). She would even agree to release Felgolos from custody.

She has no honor, however, and will break her word or attempt to reclaim what's hers as soon as the children are safely returned to her.

If any harm befalls either child, Sansuri won't rest until those responsible are crushed to a pulp. The same is true for Thullen (see area 28), who loves the children even more than his sister does.

## 24. GUARD ROOM

A **cloud giant** stands guard here at all times, peering out the arrow slit toward the gatehouse (area 10) and watching for trouble. This giant doesn't have any rocks to hurl but can substitute five-gallon flasks of acid (range 30/120 ft.), hurling one as an action and dealing 22 (4d10) acid damage on a hit. Each flask weighs 50 pounds, and there are twelve such flasks on wooden shelves about the room.

Cut into the floor in one corner of the room are six murder holes, each one big enough for a Small character to squeeze through. Next to the murder holes is a glass vat holding 30 gallons of acid. The vat weighs 400 pounds when full. If enemies enter the castle through the main door (area 11), the giant can use an action to dump the contents of the vat over the murder holes, allowing the acid to rain down on intruders in the hallway below. Any creature caught in the acid shower must make a DC 15 Dexterity saving throw, taking 44 (8d10) acid damage on a failed save, or half as much damage on a successful one. Once the vat is used, it can't be used again until it has been refilled. It takes six flasks of acid to refill the vat, and an action to pour out each flask's contents.

## 25. LOUNGE

Sansuri retires to this opulent chamber when she needs to relax and clear her mind. A 5-foot-tall table of varnished wood stands in the middle of the room. Arranged atop it are several items: a hookah, a blue crystal decanter filled with fine wine, and a wooden plate covered with a mountain of figs. Blue crystal flute glasses are stored on shelves on either side of a door that leads to the library (area 21). Two padded chairs covered in yeti hide with blue-dyed seat cushions are turned to face the table. The chairs flank a marble fireplace carved with images of birds. Above the mantelpiece is a stuffed and mounted aarakocra with blue plumage. This poor creature is the remains of Jakka (see the "Aarakocra Simulacra" section earlier in this chapter).

A *detect magic* spell reveals a faint aura of conjuration magic surrounding the fireplace. Any creature that points at the fireplace and speaks the word "ild" causes a magical, crackling fire to erupt within it. The fire lasts for 1 hour before it dies out. This property can be activated at will. Casting an *identify* spell on the fireplace reveals both its property and the command word needed to activate it.

## 26. PORT LAWN

A healthy grass lawn covers this rooftop, which is enclosed by 10-foot-high battlements. The soil beneath the grass is 2 feet deep. Unless they are drawn elsewhere, six **aarakocra simulacra** (see the "Aarakocra Simulacra" section earlier in this chapter) perch atop these battlements, half of them facing outward and half facing inward. The aarakocra have instructions to attack intruders who disturb the water in the pool (see below). They also come to the aid of the guards in area 29. They otherwise attack only in self-defense or if Sansuri commands them to.

Looking out over the battlements are three telescopes. Piles of rocks, which the giants use for ammunition, are next to two of the telescopes.

A fountain with a spout shaped like a silver dragon bound in chains feeds water into a 40-foot-diameter, 5-foot-deep pool near the western wall. Water from the spout is collected in the pool and recycled through the fountain. A **water elemental** lives in the pool and emerges to attack any intruder that disturbs the water. If the elemental is attacked, the aarakocra simulacra join the fray, coming to its defense.

Fruit trees grow in a few places, and a pumpkin patch dominates one large area. The pumpkins that grow here weigh 300 pounds each. A cloud giant can hurl a big pumpkin as far as it can throw a rock and deal as much damage.

## 27. Starboard Lawn

This rooftop garden has a lush green lawn dotted with trees and piles of rocks that cloud giants use to make ranged attacks. The soil beneath the grass is 2 feet deep. A hedge divides the yard, and inside the smaller area is a black-and-white marble chessboard. The chess pieces are all human-sized and look like decorative suits of armor, their helms sporting designs that differentiate them; for example, the kings and queens wear crowns for helms, and the knights have helms resembling griffon heads. The pawns, rooks, bishops, knights, and kings are suits of **animated armor**, thirty in all. The queens are **helmed horrors**. Since no game is in progress, all of the pieces are in their starting locations.

The constructs don't attack unless one of them is attacked first, or unless they are commanded to do so by Sansuri or Thullen. A chess piece otherwise remains still, unless Sansuri or Thullen commands it to move to a new position on the board.

## 28. Greenhouse

The door to Lyn Armaal's dome-shaped greenhouse has a delicate mithral frame set with panes of stained glass that don't hold up well to damage. A riot of flowering plants and herbs grow within the greenhouse. The plants are tended by Sansuri's younger brother, Count Thullen. If he's not here, Thullen is either in his quarters (area 20) or checking on his niece and nephew in area 23. Lurking among the flora are seven **awakened shrubs** that guard the greenhouse and protect the other plants. If an alarm sounds, Thullen heads to area 23 to make sure the children are okay, and the shrubs stay behind.

Thullen is the opposite of his sister in many ways—gentle, soft-spoken, and not easily moved to violence. Only those who harm his plants or his sister's children

stir the deep-seated rage inside him. Unlike other cloud giant nobles, Thullen doesn't wear a mask to illustrate his mood. He is a **cloud giant**, with the following changes:

- Thullen's alignment is neutral good.
- When Thullen casts *barkskin* on himself, his AC improves to 16.
- He has an Intelligence score of 18 (+4) and gains the Spellcasting action option described below.
- He speaks Common, Draconic, Druidic, and Giant.
- He has a challenge rating of 10 (5,900 XP).

***Spellcasting.*** Thullen casts one of the following spells, requiring no material components and using Wisdom as the spellcasting ability (spell save DC 15; +7 to hit with spell attacks):

At will: *druidcraft, produce flame*
2/day each: *animal messenger, barkskin, conjure animals, cure wounds, entangle, speak with plants, thunderwave*
1/day each: *call lightning, conjure elemental* (cast as 1 action), *freedom of movement, gust of wind*

### Development

Thullen isn't driven like his sister to gain and flaunt wealth and power, and thus he is lower in the cloud giant ordning and must follow her orders. However, he swore an oath to his parents to advise and protect his sister. He doesn't like making enemies, so he tries to reason with adventurers who cross his path. If all they want is Sansuri's *conch of teleportation*, he will divulge that Sansuri keeps the conch in her tower bedchamber (area 33), though he doesn't know exactly where.

If the characters seem intent on running amok, Thullen tries to defeat them quickly for the good of his family, calling on the constructs in area 27 to assist. If one or more characters surrender after causing harm to him or his family, he spares their lives but commands them to leave Lyn Armaal at once. If they refuse, or if they leave only to return at a later time, Thullen turns hostile and attacks them.

## 29. High Lawn

The roof of the main keep has a lush green lawn surrounding a squat stone building (area 30). The soil beneath the grass is 2 feet deep. A three-story tower with a conical rooftop (areas 31–33) juts upward and outward from the southeastern part of the wall, rising another 120 feet into the air. Trees and shrubs sprout from the ground here and there, and three telescopes are mounted to the battlements. A wrought iron spiral staircase descends through a hole in the ground, leading down to area 19. Near the staircase is a pile of rocks that cloud giants can use to make ranged attacks.

Perched on the battlements are six **aarakocra simulacra** (see the "Aarakocra Simulacra" section earlier in this chapter), half of them facing outward and half facing inward. They attack anyone other than Sansuri or Thullen who attempts to enter the navigation dome or Sansuri's tower. They also fight to protect themselves and one another. Two rounds after battle is joined here, the aarakocra simulacra in area 26 arrive to assist.

## 30. Navigation Dome

Sansuri has cast an *arcane lock* spell on the door to this stone building, which has no other entrances or windows. Floating 10 feet above the floor in the middle of this circular room is the castle's *navigation orb* (see appendix B), which Sansuri uses to control the movement of Lyn Armaal. The inside wall of the room is painted with a lavish mural of a cloud giant city made up of dozens of joined cloud castles. The domed ceiling is made up of overlapping shells of thin, black metal with glowing shards of crystal set into star-shaped sockets. The crystals represent the stars in the night sky, and the overlapping shells magically reposition themselves so that the artificial sky inside the dome exactly matches the night sky wherever the castle happens to be.

## 31. Hall of Masks

Masks are popular collectibles among cloud giant nobles, who wear them to reflect their moods. A cloud giant noble typically owns several, each one a valuable art object and each one's expression capturing a particular emotion, be it joy, melancholy, sorrow, anger, or something more subtle. Sansuri's collection of masks is displayed here.

This room forms the bottom floor of Sansuri's tower, with a door providing access from the rooftop lawn. If Sansuri is forced to retreat to her tower, she casts an *arcane lock* spell on the door after moving through it. A central pillar supports the roof, and an ornate, wooden spiral staircase curls up to area 32.

### Treasure

The walls of this room are festooned with masks, fifty in all, each one worth 250 gp. These nonmagical masks are sized and molded to fit Sansuri's face, and each captures a specific mood or emotion. No single artist crafted more than one mask for the countess, so each mask has a unique style. The masks rest atop narrow shelves set into the walls 10, 15, and 20 feet above the floor. A few shelves are empty, indicating that the countess has room to expand her collection.

## 32. Study

Sansuri researches new spells and hones her wizardly craft here. Furnishings include a table and a 25-foot-tall wooden cabinet with an *arcane lock* spell cast on its doors. A staircase descends to area 31 and ascends to area 33.

Two **invisible stalkers** lurk here silently and attack any creature other than a cloud giant that crosses the room.

### Treasure

The magically locked cabinet is divided into shelves and cubbyholes holding Sansuri's collection of potions and scrolls, as well as magic items obtained from adventurers who crossed paths with her and paid the ultimate price. A search of the cabinet's interior yields the following items.

- Six giant-sized potions (*clairvoyance, diminution, fire resistance, lightning resistance, storm giant strength,* and *supreme healing*). Each potion is contained in a 1-foot-tall crystal flask that weighs 15 pounds while full, or 5 pounds when empty. A giant potion must be consumed in its entirety to gain its effect, and it takes a Medium or Small character 1 minute to chug one down.

- Five spell scrolls (*animate objects*, *chain lightning*, *dominate monster*, *legend lore*, and *phantasmal killer*). Each scroll is written on a 12-foot-long, 5-foot-wide rolled sheet of vellum. Normal-sized characters can use the scrolls despite their size.
- Three normal-sized magic items. Roll on Magic Item Table F in chapter 7 of the *Dungeon Master's Guide* for the first two items and on Table G for the third.

## 33. Master Bedchamber

Sansuri has adorned her bedchamber with decorations befitting her noble status. Her mattress is filled with the softest down, and her bed's wooden frame is inlaid with gold tracery and gemstones. (These and other precious items are described in the "Treasure" section that follows.) The chamber's conical roof reaches its apex 60 feet overhead. Hanging from the rafters is Sansuri's bizarre "merry-go-round," which is made up of seven stuffed pegasi hanging from a ring-shaped "track" made of steel. The ring magically turns so that the winged horses "glide" overhead continually in a counterclockwise direction.

Hidden in the bed's headboard is a secret compartment that can be found with a DC 15 Wisdom (Perception) check. It contains a small, bejeweled chest made of gold with platinum filigree. This chest is a miniature replica of a much larger chest that Sansuri uses as the main component of a *Leomund's secret chest* spell. By touching the replica, Sansuri can recall the larger chest (see "Treasure"), causing it to appear within 5 feet of her. No other creature can summon the full-sized chest in this manner, which means the characters must persuade Sansuri to summon it for them if they want to obtain its contents (see "Development").

### Treasure

The gold tracery that adorns Sansuri's bed, if it is all pried loose, is worth only 100 gp, but the fifty gemstones embedded in the bed frame are worth 100 gp each. Prying out a single gem requires an action. Six gold-spun tapestries (each worth 2,500 gp and weighing 750 pounds) adorn the walls. Sansuri also has a freestanding mirror with an electrum frame (worth 1,500 gp and weighing 500 pounds) and a three-fold wooden privacy screen carved to look like trees with blowing leaves made of thinly pressed gold and platinum (worth 2,500 gp and weighing 500 pounds).

The full-sized *Leomund's secret chest* is worth 5,000 gp. Its smaller replica is worth 50 gp. Inside the full-sized chest are Sansuri's *conch of teleportation* (see appendix B), 500 pp, and six pieces of jewelry: four platinum bracelets (worth 750 gp each), a gold pendant necklace set with a fist-sized amethyst (worth 7,500 gp), and a diamond-encrusted diadem (worth 7,500 gp).

### Development

The characters need some kind of influence to make Sansuri use the replica chest to summon the full-size *Leomund's secret chest*. They can use a *suggestion* spell or similar magic to compel Sansuri to summon the chest. They can also hold one or both of her children hostage and use them as leverage to get what they want. If the characters defeat Sansuri in combat but keep her alive, she agrees to summon the chest and give up its contents in exchange for her life.

If the characters kill Sansuri before realizing that they need her help to obtain the *conch of teleportation*, they must either restore her to life, seek out another *conch of teleportation*, or find some other way to reach Maelstrom.

# Conquering the Castle

If Countess Sansuri dies, rightful ownership of Lyn Armaal falls to her children, but neither is old enough to rule in her stead. Their uncle, Count Thullen, assumes command of the castle if he's still alive. If the characters oppose him, Thullen tries to convince them to leave by allowing the characters to keep whatever treasures they have amassed. If they still refuse to give up control of the castle, he attacks them unless they have Sansuri's children in custody, in which case Thullen cedes control of the castle in exchange for their safe return. Thullen can use the constructs in area 27 to help him rid the castle of "small folk," should it come to that.

If the characters defeat all the cloud giants and the aarakocra simulacra, there's nothing stopping them from claiming the castle once they rid it of any remaining hostile creatures, such as the griffons in area 7 and the elementals in areas 10, 26, and 31. The dim-witted ogres in area 13 serve the characters as readily as they served the cloud giants, and the constructs in area 27 are no threat as long as they remain deactivated.

How long the characters remain in control of the castle is up to them and up to you. The characters might lose interest in it once they come to realize how inconveniently large the doors and staircases are. There are certainly other creatures in the North that might try to take it from them, including rival cloud giants and ancient dragons. Klauth, in particular, might try to seize the castle as "payment" for helping the characters earlier in the adventure; see the "Klauthen Vale" section in chapter 3 for more information on this sly old wyrm.

---

**CHARACTER ADVANCEMENT**

Once the characters obtain Sansuri's *conch of teleportation*, a character can attune to it and use it to transport the party to Maelstrom. The characters might decide not to use the conch right away, perhaps because they intend to free Felgolos but have not yet done so or because they want to clear out the castle and claim it as their own. Make sure the characters advance to 9th level before moving on to chapter 10, "Hold of the Storm Giants."

---

# CHAPTER 10: HOLD OF THE STORM GIANTS

**B**EFORE THE DISSOLUTION OF THE ORDNING, the influence of the storm giants was so great that lesser giants were compelled to abide by their decrees. The storm giants, reclusive by nature, did their best to discourage lesser giants from destroying the civilizations of the small folk. The death of Queen Neri and the disappearance of King Hekaton have left Maelstrom in disarray, allowing evil giants to run rampant.

King Hekaton saw signs that his eldest daughters were unfit to claim the *Wyrmskull Throne*, so he made his even-keeled youngest daughter, Serissa, his rightful heir. She has taken her place on the *Wyrmskull Throne*, but with the ordning shattered, she doesn't have the power to keep the evil giant lords in line. She relies on two storm giants for counsel: her uncle, Uthor (Hekaton's younger brother), and the wise, matronly Iymrith. Unfortunately, neither of them has much respect for small folk. In that regard, Serissa is alone. Like her dearly departed mother, Serissa believes that small folk are cleverer and mightier than most giants give them credit for, and as a child, she visited their shores in the company of her mother and has great affection for them.

In this part of their mission, the characters use their *conch of teleportation* (obtained in a previous chapter) to teleport to Maelstrom. Once there, they must make their way to Princess Serissa and win her confidence. She wants to believe that her father is alive. She also wants to believe that the characters are resourceful and strong enough to find and rescue King Hekaton, despite what Uthor and Iymrith whisper. If the characters convince Serissa that they can help, she shows them a clue found near the corpse of her mother: a wooden coin that leads the characters into conflict with the Kraken Society (as discussed in chapter 11, "Caught in the Tentacles").

Standing in the characters' way are Serissa's siblings, Mirran and Nym, who do everything in their power to turn Serissa against the adventurers and prove to their younger sibling that small folk can't be trusted and must be wiped out. The characters also encounter Iymrith again. To prove their true worth to the storm giants, the characters must expose the dragon who hides in their midst. The dragon flees when her true nature is revealed, and the characters don't encounter Iymrith again until they confront her in her desert lair (see chapter 12).

Characters who have no interest in intrigue might try to plunder the stronghold or do away with members of the royal family. Any such act turns Serissa against the characters and plays right into Iymrith's hands.

## STORM GIANTS

Before running this part of the adventure, review the information on storm giants in the *Monster Manual*. It will help you roleplay the storm giants in this chapter.

In addition, take another look at the "King Hekaton and His Daughters" section and the "Iymrith" section in the introduction for information on how to roleplay the sisters, Uthor, and Iymrith accurately.

## MAELSTROM: GENERAL FEATURES

Even though the storm giant stronghold Maelstrom lies deep beneath the Trackless Sea, it isn't entirely filled with water. The general features of the undersea stronghold are summarized here.

**Air-Filled and Submerged Areas.** Many chambers and corridors are filled with air that is continuously and magically replenished. On the map, air-filled areas are tinted purple. Some air-filled areas contain pools of water; a pool fills a depression in the floor and is tinted blue on the map. Submerged areas are tinted blue from wall to wall. Characters who can't breathe underwater must hold their breath in a submerged area. While submerged, they are also susceptible to the effect of water pressure (see the "Water Pressure" section). Rules for underwater combat appear in the "Underwater Combat" section in chapter 9 of the *Player's Handbook*.

**Anemone Chests.** The storm giants cultivate 10-foot-tall, 10-foot-wide anemones that can survive out of the water and have hollow cavities within them. The giants use the anemones as treasure chests and for waste disposal. Edible organic matter placed in an anemone chest is slowly digested over a period of days; inedible or inorganic matter is not.

When a storm giant touches one of these anemones, it opens at the top. Any other creature that comes into contact with an anemone must make a DC 10 Dexterity saving throw. On a failed save, the creature takes 11 (2d10) poison damage from the anemone's poisonous tendrils. A character can trick an anemone into opening by touching it and succeeding on a DC 15 Intelligence (Nature) check. If the check fails, the anemone doesn't open, and the character must make the saving throw. A chest remains open for 1 minute, then closes. An anemone chest has AC 5 and 20 hit points.

**Ceilings.** Ceilings throughout the fortress are 50 feet high in air-filled areas and 30 feet high in submerged areas unless otherwise noted. The sinkhole in the middle of the fortress is open to the sea above.

**Climbing.** The stronghold has slick, rough-hewn walls that don't offer a lot of handholds, so climbing them without gear requires a successful DC 20 Strength (Athletics) check.

**Crystal Windows.** Some rooms have oval windows made of thick, transparent crystal. These windows were designed to withstand tremendous amounts of pressure and force, and aren't easily broken. Each window has AC 15, 60 hit points, a damage threshold of 20, and immunity to psychic and poison damage. Breaking a window causes seawater to pour into the stronghold, flooding air-filled chambers and lower levels quickly. Doing this has no effect on storm giants, who can breathe water as easily as they breathe air, but creatures that can't breathe water aren't likely to survive for long without the aid of *water breathing* spells or similar magic.

**Doors and Secret Doors.** The giant-sized doors throughout Maelstrom are 30 feet tall and made of barnacle-covered stone with rusty iron hinges. Their handles are 13 feet above the floor. Secret doors are similar in size but lack visible hinges and handles. A Huge giant has no trouble opening either type of door. A smaller creature can attempt to open a door if that creature or some other helpful creature can reach the door's handle and unlatch it. While the handle is unlatched, a creature must use an action to push or pull on the heavy door, opening it with a successful DC 15 Strength (Athletics) check. On a failed check, the door doesn't open. The doors aren't airtight and can't hold back water.

Characters who have a passive Wisdom (Perception) score of 15 or higher spot a secret door as they move near its location. A character can also find it by searching for secret doors and succeeding on a DC 15 Wisdom (Perception) check.

**Giant Clams.** Giant clams appear in several of vthe stronghold's chambers. As an action, a character can pry open a giant clam with a successful DC 16 Strength (Athletics) check. Using a crowbar, a sword, or a similar tool grants advantage on the check. When a giant clam is opened, roll on the Giant Clam table to determine its contents.

### GIANT CLAM

| d100 | Treasure |
|---|---|
| 01–25 | None |
| 26–75 | A pink grapefruit-sized pearl worth 500 gp |
| 76–90 | A black grapefruit-sized pearl worth 5,000 gp |
| 91–98 | A violet grapefruit-sized *pearl of power* |
| 99–00 | A clear grapefruit-sized *crystal ball* |

**Illumination.** All interior spaces are dimly lit. Air-filled chambers have wall sconces with *continual flame* spells cast on them or oval windows of transparent crystal that allow light from the bioluminescent coral reef to enter. Bioluminescent fish dimly illuminate submerged areas.

**Oversized Furnishings and Objects.** Most of the furnishings and other items in Maelstrom are sized for storm giants. Exceptions are noted in the text. Tables, chairs, and other room fixtures are typically three times as high, long, and wide as their human-sized equivalents and roughly twenty-seven times the weight. Small and Medium creatures can scuttle under and clamber over giant-sized furniture, treating the spaces they occupy as difficult terrain.

**Portcullises.** Throughout the stronghold are iron portcullises covered in barnacles. A portcullis can be raised or lowered with a successful DC 26 Strength (Athletics) check. A Small creature can slip between the bars with ease, while a Medium creature can squeeze between the portcullis bars with a successful DC 10 Dexterity (Acrobatics) check.

**Stairs.** Staircases in the stronghold are sized for storm giants. Each step is 4 feet tall by 4 feet deep. Large and smaller creatures treat the staircases as difficult terrain.

# MAELSTROM

Maelstrom lies on the floor of the Trackless Sea, nearly 3,000 feet beneath the surface. For centuries, it has been the stronghold of the world's most powerful storm giant kings. The undersea fortress of King Hekaton is carved into a reef. Four rocky towers covered in barnacles and coral reach upward, and between them is a large sinkhole that descends into the heart of the fortress. A natural phenomenon sometimes causes the ocean currents to form a great whirlpool with enough strength to draw ships down into it. These vessels are torn apart as they are pulled down, and the wreckage is deposited at the bottom of the sinkhole, where hulking crabs pick through it for their storm giant masters.

## REACHING MAELSTROM

The easiest and safest way to reach Maelstrom (shown on maps 10.1 and 10.2) is with teleportation magic, and characters should have a *conch of teleportation* when the time comes to visit the storm giant stronghold.

## Maelstrom Roster

| Area | Creature(s) | Notes |
|---|---|---|
| 5 | 2 **hulking crabs** | The crabs scuttle out to investigate disturbances in area 1 unless the portcullis to their cave is closed. |
| 6 | 1 **killer whale** | The whale waits here for Nym. |
| 7 | 1 **roper** | The roper doesn't leave this area under any circumstances. |
| 8 | 1 **killer whale** | The whale waits here for Mirran. |
| 10 | 1 **storm giant** | The giant investigates any loud disturbance in area 8 and otherwise obeys Mirran's or Uthor's commands. |
| 11 | 1 **killer whale** | The whale waits here for Serissa. |
| 12 | 2 **storm giants** | The giants investigate any loud disturbance in area 11 and otherwise obey Serissa's or Uthor's commands. |
| 14 | Mirran, Nym, 1 **hulking crab** (pipe organ), 2 **storm giants**, 1 **cloud giant**, 1 **fire giant**, 1 **frost giant**, 1 **stone giant** | The storm giants protect Nym and Mirran, who retreat to areas 6 and 30, respectively, if seriously threatened. The crab and the other giants remain here. |
| 15 | Serissa, Uthor, Iymrith, 2 **hill giants** | Uthor protects Serissa, who retreats to area 11 if seriously threatened. Iymrith escapes through the pool if her true nature is revealed. The hill giants stand guard outside the doors at all times. |
| 19 | 10 **hunter sharks** | The sharks remain here until released, whereupon they move into the sinkhole (area 1) to hunt for prey. |
| 21, 29 | 2 **storm giants** | The giants remain here unless commanded by Uthor to go elsewhere. |
| 31 | 5 **steam mephits** | The mephits remain near the bath. |
| 33 | 1 **storm giant** | The giant remains here unless commanded by Uthor to go elsewhere. |
| 34 | 2 **storm giants**, 9 **giant crabs** | The giants and the crabs remain here until disturbed. |

Characters who teleport to Maelstrom using the conch appear atop the magical glyph in area 2.

Characters can also reach Maelstrom by ship. Maelstrom is located on the sea floor between Ruathym, the Whalebones, and the Korinn Archipelago. Any ship that sails over Maelstrom encounters a giant whirlpool, which inexorably draws the vessel into the depths. The ship's hull is torn apart, its wreckage sucked to the bottom of a sinkhole in the heart of the stronghold (area 1). Creatures aboard the vessel must make a DC 20 Constitution saving throw, taking 55 (10d10) bludgeoning damage on a failed save, or half as much damage on a successful one. There's no air in the sinkhole, so characters who survive the shipwreck must hold their breath, locate an air pocket, or use magic to breathe. Characters who are drawn down into the depths must also contend with water pressure.

### Water Pressure

Creatures and vehicles at Maelstrom's depth take 7 (2d6) force damage per minute from water pressure unless they are adapted or built to withstand this environment. Storm giants, whales, sharks, crustaceans, and aquatic invertebrates are immune to water pressure at this depth, as are vehicles with a damage threshold of 10 or higher. Other creatures might be immune to the effect of water pressure, at your discretion.

A spell that allows one to breathe underwater provides no protection against the crushing effect of water pressure unless the spell's description says otherwise. Even an *apparatus of Kwalish* isn't designed to withstand water pressure at this depth. Creatures inside an *apparatus of Kwalish* are protected from the crushing effect of the pressure while the apparatus has at least 1 hit point.

## Denizens

The Maelstrom Roster table summarizes the locations of the inhabitants when the characters approach and indicates how those creatures react when intruders are detected. Loud noises in one area of the stronghold can be heard in adjacent areas, even if there's water or a door between the locations.

Princess Serissa is the supreme authority in Maelstrom during her father's absence. She entrusts her uncle, Uthor, with command of the garrison. If the stronghold is attacked, Uthor's primary duty is to protect the princesses, Serissa first and foremost. All other storm giants—the princesses included—obey Uthor's commands when it comes to military matters.

Once Iymrith realizes that small folk have invaded the stronghold, she does everything she can to foment a war. She tries to convince Serissa that the adventurers are assassins sent to kill her ("hired by the villainous Lords' Alliance, no less," Iymrith supposes), and that every word spilling from their mouths is a lie. As a last resort, Iymrith will goad Mirran and Nym into attacking the adventurers, since she knows that Uthor and his guards will quickly turn on anyone who harms his nieces. Iymrith won't attack the adventurers herself. If her true nature is revealed, she tries to snatch the *Korolnor Scepter* (see appendix B) from Serissa's clutches before fleeing the stronghold and returning to her lair in Anauroch (see chapter 12, "Doom of the Desert").

## 1. Vortex and Sinkhole

A powerful vortex swirls above a 100-foot-deep, 180-foot-wide sinkhole on the ocean bottom. (On the surface of the water, the vortex manifests as a half-mile-wide whirlpool powerful enough to drag ships to their doom.) The sinkhole has a drain at the bottom. Plugging the drain would cause the vortex to dissipate, but the drain is 50 feet in diameter. A barnacle-covered iron grate covers the drain, and the holes between its bars are 10 feet wide. The sinkhole has three levels.

### LEVEL 1

The bottom of the sinkhole is strewn with debris—the remains of wrecked ships picked clean by the hulking crabs in area 5. The walls are covered with coral and other ocean life. Five flooded passageways lead to areas 2, 5, 6, 8, and 11.

### LEVEL 2

This level is 50 feet above the sinkhole floor. A rocky, uneven ledge clings to the outer wall of the hole and has coral, plant life, and the bones of a wrecked ship atop it. Five flooded tunnels lead to areas 15, 19, 20, 21, and 29.

### LEVEL 3

This is the top of the sinkhole. From here, an observer on the ocean floor can just barely make out a circular ledge 50 feet down, while the bottom of the sinkhole is hidden in the gloom 100 feet below. Lying around the mouth of the sinkhole are more wrecked ships, and looming above are the four coral-covered underwater spires that serve as home to the royal family. The shipwrecks have been picked clean, and anyone who lingers in the area sees sharks, whales, crabs, and other creatures moving about. These aquatic creatures mind their own business and pay little heed to surface-dwellers.

The coral on the outside of the royal spires can be harvested and sold. Someone who can withstand the pressure at this depth (see the "Water Pressure" section earlier in this chapter) can harvest 2d4 pounds of coral in an hour. Each pound is worth 50 gp. The storm giants in area 34 try to scare off anyone plundering the coral.

## 2. PORTAL CHAMBER

Anyone that teleports to Maelstrom appears atop a glowing glyph carved into the floor of an alcove in the northeast corner of this rough-hewn chamber. This is true even if the destination was elsewhere in the stronghold.

The moist walls here are covered with bioluminescent lichen, snails, starfish, and barnacles. Tiny, harmless crabs crawl across the floor, avoiding the sigil.

The first time the characters arrive in this chamber, they hear music: a powerful female voice accompanied by the deep, haunting tones of a masterfully played pipe organ. The music comes from within a spiral staircase that leads up to area 14. The two storm giants who normally stand guard at the foot of this staircase are currently in area 14, keeping an eye on some other visitors.

### POOL AND SUNKEN PASSAGE

Next to the staircase is a 40-foot-deep circular pool with a 30-foot-high passageway at the bottom. The flooded passage leads to area 1. A barnacle-covered portcullis has been lowered to block the passageway.

### NORTH AND EAST HALLWAYS

A hallway to the east ends at a life-size stone statue of a female storm giant holding a harp and wearing a gown of purple coral. Doors on the south wall of the corridor lead to area 3. Each door is made of ironbound oak, measures 15 feet tall by 7 feet wide, and has AC 15, 50 hit points, and immunity to poison and psychic damage. Neither door has a lock.

A similar hall stretches northward. The statue at the end of the north hall depicts a male storm giant blowing a pink and blue conch shell. Giant-sized doors to either side of the statue lead to more guest quarters (area 4).

### STEAM GEYSER

A narrow hall to the south leads to a circular chamber with a small steam pool at its center. Every hour on the hour, a geyser of steam shoots up from a vent in the bottom of the shallow basin, sending out a loud hissing noise as it erupts. Any creature in the small, circular room when the geyser erupts is engulfed in scalding steam and boiling water, and must make a DC 15 Dexterity saving throw, taking 22 (4d10) fire damage on a failed save, or half as much damage on a successful one.

## 3. SMALL GUEST QUARTERS

Adventurers who earn the giants' trust are quartered here during their stay. Each of these rooms contains furnishings sized for Medium and Small creatures: five comfortable beds, a circular rug, a barrel of drinking water, an empty dresser, and an empty wardrobe.

## 4. GIANT GUEST QUARTERS

Giant-sized guests are quartered here. The room to the east has a single bed, and the room to the west holds three beds. A door in the west wall opens into a storage room that holds some crates and barrels containing food and wine. No one is using these quarters at present.

## 5. CRAB PEN

A raised, barnacle-covered portcullis hangs above the entrance of this submerged cave. The cave is home to two **hulking crabs** (see appendix C). They have covered their shells with ship wreckage, and they attack anything that enters their cave unless it looks like a storm giant. From a distance of 30 feet or more, the crabs are easily mistaken for piles of debris. Any character who succeeds on a DC 15 Intelligence (Nature) check recognizes the creatures for what they are.

### TREASURE

A few treasures lie scattered across the cave floor amid rusty, barnacle-covered swords and other detritus. A thorough search yields 67 gp, a shiny electrum goblet (worth 75 gp), and 1d4 magic items. Roll on Magic Item Table G in chapter 7 of the *Dungeon Master's Guide* for the first item, and on Table F for any other items.

## 6. NYM'S WHALE

A 50-foot-deep pool takes up nearly half of this air-filled chamber. An enormous **killer whale** (144 hit points)

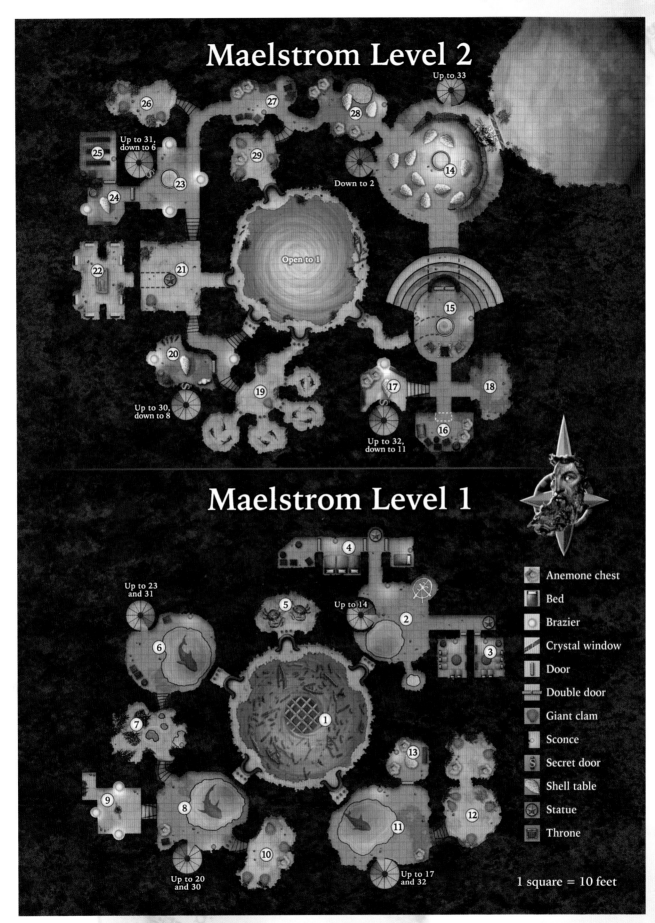

# Maelstrom Level 2

26

27

28

Up to 33

25

Up to 31,
down to 6

24

23

29

Down to 2

14

22

21

Open to 1

15

20

17

18

19

16

Up to 30,
down to 8

Up to 32,
down to 11

# Maelstrom Level 1

4

Up to 23
and 31

5

Up to 14

2

6

3

7

13

9

8

12

10

11

Up to 20
and 30

Up to 17
and 32

1 square = 10 feet

| | Anemone chest |
| | Bed |
| | Brazier |
| | Crystal window |
| | Door |
| | Double door |
| | Giant clam |
| | Sconce |
| | Secret door |
| | Shell table |
| | Statue |
| | Throne |

MAP 10.1: MAELSTROM, LEVELS 1 AND 2

swims circles in the pool, attacking any creature other than Nym that enters it. The whale is Nym's mount.

A submerged passage blocked by a lowered portcullis connects the whale's pool to the sinkhole (area 1). Crates of dead fish rest against the walls, and a spiral staircase ascends 120 feet to area 31. Halfway up the spiral staircase is a secret door that opens into area 23.

Rough-hewn stairs in the south wall descend to area 7.

### DEVELOPMENT

If Nym retreats to this chamber, she raises the portcullis, and she and the whale leave the stronghold.

## 7. CORAL GARDEN

The floor of this air-filled cave is under 5 feet of water. Staircases in the north and south walls rise up toward areas 6 and 8. Nym has turned this cave into her personal coral garden. Growths of coral sprout from walls and rock formations, all of them colorful and immense. One of the coral-covered rock formations is actually a **roper**, which Nym uses as a guardian. The roper attacks any creature other than Nym that crosses the room.

A character can harvest 2d4 pounds of coral in an hour. The coral here is worth 100 gp per pound. The garden holds 50,000 gp worth of coral.

## 8. MIRRAN'S WHALE

An enormous **killer whale** (156 hit points) swims circles in a 50-foot-deep pool here. The whale attacks any creature other than Mirran that enters the water.

A flooded passage blocked by a lowered portcullis connects the whale's pool to the sinkhole (area 1). Staircases carved into the northwest and southeast walls lead down to areas 7 and 10. An open portcullis hangs above the southeast staircase. A third stairway leads up to area 9, and a wide spiral staircase ascends 120 feet to area 30. A crate of dead fish is near the spiral staircase. Halfway up it is a secret door that opens into area 20.

### TREASURE

An anemone chest near the spiral staircase contains a shark-bladder sack with 400 pp.

### DEVELOPMENT

The storm giants sleeping in area 10 awaken and respond to any loud disturbance here.

## 9. SPARRING CHAMBER

Mirran uses this air-filled room to practice her sparring. A giant-sized dummy made from the mast, sails, and rigging of a wrecked ship stands in the middle of the room. An alcove in the northwest corner contains a stone rack that holds three quarterstaffs carved from wood.

## 10. SLEEPING GUARD

A staircase descends into a submerged chamber. A sleeping **storm giant** floats in the middle of the room, her limbs wrapped in kelp to keep from drifting.

### TREASURE

This room contains four giant clams and an anemone chest. The clams' contents are determined by the Giant Clam table (see the "Maelstrom: General Features" sidebar). The anemone chest holds four sacks made from shark bladders. Each sack contains 1d4 × 100 pp.

## 11. SERISSA'S WHALE

Serissa's pet **killer whale** (128 hit points) swims and plays in a large, 50-foot-deep pool. When the whale sees another creature, it leaps out of the water and sings for its supper. If a character throws it a dead fish or something else it can eat, the whale remembers the gift and won't attack that individual unless the character attacks it first. The pool is connected to the sinkhole (area 1) by a flooded passage with a lowered portcullis.

An anemone chest stands in the southeast corner. It contains a black sack made from a merrow's bladder. The sack is full of dead fish. Nearby a raised portcullis looms above a staircase that descends to area 12.

A spiral staircase climbs 120 feet to area 32. Halfway up the staircase is a secret door that opens into area 17.

A door set into the north wall opens into area 13.

### DEVELOPMENT

The storm giants sleeping in area 12 awaken and respond to any loud disturbance here. If Serissa retreats here, she raises the portcullis, and she and the whale leave the stronghold.

## 12. SLEEPING GUARDS

A staircase topped by a raised portcullis descends into a pair of submerged chambers filled with kelp. Two **storm giants** sleep here, one in the southernmost chamber and one in the northernmost chamber. Their limbs are wrapped in kelp to keep them from drifting. The giants are sensitive to water currents, so that any creature that swims through a giant's cave must succeed on a DC 19 Dexterity (Stealth) check to avoid waking the giant.

### TREASURE

This area contains six giant clams and two anemone chests. The clams' contents are determined by the Giant Clam table (see the "Maelstrom: General Features" sidebar). Each anemone chest holds 1d4 − 1 magic items and 1d4 shark-bladder sacks. Each sack contains 1d4 × 100 pp. Roll on Magic Item Table B in chapter 7 of the *Dungeon Master's Guide* for any magic items.

## 13. STUDY

Serissa used to come here quite often to study in solitude, but her present duties permit her no opportunity to pursue her studies. An ugly bookshelf made from ship wreckage stands against one wall, packed full of tomes that Serissa recovered from wrecked ships. The books were written by "small folk" and are sized appropriately. The covers and pages of the books are wrinkled and stained by seawater, and the writing is often smeared and illegible, but Serissa has gleaned a lot of information about humans, halflings, and other small folk from perusing the tomes. Since the books are small by Serissa's standards, she uses a spyglass to read them. The spyglass rests on top of the 20-foot-tall bookshelf.

Other furnishings include two anemone chests and a table with a concave top made from a huge mussel shell.

## TREASURE

One of the anemone chests contains dozens of worthless trinkets recovered from shipwrecks. The other contains a flag bearing the crest of Waterdeep (worth 25 gp) and a bundled-up tapestry embroidered with an image of a dashing human knight mounted on an armored white warhorse (worth 750 gp).

# 14. GREAT HALL

Music fills this hall when the characters first arrive. The room is split into two levels; a 15-foot-high raised ledge hugs the walls to the north and east, and gently sloping ramps lead up to it. The acoustics here are excellent. Barnacle-covered pillars of hewn rock rise to meet the vaulted ceiling, and a huge crystal window allows in light that casts beautiful patterns on the walls.

Under the crystal window is a **hulking crab** (see appendix C) with colored nodules and hollow flutes of beautiful coral growing out of its shell. This creature is a living instrument. When one of the nodules on its shell is tapped, the motion tickles the crab and causes it to exhale a burst of air through one of its coral pipes, producing a deep tone similar to that of a pipe organ. Any creature that has proficiency in the Performance skill can, with hours of practice, learn to play the crab organ.

Performing next to the ledge are King Hekaton's two eldest daughters, Mirran and Nym. Mirran is singing, while Nym provides instrumental accompaniment by tapping on the crab's shell with a pair of whalebone mallets. Mirran and Nym use the **storm giant** stat block, with these changes:

- Mirran and Nym are neutral evil.
- They are unarmed and unarmored (AC 12).
- They have the following additional skills: Deception +9, Performance +9.

The sisters are entertaining several high-ranking visitors: a **cloud giant** count named Vaal (neutral evil), a **fire giant** duchess named Tartha (lawful evil), a **frost giant** jarl named Hellenhild (neutral evil), and a **stone giant** thane named Braxow (neutral). These giant nobles have come to Maelstrom, using their own *conchs of teleportation*, to find out what Princess Serissa plans to do about the dissolution of the ordning, and to ascertain the extent of her power and influence. Each of them awaits an audience with the regent. The giant guests gather around mussel-shell tables and a giant coral fountain in the lower part of the room. The coral fountain spouts fresh water (see "Treasure"), which the giants drink from their conch shells. The giant visitors know better than to start a fight in here. They have no interest in hearing what the "small folk" have to say.

Watching the visitors are two **storm giants** wearing helms. If Mirran and Nym are attacked, these royal guards rush to the princesses' defense and cover their retreat to the throne room (area 15). The visiting giants join the battle on the side of the storm giants to avoid incurring the royal family's wrath.

A 40-foot-wide hall leading south ends at a guarded set of doors that open into the throne room.

## DEALING WITH MIRRAN AND NYM

The sisters end their performance when the characters appear. The guards quickly interpose themselves between the princesses and the new arrivals, but Mirran orders the guards to stand down so that she and Nym can learn "what brings these puny creatures to court."

If the characters make demands, Mirran is enraged by their insolence, while Nym gives them a cold, condescending smile. Neither sister is of a mind to facilitate a meeting between Serissa and a motley group of "small folk." If the characters are diplomatic, Mirran and Nym tell them that their young, inexperienced sister is "far too overwhelmed with important matters" to grant the characters an audience at this moment. Mirran instructs the two storm giant guards to escort the adventurers to the guest quarters (area 3), where they are to remain until summoned. If the characters allow themselves to be taken to area 3, the storm giants stand guard in area 2 to make sure they don't wander.

Meanwhile, after a private discussion, Mirran and Nym decide that the adventurers must be eliminated. Nym goes to inform Serissa that assassins have breached Maelstrom's defenses. At the same time, Mirran confronts the adventurers in area 3, tells them that their request for an audience with Serissa has been granted, and leads them into area 2, where Vaal, Tartha, Hellenhild, and Braxow wait to attack them (see "Dealing with the Giant Lords"). The storm giant guards cover Mirran's escape to area 15.

Mirran and Nym do everything possible to avoid getting entangled in melee, and they don't hesitate to turn on each other to save themselves. Neither knows that Iymrith is a blue dragon in disguise. If Iymrith's true nature is exposed, each sister blames the other for colluding with a dragon. Each feigns innocence while blaming the other for conspiring with Iymrith to murder their mother and dispose of their father.

If things go badly and the sisters have nowhere else to go, Mirran retreats to her quarters (area 30), refusing to abandon the stronghold she believes is rightfully hers, while Nym retreats to area 6 and wisely tries to flee Maelstrom on the back of her pet killer whale.

## DEALING WITH THE GIANT LORDS

Ordning or no, Count Vaal, Duchess Tartha, Jarl Hellenhild, and Thane Braxow know better than to defy the storm giants in their own stronghold. Nevertheless, a character can attempt to shift a giant lord's attitude toward the party from hostile to indifferent by succeeding on a DC 20 Charisma (Persuasion) check. A character can use an action to attempt to sway one giant lord. A failed check can't be retried against the same giant lord until 24 hours have passed. The character gains advantage on the check under the following conditions.

**Vaal.** The cloud giant count is easily swayed by bribes. If the character making the check offers to give him a rare magic item, a spellbook, or nonmagical treasure

worth a total of 10,000 gp or more, grant advantage on the check. (Vaal expects payment in short order, or he becomes hostile again.)

**Tartha.** The fire giant duchess hates dragons above all. If the character making the check claims that a dragon has infiltrated and compromised the storm giants' court, grant advantage on the check.

**Hellenhild.** The frost giant jarl respects battle prowess. If the character making the check wounds Hellenhild in melee combat, grant advantage on the check.

**Braxow.** The stone giant thane fears the giant gods. If the character making the skill check claims to have spoken with the divine oracle at the Eye of the All-Father, grant advantage on the check.

## TREASURE

Embedded in the coral fountain is a *decanter of endless water.* Anyone who inspects the fountain can, with a successful DC 20 Wisdom (Perception) check, see the decanter anchored behind coral branches, which must be smashed to free it. The sculpture stands 20 feet tall and has AC 11, 50 hit points, and immunity to psychic and poison damage. The coral itself isn't valuable.

Several of the giants carry treasure as well:

**Mirran**, the elder storm giantess, wears a gold-inlaid conch shell headdress (worth 750 gp).

**Nym**, the younger storm giantess, wears a gilded coral coronet with an anchor-like design (worth 750 gp).

**Vaal**, the cloud giant, wears a diamond-studded platinum earring (worth 7,500 gp) and a vest with platinum embroidery (worth 2,500 gp). Tied to his belt is a *conch of teleportation* (see appendix B) and a *potion of water breathing.*

**Tartha**, the fire giant, wears a necklace of gilded dragons' teeth (worth 750 gp) and has a *conch of teleportation* in an iron box chained to her belt.

**Hellenhild**, the frost giant, wears a cloak of white dragon scales (worth 2,500 gp and weighing 250 pounds) and has a *conch of teleportation* on her belt.

**Braxow**, the stone giant, has fifteen 100 gp gemstones embedded in his flesh. He carries a *conch of teleportation* in a sack.

## DEVELOPMENT

If the characters slay one or both of her sisters, Serissa is convinced that they are assassins who have been sent to finish off the royal family. She commands Uthor to marshal all of Maelstrom's defenses and destroy the adventurers. Serissa also realizes that her faith in the small folk has been misplaced. In effect, the killing Mirran or Nym gives Iymrith a major victory, so far as the act drives a wedge between giants and the small folk.

To win Serissa's trust, the characters might try to convince her that Mirran and Nym are complicit in the assassination of their mother and the abduction of their father. Without evidence or a confession from one or both evil sisters, a character must make a DC 15 Charisma (Persuasion) check to convince Serissa that one or both of her sisters should be placed under house arrest pending a full investigation. Award advantage on the check if the characters disclose that they learned of Mirran and Nym's treachery from the Eye of Annam—a source that both Serissa and Uthor trust. If the check succeeds, Serissa views the arrest of her sisters as a sensible precaution. On Serissa's orders, Uthor has Mirran and Nym confined to their towers (areas 30 and 31, respectively), with a storm giant guard placed at the top of each staircase to make sure the sisters don't leave. Each evil sister professes her innocence while proclaiming the other's treachery. If the character's Charisma (Persuasion) check fails, Serissa takes no action against her sisters. The check can be repeated, but only if new and relevant information is brought to Serissa's attention.

## 15. THRONE ROOM

If the characters approach from the north, they face the guards in front of the doors that lead to the throne room.

### TUG AND COG

Standing guard outside the throne room are two **hill giants** wearing scale mail (AC 15) and ill-fitting helms. Their names are Tug and Cog, and they are exceedingly stupid. If the characters approach from the north without a storm giant escort, Tug and Cog raise their greatclubs threateningly. Tug says, "We guard throne room!" Cog follows with, "Where your escort?"

Characters can outwit the hill giants by concocting a believable lie, such as "We are spies for Princess Serissa, come to deliver important information about her father!" or "Princess Serissa told you that we were coming, or have you forgotten?" Have the liar make a Charisma (Deception) check contested by the giants' Wisdom (Insight) check. (Roll once for both giants.) If the character wins the contest, Tug and Cog exchange glassy-eyed looks, shrug, open the doors, and allow the characters to enter the throne room. If the giants win the contest, they attack. They also attack characters who try to slip past them without a proper escort.

Tug and Cog aren't allowed to enter the throne room, nor do they leave their post to join battles in other areas, for fear of incurring Imperator Uthor's wrath.

### HALL OF THE WYRMSKULL THRONE

Maelstrom's throne room resembles an amphitheater. Stone bleachers overlook an oblong chamber with a 50-foot-deep pool of seawater near its center. In the middle of the bleachers is an archway with two doors in it. A submerged passageway that leads from the bottom of the pool to the sinkhole (area 1) is designed to serve as an escape route. At the far end of the passageway is a lowered portcullis that bars access to the sinkhole.

Facing the pool and the doors are three enormous thrones. The middle one is carved from a solid chunk of obsidian, has four blue dragon skulls affixed to its base, and floats 1 foot above the floor. Characters who succeed on a DC 18 Intelligence (Arcana) or Intelligence (History) check recognize this object as the *Wyrmskull Throne* (see appendix B). The two smaller thrones that flank it are made of coral and giant seashells.

Serissa sits on the *Wyrmskull Throne*, flanked by her two advisors, Imperator Uthor and **Iymrith** (see appendix C). Serissa wears the *Korolnor Scepter* (see "Treasure") as a pendant, tied to a kelp necklace.

Serissa is a **storm giant**, with these changes:

- She has 200 hit points and wears hide armor (AC 14).
- She wields a wooden maul made from the mast of a warship, instead of a greatsword. She has a +14 bonus to hit with the weapon, which has a reach of 10 feet and deals 30 (6d6 + 9) bludgeoning damage on a hit.
- As long as she has the *Korolnor Scepter* in her possession, she can activate the powers of the *Wyrmskull Throne*.

Uthor is a **storm giant**, with these changes:

- He has 272 hit points.
- He wields a giant-sized *trident of fish command* instead of a greatsword. Uthor has a +14 bonus to hit with the weapon, which has a reach of 10 feet and deals 19 (3d6 + 9) piercing damage on a hit, or 22 (3d8 + 9) piercing damage if used with two hands.

### DEALING WITH SERISSA

Since she has seen no evidence to the contrary, Serissa believes that her father yet lives. When she was a child, her mother would take her on trips to the Sword Coast and the Moonshae Isles, where they met small folk who were generous and kind. Serissa thinks that giants and small folk can learn to coexist peacefully, though Iymrith and Uthor would have her believe otherwise.

Serissa is mourning the death of her mother. Queen Neri's body was recovered from a cluster of islands that humans refer to as the Red Rocks. One of the storm giants who found the queen also found a wooden coin painted with a golden goose insignia and gave it to Serissa, thinking it belonged to her mother. Serissa hasn't told anyone about the coin. She doesn't know what it represents and hopes to find someone who does.

If the characters gain an audience with Serissa, she is patient and listens intently to what they have to say. If the characters express interest in bringing an end to the unrest in giant society, she hands them the wooden coin and asks them to find out where it came from. She believes that the people who murdered her mother might have also kidnapped her father, and the wooden coin is her only clue to his whereabouts. If the characters accept Serissa's quest, she leads them to the meditation cave (area 18) and uses its teleport power to transport them back to the mainland (or wherever else they wish to go). She also allows them to keep the wooden coin. The significance of the coin is revealed in chapter 11, "Caught in the Tentacles." If the characters agree to go hunting for Hekaton, Serissa suggests that they take their *conch of teleportation* with them so that they can return to Maelstrom safely. If the characters no longer have their conch for some reason, Serissa furnishes them with another one (taken from one of her guests).

If the characters attack Serissa, she uses the powers of the *Wyrmskull Throne* against them. If they make allegations against her sisters, Serissa reacts as described in the "Development" section in area 14.

### DEALING WITH UTHOR

Uthor cares deeply for Serissa and does his best not to anger, frighten, or undermine her. He advises her not to trust small folk, but otherwise doesn't interfere in her negotiations with the characters. If they harm her or any other member of the royal family, Uthor flies into a rage and attacks them until Serissa commands him to stop.

### DEALING WITH IYMRITH

In a short time, Iymrith has established herself as a surrogate mother figure to all three of Hekaton's daughters. Iymrith tries to squash any alliance between the storm giants and the small folk by telling Serissa that the adventurers can't be trusted, adding hastily, "For all we know, they're the ones who murdered your mother and abducted your father!" Iymrith realizes almost instantly that she has chosen those words poorly, for how could she know that Hekaton has been abducted? If the players fail to pick up on her self-incriminating words, have Serissa and all characters present make a DC 15 Wisdom (Insight) check. Those who succeed on the check realize that Iymrith knows more than she's letting on.

If the characters accuse Iymrith of being a dragon in disguise, she expresses outrage at the accusation and tries to convince Serissa that this claim is a ploy to sow discord in the storm giants' court. Heedless of Iymrith's words, Serissa is inclined to give the characters the benefit of the doubt. When it becomes clear to Iymrith that Serissa's fondness for small folk can't be undone with mere words, the dragon begins plotting her exit strategy.

Casting *dispel magic* on Iymrith doesn't reveal her true form, but contact with an *antimagic field* causes her to revert to her dragon form. It's unlikely that characters will have access to such powerful magic, but if all else fails, they can simply attack her. Iymrith doesn't revert to dragon form in this encounter. On her first turn in combat, she curses the characters in Draconic, declares that all giants and small folk are doomed, and snatches the *Korolnor Scepter* from around Serissa's neck. On her next turn, she teleports away. If she is unable to cast her *teleport* spell for some reason, she flees through the circular pool in the floor and swims out of the stronghold to the surface. (As long as she remains in storm giant form, Iymrith can breathe underwater.) If Serissa is seated on the *Wyrmskull Throne* when the scepter is stolen from her, Serissa is paralyzed (see the throne's description in appendix B for details).

If the characters do nothing to force Iymrith's hand, she allows them to leave and pursue Serissa's quest, convinced that they will never find King Hekaton. At the same time, Serissa's confidence in the characters' abilities sows doubt in Iymrith's mind (see "Development").

## TREASURE

Serissa wears the *Korolnor Scepter*, which allows her to sit on the *Wyrmskull Throne* and harness its magical powers. The only other treasure found here is Uthor's *trident of fish command*, which grows or shrinks to match the size of whoever attunes to it.

## DEVELOPMENT

If the characters forge an alliance with Serissa or expose Iymrith as a villainous deceiver, the blue dragon returns to her lair in the Anauroch desert and isn't encountered again until chapter 12, "Doom of the Desert."

It's possible that the characters might come into possession of a *spell scroll* of *resurrection* at some point in the adventure, in which case they could offer to cast the spell on Queen Neri and bring her back from the dead. If they make such an offer, Serissa leads them to her mother's sunken tomb (area 24) or has the queen's body brought to them. If Neri is returned to life, she replaces Iymrith as Serissa's advisor, and Serissa rewards the characters by giving them the magic items in the sea chest in the royal treasury (area 16). Queen Neri, like Serissa, has a fondness for the small folk, and she's just as eager to find out what happened to Hekaton.

## 16. ROYAL TREASURY

Thirty-four rusty anchors dangle from iron chains bolted to the 50-foot-high ceiling of this room, one above each full 10-foot square. The storm giants salvaged the anchors from wrecked ships and transported them here. Each anchor weighs roughly 3,000 pounds and is suspended 40 feet above the floor. Two of these dangling anchors are part of a trap (see "Trap").

The room holds three crates, two barrels, a massive sea chest, and two anemone chests.

### TRAP

Just inside the room, built into the floor, is a pressure plate that the storm giants avoid by stepping over it. The pressure plate fills two 10-foot squares (each marked T on the map). Anyone who searches the floor for traps before entering the room spots the pressure plate with a successful DC 17 Wisdom (Perception) check. Applying 250 pounds or more to the plate causes the anchor above each trapped square to drop, chain and all. Any creature in a trapped space must succeed on a DC 15 Dexterity saving throw or be struck by the falling anchor for 44 (8d10) bludgeoning damage. One minute after the trap triggers, a mechanism hidden in the walls and ceiling causes the iron chains to retract, pulling the anchors back up, whereupon the trap resets. As an action, a character can disable the pressure plate (by driving a wedge or iron spike into its seam to prevent the plate from moving), doing so with a successful DC 15 Dexterity check.

### TREASURE

The first crate holds six folded, giant-sized rugs made from strips of soft kelp. Each rug is 20 feet square, weighs 250 pounds, and is worth 250 gp. The second crate holds an *apparatus of Kwalish* that was recovered from the pressurized hold of a wrecked gnomish submarine. The third crate contains hundreds of trinkets recovered from the sea floor—tribute from various sea elf clans that pledge fealty to the storm giant king. The trinkets include everything from worthless baubles to fine statuary and jewelry plundered from shipwrecks. The total weight of this tribute is 100 pounds, and its total value is 10,000 gp.

The two barrels are full of exquisite wine (worth 2,500 gp each) and weigh 2,500 pounds each.

The sea chest is 12 feet long, 9 feet tall, and 9 feet deep, with a lid shaped like a half-barrel. The large padlock that hangs from its latch is too big to be picked using thieves' tools. A Small character can squeeze inside the locking mechanism and pick the lock with a successful DC 16 Dexterity check. Lifting the heavy lid requires a successful DC 20 Strength (Athletics) check. The chest holds a dozen smaller (human-made) chests that are unlocked and contain booty retrieved from the sea floor. Each small chest has 3d6 × 100 gp in mixed coinage. Lying among the chests are 1d4 + 1 magic items. Roll on Magic Item Table H in chapter 7 of the *Dungeon Master's Guide* for the first two items and on Table F for any other items.

The first anemone chest holds six grapefruit-sized pink pearls (worth 500 gp each). The second anemone chest contains six *potions of giant size* (see appendix B) in purple and green coral vials sized for Small and Medium creatures. Each coral vial is worth 25 gp.

## 17. COUNCIL ROOM

King Hekaton held private meetings here. A mussel-shell table stands in the middle of the room. Lining the walls are two giant-sized wooden bookshelves covered with nautical charts plundered from sunken ships, as well as two anemone chests (each contains 3d6 × 100 pp). A concave wall to the south has a giant-sized secret door set into the middle of it. It leads to a spiral staircase that climbs to area 32 and descends to area 11.

## 18. MEDITATION CAVE

This naturally formed cave has bioluminescent lichen, coral, snails, and starfish clinging to its damp walls. The area radiates overlapping auras of conjuration, divination, and evocation magic when scrutinized with a *detect magic* spell. Over the years, the storm giants have learned how to become attuned to the magic of this cave and harness its innate magical properties.

Becoming attuned to the cave requires a creature to spend a short rest meditating inside the cave. While meditating, the creature can't engage in any strenuous activity. If the short rest is interrupted, the attunement fails. Otherwise, at the end of the short rest, the creature becomes aware of the cave's magical properties and can use them as described here.

Only one creature can be attuned to the cave at a time. A creature's attunement to the cave ends as soon as it leaves the cave. A creature that is attuned to the cave can use an action to cast one of the following spells, requiring no material components: *clairvoyance*, *identify*, *sending*, or *teleport*.

### DEVELOPMENT

King Hekaton often used the *sending* property of the cave to arrange meetings with lesser giants and used the *teleport* property from time to time to send guests to far-flung destinations. If Serissa is on speaking terms with the party, she can use the cave's *teleport* property to send the characters wherever they wish to go, once their business in Maelstrom is concluded.

## 19. SHARK PENS

These caves are submerged. A lowered portcullis blocks the way from the main cave to the sinkhole (area 1), and lowered portcullises also confine ten **hunter sharks** to the four side caves. The sharks take advantage of any opportunity to escape from their pens, attacking any creatures other than storm giants that cross their path. The storm giants keep the sharks for defense, releasing them into the sinkhole in the event of a major attack against the stronghold. They also use shark hide to fashion apparel and shark teeth to festoon their weapons (see area 20),

### TREASURE

The main cave contains two giant clams. The clams' contents are determined by the Giant Clam table (see the "Maelstrom: General Features" sidebar).

## 20. ARMORY

A door connects this air-filled room to an air-filled passage east of it. Three descending sets of stairs lead to submerged areas southeast, north, and northeast of this location. The stairs to the southeast descend 30 feet to area 19, the stairs to the north descend 30 feet to area 21, and the stairs to the northeast descend 30 feet to a tunnel blocked by a lowered portcullis. Beyond the portcullis is the sinkhole (area 1).

The room is an armory containing weapons and armor sized for storm giants. A search of the room yields four quarterstaffs carved from sunken ship masts, a large barrel holding six tridents, an open crate containing ten coral-encrusted rocks, and a storm giant-sized mannequin wearing a golden suit of scale mail (see "Treasure"). Hanging on the walls are three enormous shields made from dragon turtle shells and six massive greatswords with coral-inlaid hilts and sharpened whalebone blades lined with shark teeth. The shields and the weapons aren't particularly valuable, especially given their weight.

A concave wall to the south has a giant-sized secret door set into it. It leads to a spiral staircase that climbs to area 30 and descends to area 8.

### TREASURE

The giant-sized suit of golden scale mail is worth 10,000 gp and weighs 1,000 pounds.

## 21. TEMPLE OF STRONMAUS

This submerged chamber has a 50-foot-high pyramidal ceiling, with walls that taper inward beginning at a height of 30 feet. Harmless bioluminescent jellyfish dimly illuminate a 40-foot-tall statue of Stronmaus, god of storm giants, standing in the middle of the room. Stronmaus looks like an imperious, bare-chested storm giant with a foamy beard, a sharp trident, and a lower body transformed into a great wave—all carved from stone. The walls of this temple are etched with images of storm giants riding whales, battling dragon turtles, and blowing conch shells to summon giant crabs, giant octopi, manta rays, and schools of fish. Harmless starfish and sea urchins cling to the walls and congregate around the base of the statue.

Characters who examine the statue and succeed on a DC 15 Wisdom (Perception) check can see marks on the rough floor, suggesting that the statue has recently been moved aside. It takes a creature as big and strong as a storm giant to slide the statue, but the characters can use ropes to pull it over with a successful DC 22 Strength (Athletics) check. Doing this breaks the statue and reveals a flooded, 15-foot-wide shaft that descends for 30 feet, then bends to the west and leads to Queen Neri's sunken tomb (area 22).

### TREASURE

A giant clam rests in the southwest corner of the room. The clam's contents are determined by the Giant Clam table (see the "Maelstrom: General Features" sidebar).

## Development

If the characters desecrate the statue of Stronmaus by breaking it, blood seems to seep from within the statue, polluting the surrounding water and attracting two **giant sharks**, which arrive 1 minute later. The sharks enter the temple through the open passage that connects with the sinkhole (area 1).

## 22. Royal Tomb

Bioluminescent fish swim about this flooded chamber, dimly illuminating an ornate sarcophagus inlaid with blue coral, its lid beautifully carved in the likeness of King Hekaton's late wife, Neri. The storm giant queen lies within, her body wrapped head to toe in black kelp. Pushing aside the sarcophagus lid requires a DC 22 Strength (Athletics) check.

Arrayed along the walls are ten upright stone sarcophagi, their barnacle-covered lids sculpted to look like regal storm giants. These airtight sarcophagi contain the lichen-covered remains and rusty greatswords of previous storm giant kings. A character can use an action to try to pry open a sarcophagus, doing so with a successful DC 20 Strength (Athletics) check. Using a crowbar or a similar tool grants advantage on the check.

### Treasure

Queen Neri is entombed with a purple coral circlet set with small black pearls (worth 7,500 gp) and a coral-and-pearl necklace (worth 2,500 gp).

## 23. Scrying Pool

The central feature of this air-filled chamber is a semicircular basin 20 feet in diameter and 10 feet deep in the middle. Fresh water fills the basin. The raised stone lip surrounding the pool is 5 feet high and equally thick. A *detect magic* spell cast on the basin reveals an aura of divination magic.

The basin has 3 charges. As long as the water in the basin is unpolluted, a creature can touch the basin and expend 1 charge to cast a *scrying* spell from the basin. The subject of the spell appears in the water's surface. The basin regains all expended charges daily at dawn.

The northwest wall has a giant-sized secret door set into it. It leads to a spiral staircase that climbs to area 31 and descends to area 6.

## 24. Study

This room contains a giant mussel-shell table and a large barrel that the giants use as a stool. High shelves made from the hull of a sunken ship stand against one wall. The shelves are lined with trinkets that the storm giants have collected from ships that were drawn down into the sinkhole (area 1).

### Treasure

A golden astrolabe of gnomish design (worth 2,500 gp) rests on a 15-foot-tall shelf, alongside fragments and bits of machinery from some sort of large device or metallic vehicle (a gnome-built submarine, although the characters have no way to know this). Resting on a 20-foot-tall

shelf is a magic item (roll on Magic Item Table G in chapter 7 of the *Dungeon Master's Guide*).

## 25. Library

This room contains sturdy, floor-to-ceiling shelves made of petrified wood. Stacked on them are scores of 4-foot-diameter, 600-pound rocks engraved with Dethek runes (the Dwarvish script). These stones have various discoveries recorded on them, including the locations of shipwrecks, sahuagin strongholds, sea elf domains, and dragon turtle lairs. These rocks also record fables that are meant to be passed down from one generation to the next, including cautionary tales about the fall of ancient Ostoria and accounts of the giants' ancient war against dragonkind. Other stones have prayers and ancient rituals inscribed on them, most having to do with the worship of Stronmaus, the patron god of storm giants. A few of the rocks have spells etched into them.

### Treasure

Five rocks have the following wizard spells inscribed on them: *antimagic field*, *conjure elemental*, *fabricate*, *legend lore*, and *stone shape*. The rocks function like pages of a spellbook, but each weighs 600 pounds. A character who has a spellbook can record these spells in it.

## 26. Uthor's Quarters

This submerged cave belongs to Imperator Uthor. Beds of kelp grow here and there, and three giant clams rest on the uneven floor. The clams' contents are determined by the Giant Clam table (see the "Maelstrom: General Features" sidebar).

## 27. Stores

If music is being played in area 14, it can be heard in this room. The storm giants keep their food supplies here, in crates, barrels, and anemone chests. Some of the food was collected from shipwrecks, some from hunts. The crates and barrels mostly contain lobsters, crabs, and fish, which the giants boil or eat raw. Food waste is put in the anemone chests to be slowly digested.

Any loud noises here awaken the giants in area 29 and alert any giants in area 14.

## 28. Kitchen

If music is being played in area 14, it can be clearly heard in this room. The storm giants prepare their own food here. The cave contains two mussel-shell tables and four anemone chests where food waste is discarded and slowly digested. Steam rises from a pool of bubbling hot water where lobsters and crabs are boiled alive.

Any loud noises here awaken the giants in area 29 and alert any giants in area 14.

## 29. Sleeping Guards

Unless they have been awakened and drawn elsewhere, two sleeping **storm giants** float in the middle of this submerged room, their limbs wrapped in kelp to keep them from drifting. They awaken if they are attacked or otherwise disturbed. The giants are sensitive to water

MAP 10.2: MAELSTROM, LEVEL 3

currents, so that any creature that swims through the cave must succeed on a DC 19 Dexterity (Stealth) check to avoid waking the giants.

### TREASURE
This room contains three giant clams and an anemone chest. The clams' contents are determined by the Giant Clam table (see the "Maelstrom: General Features" sidebar). The anemone chest holds 1d4 + 1 shark-bladder sacks. Each sack contains 1d4 × 100 pp.

## 30. MIRRAN'S TOWER

### 30A. LIVING ROOM
The walls of the living room have images of giant jelly-fish and giant eels carved into them, and bioluminescent lichen growing on the jellyfish makes them glow. A crystal window facing the interior of the stronghold provides a clear view of the swirling vortex, the sinkhole, and the other towers of Maelstrom's upper level. The mussel-shell tables in the middle of the room are covered with platters of boiled lobster, as well as edible urchins and fish, while shelves and cabinets hold various knick-knacks. Hanging on the north wall is a greatsword with a whalebone handle and a blade lined with shark's teeth.

If her life is threatened and she is forced to retreat to her tower, Mirran arms herself with the greatsword mounted on the wall, and considers her next move while gazing through the crystal window. She is too proud to flee Maelstrom and give up what she believes is her birthright.

### 30B. BEDCHAMBER
Mirran's bed has a carved coral frame and a mattress made from soft lichen, covered with dyed kelp blankets. A tall wardrobe holds her clothing, some items made from fabric and others from kelp. Mounted on the inside of the door is a coral-framed mirror.

### 30C. TREASURY
Mirran keeps her treasure here, mostly plundered from shipwrecks. The chamber has two anemone chests, four large crates, and a 500-pound barrel holding 50 gallons of ale.

One anemone chest contains seven pieces of jewelry sized for a giant, including a whalebone tiara inlaid with mother-of-pearl and precious gemstones (worth 2,500 gp), three pearl necklaces (worth 2,500 gp each), a pair of pearl-studded coral earrings (worth 1,500 gp for the pair), and a platinum necklace adorned with shark's teeth (worth 1,500 gp).

The other anemone chest contains 600 pp and 1d4 magic items. Roll on Magic Item Table G in chapter 7 of the *Dungeon Master's Guide* for the first item, and on Table D for any other items.

The first crate contains twenty bolts of fine silk (worth 250 gp each). The second crate holds a wooden chariot with gold wheel-caps (worth 500 gp). In the third crate are thirty 10-pound sacks of saffron (worth 150 gp each). The fourth crate contains a well-packed dining room furniture set consisting of a large table and eight chairs carved from dark wood and inlaid with gold; the set is worth 2,500 gp but is awkward to transport.

# 31. Nym's Tower

## 31A. Hot Bath

The walls of this room are painted to look like a bright coral forest. Five **steam mephits** swim in a pool of salt water in the floor. Their bodies generate enough heat to warm the pool. Steam fills the room and clouds the crystal window that overlooks the sinkhole to the southeast. The mephits jeer at strangers but are too lazy to fight except when forced to defend themselves.

Shelves along the walls contain various worthless knickknacks that Nym has collected from shipwrecks, including a few human skulls with barnacles on them.

## 31B. Bedchamber

The frame of Nym's bed is made from wood salvaged from shipwrecks and covered with supple, spiny octopus hide. The "mattress" is made of shark hide stuffed with lichen, covered with blankets of dyed kelp. Flanking the bed are two wardrobes. The western one holds billowy garments made of fabric and kelp. The eastern one has a coral-framed mirror hanging on the outside and holds many pairs of leather sandals (on shelves) and a large, unlocked trunk containing Nym's personal treasures.

***Treasure.*** Characters who search the trunk find 500 pp, four coral bracelets (worth 250 gp each), a black coral torc set with two red pearls (worth 2,500 gp), and 1d4 magic items. Roll on Magic Item Table G in chapter 7 of the *Dungeon Master's Guide* for the first item, and on Table B for any others.

# 32. Serissa's Tower

## 32A. Living Room

A wide crystal window offers a breathtaking view of the vortex, the sinkhole, and the other towers of the stronghold. The window has kelp curtains that are tied back with strands of rope. Hanging on the walls are tapestries made of kelp and seashells, woven by sea elf hands. A 10-foot-tall shelving unit under a tapestry on the north wall holds various knickknacks retrieved from sunken wrecks. Other furnishings include two mussel-shell tables and a pair of anemone chests. One of the anemone chests holds discarded food waste that is slowly being digested. The other is lined with a shark's bladder and contains dozens of edible sea urchins.

***Treasure.*** Characters who inspect the knickknacks on the shelves find 1d3 magic items. Roll on Magic Item Table F in chapter 7 of the *Dungeon Master's Guide* for the first item, and on Table B for any other items.

## 32B. Bedchamber

Serissa's bed is fashioned from barnacle-covered wood salvaged from a shipwreck, with sheets made from sails and a stitched-cloth mattress stuffed with roc feathers. Other furnishings include a wooden wardrobe full of clothing fit for a giant-sized princess, some items fashioned from fabric and others from kelp; a shelf lined with fifteen treasure chests recovered from shipwrecks; and a coral-framed mirror hanging on the door.

***Treasure.*** Serissa uses the treasure chests to hold her giant-sized jewelry. One chest contains two pearl necklaces (worth 2,500 gp each) given to her by her mother. Another contains a purple coral diadem adorned with pearly seashells (worth 750 gp), three matching coral bracelets (worth 750 gp each), a coral ring that magically changes color at its wearer's whim (worth 250 gp), and a kelp necklace with dangling shells (worth 25 gp).

# 33. King's Tower

This tower belongs to the storm giant king and queen. At the top of the spiral staircase is a magnificent hall with an arched ceiling, guarded by a **storm giant** who stands stiffly in the hall's middle. The giant hurls lightning at intruders before charging them with sword drawn. He remains here unless ordered elsewhere by Uthor.

Two doors on the east wall open into storage rooms (area 33A). A door on the west wall opens into the royal bedchamber (area 33B). In the southwest corner is a door leading to the king's private den (area 33C).

## 33A. Storage Rooms

Barrels of fine wine, large crates of food, and a cabinet packed with coral plates and utensils are kept here.

## 33B. Bedchamber

The frame of King Hekaton's bed is fashioned from dragon bones, with a massive coral headboard carved with a scene that depicts a storm giant king impaling an ancient blue dragon through the skull with a trident. The mattress is made of kraken hide stuffed with roc feathers, with sheets made from the sails of sunken ships. A great barrel of wine stands next to an enormous wooden wardrobe filled with royal garb fit for a king and queen.

***Treasure.*** The bed's headboard is an extraordinary work of art worth 50,000 gp intact. It is 20 feet long, 20 feet tall, and 5 feet thick, and it weighs 7,500 pounds.

## 33C. King's Den

A wide crystal window affords a majestic view of the vortex, sinkhole, and other towers of Maelstrom. Whales, sharks, and schools of fish swim impassively by. Mounted on the north wall of the den are the stuffed heads of an adult red dragon, an adult white dragon, and an adult dragon turtle. The walls are further festooned with spears, tridents, and nets sized for a storm giant, all on proud display. Other furnishings include a pair of giant mussel-shell tables, a 500-pound barrel of salt, and a crate overflowing with shucked giant oyster shells.

# 34. Guard Post

Nine **giant crabs** inhabit this underwater cave, which also serves as a watch post for two **storm giants**. The crabs pose no threat unless attacked. The giants leave periodically to patrol the waters around Maelstrom.

The cave contains three giant clams. The clams' contents are determined by the Giant Clam table (see the "Maelstrom: General Features" sidebar).

---

### CHARACTER ADVANCEMENT

The characters don't gain a level at the end of this chapter and are still 9th level when they begin chapter 11, "Caught in the Tentacles."

---

# CHAPTER 11: CAUGHT IN THE TENTACLES

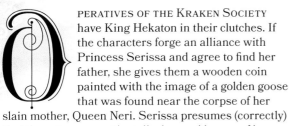PERATIVES OF THE KRAKEN SOCIETY have King Hekaton in their clutches. If the characters forge an alliance with Princess Serissa and agree to find her father, she gives them a wooden coin painted with the image of a golden goose that was found near the corpse of her slain mother, Queen Neri. Serissa presumes (correctly) that the coin was accidentally dropped by one of her mother's assassins.

The characters begin this part of their mission by tracking the gambling chip to its owner, Lord Khaspere Drylund of Yartar. The nobleman is maneuvering to become the city's new Waterbaron. He runs a gambling hall aboard a riverboat named the *Grand Dame*. Lord Drylund's wealthy patrons are the movers and shakers of Yartar, and he wants to impress them and place them in his debt. They come to his riverboat day and night, exchanging coins for wooden gambling chips called "golden geese." They dine on the finest prepared food, dance to marvelous music, and gamble away their chips at Lord Drylund's tables, all under the watchful eye of his chief of security, the wizard Pow Ming.

Tracking the wooden coin to its source requires some investigation and, perhaps, a little help from one or more factions. Once the coin is traced to a gambling hall aboard a resplendent riverboat in Yartar, the game is afoot! The characters must attack or infiltrate the riverboat to reach Lord Drylund, for only he knows where King Hekaton is kept. Drylund reveals under duress that

the storm giant king is sequestered aboard a scry-proof vessel called the *Morkoth* that circles the islands of the Trackless Sea, far from prying eyes. Drylund's betrayal immediately precedes his doom, as Slarkrethel reaches out from the depths of the Trackless Sea and slays the corrupt nobleman with a telepathic thought.

The chapter concludes with the characters' hunt for the *Morkoth* and the freeing of King Hekaton, and perhaps a terrifying encounter with the kraken itself.

## THE GOLDEN GOOSE

The wooden coin given to the characters by Princess Serissa is fairly unremarkable and easy to produce. It's half again the size of a typical gold coin, and there's nothing magical about it. A *legend lore* spell provides no clues as to its origin, since the coin isn't legendary.

Any character who has a background, a bond, or a flaw related to gambling or festhalls knows that the coin is likely a gambling chip. Ascertaining where the coin came from requires a period of downtime, during which a character can show the coin around, make inquiries at gambling houses and festhalls, and bribe local guilds for information. A character must spend a certain amount of gold per day to cover expenses. After 1d4 + 1 days, the character can make an Intelligence (Investigation) check. On a success, the character learns where the coin came from. A failed check means that the character's investigation has reached a dead end, but he or she can try again by spending the requisite amount of time

A "Golden Goose"

and gold. The DC of the check depends on where the investigation is conducted. Cities have more people to talk to and more leads to follow than towns or villages, but the expenses are higher. This information is summarized in the Finding the Golden Goose table.

You can rule that an investigation automatically fails if it is conducted in a particularly isolated location, such as the islands of Ruathym or Tuern, where it's unlikely that the characters will find anyone who is familiar with the festhalls and gambling havens of Yartar. Conversely, the Harpers, the Lords' Alliance, and the Zhentarim all have a strong presence in Yartar. Any character who belongs to one of these three factions can reach out to the organization and use this connection to gain advantage on the Intelligence (Investigation) check.

### FINDING THE GOLDEN GOOSE

| Location | Expenses per Day | Check DC |
|---|---|---|
| Yartar | 10 gp | 10 |
| City other than Yartar | 10 gp | 15 |
| Town | 5 gp | 20 |
| Village | 2 gp | 25 |

## THE GRAND DAME

The *Grand Dame* (shown on map 11.1) is an ornately decorated riverboat owned by Lord Khaspere Drylund of Yartar (NE male human). Lord Drylund is a **noble**, with these changes:

- Lord Drylund is unarmored (AC 11) and speaks Common, Dwarvish, and Elvish.
- He wields a rapier with a bejeweled octopus-shaped hilt (worth 2,500 gp).
- As long as Lord Drylund and Slarkrethel are on the same plane of existence, Lord Drylund is considered to be within range of the kraken's telepathy. While this telepathic link exists, Slarkrethel can use an action on its turn to deal 20 psychic damage to Lord Drylund. This damage is enough to kill Lord Drylund instantly.

From dawn until dusk, the flat-bottomed wooden boat is moored at the city docks. Dockworkers come and go with food and other supplies throughout the day, watched closely by crew on deck.

The ship's crew consists of a captain named Nelvin Storn (LE male human **bandit captain**) and eight deckhands (NE male and female human **bandits**). An hour before dusk, a mob of **commoners** (thirty-two rowers, six chefs, six servers, a dozen card dealers, a dozen escorts, and three musicians) arrives at the docks for inspection by the captain, who stands on the pier next to the ship's boarding ramp. Storn promises each hired worker 5 gp for good service, with payment made the next morning. Once the workers are aboard, rowers are expected to report to the lower deck (area 4), servers and chefs to the kitchen (area 8), card dealers and escorts to the casino (area 9), and musicians to the dance hall (area 14). Wealthy, well-dressed guests begin arriving around the same time as the workers. Guests are free to wander the ship but are advised to keep away from the bridge and crew quarters on the upper deck (areas 11–13). The *Grand Dame* has no living quarters for passengers, whether workers or guests.

Characters who approach the ship wearing armor or carrying unconcealed weapons are turned away. Those who threaten the ship or try to board it are attacked. A battle on the pier frightens off the workers and guests who aren't aboard. It also alerts a half dozen city **guards** patrolling the wharf, who arrive 1d4 + 2 rounds after the battle is joined and fight on the side of the ship's crew.

The adventurers might try to replace one or more of the workers or pose as wealthy guests. A character who wants to get aboard in this fashion must succeed on a Charisma (Deception) check contested by Captain Storn's Wisdom (Insight) check. A character who wins the contest can board the ship without raising suspicion. If Storn wins the contest, he views the character as suspicious and demands an explanation for the individual's presence. Storn isn't really interested in the answer; he's looking to see how the character reacts. A character who reacts in a nonthreatening manner can repeat the check. If the character wins the contest, Storn's suspicions are allayed, and the character is permitted to board. If Storn wins the contest, the character is turned away. A character who refuses to leave is attacked.

On any given night, 2d6 × 5 well-dressed aristocrats and guild members come aboard (treat these guests as unarmed and unarmored **nobles**). Guests are expected to while away the hours dining, socializing, and gambling, all under the watchful eye of Lord Drylund's banker and security officer, Pow Ming (N female human). Pow Ming is a **mage**, with these changes:

- Pow Ming speaks Common, Draconic, Dwarvish, and Elvish.
- She has the *detect thoughts* spell prepared in place of *misty step*.
- She carries a *bag of holding* and wears a *robe of serpents* (see appendix B) with six snakes.

Pow Ming keeps hundreds of golden goose chips in her *bag of holding*. The bag is also where she keeps the money she receives in trade. At any given time, the bag

# Grand Dame

1 square = 10 feet

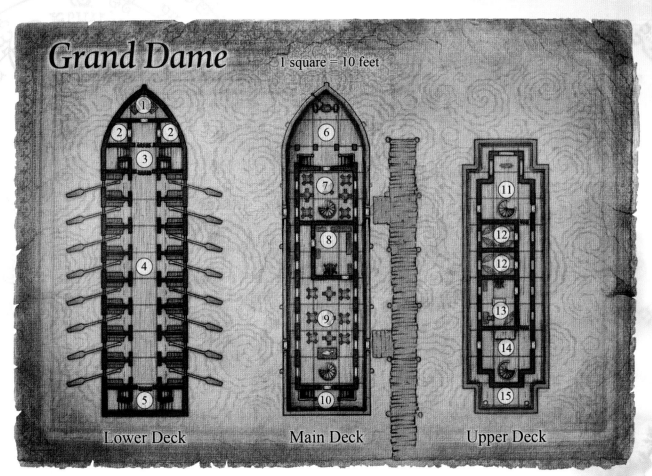

Lower Deck   Main Deck   Upper Deck

MAP 11.1: THE GRAND DAME

holds 1d10 × 100 gp. When the ship returns to port, Pow Ming pays out the winners, collects all the golden goose chips, and gives the remaining spoils to Lord Drylund, who places them in a locked chest (in area 13). If Pow Ming suspects that a guest might be cheating, she casts a *detect thoughts* spell to confirm or put to rest her suspicions. If she becomes convinced that someone is cheating, she uses her *suggestion* spell to convince the individual to take a flying leap off the deck of the ship.

Assuming that nothing happens to prevent its launch, the ship begins a slow, scenic journey upriver at dusk. Two deckhands oversee the rowers in area 4. Captain Storn and his six remaining deckhands take turns on the bridge (area 11). Pow Ming spends most of her evening in the gambling hall, keeping an eye on the guests (area 9). In the wee hours of the morning, the rowers turn the ship and head back to port so that guests and workers can disembark at dawn. Lord Drylund gives Storn money to pay the workers as they disembark.

Lord Drylund remains in his cabin (area 13) throughout the day, then emerges once the ship leaves port to greet every guest with a smile and a handshake, offering his favorites handfuls of free gambling chips. If he doesn't recognize one or more visitors, he questions them to see if they're worth keeping aboard. Drylund caters to those who have political influence in the city of Yartar, but he's eager to meet anyone with a lot of money. He expects his guests to be splendidly dressed—and unarmed. Those who are caught carrying concealed weapons are advised to cast their weapons overboard. Those who refuse to do so are unceremoniously thrown off the deck of the ship by the crew.

## 1. HOLD

Food and drink are stored in this small compartment.

## 2. HEAD

A rank odor pervades each of these small cabins, where crew members and passengers come to relieve themselves.

## 3. FORWARD STAIRS

Curtains hang over open doorways leading forward and aft. Wooden staircases lead up to the main deck.

## 4. LOWER DECK

At dusk, rowers extend the ship's oars into the water and use them to push the boat away from the dock and out into the river, while two of Captain Storn's deckhands walk up and down the hallway, barking instructions. When the ship is docked, the oars are pulled completely inside the boat.

## 5. AFT STAIRS

A curtain hangs over an open doorway leading forward. Wooden staircases lead up to the main deck.

Pow Ming

## 6. Main Deck Forward

Decorative lanterns hang from posts that support the balcony of the upper deck. A rusty winch bolted to the deck is used to raise and lower the ship's anchor. The winch is normally operated by two crew members, but a single creature can operate it with a successful DC 12 Strength (Athletics) check. It takes one action to drop the anchor and ten actions to raise it.

## 7. Dining Room

This room is full of tables and chairs, with narrow, winding avenues between them. White gossamer curtains, lush purple tablecloths, precious-looking silverware, and gaudy crystal chandeliers testify to Lord Drylund's obscenely lavish taste in decoration. A wooden spiral staircase leads up to the bridge (area 11).

Dinner is served throughout the evening, and the room is crowded from dusk until midnight. After midnight, a few occupied tables remain here and there, along with a handful of exhausted waiters.

## 8. Kitchen

Lots of clatter and yelling can be heard through the doors to this cabin, wherein hired cooks clash and bicker as they prepare meals and snacks for Lord Drylund's guests. An iron stove stands against one wall, its stovepipe piercing the ceiling. After midnight, the kitchen calms down, and the cooks spend much of their time cleaning up the mess they made and partaking of their own cuisine.

## 9. Golden Goose Casino

This large cabin has been transformed into a gambling hall, the centerpiece of which is a gold-plated wooden sculpture of a goose that rests on a table in the aft end. Glasses of fine wine, free for the taking, are arrayed around it. An unflattering portrait of a fat, foppish, grinning man (Lord Drylund) hangs on the wall across from a wooden spiral staircase that leads up to the dance hall (area 14).

Most of the floor space is taken up with tables of card games. From dusk until dawn, attractive dealers sit behind the tables, distributing cards to the players while small crowds look on. No actual currency passes into the hands of the hired help. Instead, bets are made with coin-sized wooden chips called golden geese, so named because each one bears Lord Drylund's golden goose emblem. Lord Drylund mingles with guests here, sometimes with his pet octopus on his shoulder, before retreating to his cabin (area 13) to count his money or spend time with one guest in particular—usually a "new catch" whom he tries to charm or bribe into supporting his political ambitions.

Pow Ming patrols the gambling hall in the evening, smiling at guests while watching for cheaters. She takes particular interest in customers who are on board for only the first or second time. If the characters threaten the ship or its passengers, she conjures one or more giant snakes with the aid of her *robe of serpents* and uses her spells to try to defeat them while being careful not to harm crew or passengers.

### Development

Pow Ming knows nothing about the Kraken Society or her employer's connection to the evil organization. Learning the truth wouldn't surprise her, however. Although she's not evil, Pow Ming is no saint. Her ultimate goal is to join the Arcane Brotherhood. In the meantime, she's using Lord Drylund to meet rich, influential people who might have contacts within that organization. If the characters eliminate Lord Drylund but leave Pow Ming alive and the riverboat intact, Pow Ming takes over the whole enterprise.

## 10. Main Deck Aft

Fancy lanterns dangle from the upper deck balcony overhead. Creaky staircases lead down to area 5. Guests often congregate here in the evening to schmooze and conduct illicit business dealings.

## 11. Bridge

Captain Storn and six of his deckhands are stationed here from dusk until dawn, taking turns at the wheel. If trouble arises somewhere else on the ship, the captain takes the wheel and sends one or more crew members to resolve the situation.

## 12. Crew Cabins

Each of these cabins contains four hammocks for sleeping. During the day, while the ship is docked, 1d4 deckhands can be found sleeping in each cabin. (Any deckhands not present are on the bridge, moving about the ship, or on the dock.)

## 13. Lord Drylund's Cabin

If he's not shaking hands and whispering in the ears of guests, Khaspere Drylund is here, dreaming of the day when he rules Yartar as its Waterbaron. He also receives occasional telepathic static from the kraken Slarkrethel, which leaves him with crushing headaches that last for hours.

Lord Drylund's cabin is a testament to bad taste, with its purple velvet curtains and scented candles in gaudy candelabras. In the middle of the room is a table with a large aquarium tank resting atop it. The aquarium contains a coral reef that serves as home for Lord Drylund's pet **octopus**. The octopus has bonded with its owner and can survive outside of water for 30 minutes. Beneath the aquarium, built into the table, is a shelf on which rests a locked wooden chest rigged with a poison needle trap (see the "Sample Traps" section in chapter 5 of the *Dungeon Master's Guide*). Lord Drylund hides the key inside a miniature "dead man's chest" lying inside the aquarium, and the octopus attacks any creature other than Lord Drylund that tries to reach for it.

Other furnishings include a silk hammock, a writing desk (covered with quills and loose sheets of blank parchment), a small table holding a silver wine decanter and matching goblet, and an iron stove.

### Treasure

Lord Drylund carries a rapier with a bejeweled, octopus-shaped hilt (worth 2,500 gp). The silver wine decanter and goblet are worth 25 gp each. The wooden chest contains 450 gp and a pouch containing nine 50 gp gemstones.

### Development

Lord Drylund is no match for a party of adventurers, and he knows it. If the characters corner and threaten him, he surrenders without a fight. He admits under interrogation that he's a member of the Kraken Society and reveals where King Hekaton is being kept. After he divulges that Hekaton is a prisoner aboard the *Morkoth*, which sails around the northern islands of the Trackless Sea, Lord Drylund's eyes widen in terror as he receives a telepathic message from the kraken—a wave of mind-shattering dread that deals 20 psychic damage to the nobleman. An instant later, Lord Drylund keels over dead, blood running from his nose.

## 14. Dance Hall

This smoky, dimly lit cabin features a wooden stage where musicians and other entertainers perform for the pleasure of Lord Drylund's guests. A few tables and chairs are set up along the walls, with much of the floor space kept open for dancing. A wooden spiral staircase descends to the gambling hall (area 9), and doors lead out to the upper deck balcony. Behind a curtain next to the stage is a hallway that leads to the bridge (area 11) and the crew cabins (area 12). A bronze plaque above the doorway reads "Crew Only."

Khaspere Drylund

## 15. Aft Balcony

In the evening, passengers gather here to gaze out upon the dark river and seduce one another, either for political gain or pure indulgence.

# The Hunt for Hekaton

The characters might kill Lord Drylund before he can be interrogated. If Lord Drylund dies before the characters learn King Hekaton's whereabouts, they can still learn where the storm giant king is being held by casting a *speak with dead* spell on Lord Drylund's corpse. If that option is unavailable to them, they can raise Lord Drylund from the dead. If they lack the means to do so themselves, they can bring Lord Drylund's body to a temple in any major city and pay to have the *raise dead* spell cast. The party must provide the material component of the spell (a diamond worth at least 500 gp) and make a donation of 500 gp to the temple. If one or more of the characters are members of the Lords' Alliance, they can muster the resources to acquire a *spell scroll* of *raise dead* free of charge, as long as they're in Yartar or another settlement that's part of the Lords' Alliance (see "The Lords' Alliance" section in chapter 1).

Slarkrethel has cast a powerful spell on the *Morkoth*, its crew, and their prisoner, hiding them all from divination magic. Neither the ship nor anyone aboard it can be targeted by any form of divination magic or perceived through magical scrying sensors.

# Finding the Morkoth

The *Morkoth* is sailing around a cluster of islands in the Trackless Sea known as the Purple Rocks. The ship's precise location changes from one hour to the next and is ultimately not important, nor is it imperative that the characters find the vessel quickly.

Chapter 3 describes random encounters you can use to spice up a sea voyage. To calculate how long it takes for the characters to find the *Morkoth*, ascertain the rough distance from the party's starting location to the Purple Rocks, then calculate the amount of time it would take the party's conveyance to travel that distance. Once the characters get within 100 miles of the Purple Rocks, they have a base 10 percent chance per day of locating the *Morkoth*. This chance assumes that the characters are traveling in one group or aboard multiple conveyances in fairly close formation. If multiple conveyances are searching for the *Morkoth* and they are so widespread as to be at least 30 miles apart, roll separately for each conveyance.

You can forgo precision and assume that the party spots the *Morkoth* 1d4 + 2 days after coming within 100 miles of the Purple Rocks.

## Modes of Travel

Unless the characters have the ability to cast the teleport spell or similarly powerful magic, they must rely on more conventional means to reach the *Morkoth*. The Modes of Travel table shows the number of miles a given conveyance can travel in a day, provided it has sufficient crew aboard.

### Modes of Travel

| Conveyance | Miles per Hour | Miles per Day |
|---|---|---|
| Airship | 8 | 192 |
| Cloud castle | 1 | 24 |
| Dragon mount | 8 | 192 |
| Sailing ship | 2 | 48 |

To create a more realistic journey, you can use the Weather table in chapter 5 of the *Dungeon Master's Guide* to determine the prevailing weather on a given day. If the results indicate strong wind and heavy rain, these weather conditions combine to create a storm that lasts for 1d6 hours. Once the storm has abated, the party's navigator must succeed on a DC 15 Wisdom (Survival) check to regain his or her bearings. Otherwise, the party is lost for 1 day, after which the check can be attempted again.

### Airship

If the characters have an airship (see the "Airship of a Cult" section in chapter 4), they can use it to search the Trackless Sea for the *Morkoth* while avoiding encounters with sea-bound creatures and vessels. Once the *Morkoth* is sighted, the characters can attack it from a distance or fly in close. The airship can't land on the *Morkoth*, but it can float in the water nearby or hover directly overhead, out of the line of fire of the *Morkoth*'s ship-mounted ballistae.

### Cloud Castle

If the characters gained control of a cloud castle (such as the one in chapter 9), they can fly it over the Trackless Sea and use the castle's giant telescopes to search for the *Morkoth*. Weather conditions might hinder their search, but there is no chance of the castle's being blown off course by a storm.

### Flying Mounts

Because the Trackless Sea is vast and its islands so distant, characters won't be able to reach the *Morkoth* on the backs of griffons, hippogriffs, or similar creatures, since the mounts have nowhere to land and rest when they tire. Dragons don't tire as easily and can transport characters overseas if they are sufficiently motivated. Dragons are also able to avoid and outpace storms. A friendly metallic dragon of the party's acquaintance might be persuaded to make the journey for a sizable donation to its trove. One rare magic item or 10,000 gp per passenger wouldn't be unreasonable.

### Sailing Ship

Characters can ply the Trackless Sea aboard a seafaring vessel. Since the islands of the Trackless Sea are home to predatory, seafaring Northfolk, most ship captains are unwilling to risk their vessels and lives on a fool's errand, no matter how much the characters offer to pay. Another possibility exists for characters who are associated with the Harpers, the Order of the Gauntlet, the Emerald Enclave, the Lords' Alliance, or the Zhentarim. Members in good standing of any of those groups can contact their organizations and convince them that an expedition must be mounted to find the *Morkoth*, for the sake of all civilization. Roll 2d10 for each faction that the characters approach for assistance; the result is the number of days it takes for that faction to secure and provision a sailing ship. If a deck plan of the ship becomes necessary, use the sample ship that appears in Appendix C of the *Dungeon Master's Guide*. Where the characters must go to board each vessel depends on the faction that provides the help.

The Harpers hire a brooding Waterdhavian captain named Zaldar Floshin (NG male half-elf **mage**). His ship, the *Kelpie's Kiss*, has a **sprite** named Arrow as its first mate and fifteen crewmembers (N male and female human **bandits**). A Harper agent named Ilkara Levari (CG female half-elf **spy**) serves as the ship's bosun. The ship is docked in Waterdeep.

The Order of the Gauntlet hires a merchant ship owned by a Waterdhavian noble named Arilosa Adarbrent, who supports the order financially. Her ship is the *Coin Toss*, and its captain is Tazlan Rilzeer (NG male human **bandit leader**), a fearless scoundrel with a sharp wit. His crew includes fifteen sailors (N male and female human **bandits**) and a cheery, overweight medic named Tharkil Morn (LG male human **priest** of Helm). The ship is docked in Neverwinter.

The Emerald Enclave hires the *Koalinth*, a ship under the command of a **hobgoblin captain** named Klarz and crewed by twenty **hobgoblins** and five **bugbears**. Klarz owes his life to an Emerald Enclave ranger who helped him after the two were stranded together on a monster-infested island in the Korinn Archipelago. This service repays Klarz's debt to the Emerald Enclave. Klarz's ship waits for the characters in a cove several miles north of Waterdeep.

The Lords' Alliance recently captured a pirate ship called the *Ravenous*, along with its nefarious captain, Sharlasta Stormsword (LE female human **bandit captain**). After cooling her heels in prison, Stormsword is visited by Lord Dagult Neverember, who strikes a deal with her. When she is released from custody and returned to her ship, Stormsword gathers a crew of twenty half-trained scalawags (**commoners** of various races and alignments) and whips them into shape for the voyage, the completion of which guarantees her a pardon signed by the Lords' Alliance leaders. The *Ravenous* is anchored in Neverwinter's bay.

The Zhentarim assigns Captain Drashk (N male tiefling **bandit captain**) to command a ship called the *Lost Cause* and assigns him a crew of six Zhentarim mercenaries (N male and female human **thugs** of various ethnicities) and twelve deckhands (**commoners** of various races and alignments). The eyepatch-wearing captain has an **imp** that perches on his shoulder and wreaks havoc with his moral compass. Drashk also has permission to negotiate trade deals with the storm giant king on behalf of the Black Network, should the opportunity arise. The *Lost Cause* is anchored in Waterdeep's bay.

Other ships that might be available to the characters are presented in the "Reaching Svardborg" section in chapter 7.

# THE MORKOTH

The *Morkoth* (shown on map 11.2) is a bizarre-looking yet seaworthy vessel with a hull that resembles a giant squid. As it plies the Trackless Sea, the top of the forward stabilizing fin remains above the water while the aft tentacles trail behind underwater. The *Morkoth* has the statistics of a sailing ship (see the Airborne and Waterborne Vehicles table in chapter 5 of the *Dungeon Master's Guide*). Its captain, Tholtz Daggerdark (CE male human **archmage**), is one of Slarkrethel's devoted thralls. He claims to be in constant telepathic contact with the kraken, though in truth Tholtz can only receive telepathic messages from the kraken, and such messages are rare and tend to give him nosebleeds.

Tholtz's first mate is Rool (NE male orc **assassin**), a vicious cutthroat who despises Captain Daggerdark and looks forward to gutting him like a fish one day. Rool's hatred of the wizard is well earned, for Tholtz frequently refers to the orc as a "soulless cretin" and a "bloodthirsty snake." Rool oversees a crew of twenty Kraken Society **cultists** (CE male and female humans) while Tholtz pretends to talk to Slarkrethel or raves on and on about the spells the kraken has promised to teach him. Morale aboard the ship is understandably low.

Half of the cultists are on duty at any given time, while the rest are asleep in their hammocks (area 4). When the characters first come upon the *Morkoth*, Captain Daggerdark is resting in his cabin (area 5) as well. Rool is behind the wheel atop the aft castle (area 2), and the ten awake cultists are manning the ballistae or keeping an eye on the storm giant prisoner. For ballista rules and statistics, see the "Siege Equipment" section in chapter 8 of the *Dungeon Master's Guide*.

Any loud disturbances on deck cause the captain and the sleeping cultists to awaken and investigate. Unless the characters approach the *Morkoth* invisibly, it is likely that the entire ship's crew will be armed and ready to face them in battle.

Escorting the *Morkoth* are four **merrow** loyal to Slarkrethel. These creatures swim alongside the vessel, two on each side, and use their harpoons to impale enemies and pull them into the water. Merrow harpoons have ropes made of tightly woven kelp attached to them so that they can be reeled in. If it misses with its harpoon attack, a merrow can use its next action to reel in the harpoon. If another creature is holding onto the harpoon, the merrow regains the weapon if it wins a contested Strength check. If characters take cover to avoid harpoon attacks, or if the merrow are unable to hurl their harpoons, the merrow crawl up onto the deck and attack with their teeth and claws, pursuing prey into the *Morkoth*'s lower deck if necessary.

## 1. FORECASTLE

This deck has two loaded ballistae mounted on swivel turrets. Four Kraken Society **cultists** are stationed here, ready to aim and fire the ballistae on command. Ammunition is stored in compartments under the deck boards.

## 2. AFT CASTLE

Rool, the Kraken Society **assassin**, is behind the captain's wheel, which stands in the middle of the aft castle. This flying deck sports two loaded, swivel-mounted ballistae, the ammunition for which is stored in compartments under the deck boards. Four Kraken Society **cultists** are also stationed here, ready to aim and fire the ballistae on command.

### DEVELOPMENT

If Rool finds himself in a situation where he thinks he can kill Captain Daggerdark with minimal risk to himself, he seizes the opportunity, even if it means certain defeat at the hands of his other enemies. Rool's betrayal doesn't make him friendly toward the party. Once Daggerdark is dispatched, Rool continues to fight the adventurers to the bitter end, grinning with the satisfaction that he dealt the fatal blow to his hated rival.

## 3. HEKATON IN CHAINS

Two Kraken Society **cultists** stand watch on the decks fore and aft of King Hekaton, who lies on his back in the ship's hold, wrapped in magical chains that trap him in stasis. The 28-foot-tall giant appears frozen in time, his eyes open and staring blindly into the sky. He is effectively restrained and unconscious while bound in this manner. Four chains bind him. The chains are secured to the hull and must be broken to release the giant from his stasis or free him from the ship's hold. Striking a chain alerts any *Morkoth* crew members not already engaged in battle.

# Morkoth

1 square = 5 feet

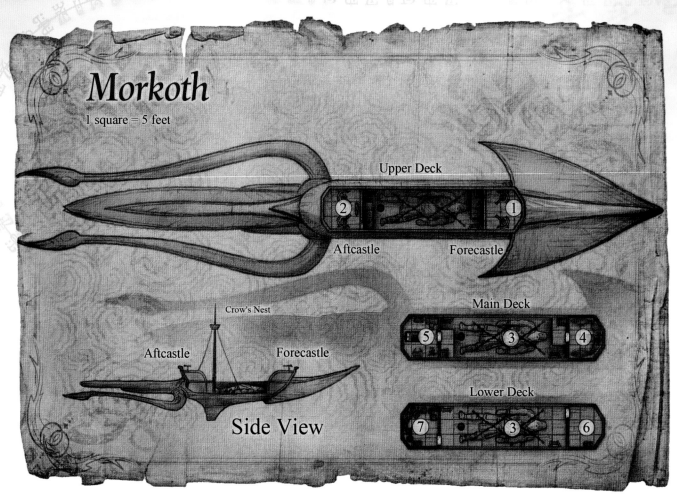

MAP 11.2: THE MORKOTH

Each chain has AC 20, 10 hit points, and immunity to all damage except bludgeoning, piercing, and slashing damage from adamantine or magic weapons. If all four chains are broken, Hekaton's stasis ends and he is no longer restrained or unconscious. If Hekaton is awakened during a battle, roll initiative for the storm giant king. Hekaton is a **storm giant**, with these changes:

- Hekaton has 330 hit points.
- He has no greatsword but can wield a length of broken chain as a melee weapon, making two attacks with it as an action on his turn. Each chain attack has a +14 bonus to hit, has a reach of 15 feet, and deals 19 (3d6 + 9) bludgeoning damage on a hit.
- He has no rocks to hurl but can pick up a shipboard ballista and use it like a heavy crossbow. The ballista gains the heavy, loading, and two-weapon properties when used in this way (see the "Weapon Properties" section in chapter 5 of the *Player's Handbook*). The weapon retains its range, attack modifier, and damage (see the "Siege Equipment" section in chapter 8 of the *Dungeon Master's Guide*).
- As a bonus action on his turn, Hekaton can shift his weight and cause any ship upon which he stands to heave to one side or the other. All other creatures standing on the ship must succeed on a DC 10 Dexterity saving throw or be knocked prone.

## DEVELOPMENT

Upon waking from his stasis, the storm giant king is disoriented, confused, and hostile toward all non-giants he sees. The last thing he remembers was being ambushed during a meeting with small folk, whom he was led to believe were representatives of the Lords' Alliance. (In fact, they were Kraken Society operatives in disguise.) The only individual aboard the *Morkoth* that Hekaton recognizes is Rool the orc, who was part of the group that ambushed him.

Hekaton rises to his full height and begins lashing out against small folk indiscriminately, shouting, "Lords' Alliance indeed! I'll see your alliance wrecked upon the waves for this treachery!" A character can use an action to try to persuade the king to stand down or not attack certain targets. That character must succeed on a DC 18 Charisma (Persuasion) check to calm down the king. If the check fails, the character's words fall on deaf ears. If the character mentions Serissa by name, the check is made with advantage.

Hekaton has no idea that his court has been thrown into upheaval and that evil forces are conspiring to usurp his throne. Only when the battle aboard the *Morkoth* has ended can the characters bring Hekaton up to date on recent developments. Regardless of what he is told, the king remains skeptical until he has had a chance to speak with his daughter, Serissa, and his brother, Uthor. He urges the characters to return to Maelstrom with him. Characters can either use Hekaton's conch to teleport themselves and the storm giant king to Maelstrom, or they can follow Hekaton as he dives into the water and swims home.

If the characters want to delay their departure, Hekaton agrees to stay around long enough for them to search the *Morkoth* or to take care of other matters. For example, the characters might need to conclude some business with the captain of the ship that brought them here, or they might need time to gather belongings from their airship. If Hekaton and the characters remain in the vicinity of the *Morkoth* for more than 1 hour, they are present when Slarkrethel shows up (see "The Kraken Cometh" section at the end of this chapter).

## 4. CREW CABIN

Ten hammocks stacked like bunk beds line the walls of this cabin. At any given time, ten Kraken Society **cultists** are asleep in these hammocks. They wake to cries of alarm and emerge from the cabin with scimitars drawn on the following round.

## 5. CAPTAIN'S CABIN

Tholtz Daggerdark's cabin is a mess. Nautical books and navigational charts are strewn across the floor, as are quills, loose sheets of blank parchment, empty wine bottles, and spilled jars of ink. Most of the furniture is bolted to the floor, including an unmade bed with a squid-shaped headboard, a writing desk stained with ink, an open trunk, a slender wardrobe stuffed with old robes, and a wooden cloak rack.

If he hasn't been disturbed, Tholtz the **archmage** is sleeping on the floor in a corner of the room, facing the cabin door. In his sleep, he used a knife to carve the words "DRAGON," "IYMRITH," "SISTERS," and "TREACHERY" into the floorboards. If he is awakened by a loud disturbance on deck, he drops the knife and leaves the cabin to investigate. He doesn't know who or what Iymrith is, nor does he know why he carved these words into the cabin floor.

Tholtz casts *mage armor* on himself before entering battle. If enemies threaten him with ranged attacks, he casts *fly* on himself, then tries to maneuver himself into a position where he can deal the most damage to them. Tholtz doesn't care if he catches his allies or King Hekaton in a spell's area.

### TREASURE

Tholtz's spellbook is locked in a desk drawer. Tholtz has the key in his possession, but the lock on the drawer is easily broken and can be just as easily picked using thieves' tools (no ability check required). The spellbook contains the following spells:

1st level: *detect magic, disguise self, identify, mage armor, magic missile, thunderwave*
2nd level: *darkvision, detect thoughts, mirror image, misty step, suggestion*
3rd level: *counterspell, fly, lightning bolt, sending, water breathing*
4th level: *arcane eye, banishment, fire shield, ice storm, stoneskin*
5th level: *cone of cone, scrying, seeming, teleportation circle, wall of force*

6th level: *chain lightning, flesh to stone, globe of invulnerability*
7th level: *prismatic spray, teleport*
8th level: *dominate monster, mind blank*
9th level: *time stop*

## 6. FIRST MATE'S CABIN

Rool's sparsely furnished cabin contains a hammock, a wooden treasure chest with a built-in lock, and a rug made from a yeti's hide.

Rool carries the key to the locked chest, which can be picked open with thieves' tools and a successful DC 15 Dexterity check. The chest is rigged with a gorgon-gas trap that triggers if an attempt is made to pick the lock. Detecting the trap requires a successful DC 20 Wisdom (Perception) check, and disabling it requires a successful DC 20 Dexterity check. If the attempt to disable the trap fails by 5 or more, the trap triggers. The green gas spills out through thin cracks in the lid and fills a 10-foot-radius sphere centered on the chest. Any creature in the area must succeed on a DC 13 Constitution saving throw or be petrified for 1 hour.

### TREASURE

Rool's chest is divided into three compartments. The first contains a sack of 180 gp. The second holds twelve nonmagical daggers that Rool has collected over the years. The third contains a deck of marked playing cards (worth 15 gp) in a wooden case, a spyglass (worth 1,000 gp), a quill, a jar of dragon blood (which Rool uses for ink), and a diary with a black leather cover.

In his diary, Rool articulately spells out why he would like to kill Captain Daggerdark and take command. The writing reveals that the captain claims to have a direct line of communication to the kraken Slarkrethel, an assertion that Rool suspects is true given that the captain is prone to headaches and nosebleeds. The diary also mentions that the captain keeps his spellbook in his desk, protected by "the worst lock I've ever seen."

### DEVELOPMENT

If the opportunity to do so arises, Rool has petrified characters thrown overboard.

## 7. HOLD

The aft compartment on the lower deck is packed with crates of rations and casks of ale and water. Four nets hold the containers in place. A few harmless **rats** creep about.

# THE KRAKEN COMETH

Khaspere Drylund's treachery convinces Slarkrethel that enemies are close to finding and freeing King Hekaton. The kraken leaves its lair in the darkest depths of the Trackless Sea and swims toward the *Morkoth*. The same magic that Slarkrethel placed on the *Morkoth* to conceal it from divination spells allows the kraken to locate the ship unerringly.

If the characters free Hekaton and leave the *Morkoth* within an hour of doing so, Slarkrethel arrives too late to stop them. If the characters are still aboard the *Morkoth* an hour after freeing Hekaton, the kraken pays them an unannounced visit. The kraken announces its arrival by wrapping its gigantic tentacles around the hull of the *Morkoth*. All creatures aboard the ship are surprised unless they are swimming beneath the vessel and can see the enormous kraken approaching from directly below the craft. Once the kraken strikes, all creatures in this encounter must roll initiative. Slarkrethel wants to terrify and humble the adventurers, not annihilate them, so it mainly uses its tentacles to crush the *Morkoth* and pull it into the depths. Under no circumstances does the kraken allow the ship to fall into enemy hands. As an action, the kraken can attack the *Morkoth* with all ten of its tentacles and deal 250 bludgeoning damage to the ship on each of its turns, accounting for the *Morkoth*'s damage threshold and the kraken's siege monster feature. Assuming the ship has all its hit points when Slarkrethel attacks, the vessel is destroyed after the kraken's second turn in combat. While crushing the ship, the kraken can't take other actions but can use its legendary actions as normal. Hekaton isn't afraid to face the kraken, and the kraken in turn has no qualms about killing the storm giant king (see "Development").

Slarkrethel is a **kraken**, with the following changes:

- Slarkrethel has a challenge rating of 25 (75,000 XP).
- It gains the Legendary Resistance trait and the Spellcasting action option described below, and it casts *foresight* on itself before it attacks.

***Legendary Resistance (3/Day).*** If Slarkrethel fails a saving throw, it can choose to succeed instead.

***Spellcasting.*** Slarkrethel casts one of the following spells, requiring no spell components and using Intelligence as the spellcasting ability (spell save DC 22):

At will: *detect magic, detect thoughts, sending*
2/day each: *control weather* (cast as 1 action), *fly, ice storm*
1/day each: *arcane eye, chain lightning, feeblemind, foresight, locate creature, mass suggestion, nondetection, power word kill, scrying* (cast as 1 action), *sequester, telekinesis, teleport*

### DEVELOPMENT

Once it sinks the *Morkoth*, the kraken withdraws into the dark depths. If Hekaton is present, the kraken tries to drag the storm giant king down with it, leaving the puny and insignificant surface-dwelling adventurers to fend for themselves. Hekaton doesn't survive long in the kraken's clutches. If the storm giant king dies, all is not lost. Characters can return to Maelstrom and report the sorry news to Serissa. Although Hekaton's death is hard on her, Serissa is determined to see the ordning restored in his name and takes her father's place in the next chapter of the adventure.

# BACK TO MAELSTROM?

The next chapter begins with the characters returning to Maelstrom, cementing their alliance with the storm giants, and plotting with the giants to take down Iymrith. If the characters fail to save King Hekaton, the adventure can proceed without him as long as the characters still have one or two allies in the court of the storm giant king. See the start of chapter 12 for details.

Failures and miscalculations on the part of the characters could create a situation in which they can't return to Maelstrom or have little reason to. For example, if they failed to rescue Hekaton from the Kraken Society's clutches and they lose the *conch of teleportation*, the characters might choose to avoid any further dealings with the storm giants and focus their attention elsewhere. The same development might ensue if the characters made enemies of Serissa and Uthor by stealing from the storm giants or harming members of the royal family. The storm giants notwithstanding, the characters might have a personal score to settle with Iymrith (a desire to avenge Harshnag, for example) and could decide to go after the dragon on their own once they find her lair. In such a case, you can time events so that the storm giants arrive at Iymrith's lair at the same time the characters do, giving the characters an opportunity to join forces with the giants and reconcile any past grievances. Conversely, the characters might choose to avoid another confrontation with Iymrith, effectively skipping chapter 12, and instead set their sights on the remaining evil giant lords. Try not to force the player characters one way or the other. Let them make the tough choices!

---

### CHARACTER ADVANCEMENT

The characters' attempt to rescue King Hekaton is more important than the outcome. As long as they try, the characters gain a level at the conclusion of this chapter and should be 10th level when they confront Iymrith in chapter 12, "Doom of the Desert." Given the danger that Iymrith poses, players might want their characters to gain more levels before facing the ancient blue dragon in her lair. The characters can go after any evil giant lords that remain, gaining a level for every two they defeat, and face Iymrith at 11th or 12th level.

---

# CHAPTER 12: DOOM OF THE DESERT

PON HIS RETURN TO MAELSTROM, KING Hekaton is quick to act against the evil that threatens all giants. With the help of his scrying pool, Hekaton figures out where Iymrith has gone to ground. Seated upon the *Wyrmskull Throne*, Hekaton summons the adventurers before him, thanks them for their help thus far, and asks them to join him as he takes the fight to Iymrith by storming the dragon's lair in the desert of Anauroch.

If the characters were unable to rescue the storm giant king, or if Hekaton didn't survive, Princess Serissa vows to avenge her father's death, swearing that Iymrith's deception will not go unpunished. She reaches out to the adventurers one more time, imploring them to join her as she confronts the dragon.

An ancient blue dragon is more than a match for a party of 10th-level adventurers, but the characters have storm giants watching their backs. Hekaton or Serissa also gives each character a *potion of giant size* (see appendix B) from the royal treasury, enabling them to face the dragon as true giants when the time comes. The storm giants describe the effect and duration of the potions, but they leave it to the characters to decide if and when to use them. The characters can quaff their potions before they enter Iymrith's lair or wait until they are about to engage the dragon in battle. Conversely, one or more characters might prefer to use the potions only as a last resort.

Hekaton or Serissa also gives the party a *claw of the wyrm rune* (see appendix B) recovered from a shipwreck near Maelstrom. Like the potions, this item is a gift; the characters can do with it what they will.

## FINDING IYMRITH

The storm giants bear the burden of finding the dragon so that the characters can focus on preparing themselves for the final showdown. Hekaton and Serissa know that blue dragons favor desert surroundings, and it doesn't take much research for them to discover that Iymrith has a reputation in the North. The storm giants learn the following facts about their nemesis:

- Iymrith is an ancient blue dragon known as the "Doom of the Desert." She is also called the "Dragon of Statues" because she creates living statues (actually gargoyles) to guard her lair.
- Her lair is a ruined amphitheater half-buried in the cold desert sands northeast of Ascore, an ancient and abandoned dwarven city.
- She is a spellcaster and, like all blue dragons, is immune to lightning damage.

Armed with this information, Hekaton (or Serissa) leaves Imperator Uthor in charge of Maelstrom and sets out with four storm giant bodyguards named Nimir, Orlekto, Shaldoor, and Vaasha (see appendix D for statistics) to confront Iymrith. The characters are invited to join them. King Hekaton has 330 hit points at full health but otherwise has the statistics of a typical storm giant. If Serissa leads the attackers, see area 15 in chapter 10 for modifications to her statistics.

The storm giants ride whales to the Whalebones. At the islands, they mount rocs and fly the remaining distance to Anauroch. Once they are within half a mile of Iymrith's lair, the storm giants dismount and approach on foot, leaving the rocs to perch atop rocky outcroppings and wait for their return. Characters can ride with the giants, or they can use some other method of conveyance—it's up to them.

Storm giants aren't stealthy and would prefer to stage a direct assault on Iymrith's lair, but they will adjust their tactics based on the desires of the characters. If the characters favor a stealthy approach, the giants offer to create a distraction so that the characters can enter Iymrith's lair undetected. Such a plan stands a better chance of succeeding if the characters refrain from drinking their *potions of giant size* until after they have infiltrated the lair.

It's best if Hekaton (or Serissa) remains an NPC under your control. You can have your players run the other storm giants if you prefer (and if they would enjoy doing so). Photocopy the storm giant stat blocks at the end of this chapter and distribute them among the players in your group. If your group includes more than four players, not every player will receive a storm giant NPC to play, and that's okay. Accompanying the giants' stat blocks are roleplaying notes that the players can use to portray the giants accurately. One of the giants (Orlekto) has sinister ulterior motives that might come into play during the events of this chapter. If you have a player who's particularly good at roleplaying underhanded characters, consider giving Orlekto to that player.

You can have all storm giants act on the same initiative count, or have the players roll initiative for each storm giant. The former approach expedites combat; the latter leads to a battle with more verisimilitude.

## IYMRITH'S LAIR

The Doom of the Desert has claimed an enormous, abandoned amphitheater in the desert as her lair (shown on map 12.1). Beneath the amphitheater lie chambers where the blue dragon sleeps and hides her treasure. When the characters approach Iymrith's lair for the first time, read or paraphrase the following boxed text aloud to the players.

> Your long journey ends here, in the desert. A churning cauldron of black clouds fills the sky as thunder peals and lightning flashes. Half buried in the cold dunes is a crumbling amphitheater adorned with statues, many of them broken, the rest worn smooth by wind and sand. Two large trebuchets stand atop the ruins. Where cheers once rang out across a great city, now a solemn fortress stands before you, waiting for you to draw near.

The dry thunderstorm is the dragon's work—a regional effect (see the blue dragon entry in the *Monster Manual*) that stretches for 6 miles in every direction. The storm has no effect on the battle as it unfolds; it's simply a reflection of Iymrith's mood.

Storm giants who stride boldly toward the amphitheater with weapons in hand draw fire from the trebuchets (see area 1). The characters can let the storm giants bear the brunt of these attacks while they approach from another direction, or they can join the giants in their direct assault. When storm giants or characters of giant size come within 1,000 feet of the amphitheater, the gargoyles notice them and fire the trebuchets. The giants can hurl lightning at the gargoyles and trebuchets once they get within 500 feet of them.

If a storm giant or a character of giant size stands in the amphitheater and loudly challenges Iymrith, the dragon's ego gets the better of her, and she responds to the challenge by crawling out of her lair to destroy her challengers. Otherwise, she remains hidden in area 3 and lets her gargoyles soften up her enemies.

Iymrith can use her lair actions within the amphitheater as well as in the dungeon underneath it. The dragon doesn't waste her lightning breath on storm giants; similarly, the storm giants know that their lightning strikes have no effect on Iymrith. The giants didn't bring any rocks with them, but they can hurl chunks of sandstone torn from Iymrith's own amphitheater.

If Iymrith is drawn to the surface and reduced to 240 hit points or fewer, she retreats to the dungeon level and makes her final stand there. She can collapse tunnels (see the "Iymrith's Lair: General Features" sidebar) as well as burrow new ones, as needed.

## 1. AMPHITHEATER AND ENVIRONS

The amphitheater once stood at the center of a magnificent city, the rest of which lies buried under the sand. The walls have abundant cracks and other handholds, enabling them to be climbed with ease. Iymrith cut a swath through the northeast section of the amphitheater, leaving a rubble-filled path that leads to an open sinkhole and conceals another one that lies along the route (see "Sinkholes").

### GARGOYLES AND TREBUCHETS

Thirty **gargoyles** inhabit the amphitheater. Twenty-two of them are perched on stone plinths, waiting to swoop down and attack intruders. The eight remaining gargoyles operate the wooden trebuchets—four per weapon. Two gargoyles use their actions to load a trebuchet

## IYMRITH'S LAIR: GENERAL FEATURES

The dragon's lair consists of a sandstone amphitheater surrounded by sand and a few ruined outbuildings, as well as a dungeon level below the amphitheater. The general features of Iymrith's lair are summarized below.

***Dungeon Architecture.*** The dungeon level contains worked areas and rough-hewn areas:

- Worked areas have flat sandstone ceilings 40 feet high, with connecting tunnels that are 20 feet high. They have brick walls with sand and clay behind them, and floors covered with sandstone tiles.
- Rough-hewn areas were excavated by the dragon from clay and sand, and have ceilings that range in height from 20 to 30 feet.

In her dragon form, Iymrith can move through passages that are 30 feet wide without impediment. She can squeeze through passages that are 20 feet wide. Openings narrower than 20 feet are too small for the dragon to squeeze through, but Iymrith can effectively burrow new passages or widen existing ones, moving through the clay and sand at her burrowing speed.

***Collapsible Passages.*** Dotted lines enclose these locations on the map. Iymrith has weakened the ceilings in these places so that she can collapse them, either to cut off escape routes or to trap intruders. A creature can trigger a collapse by dealing 10 damage or more to the ceiling with a single attack or spell effect. The collapse renders the passage impassable until the sand and stone are cleared away, which requires 250 hours of work. (Multiple creatures working together can reduce the amount of time accordingly.) Any creature in the marked section of tunnel when it collapses must make a DC 15 Dexterity saving throw. On a failed save, the creature takes 22 (4d10) bludgeoning damage from falling stone and is buried under stone and sand. While buried, the creature is prone and blinded. It also can't breathe and has total cover against attacks and other effects that might target it.

A burrowing creature (such as a blue dragon) can move through the collapsed area at its burrowing speed, leaving no tunnel in its wake as the sand fills in behind it. A buried creature that doesn't have a burrowing speed can, at the start of its turn, make a DC 15 Strength (Athletics) check. If the check succeeds, the creature can pull itself in one direction or the other at a rate of 1 foot for every 5 feet of movement spent. If that movement isn't enough to exit the collapsed area, the creature can repeat the check on its next turn. A creature standing at either end of the collapsed area can use its action to pull a buried creature out of the area, provided the buried creature is within reach (no ability check required).

***Illumination.*** Iymrith uses darkvision to see in the dungeon level. No light sources are present except for what visitors bring with them.

***Sand Dunes.*** Marked on the map are mounds of sand that range in height from 10 feet to 40 feet. They are difficult terrain for Large and smaller creatures.

while another two use their actions to aim it. Once a trebuchet is loaded and aimed, one of the gargoyles uses its next action to fire the weapon. This routine allows a trebuchet to be loaded, aimed, and fired every other round. For trebuchet rules and statistics, see the "Siege Equipment" section in chapter 8 of the *Dungeon Master's Guide.*

## MYSTICS' CAMP

Three tents surround a smoldering campfire southeast of the amphitheater. A search of the camp reveals one empty bedroll in each tent. The camp belongs to the yu-an-ti in area 3 and is currently unoccupied. Characters can follow their tracks in the sand (one wavy line left by a serpentine creature plus eight sets of footprints) to the stairs leading down to area 5 (see "Stairs Down").

## SINKHOLES

Several sinkholes lead down to the lower chambers.

- A large open sinkhole in the middle of the amphitheater drops down into area 2; Iymrith uses it to enter and exit her lair.
- Three hidden sinkholes are marked 1A, 1B, and 1C on the map.

The first creature to enter a hidden sinkhole's space causes the sinkhole to appear and must succeed on a DC 15 Dexterity saving throw or fall to the bottom of it. A creature that falls into a sinkhole lands prone but takes no damage, since the sand cushions its fall. The sinkhole remains open thereafter. Sinkhole 1A drops down into a rough-hewn passage that connects areas 4 and 5. Sinkhole 1B is directly above the purple wormling pit in area 5, and any creature falling into it is surprised and attacked by 1d4 purple wormlings. Sinkhole 1C drops down into a rough-hewn cave west of areas 2 and 3.

## STAIRS DOWN

At each end of the amphitheater's "U" shape is a tunnel staircase that descends 50 feet to a sandy passageway that leads to area 2.

The ruined building south of the amphitheatre used to be the basement of a stage. It contains a sandy, 10-foot-wide staircase that descends 50 feet to area 5.

## 2. ENTRANCE CHAMBER

Partition walls made of tight-fitting sandstone blocks support the ceiling of this chamber, which contains a 20-foot-high hill of sand. Twenty feet above the top of the mound is a gaping hole in the ceiling that leads outside. The hole lets in bright sunlight during the day and dim moonlight at night. The light doesn't extend beyond the room. Iymrith uses this hole to enter and exit her lair, and her enormous tracks can be seen coming and going from an even larger room to the north (area 3), from which chanting can be heard and torchlight seen.

## 3. SERPENTS OF THE SANDS

Two rows of sandstone pillars support the ceiling of this vast chamber. Before Iymrith claimed it as her own, this room was once a secret temple belonging to a sect of desert-dwelling yuan-ti mystics called the Serpents of the Sands. These mystics worship Dendar the Night Serpent (see the yuan-ti entry in the *Monster Manual* for more information on this deity). Iymrith invited the mystics here to contact their demon-god, hoping it might provide guidance on how to crush her enemies. Because she has become desperate, Iymrith is willing to trust the

# Iymrith's Lair

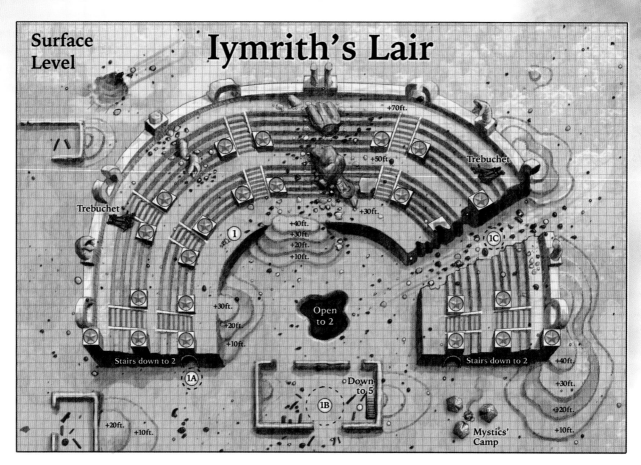

**Surface Level**

+70ft.

+50ft.

Trebuchet

+30ft.

1

Trebuchet

1C

+40ft.
+30ft.
+20ft.
+10ft.

+30ft.

Open to 2

+20ft.

+10ft.

+40ft.

Stairs down to 2

Down to 5

Stairs down to 2

+30ft.

1A

1B

+20ft.

+20ft.    +10ft.

Mystics' Camp

+10ft.

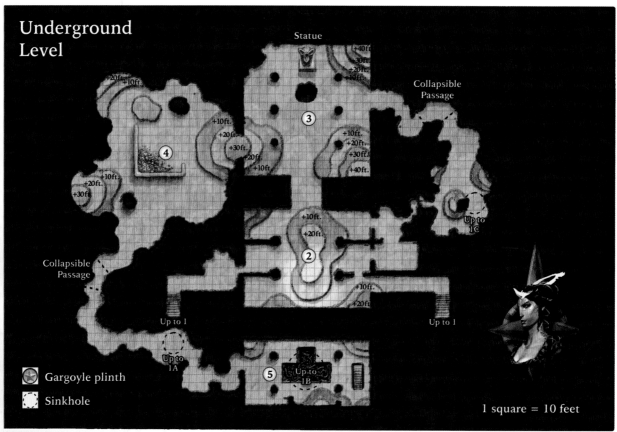

**Underground Level**

Statue

+40ft
+30ft
+20ft
+10ft

+20ft
+10ft

Collapsible Passage

3

+10ft.

4

+20ft.

+30ft.

+10ft.
+20ft.
+30ft.
+40ft.

+20ft.

+10ft.

+10ft.
+20ft.
+30ft.

Up to 1C

+30ft

Collapsible Passage

+10ft.

+20ft.

2

+10ft.

+20ft.

Up to 1

Up to 1

Up to 1A

5    Up to 1B

⬡ Gargoyle plinth

⬚ Sinkhole

1 square = 10 feet

MAP 12.1: IYMRITH'S LAIR

mystics' interpretations of the Night Serpent's whispers, which she doesn't understand.

Floor-to-ceiling piles of sand have been pushed up in three of the room's corners. One of the piles conceals a hole in the western wall (see "Dragon Bolt-Holes"). Unless Iymrith was drawn to the surface and defeated there, the ancient blue dragon is lurking under the pile of sand in the southeast corner of the room. Only her eyes and her horn are visible, and only to characters who have a passive Wisdom (Perception) score of 17 or higher. Any character who searches that corner of the room spots the dragon automatically.

**Iymrith** (see appendix C) avails herself of her lair actions here.

## DEMONIC SNAKE STATUE

At the north end of the room is an alabaster statue carved to look like the head and neck of a giant demonic snake erupting from a block of stone. The block is 10 feet high, and the serpent is another 10 feet taller still, with two gleaming eyes of polished obsidian (see "Treasure"). Its fanged mouth is open as it glares down at a 20-foot-diameter hole in the sandstone floor. The hole represents the top of an 800-foot-deep shaft, the bottom quarter of which is filled with sand and old bones (previous sacrifices to Dendar the Night Serpent). Standing around the edge of the hole are three **yuan-ti purebloods** wearing desert robes and six **yuan-ti malisons**. Two of the malisons are type 1 (human body with a snake head), two are type 2 (human head and body, with snakes for arms), and one is type 3 (human head and upper body with a serpentine lower body instead of legs). The yuan-ti chant a vile prayer, at the end of which one pureblood leaps into the shaft to his death. His sacrifice causes faint, prophetic whispers to rise from the depths, speaking in the Abyssal tongue. Any character within earshot who understands Abyssal can translate the demonic whispers:

*Wrack and ruin, flash and thunder,*
*Let them claim the dragon's plunder;*
*Death is close! Her doom has come!*
*To blade and spell she will succumb.*

Dendar the Night Serpent, having foreseen Iymrith's doom, offers her neither hope nor guidance. Once the demon-god has spoken, Iymrith calls out to the yuan-ti, demanding that they translate its words. Rather than anger her with the truth, the yuan-ti lie and tell the dragon that she must face her enemy in battle. From this, Iymrith concludes that she must kill the storm giant leader to destroy any hope of lasting peace between giants and the small folk. Once the dragon leaves, the yuan-ti attempt to flee the dragon's lair by the safest route, attacking anyone in their way.

A yuan-ti that is captured and interrogated tries to win its freedom by offering useful information about the dragon's hoard. All of the yuan-ti have, at one time or another, seen Iymrith burying or digging up sarcophagi in her treasure vault (area 4). The cultists suspect that the blue dragon keeps her most precious baubles in these sarcophagi. A yuan-ti shares this information in return for the promise of safe release.

## DRAGON BOLT-HOLES

Iymrith has broken through two walls and excavated tunnels and chambers beyond, expanding her lair.

- A 30-foot-diameter hole in the west wall is buried under a 30-foot-high mound of sand. Iymrith can burrow through the sand to reach area 4 beyond.
- A 30-foot-wide hole in the east wall is plain for all to see and leads to a rough-hewn passage that eventually connects to area 2.

### TREASURE

Any creature that can reach the statue's eyes can pry them out with a dagger, a crowbar, or a similar tool. Each eye is a 4-inch-diameter orb of polished obsidian worth 250 gp and weighing 25 pounds.

## 4. IYMRITH'S TROVE

Iymrith dug this cavern out of the sand, clay, and rock and uses it to store her treasure. In the middle of the cavern are two 10-foot-high sandstone walls. A giant pile of gold coins lies in the sand where the two walls meet.

When a creature other than Iymrith approaches within 10 feet of the treasure pile, the gold coins are swept up into four whirlwinds. These vortexes are four **air elementals** that deal extra damage because of the gold coins swirling inside them at high velocity. Each slam attack deals 18 (3d8 + 5) bludgeoning damage, and the elementals' whirlwind attack deals 20 (4d8 + 2) bludgeoning damage (half damage on a successful save, as normal). When an air elemental is destroyed, the gold coins contained within it tumble to the floor (see "Treasure").

The most prized treasures of Iymrith's hoard are contained in six stone sarcophagi buried 10 feet under the sandy floor and scattered about the room. Each sarcophagus has a *sequester* spell cast upon it, rendering it invisible and impervious to magical detection. The *sequester* spell on a given sarcophagus ends when a creature comes in direct contact with it. A creature that spends an hour digging in this cavern has a 10 percent chance of finding a sarcophagus. A group of characters working together must spend at least 10 minutes clearing the sand around the sarcophagus before it can be opened. Then and only then can a character use an action to try to pry open the lid of a sarcophagus, doing so with a successful DC 13 Strength (Athletics) check. Using a crowbar or a similar tool grants advantage on the check.

### TREASURE

Each air elemental has 2,500 gp swirling inside it.

The six sarcophagi held the mummies of dead Netherese priests, until Iymrith devoured their remains to make room for her precious loot. (She left one of the mummies intact as a surprise for would-be thieves.) The contents of the sarcophagi are described below in the order in which the sarcophagi are found. Magic items are determined by rolling on the magic item tables in chapter 7 of the *Dungeon Master's Guide*.

The first sarcophagus contains four magic items. Roll on Magic Item Table F for each item. If Iymrith stole the *Korolnor Scepter* (see appendix B) from Serissa, it is inside this sarcophagus as well.

The second sarcophagus contains three magic items. Roll on Magic Item Table G for each item.

The third sarcophagus contains two magic items. Roll on Magic Item Table H for each item.

The fourth sarcophagus contains one magic item, determined by rolling on Magic Item Table I. This item rests on a bed of 900 pp.

The fifth sarcophagus contains a bowl made from the skull of a gold dragon wyrmling (worth 25 gp) that holds twenty 500 gp gemstones. Piled around the ivory bowl are several more items: a mithral helm sculpted to look like a head of a blue dragon (worth 250 gp), a gold dragon comb set with red garnets for eyes (worth 750 gp), an eyepatch with a mock eye of blue sapphire and moonstone affixed to it (worth 2,500 gp), and a jade Dragonchess board with matching playing pieces carved to resemble metallic and chromatic dragons (worth 7,500 gp for the entire set).

The sixth and final sarcophagus contains Shaxan Kazraat, a Netherese **mummy lord** that awakens and attacks its liberators. The mummy lord was spirited from its tomb by Iymrith and can't take lair actions or cause regional effects to occur in the vicinity of the dragon's lair. Shaxan Kazraat wears a circlet of black gold formed in the shape of a cobra that has tiny black opals for eyes and ruby fangs (worth 7,500 gp). A secret compartment inside the sarcophagus contains the mummy lord's intact (yet desiccated) heart in a black cloth pouch. A character who searches the sarcophagus finds the compartment and the pouch with a successful DC 15 Wisdom (Perception) check.

## 5. Purple Wormling Nursery

Everyone needs a hobby. Iymrith's latest avocation is raising baby purple worms until they're big enough to release into the wild. She digs up purple worm nests under the sands of the desert, steals the eggs, and brings them back to her lair. When the eggs hatch, she confines the wormlings here and feeds them a healthy diet of meat so that they grow up big and strong.

Iymrith has converted a 10-foot-deep, T-shaped pit in the middle of the room into a purple wormling "playpen." The pit currently holds thirty squirming **purple wormlings** (see appendix C). Although they are too small to burrow or climb out of the pit, the wormlings eagerly attack other creatures that enter the pit, including any creature that falls in through the sinkhole above (see the "Sinkholes" section in area 1).

# Adventure Conclusion

Iymrith is too proud to abandon her lair and fights to the death to defend it. The characters' role in the death of Iymrith forces Hekaton to admit that he has misjudged the small folk. His beloved wife once told him that if giants and small folk could learn to coexist peacefully and help one another, the world would be better off. Moved by the party's heroism, Hekaton admits that he should have heeded Neri's words. "Storm giants and small folk can work together," he proclaims, "to create a better world, free from the tyranny of dragons." He vows to honor the characters and his wife by allying with the small folk against other draconic threats. This, he believes, is the test that Annam the All-Father has thrust upon him—and this alliance, he hopes, will restore the ordning as it was.

Whether or not Hekaton is correct is up to you. Seeing giants and small folk working together to destroy a common foe might inspire Annam the All-Father to elevate storm giants to the top of the ordning once more, or the order of giants might remain an open question. In any case, the death of Iymrith has no effect on the machinations of the evil giant lords of the North who aim to win their gods' favor and rise to the top of the ordning. The characters might be moved to confront and defeat these few remaining giant lords. Hekaton thinks that's a good idea and does nothing to hinder their efforts.

If Serissa participated in the battle against Iymrith in her father's place, she thanks them for their heroism and, like her father, looks forward to future cooperation between small folk and giants. Serissa likewise has no qualms about letting the characters deal with the evil giant lords who still threaten the North. She is eager to return to Maelstrom and tell the tale of Iymrith's defeat, knowing this will lure giants back to her court.

Powerful evil dragons such as Klauth and Claugiyliamatar are hardly saddened by the death of Iymrith, but they aren't pleased to see giants and small folk working together. They bide their time, as old dragons do, and wait to see how long the alliance lasts.

Although Iymrith meets her end in this adventure, the blue dragon's legacy lives on in the form of her offspring (see the "Ascore" section in chapter 3). They turn on each other, with the victor claiming Iymrith's lair and the title of "Doom of the Desert."

---

### Character Advancement

With the defeat of Iymrith, the characters gain a level. If the players are keen on defeating the remaining evil giant lords, you can continue running the adventure and allow characters to gain a level for every two additional giant lords they thwart.

---

# APPENDIX A: LINKED ADVENTURES

Wizards of the Coast has published other D&D adventures that can serve as springboards for *Storm King's Thunder*, not only getting characters to 5th level but also directing the characters toward one of the three locations described in chapter 2. If any of the characters are affiliated with a faction, such as the Harpers, you can guide them toward Bryn Shander, Goldenfields, or Triboar by having a representative of that faction give them a quest. With the growing threat of giants in the North, the quest might be as straightforward as protecting the location against a possible giant attack.

## LOST MINE OF PHANDELVER

*Lost Mine of Phandelver* is an adventure in the DUNGEONS & DRAGONS *Starter Set*, designed to take characters from 1st to 5th level. Characters who complete it are at the right level to begin *Storm King's Thunder*, and Triboar is their ideal starting point (see chapter 2). The trick is to get them from Phandalin to Triboar, which lies east along a trail that cuts across grasslands and foothills. You can simply declare that the party makes the uneventful journey, or you can offer some reason why they would want to visit Triboar. The town is a good place for them to resupply, upgrade their gear, sell their loot, and find new adventures. If those aren't reasons enough, here are a few hooks tied to NPCs in Phandalin that you can use to direct the characters toward Triboar.

### LIONSHIELD DELIVERY

Linene Graywind, who runs the trading post in Phandalin on behalf of a mercantile company, the Lionshield Coster, has a colleague, Alaestra Ulgar, who lives in Triboar with her business partner, Narth Tezrin. Linene has written a letter to her friend, describing recent tribulations in Phandalin, and asks the characters to deliver it. In a note attached to the letter, Linene asks Alaestra to reward her messengers with an old gray bag stitched with animal designs. This item is a gray *bag of tricks*.

### A DEMANDING LETTER

Harbin Wester, the pompous town master of Phandalin, asks the characters to deliver a letter to Darathra Shendrel, the lord protector of Triboar. In the letter, Harbin demands that the lord protector do a better job of patrolling the territory between their two settlements. He reprimands Darathra for allowing orcs to dwell the hills near Phandalin. Unknown to Harbin, Darathra is a member of the Harpers. She gives the characters 50 gp for having the guts to deliver the condescending letter.

### ZHENTARIM CONNECTION

The guildmaster of the Phandalin Miner's Exchange, Halia Thornton, works for the Zhentarim. If the characters impress her, she recommends that they contact Urlam Stockspool in Triboar. Urlam is always looking for adventurers to help further the Black Network's cause, and Halia vouches that "his rewards for good service are lavish." She tells the characters to look for Urlam at the office of the Triboar Travelers, a caravan company, in the heart of town.

## TYRANNY OF DRAGONS

*Tyranny of Dragons* deals with the rise of evil dragons and their attempt to free Tiamat from the Nine Hells. If you use *Tyranny of Dragons* as a springboard into this adventure, you must change the timing of events so that the *Tyranny of Dragons* story and the events that precipitate *Storm King's Thunder* happen concurrently, with Annam the All-Father breaking the ordning to stir the giants before Tiamat is brought into the world.

Early in *Tyranny of Dragons*, the characters join a caravan traveling from Baldur's Gate to Waterdeep. By the time they reach Waterdeep, they should be 5th level. You can use the party's arrival in Waterdeep to shift attention away from the *Tyranny of Dragons* story by dropping reports of giant sightings near the temple-farm of Goldenfields. The Emerald Enclave is looking for adventurers to help patrol Goldenfields' borders. If the characters take the bait, Goldenfields becomes the starting point for this adventure (see chapter 2). Although you forgo most of *Tyranny of Dragons* in favor of this new adventure, there's nothing stopping you from returning to *Tyranny of Dragons* later.

Part of *Tyranny of Dragons* takes place in Skyreach Castle, a flying fortress belonging to a cloud giant named Blagothkus. You can make him a pivotal figure in this adventure by having his castle appear when the characters are around 7th or 8th level, giving them a chance to meet the evil cloud giant and convince him to aid their cause. The characters might also want to confront him after meeting the ghost of his dead son, Eigeron, in chapter 4, "The Chosen Path." The shattering of the ordning has the following effects on Blagothkus:

- The cloud giant is eager to dispose of his Cult of the Dragon allies, use their money to buy the loyalty of lesser giants, and wage war against dragonkind. If the characters help him rid Skyreach Castle of the cultists and their white dragon ally, the giant pledges to help them in return and offers them one-third of the cult's spoils. Blagothkus honors his agreements as long as the characters pose no threat to him and he gets his way. If they have an airship with Cult of the Dragon members aboard (see the "Airship of a Cult" section in chapter 4), these cultists ally with the ones aboard Skyreach Castle.

- Blagothkus knows that King Hekaton has disappeared and suspects that dragons are somehow responsible. Although he has no proof to corroborate his suspicions, Blagothkus sees dragon conspiracies everywhere and is convinced that evil dragons would pounce on the chance to throw giant society into chaos. Although he's eager to see the ordning restored with cloud giants at its apex, he can be convinced to use his flying fortress to help the characters locate King Hekaton if he's told that one or more dragons orchestrated the king's abduction.

- Although they share a disdain for dragons, Blagothkus and Countess Sansuri are bitter rivals. If the characters intend to confront Sansuri (see chapter 9,

"Castle of the Cloud Giants"), Blagothkus offers to join the characters and help them thwart her machinations so that he, not she, can win the favor of the gods and elevate cloud giants to the top of the ordning.

Blagothkus bears no ill will toward small folk, but his desire to rekindle the ancient war between giants and dragons could have devastating consequences for small folk settlements up and down the Sword Coast.

# PRINCES OF THE APOCALYPSE

*Princes of the Apocalypse* is a stand-alone adventure that takes place in and around the Sumber Hills in the Dessarin Valley, a lightly settled region of caravan towns, isolated homesteads, and wilderness. Four evil elemental cults have taken refuge there and are building secret temples in the ruins of a dungeon complex beneath the hills. By the time the characters reach 5th level, they will have visited several settlements in the valley, explored ruins in the Sumber Hills, and defeated a number of low- to middle-rank elemental cultists.

You can transition the characters from *Princes of the Apocalypse* to this adventure by having them defend the town of Triboar from a giant attack. In this scenario, Triboar becomes the starting point for this adventure (see chapter 2), and the characters are pulled away from the threat of Elemental Evil to focus on the giant threat instead. Here are a few hooks to lure the characters to Triboar, if they aren't there already.

## HARPER SYMPATHIZER

Endrith Vallivoe, a retired caravan merchant living in the village of Red Larch, is friendly toward the Harpers. If he suspects or knows that one or more characters have ties to the Harpers, he urges them to speak to Darathra Shendrel, the lord protector of Triboar. He doesn't reveal that she's a Harper, but he's certain that she has need of adventurers in these "troubled times."

## ERRANT PRIEST

A priest of Helm, Silvarren Loomshank, is scheduled to relieve Imdarr Relvaunder, one of the priests at the Allfaiths Shrine in Red Larch. Silvarren is several days overdue, however, and Imdarr overheard a rumor that Silvarren is getting drunk nightly at the Talking Troll, a tavern in Triboar. Imdarr asks the characters to verify this rumor and, if it is true, to urge Silvarren to pull himself together and fulfill his obligations.

## HOMESTEADS IN PERIL

Herivin Dardragon, the halfling proprietor of the Harvest Inn in the town of Westbridge, has received reports that ogres and hill giants are pillaging farms along the Long Road between Westbridge and Triboar. Characters who head north to investigate can see that the reports are true. At one damaged farm, the characters encounter halflings who lost an orchard of olive trees and most of their livestock to hill giants. The Skittermarsh clan has gathered its remaining livestock (a sickly cow and four hungry goats) and packed its belongings on three mules with the intention of relocating to Triboar. The family matriarch, Misty Skittermarsh, offers the characters a 100 gp gem if they escort her family to Triboar.

---

## USING THE ELEMENTAL CULTS

Here are examples of how you can weave *Princes of the Apocalypse* and *Storm King's Thunder* together by having cultists aid the giants, as a way to hide their own plans:

- The Cult of the Black Earth sends cultists to Deadstone Cleft (see chapter 6, "Canyon of the Stone Giants"). They provide Thane Kayalithica and her stone giants with information on the defensive capabilities of nearby settlements and offer to help lay waste to them. The cultists might know about the earth primordial trapped under Deadstone Cleft and want to communicate with it.
- The Cult of the Eternal Flame helps Duke Zalto and his drow allies (see chapter 8, "Forge of the Fire Giants") steal Maegera, the fire primordial trapped in Gauntlgrym. The cultists believe that the fire primordial is the offspring of Imix, the Prince of Evil Fire, whom they worship as a god.
- The Cult of the Howling Hatred, after witnessing several cloud giant castles drifting in the skies over the Sword Coast, sends representatives to meet with the cloud giants and learn their intentions. Countess Sansuri is fascinated by the cult's ability to create *devastation orbs* and wants a demonstration. Characters who visit her castle (see chapter 9, "Castle of the Cloud Giants") might encounter a team of air cultists with a *devastation orb* in their possession.
- The Cult of the Crushing Wave might help Chief Guh and her hill giants dam the river that runs alongside her den (see chapter 5, "Den of the Hill Giants"). Water cultists might also be helping the Kraken Society guard King Hekaton (see chapter 11, "Caught in the Tentacles").

# OUT OF THE ABYSS

*Out of the Abyss* takes place almost entirely in the Underdark, a subterranean expanse of caverns, tunnels, fissures, and lakes. The characters start the adventure as prisoners of the drow and, after escaping their captors, make their way to the surface. If they succeed, they are contacted by King Bruenor Battlehammer of Gauntlgrym and asked to lead an expedition back down into the Underdark, to deal with a terrible demonic threat.

If you run that adventure as written, the characters are 8th level or thereabouts when they reach Gauntlgrym. You can plan to have them surface when they reach 5th level instead, then segue from *Out of the Abyss* to *Storm King's Thunder*. Because this adventure takes place in the lands directly above the locations in *Out of the Abyss*, you can have the characters surface near one of the three locations in chapter 2.

Once the characters become embroiled in the affairs of giants, you might want to play down the demonic threat in the Underdark. Or you can move back and forth between the two adventures, giving players the option of accepting Bruenor's quest to descend into the Underdark before returning to the surface to deal with the giants. In the latter case, it's likely that the characters will be higher level than normal, but you can make the encounters in this adventure more challenging to compensate (see the "Modifying Encounter Difficulty" section in chapter 3 of the *Dungeon Master's Guide*).

# Appendix B: Magic Items

The magic items that are introduced in this adventure are detailed here in alphabetical order.

## Banner of the Krig Rune
*Wondrous Item, Rare (Requires Attunement)*

Crafted from a thick, red fabric, this banner measures 5 feet high and 3 feet wide. The krig (war) rune is displayed on the fabric with round, metal plates sewn into it. It can be attached to a 10-foot pole to serve as a standard. Furling or unfurling the banner requires an action. The banner has the following properties.

**Mark of Courage.** As a bonus action, you can touch the unfurled banner and cause it to emanate courage. You and your allies are immune to the frightened condition while within 20 feet of it. This benefit lasts for 10 minutes or until the banner is furled. Once you use this property, you can't use it again until you finish a short or long rest.

**Sentinel Standard.** You can see invisible creatures while they are within 20 feet of the unfurled banner and within your line of sight.

**Standard's Shield.** As a bonus action, you can touch the unfurled banner and invoke this power. Any ranged attack roll that targets you or an ally of yours has disadvantage if the target is within 20 feet of the unfurled banner. This benefit lasts for 1 minute or until the banner is furled. Once you use this property, you can't use it again until you finish a short or long rest.

**Gift of Battle.** You can transfer the banner's magic to a place by tracing the krig rune on the ground with your finger. The point where you trace it becomes the center of a spherical area of magic that has a 500-foot radius and that is fixed to the place. The transfer takes 8 hours of work that requires the banner to be within 5 feet of you and during which you choose creatures, creature types, or both that will benefit from the magic. At the end, the banner is destroyed, and the area gains the following property:

> While in the 500-foot-radius sphere, the creatures you chose during the transfer process are immune to the frightened condition and gain a +1 bonus to attack rolls and AC.

## Blod Stone
*Wondrous Item, Rare (Requires Attunement)*

This diamond contains the blood of a creature—blood that appears in the form of the blod (blood) rune. While the item is on your person, you can use your action to divine the location of the creature nearest to you that is related to the blood in the item and that isn't Undead. You sense the distance and direction of the creature relative to your location. The creature is either the one whose blood is in the item or a blood relative.

This item is made from a large diamond worth at least 5,000 gp. When the blood of a creature is poured onto it during the creation process, the blood seeps into the heart of the gem. If the gem is destroyed, the blood evaporates and is gone forever. A vengeful being might use a *blod stone* to hunt down an entire bloodline. Such stones are sometimes given as gifts to siblings or handed down from parent to child.

## Claw of the Wyrm Rune
*Wondrous Item, Rare (Requires Attunement)*

This dragon's claw has been covered with a coat of molten silver, upon which has been inscribed the wyrm (dragon) rune. The claw has the following properties.

**Wyrmslayer.** As an action, you can point the claw at a Dragon within 30 feet of you. The target must then succeed on a DC 15 Constitution saving throw or gain vulnerability to all damage types until the end of your next turn. This property can be used three times. The claw regains all expended uses at the next dawn.

**Wyrm Shield.** While the claw is displayed on your person, you have resistance to the damage caused by the breath weapon of any Dragon.

**Wyrm Ward.** You can transfer the claw's magic to a place by tracing the wyrm rune on the ground with your finger. The point where you trace it becomes the center of a spherical area of magic that has a 100-foot radius and that is fixed to the place. The transfer takes 8 hours of work that requires the claw to be within 5 feet of you. At the end, the claw is destroyed, and the area gains the following property:

> While in the 100-foot-radius sphere, any Dragon has disadvantage on saving throws and can have a flying spccd no higher than 10 feet.

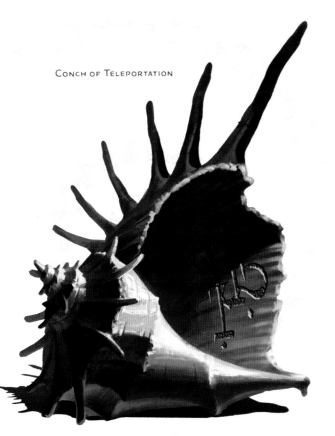

CONCH OF TELEPORTATION

## Conch of Teleportation

*Wondrous Item, Very Rare (Requires Attunement)*

This item is an ordinary, albeit rather large, conch shell that has been inscribed with the uvar rune. The conch measures 2½ feet long and weighs 20 pounds.

As an action, you can cast the *teleport* spell by blowing into the shell. The destination is fixed, and there is no chance of either a mishap or the spell being off target. Anyone teleported by the conch appears in a specific location designated by the item's creator at the time the uvar rune is inscribed on the conch. It doesn't allow teleportation to any other destination. Once its spell is cast, the conch can't be used again until the next dawn.

## Gavel of the Venn Rune

*Wondrous Item, Rare (Requires Attunement)*

This wooden gavel is small by giant reckoning but nearly the size of a warhammer in human hands. The venn (friend) rune is inscribed in mithral in the base of the haft. Among giants, this item is used as part of rituals to resolve disputes. The gavel has the following properties.

***Arbiter's Shield.*** At the start of every combat, attack rolls against you have disadvantage before the start of your first turn, provided that the gavel is on your person.

***Bond of Amity.*** As an action, you can use the gavel to strike a point on a hard surface. The first time in the next minute that a creature within 60 feet of that point deals damage to another creature with an attack that hits, the attacker takes psychic damage equal to half the damage it dealt to the target. Once you use this property, you can't use it again until you finish a long rest.

***Gift of Truth.*** You can transfer the gavel's magic to a place by tracing the venn rune on the ground with your finger. The point where you trace it becomes the center of a spherical area of magic that has a 30-foot radius and that is fixed to the place. The transfer takes 8 hours of work that requires the gavel to be within 5 feet of you. At the end, the gavel is destroyed, and the area gains the following property:

Whenever a creature utters a lie while within the 30-foot-radius sphere, that creature takes 5 psychic damage and flinches visibly.

## Gurt's Greataxe

*Weapon (Greataxe), Legendary (Requires Attunement)*

In the Year of the Icy Axe (123 DR), the frost giant lord Gurt fell to Uthgar Gardolfsson—leader of the folk who would become the Uthgardt—in a battle that marked the ascendance of humankind over the giants in the Dessarin Valley. *Gurt's greataxe* was buried in Morgur's Mound until it was unearthed and brought back to Waterdeep. After laying in the city's vaults for decades, the axe was given to Harshnag, a frost giant adventurer, in recognition of his service to Waterdeep. Uthgardt recognize the weapon on sight and attack any Giant that wields it.

You gain a +1 bonus to attack and damage rolls made with this magic weapon. It is sized for a frost giant, weighs 325 pounds, and deals 3d12 slashing damage on a hit, plus an extra 2d12 slashing damage if the target is human.

The axe sheds light as a torch when the temperature around it drops below 0 degrees Fahrenheit. The light can't be shut off in these conditions.

As an action, you can cast a version of the *heat metal* spell (save DC 13) that deals cold damage instead of fire damage. Once this power is used, it can't be used again until the next dawn.

## Ingot of the Skold Rune

*Wondrous Item, Very Rare (Requires Attunement)*

This appears to be a simple ingot of iron ore, about a foot long and a few inches across. Inspection of its surface reveals the faint, silvery outline of the skold (shield) rune. The ingot has the following properties, which work only while it's on your person.

***Runic Shield.*** You have a +1 bonus to AC.

***Shield Bond.*** As a bonus action, choose a creature that you can see within 30 feet of you, other than yourself. Until the end of your next turn, any damage the target takes is reduced to 1, but you take half the damage prevented in this way. The damage you take can't be reduced in any way. Once you use this property, you can't use it again until you finish a short or long rest.

***Shield Ward.*** You can transfer the ingot's magic to a nonmagical item—a shield or a two-handed melee weapon—by tracing the skold rune there with your finger. The transfer takes 8 hours of work that requires the two items to be within 5 feet of each other. At the end, the ingot is destroyed, and the rune appears in silver on the chosen item, which gains a benefit based on its form:

**Shield.** The shield is now a rare magic item that requires attunement. Its magic gives you a +1 bonus to AC, and the first time after each of your long rests that damage reduces you to 0 hit points, you are instead reduced to 1 hit point. You must be wielding the shield to gain these benefits.

**Weapon.** The weapon is now an uncommon magic weapon. It grants you a +1 bonus to AC while you're holding it.

## Korolnor Scepter

*Wondrous Item, Legendary (Requires Attunement)*

The *Korolnor Scepter* is one of ten Ruling Scepters of Shanatar, forged by the dwarven gods and given to the ruling houses of the ancient dwarven empire. The *Korolnor Scepter*'s location was unknown for the longest time until a storm giant queen, Neri, found it in a barnacle-covered shipwreck at the bottom of the Trackless Sea. The Ruling Scepters are all roughly the same size and shape, but their materials and properties vary.

The *Korolnor Scepter* is a tapered mithral rod as thick and long as a dwarf's forearm, with a small platinum knob at the bottom and a rounded disk adorned with a ring of seven tiny blue gems at the top.

You gain a +3 bonus to attack and damage rolls made with this scepter, which can be wielded as a magic club.

You can use the properties of the *Wyrmskull Throne*, as well as the properties of the scepter itself. The scepter has 10 charges, and it regains 1d6 + 4 expended charges at dawn. Its properties are as follows:

- If you are underground or underwater, you can use an action to expend 1 charge to determine the distance to the surface.
- As an action, you can expend 2 charges to cast the *sending* spell from the scepter.
- As an action, you can expend 3 charges to cast the *teleport* spell from the scepter. If the destination is within 60 feet of the *Wyrmskull Throne*, there is no chance of a teleport error or mishap occurring.

## NAVIGATION ORB
*Wondrous Item, Very Rare (Requires Attunement)*

A *navigation orb* is a hollow, 7-foot-diameter sphere of thin, polished mithral with a large skye (cloud) rune embossed on its outer surface. The orb levitates 10 feet above the ground and is keyed to a particular cloud castle, allowing you to control that castle's altitude and movement while the orb is inside the castle. If the orb is destroyed or removed from its castle, the castle's altitude and location remain fixed until the orb is returned or replaced.

As an action, you can cause one of the following effects to occur if you are touching the orb:

- The castle moves at a speed of 1 mph in a straight line, in a direction of your choice, until the castle stops or is made to stop, or until another action is used to change its direction. If this movement brings the castle into contact with the ground, the castle lands gently.
- The castle, if it is moving, comes to a gradual stop.
- The castle makes a slow, 90-degree turn clockwise or counterclockwise (turning a northerly view into a westerly view, for example). The castle can turn while it is moving in a straight line.

Any creature touching the orb knows the altitude of the base of the castle above the ground or water below it.

## OPAL OF THE ILD RUNE
*Wondrous Item, Rare (Requires Attunement)*

This triangular fire opal measures about three inches on each side and is half an inch thick. The ild (fire) rune shimmers within its core, causing it to be slightly warm to the touch. The opal has the following properties, which work only while it's on your person.

***Ignite.*** As an action, you can ignite an object within 10 feet of you. The object must be flammable, and the fire starts in a circle no larger than 1 foot in diameter.

***Fire's Friend.*** You have resistance to cold damage.

***Fire Tamer.*** As an action, you can extinguish any open flame within 10 feet of you. You choose how much fire to extinguish in that radius.

***Gift of Flame.*** You can transfer the opal's magic to a nonmagical item—a weapon or a suit of armor—by tracing the ild rune there with your finger. The transfer takes 8 hours of work that requires the two items to be within 5 feet of each other. At the end, the opal is destroyed, and the rune appears in red on the chosen item, which gains a benefit based on its form:

**Weapon.** The weapon is now an uncommon magic weapon. It deals an extra 1d6 fire damage to any target it hits.

**Armor.** The armor is now a rare magic item that requires attunement. You have resistance to cold damage while wearing the armor.

## ORB OF THE STEIN RUNE
*Wondrous Item, Rare (Requires Attunement)*

This orb of granite is about the size of an adult human's fist. The stein (stone) rune appears on it in the form of crystalline veins that run across the surface. The orb has the following properties, which work only while it's on your person.

***Indomitable Stand.*** As an action, you can channel the orb's magic to hold your ground. For the next minute or until you move any distance, you have advantage on all checks and saving throws to resist effects that force you to move. In addition, any enemy that moves to a space within 10 feet of you must succeed on a DC 12 Strength saving throw or be unable to move any farther this turn.

***Stone Soul.*** You can't be petrified.

***Earthen Step.*** You can cast *meld into stone* as a bonus action. Once you use this property, you can't use it again until you finish a short or long rest.

***Gift of Stone.*** You can transfer the orb's magic to a nonmagical item—a shield or a pair of boots—by tracing the stein rune there with your finger. The transfer takes 8 hours of work that requires the two items to be within 5 feet of each other. At the end, the orb is destroyed, and the rune appears in silver on the chosen item, which gains a benefit based on its form:

**Shield.** The shield is now a rare magic item that requires attunement. While you wield it, you have resistance to all damage dealt by ranged weapon attacks.

**Boots.** The pair of boots is now an uncommon magic item that requires attunement. While you wear the boots, you have advantage on Strength saving throws, and you can use your reaction to avoid being knocked prone.

## PENNANT OF THE VIND RUNE
*Wondrous Item, Very Rare (Requires Attunement)*

This blue pennant is crafted from silk and is five feet long and whips about as if buffeted by a wind. The vind (wind) rune appears on its surface, looking almost like a cloud. The pennant has the following properties, which work only while it's on your person.

**Wind Step.** As an action, you fly up to 20 feet. If you don't land at the end of this flight, you fall unless you have another means of staying aloft.

**Comforting Wind.** You can't suffocate.

**Wind's Grasp.** As a reaction when you fall, you can cause yourself to take no damage from the fall. Once you use this property, you can't use it again until you finish a short or long rest.

**Wind Walker.** While you are attuned to this rune, you can cast *levitate* as a bonus action. Once you use this property, you can't use it again until you finish a short or long rest.

**Gift of Wind.** You can transfer the pennant's magic to a nonmagical item—a suit of armor, a pair of boots, or a cloak—by tracing the vind rune there with your finger. The transfer takes 8 hours of work that requires the two items to be within 5 feet of each other. At the end, the pennant is destroyed, and the rune appears in silver on the chosen item, which gains a benefit based on its form:

**Armor.** The armor is now an uncommon magic item that requires attunement. You gain a bonus to speed of 5 feet while you wear the armor, and if it normally imposes disadvantage on Stealth checks, it no longer does so.

**Boots/Cloak.** The pair of boots or cloak is now a rare magic item that requires attunement. While wearing the item, you can convert up to 20 feet of your movement on each of your turns into flight. If you don't land at the end of this flight, you fall unless you have another means of staying aloft. You can also cast *feather fall* once from the item, and you regain the ability to do so when you finish a short or long rest.

## POTION OF GIANT SIZE
*Potion, Legendary*

When you drink this potion, you become Huge for 24 hours if you are Medium or smaller, otherwise the potion does nothing. For that duration, your Strength becomes 25, if it isn't already higher, and your hit point maximum is doubled (your current hit points are doubled when you drink the potion). In addition, the reach of your melee attacks increases by 5 feet.

Everything you are carrying and wearing also increases in size for the duration. When rolling damage for weapons enlarged in this manner, roll three times the normal number of dice; for example, an enlarged longsword would deal 3d8 slashing damage (instead of 1d8), or 3d10 slashing damage (instead of 1d10) when used with two hands.

When the effect ends, any hit points you have above your hit point maximum become temporary hit points.

This potion is a pale white liquid made from the tongue of a giant clam, with a pungent aroma akin to that of rotting algae. It tastes sweet, however, when consumed.

## ROBE OF SERPENTS
*Wondrous Item, Uncommon (Requires Attunement)*

A *robe of serpents* is a stylish silk garment that is popular among wealthy nobles and retired assassins. The robe is emblazoned with 1d4 + 3 stylized serpents, all brightly colored.

As a bonus action on your turn, you can transform one of the robe's serpents into a **giant poisonous snake**. The snake instantly falls from the robe, slithers into an unoccupied space next to you, and acts on your initiative count. The snake can tell friendly creatures from hostile ones and attacks the latter. The snake disappears in a harmless puff of smoke after 1 hour, when it drops to 0 hit points, or when you dismiss it (no action required). Once detached, a snake can't return to the robe. When all of the robe's snakes have detached, the robe becomes a nonmagical garment.

## ROD OF THE VONINDOD
*Rod, Rare (Requires Attunement)*

The fire giant duke Zalto hired a wizard to craft several of these adamantine rods. Each measures 4 feet long, weighs 100 pounds, and is sized to fit comfortably in a fire giant's hand. The rod has two prongs at one end and a molded handle grip on the opposite end.

The rod has 10 charges and regains 1d6 + 4 of its expended charges daily at dawn. As an action, you can grasp it by the handle and expend 1 charge to cast the *locate object* spell from it. When the rod is used to detect objects made of adamantine, such as fragments of the Vonindod construct, its range increases to 10 miles.

## SHARD OF THE ISE RUNE
*Wondrous Item, Very Rare (Requires Attunement)*

This shard of ice is long and slender, roughly the size of a dagger. The ise (ice) rune glows within it. The shard has the following properties, which work only while it's on your person.

**Frigid Touch.** As an action, you can touch a body of water and freeze the water in a 10-foot-radius sphere around the spot you touched. Once you use this property, you can't use it again until you finish a short or long rest.

**Frost Friend.** You have resistance to fire damage.

**Icy Mantle.** As an action, you can touch yourself or another creature with water on your finger. The water creates an icy mantle of protection. The next time within the next minute that the target takes bludgeoning, slashing, or piercing damage, that damage is reduced to 0, and the mantle is destroyed. Once you use this property, you can't use it again until you finish a short or long rest.

**Winter's Howl.** As an action, you can cast *sleet storm* (spell save DC 17). You regain this ability after you finish a short or long rest.

**Gift of Frost.** You can transfer the shard's magic to a nonmagical item—a cloak or a pair of boots—by tracing the ise rune there with your finger. The transfer takes 8 hours of work that requires the two items to be within 5 feet of each other. At the end, the shard is destroyed, and the rune appears in blue on the chosen item, which gains a benefit based on its form:

**Cloak.** The cloak is now a rare magic item that requires attunement. While wearing it, you have resistance to fire damage, and you have advantage on Dexterity (Stealth) checks made while in snowy terrain.

**Boots.** The pair of boots is now a rare magic item that requires attunement. While wearing it, you ignore difficult terrain while walking, and you can walk on water.

## WYRMSKULL THRONE

*Wondrous Item, Artifact*

Built by dwarven gods and entrusted to the rulers of Shanatar, an ancient dwarven empire, the *Wyrmskull Throne* was a symbol of dwarven power and pride for ages untold. The throne hovers a foot off the ground and is a massive thing made of polished obsidian with oversized feet—the impaled skulls of four ancient blue dragons. Runes glisten in the carved obsidian, winking to life with blue energy when the throne's powers are activated.

After the fall of Shanatar, the *Wyrmskull Throne* fell into the clutches of less honorable creatures. A band of adventurers wrested the throne from the aquatic elf tyrant Gantar Kraok and sold it to the storm giant Neri for a considerable fortune. Neri had the throne magically enlarged and gave it to her husband, King Hekaton, as a gift, along with one of the Ruling Scepters of Shanatar, which she had found in a wreck at the bottom of the Trackless Sea. Only a creature attuned to a Ruling Scepter and in possession of it can harness the powers of the *Wyrmskull Throne*, which has become the centerpiece of King Hekaton's throne room in the undersea citadel of Maelstrom. Fear of the throne's power has helped prevent evil giants from challenging or threatening Hekaton's leadership.

Any creature not attuned to a Ruling Scepter who sits on the throne is paralyzed and encased in a magical force field. While encased, the creature can't be touched or moved from the throne. Touching a Ruling Scepter to the force field dispels the field, though the creature remains paralyzed until it is separated from the throne.

Any creature seated on the throne can hear faint whispers in Draconic—the whisperings of the four blue dragons whose skulls adorn the throne. Although powerless, these spirits try to influence the decisions of the throne's master.

***Properties of the Throne.*** The throne has 9 charges and regains all expended charges daily at dawn. A creature that sits on the throne while attuned to a Ruling Scepter in its possession can harness the throne's properties, which are as follows:

- The throne gains a flying speed of 30 feet and can hover and flies where the creature wills. This property doesn't expend any charges.
- Both the throne and the creature sitting on it can move through earth and stone without disturbing the material they move through. This property doesn't expend any charges.
- As an action, the creature can expend 1 charge to cast *lightning bolt* (spell save DC 19) from the throne.

WYRMSKULL THRONE

The spell is cast as though using a 9th-level spell slot and deals 49 (14d6) lightning damage. The bolt discharges from the mouth of one of the throne's blue dragon skulls.

- As an action, the creature can expend 2 charges to cast the *globe of invulnerability* spell from the throne. The globe encloses both the creature and the throne.
- As an action, the creature can expend 3 charges to create a spectral image of an ancient blue dragon that surrounds both it and the throne. The spectral dragon lasts for 1 minute. At the end of each of the creature's turns, the spectral dragon makes one bite attack and two claw attacks against targets of the creature's choice. These attacks have the same attack bonus, reach, and damage as an ancient blue dragon's bite and claw attacks.

***Destroying the Throne.*** The *Wyrmskull Throne* can be destroyed by breaking at least five Ruling Scepters of Shanatar simultaneously on it. This fact has never been recorded or sung of among the dwarves or any bards or storytellers, and it can't be discovered with an ability check. Characters who want to destroy the throne must go on a quest to learn the method for doing so. The throne's destruction triggers an explosion, as shards of obsidian fly out in all directions. Each creature and object within a 30-foot-radius sphere centered on the throne must succeed on a DC 21 Dexterity saving throw, taking 70 (20d6) slashing damage on a failed save, or half as much damage on a successful one.

NOT ALL GIANTS WILL LIVE TO SEE
THE NORTH BURN.

# APPENDIX C: CREATURES

This appendix details the new monsters that appear in this adventure. It also provides optional actions and traits for giants.

## CRAG CAT

The creature referred to in Northlander lore as the Hunter of Men is a sure-footed predator that can be found anywhere except deep forest, preferring ledges and cliffs in the mountains. Its cry resembles a human scream of terror. It often elicits such sounds from its victims, for it prefers human flesh to all other prey.

Crag cats blend in with natural surroundings. During the winter, their fur turns white to blend in with the snow. At other times of the year, their fur is gray, enabling them to hide among the rocks more easily.

The crag cat knows its territory and often attacks when its prey is asleep, exhausted, or otherwise weakened. Although crag cats are typically solitary, they can be found in family groups of two parents and 1d4 Small noncombatant cubs in the spring, or in hungry packs in severe winter weather.

CRAG CAT

### CRAG CAT
Large Monstrosity, Unaligned

**Armor Class** 13
**Hit Points** 34 (4d10 + 12)
**Speed** 40 ft., climb 30 ft.

| STR | DEX | CON | INT | WIS | CHA |
|-----|-----|-----|-----|-----|-----|
| 16 (+3) | 17 (+3) | 16 (+3) | 4 (−3) | 14 (+2) | 8 (−1) |

**Skills** Perception +4, Stealth +7
**Senses** darkvision 60 ft., passive Perception 14
**Languages** —
**Challenge** 1 (200 XP)

***Nondetection.*** The cat can't be targeted or detected by any divination magic or perceived through magical scrying sensors.

***Pounce.*** If the cat moves at least 20 feet straight toward a creature and then hits it with a claw attack on the same turn, that target must succeed on a DC 13 Strength saving throw or be knocked prone. If the target is prone, the cat can make one bite attack against it as a bonus action.

***Spell Turning.*** The cat has advantage on saving throws against any spell that targets only the cat (not an area). If the cat's saving throw succeeds and the spell is of 7th level or lower, the spell has no effect on the cat and instead targets the caster.

### ACTIONS

***Bite.*** *Melee Weapon Attack:* +5 to hit, reach 5 ft., one target. *Hit:* 8 (1d10 + 3) piercing damage.

***Claw.*** *Melee Weapon Attack:* +5 to hit, reach 5 ft., one target. *Hit:* 7 (1d8 + 3) slashing damage.

## HULKING CRAB

Much bigger than a giant crab, a hulking crab has a body 15 to 20 feet in diameter. Its shell is often covered with coral, anemones, ship wreckage, or some other sort of detritus salvaged from the ocean floor.

### HULKING CRAB
Huge Beast, Unaligned

**Armor Class** 17 (natural armor)
**Hit Points** 76 (8d12 + 24)
**Speed** 20 ft., swim 30 ft.

| STR | DEX | CON | INT | WIS | CHA |
|-----|-----|-----|-----|-----|-----|
| 19 (+4) | 8 (−1) | 16 (+3) | 3 (−4) | 11 (+0) | 3 (−4) |

**Skills** Stealth +2
**Senses** blindsight 30 ft., passive Perception 10
**Languages** —
**Challenge** 5 (1,800 XP)

***Amphibious.*** The crab can breathe air and water.

***Shell Camouflage.*** While the crab remains motionless with its eyestalks and pincers tucked close to its body, it resembles a natural formation or a pile of detritus. A creature within 30 feet of it can discern its true nature with a successful DC 15 Intelligence (Nature) check.

### ACTIONS

***Multiattack.*** The crab makes two Claw attacks.

***Claw.*** *Melee Weapon Attack:* +7 to hit, reach 10 ft., one target. *Hit:* 20 (3d10 + 4) bludgeoning damage, and the target is grappled (escape DC 15). The crab has two claws, each of which can grapple only one target.

# IYMRITH THE DRAGON

The treacherous Iymrith is an **ancient blue dragon**, with the following changes:

- She speaks Giant and Terran in addition to Common and Draconic.
- She gains the Spellcasting and Change Shape action options, both described below.
- When she casts her *stone shape* spell, Iymrith can shape the targeted stone into a living **gargoyle** instead of altering the stone as described in the spell's description. This transformation is permanent and can't be reversed or dispelled.

**Change Shape.** Iymrith magically polymorphs into a female storm giant or back into her true form. She reverts to her true form if she dies. Any equipment she is wearing or carrying is absorbed or borne by the new form (the dragon's choice).

In storm giant form, Iymrith retains her alignment, hit points, Hit Dice, ability to speak, proficiencies, Legendary Resistance, lair actions, and Intelligence, Wisdom, and Charisma scores, as well as this action. Her statistics are otherwise replaced by those of the new form.

**Spellcasting.** Iymrith casts one of the following spells, requiring no spell components and using Charisma as the spellcasting ability (spell save DC 20):

1/day each: *detect magic, dispel magic, ice storm, stone shape, teleport*

# MAEGERA THE DAWN TITAN

Maegera is powerful Elemental that has been trapped in the forges of Gauntlgrym for millennia. About fifty years ago, Maegera briefly escaped and triggered the eruption of Mount Hotenow. Lava from the volcano flowed toward the coast, laying waste to Neverwinter. The city is still rebuilding in the wake of that catastrophe.

The fire giant duke Zalto recently sent a team of drow to infiltrate Gauntlgrym and trap Maegera in an *iron flask*. Zalto needs the primordial to ignite an adamantine forge beneath the Ice Spires. Returning Maegera to Gauntlgrym is one way to thwart the fire giant's plans.

Maegera looks like a 50-foot-tall, multi-limbed beast made of flame, with smoldering black pits for eyes.

## MAEGERA THE DAWN TITAN
*Gargantuan Elemental, Chaotic Neutral*

**Armor Class** 16
**Hit Points** 341 (22d20 + 110)
**Speed** 50 ft.

| STR | DEX | CON | INT | WIS | CHA |
|-----|-----|-----|-----|-----|-----|
| 21 (+5) | 22 (+6) | 20 (+5) | 10 (+0) | 10 (+0) | 19 (+4) |

**Saving Throws** Con +12, Wis +7, Cha +11
**Damage Resistances** bludgeoning, piercing, and slashing damage from nonmagical attacks
**Damage Immunities** fire, poison
**Condition Immunities** charmed, frightened, grappled, paralyzed, petrified, poisoned, prone, restrained
**Senses** blindsight 120 ft., passive Perception 10
**Languages** Ignan
**Challenge** 23 (50,000 XP)

**Empowered Attacks.** Maegera's slam attacks are treated as magical for the purpose of overcoming resistance and immunity to damage from nonmagical attacks.

**Fire Aura.** At the start of each of Maegera's turns, each creature within 30 feet of it takes 35 (10d6) fire damage, and flammable objects in the aura that aren't being worn or carried ignite. A creature also takes 35 (10d6) fire damage from touching Maegera or from hitting it with a melee attack while within 10 feet of it, and a creature takes that damage the first time on a turn that Maegera moves into its space. Nonmagical weapons that hit Maegera are destroyed by fire immediately after dealing damage to it.

**Fire Form.** Maegera can enter a hostile creature's space and stop there. It can move through a space as narrow as 1 inch without squeezing if fire could pass through that space.

**Illumination.** Maegera sheds bright light in a 120-foot radius and dim light for an additional 120 feet.

**Magic Resistance.** Maegera has advantage on saving throws against spells and other magical effects.

## ACTIONS

**Multiattack.** Maegera makes three Slam attacks.

**Slam.** *Melee Weapon Attack:* +12 to hit, reach 15 ft., one target. *Hit:* 15 (3d6 + 5) bludgeoning damage plus 35 (10d6) fire damage.

**Spellcasting.** Maegera casts *fireball* (spell save DC 19), requiring no material components and using Charisma as the spellcasting ability.

## LEGENDARY ACTIONS

Maegera can take 3 legendary actions, choosing from the options below. It can take only one legendary action at a time and only at the end of another creature's turn. Maegera regains spent legendary actions at the start of its turn.

**Quench Magic (Costs 1 Action).** Maegera targets one creature that it can see within 60 feet of it. Any resistance or immunity to fire damage that the target gains from a spell or a magic item is suppressed. This effect lasts until the end of Maegera's next turn.

**Smoke Cloud (Costs 2 Actions).** Maegera exhales a billowing cloud of hot smoke and embers that fills a 60-foot cube. Each creature in that area takes 11 (2d10) fire damage. The cloud lasts until the end of Maegera's next turn. Creatures completely within the cloud are blinded and can't be seen.

**Create Fire Elemental (Costs 3 Actions).** Maegera's hit points are reduced by 50 as part of it separates and becomes a **fire elemental** with 102 hit points. The elemental appears in an unoccupied space within 15 feet of Maegera and acts on Maegera's initiative count. Maegera can't use this action if it has 50 hit points or fewer. The elemental obeys Maegera's commands and fights until destroyed.

# Purple Wormling

A purple wormling is a baby purple worm no more than
six weeks old. Its rubbery body is 9 feet long and weighs
1,500 pounds. Its mouth and musculature aren't yet
strong enough to allow the wormling to burrow through
rock. The poison in its tail stinger and the acid in its
gullet are still relatively weak as well. Nevertheless, the
wormling is a voracious feeder and attacks just about
anything it can wrap its mouth around. A wormling's
gullet can hold up to four Small creatures.

# Tressym

A tressym is a mischievous winged cat as big as a house
cat, with a wingspan of 3 feet.

Thought to be the results of wizardly experimentation
on house cats, tressym are intelligent and have been
known to form strong friendships with Humanoids, particularly rangers and wizards. Tressym get along well

TRESSYM

---

## Purple Wormling
*Large Monstrosity, Unaligned*

**Armor Class** 12 (natural armor)
**Hit Points** 42 (5d10 + 15)
**Speed** 20 ft.

| STR | DEX | CON | INT | WIS | CHA |
|-----|-----|-----|-----|-----|-----|
| 16 (+3) | 7 (−2) | 16 (+3) | 1 (−5) | 6 (−2) | 2 (−4) |

**Senses** blindsight 30 ft., tremorsense 30 ft.,
  passive Perception 8
**Languages** —
**Challenge** 2 (450 XP)

### Actions

**Multiattack.** The wormling makes one Bite attack and one Tail
Stinger attack.

**Bite.** *Melee Weapon Attack:* +5 to hit, reach 5 ft., one target.
*Hit:* 7 (1d8 + 3) piercing damage, and if the target is a Small or
smaller creature, it must succeed on a DC 13 Dexterity saving
throw or be swallowed by the wormling. A swallowed creature
is blinded and restrained, it has total cover against attacks and
other effects outside the wormling, and it takes 3 (1d6) acid
damage at the start of each of the wormling's turns.

If the wormling takes 10 damage or more on a single turn
from a creature inside it, the wormling must succeed on a DC
21 Constitution saving throw at the end of that turn or regurgi-
tate all swallowed creatures, which fall prone in a space within
10 feet of the wormling. If the wormling dies, a swallowed
creature is no longer restrained by it and can escape from the
corpse by using 5 feet of movement, exiting prone.

**Tail Stinger.** *Melee Weapon Attack:* +5 to hit, reach 5 ft., one
creature. *Hit:* 5 (1d4 + 3) piercing damage, and the target
must make a DC 13 Constitution saving throw, taking 10 (3d6)
poison damage on a failed save, or half as much damage on a
successful one.

---

## Tressym
*Tiny Monstrosity, Any Alignment*

**Armor Class** 12
**Hit Points** 5 (2d4)
**Speed** 40 ft., climb 30 ft., fly 40 ft.

| STR | DEX | CON | INT | WIS | CHA |
|-----|-----|-----|-----|-----|-----|
| 3 (−4) | 15 (+2) | 10 (+0) | 11 (+0) | 12 (+1) | 12 (+1) |

**Skills** Perception +5, Stealth +4
**Damage Immunities** poison
**Condition Immunities** poisoned
**Senses** darkvision 60 ft., passive Perception 15
**Languages** understands Common but can't speak
**Challenge** 0 (10 XP)

**Detect Invisibility.** Within 60 feet of the tressym, magical invisibility fails to conceal anything from the tressym's sight.

**Keen Smell.** The tressym has advantage on Wisdom (Perception) checks that rely on smell.

**Poison Sense.** A tressym can detect whether a substance is
poisonous by taste, touch, or smell.

### Actions

**Claws.** *Melee Weapon Attack:* +0 to hit, reach 5 ft., one target.
*Hit:* 1 slashing damage.

with others of their kind, but they rarely lair or hunt together. They peacefully ignore bats, faerie dragons, and the like, but they hate stirges and evil flying monsters such as manticores. They also enjoy teasing dogs.

Tressym feed on small rodents, birds, and insects, stalking and pouncing on prey much as normal cats do, but with the added advantage of flight. Tressym don't, however, attack nestlings or despoil eggs.

Tressym mate with others of their kind, but they don't mate for life. A tressym can also mate with a normal cat, though only one out of every ten of their offspring will be a tressym; the others will be normal cats.

Tressym have good memories, particularly when it comes to danger. For example, a tressym that sees a human use a *wand of lightning bolts* remembers the danger of "sticks of wood held by humans" for the rest of its life. A lucky, healthy tressym can live to be 20 years old.

With the DM's permission, a person who casts the *find familiar* spell can choose to conjure a tressym instead of a normal cat.

# UTHGARDT SHAMAN

The Uthgardt are suspicious and resentful of most kinds of magic. Seldom do they choose to become shamans. Instead, the role is thrust upon those who are born with a strong connection to the spirit world. To be a shaman is to stand with one foot in the land of the living and the other in the land of the dead. Those who walk the shadowed path between two lands do so because the spirits of the dead compel them. Other Uthgardt fear and respect a shaman's power.

An Uthgardt shaman must possess a sacred bundle to cast spells. A sacred bundle is made up of sticks, bones, feathers, tufts of fur, and stones that have been "touched" by spirits. It takes a month for a shaman to assemble a sacred bundle, and a shaman can use only one such bundle at a time. A sacred bundle benefits only the shaman who created it, and it doesn't replace the normal components of a spell.

UTHGARDT
SHAMAN

---

> ## UTHGARDT SHAMAN TRIBAL SPELLS
>
> Depending on an Uthgardt shaman's tribe, the shaman's Spellcasting action gains additional spells, each of which the shaman can cast once per day.
>
> **Black Lion:** *feign death, revivify*
> **Black Raven:** *animal messenger* (raven only), *polymorph* (self only; into a raven only)
> **Blue Bear:** *enhance ability* (bear's endurance only), *heroism*
> **Elk:** *find steed* (cast as 1 action; elk only), *haste*
> **Gray Wolf:** *beast sense* (wolf or dire wolf only), *speak with animals* (wolf or dire wolf only)
> **Great Worm:** *crusader's mantle, hypnotic pattern*
> **Griffon:** *beast sense* (birds only), *fly*
> **Red Tiger:** *enhance ability* (cat's grace only), *jump*
> **Sky Pony:** *gust of wind, witch bolt*
> **Thunderbeast:** *enhance ability* (bull's strength only), *pass without trace*
> **Tree Ghost:** *barkskin, speak with plants*

---

## UTHGARDT SHAMAN

*Medium Humanoid (Human), Any Alignment*

---

**Armor Class** 13 (hide armor)
**Hit Points** 38 (7d8 + 7)
**Speed** 30 ft.

---

| STR | DEX | CON | INT | WIS | CHA |
|-----|-----|-----|-----|-----|-----|
| 14 (+2) | 12 (+1) | 13 (+1) | 10 (+0) | 15 (+2) | 12 (+1) |

---

**Skills** Medicine +4, Nature +4, Perception +4, Survival +6
**Senses** passive Perception 14
**Languages** Bothii, Common
**Challenge** 2 (450 XP)

---

### ACTIONS

***Spear.*** *Melee or Ranged Weapon Attack:* +4 to hit, reach 5 ft. or range 20/60 ft., one target. *Hit:* 5 (1d6 + 2) piercing damage, or 6 (1d8 + 2) piercing damage if used with two hands to make a melee attack.

***Shortbow.*** *Ranged Weapon Attack:* +3 to hit, range 80/320 ft., one target. *Hit:* 4 (1d6 + 1) piercing damage.

***Spellcasting (Requires a Sacred Bundle).*** The shaman casts one of the following spells, using Wisdom as the spellcasting ability (spell save DC 12; +4 to hit with spell attacks):

At will: *dancing lights, mage hand, message, thaumaturgy*
1/day each: *augury* (cast as 1 action), *bestow curse, cordon of arrows, detect magic, speak with dead, spirit guardians*

In addition to the spells that all Uthgardt shamans can cast, a shaman of a particular tribe gains additional spells based on tribal affiliation (see the "Uthgardt Shaman Tribal Spells" sidebar).

By communing with their ancestors' spirits, Uthgardt shamans can also learn secret rituals. These rituals almost always require some sort of blood sacrifice, and their effects are usually transformative. For example, some Black Raven shamans know a ritual that allows them to hatch giant ravens from normal raven eggs, and some shamans of the Griffon tribe can transform themselves into griffons by performing a ritual that requires them to drink copious amounts of horse blood.

## YAKFOLK WARRIOR

*Large Monstrosity, Typically Neutral Evil*

**Armor Class** 11 (leather armor)
**Hit Points** 60 (8d10 + 16)
**Speed** 30 ft.

| STR | DEX | CON | INT | WIS | CHA |
|-----|-----|-----|-----|-----|-----|
| 18 (+4) | 11 (+0) | 15 (+2) | 14 (+2) | 15 (+2) | 14 (+2) |

**Skills** Deception +4, Survival +4
**Senses** passive Perception 12
**Languages** Common, Yikaria
**Challenge** 3 (700 XP)

***Possession (Recharges after a Short or Long Rest).*** The yakfolk attempts to magically possess a Humanoid or Giant. The yakfolk must touch the target throughout a short rest, or the attempt fails. At the end of the rest, the target must succeed on a DC 12 Constitution saving throw or be possessed by the yakfolk, which disappears with everything it is carrying and wearing. Until the possession ends, the target is incapacitated, loses control of its body, and is unaware of its surroundings. The yakfolk now controls the body and can't be targeted by any attack, spell, or other effect, and it retains its alignment; its Intelligence, Wisdom, and Charisma scores; and its proficiencies. It otherwise uses the target's statistics, except the target's knowledge, class features, feats, and proficiencies.

The possession lasts until either the body drops to 0 hit points, the yakfolk ends the possession as an action, or the yakfolk is forced out of the body by an effect such as the *dispel evil and good* spell. When the possession ends, the yakfolk reappears in an unoccupied space within 5 feet of the body and is stunned until the end of its next turn. If the host body dies while it is possessed by the yakfolk, the yakfolk dies as well, and its body doesn't reappear.

### ACTIONS

***Multiattack.*** The yakfolk makes two Greatsword or Longbow attacks.

***Greatsword.*** *Melee Weapon Attack:* +6 to hit, reach 5 ft., one target. *Hit:* 18 (4d6 + 4) slashing damage.

***Longbow.*** *Ranged Weapon Attack:* +2 to hit, range 150/600 ft., one target. *Hit:* 9 (2d8) piercing damage.

# YAKFOLK (YIKARIA)

Yakfolk, known among themselves as Yikaria ("the Lucky Chosen" in their language), are ogre-sized bipeds with curved horns and dour expressions. Their hulking bodies are coated with thick fur and hair, and many outsiders can't tell the males and females apart.

***Servants of the Forgotten God.*** Yakfolk are the creations of a malevolent deity they call the Forgotten God. The worship of this nameless deity directs their lives. The deity takes the form of a male Yikaria, but its face is worn smooth into a featureless mask. The deity is appeased by sacrifice, which its followers carry out by capturing Humanoids and putting them to death by fire (immolation), earth (live burial), water (drowning), or air (throwing the victims off a great height). Sacrifices ensure the Forgotten God's benevolence.

The Forgotten God enabled the yakfolk to enslave dao for a time. It is said that the Forgotten God journeyed to the Elemental Plane of Earth and, through guile and deception, defeated the Grand Khan of the dao. The price of that defeat was harsh: the dao were forced to serve the Forgotten God and its minions—and forbidden to attack them—"for a thousand years and a year." The sentence has since expired, and yakfolk can no longer summon dao as they once did, but fear of the Forgotten God has kept the dao from seeking vengeance.

YAKFOLK
WARRIOR

## Yakfolk Priest

*Large Monstrosity, Typically Neutral Evil*

**Armor Class** 12 (hide armor)
**Hit Points** 52 (7d10 + 14)
**Speed** 30 ft.

| STR | DEX | CON | INT | WIS | CHA |
|-----|-----|-----|-----|-----|-----|
| 16 (+3) | 11 (+0) | 15 (+2) | 14 (+2) | 18 (+4) | 14 (+2) |

**Skills** Deception +4, Medicine +6, Survival +6
**Senses** passive Perception 14
**Languages** Common, Yikaria
**Challenge** 4 (1,100 XP)

**Possession (Recharges after a Short or Long Rest).** The yakfolk attempts to magically possess a Humanoid or Giant. The yakfolk must touch the target throughout a short rest, or the attempt fails. At the end of the rest, the target must succeed on a DC 12 Constitution saving throw or be possessed by the yakfolk, which disappears with everything it is carrying and wearing. Until the possession ends, the target is incapacitated, loses control of its body, and is unaware of its surroundings. The yakfolk now controls the body and can't be targeted by any attack, spell, or other effect, and it retains its alignment; its Intelligence, Wisdom, and Charisma scores; and its proficiencies. It otherwise uses the target's statistics, except the target's knowledge, class features, feats, and proficiencies.

The possession lasts until either the body drops to 0 hit points, the yakfolk ends the possession as an action, or the yakfolk is forced out of the body by an effect such as the *dispel evil and good* spell. When the possession ends, the yakfolk reappears in an unoccupied space within 5 feet of the body and is stunned until the end of its next turn. If the host body dies while it is possessed by the yakfolk, the yakfolk dies as well, and its body doesn't reappear.

### Actions

**Multiattack.** The yakfolk makes two Quarterstaff attacks.

**Quarterstaff.** *Melee Weapon Attack:* +5 to hit, reach 5 ft., one target: *Hit:* 10 (2d6 + 3) bludgeoning damage, or 12 (2d8 + 3) bludgeoning damage if used with two hands.

**Spellcasting.** The yakfolk casts one of the following spells, using Wisdom as the spellcasting ability (spell save DC 14; +6 to hit with spell attacks):

At will: *light, sacred flame, thaumaturgy*
1/day each: *augury* (cast as 1 action), *bane, banishment, bestow curse, command, cure wounds, hold person, protection from energy, sending*

**Summon Earth Elemental (1/Day).** The yakfolk summons an **earth elemental**. The summoned elemental appears in an unoccupied space within 60 feet of its summoner and acts as an ally of the summoner. It remains for 10 minutes, until it dies, or until its summoner dismisses it as an action.

**Yakfolk Society.** Yakfolk dwell in secluded settlements sheltered from the worst of nature's abuse, including mountain valleys, soaring plateaus, and desert oases. Outsiders that stumble into an enclave of yakfolk are usually surprised and pleased to find what appears to be a utopia, and the yakfolk foster that image until the strangers can be disarmed and taken prisoner.

In their seemingly idyllic hideaways, the yakfolk rule with iron fists, and for all their learning and culture, they are enormously evil overlords. Yakfolk care for their hapless prisoners only to the extent that a live one is more useful than a dead one, and putting a prisoner to work is easier than laboring oneself. It's not that yakfolk are lazy—quite the contrary. They simply consider most menial tasks beneath them.

Yakfolk have a drive for learning, particularly when it comes to the secrets of elemental magic and dark knowledge that might serve to corrupt or dominate others. Knowledge that the yakfolk can't gain or use is to be destroyed. Unsentimental by nature, yakfolk parents pack children off to communal creches once they are weaned, never to recognize them again. Yakfolk feel no loyalty to their families—only to their god and race.

**Skin Crawlers.** A yakfolk's most frightening weapon is its ability to magically crawl under another creature's skin, control its body, and suppress its mind. The yakfolk use this ability to spy on enemies, rob them, murder their leaders, and kidnap their young.

## New Giant Options

You can customize any of the giants in this adventure by giving them features beyond what's presented in the *Monster Manual*. This section gives new options for all six kinds of giants.

### Cloud Giants

Some adult cloud giants have the magical ability to create barriers of gale-force wind around themselves that can deflect incoming missiles. Others like to fling enemies through the air. These abilities are represented by the following action options.

**Fling.** The giant tries to throw a Small or Medium creature within 10 feet of it. The target must succeed on a DC 20 Dexterity saving throw or be hurled up to 60 feet horizontally in a direction of the giant's choice and land prone, taking 1d8 bludgeoning damage for every 10 feet it was thrown.

**Wind Aura.** A magical aura of wind surrounds the giant. The aura is a 10-foot-radius sphere that lasts as long as the giant maintains concentration on it (as if concentrating on a spell). While the aura is in effect, the giant gains a +2 bonus to its AC against ranged weapon attacks, and all open flames within the aura are extinguished unless they are magical.

### Fire Giants

Some adult fire giants are trained to lay siege to strongholds and break through enemy lines. These abilities are represented by the following traits.

**Siege Monster.** The giant deals double damage to objects and structures.

**Tackle.** When the giant enters any enemy's space for the first time on a turn, the enemy must succeed on a DC 19 Strength saving throw or be knocked prone.

## FROST GIANTS

Some adult frost giants are skilled hunters who construct and hurl nets weighted down with fragments of metal or bone. This ability is represented by the following action option.

**Weighted Net.** *Ranged Weapon Attack:* +5 to hit, ranged 20/60 ft., one Small, Medium, or Large creature. *Hit:* The target is restrained until it escapes the net. Any creature can use its action to make a DC 17 Strength check to free itself or another creature in the net, ending the effect on a success. Dealing 15 slashing damage to the net (AC 12) destroys the net and frees the target.

## HILL GIANTS

Some adult hill giants like to hurl themselves bodily at smaller foes and crush them beneath their bulk. This ability is represented by the following action option.

**Squash.** *Melee Weapon Attack:* +8 to hit, reach 5 ft., one Medium or smaller creature. *Hit:* 26 (6d6 + 5) bludgeoning damage, the giant lands prone in the target's space, and the target is grappled (escape DC 15). Until this grapple ends, the target is prone. The grapple ends early if the giant stands up.

## STONE GIANTS

Some adult stone giants like to grab enemies and fling them through the air. They can also roll boulders across the ground, striking multiple enemies in a line. These abilities are represented by the following action options.

**Fling.** The giant tries to throw a Small or Medium creature within 10 feet of it. The target must succeed on a DC 17 Dexterity saving throw or be hurled up to 60 feet horizontally in a direction of the giant's choice and land prone, taking 1d6 bludgeoning damage for every 10 feet it was thrown.

**Rolling Rock.** The giant sends a rock tumbling along the ground in a 30-foot line that is 5 feet wide. Each creature in that line must make a DC 17 Dexterity saving throw, taking 22 (3d10 + 6) bludgeoning damage and falling prone on a failed save.

## STORM GIANTS

Some adult storm giants can channel thunderous power through their bodies and release it with a deafening stomp. This ability is represented by the following action option.

**Thunderous Stomp (Recharge 6).** The storm giant stomps the ground, triggering a thunderclap. All other creatures within 15 feet of the giant must succeed on a DC 17 Constitution saving throw or take 33 (6d10) thunder damage and be deafened until the start of the giant's next turn. On a successful save, a creature takes half as much damage and isn't deafened. The thunderclap can be heard out to a range of 1,200 feet.

# APPENDIX D: SPECIAL NPCs

## AUGREK BRIGHTHELM
*Medium Humanoid (Dwarf), Lawful Good*

**Armor Class** 15 (chain shirt, shield)
**Hit Points** 13 (2d8 + 4)
**Speed** 25 ft.

| STR | DEX | CON | INT | WIS | CHA |
|---|---|---|---|---|---|
| 14 (+2) | 11 (+0) | 15 (+2) | 10 (+0) | 11 (+0) | 11 (+0) |

**Skills** Athletics +4, Perception +2
**Damage** Resistances poison
**Senses** darkvision 60 ft., passive Perception 12
**Languages** Common, Dwarvish

*Dwarven Resilience.* Augrek has advantage on saving throws against poison.

### ACTIONS

*Warhammer. Melee Weapon Attack:* +4 to hit, reach 5 ft., one target. *Hit:* 6 (1d8 + 2) bludgeoning damage, or 7 (1d10 + 2) bludgeoning damage if used with two hands.

*Heavy Crossbow. Ranged Weapon Attack:* +2 to hit, range 100/400 ft., one target. *Hit:* 5 (1d10) piercing damage. Augrek carries ten crossbow bolts.

### ROLEPLAYING INFORMATION

Sheriff's deputy Augrek guards the southwest gate of Bryn Shander and welcomes visitors to town. She has a good heart.

**Ideal:** "You'll get farther in life with a kind word than an axe."
**Bond:** "Bryn Shander is my home. It's my job to protect her."
**Flaw:** "I'm head over heels in love with Sheriff Southwell. One day I hope to marry him."

## SIRAC OF SUZAIL
*Medium Humanoid (Human), Lawful Good*

**Armor Class** 14 (leather)
**Hit Points** 22 (5d8)
**Speed** 30 ft.

| STR | DEX | CON | INT | WIS | CHA |
|---|---|---|---|---|---|
| 14 (+2) | 17 (+3) | 11 (+0) | 12 (+1) | 13 (+1) | 16 (+3) |

**Skills** Athletics +4, Insight +3, Survival +3
**Senses** passive Perception 11
**Languages** Common, Orc

### ACTIONS

*Shortsword. Melee Weapon Attack:* +5 to hit, reach 5 ft., one target. *Hit:* 6 (1d6 + 3) piercing damage.

*Dart. Ranged Weapon Attack:* +5 to hit, range 20/60 ft., one target. *Hit:* 5 (1d4 + 3) piercing damage. Sirac carries six darts.

### REACTIONS

*Parry.* Sirac adds 2 to his AC against one melee attack that would hit him. To do so, Sirac must see the attacker and be wielding a melee weapon.

### ROLEPLAYING INFORMATION

An acolyte of Torm, Sirac grew up on the streets of Suzail, the capital of Cormyr. He came to Icewind Dale to become a knucklehead trout fisher but instead found religion. The misbegotten son of Artus Cimber, a renowned human adventurer, Sirac hasn't seen his father since he was a baby.

**Ideal:** "Without duty or loyalty, a man is nothing."
**Bond:** "Icewind Dale is where I belong for the rest of my life."
**Flaw:** "I am honest to a fault."

## DUVESSA SHANE

*Medium Humanoid (Human), Lawful Good*

**Armor Class** 10
**Hit Points** 9 (2d8)
**Speed** 30 ft.

| STR | DEX | CON | INT | WIS | CHA |
|-----|-----|-----|-----|-----|-----|
| 10 (+0) | 11 (+0) | 10 (+0) | 16 (+3) | 14 (+2) | 16 (+3) |

**Skills** Deception +5, Insight +4, Persuasion +5
**Senses** passive Perception 12
**Languages** Common, Dwarvish, Giant, Orc

### ACTIONS

***Dagger.*** *Melee or Ranged Weapon Attack:* +2 to hit, reach 5 ft. or range 20/60 ft., one target. *Hit:* 2 (1d4) piercing damage. Duvessa carries only one dagger.

### REACTIONS

***Parry.*** Duvessa adds 2 to her AC against one melee attack that would hit her. To do so, Duvessa must see the attacker and be wielding a melee weapon.

### ROLEPLAYING INFORMATION

The daughter of a Waterdhavian trader and a tavern server, Duvessa has her mother's talent for negotiation and her father's charm. As the first woman to serve as Town Speaker of Bryn Shander, and a young one at that, she has much to prove.

**Ideal:** "The people of Icewind Dale are survivors. They can weather any storm."
**Bond:** "My mother taught me what it means to be a good leader. I won't disappoint her."
**Flaw:** "I don't give an inch in any argument or conflict."

## MARKHAM SOUTHWELL

*Medium humanoid (Human), Lawful Good*

**Armor Class** 17 (splint)
**Hit Points** 58 (9d8 + 18)
**Speed** 30 ft.

| STR | DEX | CON | INT | WIS | CHA |
|-----|-----|-----|-----|-----|-----|
| 15 (+2) | 13 (+1) | 14 (+2) | 11 (+0) | 16 (+3) | 14 (+2) |

**Skills** Perception +5, Survival +5
**Senses** passive Perception 15
**Languages** Common

### ACTIONS

***Multiattack.*** Markham makes two Longsword attacks.

***Longsword.*** *Melee Weapon Attack:* +4 to hit, reach 5 ft., one target. *Hit:* 6 (1d8 + 2) slashing damage, or 7 (1d10 + 2) slashing damage if used with two hands.

***Heavy Crossbow.*** *Ranged Weapon Attack:* +3 to hit, range 100/400 ft., one target. *Hit:* 6 (1d10 + 1) piercing damage. Markham carries twenty crossbow bolts.

### ROLEPLAYING INFORMATION

Sheriff Markham of Bryn Shander is a brawny, likable man of few words. Nothing is more important to him than protecting Icewind Dale. He judges others by their actions, not their words.

**Ideal:** "All people deserve to be treated with dignity."
**Bond:** "Duvessa is a natural leader, but she needs help. That's my job."
**Flaw:** "I bury my emotions and have no interest in small talk."

# BELDORA

*Medium Humanoid (Human), Chaotic Good*

**Armor Class** 12
**Hit Points** 18 (4d8)
**Speed** 30 ft.

| STR | DEX | CON | INT | WIS | CHA |
|-----|-----|-----|-----|-----|-----|
| 10 (+0) | 14 (+2) | 10 (+0) | 16 (+3) | 12 (+1) | 16 (+3) |

**Skills** Deception +5, Insight +3, Investigation +5, Perception +3, Persuasion +5
**Senses** passive Perception 13
**Languages** Common, Draconic, Dwarvish, Halfling

## ACTIONS

***Shortsword.*** *Melee Weapon Attack:* +4 to hit, reach 5 ft., one target. *Hit:* 5 (1d6 + 2) piercing damage.

***Hand Crossbow.*** *Ranged Weapon Attack:* +4 to hit, range 30/120 ft., one target. *Hit:* 5 (1d6 + 2) piercing damage. Beldora carries ten crossbow bolts.

## REACTIONS

***Duck and Cover.*** Beldora adds 2 to her AC against one ranged attack that would hit her. To do so, Beldora must see the attacker and can't be grappled or restrained.

## ROLEPLAYING INFORMATION

Beldora is a member of the Harpers who survives using her wits and wiles. She looks like a homeless waif, but she's a survivor who shies away from material wealth.

**Ideal:** "We should all strive to help one another."
**Bond:** "I'll risk my life to protect the powerless."
**Flaw:** "I like lying to people. Makes life more interesting, no?"

# SIR BARIC NYLEF

*Medium Humanoid (Human), Lawful Good*

**Armor Class** 18 (plate)
**Hit Points** 52 (8d8 + 16)
**Speed** 30 ft.

| STR | DEX | CON | INT | WIS | CHA |
|-----|-----|-----|-----|-----|-----|
| 18 (+4) | 11 (+0) | 14 (+2) | 11 (+0) | 15 (+2) | 15 (+2) |

**Skills** Insight +4, Investigation +2, Medicine +4, Survival +4
**Senses** passive Perception 12
**Languages** Common

***Brave.*** Baric has advantage on saving throws against being frightened.

## ACTIONS

***Maul.*** *Melee Weapon Attack:* +6 to hit, reach 5 ft., one target. *Hit:* 11 (2d6 + 4) bludgeoning damage.

***Heavy Crossbow.*** *Ranged Weapon Attack:* +2 to hit, range 100/400 ft., one target. *Hit:* 5 (1d10) piercing damage. Baric carries twenty crossbow bolts.

## ROLEPLAYING INFORMATION

As a knight of the Order of the Gauntlet, Sir Baric has sworn oaths to catch evildoers and bring them to justice. His current quarry is a dwarf brigand, Worvil "the Weevil" Forkbeard, who is rumored to be hiding in Icewind Dale. In addition to his gear, Sir Baric has an unarmored **warhorse**, Henry.

**Ideal:** "Evil must not be allowed to thrive in this world."
**Bond:** "Tyr is my lord; the order, my family. Through my actions, I shall honor both."
**Flaw:** "I'm not afraid to die. When Tyr finally calls me, I'll go to him happily."

# SHALVUS MARTHOLIO

*Medium Humanoid (Human), Neutral*

**Armor Class** 13 (leather)
**Hit Points** 27 (6d8)
**Speed** 30 ft.

| STR | DEX | CON | INT | WIS | CHA |
|-----|-----|-----|-----|-----|-----|
| 10 (+0) | 15 (+2) | 10 (+0) | 12 (+1) | 14 (+2) | 14 (+2) |

**Skills** Deception +4, Insight +4, Investigation +3, Perception +4, Sleight of Hand +4, Stealth +4
**Senses** passive Perception 12
**Languages** Common, Elvish

***Sneak Attack (1/Turn).*** Shalvus deals an extra 7 (2d6) damage when he hits a target with a weapon attack and has advantage on the attack roll, or when the target is within 5 feet of an ally of Shalvus that isn't incapacitated and Shalvus doesn't have disadvantage on the attack roll.

## ACTIONS

***Quarterstaff.*** *Melee Weapon Attack:* +2 to hit, reach 5 ft., one target. *Hit:* 3 (1d6) bludgeoning damage, or 4 (1d8) bludgeoning damage if used with two hands.

***Hand Crossbow.*** *Ranged Weapon Attack:* +4 to hit, range 30/120 ft., one target. *Hit:* 5 (1d6 + 2) piercing damage. Shalvus carries ten crossbow bolts.

## ROLEPLAYING INFORMATION

Nalaskur Thaelond of Bargewright Inn has entrusted the shepherd Shalvus with an important assignment: to figure out the best way by which Goldenfields can be brought under the Black Network's control. Shalvus believes that success will ensure his swift rise through the Zhentarim ranks.

**Ideal:** "I'll do what it takes to prove myself to the Zhentarim."
**Bond:** "I love animals, and I'm very protective of them."
**Flaw:** "I can't resist taking risks to feed my ambitions."

# LIFFERLAS

*Huge Plant, Unaligned*

**Armor Class** 13 (natural armor)
**Hit Points** 59 (7d12 + 14)
**Speed** 20 ft.

| STR | DEX | CON | INT | WIS | CHA |
|-----|-----|-----|-----|-----|-----|
| 19 (+4) | 6 (–2) | 15 (+2) | 10 (+0) | 10 (+0) | 7 (–2) |

**Damage Vulnerabilities** fire
**Damage Resistances** bludgeoning, piercing
**Senses** passive Perception 10
**Languages** Common

***False Appearance.*** While Lifferlas remains motionless, it is indistinguishable from a normal tree.

## ACTIONS

***Multiattack.*** Lifferlas makes two Slam attacks.

***Slam.*** *Melee Weapon Attack:* +6 to hit, reach 10 ft., one target. *Hit:* 14 (3d6 + 4) bludgeoning damage.

## ROLEPLAYING INFORMATION

A druid of the Emerald Enclave awakened the tree Lifferlas with a spell. Goldenfields is his home, its people his friends. Children like to carve their names and initials into his body and hang from his boughs, and he's happy with that.

**Ideal:** "I exist to protect the people and plants of Goldenfields."
**Bond:** "Children are wonderful. I would do anything to make them feel happy and safe."
**Flaw:** "I can't remember people's names and often get them mixed up."

# ZI LIANG

*Medium Humanoid (Human), Chaotic Good*

---

**Armor Class** 15
**Hit Points** 22 (5d8)
**Speed** 40 ft.

| STR | DEX | CON | INT | WIS | CHA |
|-----|-----|-----|-----|-----|-----|
| 12 (+1) | 15 (+2) | 11 (+0) | 14 (+2) | 16 (+3) | 11 (+0) |

**Skills** Acrobatics +4, Athletics +3, Perception +5, Stealth +4
**Senses** passive Perception 15
**Languages** Common, Elvish, Goblin

---

***Unarmored Defense.*** While Zi is wearing no armor and wielding no shield, her AC includes her Wisdom modifier.

## ACTIONS

***Multiattack.*** Zi makes two Quarterstaff attacks.

***Quarterstaff.*** *Melee Weapon Attack:* +3 to hit, reach 5 ft., one target. *Hit:* 4 (1d6 + 1) bludgeoning damage, or 5 (1d8 + 1) bludgeoning damage if used with two hands.

***Sling.*** *Ranged Weapon Attack:* +4 to hit, range 30/120 ft., one target. *Hit:* 4 (1d4 + 2) bludgeoning damage. Zi carries twenty sling stones.

## ROLEPLAYING INFORMATION

Zi Liang is a devout worshiper of Chauntea, the Earth Mother. She has considerably less faith in Goldenfields' defenders, so she patrols the temple-farm during her off-duty hours.

**Ideal:** "If we faithfully tend to our gardens and our fields, Chauntea will smile upon us."
**Bond:** "Goldenfields is the breadbasket of the North. People depend on its safety and prosperity, and I'll do what must be done to protect it."
**Flaw:** "I don't trust authority. I do what my heart says is right."

---

# MIROS XELBRIN

*Medium Humanoid (Human), Neutral Good*

---

**Armor Class** 10
**Hit Points** 22 (4d8 + 4)
**Speed** 30 ft.

| STR | DEX | CON | INT | WIS | CHA |
|-----|-----|-----|-----|-----|-----|
| 16 (+3) | 10 (+0) | 15 (+2) | 11 (+0) | 12 (+1) | 14 (+2) |

**Skills** Intimidation +4, Perception +3
**Senses** passive Perception 13
**Languages** Common

---

## ACTIONS

***Bearhug.*** *Melee Weapon Attack:* +5 to hit, reach 5 ft., one creature. *Hit:* 5 (1d4 + 3) bludgeoning damage, and the target is grappled (escape DC 13) and takes 5 (1d4 + 3) bludgeoning damage at the start of each of Miros's turns until the grapple ends. Miros cannot make attacks while grappling a creature.

***Club.*** *Melee Weapon Attack:* +5 to hit, reach 5 ft., one target. *Hit:* 5 (1d4 + 3) bludgeoning damage.

***Heavy Crossbow.*** *Ranged Weapon Attack:* +2 to hit, range 100/400 ft., one target. *Hit:* 5 (1d10) piercing damage. Miros carries ten crossbow bolts.

## ROLEPLAYING INFORMATION

Innkeeper Miros is a retired carnival attraction, dubbed "the Yeti" because of his barrel-shaped body and the thick, white hair covering his arms, chest, back, and head. When Goldenfields suffers, so does his business, so he takes strides to protect the compound.

**Ideal:** "As does the Emerald Enclave, I believe that civilization and the wilderness need to learn to coexist."
**Bond:** "Make fun of me all you like, but don't speak ill of my inn or my employees!"
**Flaw:** "When something upsets me, I have a tendency to fly into a rage."

# NAXENE DRATHKALA

*Medium Humanoid (Human), Neutral Good*

**Armor Class** 10 (13 with *mage armor*)
**Hit Points** 27 (6d8)
**Speed** 30 ft.

| STR | DEX | CON | INT | WIS | CHA |
|-----|-----|-----|-----|-----|-----|
| 8 (–1) | 11 (+0) | 11 (+0) | 17 (+3) | 12 (+1) | 11 (+0) |

**Skills** Arcana +5, History +5
**Senses** passive Perception 11
**Languages** Common, Draconic, Dwarvish, Elvish

## ACTIONS

***Staff.*** *Melee Weapon Attack:* +1 to hit, reach 5 ft., one target. *Hit:* 2 (1d6 – 1) bludgeoning damage, or 3 (1d8 – 1) bludgeoning damage if used with two hands.

***Spellcasting.*** Naxene casts one of the following spells, using Intelligence as the spellcasting ability (spell save DC 13; +5 to hit with spell attacks):

At will: *fire bolt* (1d10 fire damage), *light*, *mage hand*
1/day each: *mage armor*, *magic missile*, *suggestion*

## ROLEPLAYING INFORMATION

Goldenfields' crops are vital to Waterdeep's survival, which is why the Watchful Order of Magists and Protectors sent Naxene to make sure the temple-farm is adequately defended. At first she regarded the task as a punishment, but now she appreciates the peace and quiet.

**Ideal:** "There's no problem that can't be solved with magic."
**Bond:** "I have great respect for Lady Laeral Silverhand of Waterdeep. She and the Lords' Alliance are going to bring some much-needed order to this lawless land."
**Flaw:** "I'm too smart to be wrong about anything."

# OREN YOGILVY

*Small Humanoid (Halfling), Chaotic Good*

**Armor Class** 11
**Hit Points** 9 (2d6 + 2)
**Speed** 25 ft.

| STR | DEX | CON | INT | WIS | CHA |
|-----|-----|-----|-----|-----|-----|
| 8 (–1) | 13 (+1) | 12 (+1) | 11 (+0) | 10 (+0) | 16 (+3) |

**Skills** Perception +2, Performance +7, Persuasion +5
**Damage Resistances** poison
**Senses** passive Perception 12
**Languages** Common, Halfling

***Halfling Nimbleness.*** Oren can move through the space of any creature that is of a size larger than his.

***Lucky.*** When Oren rolls a 1 on an attack roll, ability check, or saving throw, he can reroll the die and must use the new roll.

***Stout Resilience.*** Oren has advantage on saving throws against poison.

## ACTIONS

***Dagger.*** *Melee or Ranged Weapon Attack:* +3 to hit, reach 5 ft. or range 20/60 ft., one target. *Hit:* 3 (1d4 + 1) piercing damage. Oren carries four daggers.

## ROLEPLAYING INFORMATION

Oren came to Northfurrow's End looking for easy work and found it. He sings for his supper, drinks like a fish, and wanders the fields at night dreaming up new lyrics to entertain the inn's other guests. Oren likes to stir up trouble from time to time, but he doesn't have a mean bone in his body.

**Ideal:** "Music is food for the soul."
**Bond:** "You had me at 'Can I buy you a drink?'"
**Flaw:** "I have a knack for putting myself in harm's way. Good thing I'm lucky!"

# Darathra Shendrel

*Medium Humanoid (Human), Lawful Good*

**Armor Class** 14 (breastplate)
**Hit Points** 52 (8d8 + 16)
**Speed** 30 ft.

| STR | DEX | CON | INT | WIS | CHA |
|---|---|---|---|---|---|
| 16 (+3) | 11 (+0) | 14 (+2) | 11 (+0) | 11 (+0) | 15 (+2) |

**Skills** History +2, Intimidation +4, Investigation +2, Perception +2, Persuasion +4
**Senses** passive Perception 12
**Languages** Common

***Brave.*** Darathra has advantage on saving throws against being frightened.

## Actions

***Multiattack.*** Darathra makes two Greatsword attacks.

***Greatsword.*** *Melee Weapon Attack:* +5 to hit, reach 5 ft., one target. *Hit:* 10 (2d6 + 3) slashing damage.

***Heavy Crossbow.*** *Ranged Weapon Attack:* +2 to hit, range 100/400 ft., one target. *Hit:* 5 (1d10) piercing damage. Darathra carries twenty crossbow bolts.

## Roleplaying Information

As the Lord Protector of Triboar and a secret agent of the Harpers, Darathra has sworn an oath to defend the town. She takes her duty very seriously. In addition to her gear, Darathra has an unarmored warhorse named Buster.

**Ideal:** "Good people should be given every chance to prosper, free of tyranny."
**Bond:** "I'll lay down my life to protect Triboar and its citizens."
**Flaw:** "I refuse to back down. Push me, and I'll push back."

# Darz Helgar

*Medium Humanoid (Human), Neutral*

**Armor Class** 12
**Hit Points** 27 (5d8 + 5)
**Speed** 30 ft.

| STR | DEX | CON | INT | WIS | CHA |
|---|---|---|---|---|---|
| 15 (+2) | 15 (+2) | 12 (+1) | 10 (+0) | 11 (+0) | 11 (+0) |

**Skills** Intimidation +2, Sleight of Hand +4, Stealth +4
**Senses** passive Perception 10
**Languages** Common

***Sneak Attack (1/Turn).*** Darz deals an extra 7 (2d6) damage when he hits a target with a weapon attack and has advantage on the attack roll, or when the target is within 5 feet of an ally of Darz that isn't incapacitated and Darz doesn't have disadvantage on the attack roll.

## Actions

***Shortsword.*** *Melee Weapon Attack:* +4 to hit, reach 5 ft., one target. *Hit:* 5 (1d6 + 2) piercing damage.

***Sling.*** *Ranged Weapon Attack:* +4 to hit, range 30/120 ft., one target. *Hit:* 4 (1d4 + 2) bludgeoning damage. Darz carries twenty sling stones.

## Roleplaying Information

In his youth, Darz was a member of the Xanathar Thieves' Guild in Waterdeep. After serving ten years in prison for his crimes, he cut all ties to the city and moved north to be a campground caretaker.

**Ideal:** "You can run from your past, but you can't hide from it."
**Bond:** "I've made a new life in Triboar. I'm not gonna run away this time."
**Flaw:** "I have no regrets. I do whatever it takes to survive."

# NARTH TEZRIN
*Medium Humanoid (Human), Chaotic Good*

**Armor Class** 12
**Hit Points** 18 (4d8)
**Speed** 30 ft.

| STR | DEX | CON | INT | WIS | CHA |
|-----|-----|-----|-----|-----|-----|
| 10 (+0) | 15 (+2) | 10 (+0) | 12 (+1) | 14 (+2) | 16 (+3) |

**Skills** Insight +4, Investigation +3, Perception +6, Persuasion +5
**Senses** passive Perception 16
**Languages** Common, Dwarvish

***Cunning Action.*** On each of his turns, Narth can use a bonus action to take the Dash, Disengage, or Hide action.

## ACTIONS

***Shortsword.*** *Melee Weapon Attack:* +4 to hit, reach 5 ft., one target. *Hit:* 5 (1d6 + 2) piercing damage.

***Hand Crossbow.*** *Ranged Weapon Attack:* +4 to hit, range 30/120 ft., one target. *Hit:* 5 (1d6 + 2) piercing damage. Narth carries twenty crossbow bolts.

## ROLEPLAYING INFORMATION

Narth sells gear to adventurers, and he also has an adventurous spirit. The Lionshield Coster pays him well, but he longs to make a name for himself. At the same time, he runs a business with his partner Alaestra and knows she wouldn't forgive him if he ran off and never returned.

**Ideal:** "The bigger the risk, the greater the reward."
**Bond:** "I adore my colleague Alaestra, and I'd like to do something to impress her."
**Flaw:** "I'll risk life and limb to become a legend."

# URGALA MELTIMER
*Medium Humanoid (Human), Lawful Good*

**Armor Class** 12 (leather)
**Hit Points** 58 (9d8 + 18)
**Speed** 30 ft.

| STR | DEX | CON | INT | WIS | CHA |
|-----|-----|-----|-----|-----|-----|
| 16 (+3) | 13 (+1) | 14 (+2) | 12 (+1) | 14 (+2) | 13 (+1) |

**Skills** Athletics +5, Intimidation +3
**Senses** passive Perception 12
**Languages** Common, Giant

***Giant Slayer.*** Any weapon attack that Urgala makes against a Giant deals an extra 7 (2d6) damage on a hit.

## ACTIONS

***Multiattack.*** Urgala makes two Morningstar or Shortbow attacks.

***Morningstar.*** *Melee Weapon Attack:* +5 to hit, reach 5 ft., one target. *Hit:* 7 (1d8 + 3) piercing damage.

***Shortbow.*** *Ranged Weapon Attack:* +3 to hit, range 80/320 ft., one target. *Hit:* 5 (1d6 + 1) piercing damage. Urgala carries a quiver of twenty arrows.

## ROLEPLAYING INFORMATION

A retired adventurer, Urgala owns a respectable inn, the Northshield House, and she doesn't want to see it or her neighbors' homes destroyed. She has no tolerance for monsters or bullies.

**Ideal:** "We live in a violent world, and sometimes violence is necessary for survival."
**Bond:** "My home is my life. Threaten it, and I'll hurt you."
**Flaw:** "I know how treacherous and greedy adventurers can be. I don't trust them—any of them."

# OTHOVIR
*Medium Humanoid (Human), Lawful Neutral*

**Armor Class** 10 (13 with *mage armor*)
**Hit Points** 16 (3d8 + 3)
**Speed** 30 ft.

| STR | DEX | CON | INT | WIS | CHA |
|-----|-----|-----|-----|-----|-----|
| 11 (+0) | 10 (+0) | 13 (+1) | 12 (+1) | 14 (+2) | 16 (+3) |

**Skills** Deception +5, Insight +4, Persuasion +5
**Senses** passive Perception 12
**Languages** Common, Elvish

## ACTIONS

***Rapier.*** *Melee Weapon Attack:* +2 to hit, reach 5 ft., one target. *Hit:* 4 (1d8) piercing damage.

***Spellcasting.*** Othovir casts one of the following spells, using Charisma as the spellcasting ability (spell save DC 13; +5 to hit with spell attacks):

At will: *fire bolt* (1d10 fire damage), *prestidigitation*
1/day each: *mage armor*, *thunderwave*, *witch bolt*

## REACTIONS

***Parry.*** Othovir adds 2 to his AC against one melee attack that would hit him. To do so, Othovir must see the attacker and be wielding a melee weapon.

## ROLEPLAYING INFORMATION

Othovir is a gifted harness-maker who doesn't talk about his family or where he came from. He cares about his business, his clients, and his good name.

**Ideal:** "Find what you do well, and do it to the best of your ability."
**Bond:** "I won't allow my name to be tarnished."
**Flaw:** "I get angry when others pry into my private life."

# GHELRYN FOEHAMMER
*Medium Humanoid (Dwarf), Lawful Good*

**Armor Class** 14 (breastplate, shield)
**Hit Points** 30 (4d8 + 12)
**Speed** 25 ft.

| STR | DEX | CON | INT | WIS | CHA |
|-----|-----|-----|-----|-----|-----|
| 18 (+4) | 7 (−2) | 17 (+3) | 10 (+0) | 11 (+0) | 11 (+0) |

**Skills** Athletics +6, Intimidation +2, Perception +2
**Damage Resistances** poison
**Senses** darkvision 60 ft., passive Perception 12
**Languages** Common, Dwarvish

***Dwarven Resilience.*** Ghelryn has advantage on saving throws against poison.

***Giant Slayer.*** Any weapon attack that Ghelryn makes against a giant deals an extra 7 (2d6) damage on a hit.

## ACTIONS

***Multiattack.*** Ghelryn makes two Battleaxe attacks.

***Battleaxe.*** *Melee Weapon Attack:* +6 to hit, reach 5 ft., one target. *Hit:* 8 (1d8 + 4) slashing damage, or 9 (1d10 + 4) slashing damage if used with two hands.

## ROLEPLAYING INFORMATION

The blacksmith Ghelryn has a good heart, but he hates orcs and giants—hates them with a fiery passion. He considers it the solemn duty of all dwarves to cave in their skulls!

**Ideal:** "It is incumbent upon every dwarf to forge a legacy."
**Bond:** "I stand for Clan Foehammer and all dwarvenkind."
**Flaw:** "I never run from a fight, especially if it involves killing orcs or giants."

## Instructions for the DM

If you want your players to run the storm giant NPCs in chapter 12, make four copies of the **storm giant** stat block on this page and distribute these stat blocks among your players. If you have more than four players, not every player will get a storm giant NPC to play.

Each player who receives a stat block should also receive a copy of one of the four smaller cards on this page. Each card provides skill proficiencies and role-playing information for a specific storm giant. There is one card each for Nimir, Orlekto, Shaldoor, and Vaasha. Make sure that the player who receives Orlekto's card is comfortable running an evil, treacherous NPC.

## Storm Giant
*Huge Giant*

---

**Armor Class** 16 (scale mail)
**Hit Points** 230 (20d12 + 100)
**Speed** 50 ft., swim 50 ft.

---

| STR | DEX | CON | INT | WIS | CHA |
|-----|-----|-----|-----|-----|-----|
| 29 (+9) | 14 (+2) | 20 (+5) | 16 (+3) | 18 (+4) | 18 (+4) |

---

**Saving Throws** Str +14, Con +10, Wis +9, Cha +9
**Damage Resistances** cold
**Damage Immunities** lightning, thunder
**Senses** passive Perception 19
**Languages** Common, Giant

---

**Amphibious.** The giant can breathe air and water.

### Actions

**Multiattack.** The giant makes two Greatsword attacks.

**Greatsword.** *Melee Weapon Attack:* +14 to hit, reach 10 ft., one target. *Hit:* 30 (6d6 + 9) slashing damage.

**Rock.** *Ranged Weapon Attack:* +14 to hit, range 60/240 ft., one target. *Hit:* 35 (4d12 + 9) bludgeoning damage.

**Lightning Strike (Recharges after a Short or Long Rest).** The giant hurls a magical lightning bolt at a point it can see within 500 feet of it. Each creature within 10 feet of that point must make a DC 17 Dexterity saving throw, taking 54 (12d8) lightning damage on a failed save, or half as much damage on a successful one.

**Spellcasting.** The giant casts one of the following spells, requiring no material spell components and using Charisma as the spellcasting ability (spell save DC 17):

At will: *detect magic*, *levitate*, *light*
1/day each: *control weather* (cast as 1 action), *water breathing*

## Nimir
*Lawful Good Storm Giant (Male)*

---

**Skills** Athletics +14, Insight +8, Perception +9

### Roleplaying Information

Nimir is an insightful, even-keeled storm giant who believes that a lasting alliance between giants and small folk can make the world a safer, more enlightened place. He believes King Hekaton was wise to choose Princess Serissa as his heir apparent, and it would never occur to him to question their orders.

**Ideal:** "It's the duty of the big to protect the small."
**Bond:** "I'd give my life to defend my king and his royal line."
**Flaw:** "I never question orders."

## Orlekto
*Chaotic Evil Storm Giant (Male)*

---

**Skills** Athletics +14, Deception +14, Perception +9

### Roleplaying Information

Orlekto is in love with Princess Mirran and wants to see her become Queen of the *Wyrmskull Throne*. (If Mirran is dead, Orlekto aims to avenge her.) If the opportunity to eliminate Hekaton or Serissa presents itself, Orlekto seizes it. Until then, he conceals his treacherous nature.

**Ideal:** "Storm giants should rule the world. Weak leaders have let dragons and others steal what the gods gave to us!"
**Bond:** "I serve Princess Mirran and her alone."
**Flaw:** "For Mirran's love or my revenge, I'd betray my king and my honor."

## Shaldoor
*Chaotic Good Storm Giant (Female)*

---

**Skills** Animal Handling +9, Athletics +14, Perception +9

### Roleplaying Information

A skilled rider of rocs and whales, Shaldoor believes that Annam the All-Father shattered the ordning to push giants into war against the dragons. She is thrilled to be on the front lines in this great conflict!

**Ideal:** "Giants are made for war—storm giants most of all!"
**Bond:** "Ostoria is gone, yet I long for the return of a mighty giant empire."
**Flaw:** "I like to rain destruction down upon my enemies, and I never show them mercy."

## Vaasha
*Neutral Good Storm Giant (Female)*

---

**Skills** Athletics +14, Perception +9, Survival +14

### Roleplaying Information

Vaasha is a skilled hunter and tracker who doesn't charge into danger without first assessing the risks. She's not afraid to speak her mind, even to her king. To her, a worthy leader values the truth, no matter how painful it is.

**Ideal:** "I want this conflict over with so that I can return to the quiet stillness of the ocean depths."
**Bond:** "I'll protect this beautiful world from the ravages of evil with my dying breath."
**Flaw:** "I don't care if my words hurt others' feelings."